MediaShare for Business offers a curated collection of business videos that provide customizable, auto-scored assignments. Media-Share for Business helps students understand why they are learning key concepts and how they will **apply** those in their careers.

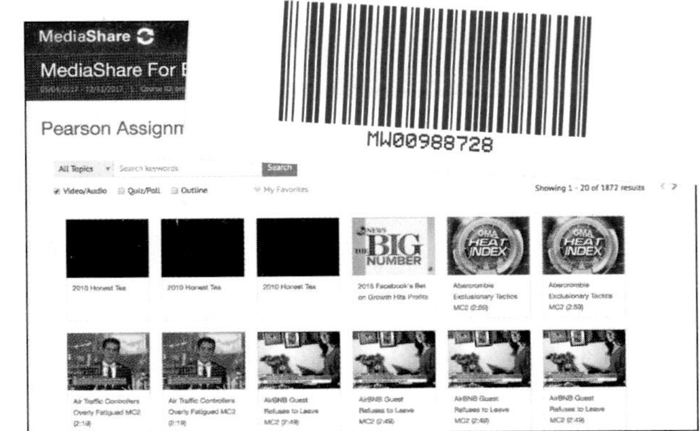

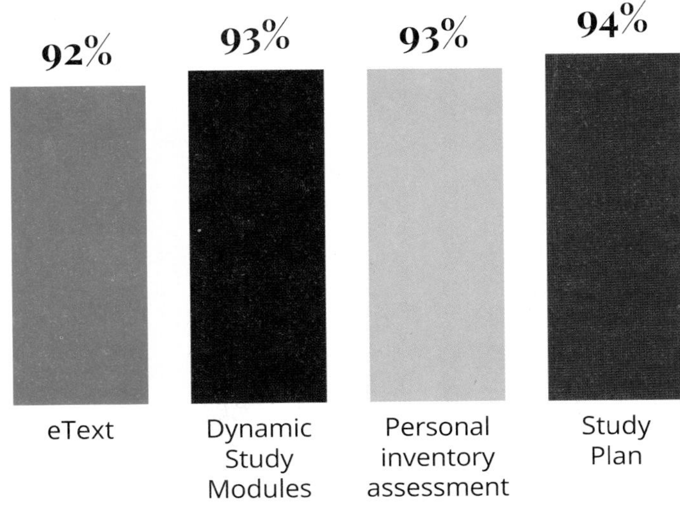

Pearson eText enhances student learning—both in and outside the classroom. Take notes, highlight, and bookmark important content, or engage with interactive lecture and example videos that bring learning to life (available with select titles). Accessible anytime, anywhere via MyLab or the app.

% of students who found learning tool helpful

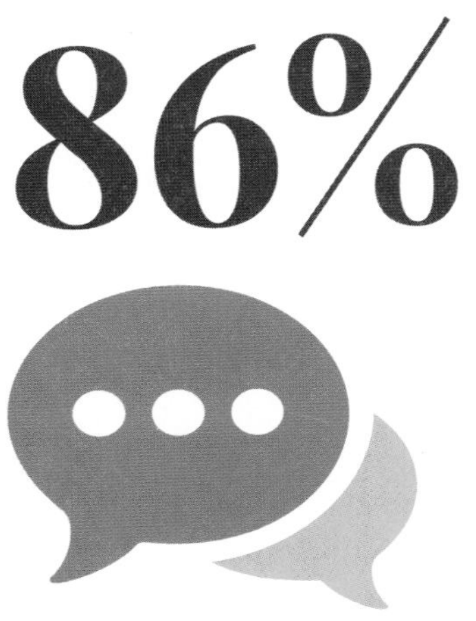

of students would tell their instructor to keep using MyLab Management

The **MyLab Gradebook** offers an easy way for students and instructors to view course performance. Item Analysis allows instructors to quickly see trends by analyzing details like the number of students who answered correctly/incorrectly, time on task, and median time spend on a question by question basis. And because it's correlated with the AACSB Standards, instructors can track students' progress toward outcomes that the organization has deemed important in preparing students to be **leaders.**

"I was able to find myself actually learning at home rather than memorizing things for a class."
— Katherine Vicente, Student at County College of Morris

For additional details visit: www.pearson.com/mylab/management

Human Resource Management

Joseph J. Martocchio

Fifteenth Edition

New York, NY

Vice President, Business, Economics, and UK Courseware: Donna Battista
Director of Portfolio Management: Stephanie Wall
Editorial Assistant: Linda Siebert Albelli
Vice President, Product Marketing: Roxanne McCarley
Product Marketer: Kaylee Claymore
Product Marketing Assistant: Marianela Silvestri
Manager of Field Marketing, Business Publishing: Adam Goldstein
Field Marketing Manager: Nicole Price
Vice President, Production and Digital Studio, Arts and Business: Etain O'Dea
Director of Production, Business: Jeff Holcomb
Managing Producer, Business: Melissa Feimer
Content Producer: Yasmita Hota
Operations Specialist: Carol Melville
Design Lead: Kathryn Foot
Manager, Learning Tools: Brian Surette
Content Developer, Learning Tools: Lindsey Sloan
Managing Producer, Digital Studio and GLP, Media Production and Development: Ashley Santora
Managing Producer, Digital Studio: Diane Lombardo
Digital Studio Producer: Monique Lawrence
Digital Studio Producer: Alana Coles
Project Manager: Nicole Suddeth and Raja Natesan, SPi Global
Interior Design: SPi Global
Cover Design: SPi Global
Cover Art: A-Digit/DigitalVision Vectors/Getty Images
Printer/Binder: LSC Communications, Inc./Menasha
Cover Printer: Phoenix Color/Hagerstown

Library of Congress Cataloging-in-Publication Data
Names: Martocchio, Joseph J., author. | Mondy, R. Wayne, 1940- Human resource management.
Title: Human resource management / Joseph J. Martocchio.
Description: Fifteenth Edition. | Boston : Pearson, [2017] | Revised edition of Human resource management, [2016]
Identifiers: LCCN 2017037154| ISBN 9780134739724 | ISBN 0134739728
Subjects: LCSH: Personnel management—United States. | Personnel management.
Classification: LCC HF5549.2.U5 M66 2017 | DDC 658.3—dc23 LC record available at https://lccn.loc.gov/2017037154

2 18

Pearson

ISBN 10: 0-13-473972-8
ISBN 13: 978-0-13-473972-4

To my parents—for their sacrifices which have provided me with great opportunities.

Brief Contents

Contents

Preface

New to this Edition

Four new features appear in each chapter that enable students to integrate knowledge and valuable skills regardless whether choosing a career in the HRM profession or other business function in smaller or larger organizations, all available in MyLab.

> HRM Is Everyone's Business
>
> Most company leaders and employees will face ethical challenges at one time or another. Some employees will intentionally commit ethics violations for personal gain. Other employees may unknowingly do so. Whether you are a manager or HR professional—an employee may bring concerns about possible ethical violations to your attention or you may observe them yourself. Once you are aware of a situation where ethics are in question, you are obligated to respond.
>
> **Action checklist for managers and HR—responding to allegations of unethical behavior**
>
> **HR takes the lead**
>
> ☑ Work with managers to ensure that they understand the company's code of ethics and communicate the procedures for addressing instances of potential ethical violations.
> ☑ Encourage managers to share the company's code of ethics with employees, lead open discussions about everyone's obligation to behave ethically, and create a safe environment for employees to report their concerns about possible ethical violations to the appropriate authority.
> ☑ Guide managers through the process of handling employees who are suspected of committing ethical violations.
>
> **Managers take the lead**
>
> ☑ Educate HR on certain aspects of employee roles to better understand how unethical behavior may manifest in your department. Bringing HR up to speed creates a partnership for more effectively responding to possible ethical violations.
> ☑ Discuss concerns with HR about possible ethical violations and follow through based on company policy and procedures.
> ☑ Work together with HR to implement a training plan on the company's code of ethics and creating hypothetical scenarios illustrating ethical and unethical behavior relevant to your departmental activities.

- HRM Is Everyone's Business. This feature explains how HR professionals and managers throughout the organization work together to address important workplace issues by highlighting specific connections and the reality that HR activities are never performed in isolation.

- HRM by the Numbers. This feature provides an excellent opportunity to think through concepts and their applications as well as analyze quantitative data to facilitate problem solving.

> HRM by the Numbers
>
> **Paying the Price for Underpaying Workers**
>
> *An additional HRM by the Numbers exercise can be found on MyLab Management.*
>
> HR professionals should ensure that workers are paid for their work on a timely basis. Sometimes, companies pay workers less than what they should and there are various possible reasons such as intent to save money or in error. Either way, paying employees lesser amounts than owed may violate the law. For instance, the Fair Labor Standards Act (FLSA), which we will discuss in Chapter 3, requires employers to pay eligible workers a higher pay for overtime work. Specifically, the overtime pay rate equals 1.5 times the regular hourly pay rate for each additional hour exceeding 40 in a work week.
>
> You've learned that the company has not been paying employees appropriately for overtime work hours. It is your responsibility to calculate the amount of overtime pay owed to workers. After reviewing the payroll records, you discovered the following details:
>
> 1. Group 1: 225 workers. Each worker earns a regular hourly pay rate of $18.00. For each of the past 15 work weeks, everyone worked 45 hours.
> 2. Group 2: 310 workers. Each worker earns a regular hourly pay rate of $21.00. For each of the past 20 work weeks, everyone worked 47 hours.
>
> Every worker received regular pay for all their hours worked, but they did not receive an additional overtime pay amount.
>
> **Questions**
>
> **2-13.** Calculate the hourly overtime pay rate for each worker in (a) group 1 and (b) group 2.
> **2-14.** How much money does the company owe all the workers in (a) group 1 over 15 weeks and (b) group 2 over 20 weeks?
> **2-15.** How much money did the company save by not paying all the workers (groups 1 and 2 combined) overtime pay?

> Working Together: Team Exercise
>
> In small groups of three or four, come up with specific answers to the following questions. Talk through your perspectives and come up with a brief team response. Be prepared to share your ideas with the class.

- Working Together. This feature offers opportunities for students to collaborate through sharing ideas, listening to others' ideas, and coming up with a cohesive team response to the assignment.

- FYI. This feature provides tidbits of information from survey research and extensive databases (e.g., employment statistics) that illuminate trends, opinions, and the use of specific HR practices.

> **FYI**
>
> The 2017 Global 100 Most Sustainable Corporations were most commonly found in the following countries:
>
> - United States: 19 companies
> - France: 12 companies
> - United Kingdom: 11 companies
> - Canada and Germany: 6 companies
> - Netherlands: 5 companies[105]

Updates to the 15th Edition

There are three significant updates made to this edition of the textbook; revised learning objectives, updates to HRM practices, and new content in the majority of special features. First, the learning objectives in each chapter have been revised to be consistent across chapters (there are now six learning objectives per chapter with the exception of chapter 1) in order to better integrate the chapter material together in a more effective manner to improve learning.

Second, there are substantial updates that highlight evolving HRM practices, statistics, and business professionals' perspectives. For instance, Chapter 7 (performance management and performance appraisal) includes a section on trends in performance appraisal practice. In a nutshell, some companies are providing performance feedback more frequently and as needed on a less structured basis rather than putting off providing feedback until structured annual reviews are given. This section also addresses the pros and cons of this more contemporary thinking as well the same of longstanding approaches to provide students a balanced view.

Third, fifty percent of the *Ethics Dilemma* and fifty percent of the *Incident* features are new. Business ethics are sets of guiding principles that influence the way individuals and organizations behave within the society that they operate. Analysis of the incidents, which depict realistic scenarios, requires interpretation and proposed actionable responses. Many new *Watch It!* videos appear throughout this edition.

Solving Teaching and Learning Challenges

Increasingly, students expect to see the applicability of their coursework to life and work after graduation. When the connection is not clear to students, many may lose interest and, perhaps, choose to do as little as possible to earn a good enough grade on quizzes and exams. How the author conveys content and the choice of pedagogical features can pique interest in the subject matter and enhance learning and development of seven critical employability skills, which I have discussed in the Developing Employability Skills section in Chapter 1.

I approach the study of HRM in a realistic, practical, interesting, and stimulating manner. I focus on showing how HRM is practiced in the real world. Throughout the book, you will see examples of how organizations practice HRM. In explaining a concept, I often quote HRM professionals and other business professionals, yet all HRM discussion is based on sound theoretical concepts and practice. Where appropriate, the strategic role of HRM is apparent in the discussion of each major HRM function. In addition, I show how HRM topics are related to other HRM topics. For instance, a firm that emphasizes recruiting top-quality candidates but neglects to provide satisfactory compensation is wasting time, effort, and money. If a firm's compensation system pays below-market wages, the firm will always be hiring and training new employees only to see the best leave for a competitor's higher wages. Besides this one example, the interrelationship of HRM practices set in a dynamic business environment will become more obvious as these topics are addressed throughout the book. These interrelationships are also shown to be important as organizations operate within the global environment. I included several features that appear in the textbook and MyLab, designed to enhance student learning by actively engaging students.

Learn It
If your professor has chosen to assign this, go to **www.pearson.com/mylab/management** to see what you should particularly focus on and to take the Chapter 2 Warm-Up.

Learn It Practice

Students can be assigned the Chapter Warm-Up before coming to class. Assigning these questions ahead of time will ensure that students are coming to class prepared.

Watch It Videos

Recommends a video clip that can be assigned to students for outside classroom viewing or that can be watched in the classroom. The video corresponds to the chapter material and is accompanied by multiple choice questions that reinforce student's comprehension of the chapter content.

Watch It I
If your instructor has assigned this, go to **www.pearson.com/mylab/management** to watch a video titled Patagonia: Ethics and Social Responsibility and to respond to questions.

> **Try It!**
> If your instructor has assigned this, go to **www.pearson.com/mylab/management** to complete the Management & Ethics simulation and test your application of these concepts when faced with real-world decisions.

Try It Mini Simulations

Recommends a mini simulation that can be assigned to students as an outside classroom activity or it can be done in the classroom. As the students watch the simulation they will be asked to make choices based on the scenario presented in the simulation. At the end of the simulation the student will receive immediate feedback based on the answers they gave. These simulations reinforces the concepts of the chapter and the students' comprehension of those concepts.

HR Bloopers Exercises

HR Bloopers present scenarios that describe potential mistakes that may occur in HR practice. Questions that follow in MyLab Management provide students with the opportunity to test their understanding and recall of the chapter material based on the information contained in the scenarios.

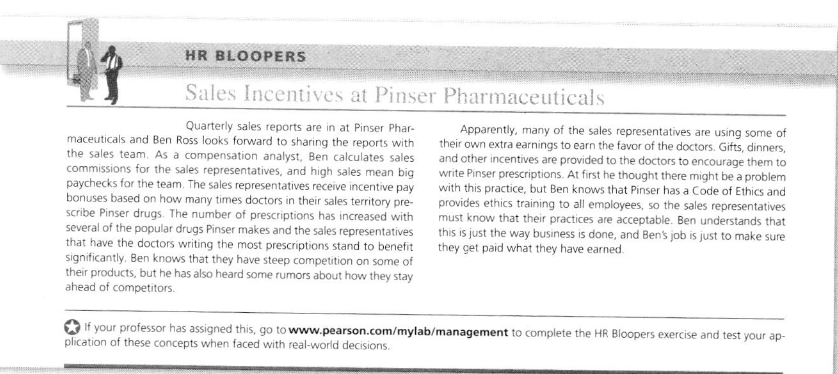

HR BLOOPERS

Sales Incentives at Pinser Pharmaceuticals

Quarterly sales reports are in at Pinser Pharmaceuticals and Ben Ross looks forward to sharing the reports with the sales team. As a compensation analyst, Ben calculates sales commissions for the sales representatives, and high sales mean big paychecks for the team. The sales representatives receive incentive pay bonuses based on how many times doctors in their sales territory prescribe Pinser drugs. The number of prescriptions has increased with several of the popular drugs Pinser makes and the sales representatives that have the doctors writing the most prescriptions stand to benefit significantly. Ben knows that they have steep competition on some of their products, but he has also heard some rumors about how they stay ahead of competitors.

Apparently, many of the sales representatives are using some of their own extra earnings to earn the favor of the doctors. Gifts, dinners, and other incentives are provided to the doctors to encourage them to write Pinser prescriptions. At first he thought there might be a problem with this practice, but Ben knows that Pinser has a Code of Ethics and provides ethics training to all employees, so the sales representatives must know that their practices are acceptable. Ben understands that this is just the way business is done, and Ben's job is just to make sure they get paid what they have earned.

If your professor has assigned this, go to **www.pearson.com/mylab/management** to complete the HR Bloopers exercise and test your application of these concepts when faced with real-world decisions.

> PREPARING FOR MY CAREER
>
> P I A Personal Inventory Assessment
>
> *An additional Personal Inventory Assessment can be found on MyLab Management.*
>
> **Ethical Leadership Assessment**
>
> Organizations need ethical leadership from all employees, but especially from managers. In this PIA, you'll see how much thought and effort goes into being ethical in your workplace behavior.

Personal Inventory Assessments

The *Personal Inventory Assessment* feature, included in most chapters, gives students the opportunity for self-assessment and personal reflection. Understanding yourself and finding your voice will help you approach situations within and outside the employment setting with greater confidence.

HRM Is Everyone's Business

As noted earlier, *HRM Is Everyone's Business* explains how HR professionals and managers throughout the organization work together to address important workplace issues. This feature highlights some of the specific connections between managers and HR professionals, and the reality that HR activities are never performed in isolation.

> HRM Is Everyone's Business
>
> In Chapter 5, we explained the role of HR professionals and managers in the recruitment process. Together, identified the best approaches to building a pool of qualified candidates. Now, it's time to make selection (hiring) decisions. Successful selection decisions are based on the collaboration between HR professionals and hiring managers who bring complementary expertise and perspectives to the task. HR professionals are experts on every aspect of the selection process (e.g., reliability and validity), and hiring managers are most well-acquainted with their staffing needs.
>
> **Action checklist for managers and HR—understanding and applying selection concepts and methods**
>
> **HR takes the lead**
>
> - ☑ Review the appropriate guidelines for evaluating applications and résumés. Communicate what should and should not be considered. For example, some people list birthdate or marital status on their résumés and this information should never be considered when formulating interview questions or making the selection decision.
> - ☑ Discuss whether testing will add useful information for making more accurate selection decisions.
> - ☑ Review the guidelines for conducting effective interviews and coordinate the types of interview questions that will be asked by HR and the questions that will be asked by managers.
> - ☑ HR professionals conduct background checks.
> - ☑ HR professionals share their evaluations of the job candidates, and inform managers whether the results of the background check warrant further consideration.
>
> **Managers take the lead**
>
> - ☑ Review the top candidates with HR after prescreening applications and résumés.
> - ☑ If testing is considered relevant, explain the minimum performance standards expected of successful employees.
> - ☑ Share interview questions with HR to ensure job-relatedness.
> - ☑ Consider all the job-related information and discuss whether a job offer should be made.

> HRM by the Numbers
>
> **Detecting Adverse Impact**
>
> *An additional HRM by the Numbers exercise can be found on MyLab Management.*
>
> Adverse impact *usually* takes place when an employment decision, practice, or policy has a disproportionately negative effect on a protected group. HR professionals rely on the "four-fifths" or "80 percent" rule to judge whether adverse impact may have occurred. Consider the situation for men and for women:

Sex	*Total Applicants*	*Selected Applicants*	*Selection Rate*
Female	750	375	
Male	1,050	450	
Total	1,800	825	

> **3-18.** Calculate (a) the selection rate for females and (b) the selection rate for males.
> **3-19.** What is the ratio of the female selection rate to the male selection rate?
> **3-20.** Based on your answer to question 3-19, is there evidence of possible adverse impact?

HRM By The Numbers Exercises

As noted earlier, *HRM by the Numbers* provides an excellent opportunity to sharpen problem solving skills through the analysis of numerical data, creating the foundation for quantifying HRM concepts and practices. There are two data-driven exercises per chapter, one in the book and both in MyLab Management. Answers are found in the Instructor's Manual and in MyLab Management.

Working Together Exercise

As noted earlier, *Working Together* offers opportunities for students to collaborate through sharing ideas, listening to others' ideas, and coming up with a cohesive team response to the assignment. If assigned by the instructor, students may make brief oral presentations of their ideas to the class, creating an additional opportunity for working together.

Assisted Graded Writing Questions

These are short essay questions which the students can complete as an assignment and submit to you, the professor for grading.

MyLab Management

Reach every student with MyLab

MyLab is the teaching and learning platform that empowers you to reach *every* student. By combining trusted author content with digital tools and a flexible platform, MyLab personalizes the learning experience and improves results for each student. Learn more at MyLab Management.

Deliver trusted content

You deserve teaching materials that meet your own high standards for your course. That's why we partner with highly respected authors to develop interactive content and course-specific resources that you can trust — and that keep your students engaged.

Empower each learner

Each student learns at a different pace. Personalized learning pinpoints the precise areas where each student needs practice, giving all students the support they need — when and where they need it — to be successful.

Teach your course your way

Your course is unique. So whether you'd like to build your own assignments, teach multiple sections, or set prerequisites, MyLab gives you the flexibility to easily create *your* course to fit *your* needs.

Improve student results

When you teach with MyLab, student performance improves. That's why instructors have chosen MyLab for over 15 years, touching the lives of over 50 million students. Learn more.

Developing Employability Skills

For students to succeed in a rapidly changing job market, they should be aware of their career options and how to go about developing a variety of skills. In this book and MyLab, I focus on developing these skills in the following ways: In this course, and, specifically in this text, students will have the opportunity to develop and practice seven important skills based on various learning features that are summarized in the matrix and subsequently illustrating some of the connections between the employability skills and learning features:

	Communication	Critical Thinking	Collaboration	Knowledge Application and Analysis	Business Ethics and Social Responsibility	Information Technology and Computing Skills	Data Literacy
FYI				✓			✓
Watch It!		✓		✓			
Try It! Simulation	✓	✓		✓	✓		
HR Bloopers		✓	✓	✓	✓		
Chapter Review		✓		✓			
Personal Inventory Assessment			✓	✓			
Ethics Dilemma		✓		✓	✓		
HRM Is Everyone's Business	✓		✓	✓			
HRM by the Numbers		✓		✓		✓	✓
Working Together	✓		✓	✓			
Case Incident 1		✓		✓	✓		
Case Incident 2		✓		✓	✓		

Instructor Teaching Resources

Human Resource Management comes with the following teaching resources.

Supplements available to instructors at www.pearsonhighered.com/	Features of the Supplement
Instructor's Manual	• Chapter-by-chapter summaries • Examples and activities not in the main book • Teaching outlines • Solutions to all questions and problems in the book
Test Bank	More than 2,000 multiple-choice, true/false, and short-answer questions with these annotations: • Difficulty level (1 for easy, 2 for moderate, 3 for difficult) • Type (Multiple-choice, true/false, short-answer, essay • Topic (The term or concept the question supports) • Learning outcome • AACSB learning standard (Written and Oral Communication, Ethical Understanding and Reasoning; Analytical Thinking; Information Technology; Diverse and Multicultural Work; Reflective Thinking; Application of Knowledge; Interpersonal Relations and Teamwork)
Computerized TestGen	TestGen allows instructors to: • Customize, save, and generate classroom tests • Edit, add, or delete questions from the Test Item Files • Analyze test results • Organize a database of tests and student results.
PowerPoints	Slides include many of the figures and table in the textbook PowerPoints meet accessibility standards for students with disabilities. Features include, but not limited to: • Keyboard and Screen Reader access • Alternative text for images • High color contrast between background and foreground colors

Acknowledgments

I wish to give a special thank you to R. Wayne Mondy whose dedication and expertise in the first 14 editions have positively impacted thousands of students' educational experiences. I am thrilled and honored to carry the torch forward in pursuit of doing the same for thousands more.

At Pearson, I wish to thank my editor, Dan Tylman, who provided excellent insights throughout the preparation of this edition. Many others at Pearson provided excellent advice throughout the process and project management oversight, including Yasmita Hota, Ashley Santora, Melissa Feimer, and Stephanie Wall. At SPi Global, I thank Raja Natesan and Nicole Suddeth. In addition, student feedback has made this book an invaluable resource. Finally, the support and encouragement of many practicing HRM professionals and faculty members has helped to make this book possible.

About Joseph J. Martocchio

My interest in the human resource management field began while I was a junior at Babson College. I found myself wanting to practice in the field as well as to become a university professor and researcher. I pursued both professional desires starting with employment at Cameron and Colby (a reinsurance company) in Boston and General Electric's Aerospace business group in Valley Forge, Pennsylvania.

I advanced my education in the human resource management (HRM) field by earning a master's degree and Ph.D. degree at Michigan State University. My master's degree enabled me to build an even stronger foundation in practice and my doctoral degree provided me with the skills to conduct scholarly research and teach college-level courses. Since earning my graduate degrees, I have been a professor in the School of Labor and Employment Relations at the University of Illinois, Urbana–Champaign and assumed administrative roles as a Provost Fellow, Associate Dean for Academic Affairs, and Interim Dean. All the while, I have taught a variety of courses in the HRM field. These include compensation systems, employee benefits, employment systems (HRM and labor relations), HR planning and staffing, and statistics. I also teach the compensation and statistics courses online. For many years, I served as the faculty advisor to the student chapter of the Society for Human Resource Management at the University of Illinois during which time students earned Merit Awards and Superior Merit awards on multiple occasions.

As a researcher, I have studied a variety of topics that include employee absenteeism, employee training and development, compensation systems, employee benefits, and generational diversity. My work appears in leading scholarly journals such as *Academy of Management Journal*, *Academy of Management Review*, *Journal of Applied Psychology*, *Journal of Management*, and *Personnel Psychology*. I received the Ernest J. McCormick Award for Distinguished Early Career Contributions from the Society for Industrial and Organizational Psychology (SIOP), and I was subsequently elected as a Fellow in both the American Psychological Association and SIOP. Following the attainment of this recognition, I served as the Chair of the HR Division of the Academy of Management as well as in various other leadership roles within that organization.

Besides writing scholarly articles and *Human Resource Management*, I have two sole-authored textbooks: *Strategic Compensation: A Human Resource Management Approach* (Pearson Higher Education), which is in its 9th edition, and *Employee Benefits: A Primer for Human Resource Professionals* (McGraw-Hill), which is in its 6th edition.

Part One
Setting the Stage

Chapter 1
Human Resource Management: An Overview

Chapter 2
Business Ethics, Corporate Social Responsibility, and Sustainability

Chapter 3
Equal Employment Opportunity, Affirmative Action, and Workforce Diversity

1

Human Resource Management: An Overview

LEARNING OBJECTIVES After completing this chapter, students should be able to:

1.1 Define human resource management (HRM) and the importance of studying it.

1.2 Describe who performs HRM.

1.3 Explain how the HRM function serves as a strategic business partner and the elements of the dynamic HRM environment.

1.4 Discuss the role of HRM in building corporate culture and employer branding.

1.5 Summarize HRM issues for small businesses.

1.6 Identify ways that country culture influences global business.

1.7 Explore essential skills for developing your career in HR or any other career path.

MyLab Management

Improve Your Grade!

If your professor is using MyLab Management, visit **www.pearson.com/mylab/management** for videos, simulations, and writing exercises.

Learn It

If your professor has chosen to assign this, go to **www.pearson.com/mylab/management** to see what you should particularly focus on and to take the Chapter 1 Warm-Up.

Like many students, you've probably had a job (or two) at some time or another while working on your degree. Your work experiences are likely to have been influenced by the knowledge and skills of a human resource (HR) manager and your manager. Both HR professionals and managers work together to recruit and hire the right individuals as well as evaluating and rewarding job performance. This textbook is about the important work that HR managers accomplish and how they work with managers and employees to promote a mutually beneficial employment experience. Mutually beneficial employment experiences can be described by goal-directed managers who create a positive environment for you to achieve exemplary job performance, which, together with other employees, will help the company meet its strategic objectives.

This chapter will enable you to describe and understand the human resource management function and why it is worthwhile to study it. In the sections that follow, we introduce you to the functions that make up human resource management (HRM) and identify who is responsible for managing it. Next, we discuss HRM as a strategic business partner and the dynamic role of the environment that influences HRM practice, followed by considering the role of HRM in building corporate culture and employer branding. Then, we turn our attention to HRM in small businesses and the influence of country culture on global business. Finally, we explore essential skills for developing your career in HR or any other career path.

1.1 Define human resource management (HRM) and the importance of studying it.

Human Resource Management: What It is and Why It is Important

human resource management (HRM)
Utilization of individuals to achieve organizational objectives.

Human resource management (HRM) is the use of individuals to achieve organizational objectives. Basically, all managers get things done through the efforts of others. Consequently, managers at every level must concern themselves with HRM. Individuals dealing with human resource matters face a multitude of challenges, ranging from a constantly changing workforce to ever-present government regulations, a technological revolution, and the economy of the United States and the world. Furthermore, global competition has forced both large and small organizations to

be more conscious of costs and productivity. Because of the critical nature of human resource issues, these matters must receive major attention from upper management.

Why Study HRM?

Many of you plan to seek a career in HRM; others do not. Even if you don't, HRM is everyone's business. Why should you care about studying HRM if you plan to work in accounting, finance, marketing, operations, or starting your own business? Here are two things to consider. First, understanding HRM will give you a solid foundation for understanding your rights and responsibilities as an employee. For instance, you will be more informed about whether the employer is evaluating your performance relative to other employees' performance or on an absolute standard. Knowing about the Fair Labor Standards Act primes an understanding about whether you qualify for overtime pay. The list goes on and on. Just read the book!

Second, at some point in the future, you will probably have the opportunity to supervise employees or lead a department. When you do, you will need to have the most qualified employees on your team; and, you will want to ensure that they are achieving exemplary performance by providing regular feedback and rewarding excellence. Also, when employees are not performing to standard, you will be responsible for identifying strategies for improvement, perhaps by recommending participation in a training program or two, or deciding to terminate employment. You will seek guidance from HR professionals and they will work with you to use appropriate methods to recruit, select, evaluate, and reward employees. In the end, success in your career will not only depend on your expertise, but also on having good employees.

Human Resource Management Functions

People who manage HRM develop and work through an integrated HRM system. As Figure 1-1 shows, six functional areas are associated with effective HRM: staffing, human resource development, performance management, compensation, safety and health, and employee and labor relations. These functions are discussed next.

staffing
Process through which an organization ensures that it always has the proper number of employees with the appropriate skills in the right jobs, at the right time, to achieve organizational objectives.

STAFFING **Staffing** is the process through which an organization ensures that it always has the proper number of employees with the appropriate skills in the right jobs, at the right time, to achieve organizational objectives. Staffing involves job analysis, human resource planning, recruitment, and selection, all of which are discussed in this text.[1]

Job analysis is the systematic process of determining the skills, duties, and knowledge required for performing jobs in an organization. It impacts virtually every aspect of HRM, including planning, recruitment, and selection. *Human resource planning* is the systematic process of

FIGURE 1-1
Human Resource Management Functions

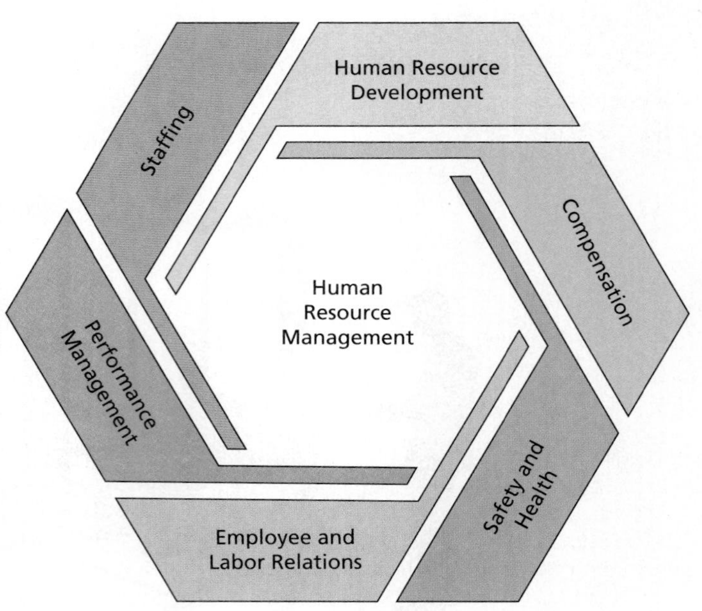

matching the internal and external supply of people with job openings anticipated in the organization over a specified period. The data provided set the stage for recruitment or other HR actions. *Recruitment* is the process of attracting individuals on a timely basis, in sufficient numbers, and with appropriate qualifications to apply for jobs with an organization. *Selection* is the process of choosing the individual best suited for a position and the organization from a group of applicants. Successful accomplishment of the staffing function is vital if the organization is to effectively accomplish its mission. These topics are collectively often referred to as staffing.

performance management (PM)
Goal-oriented process directed toward ensuring that organizational processes are in place to maximize the productivity of employees, teams, and ultimately, the organization.

PERFORMANCE MANAGEMENT **Performance management (PM)** is a goal-oriented process that is directed toward ensuring that organizational processes are in place to maximize the productivity of employees, teams, and ultimately, the organization. *Performance appraisal* is a formal system of review and evaluation of individual or team task performance. It affords employees the opportunity to capitalize on their strengths and overcome identified deficiencies, thereby helping them to become more satisfied and productive employees.

human resource development (HRD)
Major HRM functions consisting not only of training and development but also of individual career planning and development activities, organization development, and performance management and appraisal.

HUMAN RESOURCE DEVELOPMENT **Human resource development (HRD)** is a major HRM function consisting not only of training and development but also of career planning and development activities, organization development, and performance management and appraisal. *Training* is designed to provide learners with the knowledge and skills needed for their present jobs. *Development* involves learning that goes beyond today's job and has a more long-term focus.

Organization development (OD) is planned and systematic attempts to change the organization (corporate culture), typically to a more behavioral environment. OD applies to an entire system, such as a company or a plant. Numerous OD methods are discussed that serve to improve a firm's performance.

Career planning is an ongoing process whereby an individual sets career goals and identifies the means to achieve them. According to the U.S. Bureau of Labor Statistics, today's employees will work for approximately 7 to 10 companies during their careers based on the assumption that most people will work 30 to 40 years.[2] A survey conducted by LinkedIn revealed that on average, individuals under the age of 32 change jobs four times.[3] Employee loyalty loses its meaning in this environment.

Career development is a formal approach used by the organization to ensure that people with the proper qualifications and experiences are available when needed. Individual careers and organizational needs are not separate and distinct. Organizations should assist employees in career planning so the needs of both can be satisfied.

COMPENSATION The question of what constitutes a fair day's pay has plagued management, unions, and workers for a long time. A well-thought-out compensation system provides employees with adequate and equitable rewards for their contributions to meeting organizational goals. As used in this book, the term *compensation* includes the total of all rewards provided to employees in return for their services. The rewards may be one or a combination of the following:

direct financial compensation (monetary compensation)
Pay that a person receives in the form of wages, salary, commissions, and bonuses.

indirect financial compensation (employee benefits)
All financial rewards that are not included in direct financial compensation.

non-financial compensation
Satisfaction that a person receives from the job itself or from the psychological and/or physical environment in which the person works.

- **Direct Financial Compensation (Monetary Compensation)**: Pay that a person receives in the form of wages, salaries, commissions, and bonuses.
- **Indirect Financial Compensation (Employee Benefits)**: All financial rewards that are not included in direct compensation, such as paid vacations, sick leave, holidays, and medical insurance.
- **Non-financial Compensation**: Satisfaction that a person receives from the job itself or from the psychological or physical environment in which the person works.[4]

EMPLOYEE AND LABOR RELATIONS Businesses are required by law to recognize a union and bargain with it in good faith if the firm's employees want the union to represent them. In the past, this relationship was an accepted way of life for many employers, but most firms today would rather have a union-free environment. As a starting point, union wages and benefits are on average 54 percent higher than nonunion wages and benefits.[5] When a labor union represents a firm's employees, the human resource activity is often referred to as labor relations, which handles the job of collective bargaining (i.e., negotiating employment terms such as work hours). Internal employee relations comprise the HRM activities associated with the movement of employees within the organization such as promotions, demotion, termination, and resignation.

safety
Protection of employees from injuries caused by work-related accidents.

health
Employees' freedom from physical or emotional illness.

SAFETY AND HEALTH **Safety** involves protecting employees from injuries caused by work-related accidents. **Health** refers to the employees' freedom from physical or emotional illness. These aspects of the job are important because employees who work in a safe environment and enjoy good health are more likely to be productive and yield long-term benefits to the organization. For instance, one survey showed that the injury rate in highly productive organizations was 18 times lower than in average performing companies and 60 percent lower than in less productive organizations.[6] Today, because of federal and state legislation that reflect societal concerns, most organizations have become attentive to their employees' safety and health needs.

HUMAN RESOURCE DATA ANALYTICS Although human resource data analytics is not a traditional HRM function, it pervades all functional areas. Analyzing employment data (e.g., employee productivity) and business outcomes (e.g., profits) has empowered HR professionals to quantify its influence. In 2016, 51 percent of companies correlated business outcomes with HR programs, which is up from 38 percent just one year earlier.[7] Data analytics go a long way toward establishing the HRM function as a strategic business partner.

The scope of data analytics is growing rapidly. No longer do HR professionals limit analyses to internal data. Nowadays, they leverage technology, which has given unfettered access to external data. (We discuss the available technology as part of the dynamic HRM environment later in this chapter.) Internally, research on job safety may identify the causes of certain work-related accidents. The reasons for problems such as excessive absenteeism or excessive grievances may not be clear. However, when such problems occur, HR analytics can help HR professionals find the causes and offer possible solutions. Externally, data gathered through social media outlets, demographic information, hiring patterns, and turnover can help HR professionals develop strategies for attracting top talent.[8]

HR professionals should not rely exclusively on data analytics for making decisions. Because data, no matter how comprehensive or well analyzed, needs to be tempered by good judgment. For instance, a recent government report states: "Companies should remember that while big data is very good at detecting correlations, it does not explain which correlations are meaningful."[9] For example, researchers have generally established a correlation between pay and turnover (lower pay rates are associated with higher turnover rates). However, it certainly is not the case that every person with low pay will leave the company. Some may stay because they have supportive managers or commute times are short. When making decisions, it is important to remember that correlation does not equate with cause and effect.

INTERRELATIONSHIPS OF HUMAN RESOURCE MANAGEMENT FUNCTIONS All HRM functional areas are highly interrelated. Management must recognize that decisions in one area will affect other areas. For instance, a firm that emphasizes recruiting top-quality candidates but neglects to provide satisfactory compensation is wasting time, effort, and money. If a firm's compensation system pays below-market wages, the firm will always be hiring and training new employees only to see the best leave for a competitor's higher wages. For instance, Walmart raised the starting pay rate for store associates to $9 per hour. Walmart executives reasoned that raising pay is a good business decision because it should promote better customer service, higher sales, and lower expenses.[10] The interrelationships among the HRM functional areas will become more obvious as these topics are addressed throughout the book.

1.2 Describe who performs HRM activities

Who Performs Human Resource Management Activities?

The person or units who perform the HRM tasks have changed dramatically in recent years, and today there is no typical HR department. Many of these changes are being made so that HR professionals can accomplish a more strategic role. Still, most organizations continue to perform most HR functions within the firm. However, as companies reexamine internal operations, questions are raised, such as: Can some HR tasks be performed more efficiently by line managers or outside vendors? Can some HR tasks be centralized or eliminated altogether? Can technology improve the productivity of HR professionals? One apparent fact is that all functions within today's organizations are being scrutinized for cost cutting, including HR. All units must operate under a lean budget in this competitive global environment, and HR is no exception.

Evidence provided by The Hackett Group shows that the HR functions have been impacted more than other functions with regard to reductions in staff and operating budgets.[11] In fact, the most efficient companies typically spend nearly 30 percent less per employee on HR and operate with 25 percent fewer HR employees.[12] Mobile HR has been a major factor in this trend as we discuss later in the chapter. Also, many HR departments continue to get smaller because others outside the HR department now perform certain functions. For instance, HR outsourcing, shared service centers, professional employer organizations, and line managers now assist in the accomplishment of many traditional HR activities.

Human Resource Management Professional

human resource management professional
Individual who normally acts in an advisory or staff capacity, working with other professionals to help them deal with human resource matters.

Historically, the HR manager was responsible for each of the six HR functions. A **human resource management professional** is an individual who normally acts in an advisory or staff capacity, working with other managers to help them address human resource matters. Often, HR departments are created, with the central figure being the HR manager or executive. The HRM professional is primarily responsible for coordinating the management of HR to help the organization achieve its goals. We say more about the work of HR professionals later in the chapter before looking at HRM as a strategic business partner. In the meantime, Figure 1-2 displays a summary of a typical human resource professional's job along with their usual duties. The typical tasks performed by these professionals.

Line Managers

line managers
Individuals directly involved in accomplishing the primary purpose of the organization.

All managers get things done through the efforts of others. Consequently, managers at every level naturally concern themselves with HRM, for example, making decisions about which job candidates are likely to meet the needs of company, conducting employee performance evaluations, and determining pay raise amounts. Individuals directly involved in accomplishing the primary purpose of the organization are **line managers**. As the traditional work of HR managers evolves, line managers have assumed some tasks typically done by HR professionals.[13] Automation has assisted greatly in this process. Managers are being assisted by manager self-service, the use of software, and the corporate network to automate paper-based human resource processes that require a manager's approval, recordkeeping or input, and processes that support the manager's job. Everything from recruitment, selection, and performance appraisal to employee development has been automated to assist line managers in performing traditional HR tasks.

FIGURE 1-2
Human Resource Professional Job Description

Source: National Center for O*NET Development. 11-3121.00. *O*NET OnLine*. Retrieved January 2, 2017, from http://www.onetonline.org/link/summary/11-3121.00

Plan, direct, or coordinate HR activities and staff of an organization.
Sample of reported job titles: Human Resources Manager (HR Manager), Director of Human Resources, Human Resources Director (HR Director), Employee Benefits Manager, Human Resources Vice President, Employee Relations Manager

Tasks

- Serve as a link between management and employees by handling questions, interpreting and administering contracts, and helping resolve work-related problems.
- Analyze and modify compensation and benefits policies to establish competitive programs and ensure compliance with legal requirements.
- Advise managers on organizational policy matters such as equal employment opportunity and sexual harassment, and recommend needed changes.
- Perform difficult staffing duties, including dealing with understaffing, refereeing disputes, firing employees, and administering disciplinary procedures.
- Plan and conduct new employee orientation to foster a positive attitude toward organizational objectives.
- Identify staff vacancies and recruit, interview, and select applicants.
- Plan, direct, supervise, and coordinate work activities of subordinates and staff relating to employment, compensation, labor relations, and employee relations.
- Plan, organize, direct, control, or coordinate the personnel, training, or labor relations activities of an organization.
- Represent organization at personnel-related hearings and investigations.
- Administer compensation, benefits and performance management systems, and safety and recreation programs.

There is a shared responsibility between line managers and HR professionals. Frequently, the line manager looks to HR for guidance in topics such as selection, training, promotion, and taking disciplinary action. The relationship between HR professionals and line managers is illustrated by the following account:

Bill Brown, the production supervisor for Ajax Manufacturing, has just learned that one of his machine operators has resigned. He immediately calls Sandra Williams, the HR manager, and says, "Sandra, I just had a Class A machine operator quit down here. Can you find some qualified people for me to interview?" "Sure Bill," Sandra replies. "I'll send two or three down to you within the week, and you can select the one that best fits your needs."

In this instance, both Bill and Sandra are concerned with accomplishing organizational goals, but from different perspectives. As an HR manager, Sandra identifies applicants who meet the criteria specified by Bill. Yet, Bill will make the final decision about hiring because he is responsible for the machine operators' performance. His primary responsibility is production; hers is human resources. As an HR manager, Sandra must constantly deal with the many problems related to HR that Bill and the other managers face. Her job is to help them meet the human HR needs of the entire organization.

FYI

- The HR outsourcing industry in 2020 is expected to generate $53.9 billion in revenue, up from $42.6 billion in 2015.[14]
- The industry's expected future annual global growth is nearly 13 percent.[15]

Human Resources Outsourcing

HR outsourcing (HRO)
Process of hiring external HR professionals to do the HR work that was previously done internally.

HR outsourcing (HRO) is the process of hiring external HR professionals to do the HR work that was previously done internally. In the early days of HRO, cost savings was the primary driver in determining which activities to outsource. Today, outsourcing agreements are focusing more on quality of service and saving time, which is often more important than saving money.[16] In addition, HRO enables HR to serve as strategic business partners. Paul Belliveau, global advisor at Avance Human Capital Management Advisors, said "Fundamentally, this is about the transformation of HR. Wherever there's transformation, you have to take away things HR shouldn't be doing anymore so they can be more strategic."[17] As will be stressed throughout the text, strategic HR has become a major driver for HR professionals.[18]

Discrete services outsourcing involves one element of a business process or a single set of high-volume repetitive functions to be outsourced.[19] Benefits have often been the HR task most likely to be outsourced. Dan Thomas, president of Trivalent Benefits Consulting Inc., said, "Benefits administration has become so complex that it really takes someone who works with it every single day to keep track of all of the different laws and changes that are going on."[20] For example, a survey conducted by The Prudential Financial and CFO research revealed that the complexity of employee benefits regulation has prompted companies to outsource or consider outsourcing parts of their benefits function: 46 percent (Affordable Care Act), 40 percent (Americans with Disabilities Act), and 38 percent (Family and Medical Leave Act).[21]

Business process outsourcing (BPO) is the transfer of the majority of HR services to a third party. Typically, larger companies are involved with BPO, both as a provider and a user. A major HR outsourcer is Accenture that has more than $32 billion in revenue.[22] For instance, Levi Strauss & Company signed a multiyear BPO agreement in which Accenture took over recruitment and hiring for all of Levi Strauss' 55,000 retail outlets in more than 110 countries.[23] Florida created a Web-based HR information system and outsourced administration of most HR functions for approximately 240,000 state employees and retirees. Outsourced services included recruiting, payroll, and HR administration services and benefits administration.[24]

Human Resources Shared Service Centers

shared service center (SSC)
A center that takes routine, transaction-based activities dispersed throughout the organization and consolidates them in one place.

A **shared service center (SSC)**, also known as a center of expertise, takes routine, transaction-based activities dispersed throughout the organization and consolidates them in one place. For example, a company with 20 strategic business units might consolidate routine HR tasks and perform them in one location. Shared service centers provide an alternative to HRO and can often provide the same cost savings and customer service. Fewer HR professionals are needed when shared service centers are used, resulting in significant cost savings. The most common HR functions that use SSCs are benefits and pension administration, payroll, relocation assistance and recruitment support, global training and development, succession planning, and talent retention.

Professional Employer Organizations

professional employer organization (PEO)
A company that leases employees to other businesses.

A **professional employer organization (PEO)** is a company that leases employees to other businesses. When a decision is made to use a PEO, the company releases its employees, who are then hired by the PEO. The PEO then manages the administrative needs associated with employees. It is the PEO that pays the employees' salaries; it also pays workers' compensation premiums, payroll-related taxes, and employee benefits. The PEO is responsible to the Internal Revenue Service (IRS) if, for example, the payroll taxes go unpaid. The company reimburses the PEO, which typically charges a fee of from 2 to 7 percent of the customer's gross wages, with percentages based on the number of leased employees. Because the PEO is the employees' legal employer it has the right to hire, fire, discipline, and reassign an employee. However, the client company maintains enough control so it can run the day-to-day operations of its business. Although PEOs have been available since the early 1980s, they have recently become a multi-billion dollar industry. The industry size is valued between $136 billion and $156 billion.[25] In fact, there is an estimated two to three million U.S. workers employed under a PEO-type arrangement, and that number is certain to grow.[26] PEOs permit business owners to focus on their core business, whereas the PEO handles HR activities.[27] Companies using a PEO typically have a high level of benefits and greater HR expertise than they could possibly have had on their own.

More about HR Professionals

executive
A top-level manager who reports directly to a corporation's chief executive officer or to the head of a major division.

generalist
A person who may be an executive and performs tasks in a variety of HR-related areas.

specialist
An individual who may be a human resource executive, a human resource manager, or a nonmanager, and who is typically concerned with only one of the six functional areas of human resource management.

Various designations are used within the HR profession; among these are HR executives, generalists, and specialists. An **executive** is a top-level manager who reports directly to the corporation's chief executive officer (CEO) or to the head of a major division. A **generalist**, who may be an executive, performs tasks in a variety of HR-related areas. The generalist is involved in several, or all, of the six HRM functions. A **specialist** may be an HR executive, manager, or nonmanager who is typically concerned with only one of the six functional areas of HRM. Figure 1-3 helps clarify these distinctions.

The vice president of industrial relations, shown in Figure 1-3, specializes primarily in union-related matters. This person is both an executive and a specialist. An HR vice president is both an executive and a generalist, having responsibility for a wide variety of functions. The compensation manager is a specialist, as is the benefits analyst. Whereas a position level in the organization identifies an executive, the breadth of such positions distinguishes generalists and specialists.

HR BLOOPERS

Staffing Stone Consulting

Business at Stone Consulting is growing faster than Shelly Stone expected. She just signed a contract on another big project that she believes secures her future in the consulting business.

However, she has been so busy selling the firm's services that she has put little thought into how she is going to staff the projects she has recently sold. She opened the firm more than a year ago and quickly hired five consultants and an office manager to help her get the business off the ground.

Unfortunately, one of the consultants has already left the firm after making a huge mistake that caused Shelly to lose a client. Some of the other consultants have raised some concerns with Shelly as well. They've asked about pay increases and also her promise to eventually provide them with health insurance. However, she hasn't had time to even think about these issues because she has focused her attention on finding new clients. As she looks over her project list she realizes she needs to start thinking about staffing fast. Her current team is already committed to other projects and the new projects she has secured need to get started right away. The office manager interrupts her thoughts to tell her a potential client is on the line. Excited about yet another opportunity, Shelly jumps on the call, quickly forgetting her staffing concerns.

If your professor has assigned this, go to **www.pearson.com/mylab/management** to complete the HR Bloopers exercise and test your application of these concepts when faced with real-world decisions.

FIGURE 1-3
Human Resource Executives, Generalists, and Specialists

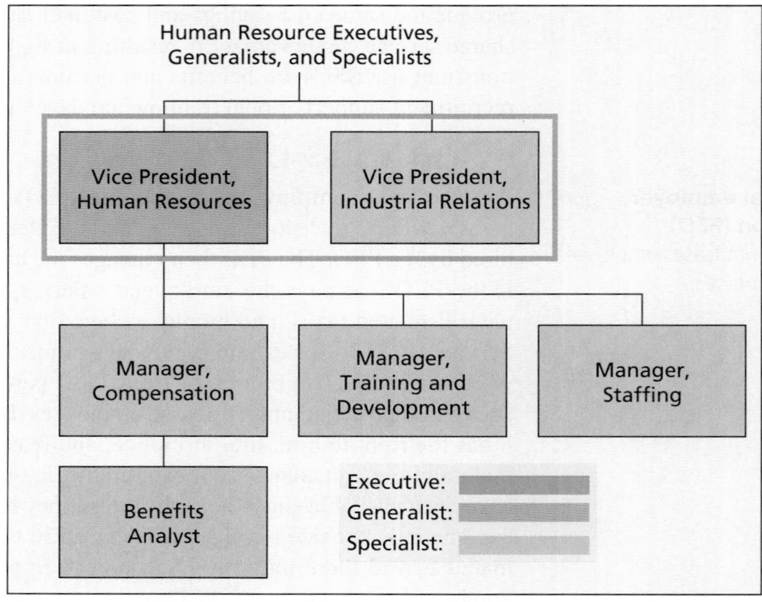

profession
Vocation characterized by the existence of a common body of knowledge and a procedure for certifying members.

A **profession** is a vocation characterized by the existence of a common body of knowledge and a procedure for certifying members. Performance standards are established by members of the profession rather than by outsiders; that is, the profession is self-regulated. Most professions also have effective representative organizations that permit members to exchange ideas of mutual concern. These characteristics apply to the field of HR, and several well-known organizations serve the profession. Among the more prominent is the Society for Human Resource Management (www.shrm.org), the Human Resource Certification Institute (www.hrci.org), the Association for Talent Development (ATD, http://www.td.org), and WorldatWork (www.worldatwork.org). The HR profession is based on a variety of competencies. Figure 1-4 lists five competencies and brief descriptions. We will see throughout this book that effective HR professionals demonstrate these competencies. For example, we will look at the advocate competency, particularly, in Chapter 2 as it applies to ethics, corporate social responsibility, and sustainability. The HR expert competency includes all of the knowledge we have already studied and to come in the remainder of this book, for example, staffing, training, and employee relations.

HR Web Wisdom
Human Resource Certification Institute (HRCI)
www.hrci.org
A Professional Certification Program in HR Management is for individuals seeking to expand their formal HR training.

Opportunities for employment in the HRM profession are growing. According to the U.S. Bureau of Labor Statistics:

> *Employment of human resources managers is projected to grow 9 percent from 2014 to 2024, faster than the average for all occupations.*
>
> *Employment growth largely depends on the performance and growth of individual companies. However, as new companies form and organizations expand their operations, they will need more human resources managers to oversee and administer their programs.*
>
> *Managers will also be needed to ensure that firms adhere to changing, complex employment laws regarding occupational safety and health, equal employment opportunity, healthcare, wages, and retirement plans. For example, adoption of the Affordable Care Act may spur the need to hire more managers to help implement this program.*
>
> *Although job opportunities are expected to vary based on the staffing needs of individual companies, very strong competition can be expected for most positions.*
>
> *Job opportunities should be best in the management of companies and enterprises industry as organizations continue to use outside firms to assist with some of their human resources functions.*
>
> *Candidates with certification or a master's degree—particularly those with a concentration in human resources management—should have the best job prospects. Those with a solid background in human resources programs, policies, and employment law should also have better job opportunities.*[28]

The median annual compensation for HR managers was $106,910, which is nearly three times the median annual earnings for all jobs. Human resource specialist median salaries ranged

FIGURE 1-4

Model of Human Resources Competencies

Source: U.S. Office of Personnel Management. Online: http://archive.opm.gov/studies/transapp.pdf. Accessed January 2, 2017.

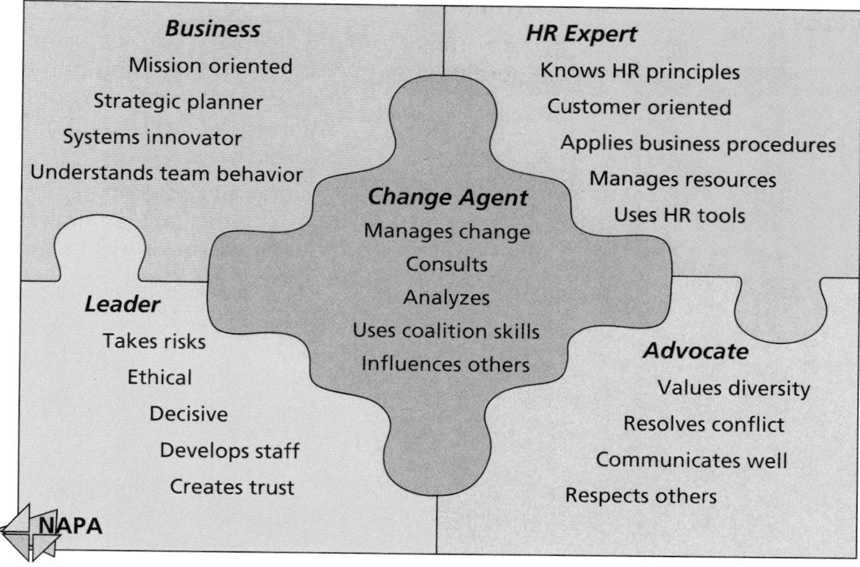

between $59,020 for training and development specialists to $116,240 for compensation and benefits managers. Figure 1-5 lists the median annual salaries for various jobs in the HRM profession. The salary levels vary on a number factors, including relevant work experience, educational credentials, and industry. For example, median annual salaries for HR managers were substantially higher in the management of companies and enterprises industry ($118,320) than in the health care and social assistance industry ($89,090).

FIGURE 1-5

HR Professional Annual Salaries

Source: U.S. Bureau of Labor Statistics, "Human Resources Managers," *Occupational Outlook Handbook, 2016–17 Edition*," Accessed January 2, 2017, at : www.bls.gov/ooh/management/human-resources-managers.htm.

Occupation	Job Duties	2016 Median Pay
Compensation and Benefits Managers	Compensation managers plan, direct, and coordinate how much an organization pays its employees and how employees are paid. Benefits managers plan, direct, and coordinate retirement plans, health insurance, and other benefits that an organization offers its employees.	$116,240
Compensation, Benefits, and Job Analysis Specialists	Compensation, benefits, and job analysis specialists help conduct an organization's compensation and benefits programs. They also evaluate job positions to determine details such as classification and salary.	$62,080
Human Resources Managers	Human resources managers plan, direct, and coordinate the administrative functions of an organization. They oversee the recruiting, interviewing, and hiring of new staff; consult with top executives on strategic planning; and serve as a link between an organization's management and its employees.	$106,910
Human Resources Specialists and Labor Relations Specialists	Human resources specialists recruit, screen, interview, and place workers. They often handle other human resources work, such as those related to employee relations, payroll and benefits, and training. Labor relations specialists interpret and administer labor contracts regarding issues such as wages and salaries, employee welfare, healthcare, pensions, and union and management practices.	$59,180

FIGURE 1-5 (Continued)

Occupation	Job Duties	2016 Median Pay
Instructional Coordinators	Instructional coordinators oversee school curriculums and teaching standards. They develop instructional material, coordinate its implementation with teachers and principals, and assess its effectiveness.	$62,460
Training and Development Specialists	Training and development specialists help plan, conduct, and administer programs that train employees and improve their skills and knowledge.	$59,020

FYI

HR is now more likely to serve on a company's board of directors or hold an executive position:

- 2014 to 2015: 66 percent
- 2004: 41 percent[29]

1.3 Explain how the HRM function serves as a strategic business partner and the elements of the dynamic HRM environment.

Human Resources as a Strategic Business Partner in a Dynamic Environment

In the environment presently confronting HR, many HR professions are increasingly taking on the role of being a strategic partner with upper management.[30] As a strategic business partner, HR professionals are able to focus on matters that are truly important to the company as a whole.[31] For example, increasing sales and building customer loyalty to the brand are important goals of soft drink companies such as Coca Cola and PepsiCo. Increasing sales require hiring highly dedicated and motivated sales and distribution employees. As a strategic business partner, HR helps to identify and develop the employees necessary for excellent performance, builds recruitment systems, training programs for product distribution and interactions with customers, constructs performance management, and structures compensation programs that will greatly incentivize these employees to excel. The rapidly evolving world of HR will increasingly require HR professionals to thoroughly understand all aspects of what the companies they work for do. Essentially, they must know more than just HR work.[32] In moving from a transactional to a strategic model, HR professionals work toward solving strategic problems in the organization. No longer is an administrative and compliance role appropriate as their primary jobs. For instance, preparing the company's affirmative action plan or administering the payroll system are compliance and administrative tasks. HR executives today need to think like the CEO to become a strategic partner in achieving organizational plans and results.[33] In doing so, they understand the production side of the business and help to determine the strategic capabilities of the company's workforce, both today and in the future. HR professionals need to be agile in their thinking as they adapt to the ebbs and flows of business. Therefore, HR executives are ensuring that human resources support the firm's mission.

HR professionals have changed the way they work. Working as a strategic business partner requires a much deeper and broader understanding of business issues.[34] What strategically should HR be doing exactly? Possible strategic tasks for HR include making workforce strategies fundamental to company strategies and goals; increasing HR's role in strategic planning, mergers, and acquisitions; developing awareness or an understanding of the business; and, helping line managers achieve their goals as in the previous example of soft drink companies.

HR professionals can give the CEO and chief financial officer (CFO) a powerful understanding of the role that employees play in the organization and the way it combines with business processes to expand or shrink shareholder value. HR professionals are integrating the goals of HR with the goals of the organization and focusing on expanding its strategic and high-level corporate participation with an emphasis on adding value. In doing so, HR is demonstrating that it can produce a return on investment for its programs. It analyzes HR activities to determine whether they are maintaining acceptable profit margins. For example, HR professionals strive to develop cost-effective training strategies that boost sales revenue that far exceeds the cost of training. The CEO needs help in matters that HR professionals are qualified to handle. HR professionals are the enablers; they are the ones who should know about change and develop strategies to make it work.

Capital and Human Capital

A useful way to better understand *how* HR serves as a strategic business partner is to think about the use of capital for value creation. **Capital** refers to the factors that enable companies to generate income, higher company stock prices, economic value, strong positive brand identity, and reputation. There is a variety of capital that companies use to create value, including financial capital (cash) and capital equipment (state-of-the-art robotics used in manufacturing).

human capital
As defined by economists, human capital refers to sets of collective skills, knowledge, and ability that employees can apply to create economic value for their employers.

Employees represent a specific type of capital called human capital. **Human capital**, as defined by economists, refers to sets of collective skills, knowledge, and ability that employees can apply to create value for their employers. Companies purchase the use of human capital by paying employees an hourly wage, salary, or bonuses and providing benefits such as paid vacation and health insurance. Also, companies help develop human capital to their advantage by offering training programs aimed at further boosting employee productivity.

The meaning of value creation differs according to a company's mission. It is useful to think about the differences between for-profit and not-for-profit organizations. For example, Microsoft and Frito Lay are for-profit companies that strive to generate annual earnings for company shareholders. These companies promote profit generation by selling quality software and quality snack products, respectively. The American Red Cross is an illustration of a not-for-profit organization that relies on charitable monetary contributions and grant money to create societal value. The people who contribute money and other resources do not seek monetary gain. Instead, they value supporting humanitarian causes such as disaster relief. The American Red Cross provides disaster relief after the occurrence of devastating events, including the wildfires in California, earthquakes in Oklahoma, and tornadoes in Florida.

Every organization relies on capital to create value, but the combination of capital used to create value differs from company to company. For example, Frito Lay uses state-of-the-art manufacturing equipment, and the American Red Cross does not. However, every organization shares in common the employment of individuals and the necessity of managing employees to successfully create value. Indeed, HRM is the business function of managing employees to facilitate an organization's efforts to create value.

Dynamic Human Resource Management Environment

Many interrelated factors affect HRM practice within and outside the organization. As illustrated in Figure 1-6, environmental factors include legal considerations, labor market, society, political parties, unions, shareholders, competition, customers, technology, the economy, and unanticipated events. Each factor, either separately or in combination with others, can create constraints or opportunities for HRM.

LEGAL CONSIDERATIONS A significant external force affecting HRM relates to federal, state, and local legislation and the many court decisions interpreting this legislation. For example, the Age Discrimination in Employment Act is an example of a federal law that protects older workers from illegal discrimination. In addition, presidential executive orders have had a major impact on HRM. Executive Order 13145 protects all qualified individuals in federal employment based on protected genetic information, or information about a request for or the receipt of genetic services. These legal considerations affect virtually the entire spectrum of human resource policies. Laws, court decisions, and executive orders affecting other HRM activities will be described in the appropriate chapters.

LABOR MARKET Potential employees located within the geographic area from which employees are normally recruited comprise the *labor market*. The capabilities of a firm's employees determine, to a large extent, how well the organization can perform its mission. Because new employees are hired from outside the firm, the labor market is considered an important environmental factor. The labor market is always changing, and these shifts inevitably cause changes in the workforce of an organization. For example, members of the aging baby boom cohort, the largest current

FIGURE 1-6
Environment of Human Resource Management

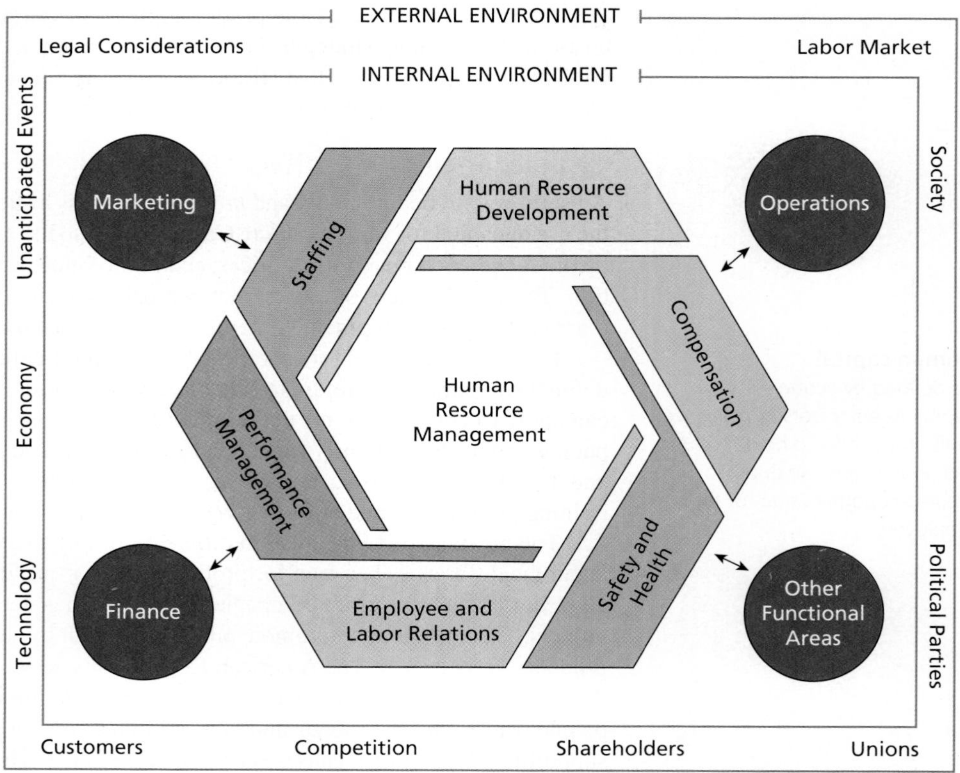

generation of employees, are retiring in large numbers; however, younger generations are smaller and less well-prepared to assume leadership roles because they have had much less time in the workforce to develop them.

SOCIETY Society may also exert pressure on HRM. The public is no longer content to accept, without question, the actions of business. To remain acceptable to the public, a firm must accomplish its purpose while complying with societal norms.

Ethics is the discipline dealing with what is good and bad, or right and wrong, or with moral duty and obligation. *Corporate social responsibility (CSR)* is closely related to ethics. CSR is the implied, enforced, or felt obligation of managers, acting in their official capacity, to serve or protect the interests of groups other than themselves.[35] We take up these subjects in Chapter 2.

POLITICAL PARTIES Closely related to society, but not the same, are political parties. The Democratic and Republican parties are the two major political parties in the United States. These parties often have differing opinions on how HRM should be accomplished. For example, Democrats tend to favor more government regulation that protects the rights of virtually all employees to receive at least a minimum wage (the Fair Labor Standards Act) and unpaid family leave (the Family and Medical Leave Act). Republicans, on the other hand, tend to favor less government regulation, believing that businesses should have as much flexibility as possible to operate profitably.

union
Consists of employees who have joined together for the purpose of negotiating terms of employment, such as wages and work hours.

UNIONS Wage levels, benefits, and working conditions for millions of employees reflect decisions made jointly by unions and management. A **union** consists of employees who have joined together for the purpose of negotiating terms of employment such as wages and work hours. The United Auto Workers is an example of a large labor union. Unions are treated as an environmental factor because, essentially, they become a third party when dealing with the company.

shareholders
Owners of a corporation.

SHAREHOLDERS The owners of a corporation are called **shareholders**. Because shareholders, or stockholders, have invested money in the firm, they may at times challenge programs considered by management to be beneficial to the organization. Stockholders are wielding increasing influence, and management may be forced to justify the merits of a program in terms of how it will affect future projects, costs, revenues, profits, and even benefits to society as a whole.[36] Considerable pressure has recently been exerted by shareholders and lawmakers to control the salaries of corporate executives as we shall see in the discussion of the Dodd-Frank Act in Chapters 2 and 9.[37]

COMPETITION Firms may face intense global competition for both their product or service and labor markets. Unless an organization is in the unusual position of monopolizing the market it serves, other firms will be producing similar products or services. A firm must also maintain a supply of competent employees if it is to succeed, grow, and prosper. But other organizations are also striving for that same objective. A firm's major task is to ensure that it obtains and retains a sufficient number of employees in various career fields to allow it to compete effectively. A bidding war often results when competitors attempt to fill certain critical positions in their firms. Even in a depressed economy, firms find creative ways to recruit and retain such employees. For example, a company may offer a signing bonus (that is, a one-time monetary payment) to offset lower pay.

CUSTOMERS The people who use a firm's goods and services also are part of its external environment. Because sales are crucial to the firm's survival, management has the task of ensuring that its employment practices provide excellent customer support service. Customers constantly demand high-quality products and after-purchase service. Therefore, a firm's workforce should provide top-quality goods and after-sale customer support. These conditions relate directly to the skills, qualifications, and motivations of the organization's employees.

FYI

- In a survey of HR professionals, 36 percent have disqualified a job candidate because of troubling information discovered on a public social media profile.[38]

HR TECHNOLOGY The rate of technological change is staggering. The development of technology has created new roles for HR professionals but also places additional pressures on them to keep abreast of the technology. As noted earlier, leveraging technology can help HR professionals to consider both internal and external data to aid in decision making. We will briefly review three applications: human resource information systems, cloud computing, and social media.

human resource information system (HRIS)
Any organized approach for obtaining relevant and timely information on which to base HR decisions.

With the increased technology sophistication has come the ability to design a more useful **human resource information system (HRIS)**, which is any organized approach for obtaining relevant and timely information on which to base HR decisions. The HRIS brings under one encompassing technology system many human resource activities. Think of an HRIS as an umbrella for merging the various subsystems discussed throughout this text. Today, mainstay HR responsibilities such as planning, recruitment, selection, oversight of legal and regulatory compliance, benefits administration, and the safeguarding of confidential employee information cannot be carried out effectively without an HRIS. Throughout the text, topics will be highlighted that are part of an HRIS. In addition, all of the HRIS applications may be accessed through cloud computing.

A rapidly developing trend is the increased mobility of tasks performed by HR professionals.[39] A major factor contributing to HR mobility is *cloud computing*, a means of providing software and data via the Internet. Cloud computing and the use of mobile devices are changing the way HR work is performed, and the change is moving at an amazing pace.[40] With the cloud there is no more expensive, capital-intensive hardware and infrastructure and no more expensive, time-consuming, staff-intensive upgrades.[41] Cloud computing permits businesses to buy and use what they need, when they need it. It allows large organizations to move away from managing their own computer centers and focus on the core competencies of the firm. Cloud users can access the application securely from anywhere in the world.[42] HR professionals can be virtually anywhere and access the cloud, all through any standard Web.

HR departments are leveraging the increasing popularity of *social media*, including LinkedIn, Facebook, YouTube, and Twitter. In a 2015 Society for Human Resource Management survey, HR professionals revealed that social networking is an important tool for recruiting passive and active applicants. Most respondents, 84 percent, say that their organizations currently use social media and 9 percent plan to use it.[43] There are two additional applications of social media. First, companies may use social media to promote knowledge sharing as well as training and development. Second, social media is often used to reinforce identification with the organization and promoting the brand.

ECONOMY The economy of the nation and world is a major environmental factor affecting HRM. As a generalization, when the economy is booming, it is more difficult to recruit qualified workers. On the other hand, when a downturn is experienced, more applicants are typically available. To complicate this situation even further, one segment of the country may be experiencing an economic downturn, another a slow recovery, and another a boom. A major challenge facing HR is working within this dynamic, ever-changing economic environment because it impacts every aspect of HRM.[44]

UNANTICIPATED EVENTS Unanticipated events are occurrences in the environment that cannot be foreseen. The *Deepwater Horizon* oil spill off the Gulf Coast in 2010 caused major modifications in the performance of many HR functions. Every disaster—whether human-made or natural—likely requires a tremendous amount of adjustment with regard to HRM. For example, after Hurricane Katrina, Tulane University reduced their number of employees. On a global perspective, think of the many different ways HR was affected by the tsunami in Japan. Japanese automobile plants in the United States were forced to temporarily shut down because of a lack of parts produced in Japan. Other recent disasters, such as heat waves, earthquakes, tornadoes, floods, and fires have created their own type of difficulty.

1.4 Discuss the role of HRM in building corporate culture and employer branding.

The Role of HRM in Building Corporate Culture and Employer Branding

FYI

- A survey of more than 7,000 CEOs and HR leaders revealed that 82 percent consider culture a source of competitive advantage.[45]

corporate culture
System of shared values, beliefs, and habits within an organization that interacts with the formal structure to produce behavioral norms.

employer branding
Firm's corporate image or culture created to attract and retain the type of employees the firm is seeking.

As an internal environment factor affecting HRM, corporate culture refers to the firm's social and psychological climate. **Corporate culture** is defined as the system of shared values, beliefs, and habits within an organization that interacts with the formal structure to produce behavioral norms. Employer branding is an extension of product or business branding. **Employer branding** is the firm's corporate image or culture created to attract and retain the type of employees the firm is seeking. It is what the company stands for in the public eye.[46] Establishing a positive corporate culture and brand is another way HR professionals contribute to a company's success. We discuss corporate culture and employer branding next.

Corporate Culture

Culture gives people a sense of how to behave and what they ought to be doing. Each individual gradually forms such perceptions over a period of time as the person performs assigned activities under the general guidance of a superior and a set of organizational policies. The culture existing within a firm influences the employees' degree of satisfaction with the job as well as the level and quality of their performance. The assessment of how desirable the organization's culture is may differ for each employee. One person may perceive the environment as bad, and another may see the same environment as positive. An employee may actually leave an organization in the hope of finding a more compatible culture. Max Caldwell, a managing director at Towers Watson, said, "Maybe the best definition of company culture is what everyone does when no one is looking."[47] Topics related to corporate culture are presented throughout this text. Some corporate culture topics include the following:

- *Employer branding* is the firm's corporate image or culture created to attract and retain the type of employees the firm is seeking. It is what the company stands for in the public eye.
- *Diversity management* is about pursuing an inclusive corporate culture in which newcomers feel welcome and everyone sees the value of his or her job.
- *Organizational fit* refers to management's perception of the degree to which the prospective employee will fit in with the firm's culture or value system. A good Web site should provide a feeling of the kind of corporate culture that exists within the company.
- *New hire orientation* reflects the firm's corporate culture by showing in effect, "How we do things around here."

- *Talent management* is a strategic endeavor to optimize the use of employees and enables an organization to drive short- and long-term results by building culture, engagement, capability, and capacity through integrated talent acquisition, development, and deployment processes that are aligned to business goals.
- *Organization development* is a major means of achieving change in the corporate culture.
- Anything that the company provides an employee is included in compensation, from pay and benefits to the organization's culture and environment.
- A corporate culture that does not consider the needs of employees as individuals makes the firm ripe for unionization.
- Retaining the best employees often rests with the corporate culture that exists within the organization.
- Accident rates decline when the corporate culture encourages workers consciously or subconsciously to think about safety.
- A **country's culture** is the set of values, symbols, beliefs, languages, and norms that guide human behavior within the country. Cultural differences are often the biggest barrier to doing business in the world market. Many of the global topics discussed throughout your text are influenced by the issue of corporate culture or country culture.

country's culture
Set of values, symbols, beliefs, language, and norms that guide human behavior within the country.

Employer Branding

A colleague shared a memory about his mother, which bears directly on this subject. His mother would always buy a certain brand of canned fruit even though it was more expensive. The brand name itself caused her to buy a product that although higher priced was probably the same or similar quality as less expensive brands. The company had created a positive image that made her want to use the product. As with the canned fruit, companies want a brand that will entice individuals to join and remain with the firm.[48] HR professionals play an essential role in creating and promoting a company's brand. Effective branding communicates why the company is a cut above other workplaces by providing persuasive reasons for job seekers to choose the company over others.[49] As such, the focus on employer branding has become increasingly important for organizations. Jeffrey St. Amour, national practice leader for PricewaterhouseCoopers' HR Services strategic communication group said, "They're both trying to create the same thing, which is product loyalty or a feeling that this is a high-quality company."[50] Employer branding has become a major recruitment and retention strategy and everyone in the company works to promote the image of the firm.[51]

Brands imply what employees will get from working there and why working for the company is a career and not just a job. For example, consulting firm PwC emphasizes its commitment to career development as part of its recruitment strategy: "Every career path is different. That's why we help you design your own."[52] As more Gen-Yers enter the workforce, firms may need to alter their brand to attract and retain these young people who view having fun in an engaging work environment as important as a good salary. A well-paying job that is boring will not keep them for long. Cosmetic company L'Oréal understands this expectation. The company takes time to understand what employees value in their work experiences, and they incorporate much of these values in an employee value proposition. L'Oréal promises prospective employees a "thrilling experience" and an "environment that will inspire you."[53]

An employer brand embodies the values and standards that guide people's behavior. Through employer branding, people get to know what the company stands for, the people it hires, the fit between jobs and people, and the results it recognizes and rewards. Every company has a brand, which could be the company of choice or one of last resort. A robust employment brand attracts people and makes them want to stay. In fact, most workers want to belong to an organization that embraces the ideas and principles they share.[54] Employer branding has become a driving force to engage and retain the firm's most valuable employees.[55] As the economy prospers, firms vigorously seek talent, and, employer branding is attracting more attention.

Achieving acknowledgment by an external source is a good way for a brand to be recognized. Being listed on *Fortune* magazine's 100 Best Companies to Work For is so desirable that some organizations try to change their culture and philosophies to get on the list. Think about how being on the following lists might assist in a company's recruitment and retention programs:

- *Black Enterprise* list of Best Companies for Diversity
- *Business Ethics* magazine list of 100 Best Corporate Citizens
- *Computerworld* list of Best Places to Work

- *Forbes* magazine list of Best Companies for Work-Life Balance
- *Fortune* magazine list of 100 Fastest-Growing Companies in the United States
- *Training* magazine list of 125 Best Companies for Employee Development
- *Working Mother* list of 100 Best Companies

As the previous discussion indicates, many companies embrace creating and maintaining a positive work culture, and they recognize it is "good" business because they are better able to recruit and retain valued employees. A company named Patagonia also recognizes the benefits of a positive work culture from the perspective of employees. The following Watch It video describes Patagonia's efforts to maintain a positive work culture that emphasizes a culture of personal responsibility, flexibility, and development.

Watch It 1

If your instructor has assigned this, go to **www.pearson.com/mylab/management** to watch a video titled Patagonia: Human Resource Management and to respond to questions.

1.5 Summarize human resource management issues for small businesses.

HR Web Wisdom

U.S. Small Business Administration

www.sba.gov/

Small business is the most powerful engine of opportunity and economic growth in the United States. SBA offers a variety of programs and support services to help owners navigate the issues they face with initial applications and resources to help after they open for business. Virtually all HR topics can be addressed from a small business standpoint.

Human Resource Management in Small Businesses

The Small Business Administration (SBA) defines a small business as one that is independently owned and operated, is organized for profit, and is not dominant in its field. More than 99 percent of the businesses in the United States are classified as small businesses and they are responsible for at least half of private sector employment.[56] The discussion throughout this text has historically focused primarily on how HR is practiced with major corporations. However, today, many college graduates obtain jobs in small businesses. In fact, growth of small business is often a primary driver for the economy. Therefore, the practice of HR as it is conducted in small businesses is discussed at various times in your text.

Typically, the same HR functions previously identified must be accomplished by small business, but the manner in which they are accomplished may be altered.[57] Small businesses often do not have a formal HR unit or an HRM specialist. Rather, line managers often handle the HR functions. The focus of their activities is generally on hiring and retaining capable employees. Some aspects of HR functions may actually be more significant in smaller firms than in larger ones. For example, a staffing mistake in hiring an incompetent employee who alienates customers may cause the business to fail. In a larger firm, such an error might be much less harmful. As the business grows, the need for a more sophisticated HR function usually is needed.[58] This move typically occurs at the 25-employee level when concerns about compliance with labor laws often begin.[59] Also, new small businesses are faced with a host of federal and state government regulatory requirements, tax laws, and compensation demands.

Watch It 2

If your instructor has assigned this, go to **www.pearson.com/mylab/management** to watch a video titled Blackbird Guitars: Managing Human Resources in Entrepreneurial Firms and to respond to questions.

1.6 Identify ways that country culture influences global business.

Country Culture and Global Business

A country's culture is the set of values, symbols, beliefs, languages, and norms that guide human behavior within the country. It is learned behavior that develops as individuals grow from childhood to adulthood. As one goes from one side of this country to the other, a wide range of cultural differences will be experienced. The same can be said in traveling from north to south. Then, think about the cultural differences that exist in going from this country to another. Americans' use of colloquialisms often creates cultural barriers. Perhaps surprisingly, misunderstanding can occur between two countries that share the same language such as is the case for the United States and the United Kingdom. For instance, Martin Brooks, Production and Export Manager of pet nutrition company Hilton Herbs considers the United States as one of the most challenging. "As an example, we had a product for older horses and dogs called Veteran," he says.[60] Sales were flat until the company replaced the word "veteran" with "senior," following the way people in the United States refer to older pets. Veteran is a commonplace descriptor in the UK. If a significant cultural divide can exist between two countries that share a common language, how much wider must the contrast be between countries that speak different languages? No doubt quite significant.

Even though the language may be the same, such as is the case with the United States and the United Kingdom, major cultural differences do exist. Dean Foster, a New York-based consultant on intercultural business issues said, "The United Kingdom really is a foreign country—and HR departments that ignore that fact are at their peril. It's that expectation of similarity that throws everyone off."[61] A businessperson who travels from Switzerland to Italy goes from a country where meetings tend to be highly structured and expected to start on time to one where meetings can be more informal and punctuality is less important.[62] Many believe that China has the most different culture for Americans to deal with.[63]

Throughout this text, cultural differences between countries will be identified as a major factor influencing global business. This borderless world adds dramatically to the difficulty of managing employees. Cultural differences reveal themselves in everything from the workplace environments to differences in the concept of time, space, and social interaction.[64] Companies operating in the global environment recognize that national cultures differ and that such differences cannot be ignored.[65]

Getting work done is less likely when individuals from one culture are tone deaf to cultural norms elsewhere. For example, L'Oréal's decision making culture encourages open debate, which management maintain generates creativity.[66] However, that style probably does not fit well with cultural differences in other countries. The company's confrontational approach is inconsistent with the cultural values in Southeast Asia, which is a region where they conduct business. An Indonesian employee said, "To an Indonesian person, confrontation in a group setting is extremely negative, because it makes the other person lose face. So it's something that we try strongly to avoid in any open manner."[67]

Getting work done becomes especially more challenging when companies of different country origins merge. For instance, Chrysler Corporation employees have gone through major cultural changes in the last several years.[68] The misfortune cost Daimler nearly $36 billion over a decade, which amounted to a loss of almost $10 million per day for 10 years.[69] First, they were merged into a German firm, Daimler-Benz, then they were sold back to a U.S. company, and they are now merged into Fiat, an Italian firm. Each ownership change brought new cultural rules with which employees had to deal. Certainly, the Germans and Italians have two distinct cultures.[70] InBev, based in Leuven, Belgium, purchased Anheuser-Busch several years ago, making it the leading global brewer and one of the world's top five consumer products companies (AB InBev). Merging two large corporate cultures after an acquisition is often not easy. In fact, InBev's purchase of Anheuser-Busch was particularly difficult, even two-and-a-half years after the $52 billion deal closed, the story continues.[71] AB InBev reached an agreement, valued at $100 billion, to acquire beer brewer SABMiller. No doubt, the companies will face further challenges as they merge their workforces and operations. For instance, AB InBev's CEO Carlos Brito once said that he does not "like people at the company to have fun."[72] Brito's sentiment does not fit with SABMiller's work culture, which reportedly is more casual.

The cultural norms of Japan promote loyalty and teamwork. The work culture there is one in which honesty and hard work are prized assets. In Japan, most managers tend to remain with the same company for life. In the United States, senior executives often change companies, but the Japanese believe strongly that leaving a job is to be avoided out of respect for the business team.[73] In Japan, if a boss gives detailed instructions to a subordinate, it is like saying the person is incompetent.[74] Japan is not the only Asian country that promotes worker respect for their bosses and a team work ethic. For example, norms in Korean culture pressure workers to "pull late nights" because they feel the need to please their superiors. One observer described these workers: "They just sit in their chairs and they just watch their team leaders, and they're thinking, 'What time is he going to leave the office?'"[75] Then, there is an expectation that the boss and employees will go out for drinks, and it is important that employees participate. In Korea, drinking together helps build workplace camaraderie and trust.[76]

Cultural misunderstandings are common, but they can be hazards to executives managing global workforces. Samuel Berner, head of HR of the private banking Asia Pacific division in

Singapore for Credit Suisse AG said, "Things that are perfectly natural in one culture offend in another."[77] Eric Rozenberg, CMM, CMP, president, Ince&Tive, of Brussels, Belgium, stated, "Even though people are aware that there are cultural differences between various nationalities, they're still uncomfortable with it and are afraid of making mistakes."[78]

Try It!

If your instructor has assigned this, go to **www.pearson.com/mylab/management** to complete the Human Resource Management simulation and test your application of these concepts when faced with real world decisions.

1.7 Explore essential skills for developing your career in HR or any other career path.

Developing Skills for Your Career

If you're not an HRM major, you may be thinking that this section isn't relevant to you. Let me assure you, it is. Whether or not you plan on a career in HRM, the lessons you learn in this course will help you in business and in your life. Also, it is only through the aggregate of your educational experience that you will have the opportunity to develop many of the skills that employers have identified as critical to success in the workplace. In this course, and, specifically in this text, you'll have the opportunity to develop and practice seven important skills in the following ways: communication, critical thinking, collaboration, knowledge application and analysis, business ethics and social responsibility, information technology application and computing skills, and data literacy.

Communication

Communication is defined as effective use of oral, written, and nonverbal skills for multiple purposes (e.g., to inform, instruct, motivate, persuade, and share ideas); effective listening; using technology to communicate; and being able to evaluate the effectiveness of communication efforts—all within diverse contexts. The *Working Together* feature offers opportunities to collaborate through sharing ideas, listening to others' ideas, and coming up with a cohesive team response to the assignment. If assigned by your instructor, you may make brief oral presentations, creating an additional opportunity for working together. All the while, you will gain insight into your and your group members' strengths and weaknesses pertaining to communication (and collaboration) skills. Never pass up an opportunity to hone these skills.

Critical Thinking

Critical thinking involves purposeful and goal-directed thinking used to define and solve problems, make decisions or form judgments related to a situation or set of circumstances. The *Chapter Review* questions and a new feature in this edition, *HRM by the Numbers*, provide you with an excellent opportunity to think through concepts and their applications. *HRM by the Numbers* will also give you the chance to analyze quantitative data to facilitate problem solving. Analysis of the *Incidents*, which depict realistic scenarios that you will likely encounter in the workplace, requires your interpretation and an actionable response. Similarly, you will have the chance to think through and discuss your responses to common *Ethics Dilemmas*. More about the ethics dilemmas shortly. Critically thinking about situations is just one part of the story. The *Personal Inventory Assessment* feature, included in most chapters, gives you the opportunity for self-assessment and personal reflection. Understanding yourself and finding your voice will help you approach situations within and outside the employment setting with greater confidence.

Collaboration

Collaborative learning takes place in a situation in which individuals actively work together on a task, constructing meaning and knowledge as a group through dialogue and negotiation resulting in a final product reflective of their joint, interdependent actions. I've already made the case for *Working Together*. Your professor may similarly ask you to analyze *Incidents* in small groups. Another feature new in this edition, *HRM is Everyone's Business*, explains how HR professionals and managers throughout the organization work together to address important workplace issues. This feature highlights the connections between managers and HR professionals, and the reality that work is rarely performed in isolation.

Knowledge Application and Analysis

Knowledge application and analysis is defined as the ability to learn a concept and then appropriately apply that knowledge in another setting to achieve a higher level of understanding. All the activities discussed in this section provide you with multiple opportunities to think through solutions to specific problems and generalize these processes to other situations you will likely encounter in the future. Two additional features further help you develop this skill. *Try It* directs you to mini simulations and, in *Watch It*, you will review video clips that require a response to important workplace challenges.

Business Ethics and Social Responsibility

Business ethics are sets of guiding principles that influence the way individuals and organizations behave within the society that they operate. Two additional issues require everyone's attention. The first, CSR is the implied, enforced, or felt obligation of managers, acting in their official capacity, to serve or protect the interests of groups other than themselves. Second, corporate sustainability focuses on the possible future impact of an organization on society, including social welfare, the economy, and the environment. Both issues are like ethics; however, ethics also focuses on individual decision making and behavior as well as the impact of ethical choices on employee welfare. The review questions, particularly in Chapter 2 on ethics, social responsibility, and sustainability, and the Ethics Dilemmas throughout your textbook, will keep these important matters in the forefront as you move ahead in your career.

Information Technology Application and Computing Skills

Information technology application and computing skills are defined as the ability to select and use appropriate technology to accomplish a given task. The individual is also able to apply computing skills to solve problems. *HRM by the Numbers* gives you the opportunity to develop these skills.

Data Literacy

Data literacy is the ability to access, assess, interpret, manipulate, summarize, and communicate data. Throughout this book, the newly created feature titled *FYI* provides tidbits of information from survey research and extensive databases (e.g., employment statistics) that illuminate trends, opinions, and the use of specific HR practices. These data should enable you to translate quantitative information for placement into the employment context. Further, you can expand this skill by thinking through when and how to create new policies or modify existing ones.

In summary, you will find opportunities throughout this book to develop several critical skills that provide a foundation of success on any career path that you follow. As you learn about HRM, consider how you can generalize these skills to other workplace situations. Best of luck whether you are preparing for the start of your career or are in the process of changing career paths!

SCOPE OF THIS BOOK

Effective HRM is crucial to the success of every organization. To be effective, managers must understand and competently practice HRM. This book was designed to give you the following:

- An insight into the role of strategic HRM in today's organizations and the strategic role of HR functions
- An appreciation of the value of employees as human capital
- An awareness of the importance of business ethics and corporate social responsibility
- An understanding of job analysis, HR planning, recruitment, and selection
- An awareness of the importance of HR development, including training and developing, for employees at all levels
- An understanding of performance appraisal and its role in performance management
- An appreciation of how compensation and employee benefits programs are formulated and administered
- An opportunity to understand employee and labor relations
- An understanding of safety and health factors as they affect the firm's profitability

An appreciation of the global impact on HRM This book is organized in six parts, as shown in Figure 1-7; combined, they provide a comprehensive view of HRM. As you read it, hopefully you will be stimulated to increase your knowledge in this rapidly changing and challenging field.

FIGURE 1-7
Organization of This Book

HUMAN RESOURCE MANAGEMENT, 15TH EDITION

PART ONE: SETTING THE STAGE
Chapter 1: Human Resource Management: An Overview
Chapter 2: Business Ethics, Corporate Social Responsibility, and Sustainability
Chapter 3: Equal Employment Opportunity, Affirmative Action, and Workforce Diversity

PART TWO: STAFFING
Chapter 4: Strategic Planning, Human Resource Planning, and Job Analysis
Chapter 5: Recruitment
Chapter 6: Selection

PART THREE: PERFORMANCE MANAGEMENT AND TRAINING
Chapter 7: Performance Management and Appraisal
Chapter 8: Training and Development

PART FOUR: COMPENSATION
Chapter 9: Direct Financial Compensation (Monetary Compensation)
Chapter 10: Indirect Financial Compensation (Employee Benefits)

PART FIVE: LABOR RELATIONS, EMPLOYEE RELATIONS, SAFETY AND HEALTH
Chapter 11: Labor Unions and Collective Bargaining
Chapter 12: Internal Employee Relations
Chapter 13: Employee Safety, Health, and Wellness

PART SIX: OPERATING IN A GLOBAL ENVIRONMENT
Chapter 14: Global Human Resource Management

PREPARING FOR EXAMS/QUIZZES

Chapter Summary by Learning Objectives

1. ***Define* human resource management *and the importance of studying it.*** *Human resource management (HRM)* is the utilization of employees to achieve organizational objectives. It is the business function of managing employees. HRM professionals embrace the idea that employees are essential to the success of organizations, and as such, they view employees as assets or human capital. Studying HRM is a worthwhile endeavor, whether you plan to become an HR professional. Possessing knowledge about HRM principles and practices will help you understand your rights and responsibilities as an employee. Also, if you eventually lead a department or supervise employees, you will seek guidance on issues such as appraising job performance. There are six functional areas associated with effective HRM: staffing, HR development, performance management, compensation, safety and health, and employee and labor relations.
2. ***Describe who performs HRM.*** *Human resource managers* are individuals who normally act in an advisory or staff capacity, working with other managers to help them deal with human resource matters. *HR outsourcing* is the process of hiring an external provider to do the work that was previously done internally. *HR shared service centers* take routine, transaction-based activities that are dispersed throughout the organization and consolidate them in one place. A *professional employer organization* is a company that leases employees to other businesses. *Line managers* in certain firms are being used more frequently than before to deliver HR services.

   Various designations are used within the HR profession; among these are HR executives, generalists, and specialists. A *profession* is a vocation characterized by the existence of a common body of knowledge and a procedure for certifying members.

   Executives are top-level managers who report directly to the corporation's CEO or the head of a major division. *Generalists* (who are often executives) are persons who perform tasks in a wide variety of HR-related areas. A *specialist* may be an HR executive, manager, or non manager who typically is concerned with only one of the functional areas of HRM.

   Several well-known organizations serve the profession. Among the more prominent are the Society for Human Resource Management (SHRM), the Human Resource Certification Institute (HRCI), the Association for Talent Development (ATD), and WorldatWork.
3. ***Explain how the HRM function serves as a strategic business partner and the elements of the dynamic HRM environment.*** Working as a strategic business partner requires a much deeper and broader understanding of

business issues. Possible strategic tasks for HR include making workforce strategies fundamental to company strategies and goals; increasing HR's role in strategic planning, mergers, and acquisitions; developing awareness or an understanding of the business; and helping line managers achieve their goals. Also, as a strategic business partner, HR helps to identify and develop the human capital necessary for excellent performance, builds recruitment systems, training programs for product distribution and interactions with customers, constructs performance management, and structures compensation programs that will greatly incentivize these employees to excel. In the end, if HR is to be a strategic partner, HR executives must work with top management in achieving concrete plans and results. Factors include legal considerations, the labor market, society, political parties, unions, shareholders, competition, customers, technology, economy, and unanticipated events.

4. ***Discuss the role of HRM in building corporate culture and employer branding.*** *Corporate culture* is the system of shared values, beliefs, and habits within an organization that interacts with the formal structure to produce behavioral norms. Culture gives people a sense of how to behave and what they ought to be doing. It often affects job performance throughout the organization and consequently affects profitability. *Employer branding* is the firm's corporate image or culture created to attract and retain the type of employees the firm is seeking. It is what the company stands for in the public eye.
5. ***Summarize HRM issues for small businesses.*** Often the same HR functions previously identified must be accomplished by small business, but the manner in which they are accomplished may be altered. Small businesses often do not have a formal HR unit or HRM specialists. Rather, other line managers in the company handle HR functions.
6. ***Identify ways that country culture influences global business.*** Cultural differences reveal themselves in everything from the workplace environments to differences in the concepts of time, space, and social interaction. Cultural differences are often the biggest barrier to doing business in the world market.
7. ***Explore essential skills for developing your career in HR or any other career path.*** Whether you are embarking on a career in HRM on another path, there are seven essential skills needed for success: communication, critical thinking, collaboration, knowledge application and analysis, business ethics and social responsibility, information technology application and computing skills, and data literacy.

Key Terms

human resource management (HRM) 3
staffing 4
performance management 5
human resource development (HRD) 5
direct financial compensation 5
indirect financial compensation (benefits) 5
nonfinancial compensation 5
safety 6
health 6
human resource management professional 7
line managers 7
HR outsourcing (HRO) 8
shared service center (SSC) 9
professional employer organization (PEO) 9
executive 9
generalist 9
specialist 10
profession 10
capital 13
human capital 13
union 15
shareholders 15
human resource information system (HRIS) 15
corporate culture 16
country's culture 17
employer branding 16

MyLab Management

If your instructor is using MyLab Management, go to **www.pearson.com/mylab/management** to complete the problems marked with this icon ✪.

Questions for Review

✪1-1. Define *human resource management*. What HRM functions must be performed regardless of the organization's size?

1-2. Define *profession*. Do you believe that the field of HRM is a profession? Explain your answer.

✪1-3. What are the environmental factors that affect HRM? Describe each one.

✪1-4. How might HR technology affect the various HR functions?

1-5. Define *corporate culture*. Explain why corporate culture is a major internal environment factor.

1-6. This chapter describes HR's changing role in business. Describe each component that is involved in HRM.

1-7. How does HRM become more complex as a company's workforce reaches 25 employees?

✪1-8. What are the various designations associated with the HRM profession?

1-9. What has been the evolution of HRM?

1-10. Explain how the seven employability skills matter regardless of your career aspirations.

PREPARING FOR MY CAREER

Personal Inventory Assessment

Additional Personal Inventory Assessments can be found on MyLab Management.

What's My Comfort with Change?

Change is a big part of the external environment and an organization's culture. This PIA will assess how comfortable you are with change.

ETHICS DILEMMA

Broken Promises

You've recently joined the HR department and noticed that employee turnover has been higher than usual. Most of the departing employees are star performers who worked in the marketing department. Naturally, losing too many high performers is a detriment to the company's efforts to meet its strategic objectives. You've decided to investigate the possible reasons for higher turnover and learned some unsettling facts. One of the recruiters entices top job candidates to join the company by conveying its commitment to career development when, in fact, the company does not provide any career development opportunities. You also learned that most of these job candidates possessed other job offers that they turned down on the promise of career development opportunities in your company.

1-11. What would you do?

1-12. What factors in this ethics dilemma might influence a person to make a less-than-ethical decision?

HRM Is Everyone's Business

Many companies have moved from the personnel management model to the HR business partner model; however, some still look to HR to guarantee that policies are being enforced and the company mitigates legal risk. Depending on the company where you are employed—and whether you are a manager or HR professional—you may find yourself in a position to understand the competitive strategy of the business and align HR practices with the strategic thrust of the business.

Action checklist for managers and HR—aligning HR practice with competitive strategy

HR takes the lead

- ☑ Work with managers to fully understand which roles and types of employees will best support the execution of company strategy.
- ☑ Collaborate with managers to run an analysis of market factors (e.g., competitors, industry standards, local labor market) to get indicators of norms and standards in order to keep your company's HR practices competitive.
- ☑ Create, together with managers, job structures wherein roles are placed into the organizational structure. Each job structure will have tailored pay ranges, performance standards, and training guidelines to help employees advance in the organization.

Managers take the lead

- ☑ Educate employees, along with other managers and supervisors, about the company's strategy and how everyone contributes to meeting strategic objectives.
- ☑ Educate HR on certain aspects of roles (e.g., autonomy, skill variety, task significance, etc.) that, when enhanced, could improve motivation; thus, leading to benefits for employees and employers.
- ☑ Work together with HR to implement a plan that promotes successful recruitment, training, and development, ensuring that the company is retaining the talent that is critical to the implementation and delivery of the strategic objectives.

HRM by the Numbers

Making a Sufficient Number of Job Offers to Maintain Staffing Levels

An additional HRM by the Numbers exercise can be found on MyLab Management.

HR professionals and other managers work together to calculate the number of employees needed to meet objectives. For instance, they determined that 100 full-time production workers are needed to assemble 2,500 children's bicycles each day. Each year, a total of 20 percent of these workers are either promoted or they leave the company due to poor performance or better job opportunities elsewhere. Management can use your help in understanding the impact of understaffing on meeting production goals as well as calculating the number of job offers needed to maintain the necessary staffing level.

Questions

1-13. If the company does not replace the workers who leave, how many bikes must each employee produce on a given day (assume that on any given day, there are 20 percent fewer workers than needed to meet the production goal)?

1-14. Assume that each job candidate accepts the company's job offer. Calculate the number of job offers necessary to maintain the required staffing level of 100 employees on an annual basis.

1-15. Instead, assume that only 50 percent of the job candidates accept a job offer. Calculate the number of job offers necessary to maintain the required staffing level of 100 employees on an annual basis.

Working Together: Team Exercise

In small groups of three or four, come up with specific answers to the following questions. Talk through your perspectives as you prepare your answers. Be prepared to share your ideas with the class.

As a group, identify a company with which members are familiar. On the company's website, review its mission, products or services, and career opportunities.

1-16. How would you describe the company's employment brand to your friends?

1-17. What information might lead you to choose working for the company?

INCIDENT 1 HR After a Disaster

After Hurricane Rita struck Lake Charles in southwest Louisiana, many businesses wondered if they would ever return to their former selves. Massive destruction was everywhere. Lake Charles, known for its large and beautiful oak and pine trees, now had the job of removing those downed trees from homes, businesses, and lots. You could see for miles through what used to be thick forests. Huge trucks designed for removing massive tree trunks were everywhere. While driving down a street, downed trees could be seen stacked two stories high, waiting to be picked up. The town grew rapidly in size because of the increased number of repair crews working on recovery operations. The noise created by their chain saws could be heard from daylight until dark. The sounds of hammers were everywhere as homeowners scrambled to get their roofs repaired. Often repair crews would just find an empty lot and set up tents for the night because all motels were full. Traffic was unbelievably slow, and it appeared as if everyone was attempting to get on the road at the same time. Just driving from Point A to Point B could often be quite an adventure. As might be expected in conditions such as these, accidents were numerous. Often police did not have the resources to ticket every fender bender, so unless there were injuries, insurance cards were exchanged and the police went on to the next accident.

Months after Hurricane Rita struck, large and small businesses were still frantically trying to find workers so they could start up again. It appeared that every business in the town had a "Help Wanted" sign out front. Individuals who wanted a job could get one and could command a premium salary. Walmart, known for remaining open 24 hours a day, could only stay open on an abbreviated schedule. Employers often had to bus employees from locations not affected by the hurricane each morning and returned them at night because there were not enough workers available in the local area. Restaurants that normally remained open late into the evening closed at 6:00 p.m., if they opened at all. Compensation scales that were in use before the hurricane had to be thrown out and new plans implemented. Minimum-wage jobs were nonexistent. Employees who earned minimum wage before the storm could now command $10 per hour just for being a flagger (a person who directs traffic). Fast-food restaurants that normally paid minimum wage now paid $10 or $11. Burger King was even offering a $1,500 bonus for entry-level workers. Upscale restaurants that normally paid minimum wage plus tips now paid premium rate plus tips. Restaurants that remained open often had a much younger staff, and it was evident that the managers and assistant managers were working overtime to train these new workers. Restaurant patrons had to learn patience because there would be mistakes by these eager, but largely untrained workers.

Questions

1-18. Which environment factor(s) did Hurricane Rita affect? Discuss.

1-19. How were the HR functions affected by Hurricane Rita?

1-20. Do you believe the HR situations described regarding Hurricane Rita would be typical in a disaster? Explain.

INCIDENT 2 Parental Leave at Yahoo

Employer branding is an ongoing effort that requires a company to "puts its money where its mouth is." In other words, building and maintaining a positive employer brand goes beyond written policy and good media coverage. Successful branding starts with executive leadership setting an example for employees. Take the Internet company Yahoo. Yahoo has a policy that provides generous paid parental leave and permits employees to work from home. The company had a golden opportunity to demonstrate commitment to its family leave policy after then CEO Marissa Mayer gave birth to her baby in 2012. Rather than taking several weeks to work from home, she built a nursery next to her office where she could be close to the baby. Then, in 2013, a leaked internal memo revealed that Yahoo would terminate its telecommuting policy that allowed employees to work from home. In the memo, she stated: "Speed and quality are often sacrificed when we work from home."[79] In addition, "We need to be one Yahoo, and that starts with physically being together." Media responses were mixed. On one hand, Mayer showed that she could continue to lead Yahoo as a new mother. On the other hand, media reports criticized her "for failing to set a realistic expectation for America's working moms."[80] Since then, Yahoo expanded its parental leave policy for the birth or adoption of a child, foster child placement, or surrogacy.

1-21. How do these changes at Yahoo influence the company's employment branding?

1-22. As an HR professional, what would you have done after Mayer chose not to take more time allowed under Yahoo's parental leave policy?

MyLab Management

If your instructor is using MyLab Management, go to **www.pearson.com/mylab/management** for Auto-graded writing questions as well as the following Assisted-graded writing questions:

1-23. What is employer branding? How might employer branding affect a company's ability to recruit?

1-24. How might a country's culture be a barrier to global business?

Endnotes

1 Jean M. Phillips and Stanley M. Gully, *Strategic Staffing*, 3rd ed. (Hoboken, NJ: Prentice Hall, 2015).

2 U.S. Bureau of Labor Statistics, *Employee Tenure in 2016* (September 22, 2016). USDL: 16-1867. Accessed January 2, 2017, at www.bls.gov/.

3 Heather Long, "The New Normal: 4 Job Changes by the Time You're 32," *CNN Money* online (April 12, 2016). Accessed on January 3, 2017, at www.money.cnn.com.

4 Joseph J. Martocchio, *Strategic Compensation*, 9th ed. (Hoboken, NJ: Pearson Education, 2017).

5 U.S. Bureau of Labor Statistics, *Employer Costs for Employee Compensation–September 2016* (December 8, 2016). USDL: 16-2255. Accessed January 2, 2017, at www.bls.gov/.

6 Travis Hessman, "Safety Is Productivity," *EHS Today* (December 12, 2014). Accessed on January 3, 2017, at http://ehstoday.com/safety-leadership-conference-2015/safety-productivity.

7 "The New Organization: Different by Design," *Global Human Capital Trends 2016* (2016). Accessed December 20, 2016, https://www2.deloitte.com/us/en/pages/human-capital/articles/introduction-human-capital-trends.html.

8 Ibid.

9 U.S. Federal Trade Commission, "Big Data: A Tool for Inclusion or Exclusion," (January 2016): 29.

10 Lauren Weber, "One Reason Wal-Mart Is Raising Pay: Turnover," *The Wall Street Journal* online (February 19, 2015). Accessed January 2, 2017, at http://www.wsj.com.

11 Eric Krell, "Change Within," *HR Magazine* 56 (August 2011): 42–50.

12 "Despite Recession, World-Class HR Organizations Reduce Costs by 13 Percent," *Controller's Report* 2011 (August 2011): 1–19.

13 Jon Severs, "Supervisors on the Front Line," *PrintWeek* (January 21, 2011): 20–21.

14 Mark Feffer, "More HR Professionals Are Striking Out on Their Own to Work as Independent Contractors," *HR Magazine*, (July/August 2016): 55–61.

15 "Focus on Cost Effective People Management Drives Adoption of Human Resource Outsourcing, According to a New Report by Global Industry Analysts, Inc," Global Industry Analysts, Inc. (Web site). Accessed January 2, 2017, at www.strategyr.com/pressMCP-1516.asp.

16 Accenture Inc., "Achieving High Performance in BPO: Research Report," (2012). Accessed December 30, 2013, at www.accenture.com.

17 Mark Feffer, "Meet the People Behind Your HR Outsourcing," *HR Magazine* (July/August 2016) online. Accessed January 2, 2017, at www.shrm.org/hr-today/news/hr-magazine/0716/Pages/meet-the-people-behind-your-hr-outsourcing.aspx.

18 Erika Andersen, "4 Ways to Become a Strategic Business Partner (And Why You Should Want to): *Forbes* (September 6, 2013). Accessed October 10, 2013, at www.forbes.com.

19 Eric Krell, "Amid Consolidation, Clients Grow Selective," *HR* Magazine 58 (July 2013): 49–51.

20 Joel Berg, "Employers Outsource HR Work in Recession," *Central Penn Business Journal* 25 (November 13, 2009): 17–21.

21 CFO Research, "A Rising Interest in Outsourcing Benefits Administration," (2016 Research Report). Accessed January 2, 2017, at http://research.prudential.com/documents/rp/CFO_Prudential_ADA_Report5_4_19.pdf.

22 "Leading in the New," Accenture Annual Report 2016," Accessed January 2, 2017, at www.accenture.com/t20161030T213116__w__/us-en/_acnmedia/PDF-35/Accenture-2016-Shareholder-Letter10-K006.pdf#zoom=50.

23 "Levi Strauss: Recruitment Process Outsourcing," (Case Study). Accessed January 2, 2017, at https://acn-uat.ciotest.accenture.com/ng-en/success-levi-strauss-recruitment-process-outsourcing.

24 Bill Leonard, "Salvage, Don't Scrap," *HR Magazine* 56 (June 2011): 74–77.

25 Laurie Bassi and Dan McMurrer, "The State of the PEO Industry 2016: Markets, Value, and Trends," National Association of Professional Employer Organizations (September 2016). Accessed January 3, 2017, at www.napeo.org.

26 Ibid.

27 David Imbrogno, "The Outsourcing of HR," *Quality* 49 (December 2010): 34–35.

28 U.S. Bureau of Labor Statistics, "Human Resources Mangers," *Occupational Outlook Handbook, 2016–17 Edition*." Accessed January 2, 2017, at www.bls.gov/ooh/management/human-resources-manages.htm.

29 Henry G. Jackson, "Being Strategic Is Not Optional," *HR Magazine*, (November 2015): 6.

30 Adrienne Fox, "Reach New Height," *HR Magazine* (July 2012): 34–39.

31 Edward E. Lawler III and John W. Boudreau, "Creating an Effective Human Capital Strategy," *HR Magazine* 57 (August 2012): 57–59.

32 "HR in 2020 Should Understand Clearly All Aspects of Business," *HR Focus* 90 (February 2013): 8–9.

33 "Attorney Urges HR Professionals to Think Like the CEO," *HR Focus* 89 (April 2012): 10.

34 Cam Caldwell, Do X. Truong, Pham T. Linh, and Anh Tuan, "Strategic Human Resource Management as Ethical Stewardship," *Journal of Business Ethics* 98 (January 2011): 171–182.

35 Kenneth E. Goodpaster and John B. Matthews, Jr., "Can a Corporation Have a Conscience?" *Harvard Business Review* 60 (January–February 1982): 132–141.

36 Steve Bates, "Report: Prepare for Increased Shareholder Activism," *HR Magazine* 54 (June 2009): 32.

37 Joseph J. Martocchio, *Strategic Compensation*, 9th ed. (Hoboken, NJ: Pearson Education, Inc., 2017).

38 Society for Human Resource Management, "Using Social Media for Talent Acquisition—Recruitment and Screening," (January 7, 2016). Accessed January 3, 2017, at www.shrm.org.

39 Jennifer Schramm, "A Cloud of Workers," *HR Magazine* 58 (March 2013): 80; Bill Goodwin, "The Emerging Technologies Transforming How HR Works," *Computer Weekly* (July 16, 2013): 16–18.

40 Katherine Noyes, "How the Cloud Is Transforming HR," *PC World* (March 30, 2016). Accessed January 3, 2017, at http://www.pcworld.com/article/3049645/how-the-cloud-is-transforming-hr.html; Bill Roberts, "The Grand Convergence," *HR Magazine* 56 (October 2011): 39–46.

41 Jane Ward, "Structuring Your Selection Process," *Human Resources Magazine* 16 (February/March 2012): 22–23.

42 Susan Galer, "3 Benefits of Cloud Computing for Human Resources," *Forbes* online (March 26, 2015). Accessed January 3, 2017, at www.forbes.com; Michael Custers, "HR Technologies Guide Employers to Better Benefits Offerings," Employee Benefit Plan Review 67 (February 2013): 20–21.

43 Society for Human Resource Management, "Using Social Media for Talent Acquisition—Recruitment and Screening," (January 7, 2016). Accessed January 3, 2017, at www.shrm.org.

44 "As Economy Recovers, HR Will Have More Opportunities to Show Value," *HR Focus* 89 (February 2012): 6.

45 "The New Organization: Different by Design," *Global Human Capital Trends 2016* (2016). Accessed December 20, 2016, www2.deloitte.com/us/en/pages/human-capital/articles/introduction-human-capital-trends.html.

46 Bob Duffy, "Rethinking Employer Brands," *Journal of Corporate Recruiting Leadership* 5 (June 2010): 10–15.

47 Lydell C. Bridgeford, "Blinding Them with Science," *Employee Benefit News* 25 (January 2011): 8–9.

48 Paul Jacobs, "Emergence of Human Techsourcing," *Human Resources Magazine* 16 (February/March 2012): 14–15.

49 Brandon Rigoni and Jim Asplund, "Strengths-Based Cultures Attract Top Talent," *Gallup* (Web site), (January 3, 2017). Accessed January 4, 2017, www.gallup.com/businessjournal/200123/strengths-based-cultures-attract-top-talent.aspx?utm_source=alert&utm_medium=email&utm_content=morelink&utm_campaign=syndication.

50 Soumya Gaddam, "Modeling Employer Branding Communication: The Softer Aspect of HR Marketing Management," ICFAI Journal of Soft Skills 2 (2008): 45–55.

51 Kelly Borth, "Live Your Brand," Smart Business Columbus 19 (March 2011): 6.

52 "Career Growth," *PwC* Web site. Accessed January 3, 2017, at www.pwc.com/us/en/careers/campus/why-pwc/career-growth.html.

53 "How L'Oréal developed a New Employee Value Proposition (EVP)," *Link Human* (Web site). Accessed January 3, 2017, at http://linkhumans.com/employer-branding/loreal-employer-value.

54 Ronald J. Alsop, "Cultural Awareness," *Workforce Management* 90 (July 2011): 42.

55 Brett Minchington, "Where to Next for Employer Branding?" *Human Resources Magazine* 16 (October/November 2011): 22.

56 Small Business Association, "Small Business Profile, 2016." Accessed January 3, 2017, at www.sba.gov/sites/default/files/advocacy/all_profiles_10_18_16.pdf.

57 Kelly Brent Massey and Nathanael Campbell, "Human Resource Management: Big Problem for Small Business," *Entrepreneurial Executive* 18 (2013): 77–88.

58 Dan Emerson, "When to Outsource HR Duties and When to Hire," *Finance & Commerce* (February 20 2013). Accessed May 7, 2014, at http://finance-commerce.com/2013/02/when-to-outsource-hr-duties-and-when-to-hire/.

59 Susan J. Wells, "Big Fish, Small Ponds," *HR Magazine* 58 (July 2013): 30–36.

60 Jenny Hirschkorn, "Business Etiquette: The Importance of Cultural Sensitivity," *The Telegraph* online (January 30, 2014). Accessed January 5, 2017, at www.telegraph.co.uk.

61 DeeDee Doke, "Perfect Strangers," *HR Magazine* 49 (December 2004): 62–68.

62 Richard Miller, "Taste for Risk Varies Across Europe," *Business Insurance* 43 (September 28, 2009): 9–10.

63 Stanley Bing, "Big Questions in the Middle Kingdom," *Fortune* 167 (January 14, 2013): 100.

64 Norm Kamikow, "Lost in Translation," *Chief Learning Officer* 8 (September 2009): 4.

65 Pankaj Ghemawat, "The Cosmopolitan Corporation," *Harvard Business Review* 89 (May 2011): 92–99.

66 Erin Meyer, "When Culture Doesn't Translate," *Harvard Business Review*, October 2015, p. 6.

67 Ibid.

68 "Cultural Gaps Can Spell Merger Disaster," *Executive Leadership* 28 (March 2013): 4.

69 Robert Whipple, "Avoid Common Major Pitfalls of Restructuring," *T+D* 67 (September 2013): 60–63.

70 John Freivalds, "Nokia Comes to the US: Cultural Differences," *MultiLingual* 20 (September 2009): 30–31.

71 David Kesmode, "Bitter Brew: The Continued Budweiser/InBev Culture Clash," *Wall Street Journal* online (May 2, 2011). Accessed May 7, 2014, at http://blogs.wsj.com/deals/2011/05/02/bitter-brew-the-continued-budweiserinbev-culture-clash/.

72 Matthew Boyle, Matthew Campbell, and Thomas Buckley, "SABMiller Better Get Ready for a CEO Who Doesn't Like to Have Fun," *Bloomberg* online (October 9, 2015). Accessed January 5, 2017, at www.bloomberg.com.

73 Anumeha Chaturvedi, "Loving It in Tokyo," *Business Today* 20 (August 21, 2011): 127.

74 Brad Klontz, "Multi-Culti Competence," *On Wall Street* 23 (August 2013): 32–34.

75 Kathy Novak, "Never Say No! South Korea's Pressure-Cooker Work Culture," *CNN* (July 23, 2015). Accessed January 5, 2017, at www.cnn.com.

76 "South Korea's Hangover," *Al Jazeera* (February 5, 2016). Accessed January 5, 2017, at www.aljazeera.com.

77 Kathryn Tyler, "What Are Global Cultural Competencies?" *HR Magazine* 56 (May 2011): 44–46.

78 Julie Barker, "The Cultural Divide," *Incentive* 182 (March 2008): 2–6. Cultural barriers are not easily overcome.

79 Susan Rohwer, "Balancing Family and Work Shouldn't Be Hazardous to Your Employment," *The Los Angeles Times* online (February 19, 2014). Accessed January 17, 2017, at www.latimes.com.

80 Lisa Fernandez and John Schuppe, "Yahoo Expands Maternity Leave After Banning Telecommuting," *CNBC* online (April 30, 2013). Accessed January 17, 2017, at http://www.cnbc.com/id/100689956.

2 Business Ethics, Corporate Social Responsibility, and Sustainability

LEARNING OBJECTIVES After completing this chapter, students should be able to:

2.1 Discuss what ethics means and the sources of ethical guidance.

2.2 Explore human resource management's (HRM) role in creating an ethical culture and a code of ethics.

2.3 Define human resource ethics.

2.4 Explain the concepts and practices related to corporate social responsibility and corporate sustainability.

2.5 Describe a social audit.

MyLab Management

Improve Your Grade!

If your professor is using MyLab Management, visit **www.pearson.com/mylab/management** for videos, simulations, and writing exercises.

Learn It

If your professor has chosen to assign this, go to **www.pearson.com/mylab/management** to see what you should particularly focus on and to take the Chapter 2 Warm-Up.

Choosing *how* ethical and socially responsible an organization needs to be and *when* it should be brings up difficult issues all managers may have to address as they perform their duties. These issues can and do shape their decisions. HR professionals play a significant role in helping organizations start and stay on a path of ethical practice, corporate social responsibility, and sustainability. Let's explore the role of HR professionals in managing ethical obligations and considerations related to corporate social responsibility and sustainability.

2.1 Discuss what ethics means and the sources of ethical guidance.

Defining Ethics and the Sources of Ethical Guidance

ethics
Discipline dealing with what is good and bad, or right and wrong, or with moral duty and obligation.

Ethics is the discipline dealing with what is good and bad, right and wrong, or with moral duty and obligation. Ethics at times may appear to be complicated because businesses are created to produce a short-term profit, which could potentially conflict with ethical behavior.[1] Today most executives have a different view in that integrity and ethical values have an important place in business and should form the foundation of a company's culture.[2] Unfortunately, some companies and individuals still behave unethically, perhaps, because ethics moves to the back burner while executives focus on what they believe to be more important concerns.

Business Ethics

The past corrupt conduct of corporations such as WorldCom and Enron and the senior managers who led them provides deplorable examples of just how unethical company leadership can be. We also forgot to guard against the type of ethical abuses that ultimately bankrupted companies such as Bear Stearns and Lehman Brothers. Unfortunately, unethical behavior manifests in other ways. For example, Volkswagen (VW) distinguished itself from the competition when it developed the so-called clean diesel engine. The company falsely advertised these engines as good for the environment

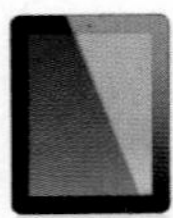

HR Web Wisdom

International Business Ethics Institute

www.business-ethics.org

The Institute was founded in 1994 in response to the growing need for transnational organizations in the field of business ethics.

because they emitted low levels of harmful nitrogen oxides. However, it was revealed that VW knowingly installed software, which, when the car was being tested for emissions, cleaned these pollutants from the exhaust. U.S. law enforcement agencies determined that the deception started in 1991 involving not only top executives but also lower level engineers.[3] Since the news came to light, VW's CEO resigned and numerous engineers were fired.[4] Andrew McCabe, FBI deputy director, stated "It is now clear that Volkswagen's top executives knew about this illegal activity and deliberately kept regulators, shareholders and consumers in the dark—and they did this for years."[5]

CEOs should be clear that unethical behavior is not acceptable. In one survey, 67 percent of investors said they would move their account if they discovered the company was involved in unethical behavior.[6] Jeff Immelt, General Electric's (GE) CEO, begins and ends each annual meeting of 220 officers and 600 senior managers by restating the company's fundamental integrity principles: "GE's business success is built on our reputation with all stakeholders for lawful and ethical behavior."[7] At GE, when it comes to integrity violations, it is one strike and you are out. There are no second chances.[8] The focus should be on just doing the right thing. The image of the business world would be in much better shape if this simple advice were followed. Hopefully, ethical standards are improving.

Most of the 500 largest corporations in the United States now have a code of ethics, which encompasses written conduct standards, internal education, and formal agreements on industry standards, ethics offices, social accounting, and social projects. Even so, business ethics scandals continue to be headline news. Lying on résumés, obstruction of justice, destruction of records, stock price manipulation, cutting corners to meet Wall Street's expectations, fraud, waste, and abuse are unfortunately occurring all too often when those in business decide to make poor ethical choices. Then, there are the corporate executives that took home millions even though their company failed and employees were laid off. Even more noteworthy is that some are rewarded for bad behavior. For instance, Jeff Smisek, former CEO of United Continental Holdings, was paid a severance package worth a whopping $36.8 million. He left the airline following alleged participation in a corruption scandal.[9]

However, business is not alone. There is virtually no occupation that has not had its own painful ethical crises in recent years. There were the teachers who provided answers on standardized tests to improve their schools' performance scores. Doctors who make money by falsely billing Medicare do not even make the headlines anymore. Certainly, a devastating blow to society has been dealt by business, and ethical breaches in business continue today.

Compliance with the law sets the minimum standard for ethical behavior; ethics, however, is much more. There must be leaders who are able and willing to instill ethics throughout the culture of the organization. Ethics is about deciding whether an action is good or bad and what to do about it if it is bad. Ethics is a philosophical discipline that describes and directs moral conduct. Those in management make ethical (or unethical) decisions every day. Do you hire the best-qualified person, who is a minority? Do you forget to tell a candidate about the dangerous aspect of a certain job? Some ethical decisions are major and some are minor. But decisions in small matters often set a pattern for the more important decisions a manager makes. Attitudes such as "It's standard practice," "It's not a big deal," "It's not my responsibility," and "I want to be loyal" are simply not acceptable.[10] The Roman philosopher Cicero echoed this when he said, "It is a true saying that one falsehood leads easily to another."[11] In the sixteenth century, Sir Thomas More said, "If virtue were profitable, common sense would make us good and greed would make us saintly."[12] More knew that virtue is not profitable, so people must make hard choices from time to time.

Sources of Ethical Guidance

The sources of ethical guidance should lead to our beliefs or a conviction about what is right or wrong. Most would agree that people have a responsibility to avail themselves to these sources of ethical guidance. In short, individuals should care about what is right and wrong and not just be concerned with what is expedient. One might use several sources to determine what is right or wrong, good or bad, and moral or immoral. These sources include the Bible and other holy books. They also include the small voice that many refer to as conscience. Many believe that conscience is a gift of God or the voice of God. Others see it as a developed response based on the internalization of societal mores. Another source of ethical guidance is the behavior and advice of the people psychologists call "significant others"—our parents, friends, and role models and members of our churches, clubs, and associations.

Laws also offer guidance to ethical behavior, prohibiting acts that can be especially harmful to others. They codify what society has deemed to be unacceptable.[13] If a certain behavior is illegal, most would consider it to be unethical as well. There are exceptions, of course. For example, through the 1950s, laws in most southern states relegated black Americans to the backs of buses and otherwise assigned them inferior status. Martin Luther King Jr. resisted such laws and, in fact, engaged in civil disobedience and other nonviolent forms of resistance to their enforcement. King won the Nobel Peace Prize for his efforts.

Two conditions must exist if an individual or organization is to be considered ethical. First, ethics consists of the strength of the relationship between what an individual or an organization believes to be moral and correct and what available sources of guidance suggest is morally correct. For example, suppose a manager believes it is acceptable not to hire minorities, even though almost everyone condemns this practice. This person would not be considered ethical. Having strong beliefs about what is right and wrong and basing them on the proper sources may have little relationship to what one does.

Second, ethics consists of the strength of the relationship between what one believes and how one behaves. For example, if a manager knows that it is wrong to discriminate but does so anyway, the manager is also unethical. If a board of directors considers it wrong to pay excessively high salaries relative to the CEO's job performance, yet pays salaries that are excessive in this context, this behavior is also unethical. Generally, a person is not considered ethical unless the person satisfies both conditions.

For most professionals, there are codes of ethics that prescribe certain behavior. Without this conscience that has developed, it might be easy to say, "Everyone does it," "Just this once won't hurt," or "No one will ever know." Some still believe that greed is acceptable if the Equal Employment Opportunity Commission (EEOC) or other regulatory agencies do not find out.[14] Fortunately, the HRM profession subscribes to a code of ethics, which we discuss later in this chapter.

Legislating Ethics

In 1907, Teddy Roosevelt said, "Men can never escape being governed. If from lawlessness or fickleness, from folly or self-indulgence, they refuse to govern themselves, then in the end they will be governed [by others]."[15] Many contend that ethics cannot be legislated. Although laws cannot mandate ethics, they may be able to identify the baseline separating what is good and what is bad. Much of the current legislation was passed because of business ethics breakdowns. There have been at least four attempts to legislate business ethics since the late 1980s. We discuss some of these laws next.

PROCUREMENT INTEGRITY ACT The Procurement Integrity Act of 1988 prohibits the release by government employees of source selection and contractor (for the purposes of this act, a business that enters into contracts with government to provide goods or services) bid or proposal information. Examples of information contained in bids include employee pay rates and proprietary information about the contractor's business processes. Further, this act applies this restriction to non-government employees who provided consulting services on procurement matters. Finally, a former government employee who served in certain positions on a procurement action or contract more than $10 million is barred from receiving compensation as an employee or consultant from that contractor for one year. The act was passed after there were reports of military contracts for $500 toilet seats. There was also a $5,000 hammer.

FEDERAL SENTENCING GUIDELINES FOR ORGANIZATIONS ACT The second attempt occurred with the passage of the 1992 Federal Sentencing Guidelines for Organizations (FSGO) Act, which outlined an effective ethics training program and explained the seven minimum requirements for an effective program to prevent and detect violations.[16] The FSGO promised softer punishments for wayward corporations that already had ethics programs in place. In the law were recommendations regarding standards, ethics training, and a system to anonymously report unacceptable conduct. Executives were supposed to be responsible for the misconduct of those lower in the organization. If executives were proactive in their efforts to prevent white-collar crime, it would lessen a judgment against them and reduce the liability. Organizations responded by creating ethics officer positions, installing ethics hotlines, and developing codes of ethics. But it is one thing to have a code of ethics and quite another to have this code instilled in all employees from top to bottom.

CORPORATE AND AUDITING ACCOUNTABILITY, RESPONSIBILITY, AND TRANSPARENCY ACT The third attempt at legislating business ethics was the Corporate and Auditing Accountability, Responsibility and Transparency Act of 2002, which criminalized many corporate acts that were previously relegated to various regulatory structures. Known as the Sarbanes–Oxley Act, its primary focus is to redress accounting and financial reporting abuses in light of corporate scandals.[17] The Sarbanes–Oxley Act was intended to eliminate or at least reduce conflicts of interest by requiring audit-committee-level pre-approval for non-audit services auditors at companies they audit and enforcing a code of ethics on senior client financial management.[18] The act contains broad employee whistle-blower protections that subject corporations and their managerial personnel to significant civil and criminal penalties for retaliating, harassing, or discriminating against employees who report suspected corporate wrongdoing. The whistle-blower protections of the act apply to corporations listed on U.S. stock exchanges; companies otherwise obligated to file reports under the Securities and Exchange Act; and officers, employees, contractors, subcontractors, and agents of those companies.

The act states that management may not discharge, demote, suspend, threaten, harass, or in any other manner discriminate against an employee protected by the act. It protects any employee who lawfully provides information to governmental authorities concerning conduct he or she reasonably believes constitutes mail, wire, or securities fraud; violations of any rule or regulation issued by the Securities and Exchange Commission (SEC); or violations of any other federal law relating to fraud against shareholders. The act evidently has teeth because in the *Bechtel v. Competitive Technologies Inc.* (2003) Supreme Court case involving wrongful termination under Sarbanes–Oxley's whistle-blower protection rule, the Court ruled that the company violated the act by firing two employees and ordered them reinstated. They were fired because during a meeting they had raised concerns about the company's decision not to report, on its SEC filing, an act they thought should have been disclosed.[19]

The law prohibits loans to executives and directors. It requires publicly traded companies to disclose whether they have adopted a code of ethics for senior officers. The act does not require banks and bank-holding companies that report to the SEC to have a code of ethics, but if an SEC reporting company does not have one, it must explain why.[20] However, as former SEC Chairman Arthur Levitt said, "While the Sarbanes–Oxley Act has brought about significant change, the greatest change is being brought about not by regulation or legislation, but by humiliation and embarrassment and private rights of action."[21]

DODD–FRANK WALL STREET REFORM AND CONSUMER PROTECTION ACT The fourth, the Wall Street Reform and Consumer Protection Act (Dodd–Frank Act), was signed into law in 2010. The act was brought on by the worst financial crisis since the Great Depression, which resulted in the loss of 8 million jobs, failed businesses, a drop in housing prices, and wiped out personal savings of many workers. As the financial crisis advanced, it became clear that executive compensation played a major role in the financial services sector as well as in the capital markets following the collapse of investment services firms such as Lehman Brothers, Merrill Lynch, Bear Stearns, and AIG.[22] The Dodd–Frank Act enhances the transparency of executive compensation practices. The act requires the companies that trade stock on public exchanges to comply with several provisions of which we describe three. The first provision requires say on pay. Say on pay gives company shareholders the right to vote yes or no on executive compensation. Although the say on pay provision guarantees shareholders the right to vote on executive compensation proposals, the vote is non-binding. The non-binding vote advises the company's board of directors of possible concerns about the structure of executive compensation packages, including excessive perks and the lack of clarity between compensation and business results. The board may choose to modify the proposed compensation package.

The second provision details independence requirements for compensation committee members and their advisors, such as compensation consultants and legal counsel. Members of compensation committees typically receive compensation for their services, and this practice is acceptable. However, possible violations of the Dodd–Frank independence requirement may arise when at least one committee member also receives compensation as a company employee. For example, a compensation committee member who also serves as the company's executive vice president may be considered violating the independence requirement.

The third provision addresses whistle-blower protection. In the legal use of the term, a whistle-blower is someone who participates in an activity that is protected. Corporate whistleblowing involves ethics, a topic of this chapter. It requires an individual to choose between personal ethics and the status quo. Often whistle-blowers view themselves as the company's conscience.[23] The use of whistle-blowers has been around since 1863 when President Abraham Lincoln signed into law the Federal False Claims Act, which was designed to protect the United States from purchases of fake gunpowder during the Civil War.[24] The number of whistle-blower suits has increased dramatically in recent years under federal and state laws aimed at uncovering fraud and protecting the public. Since 2007, the Justice Department recovered more than $3 billion in taxpayer funds thanks to whistle-blowers, who originated hundreds of lawsuits.[25] In 2015 alone, whistle-blowers shared $501 million of the proceeds.[26]

FYI

The number of whistle-blower tips has increased dramatically since the passage of the Dodd–Frank Act:

- Fiscal Year 2011: 334
- Fiscal Year 2012: 3,001
- Fiscal Year 2013: 3,238
- Fiscal Year 2014: 3,620
- Fiscal Year 2015: 3,923
- Fiscal Year 2016: 4,218[27]

The Dodd–Frank Act contains a whistle-blower protection provision, which is shaped after the successful IRS program. In passing the act, Congress believed that award programs were a good method to get people to provide fraud information to responsible law enforcement officials. The act requires the Securities SEC to give an award to qualified whistle-blowers of between 10 and 30 percent of the total amount obtained if the information is voluntarily provided and leads to a successful enforcement or related action. The act also improves whistle-blowers' retaliation protection from their employers through the expansion of the whistle-blower protections of the Sarbanes–Oxley Act of 2002. Firms may not directly or indirectly discharge, demote, suspend, threaten, harass, or in any way discriminate against whistle-blowers that provide information to the SEC as specified in the program.[28] This is important because in the past whistle-blowers often were fired, demoted, blacklisted, or quit under duress. Former SEC Chair Mary L. Schapiro said, "While the SEC has a history of receiving a high volume of tips and complaints, the quality of the tips we have received has been better since Dodd–Frank became law, and we expect this trend to continue."[29] The most common complaint categories reported by whistle-blowers were corporate disclosures and financials (22 percent), fraud offerings (156 percent), and manipulation (11 percent).[30] Until the end of 2016, the largest award to a whistle-blower totaled $30 million.[31]

Many believe that information provided by whistle-blowers is much more effective in uncovering wrongdoings than are external auditors. In testimony to the Senate Banking Committee, Certified Fraud Examiner Harry Markopolos stated that "whistle-blower tips detected 54.1 percent of uncovered fraud schemes in public companies. External auditors detected a mere 4.1 percent of fraud schemes."[32]

Companies have some uneasiness regarding the whistle-blower provision of the Dodd–Frank Act.[33] A recent survey of senior legal, compliance, and HR executives at publicly traded or highly regulated companies found that 96 percent expressed either moderate or great concerns about potential whistle-blower complaints.[34] The major concern is that the rules run counter to a firm's internal compliance efforts.[35] Companies are afraid that employees will not go through internal channels first and instead go directly to government authorities to collect the reward.[36] Another fear is that an employee might have another grievance with the company and use the whistle-blower provision to get back at the company.

2.2 Explore human resource management's (HRM) role in creating an ethical culture and a code of ethics.

Creating an Ethical Culture and a Code of Ethics

Ethics is an important component of an organization's culture. And it's turning out to be more key for organizations to conduct business in an ethical fashion. Why? The public insists on it. Customers call for it. Most companies that take ethics seriously have a code of ethics that codifies ethical principles and guides employees to behave ethically. Let's explore HR professionals' roles in facilitating ethical cultures and codes of ethics.

Ethical Culture

Mark Twain once said, "Always do right. This will gratify some people and astonish the rest."[37] This is certainly good advice for both employees and employers if the firm wants to create an ethical culture. Saying that a company has an ethical culture and having one may be two different things. Culture is concerned with the way people think, which affects the way that they act. Changing an organization's culture thus requires modifying the common way of thinking of its members.[38] Organizations with strong ethical cultures take steps to ensure that their standards are widely accessible, promoted, and followed by their leaders and employees.[39] For example, the Volkswagen debacle was not supposed to happen. The Volkswagen Code of Conduct was 24 pages long and had a foreword by Martin Winterkorn, who was then the company's CEO, and other top executives saying, "We stand for respectable, honest, and actions in everyday business that are in accordance with rules, and we commit ourselves to the following Code of Conduct."[40] Even with the ethical code, it is apparent that Volkswagen's top management pursued business as usual.

One way for a firm to create and sustain an ethical culture is to audit ethics, much like a company audits its finances each year.[41] An ethics audit is simply a systematic, independent, and documented process for obtaining evidence regarding the status of an organization's ethical culture. It takes a closer look at a firm's ethical culture instead of just allowing it to remain unexamined. An ethical culture is made up of factors such as ethical leadership, accountability, and values. The climate with top management is fundamental to a company's ethical culture.[42] Ethical leadership begins with the board of directors and CEO and continues to middle managers, supervisors, and employees.[43] Building an ethical culture that lasts requires a foundation of practices that continue even when leaders change.[44] The following Watch It video illustrates how employees and members of management are brought together to enact a change within the company. Their goal is to limit the negative environmental impacts of their company as much as possible by applying the best practices concept to their everyday activities.

Watch It 1

If your instructor has assigned this, go to **www.pearson.com/mylab/management** to watch a video titled Patagonia: Ethics and Social Responsibility and to respond to questions.

According to the Corporate Executive Board in Arlington, Virginia, companies with weak ethical cultures experience 10 times more misconduct than companies with strong ethical cultures.[45] In workplaces with a strong ethical culture, only 4 percent of employees feel pressure to compromise standards and commit misconduct compared to 15 percent in a weaker culture.[46] That's a noteworthy difference. As important as endorsing ethical cultures is, more companies need to get on board. A survey of compliance and ethics professionals revealed that only half maintain that promoting an ethical culture is a priority.[47] Perhaps this is the case because only 13.3 percent believe that management embraces an ethical culture as a primary objective of ethics programs. The results are not much better when it comes to their view of the board of directors' values. Only 15.6 percent of the respondents saw creating an ethical culture as the board's primary objective.

For organizations to grow and prosper, good people must be employed. Recent studies suggest that six personality characteristics are useful predictors of ethical individuals.[48] Individuals who are *conscientious* and *morally attentive* are more likely to recognize whether activities are ethical. *Dutiful* employees and those who are *customer-oriented* are more likely to take ethical challenges seriously. Individuals who are highly *proactive* and *assertive* are more likely motivated to rectify them. Dov Seidman, a management guru who advocates corporate virtue to many companies, believes that companies that "outbehave" their competitors ethically will generally outperform them financially.[49] Further, according to the National Association of Colleges and Employers, the ethical—or unethical—behavior of an organization is a critical factor for new college graduates seeking jobs.[50]

Selecting the right people doesn't ensure a strong ethical culture. Unfortunately, good people sometimes make unethical choices because the organization has allowed and reinforced dysfunctional behavior. A body of research suggests that there are five common ways that companies may lead good employees to make unethical choices:

- It is psychologically unsafe to speak up.
- There is excessive pressure to reach unrealistic performance targets.
- Conflicting goals provoke a sense of unfairness.
- Ethical behavior is not part of the routine conversation.
- A positive example isn't being set.[51]

Organizations need to be willing to change their ways. By fostering a strong ethical culture, firms are better able to gain the confidence and loyalty of their employees and other stakeholders, which can result in reduced financial, legal, and reputation risks, as well as improvements in organizational performance. Organizations are redesigning their ethics programs to facilitate a broader and more consistent process that incorporates the analysis of outcomes and continual improvement. To build and sustain an ethical culture, organizations need a comprehensive framework that encompasses communication of behavior expectations, training on ethics and compliance issues, stakeholder input, resolution of reported matters, and analysis of the entire ethics program. Well-designed training programs can educate employees about what is and is not ethical. Effective training starts with the recognition that problems such as conflicts of interest are not recognizable to many employees.[52] Oftentimes, companies just assume that employees naturally know the difference, which is not always the case. To make it work, involvement by top management is certainly necessary.

Code of Ethics

code of ethics
Establishes the rules that the organization lives by.

A distinction needs to be made between a code of conduct and a code of ethics; the former should tell employees what the rules of conduct are. A **code of ethics** establishes the rules that the organization lives by. It helps employees know what to do when there is not a rule for something.[53] Jim Ward, associate vice president of ethics and compliance at Georgetown University, summed it up by saying, "You can't draft enough rules to cover everything."[54] A broad-based participation of those subject to the code is important. For a company to behave ethically, it must live and breathe its code of ethics, train its personnel, and communicate its code through its vision statements. It cannot just print a manual that sits on a corporate shelf. The code is a statement of the values adopted by the company, its employees, and its directors and sets the official tone of top management regarding expected behavior. Many industry associations adopt such codes, which are then recommended to members. There are many kinds of ethical codes. An excellent example of a code of ethics was developed by the Society for Human Resource Management (SHRM). The six core provisions in the SHRM code of ethics are professional responsibility, professional development, ethical leadership, fairness and justice, conflicts of interest, and use of information.[55] Another excellent example is the code of ethics developed by the International Ethics Standards Board for Accountants (IESBA). The IESBA recognizes that accountants and auditors feel bound by client confidentiality rules, making them reluctant to report any wrong doing. These ethical standards are designed to guide accountants who face such conflicts of interest. Stavros Thomadakis, chairman of the IESBA, stated that "It's trying to bring about early, early detection, if you will, but also early action by management authorities."[56]

There are good reasons to encourage industry associations to develop and promote codes of ethics. It is difficult for a single firm to pioneer ethical practices if its competitors take advantage of unethical shortcuts. For example, U.S. companies must comply with the Foreign Corrupt Practices Act (FCPA), which prohibits bribes of foreign government officials or business executives. Obviously, this law does not prevent foreign competitors from bribing government or business officials to get business, and such practices are common in many countries. This reality sometimes puts U.S. companies at a disadvantage. For instance, Johnson Controls violated the FCPA because one of its Chinese subsidiaries made nearly $5 million in illegal payments to employees of Chinese government-owned shipyards. The company avoided charges for its violations because it took immediate actions to rectify the problem. Johnson Controls' CEO Alex Molinaroli showed that the company is poised to address ethical problems. He said: "The ability to identify and address issues when they do occur, reflects the company's commitment to ethics, responsible management practices and the good governance systems that uphold them."[57]

Just what should be included in a code of ethics? Topics typically covered might be business conduct, fair competition, and workplace and HR issues. For example, employees in purchasing would be shown what constitutes a conflict of interest. The same would occur for sales. At Walmart, it is considered unethical to accept gifts from suppliers. Gifts are either destroyed or given to charity. Fidelity International recently fired two Hong Kong-based fund managers over breaches of its internal code of ethics. Fidelity said, "Our routine checks discovered a pattern of behavior that breached our internal policies."[58] Some companies even include the subject of romantic relationships, which can sometimes lead to conflicts of interest. For instance, Fifth Third Bancorp fired its general counsel because she was engaged in a romantic relationship with Fannie Mae's CEO. Fifth Third's code of ethics states: "We all must avoid actual or apparent conflict of interest with Fifth Third or its Customers."[59] Fifth Third Bancorp's leadership considered the relationship a possible conflict of interest because both companies conduct business with each other, and the appearance of conflict of interest even where one has not occurred could lead to public perception of impropriety. Fannie Mae's approach was less punitive because it did not fire its CEO. Instead, the company's board of directors prohibited the CEO from conducting any business transactions with Fifth Third Bancorp.

To keep the code on the front burner for employees, larger firms appoint an ethics officer. The ethics officer is the point person in guiding everyone in the company toward ethical actions. This individual should be a person who understands the work environment. To obtain the involvement of others within the organization, an ethics committee is often established.

Even the criteria for winning the Malcolm Baldrige National Quality Award have changed, and an increased emphasis on ethics in leadership is now stressed. The criteria say senior leaders should serve as role models for the rest of their organizations. Baldrige applicants are asked questions about how senior leaders create an environment that fosters legal and ethical behavior. They need to show how the leaders address governance matters such as fiscal accountability and independence in audits.

We have made a case for creating both an ethical culture and code of ethics. Is one more important than the other in promoting ethical business practice and employee behavior? Not surprisingly, there are differing opinions. Some business experts weigh culture as more important. For instance, Melissa Stapleton Barnes, chief ethics and compliance officer at Eli Lilly, maintains that emphasizing rules over culture can be detrimental to the organization because employees might seek loopholes to get around them.[60] Rather, she believes that promoting an ethical culture motivates employees to seek ways to act ethically. Others assert that culture is too vague and should not be relied on to guide ethical behavior. Brian Beeghly, vice president of compliance at Johnson Controls, suggests that culture should be aligned with concrete practices, including compliance programs, training, policies, and procedures.[61] Perhaps maintaining an ethical culture and enforcing a code of ethics are likely to provide the best outcomes.

2.3 Define human resource ethics.

Human Resource Ethics

human resource ethics
Application of ethical principles to human resource relationships and activities.

Human resource ethics is the application of ethical principles to HR relationships and activities. It is vitally important that HR professionals know the practices that are acceptable and unacceptable and work to ensure that organizational members also have this awareness in dealing with others.

Some believe that those in HR have a great deal to do with establishing an organization's conscience.[62] In fact, according to a SHRM report, integrity and ethical behavior rank in the top five competencies needed for senior HR leaders.[63] Certainly ethics is a quality the HR professionals should possess; it is the duty of HR professionals to help create an ethical climate in their organization.[64]

HR professionals can help foster an ethical culture, but that means more than just hanging the ethics codes posters on walls. Instead, because the HR professionals' primary job is dealing with people, they must help to instill ethical practices into the corporate culture. Those values must be clearly communicated to all employees, early and often, beginning with the interview process, reinforced during employee orientation, and regularly recognized during performance reviews, public ceremonies, celebrations, and awards. They need to help establish an environment in which employees throughout the organization work to reduce ethical lapses. The ethical bearing of those in HR goes a long way toward establishing the credibility of the entire organization.

There are many topics through which HR professionals can have a major impact on ethics, and therefore, on creating an ethical corporate culture. Some ethical questions that might be considered include:

- Do you strive to create a diverse workforce?
- Do you insist that job descriptions are developed to accurately depict jobs that are dangerous or hazardous?
- Do you strive to recruit and select the best-qualified applicant for the job?
- Are your training initiatives geared so that everyone will have an opportunity to receive the best training and development possible?
- Is your performance management and appraisal system able to identify those who are indeed the best producers and rewarded accordingly?
- Is your compensation and benefit system developed so that employees will view it as fair and impartial?
- Does your organization make a sincere attempt to provide a safe and healthy work environment?
- Does your organization attempt to develop a work environment in which employees will not feel compelled to join a union?
- Are you fair and impartial when dealing with disciplinary action, promotion, transfer, demotion, resignation, discharge, layoff, and retirement?
- Does your firm adhere to ethical norms when operating in the global environment?

HR should review, develop, and enforce organizational policies to ensure a high level of ethics throughout the organization. All employees should know what is ethical and unethical in their specific area of operations. It is insufficient to say that everyone should behave ethically. Let's turn our attention to two areas where HR professionals use their expertise to promote practices and employee behavior in organizations: pay and training.

Linking Pay to Ethical Behavior

The City of Los Angeles sued Wells Fargo Bank based on allegations that the company engaged in unlawful and fraudulent conduct. Bank employees routinely opened customer accounts without their authorization, and those accounts came with monthly fees. Los Angeles City Attorney Michael Feuer maintained that bank management was regularly, "abusing employees and telling them 'to do whatever it takes' to reach quotas on the number of new accounts they must open."[65] Shortly after the suit was filed, Wells Fargo agreed to settle the case out of court without admitting wrongdoing.[66] The bank also agreed to reimburse customers for all of the fees associated with accounts the accounts in question. Clearly, management sent the signal that performance would be rewarded based on opening a highly unrealistic number of new accounts, and employees felt pressure to perform. Since this incident took place, Wells Fargo restructured its compensation plan. Spokeswoman Mary Eshet stated that the new compensation plan, "eliminates sales goals, measures performance based on customer experience and adds more oversight and risk management."[67]

Wells Fargo is just one of many companies where the ethics of pay practices are in question, highlighting the importance of linking pay to performance when discussing ethics. It is well known in the compensation world that "what you reward is what you get." If the statement is correct, then a problem exists because most companies do not link pay to ethical behavior but base pay on entitlement and custom.[68] A survey of 358 compliance and ethics professionals by the Society of Corporate Compliance and Ethics (SCCE) and Health Care Compliance Association found that only a few companies have made ethics and compliance a process for determining how employees are compensated, and only about one company in six ties employee bonuses and incentives to ethical performance.[69] In another survey, when asked how much impact the ethics and compliance function has on the compensation process for executives, just 34 percent of respondents said it had some or a great deal of impact. The majority indicated that compliance and ethics played very little (27 percent) or no role (29 percent), and the balance was unsure of the role of ethics and compliance.[70] CEO Roy Snell of SCCE said, "The net result is that there is more work to be done in aligning business practices with stated commitment to compliant, ethical behavior."[71] For example, ethical expectation could be made part of the performance review and the results tied to pay raises.[72] As one author recently stated, "When employees behave in undesirable ways, it's a good idea to look at what you're encouraging them to do."[73]

FYI

- Eighty-one percent of companies provide ethics training.[74]

Ethics Training

The FSGO Act outlined an effective ethics training program and explained the seven minimum requirements for an effective program to prevent and detect violations. The fourth requirement stated, "Educate employees in the company's standards and procedures through publications and training." Companies train employees on many topics, but ethics training is often not considered, which is a major oversight. Because of its inclusion within the FSGO, a brief discussion of ethics training will be provided in this chapter.

Companies that consistently rank high on the lists of best corporate citizens tend to make ethics training part of a company-wide initiative to promote integrity.[75] Ethics training should be part of a proactive, not reactive, strategy. Regular training builds awareness of common ethical issues and provides tools for effective problem solving. Warren Buffett once said, "Pick out associates whose behavior is better than yours and you'll drift in that direction."[76] Ethics training should begin at the top and continue through all levels in the organization.[77] Ethics training should also take into consideration the differences in these levels. Although boards of directors and top management set the ethical tone, middle managers are the ones who will likely be the first to receive reports of unethical behavior. Unfortunately, many companies do not follow this prescription. A survey of ethics and compliance officers revealed that board members receive less training about important matters including cybersecurity, workplace harassment, and conflicts of interest than others in the company.[78] For instance, only 12 percent provides training to board members about workplace harassment versus 76 percent for employees.

KPMG believes that there are three fundamental factors in handing ethics issues: provide multiple channels for raising alarms, eliminate fear of retaliation for those who raise questions, and ensure consistent investigation and resolution of all matters reported. Individuals who report potential ethics violations could be subject to retaliation, so KPMG monitors performance reviews and other metrics to proactively identify retaliatory behavior. The credibility of the program requires all reports to be consistently investigated and resolved.[79]

Cisco created a unique ethics training program that showcased cartoon contestants singing about various ethical workplace situations found in Cisco's *Code of Business Conduct*. Jeremy Wilson, manager, ethics office for Cisco Systems, Inc., said, "We wanted what was right for our employees, based upon our own risk analysis." When Cisco created its program, it invited input

HR BLOOPERS

Sales Incentives at Pinser Pharmaceuticals

Quarterly sales reports are in at Pinser Pharmaceuticals and Ben Ross looks forward to sharing the reports with the sales team. As a compensation analyst, Ben calculates sales commissions for the sales representatives, and high sales mean big paychecks for the team. The sales representatives receive incentive pay bonuses based on how many times doctors in their sales territory prescribe Pinser drugs. The number of prescriptions has increased with several of the popular drugs Pinser makes and the sales representatives that have the doctors writing the most prescriptions stand to benefit significantly. Ben knows that they have steep competition on some of their products, but he has also heard some rumors about how they stay ahead of competitors.

Apparently, many of the sales representatives are using some of their own extra earnings to earn the favor of the doctors. Gifts, dinners, and other incentives are provided to the doctors to encourage them to write Pinser prescriptions. At first he thought there might be a problem with this practice, but Ben knows that Pinser has a Code of Ethics and provides ethics training to all employees, so the sales representatives must know that their practices are acceptable. Ben understands that this is just the way business is done, and Ben's job is just to make sure they get paid what they have earned.

If your professor has assigned this, go to **www.pearson.com/mylab/management** to complete the HR Bloopers exercise and test your application of these concepts when faced with real-world decisions.

from more than 120 people from departments across the organization, including legal, human resources, IT security, and records management.[80]

Ethics training for global organizations is more complicated than preparing the training for U.S. employees. One must also train for the country in which the global company operates. Since 1994, LRN has helped 15 million people at 700 companies across the world simultaneously navigate legal and regulatory environments and foster ethical cultures.[81] A few of their customers include CBS, Dow Chemical, eBay, 3M, and Siemens. Chris Campbell, creative director at LRN, says, "Localization is as important as the accuracy of the translation process. Learners need to be able to connect in a way that is believable to them."[82]

2.4 Explain the concepts and practices related to corporate social responsibility and corporate sustainability.

Corporate Social Responsibility and Sustainability

Related to ethics are the concepts of corporate social responsibility and corporate sustainability. **Corporate social responsibility (CSR)** is the implied, enforced, or felt obligation of managers, acting in their official capacity, to serve or protect the interests of groups other than themselves, and **corporate sustainability** focuses on the possible future impact of an organization on society, including social welfare, the economy, and the environment. CSR and corporate sustainability differ from ethics in an important way. Ethics focus on individual decision making and behavior and the impact of ethical choices on employee welfare. As noted, CSR and corporate sustainability consider the broader impact of corporate activities on society.

corporate social responsibility (CSR)
Implied, enforced, or felt obligation of managers, acting in their official capacity, to serve or protect the interests of groups other than themselves.

corporate sustainability
Concerns with possible future impact of an organization on society, including social welfare, the economy, and the environment.

Ethics, CSR, and corporate sustainability are everyone's business. HR professionals particularly concern themselves with establishing policies to promote ethical behavior and discourage unethical behavior. In addition, the HRM function's leadership works with other executive leadership to identify training opportunities for educating employees about how they may make positive contributions to these objectives and developing performance-based pay programs that align employee performance with CSR and social responsibility goals.

FYI

- Eighty-eight percent feel their job is more fulfilling when they are provided opportunities to make a positive impact on social or environmental issues.[83]

Corporate Social Responsibility

As previously stated, CSR is the implied, enforced, or felt obligation of managers, acting in their official capacity, to serve or protect the interests of groups other than themselves. A recent survey revealed that 86 percent of consumers wanted companies to tell them more about the results of CSR efforts.[84] Another survey revealed that 58 percent of respondents consider a company's social and environmental commitments when deciding where to work: 58 percent said they would choose to work for a socially responsible company, even if the salary was less, and 51 percent indicated they won't work for a company that doesn't have strong social or environmental commitments.[85] Many companies are listening. About 60 percent of companies offer workers paid time off to volunteer, and 33 percent of them volunteered in 2015—up from 28 percent in 2013.What do the following U.S. companies have in common: Johnson & Johnson, Cisco Systems, Inc., McCormick & Co, Inc., Allergan, plc, and Prologis Inc.? They have been identified as having a commitment to excellence in CSR and are included in the 2017 Global 100 Most Sustainable Corporations in the World.[86] These companies have demonstrated the ability to manage the "triple bottom line" of social responsibility (society, environment, and economy).[87] They represent the top 5 percent of socially responsible companies.

HR Web Wisdom

Business for Social Responsibility

www.bsr.org

This is a global organization that helps member companies achieve success in ways that respect ethical values, people, communities, and the environment.

CSR is the model in which economic, social, and environmental responsibilities are satisfied concurrently.[88] Figure 2-1 illustrates the layers of responsibility associated with CSR. When a corporation behaves as if it has a conscience, it is said to be socially responsible. CSR considers the overall influence of corporations on society at large and goes beyond the interests of shareholders. It is how a company behaves toward society. In many companies, social responsibility has moved from nice to do to must do.[89] More and more companies are issuing CSR reports that detail their environmental, labor, and corporate-giving practices. Some firms, such as Burger King, have created the position of director of CSR.

Apparently, socially responsible behavior pays off on the bottom line. When GE CEO Jeffrey Immelt announced that the company would double its spending on green technology research, it was no grand attempt to save the planet; it was an example of astute business strategy. Immelt said, "We plan to make money doing it."[90] Social responsibility has also impacted the recruiting process. College graduates of today often seek out corporations that have a reputation for being socially responsible, which was not often the case in the past. In fact, job seekers overall tend to be more attracted to organizations known for CSR.[91]

Procter & Gamble (P&G) has long believed it has a responsibility for the long-term benefit of society as well as the company. Over the years, P&G has pursued programs to strengthen U.S. education, to encourage employment opportunities for minorities and women, to develop and implement environment-protection technology, and to encourage employee involvement in civic activities and the political process.

Deborah Leipziger, an Ethical Corporation Institute researcher, said, "The more credible efforts tend to be led by key players within a company."[92] An organization's top executives usually determine a corporation's approach to social responsibility. For example, under executive chairman and (former) CEO Howard Schultz, Starbucks Coffee focuses its corporate responsibility

FIGURE 2-1

Carroll's Pyramid of Corporate Social Responsibility

Source: SHRM Foundation, "*HRM's Role in Corporate Social Responsibility and Environmental Sustainability*," 2012, Alexandria, VA: SHRM Foundation, page 4. Accessed January 14, 2017, at www.shrmfoundation.org.

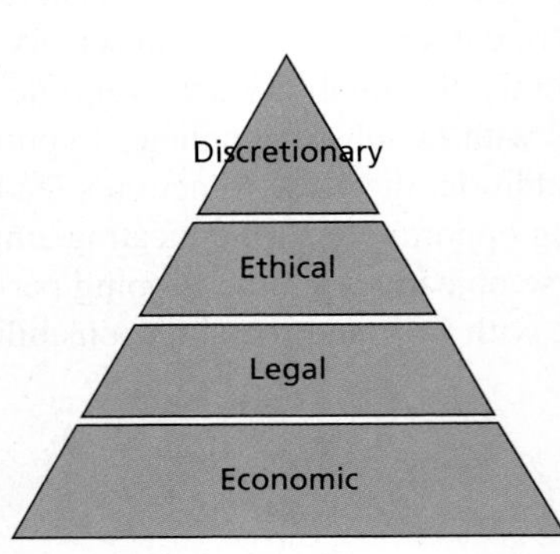

- **Discretionary responsibilities:** The fourth layer of responsibility is to proactively seek opportunities to make a positive contribution to society beyond profitability, compliance, and business ethics. At the discretionary, or voluntary level, organizations have a responsibility to understand broad stakeholder needs and to address societal concerns though their business practices.
- **Ethical responsibilities:** The third layer of the pyramid requires organizations to consider social and environmental impacts of their operations and, as far as possible, to do no harm while pursuing business interests.
- **Legal responsibilities:** The second aspect of responsibility requires that organizations operate within the law at all locations in which they do business.
- **Economic responsibilities:** The first responsibility of any organization is to deliver an acceptable return for shareholders (while contributing to local and global economies through their core business).

efforts on three main areas: ethical sourcing, environmental stewardship, and community involvement.[93] Starbucks approaches ethical sourcing by helping the farmers and suppliers who grow and produce their products use responsible growing methods. Environmental stewardship has been one of the more difficult activities for Starbucks. After all, Starbucks sells billions of beverages in disposable cups each year in the United States, most of which end up in landfills. The company has invested substantial amounts of money to come up with recyclable cups—one that can be recycled into other paper products again and again. Not only has this process been time consuming and expensive, but Starbucks has had to devote substantial time and resources to educating its customers and encourage responsible disposal of empty cups. In addition, Starbucks also looks after the communities where stores are located. It provides financial support and employees are encouraged to get involved in volunteering in their communities. For instance, Starbucks spearheaded the 100,000 Opportunities Hiring Initiative, which is a coalition of companies that offer meaningful work to youths.

The same can be said about leadership's role in supporting environmental sustainability. For instance, SC Johnson Company collaborated with a European company to develop an environmentally friendly alternative to the original formulation of Saran Wrap, which had come under criticism for containing polyvinyl chloride and is known to have ill side effects. Even though the reformulated Saran Wrap product does not work as well as the original, the company's leadership decided not to return to the original formulation despite consumer preferences. SC Johnson's CEO Fisk Johnson III and leadership team faced a dilemma: jeopardize losing customers and market share by replacing the original product with a lesser one or the goodwill the company had developed over the years with consumers and other stakeholders.[94] Ultimately, the company sacrificed substantial market share and profits in favor of helping to protect the environment.

One of the best benchmarks for defining social responsibility in manufacturing is the one-page set of operating principles developed 60 years ago by Robert Wood Johnson, then Johnson & Johnson's chairman of the board. The document is still in use today and addresses supporting good works and charities.[95]

During the Vietnam War, Dow Chemical gained a bad reputation for not being socially responsible because it produced the deadly chemical agent napalm. As a result, Dow had difficulty recruiting the best scientists and other professionals. To overcome this image, Dow built a campaign that highlighted how Dow has benefitted agricultural production. Once people saw the positive side of Dow, its ability to recruit and retain the best chemists improved.[96] However, the chemical industry continues to face widespread public mistrust despite being an enabler of advances that are vital to solving global challenges as well as efforts to improve product and process safety.[97]

Thus far, only the virtues of CSR have been provided. However, the question of whether businesses should promote CSR is at times hotly debated and not all companies have embraced the concept.[98] Some have challenged the concept that doing well is doing good (DWDG). They believe that although appealing to some, DWDG is also profoundly wrong.[99] Milton Friedman was a U.S. economist, statistician, academic, and author who taught at the University of Chicago for more than three decades and was a recipient of the Nobel Memorial Prize in Economic Sciences. In his book *Capitalism and Freedom*, he argued that the only social responsibility of business was to increase its profits. According to Friedman, as a firm creates wealth for its shareholders, society will also be benefited.[100] Friedman disciples continue to condemn CSR as a hodgepodge of "value-destroying nonsense."[101]

These days, more employers are publicly endorsing a culture of ethics and social responsibility. However, some believe that it is being done more as a public relations campaign. For instance, the Wounded Warrior Project is a not-for-profit organization that helps wounded military service members, particularly facilitating access to mental health services. Television campaigns that showcase service members' testimonial about how they (and their families) have benefited from the organization's generosity. However, several employees claimed that the organization's leadership routinely diverted money away from helping wounded service members to throw lavish parties and executives of the organization were subsequently fired. Certainly, Wounded Warrior is a legitimate organization; however, this incident illustrates that leaders' behavior may sometimes be inconsistent with the mission they declare to uphold.

Also, long before the enormous oil spill in 2010, BP promoted itself as being eco-friendly. Its literature stated that BP stood for "Beyond Petroleum." BP marketed itself as a producer of alternative energies, an image that was seriously damaged by the devastating oil spill in the Gulf of Mexico in 2010. Instead of spending billions on eco-friendly energy and building an employer brand campaign around it, many believe that BP would have been much better off if it had spent more time and effort in training its employees on its oil drilling platforms, establishing stronger safety protocols, and waiting until they were safe to operate. Even during this public relations campaign, BP had a history of safety violation. BP had been "fined more than $100 million for safety violations that led to deaths of workers, explosions of refineries, and leaking pipelines."[102] The following Watch It video describes the environmental impact of another oil company's spill and leadership's reaction to the disaster.

Watch It 2

If your instructor has assigned this, go to **www.pearson.com/mylab/management** to watch a video titled Co Responsible for Oil Spill Under Fire and to respond to questions.

Brighter Planet, a sustainability technology company, discovered in a recent survey that although more firms are engaging in green activities, the effectiveness of these efforts has declined.[103] Some believe that the problem with CSR is that it consists of a universal set of guidelines such as the "triple bottom line" (society, environment, and economy) mentioned previously. To be "socially responsible," each firm should follow the same guidelines instead of what would be the most appropriate strategy for each firm. Using this logic, it would be more logical for oil companies such as BP to focus on being profitable, yet be an environmentally conscious oil company. Fast-food restaurants such as McDonald's and retailers such as Walmart should each use a different set of rules to do the same thing in their own industries.

There are those who believe that all shareholders should not be required to be involved in CSR investments. They think that only investors who want to be involved should participate. These investors would do so with the understanding that the objective is not just to make money but also to do good. For example, an oil company such as Exxon could establish an alternative-energy subsidiary. Exxon would own a controlling stake, but funding would come from new investors who want to support alternative energy and thus be socially responsible. If the subsidiary was unsuccessful, the losses would be confined to the new investors. If it succeeded, the profits would be shared by all shareholders.[104]

FYI

The 2017 Global 100 Most Sustainable Corporations were most commonly found in the following countries:

- United States: 19 companies
- France: 12 companies
- United Kingdom: 11 companies
- Canada and Germany: 6 companies
- Netherlands: 5 companies[105]

Corporate Sustainability

Corporate sustainability has evolved from the more traditional view of CSR. According to the World Commission on Environment and Sustainability, the narrow definition of sustainability is, "meeting the needs of the present without compromising the ability of future generations to meet their own needs."[106] The Dow Jones World Sustainability Index (DJSI) provides a good working definition of this term. They define it as, "An approach to creating long-term shareholder value by embracing opportunities and managing risks deriving from economic, environmental and social trends and challenges."[107] In recent years, sustainability has been expanded to include the social, economic, environmental, and cultural systems needed to support an organization. This type of organization can continue both now and in the future. A recent study revealed that 90 percent of the 250 world's largest companies reported information about their corporate responsibility initiatives.[108] Also, 154 U.S. companies voluntarily signed the American Business Act on Climate Pledge to demonstrate their additional commitment to promoting environmental sustainability.[109] Among the companies signing the pledge, Berkshire Hathaway Energy promised to retire more than 75 percent of its coal-fueled generating capacity in Nevada by 2019.

Corporate sustainability may be thought of as being a business and investment approach that strives to use the best business practices to meet the needs of current and future shareholders. According to Louis D. Coppola, executive vice president of the Government & Accountability Institute, "Leaders increasingly understand the critical importance of adopting and implementing strategies, products, services, programs and initiatives that reflect the twenty-first century business environment, and the interest of investors and important stakeholders."[110] HR professionals play an important role in promoting corporate sustainability objectives. Figure 2-2 illustrates how HR professionals can use their expertise toward this end. Today it relates to how an organization's decisions could affect society and the environment. Essentially it is about how a firm handles its business while understanding how these decisions may affect others. One could think of corporate sustainability in a business sense as providing long-term profitability. Thus, sustainability should be a fundamental part of business strategy, product development, talent development, and capital investment. Some organizations have emphasized the importance of corporate sustainability by establishing the position of chief sustainability officer.[111]

HR Web Wisdom

Deloitte Sustainability Are You Overlooking Opportunities?

www.deloitte.com/us/sustainability

Many executives are turning to sustainability to help improve the bottom line.

Others such as Johnson & Johnson prefer to see it developed into the overall culture of the firm. Tish Lascelle, Johnson & Johnson's senior director of environment, said, "Sustainability is embedded in our culture. It's been a part of who we are for more than 65 years, long before the notion of sustainability became trendy."[112] The following Watch It video illustrates how a company has taken to become, and remain, a "mission-driven business" with corporate social responsibility as one of its mission's core values.

Watch It 3

If your instructor has assigned this, go to **www.pearson.com/mylab/management** to watch a video titled Honest Tea: Corporate Social Responsibility and to respond to questions.

FIGURE 2-2

How to Embed Sustainability Using HRM Tools

Source: SHRM Foundation, "*HRM's Role in Corporate Social Responsibility and Environmental Sustainability*," 2012, Alexandria, VA: SHRM Foundation, page 8. Accessed January 14, 2017, at www.shrmfoundation.org.

- Employee attraction: Using the organization's commitment to sustainability in recruitment helps attract more applicants and at the same time ensures the right "fit" with the company's sustainability goals.
- Employee attitudes: Although the research is unclear whether an organization's commitment to sustainability leads to higher employee retention, it does have positive effects on employee commitment and job satisfaction.
- Employee skills and knowledge: Many organizations provide initial and ongoing training and development on the knowledge and skills needed to achieve their sustainability goals, although the research on the impact of achieving sustainability goals is still limited.
- Employee sustainability goal attainment: Including sustainability targets in evaluation and compensation systems can lead to greater attention to and achievement of those goals.
- Sustainability organizational climate: Though the research is lacking in this area, a sustainability strategy will likely fail if the company's organizational climate does not appropriately support it.
- Employee sustainability behaviors: Supervisory and organizational support can lead to more sustainability behaviors in employees.

Numerous companies are working toward becoming eco-friendly. In 2016, approximately 81 percent of the S&P 500 Index companies reported having an active sustainability program in place, up from 20 percent in 2011.[113] For instance, Unilever has placed sustainability at the core of its business. The company promised by 2020 to double its sales even as it cuts its environmental footprint in half and sources all its agricultural products in ways that don't degrade the Earth.[114] Target's waste-reduction efforts have cut waste by 70 percent. Home Depot attempts to make sure that wood and lumber sold in its stores come from sustainable forests. Corporate environmental responsibility for McDonald's focuses on energy efficiency, sustainable packing and waste management, and green restaurant design.[115] McDonald's has eliminated the use of containers made with ozone-depleting chlorofluorocarbons, cut down on the amount and type of packaging it uses, and implemented a program of purchasing goods made from recycled materials. Walmart is working on sustainable initiatives. Solar panels are being installed in all the retailer's super centers with unused energy being sold back into the energy grid, a cost-saving move for the community.[116]

Increasingly, environmentally sound and cost-cutting operating procedures are being included in firms' business plans not only for their own employees, products, and facilities, but also for suppliers and trade partners. Walmart Stores Inc. has initiated and promoted sustainability not only in its own stores and production facilities, but also for its U.S. and global suppliers.[117] Frito-Lay, which operates the world's seventh-largest private delivery fleet, has put 176 all-electric box trucks on the road in places such as California, Texas, and the Pacific Northwest. The trucks are expected to cut diesel consumption by 500,000 gallons a year while limiting greenhouse emissions by 75 percent compared with combustion engines. The trucks will also cut annual maintenance costs by as much as $700,000.[118] Coca-Cola Enterprises Corporate Responsibility and Sustainability Report stated that they have taken steps to reduce the number of calories per liter by 10 percent by 2020.[119]

PPG Industries recently issued a corporate sustainability report that provides information about the company's financial performance, environmental metrics such as greenhouse gas emissions and energy use, safety statistics, stakeholder engagement, philanthropic activities, and awards and recognition. In the report, Charles E. Bunch, PPG chairman and CEO, said, "Sustainability is business as usual at PPG. An underlying principle for the company since its founding in 1883, a commitment to sustainability has been crucial to our long-term success."[120] Leading up to 2020, PPG will strive to reduce environmental impact, improve employees' safety, health and well-being and encourage and report employee charitable donations and volunteerism.[121] Dow Chemical's way of thinking regarding sustainability is, "If you can't do it better, why do it?" This philosophy is at the very heart of sustainability at Dow. Every decision is made with the future in mind.[122]

Institutional investors managing more than $1.6 trillion in assets are starting to put pressure on the world's 30 largest stock exchanges to force companies to improve their sustainability reporting. Twenty-four institutional shareholders said they want it to be easier to judge the environmental, social, and governance risks of the firms in which they invest.[123]

Sustainability has also become extremely popular for companies operating in the global environment. Recently, Danone's German division switched to a plastic made from plants (not oil) for its Activia yogurt packaging sold in Germany.[124] Coca-Cola Enterprises in Great Britain has cut its carbon emissions by 470,000 tons, which is about a third of its 2020 target. It is also recycling 99 percent of the factory waste it produces, with five out of six of its production sites sending zero waste to landfills.[125] Global polystyrene leader Styron LLC has more than 2,000 employees at 20 plants worldwide with annual sales of $5 billion. It begins each corporate meeting with the topic of sustainability. Employees' bonuses are tied in to meeting sustainability goals. Recently, Styron introduced a recycled-content grade of polycarbonate at the Chinaplas trade show in Guangzhou, China.[126] Renault partnered with Veolia Environment to build the world's first zero-emissions, 100-percent renewable energy-reliant car manufacturing plant in Morocco.[127]

2.5 Describe a social audit.

Conducting a Social Audit

To overcome the negative publicity of corporate misdeeds and to restore trust, businesses are now conducting audits of their social responsibility activities and not just financial audits. A **social audit** is a systematic assessment of a company's activities in terms of its social impact.

social audit
Systematic assessment of a company's activities in terms of its social impact.

Some of the topics included in the audit focus on core values such as social responsibility, open communication, treatment of employees, confidentiality, and leadership. Firms are now acknowledging responsibilities to various stakeholder groups other than corporate owners.[128]

Some audits even set specific objectives in social areas. They are attempting to formally measure their contributions to various elements of society and to society. An increasing number of companies, as well as public and voluntary sector organizations, are trying to assess their social performance systematically. Three types of social audits are currently being used: (1) simple inventory of activities; (2) compilation of socially relevant expenditures; and (3) determination of social impact. The inventory is generally a good starting place. It consists of a listing of socially oriented activities undertaken by the firm. Here are some examples: minority employment and training, support of minority enterprises, pollution control, corporate giving, involvement in selected community projects by executives, and a hard-core unemployment program. The ideal social audit would go well beyond a simple listing and involve determining the true benefits to society of any socially oriented business activity.

Try It!

If your instructor has assigned this, go to **www.pearson.com/mylab/management** to complete the Management & Ethics simulation and test your application of these concepts when faced with real-world decisions.

PREPARING FOR EXAMS/QUIZZES

Chapter Summary by Learning Objectives

1. ***Discuss what* ethics *means and the sources of ethical guidance.*** *Ethics* is the discipline dealing with what is good and bad, right and wrong, or with moral duty and obligation. Business ethics addresses matters of choices about right and wrong made by business leaders. One might use numerous sources to determine what is right or wrong, good or bad, and moral or immoral, such as holy books or one's conscience. Another source of ethical guidance is the behavior and advice of people, including our parents, friends, and role models and members of our churches, clubs, and associations. For most professionals, there are codes of ethics that prescribe certain behavior.
2. ***Explore human resource management's (HRM) role in creating an ethical culture and a code of ethics.*** An ethical culture is made up of factors such as ethical leadership, accountability, and values. The climate at the top is fundamental to a company's ethical culture. Ethical leadership begins with the board of directors and CEO and continues to HR managers, all other managers, and supervisors. Building an ethical culture that lasts requires a foundation of practices that continue even when leaders change.

   A *code of ethics* establishes the rules that the organization lives by. Only a few companies have made ethics and compliance a process for determining how employees are compensated.
3. ***Define* human resource ethics.** *Human resource ethics* is the application of ethical principles to HR relationships and activities.
4. ***Explain the concepts and practices related to corporate social responsibility and corporate sustainability.*** *Corporate social responsibility* is the implied, enforced, or felt obligation of managers, acting in their official capacity, to serve or protect the interests of groups other than themselves, and *corporate sustainability* focuses on the possible future impact of an organization on society, including social welfare, the economy, and the environment. According to the World Commission on Environment and Sustainability, the narrow definition of sustainability is, "meeting the needs of the present without compromising the ability of future generations to meet their own needs." In recent years, sustainability has been expanded to include the social, economic, environmental, and cultural systems needed to support an organization.
5. ***Describe a social audit.*** A *social audit* is a systematic assessment of a company's activities in terms of its social impact.

Key Terms

ethics 29
code of ethics 35
human resource ethics 36
corporate social responsibility (CSR) 39
corporate sustainability 39
social audit 44

MyLab Management

If your instructor is using MyLab Management, go to **www.pearson.com/mylab/management** to complete the problems marked with this icon ✪.

Questions for Review

2-1. What are ethics and business ethics?
2-2. What are some sources of ethical guidance?
2-3. What laws have been passed to legislate ethics?
2-4. Why is it important to have a code of ethics?
✪ **2-5.** Regarding business ethics, what does the statement "what you reward is what you get" mean?
2-6. What are HR ethics?
✪ **2-7.** What are the areas in which HR professionals can have a major impact on ethics?
2-8. What is corporate social responsibility?
✪ **2-9.** What does corporate sustainability mean?
2-10. What are some of the practices companies can use to promote sustainability?

PREPARING FOR MY CAREER

P I A Personal Inventory Assessment

✪ *An additional Personal Inventory Assessment can be found on MyLab Management.*

Ethical Leadership Assessment

Organizations need ethical leadership from all employees, but especially from managers. In this PIA, you'll see how much thought and effort goes into being ethical in your workplace behavior.

ETHICS DILEMMA

A Selection Quandary

You are being promoted to a new assignment within your company, and your boss has asked you to nominate one of your subordinates as your replacement. The possible candidates are Randy Carlton, who is obviously more qualified, and James Mitchell, who, though not as experienced, is much better liked by the workers. If Randy is given the promotion, you are not certain the workers will accept him as their leader. James, on the other hand, is a hard worker and is well liked and respected by the others, including Randy. As you labor over the decision, you think about how unfair it would be to Randy if the feelings of the other workers kept him from getting a deserved promotion. At the same time, you feel that your primary responsibility should be to maintain the productivity of the work unit. If your former division fell apart after your departure, it would hurt your reputation, not to mention the company.

2-11. What would you do?
2-12. What factor(s) in this ethics dilemma might influence a person to make a less-than-ethical decision?

HRM Is Everyone's Business

Most company leaders and employees will face ethical challenges at one time or another. Some employees will intentionally commit ethics violations for personal gain. Other employees may unknowingly do so. Whether you are a manager or HR professional—an employee may bring concerns about possible ethical violations to your attention or you may observe them yourself. Once you are aware of a situation where ethics are in question, you are obligated to respond.

Action checklist for managers and HR—responding to allegations of unethical behavior

HR takes the lead

- ☑ Work with managers to ensure that they understand the company's code of ethics and communicate the procedures for addressing instances of potential ethical violations.
- ☑ Encourage managers to share the company's code of ethics with employees, lead open discussions about everyone's obligation to behave ethically, and create a safe environment for employees to report their concerns about possible ethical violations to the appropriate authority.
- ☑ Guide managers through the process of handling employees who are suspected of committing ethical violations.

Managers take the lead

- ☑ Educate HR on certain aspects of employee roles to better understand how unethical behavior may manifest in your department. Bringing HR up to speed creates a partnership for more effectively responding to possible ethical violations.
- ☑ Discuss concerns with HR about possible ethical violations and follow through based on company policy and procedures.
- ☑ Work together with HR to implement a training plan on the company's code of ethics and creating hypothetical scenarios illustrating ethical and unethical behavior relevant to your departmental activities.

HRM by the Numbers

Paying the Price for Underpaying Workers

✪ *An additional HRM by the Numbers exercise can be found on MyLab Management.*

HR professionals should ensure that workers are paid for their work on a timely basis. Sometimes, companies pay workers less than what they should and there are various possible reasons such as intent to save money or in error. Either way, paying employees lesser amounts than owed may violate the law. For instance, the Fair Labor Standards Act (FLSA), which we will discuss in Chapter 3, requires employers to pay eligible workers a higher pay for overtime work. Specifically, the overtime pay rate equals 1.5 times the regular hourly pay rate for each additional hour exceeding 40 in a work week.

You've learned that the company has not been paying employees appropriately for overtime work hours. It is your responsibility to calculate the amount of overtime pay owed to workers. After reviewing the payroll records, you discovered the following details:

1. Group 1: 225 workers. Each worker earns a regular hourly pay rate of $18.00. For each of the past 15 work weeks, everyone worked 45 hours.
2. Group 2: 310 workers. Each worker earns a regular hourly pay rate of $21.00. For each of the past 20 work weeks, everyone worked 47 hours.

Every worker received regular pay for all their hours worked, but they did not receive an additional overtime pay amount.

Questions

2-13. Calculate the hourly overtime pay rate for each worker in (a) group 1 and (b) group 2.
2-14. How much money does the company owe all the workers in (a) group 1 over 15 weeks and (b) group 2 over 20 weeks?
2-15. How much money did the company save by not paying all the workers (groups 1 and 2 combined) overtime pay?

Working Together: Team Exercise

In small groups of three or four, come up with specific answers to the following questions. Talk through your perspectives and come up with a brief team response. Be prepared to share your ideas with the class.

As a group, identify a company that has been in the news for committing ethical violations, exhibiting poor social responsibility, or engaging in practices that harmed the environment (sustainability). Consider those issues. In addition, review the company's position on ethics, social responsibility, and sustainability (perhaps from its website).

2-16. What are the main issues pertaining to lapses in ethical practice, failure to be socially responsible, or harmful environmental practices that were reported in the news about this company?

2-17. How does the company's stated position on ethics, social responsibility, and sustainability (found on the website) differ from what you have read in the news? Explain.

INCIDENT 1 An Ethical Flaw

Amber Davis had recently graduated from college with a degree in general business. Amber was quite bright, although her grades did not reflect this. She had thoroughly enjoyed school, dating, playing tennis, and swimming, but found few stimulating academic endeavors. When she graduated, she had not found a job. Her dad was extremely upset when he discovered this, and he took it upon himself to see that Amber became employed.

Amber's father, Allen Davis, was executive vice president of a medium-sized manufacturing firm. One of the people he contacted in seeking employment for Amber was Bill Garbo, the president of another firm in the area. Mr. Davis purchased many of his firm's supplies from Garbo's company. After telling Bill his problem, Allen was told to send Amber to Bill's office for an interview. Amber went, as instructed by her father, and before she left Bill's firm, she was surprised to learn that she had a job in the accounting department. Amber may have been lazy, but she certainly was not stupid. She realized that Bill had hired her because he hoped that his action would lead to future business from her father's company. Although Amber's work was not challenging, it paid better than the other jobs in the accounting department.

It did not take long for the employees in the department to discover the reason she had been hired; Amber told them. When a difficult job was assigned to Amber, she normally got one of the other employees to do it, implying that Mr. Garbo would be pleased with that person if he or she helped her out. She developed a pattern of coming in late, taking long lunch breaks, and leaving early. When the department manager attempted to reprimand her for these unorthodox activities, Amber would bring up the close relationship that her father had with the president of the firm. The department manager was at the end of his rope.

Questions

2-18. From an ethical standpoint, how would you evaluate the merits of Mr. Garbo's employing Amber? Discuss.

2-19. Now that she is employed, what course would you follow to address her on-the-job behavior?

2-20. It may be that Mr. Garbo viewed the hiring of Amber as strictly a business decision that would ensure receiving continued business from Amber's father. What might be some negative results of this questionable ethical decision?

INCIDENT 2 Illegal Hiring

The Foreign Corrupt Practices Act (FCPA) prohibits U.S. companies from bribing foreign officials; yet, the number of violations each year is staggering. Some violations center on the use of unethical HR practices. For example, the banking industry has been investigated for its internship and full-time employment hiring practices. The Bank of New York Mellon Corp. (BNY Mellon) gave internships to family members of foreign government officials. The bank's leadership intended to maintain or increase business with a Middle Eastern sovereign wealth fund. Internship programs are legal and BNY Mellon has a legitimate internship program, but these internships were awarded outside the accepted procedures and criteria used in its program. The U.S. SEC issued a cease-and-desist order, stating that "Delivering them [internships] 'was seen by certain relevant [bank] employees as a way to influence the officials' decisions."[129] This is the first cease-and-desist order of which internship hiring was the subject. Phillip Bezanson, a Bracewell & Giuliani Law LLP (firm) partner stated that "the concept of 'anything of value' under the FCPA can be 'really abstract.'. . ."[130] In the end, the bank agreed to pay a $5 million penalty, give up $8.3 million, and pay $1.5 million in interest.[131]

2-21. What would you have done in response to learning about these facts?

2-22. What factors in this situation might influence a company to make less-than-ethical decisions?

MyLab Management

If your instructor is using MyLab Management, go to **www.pearson.com/mylab/management** for Auto-graded writing questions as well as the following Assisted-graded writing questions:

2-23. Why should a firm want to create an ethical culture?

2-24. Why is everyone not on board about corporate social responsibility?

Endnotes

1 Kyle Scott, "Business Ethics: Do What's Right, or What's Right Now?" *Supervision* 72 (July 2011): 8–9.

2 Richard M. Steinberg, "Does Integrity and Ethical Behavior Pay Off?" *Compliance Week* 10 (June 2013): 44–45.

3 William Boston, Arian Campo-Flores, and Aruna Viswanatha, "FBI Arrests Volkswagen Executive in Emissions Scandal," *The Wall Street Journal* online (January 9, 2017). Accessed January 10, 2017, at www.wsj.com; Aruna Viswanatha and Mike Spector, "VW Emissions Cheating Ran Deep and Wide, State Alleges," *The Wall Street Journal* online (July 19, 2016). Accessed January 10, 2017, at www.wsj.com.

4 Winthrop Quigley, "VW Case Shows Need for Ethics in Cost-Benefit Toolkit," *Albuquerque Journal* online (October 15, 2015). Accessed December 1, 2016, at www.abqjournal.com; J. Plungis and D. Hull, "VW's Emissions Cheating Found by Curious Clean-Air Group," *Bloomberg Business* online (September 19, 2015). Accessed January 10, 2017, at www.bloomberg.com.

5 "6 VW Execs Indicted as Carmaker Agrees to $4.3 billion Diesel Cheat Settlement," *Fortune* online (January 12, 2017). Accessed January 15, 2017, at www.fortune.com.

6 "Investors Are Looking Closely at Corporate Ethics," *Corporate Board* 28 (September 2007): 28.

7 Ben W. Heineman, Jr., "Avoiding Integrity Land Mines," *Harvard Business Review* 85 (April 2007): 100–108.

8 Steve Steckler, "The Leadership Challenges Facing HR: Top CHROs Share Learnings and Advice on What's Next," *People & Strategy* 33 (2010): 14–21.

9 Becky Yerak, "Ex-United CEO Got $36.8 Million Severance Package," *Chicago Tribune* online (May 2, 2016). Accessed January 10, 2017, at www.chicagotribune.com.

10 Mary C. Gentile, "Keeping Your Colleagues Honest," *Harvard Business Review* 88 (March 2010): 114–117.

11 T. L. Stanley, "Ethics in Action," *Supervision* 69 (April 2008): 14–16.

12 Quoted in Robert Bolt, *A Man for All Seasons*. (New York: Random House) 1962.

13 Bill Streeter, "Regulation Is Not Ethics," *ABA Banking Journal* 104 (January 2012): 6.

14 Ikujiro Nonaka and Hirotaka Takeuchi, "The Wise Leader," *Harvard Business Review* 89 (May 2011): 58–67.

15 Kenneth D. Lewis, "The Responsibility of the CEO: Providing Ethical and Moral Leadership," *Vital Speeches of the Day* 69 (October 15, 2002): 6–9.

16 Sheryl L. Hopkins, "How Effective Are Ethics Codes and Programs?" *Financial Executive* 29 (March 2013): 42–45.

17 Patrick Moran, "Executive Perspective: What We've Learned from Sarbanes-Oxley," *Pennsylvania CPA Journal* 84 (Summer 2013): 32–35.

18 Thomas M. Behmer, "Sarbanes-Oxley Fails on Auditor Independence," *Accounting Today* 27 (January 2013): 13–14.

19 Cathleen Flahardy, "SOX Gives DOL Power to Reinstate Whistleblowers," *Corporate Legal Times* 15 (August 2005): 24–26.

20 Melissa Klein Aguilar, "Questions Arise on Timely Ethics Disclosure," *Compliance Week* 7 (March 2010): 58–59.

21 Howard Stock, "Ethics Trump Rules, Levitt Says," *Investor Relations Business* (April 7, 2003): 1.

22 Paul Schneider, "Dodd–Frank Financial Reform Legislation Addresses Executive Compensation," *Journal of Financial Service Professionals* 65 (January 2011): 27–31.

23 Dave Rebbitt, "The Dissenting Voice," *Professional Safety* 58 (April 2013): 58–61.

24 Jonathan Lawner and Denise Dickins, "Will There Be Whistleblowers?" *Regulation* 34 (Summer 2011): 36–40.

25 "IRS Whistleblower Program," Fiscal Year 2015 Annual Report to Congress (Publication 5241).

26 Ibid.

27 "2016 Annual Report to Congress on the Dodd-Frank Whistleblower Program," *U.S. Securities and Exchange Commission* (2016). Accessed January 3, 2017, at www.sec.gov/whistleblower/reportspubs/annual-reports/owb-annual-report-2016.pdf.

28 Eileen Z. Taylor and Jordan A. Thomas, "Enhanced Protections for Whistleblowers under the Dodd-Frank Act," *CPA Journal* 83 (January 2013): 66–71.

29 Curtis C. Verschoor, "New Whistleblower Rules Broaden Opportunities," *Strategic Finance* 93 (September 2011): 13–69.

30 Ibid.

31 "Whistleblower Gets $22 Million from SEC in Second-Biggest Award," (August 30, 2016). Bloomberg Web site. Accessed January 10, 2017, at www.bloomberg.com.

32 Anthony M. Alexis, Marcia E. Goodman, and Scott A. Clafee, "New Whistleblower Provisions Provide Bounty Incentives and Greatly Expanded Protections," *Insights: The Corporate & Securities Law Advisor* 24 (September 2010): 45–50.

33 "Companies Anticipate an Increase in Whistleblower Claims," *Corporate Board* 32 (January/February 2012): 28–29.

34 "Whistleblower Claims in Dodd–Frank Era Expected," *Financial Executive* 28 (January/February 2012): 11.

35 Jason C. Schwartz and Porter N. Wilkinson, "2011 Year-End Update on Dodd–Frank and SOX Employee Whistleblower Provisions," *Insights: The Corporate & Securities Law Advisor* 26 (January 2012): 15–22.

36 Michael Washburn, "Former SEC Counsel: Whistleblower Program Shortcomings," *International Financial Law Review* (February 2013): 22.

37 Shele Bannon, Kelly Ford, and Linda Meltzer, "How to Instill a Strong Ethical Culture," *CPA Journal* 80 (July 2010): 56–58.

38 Jean Francois Manzoni, "Nurturing a High Integrity Culture," *Rotman Magazine* (Winter 2013): 22–27.

39 Janice Block, "Ethical Culture," *Inside Counsel* 24 (April 2013): 10.

40 "The Volkswagen Group Code of Conduct," (not dated). Accessed January 15, 2017, at http://en.volkswagen.com/content/medialib/vwd4/de/Volkswagen/Nachhaltigkeit/service/download/corporate_governance/Code_of_Conduct/_jcr_content/renditions/rendition.file/the-volkswagen-group-code-of-conduct.pdf.

41 Eric Krell, "How to Conduct an Ethics Audit," *HR Magazine* 55 (April 2010): 48–51.

42 Steve Watkins, "Build Top Ethical Culture," *Investor's Business Daily* (March 30, 2012): 3.

43 "High Levels of Corporate Stress, Flawed Remuneration Policies, Excessive Reliance on Takeovers, and Lax Financial Discipline May Indicate Poor Corporate Culture—New Report Concludes," *The Governance Institute* (press release, March 7, 2016). Accessed January 13, 2017, at www.ibe.org.uk/userassets/pressreleases/icgn_ibe_icsa_pressrelease.pdf.

44 Patricia Harned, "Beyond Tone at the Top," *Boardroom Briefing* 7 (Fall 2010): 39–40.

45 Dori Meinert, "Strong Ethical Culture Helps Bottom Line," *HR Magazine* 55 (December 2010): 21.

46 Curtis C. Verschoor, "Top-Management Example and Peer Pressures Bring Benefits," *Strategic Finance* 92 (September 2010): 15–63.

47 "2016 Compliance and Ethics Program Objectives Survey," The Society of Corporate Compliance and Ethics and the Health Care Compliance Association (July 2016). Accessed January 13, 2017, at www.corporatecompliance.org.

48 David De Cremer, "6 Traits That Predict Ethical Behavior at Work," *Harvard Business Review* online (December 22, 2016). Accessed January 13, 2017, at www.hbr.org.

49 Richard McGill Murphy, "Why Doing Good Is Good for Business," *Fortune* 161 (February 8, 2010): 90–95.

50 "Ethics as Recruiting Tool," *Journal of Accountancy* 207 (January 2009): 21.

51 Ron Carucci, "Why Ethical People Make Unethical Choices," *Harvard Business Review* online (December 16, 2016). Accessed January 13, 2017, at www.hbr.org.

52 Ben Dipietro, "The Morning Risk Report: Report Details 'Right Way' to Teach Ethics," *The Wall Street Journal* online (April 13, 2016). Accessed January 13, 2017, at www.wsj.com.

53 Christopher Bauer, "Baking Ethics into Company Culture," *Financial Executive* 25 (May 2009): 18–21.

54 Jaclyn Jaeger, "The ROI of a Strong Ethical Culture," *Compliance Week* 10 (February 2013): 34–36.

55 Society for Human Resource Management, "SHRM Code of Ethics." Accessed February 3, 2014, at www.shrm.org/about/Pages/code-of-ethics.aspx.

56 Richard Teitelbaum, "Accountants, Auditors to Get a New Ethics Rule Book," *The Wall Street*

Journal online (July 11, 2016). Accessed January 10, 2017, at www.wsj.com.

57 Stephen Dockery, "Johnson Controls Settles China Corruption Case with SEC," *The Wall Street Journal* online (July 11, 2016). Accessed January 10, 2017, at www.wsj.com.

58 "Fidelity Fires Hong Kong Managers," *Fund Action* (February 22, 2010): 76.

59 Emily Glazer, Rachel Louise Ensign, and Nick Timiraos, "Romantic Relationships with Fannie Mae CEO Prompted Firing of Fifth Third Lawyer," *The Wall Street Journal* online (August 10, 2016). Accessed January 13, 2017, at www.wsj.com.

60 Ben Dipietro, "What Matters More: Focusing on Rules or Creating Ethical Culture?" *The Wall Street Journal* online (March 15, 2016). Accessed January 10, 2017, at www.wsj.com.

61 Ibid.

62 Kathryn Mayer, "HR Is the 'Conscience' of Workplace Culture," BenefitsPro (Web site, June 29, 2015). Accessed January 13, 2017, at www.benefitspro.com.

63 "Competencies Senior HR Pros Need Now, in Five Years," *HR Focus* 87 (June 2010): 12–13.

64 Ken Sloan and Joanne H. Gavin, "Human Resource Management: Meeting the Ethical Obligations of the Function," *Business & Society Review* 115 (Spring 2010): 57–74.

65 Peter Rudegeair, "Los Angeles Sues Wells Fargo Over Sales Tactics," *The Wall Street Journal* online (May 5, 2015). Accessed January 7, 2017, at www.wsj.com.

66 James Rufus Koren, "Wells Fargo to Pay $185 Million Settlement for 'Outrageous' Sales Culture," *LA Times* online (September 8, 2016). Accessed January 6, 2017, at www.latimes.com.

67 Emily Glazer, "Wells Fargo to Roll Out New Compensation Plan to Replace Sales Goals," *The Wall Street Journal* online (January 6, 2017). Accessed January 6, 2017, at www.wsj.com.

68 Darnell Lattel, "The Slippery Slope," *T+D* 66 (March 2012): 22.

69 Sven Erik Holmes, "Under Pressure: Maintaining an Effective Ethics and Compliance Program," *Directorship* 35 (October/November 2009): 72.

70 "Few Tie Executive Pay or Bonuses to Compliance," *Compliance Week* 6 (July 2009): 10.

71 S. Steffee, "Weak Link between Business Ethics and Executive Compensation," *Internal Auditor* 66 (August 2009): 16.

72 Patricia J. Harned, "Encourage Ethical Behavior as Economy Recovers," *HR Specialist: Compensation & Benefits* 5 (January 2010): 5.

73 Max H. Bazerman and Ann E. Tenbrunsel, "Ethical Breakdowns," *Harvard Business Review* 89 (April 2011): 58–65.

74 National Business Ethics Survey of the U.S. Workforce, 2013, Ethics Resource Center, www.ethics.org/nbes, 2014.

75 Luis Ramos, "Outside-the-Box Ethics," *Leadership Excellence* 26 (April 2009): 19.

76 Craig Mindrum, "Imitating Virtuous Behaviors," *Chief Learning Officer* 12 (April 2013): 34–37.

77 Karen Kroll, "Ethics & Compliance Training for Hourly Workers," *Compliance Week* 10 (June 2013): 42–66.

78 Ben Dipietro, "Survey Roundup: Companies Lagging on Training Directors," *The Wall Street Journal* online (July 29, 2016). Accessed January 13, 2017, at www.wsj.com.

79 Jerry Maginnis and Joseph P. Charles, "Build a Strong Ethical Culture," *Pennsylvania CPA Journal* 80 (Summer 2009): 1–2.

80 Cynthia Kincaid, "Corporate Ethics Training: The Right Stuff," *Training* 46 (May 2009): 35.

81 LRN Corporation, "Who We Are." Accessed February 21, 2012, at www.lrn.com/who-we-are.

82 Ron Miller, "It's a Small World After All," *EContent* 31 (January/February 2008): 26–31.

83 "2016 Cone Communications: Employee Engagement Study," (2016), Cone Communications. Accessed December 20, 2016 at www.conecomm.com/research-blog/2016-employee-engagement-study.

84 Brittaney Kiefer, "CSR Moves from Planting Trees to Credible Business Strategies," *PRWeek* 16 (February 2013): 12.

85 "2016 Cone Communications: Employee Engagement Study," (2016), Cone Communications. Accessed December 20, 2016 at www.conecomm.com/research-blog/2016-employee-engagement-study.

86 "The Results for the 2017 Global 100 Most Sustainable Corporations in the World Index," *Corporate Knights* (Web site)." Accessed January 27, 2017, www.corporateknights.com/reports/2017-global-100/.

87 Nguyen Thi Hong Ngoc, "Being Socially Responsible and Environmentally Friendly Improves the Corporate Competitiveness and Profitability?" *Advances in Management* 4 (March 2011): 21–25.

88 Paul Shum and Sharon Yam, "Ethics and Law: Guiding the Invisible Hand to Correct Corporate Social Responsibility Externalities," *Journal of Business Ethics* 98 (February 2011): 549–571.

89 Mikhail Reider-Gordon, "Understanding Foreign States' Mandatory Corporate Social Responsibility Reporting," *Litigation* 39 (Winter 2013): 61–63.

90 Simon Zadek, "Responsibility Isn't a Blame Game," *Fortune (Europe)* 152 (October 3, 2005): 70–73.

91 Rachel Feintzeig, "Firms, Workers Boost Their Giving," *The Wall Street Journal* online (June 8, 2016). Accessed January 13, 2017, at www.wsj.com.

92 John S. McClenahen, "Defining Social Responsibility," *Industry Week* 254 (March 2005): 64–65.

93 "2015 Global Sustainability Report," Starbucks Corporation (Web site), Accessed January 14, 2017, at www.starbucks.com/responsibility/global-report.

94 Fisk Johnson, "SC Johnson's CEO on Doing the Right Thing, Even When It Hurts Business," *Harvard Business Review* online (April 2015). Accessed January 13, 2017, at www.hbr.org.

95 Z. Jill Barclift, "Corporate Social Responsibility and Financial Institutions: Beyond Dodd–Frank," *Banking & Financial Services Policy Report* 31 (January 2012): 13–19.

96 Aneel Karnani, "Doing Well by Doing Good: The Grand Illusion," *California Management Review* 53 (Winter 2011): 69–86.

97 Rebecca Coons, "Corporate Social Responsibility: Pursuing the Triple Bottom Line," *Chemical Week* 175 (May 27, 2013): 21–23.

98 V. Sivarama Krishnan, "In Defense of Social Responsibility of Business," *Journal of Business & Ethics* (2011): 31–37.

99 "Milton Friedman Goes on Tour," *Economist* 398 (January 29, 2011): 63.

100 Ronald J. Alsop "Cultural Awareness," *Workforce Management* 90 (July 2011): 42.

101 "Corporate Social Responsibility Heads for Oblivion," *Trends Magazine* 94 (February 2011): 10–14.

102 "Corporate Social Responsibility Heads for Oblivion," *Trends Magazine* 94 (February 2011): 10–14.

103 Adam Werbach, "Learning to Be Sustainable," *Chief Learning Officer* 10 (May 2011): 46–49.

104 Lilli Monolis, "Sustainability: It Will Change Your Business . . . If It Hasn't Already," *Plastics Technology* 58 (January 2012): 34–63.

105 "The Results for the 2017 Global 100 Most Sustainable Corporations in the World Index," *Corporate Knights* (Web site)." Accessed January 27, 2017, www.corporateknights.com/reports/2017-global-100/.

106 "Johnson & Johnson: Sustainability Is Mission-Critical," *Site Selection* 57 (January/February 2012): 42.

107 Alexandra R. Lajoux and Cheryl Soltis Martel, "Sustainability Rising," *NACD Directorship* 39 (March/April 2013): 24–35.

108 "Currents of Change: The KPMG Survey of Corporate Responsibility Reporting," (2015). *KPMG*. Accessed December 1, 2016, at www.kpmg.com.

109 White House Announces Additional Commitments to the American Business Act on Climate Package," *White House*. Accessed December 1, 2015, at www.whitehouse.gov.

110 "CSR's Mainstream Shift: 81 Percent of Leading Companies Published Corporate Sustainability Reports in 2015," *Bulldog Reporter* (Web site, March 16, 2016). Accessed January 13, 2017, at www.bulldogreporter.com/csrs-mainstream-shift-81-of-leading-companies-published-corporate-sustainability-reports-in-2015/.

111 Nguyen Thi Hong Ngoc, "Profitability?" *Advances in Management* 4 (March 2011): 21–25.

112 Michael Laff, "Triple Bottom Line," *T+D* 63 (February 2009): 34–39.

113 "CSR's Mainstream Shift: 81 Percent of Leading Companies Published Corporate Sustainability Reports in 2015," *Bulldog Reporter* (Web site, March 16, 2016). Accessed January 13, 2017, at www.bulldogreporter.com/csrs-mainstream-shift-81-of-leading-companies-published-corporate-sustainability-reports-in-2015/.

114 Marc Gunther, "Unilever's CEO Has a Green Thumb," *Fortune* 167 July 10, 2013): 124.

115 Jaclyn Jaeger, "Choosing Among a Vast Array of CSR Initiatives," *Compliance Week* 6 (October 2009): 60–70.

116 "Social Responsibility: An Ongoing Mission for a Good Corporate Citizen," *Nation's Restaurant News* (April 11, 2005): 60–66.

117 Sean Milmo, "LCA Plays Key Role for Sustainability," *ICIS Chemical Business* 280 (October 3, 2011): 13.

118 "Institutional Investors Push for Increased Corporate Sustainability Reporting," *Business & the Environment with ISO 14000 Updates* 22 (April 2011): 5–6.

119 "Coca-Cola Enterprises Corporate Responsibility & Sustainability Report 2015/2016," Accessed January 13, 2017, at www.coca-colacompany.com/stories/sustainability-reports.

120 "Corporate Sustainability," *Industry Week* 260 (February 2011): 49.

121 "PPG Launches New Sustainability Framework, Issues 2012 Sustainability Report," *Paintindia* 63 (May 2013): 145.

122 "Sustainability by the Numbers," *Business & the Environment with ISO 14000 Updates* 22 (July 2011): 13–14.

123 "PPG Issues 2010 Corporate Sustainability Report," *Paintindia* 61 (May 2011): 128–130.

124 Jim Carper, "Danone Uses Plant-based Packaging for Activia Yogurt in Germany," *Dairy Foods* 112 (August 2011): 10–11.

125 "Coca-Cola: Manufacturers Will Never Win the Battle of the Biodegradable Bottle," *Food Manufacture* 86 (August 2011): 7.

126 Frank Esposito, "Styron's Sustainability Goals, Progress Detailed in Report," *Plastics News* 23 (July 18, 2011): 4.

127 Ann Moline, "Not Your Father's Recycling Program," *Site Selection* 57 (January/February 2012): 41–45.

128 John Peloza, "Using Corporate Social Responsibility as Insurance for Financial Performance," *California Management Review* 48 (Winter 2006): 52–72.

129 S. Rubenfeld, "Bank of New York Mellon Settles SEC Bribery Charges," *The Wall Street Journal* online, www.wsj.com, August 18, 2015.

130 S. Rubenfeld, "The Morning Risk Report: Internships are Bribes in BNY Mellon Case," *The Wall Street Journal* online, www.wsj.com, August 19, 2015.

131 S. Rubenfeld, "Bank of New York Mellon Settles SEC Bribery Charges," *The Wall Street Journal* online, www.wsj.com, August 18, 2015.

3

Equal Employment Opportunity, Affirmative Action, and Workforce Diversity

LEARNING OBJECTIVES After completing this chapter, students should be able to:

3.1 Explain the concept of equal employment opportunity (EEO) and identify the federal laws affecting EEO.

3.2 Discuss who is responsible for ensuring equal employment opportunity.

3.3 Define the types of illegal employment discrimination and discuss affirmative action.

3.4 Explain the *Uniform Guidelines* related to various types of illegal employment discrimination, including sexual harassment, national origin, religion, and caregiver (family responsibility) discrimination.

3.5 Describe the concept of diversity and diversity management.

3.6 Explain the various elements of a diverse workforce.

MyLab Management

Improve Your Grade!

If your professor is using MyLab Management, visit **www.pearson.com/mylab/management** for videos, simulations, and writing exercises.

Learn It

If your professor has chosen to assign this, go to **www.pearson.com/mylab/management** to see what you should particularly focus on and to take the Chapter 3 Warm-Up.

equal employment opportunity (EEO)
The set of laws and policies that requires all individuals' rights to equal opportunity in the workplace, regardless of race, color, sex, religion, national origin, age, or disability.

affirmative action
Refers to the expectation and program requirements that companies make a positive effort to recruit, hire, train, and promote employees from groups who are underrepresented in the labor force.

diversity
Any perceived difference among people: age, race, religion, functional specialty, profession, sexual orientation, geographic origin, lifestyle, tenure with the organization or position, and any other perceived difference.

The workforce of today has become truly diverse. But this was not the case in the early 1960s; in fact, little of the workforce of those days remotely resembled that of today. Then, few mainstream opportunities were available to women, minorities, and those with disabilities. The Civil Rights Movement in the 1960s during which time blacks sought equality in employment and other areas of society led to a series of laws and executive orders, starting with Equal Employment Opportunity laws passed by the U.S. federal government. **Equal Employment Opportunity (EEO)** refers to the set of laws and policies that requires all individuals' rights to equal opportunity in the workplace, regardless of race, color, sex, religion, national origin, age, disability, or genetic information. Additional requirements, known as Affirmative Action, were established. **Affirmative Action** creates the expectation and program requirements that companies make a positive effort to recruit, hire, train, and promote employees from groups who are underrepresented in the labor force.

Since the Civil Rights movement and the passage of EEO laws, most companies have chosen to embrace the idea of promoting diversity in the workplace. **Diversity** refers to *any* actual or perceived difference among people: age, race, religion, functional specialty, profession, sexual orientation, gender identity, geographic origin, lifestyle, tenure with the organization or position, and any other perceived difference, including values and nontraditional work experiences. As you can see, characteristics of diversity go well beyond protected classes such as race in EEO law. Unlike EEO and Affirmative Action, promoting a diverse workforce is not required by law. Companies choose to embrace workforce diversity as a strategic choice. Capitalizing on a diverse workforce may be seen as contributing to a company's objectives such as profit, productivity, and morale. Diversity is inclusive, encompassing everyone in the workplace. Diversity management is aimed at creating a workplace in which every employee fits, feels accepted, has value, and contributes.

The purpose of this chapter is to explore EEO and Affirmative Action requirements. Then, we will take up the subject of workplace diversity.

3.1 Explain the concept of equal employment opportunity (EEO) and identify the federal laws affecting EEO.

Equal Employment Opportunity and the Federal Laws Affecting EEO

Legislation (federal, state, and local), Supreme Court decisions, and executive orders have required both public and private organizations to tap the abilities of a workforce that was largely underused before the mid-1960s. The concept of EEO has undergone much modification and fine-tuning since the passage of the Equal Pay Act of 1963, the Civil Rights Act of 1964, and the Age Discrimination in Employment Act of 1967.

Numerous amendments to these acts have been passed, as well as other acts in response to oversights in the initial legislation. Major Supreme Court decisions interpreting the provisions of the acts have also been handed down. A presidential executive order was signed into law that provided for affirmative action. More than five decades have passed since the introduction of the first legislation, and EEO has become an integral part of the workplace.

Although EEO has come a long way since the 1960s, continuing efforts are required because many problems still exist. Although perfection is elusive, most businesses today do attempt to make employment decisions based on who is the best qualified, as opposed to whether an individual is of a certain gender, race, religion, color, national origin, or age, or is disabled. Hiring standards to avoid will be identified based on some of the laws and executive orders that have had a major impact in creating this diverse workforce.

Numerous federal laws have been passed that have had an impact on EEO. The passage of these laws reflects society's attitude toward the changes that should be made to give everyone an equal opportunity for employment. The most significant of these laws will be described in the following sections after clarifying the sources of legislation based on the unit of government—federal government, state government, and local government. The federal government enacts and passes laws that apply throughout the entire United States. State government (for example, the states of Illinois and Louisiana) enacts legislation that applies throughout its jurisdiction within the state border. Local government may oversee the activities of a county or municipality within the state (e.g., Suffolk County in Massachusetts or New York City in New York). Our focus will be on federal laws, and we will make reference to state and local laws as necessary.

Constitutional Amendments and the Civil Rights Act of 1866

Although not an EEO law, one could say that the oldest federal legislation affecting staffing is the Civil Rights Act of 1866, which is based on the Thirteenth Amendment to the U.S. Constitution. The Thirteenth Amendment abolished slavery in the United States and provides that, "Neither slavery nor involuntary servitude, except as a punishment for crime whereof the party shall have been duly convicted, shall exist within the United States, or any place subject to their jurisdiction." The Civil Rights Act of 1866 granted citizenship and the same rights enjoyed by white citizens to all male persons in the United States, "without distinction of race or color, or previous condition of slavery or involuntary servitude." Subsequently, the Fourteenth Amendment to the U.S. Constitution was enacted to ensure that the Civil Rights Act passed in 1866 would remain valid ensuring that, "all persons born in the United States . . . excluding Indians not taxed. . . . " were citizens and were to be given, "full and equal benefit of all laws."

Title VII of the Civil Rights Act of 1964, Amended in 1972

The statute that has had the greatest impact on EEO is Title VII of the Civil Rights Act of 1964, as amended by the Equal Employment Act of 1972. Under Title VII, it is illegal for an employer to discriminate in hiring, firing, promoting, compensating, or in terms, conditions, or privileges of employment based on race, color, sex, religion, or national origin. The act also forbids retaliation against an employee who has participated in an investigation, proceeding, or hearing. For instance, Merrill Lynch & Co. paid $160 million to settle an employment discrimination lawsuit filed by black broker George McReynolds on behalf of 700 black brokers who worked for Merrill (*McReynolds, et al. v. Merrill Lynch & Co*). McReynolds claimed that the company gave white brokers more lucrative accounts while also denying black employees equal pay and career advancement opportunities.

Since the passage of this law, the Equal Employment Opportunity Commission (EEOC, discussed shortly), broadened its interpretation of sex discrimination and "enforces Title VII's prohibition of sex discrimination as forbidding any employment discrimination based on sexual orientation or gender identity."[1] In recent years, the EEOC has filed lawsuits in various courts tackling an assortment of LGBT discrimination-related issues including sexual orientation and transgender employees. For example, in *EEOC v. Pallet Companies d/b/a IFCO Sys. North Am., Inc.*, the EEOC alleged that Pallet Companies illegally terminated a lesbian employee based on sexual orientation after she complained about harassment. Discrimination cases involving transgender employees are becoming increasingly common. For instance, in *EEOC v. Lakeland Eye Clinic, P.A.*, the EEOC alleged that Lakeland Eye Clinic discriminated based on sex because it fired an employee who was transitioning from male to female and did not conform to gender-based expectations. In both cases, the employees' job performance was satisfactory. The companies in each case settled the claims out of court. Issues such as these can present challenges in terms of how we perceive ourselves and those around us. The following Watch It video looks at ways in which managers may react to an employee's gender transitioning.

Watch It 1

If your instructor has assigned this, go to **www.pearson.com/mylab/management** to watch a video titled TLM-Workforce Diversity and to respond to questions.

Title VII covers employers engaged in or affecting interstate commerce who have 15 or more employees for each working day in each of 20 calendar weeks in the current or preceding calendar year. Also, included in the definition of employers are state and local governments, schools, colleges, unions, and private employment agencies with 15 or more employees. All private employers who are subject to the Civil Rights Act of 1964 as amended with 100 employees or more must annually submit an EEO-1 report (see Figure 3-1). The EEO-1 reports information about the number of employees by job category (e.g., professional employees), by sex and race or ethnicity, and pay data and hours worked. Just as this book went to press, the requirements of reporting pay data and hours worked were suspended, at least for a time.

Three notable exceptions to discrimination as covered by Title VII are bona fide occupational qualifications (BFOQs), seniority and merit systems, and testing and educational requirements. According to the act, it is not an unlawful employment practice for an employer to hire and employ employees based on his or her religion, sex, or national origin in those certain instances where religion, sex, or national origin is a BFOQ reasonably necessary to the normal operation of the business or enterprise. For example, religious institutions, such as churches or synagogues, may legally refuse to hire teachers whose religious conviction is different from that of the hiring institution. Likewise, a maximum-security correctional institution housing only male inmates may decline to hire females as security guards. The concept of BFOQ was designed to be narrowly, not broadly, interpreted and has been so interpreted by the courts in many cases. For instance, historically women sales representatives were barred from working in a male clothing store because it was thought that men would not purchase from them. This stereotype has certainly been overcome because men regularly see female salespersons working in men's clothing stores. The burden of proving necessity rests entirely on the employer.

The second exception to discrimination under Title VII is a bona fide seniority system such as the type normally contained in a union contract. Differences in employment conditions among workers are permitted, if such differences are not the result of an intention to discriminate because of race, color, religion, sex, or national origin. Even if a bona fide seniority system has an adverse impact on those individuals protected by Title VII, the system can be invalidated only by evidence that the actual motives of the parties to the agreement were to discriminate.

Finally, in the matter of testing and educational requirements, Title VII states that it is not, "an unlawful employment practice for an employer to give, and to act upon, the results of any professionally developed ability test if such test, its administration, or action upon the results is not designed, intended or used to discriminate because of race, color, religion, sex, or national origin." Employment testing and educational requirements must be job related, and when adverse impact is shown, the burden of proof is on the employer to establish that a demonstrable relationship exists between actual job performance and the test or educational requirement. For instance, the EEOC charged retailer Target Corporation for illegal discrimination based on race and sex. It claimed that the company's hiring techniques disproportionately screened out racial minority and female applicants for professional positions.[2] Target chose to discontinue using the hiring practices in question and agreed to conduct validation studies to establish whether the practices were related to job performance and whether the practices have potential to disproportionately exclude qualified applicants based on race, ethnicity, and gender.

The Civil Rights Act of 1964 also created the Equal Employment Opportunity Commission (EEOC) and assigned enforcement of Title VII to this agency. Consisting of five members appointed by the president, the EEOC is empowered to investigate, conciliate, and litigate charges of discrimination arising under provisions of Title VII. In addition, the commission has the responsibility of issuing procedural regulations and interpretations of Title VII and the other statutes it enforces. The most significant regulation issued by EEOC is the *Uniform Guidelines on Employee Selection Procedures*. The EEOC enforces other EEO laws, with exceptions noted when those laws are discussed next.

FIGURE 3-1
Equal Employment Opportunity Employer Information Report

SECTION A - TYPE OF REPORT

1. Indicate by marking in the appropriate box the type of reporting unit for which this copy of the form is submitted (MARK ONLY ONE BOX).

☐ Single-establishment Employer Report

Multi-establishment Employer:
☐ Consolidated Report (Required)
☐ Headquarters Unit Report (Required)
☐ Individual Establishment Report (submit one for each establishment with 50 or more employees)
☐ Special Report

2. Total number of reports being filed by this Company (Answer on Consolidated Report only):

SECTION B - COMPANY IDENTIFICATION

1. Name of parent company that owns or controls establishment in item 2 (omit if same as above).

a. Parent Company:

Address (Number and Street):

City or Town: State: ZIP code:

2. Establishment for which this report is filed (omit if same as above)

a. Name of Establishment:

Address (Number and Street):

City or Town: County: State: ZIP code:

b. Employer identification No. (IRS 9-DIGIT TAX NUMBER):

c. Was an EEO-1 report filed for this establishment last year?
☐ Yes ☐ No

SECTION C - EMPLOYERS WHO ARE REQUIRED TO FILE

1. Does the entire company have at least 100 employees in the payroll period for which you are reporting?
☐ Yes ☐ No

2. Is your company affiliated through common ownership and/or centralized management with other entities in an enterprise with a total employment of 100 or more?
☐ Yes ☐ No

3. Does the company or any of its establishments (a) have 50 or more employees AND (b) is not exempt as provided by 41 CFR 60-1.5, AND either (1) is a prime government contractor or first-tier subcontactor, and has a contract, subcontract, or purchase order amounting to $50,000 or more, or (2) serves as a depository of Government funds in any amount or is a financial institution which is an issuing and paying agent for U.S. Savings Bonds and Savings Notes?
☐ Yes ☐ No

4. If the response to the above question (C - 3) is Yes, please enter your Dun and Bradstreet identification number (if you have one):

FIGURE 3-1
(*Continued*)

SECTION D - EMPLOYMENT DATA

Employment at this establishment - Report all permanent full- and part-time employees including apprentices and on-the-job trainees unless specifically excluded as set forth in the instructions. Enter the appropriate figures on all lines and in all columns. Blank spaces will be considered as zeros.

Job Categories	Annual Salary in Thousands	Number of Employees (Report employees in only one category)														
		Race/Ethnicity														Total Col A-N
		Hispanic or Latino		Non/Hispanic or Latino												
				Male						Female						
		Male	Female	White	Black or African American	Native Hawaiian or Pacific Islander	Asian	Native American or Alaska Native	Two or More races	White	Black or African American	Native Hawaiian or Pacific Islander	Asian	Native American or Alaska Native	Two or More races	
		A	B	C	D	E	F	G	H	I	J	K	L	M	N	O
	1. $19,239 and under															
	2. $19,240 - $24,439															
	3. $24,440 - $30,679															
	4. $30,680 - $38,999															
	5. $39,000 - $49,919															
Executive/Senior Level Officials and Managers 1.1	6. $49,920 - $62,919															
	7. $62,920 - $80,079															
	8. $80,080 - $101,919															
	9. $101,920 - $128,959															
	10. $128,960 - $163,799															
	11. $163,800 - $207,999															
	12. $208,000 and over															
	13. $19,239 and under															
	14. $19,240 - $24,439															
	15. $24,440 - $30,679															
	16. $30,680 - $38,999															
	17. $39,000 - $49,919															
First/ Mid-Level Officials and Managers 1.2	18. $49,920 - $62,919															
	19. $62,920 - $80,079															
	20. $80,080 - $101,919															
	21. $101,920 - $128,959															
	22. $128,960 - $163,799															
	23. $163,800 - $207,999															
	24. $208,000 and over															
	25. $19,239 and under															
	26. $19,240 - $24,439															
	27. $24,440 - $30,679															
	28. $30,680 - $38,999															
	29. $39,000 - $49,919															
Professionals 2	30. $49,920 - $62,919															
	31. $62,920 - $80,079															
	32. $80,080 - $101,919															
	33. $101,920 - $128,959															
	34. $128,960 - $163,799															
	35. $163,800 - $207,999															
	36. $208,000 and over															

FYI

The gender wage gap is substantial:

- All women working full time earn 79 percent of similar men's earnings.
- Hispanic women earn 55 percent of white men's earnings.
- African-American women earn 60 percent of white men's earnings.
- Asian women earn 84 percent of white men's earnings.[3]

Equal Pay Act of 1963, Amended in 1972

Passed as an amendment to the Fair Labor Standards Act, the Equal Pay Act (EPA) of 1963 prohibits an employer from paying women less money than men if both employees do work that is substantially the same. The EPA was passed largely to overcome the outdated belief that a man should be paid more than a woman because he was the primary breadwinner. The pay gap has declined through the years; however, one still exists as indicated in the FYI feature.

The EPA covers work within the same physical place of business. For example, an employer could pay a female more in San Francisco than a male working in the same position in Slippery Rock, Pennsylvania, even if the jobs were substantially the same, because of the cost-of-living difference. A key point to remember is that the pay difference must be substantial and that small pay differences might be acceptable. Four exceptions that permit unequal pay for equal work include:

- Seniority system
- Merit system
- System that measures earnings by quantity or quality of production
- Any other factor other than sex

More recently, new approaches to minimize the pay gap between women and men performing comparable work are being undertaken. For instance, Massachusetts' Pay Equity Act prohibits companies from inquiring about an applicant's pay history on job applications, interviews, and during pay negotiations. Companies are also prohibited from asking previous employers to verify pay amount prior to making a job offer. This law does have the potential to reduce the pay gap. For example, let's say that an employer's policy is to offer a salary that is 10 percent higher than the applicant's previous salary. And, for this illustration, a female applicant making $50,000 would receive a salary offer of $55,000 under the company's policy. A male applicant whose current salary is $75,000 would receive a salary offer of $82,500, thus, perpetuating the pay gap. Prohibiting questions about salary history helps companies to focus on the market value of the job.

Some companies voluntarily attempt to reduce the pay gap by prohibiting salary negotiations. These actions are based on the belief that most men are presumably better negotiators than women. One such company known for prohibiting salary negotiations is Reddit. In the following Watch It video, (former) CEO Ellen Pao further discusses the rationale for choosing not to negotiate job offers with applicants.

Watch It 2

If your instructor has assigned this, go to **www.pearson.com/mylab/management** to watch a video titled Reddit's Ellen Pao Bans Salary Negotiations and to respond to questions.

The EEOC enforces the EPA. The EEOC possesses the authority to investigate and reconcile charges of illegal discrimination. Title VII protects employees who work for all private sector employers; local, state, and federal governments; and educational institutions that employ 15 or more individuals. Title VII also applies to private and public employment agencies, labor organizations, and joint labor management committees controlling apprenticeship and training. It should be noted that the remaining laws that follow are also enforced by the EEOC.

Lilly Ledbetter Fair Pay Act of 2009

Lilly Ledbetter worked as a supervisor for Goodyear Tire from 1979 until 1998. Just before retirement, she received information that compared her salary with salaries of male coworkers. She was earning $3,727 monthly compared with 15 male coworkers who earned between $4,286 and $5,236. She sued, claiming pay discrimination under Title VII of the Civil Rights Act of 1964 and the Equal Pay Act of 1963.[4] In the 2007 Supreme Court case of *Ledbetter v. Goodyear Tire & Rubber Co., Inc.*, the Court said that discrimination charges must be filed within 180 days after the allegedly discriminatory pay decision. Lilly Ledbetter had worked for Goodyear for many years but she did not realize until she was close to retirement that she was being discriminated against because of pay. Because she did not file a discrimination charge within 180 days of her employment, the Supreme Court ruled against her. To reverse the Ledbetter decision, the Lilly Ledbetter Fair Pay Act was passed by Congress and signed into law in 2009. The law creates a rolling or open time frame for filing wage discrimination claims. Each paycheck that unfairly pays a worker less than it should is a discriminatory act. The act gives the worker a fresh 180-day period (300 days in some states) to file a charge of discrimination with the EEOC.

Pregnancy Discrimination Act of 1978

Prior to the passage of the Pregnancy Discrimination Act (PDA), most pregnant women did not receive the same protections afforded to others under Title VII. Many women argued that pregnancy should be specified as a protected class in Title VII. Efforts to amend Title VII were met with resistance by lawmakers, particularly following the Supreme Court decision in 1976. In *General Electric v. Gilbert*, the court ruled that excluding pregnancy as a condition qualifying for coverage under a disability plan did not constitute sex discrimination. Excluding pregnancy divided employees into two groups, one that was exclusively women and the other that included both women and men; thus, the distinction was not mainly sex-based. Members of the feminist movement and civil rights activists refused to accept this ruling, pressuring Congress to amend Title VII and overturn the Gilbert decision. Their efforts were successful. In 1978, Congress passed the PDA.

The Pregnancy Discrimination Act prohibits discrimination in employment based on pregnancy, childbirth, or related medical conditions. The basic principle of the act is that women affected by pregnancy and related conditions must be treated the same as other applicants and employees based on their ability or inability to work. A woman is therefore protected against such practices as being fired or refused a job or promotion merely because she is pregnant or has had an abortion. She usually cannot be forced to take a leave of absence if she can work. If other employees on disability leave are entitled to return to their jobs when they can work again, so too are women who have been unable to work because of pregnancy. Also, limiting job advancement opportunities while a woman is pregnant may be a violation of the act. Questions regarding a woman's family and childbearing plans should not be asked. Such questions may be viewed as discriminatory because they are not asked of men.

The same principle applies in the employee benefits area, including disability benefits, sick leave, and health insurance. A woman unable to work for pregnancy-related reasons is entitled to disability benefits or sick leave on the same basis as employees unable to work for other medical reasons. Also, any health insurance provided must cover expenses for pregnancy-related conditions on the same basis as expenses for other medical conditions.

Civil Rights Act of 1991

During 1988–1989, the Supreme Court rendered six employment discrimination decisions of such magnitude that a congressional response was required to overturn these decisions. The result was passage of the Civil Rights Act of 1991. The act amended five statutes: (1) the Civil Rights Act of 1866; (2) Title VII of the Civil Rights Act of 1964, as Amended; (3) the Age Discrimination in Employment Act of 1967, as Amended; (4) the Rehabilitation Act of 1973; and (5) the Americans with Disabilities Act of 1990.

The Civil Rights Act of 1991 had the following purposes:

- To provide appropriate remedies for intentional discrimination and unlawful harassment in the workplace.
- To codify the concepts of *business necessity* and *job-relatedness* pronounced by the Supreme Court in *Griggs v. Duke Power Company*.
- To confirm statutory authority and provide statutory guidelines for the adjudication of disparate impacts under Title VII of the Civil Rights Act of 1964. Disparate impact occurs when certain actions in the employment process work to the disadvantage of members of protected groups. Disparate impact will be discussed under the heading, "Adverse Impact."
- To respond to decisions of the Supreme Court by expanding the scope of relevant civil rights statutes to provide adequate protection to victims of discrimination.

Under this act, a complaining party may recover punitive damages if the complaining party demonstrates that the company engaged in a discriminatory practice with malice or with reckless indifference to the law. However, the following limits, based on the number of people employed by the company, were placed on the amount of the award:

- Between 15 and 100 employees—$50,000
- Between 101 and 200 employees—$100,000
- Between 201 and 500 employees—$200,000
- More than 500 employees—$300,000

In each case, aggrieved employees must be with the firm for 20 or more calendar weeks in the current or preceding calendar year.

Regarding burden of proof, a complaining party must show that an employment practice causes a disparate impact based on race, color, religion, sex, or national origin. It must also be shown that the company is unable to demonstrate that the challenged practice is job related for the position in question and consistent with business necessity. The act also extends the coverage of the Civil Rights Act of 1964 to extraterritorial employment. However, the act does not apply to U.S. companies operating in other countries if compliance, "would cause such employer, or a corporation controlled by such employer, to violate the laws of the country in which such workplace is located."[5] The act also extends the nondiscrimination principles to Congress and other government agencies, such as the General Accounting Office.

Age Discrimination in Employment Act of 1967, Amended in 1978, 1986, and 1990

Older workers were often discriminated against by employers based on the belief that they were less able to perform as well as younger workers. Also, many companies avoided hiring older workers because they expected to receive a lower return on investment from training. Statistically speaking, older workers will have fewer years remaining on the job than younger workers. In 2015, the median age of the labor force was 42.3 years, and nearly 55 percent of them were at least 40 years old.[6] The number of older individuals will increase for many years to come, particularly among individuals at least 55 years of age.[7]

As originally enacted, the Age Discrimination in Employment Act (ADEA) prohibited employers from discriminating against individuals who were 40 to 65 years old. The 1978 amendment provided protection for individuals who were at least 40, but less than 70 years old. In a 1986 amendment, employer discrimination against anyone age 40 or older is illegal. Questions asked about an applicant's age or date of birth may be ill-advised. Also, if only younger applicants are more eager and ready to learn new technology may bring an age discrimination suit because people of any age may possess these qualities. However, a firm may ask for age information to comply with the child labor law. For example, the question could be asked, "Are you under the age of 18?" Nonetheless, questions about the ages of children, if any, could be potentially discriminatory because a close approximation of the applicant's age often is obtained through knowledge of the ages of the applicant's children.

The Older Workers Benefit Protection Act—the 1990 amendment to the ADEA—focused on employer benefits practices. When employers require that all employees contribute toward coverage of benefits, under circumstances, they can also require older employees to pay more for health care, disability, or life insurance than younger employees. This is the case because these benefits generally become costlier with age (e.g., older workers may be more likely to incur serious illnesses, thus, insurance companies may charge employers higher rates). However, an older employee may not be required to pay more for the benefit *as a condition of employment*. Where the premium has increased for an older employee, the employer must provide three options to older workers. First, the employee has the option of withdrawing from the benefit plan altogether. Second, the employee has the option of reducing his or her benefit coverage to keep the same cost. Third, an older employee may be offered the *option* of paying more for the benefit to avoid otherwise justified reductions in coverage.

The EEOC is responsible for administering the ADEA. This act pertains to employers who have 20 or more employees for 20 or more calendar weeks (either in the current or preceding calendar year); unions with 25 or more members; employment agencies; and federal, state, and local government subunits.

Enforcement begins when a charge is filed, but the EEOC can review compliance even if no charge is filed. The ADEA differs from Title VII of the Civil Rights Act because it provides for a trial by jury and carries possible criminal penalty for violation of the act. The trial-by-jury provision is important because juries are thought to have great sympathy for older people who may have been discriminated against. The criminal penalty provision means that a person may receive more than lost wages if discrimination is proved. Further, an employer found to have wilfully violated the ADEA can be liable to the victimized person for "liquidated damages" or double damages.[8] The 1978 amendment also makes class action suits possible.

Age Can Actually Be a Bona Fide Occupational Qualification

Age can be a BFOQ when it is reasonably necessary to the essence of the business, and the employer has a rational or factual basis for believing that all, or substantially all, people within an age class would not be able to perform satisfactorily. Courts have continued to rule that the Federal

HR Web Wisdom

Office of Contract Compliance Programs

www.dol.gov/ofccp/

Home page for the OFCCP, the agency responsible for ensuring that employers doing business with the federal government comply with the laws and regulations requiring nondiscrimination and affirmative action.

Aviation Administration adequately explained its long-standing rule that it can force commercial pilots to retire at age 60. The age 60 rule was first imposed in 1959 and was long controversial. However, in 2007, the retirement age for commercial pilots was raised to 65.

This ruling supported the 1974 Seventh Circuit Court decision that Greyhound did not violate the ADEA when it refused to hire persons 35 years of age or older as intercity bus drivers. Again, the likelihood of risk or harm to its passengers was involved. Greyhound presented evidence concerning degenerative physical and sensory changes that humans undergo at about age 35 that have a detrimental effect on driving skills, and that the changes are not detectable by physical tests. These skills would gradually deteriorate with increased age.

Rehabilitation Act of 1973

The Rehabilitation Act prohibits discrimination against disabled workers who are employed by certain government contractors and subcontractors and organizations that receive federal grants more than $2,500. Individuals are considered disabled if they have a physical or mental impairment that substantially limits one or more major life activities or if they have a record of such impairment. Protected under the act are diseases and conditions such as epilepsy, cancer, cardiovascular disorders, AIDS, blindness, deafness, mental retardation [language stated in the act], emotional disorders, and dyslexia.

There are two primary levels of the act. All federal contractors or subcontractors exceeding the $2,500 base are required to post notices that they agree to take affirmative action to recruit, employ, and promote qualified disabled individuals. If the contract or subcontract exceeds $50,000, or if the contractor has 50 or more employees, the employer must prepare a written affirmative action plan for review by the Office of Federal Contract Compliance Programs (OFCCP), which administers the act. In it, the contractor must specify that reasonable steps are being taken to hire and promote disabled persons.

In an interpretation of Section 8 of the Rehabilitation Act, federal technology buyers are forced to think about people who are blind, deaf, paralyzed, or have other disabilities before they buy software, computers, printers, copiers, fax machines, kiosks, telecommunications devices, or video and multimedia products. Federal employees with disabilities must have access to and use of information and data that is comparable to the access and use by federal employees who are not individuals with disabilities, unless an undue burden would be imposed on the agency.

Vietnam Era Veteran's Readjustment Assistance Act of 1974

The Vietnam Era Veterans' Readjustment Assistance Act (VEVRAA) requires covered federal government contractors and subcontractors to take affirmative action to employ and advance in employment specified categories of veterans protected by the act and prohibits discrimination against such veterans. In addition, VEVRAA requires contractors and subcontractors to list their employment openings with the appropriate employment service delivery system and that covered veterans receive priority in referral to such openings. Further, VEVRAA requires federal contractors and subcontractors to compile and submit annually a report on the number of current employees who are covered veterans. The affirmative action and mandatory job-listing provisions of VEVRAA are enforced by the Employment Standards Administration's Office of Federal Contract Compliance Programs (OFCCP) within the U.S. Department of Labor (DOL). DOL's Veterans' Employment and Training Service (VETS) administers the veterans' employment reporting requirement.

Vietnam Era Veterans' Readjustment Assistance Act of 1974, as Amended

Under VEVRAA, federal contractors and subcontractors are required to take affirmative action in hiring covered veterans. VEVRAA prohibits federal contractors from discriminating against specified categories of veterans and requires them to take affirmative action to recruit, employ, and promote protected veterans. Contractors with 50 or more employees (and $100,000 in federal contracts made on or after December 1, 2003) must maintain a written affirmative action plan.[9] As originally passed, only covered honorably discharged persons who served more than 18 days on active duty between August 5, 1964, and May 7, 1975. Now the definition of "protected" or "covered" veteran has been expanded to include those who have served in a campaign or expedition for which a campaign badge was issued.[10] This includes campaigns such as current engagements in the Middle East.

Recently, there have been rather significant changes in the OFCCP requirement regarding the Rehabilitation Act and the VEVRAA. The final regulations require contractors to establish a nationwide 7 percent utilization goal for disabled individuals and veterans in each job group of their workforce. If a contractor has less than 100 employees, the final rule requires the 7 percent goal to be applied to the entire workforce. In addition, OFCCP's final rules provide two methods for contractors to establish hiring benchmarks for disabled individuals and veterans based on either the current national percentage of veterans in the workforce, which currently stands at 8 percent, or their own benchmark based on the best available data. The OFCCP stresses that goal is not a rigid and inflexible quota which must be met.

Americans with Disabilities Act of 1990

The U.S. Bureau of Labor Statistics estimated that approximately 9.8 million disabled individuals were employed.[11] The Americans with Disabilities Act (ADA) prohibits discrimination against qualified individuals with disabilities. The ADA prohibits discrimination in all employment practices, including job application procedures, hiring, firing, advancement, compensation, training, and other terms, conditions, and privileges of employment. It applies to recruitment, advertising, tenure, layoffs, leaves, benefits, and all other employment-related activities. The employment provisions apply to private employers, state and local governments, employment agencies, and labor unions. Persons discriminated against because they have a known association or relationship with a disabled individual are also protected. Employers with 15 or more employees are covered. The ADA defines an individual with a disability as a person who has, or is regarded as having, a physical or mental impairment that *substantially limits* one or more major life activities and has a record of such an impairment or is regarded as having such an impairment.

Americans with Disabilities Act Amendments Act of 2008

The Americans with Disabilities Act Amendments Act (ADAAA) brings millions more people within the ADA's protection. The ADAAA expands the definition of "disability," so that many more applicants and employees are eligible for reasonable accommodations.[12] The ADAAA broadened the ADA's definition of disability by expanding the term "major life activities," doing away with the "substantially limited" requirement (previously mentioned) for those regarded as having a disability, and overturning two U.S. Supreme Court decisions that interpreted the ADA's definition of disability narrowly.

According to the EEOC, one of the purposes of the ADAAA is the reinstatement of a broad scope of protection by expanding the definition of the term *disability*. Congress found that persons with many types of impairments—including epilepsy, diabetes, multiple sclerosis, major depression, and bipolar disorder—had been unable to bring ADA claims because they were found not to meet the ADA's definition of disability. The ADA still covers only qualified individuals with disabilities and provides that to be disabled, an individual must have "a physical or mental impairment that substantially limits one or more major life activities," must have a record of such an impairment, or must be regarded as having such an impairment. The ADAAA also defines and vastly expands the term *major life activities* as including caring for oneself, performing manual tasks, seeing, hearing, eating, sleeping, walking, standing, lifting, bending, speaking, breathing, learning, reading, concentrating, thinking, communicating, and working. The amendment states that major life activities include the operation of a major bodily function, such as functions of the immune system, normal cell growth, digestive, bowel, bladder, neurological, brain, respiratory, circulatory, endocrine, and reproductive functions. The only exception to this rule is that if a person's vision can be corrected with eyeglasses or contact lenses, he or she will not be considered disabled.

Questions about possible weight discrimination under this law have been raised, and it is not surprising. Obesity in the United States is on the rise. Overall, 38 percent of adults are obese and 17 percent of teenagers are as well.[13] Federal court rulings and the EEOC do not consider "regular" obesity as a disability; however, morbid obesity is. The EEOC generally considers an individual to be morbidly obese when body weight is at least double the normal amount *and* substantially limits the person's ability to walk, stand, kneel, stoop, and breathe. This guideline is not set in stone because a lesser overweight person could have these limitations. Also, employers should not discriminate against obese applicants or employees simply because they believe they cannot perform their jobs. According to EEOC General Counsel David Lopez, "All people with a disability who are qualified for their position are protected from unlawful discrimination."[14] He went on to say that, "Severe obesity is no exception. It is important for employers to realize that stereotypes, myths, and biases about that condition should not be the basis for employment decisions." Employers would be prudent to consider requests for reasonable accommodation for obesity just as they would for other types of disabilities.

Immigration Reform and Control Act of 1986

The Immigration Reform and Control Act (IRCA) makes it illegal for certain employers to fire or refuse to hire a person based on that person's national origin or citizenship. This law also makes it illegal for an employer to request employment verification only from people of a certain national origin or only from people who appear to be from a foreign country. An employer who has citizenship requirements or gives preference to U.S. citizens also may violate IRCA.

Uniformed Services Employment and Reemployment Rights Act of 1994

The Uniformed Services Employment and Reemployment Rights Act (USERRA) provides protection to Reserve and National Guard members. Under the USERRA, those workers are entitled to return to their civilian employment after completing their military service. The USERRA is intended to eliminate or minimize employment disadvantages to civilian careers that can result from service in the uniformed services. The USERRA was enacted to protect the reemployment benefits and nondiscrimination rights of individuals who voluntarily or involuntarily take a leave of absence from employment to serve in the military. As a rule, a returning employee is entitled to reemployment in the same job or position that he or she would have attained with reasonable certainty if not for the absence to serve in the military. Known as the *escalator principle*, this requirement is designed to ensure that a returning employee is not penalized (by losing a pay raise, promotion, etc.) for the time spent on active duty, not exceeding five years. To accomplish this, organizations should track factors ranging from compensation to promotions that employees would have received had they not been on military leave.[15] There are no special rights under USERRA for temporary workers or the new hires taking over the Reserve or National Guide members' jobs.

The Veterans Opportunity to Work (VOW) Act passed in 2011 amended the USERRA. It is now easier for employees to sue employers based on hostile work environment claims related to an employee's military status. In 2015, 39.6 percent of USERRA cases contained allegations of discrimination based on past, present or future military service or status, and 18.7 percent involved allegations of improper reinstatement into civilian jobs following military service.[16] USERRA is administered by the U.S. Department of Labor.

Genetic Information Nondiscrimination Act of 2008

The Genetic Information Nondiscrimination Act (GINA) of 2008 protects job applicants, current and former employees, labor union members, and apprentices and trainees from discrimination based on their genetic information by making unlawful the misuse of genetic information to discriminate in health insurance and employment. GINA contains two titles.

Title I of GINA applies to employer-sponsored group health plans. This title generally prohibits discrimination in group premiums based on genetic information and the use of genetic information as a basis for determining eligibility or setting health insurance premiums. Title I also places limitations on genetic testing and the collection of genetic information.

Title II of GINA prohibits the use of genetic information in the employment setting for making employment decisions such as hiring decisions, compensation, training, and termination. GINA further restricts the deliberate acquisition of genetic information by employers and others covered by Title II and strictly limits disclosing genetic information.

State and Local Laws

Numerous state and local laws also affect EEO. Many states and some cities have passed fair employment practice laws prohibiting discrimination on the basis of race, color, religion, sex, or national origin. Even prior to federal legislation, several states had antidiscrimination legislation relating to age and gender. For instance, New York protected individuals between the ages of 18 and 65 prior to the passing of the ADEA, and California had no upper limit on protected age. San

Francisco has voted to ban weight discrimination. The Board of Supervisors added body size to city laws that already bar discrimination based on race, color, religion, age, ancestry, sex, sexual orientation, disability, place of birth, or gender identity. The state of California has a law that requires sexual harassment prevention training. Recently, New York City passed a law designed to protect unemployed job seekers from discrimination by employers.[17] When EEOC regulations conflict with state or local civil rights regulations, the legislation more favorable to women and minorities applies. Of late, state laws have addressed drug and alcohol testing, EEO, human trafficking, immigration, time off, wages paid, and worker privacy.[18]

3.2 Discuss who is responsible for ensuring equal employment opportunity.

Who's Responsible for Ensuring Equal Employment Opportunity?

The main groups that take responsibility for establishing and supporting EEO include the government (EEOC and OFCCP) and employers.

FYI

There were 91,503 charges of illegal discrimination in fiscal year 2016, of which are:

- Retaliation: 45.9 percent
- Race: 35.3 percent
- Disability: 30.7 percent
- Sex: 29.4 percent
- Age: 22.8 percent
- National Origin: 10.8 percent
- Religion: 4.2 percent
- Color: 3.4 percent
- Equal Pay Act: 1.2 percent
- Genetic Information Non-Discrimination Act: 0.3 percent[19]

Equal Employment Opportunity Commission

Title VII of the Civil Rights Act, as amended, created the EEOC, which is charged with administering most of the aforementioned laws. Under Title VII, filing a discrimination charge initiates EEOC action. The EEOC continually receives complaints. As shown in the FYI, employees filed 91,503 workplace discrimination charges in 2016. In 2016, the EEOC obtained approximately $52.2 million in monetary relief for thousands of discrimination victims as well as significant nonmonetary remedies from employers.[20]

Charges may be filed by one of the presidentially appointed EEOC commissioners, by any aggrieved person, or by anyone acting on behalf of an aggrieved person. Charges must be filed within 180 days of the alleged act; however, the time is extended to 300 days if a state or local agency is involved in the case.

Notice in Figure 3-2 that when a charge is filed, the EEOC first attempts a no-fault settlement. Essentially, the organization charged with the violation is invited to settle the case with no admission of guilt. Most charges are settled at this stage. Failing settlement, the EEOC investigates the charges. Once the employer is notified that an investigation will take place, no records relating to the charge may be destroyed. During the investigative process, the employer is permitted to present a position statement. After the investigation, the district director of the EEOC will issue a probable cause or a no probable cause statement.

In the event of a probable cause statement, the next step involves attempted conciliation. In the event this effort fails, the case will be reviewed for litigation potential. Some of the factors that determine whether the EEOC will pursue litigation are (1) the number of people affected by the alleged practice; (2) the amount of money involved in the charge; (3) other charges against the employer; and (4) the type of charge. Recommendations for litigation are then passed on to the general counsel of the EEOC. If the recommendation is against litigation, a right-to-sue notice will be issued to the charging party.

FIGURE 3-2
EEOC Procedure Once a Charge Is Filed

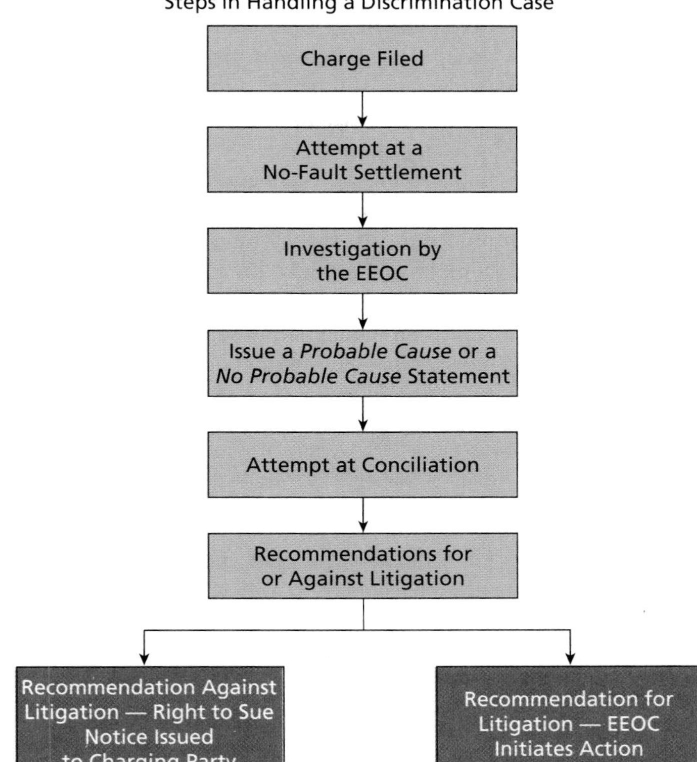

HR Web Wisdom

EEOC

www.eeoc.gov

The home page for the Equal Employment Opportunity Commission.

Office of Federal Contract Compliance Programs

The purpose of the OFCCP is to enforce the requirements of affirmative action and EEO required of those who do business with the federal government. The OFCCP is an agency within the U.S. DOL. According to the U.S. DOL, the OFCCP uses the following enforcement procedures:[21]

- Offers technical assistance to federal contractors and subcontractors to help them understand the regulatory requirements and review process.
- Conducts compliance evaluations and complaint investigations of federal contractors and subcontractors personnel policies and procedures.
- Obtains conciliation agreements from contractors and subcontractors who are in violation of regulatory requirements. When a compliance review discloses problems, OFCCP attempts to work with the contractor, often entering into a conciliation agreement. A conciliation agreement may include back pay, job offers, seniority credit, promotions or other forms of relief for victims of discrimination. It may also involve new training programs, special recruitment efforts, or other affirmative action measures
- Monitors contractors and subcontractors progress in fulfilling the terms of their agreements through periodic compliance reports.
- Forms linkage agreements between contractors and DOL job training programs to help employers identify and recruit qualified workers.
- Recommends enforcement actions to the Solicitor of Labor.
- The ultimate sanction for violations is debarment—the loss of a company's federal contracts. Other forms of relief to victims of discrimination may also be available, including back pay for lost wages.

Employers

Much has occurred since the first piece of EEO legislation was enacted approximately 50 years ago, and the basic hiring standards to avoid are largely understood by those in the workforce. In a perfect world, discrimination, retaliation, and harassment would not exist. However, despite a company's best efforts to treat employees fairly, suits are still brought and won because of mistakes in adherence to these standards.[22] Perhaps, it was only a temporary lapse where a manager knowingly decides to hire a less-qualified friend over a qualified member of a protected group. Or the manager may sincerely believe that he or she has the best intention of abiding by the law but still makes a mistake perhaps because of some complexity in the law.

To limit the prospect of an EEO lawsuit, an organization can do a few things. First, and foremost, it must have and enforce a strong EEO policy against discrimination. This policy must begin with top management and filter down to everyone in the organization. This policy should clearly spell out what standards are to be avoided. It should also conspicuously describe the complaint procedure and the various avenues that can be followed if the person in charge is the cause of the complaint. Certainly, the policy should provide a strong anti-retaliation clause. Workers need to believe that a complaint will result in immediate and appropriate action.

Even with a policy such as the one described, there may still be breakdowns. When they do occur, it becomes an opportunity to train employers how to handle an employee-relations problem better the next time. By taking the high road in the solution of a suit, it provides a means of reinforcing the seriousness of the nondiscrimination policy.[23]

3.3 Define the types of illegal employment discrimination and discuss affirmative action.

Illegal Discrimination and Affirmative Action

Unfortunately, we hear about *illegal discrimination* in the workplace all too often in the news, through friends or family who may have been victims, or personally. At minimum, every employee should possess an awareness of how the law defines illegal workplace discrimination. Even a basic understanding may help employers and employees to minimize the prevalence of illegal discriminatory acts through self-monitoring or reporting concerns of possible illegal discrimination to human resource management professionals.

Uniform Guidelines on Employee Selection Procedures

Prior to 1978, employers were faced with complying with several different selection guidelines. In 1978, the EEOC, the Civil Service Commission, the Department of Justice, and the DOL adopted the *Uniform Guidelines on Employee Selection Procedures*. These guidelines cover several federal EEO statutes and executive orders, including Title VII of the Civil Rights Act, EO 11246, and the Equal Pay Act.

Uniform Guidelines
Provide a single set of principles that were designed to assist employers, labor organizations, employment agencies, and licensing and certification boards in complying with federal prohibitions against employment practices that discriminate on the basis of race, color, religion, sex, and national origin.

The ***Uniform Guidelines*** provide a single set of principles that were designed to assist employers, labor organizations, employment agencies, and licensing and certification boards in complying with federal prohibitions against employment practices that discriminate on the basis of race, color, religion, sex, and national origin. The *Uniform Guidelines* provide a framework for making legal employment decisions about hiring, promotion, demotion, referral, retention, licensing and certification, the proper use of tests, and other selection procedures. Under the *Uniform Guidelines*, recruiting procedures are not considered selection procedures and therefore are not covered.

Regarding selection procedures, the *Uniform Guidelines* state that a test is any measure, combination of measures, or procedures used as a basis for any employment decision. Selection procedures include the full range of assessment techniques from traditional paper-and-pencil tests, performance tests, testing programs or probationary periods, and physical, education, and work experience requirement through informal or casual interviews and unscored application forms.

Using this definition, virtually any instrument or procedure used in the selection decision is considered a test.

Types of Unlawful Employment Discrimination

Unlawful employment discrimination, as established through various Supreme Court decisions, can be divided into two broad categories: disparate treatment and adverse impact. We will review each type next.

disparate treatment
Employer treats some people less favorably than others because of race, religion, color, sex, national origin, or age.

DISPARATE TREATMENT **Disparate treatment** means that an employer treats some employees less favorably than others because of race, religion, color, sex, national origin, or age. It is the most easily understood form of discrimination.

For example, males are treated differently from females; Caucasians are treated differently from non-Caucasians. The crux of disparate treatment is different treatment based on some non-allowable criterion. It may be thought of as *intentional discrimination*. Common forms of disparate treatment include selection rules with a racial, sexual, or other premise; prejudicial action; unequal treatment on an individual basis; and different hiring standards for different groups. *McDonald v. Santa Fe Trail Transportation Company* offers an example of disparate treatment. Three of the company's employees, two white people and one black person, had allegedly misappropriated 60 gallons of antifreeze. Santa Fe took disciplinary action against the workers by terminating the two white employees, but not the black employee. The discharged white workers filed suit against the company, charging that their termination violated both Title VII and the Civil Rights Act of 1866. The Supreme Court agreed with the plaintiffs that they had been the recipients of unequal treatment based on their race. Central to disparate treatment is the matter of proof. The plaintiff must first be able to establish a prima facie case (i.e., the appearance of possible illegal discrimination), and second, can establish that the employer was acting based on a discriminatory motive.

adverse impact
takes place when an employment decision, practice or policy has a disproportionately negative effect on a protected group. Oftentimes, it may be thought of as *unintentional discrimination*.

ADVERSE IMPACT Before the issuance of the *Uniform Guidelines*, the only way to prove job-relatedness was to validate each test. The *Uniform Guidelines* do not require validation in all cases. Essentially, it is required only in instances in which the test or other selection device produces an adverse impact on a minority group. **Adverse impact** takes place when an employment decision, practice or policy has a disproportionately negative effect on a protected group. Oftentimes, it may be thought of as *unintentional discrimination*. According to the *Uniform Guidelines*, adverse impact is said to occur if, "a substantially different rate of selection in hiring, promotion or other employment decision which works to the disadvantage of members of a race, sex or ethnic group" is evident.[24] In practical terms, adverse impact may have occurred when women and minorities are not hired at the rate of at least 80 percent of the best-achieving group. This formula has also been called the "four-fifths" or "80 percent" rule, which is a guideline subject to interpretation by the EEOC.

Under the *Uniform Guidelines*, adverse impact has been described in terms of selection rates, the selection rate being the number of qualified applicants hired or promoted, divided by the total number of applicants in a particular group. The groups identified for analysis under the guidelines are (1) African Americans, (2) American Indians (including Alaskan natives), (3) Asians, (4) Hispanics, (5) Caucasian, (6) women, and (7) men.

The following formula is used to compute adverse impact for ethnic or racial group (numbers 1 through 4):

$$\frac{\text{Selection rate for ethnic or racial minority applicants}}{\text{Selection rate for Caucasian applicants}} = \text{Assessment of possible adverse impact}$$

For sex (group 6):

$$\frac{\text{Selection rate for female applicants}}{\text{Selection rate for male applicants}} = \text{Assessment of possible adverse impact}$$

The selection rate for the female or ethnic or racial minority group is determined by dividing the number of members of females, members of an ethnic group, or members of a racial group hired in a period by the number of applicants in the same group for the same period. The selection rate for the male or Caucasian group is determined by dividing the number of males or Caucasians hired in a period by the number of applicants in the same group for the same period.

Using the formula, let us determine whether there has been adverse impact in the following case. During 2017, 400 people were hired to fill as many vacant positions. Of the total number hired, 300 were Caucasian and 100 were African American. There were 1,500 applicants for these jobs, of whom 1,000 were Caucasian and 500 were African American. The selection rate for African Americans equals 0.2 (that is, 100/500). The selection rate for Caucasians is 0.3 (that is, 300/1,000). Using the adverse impact formula, you have:

$$\frac{100/500}{300/1{,}000} = \frac{0.2}{0.3} = 66.67\%$$

Thus, adverse impact likely exists because the ratio falls below the 80 percent guideline.

Therefore, firms must monitor their recruitment efforts carefully. Obviously, firms should attempt to recruit qualified individuals because once in the applicant pool, they will be used in computing whether adverse impact is evident.

If adverse impact is shown, employers have two avenues available to them if they still desire to use a particular selection standard. First, the employer may validate a selection device by showing that it is indeed a predictor of success. For instance, the employer may be able to show a strong relationship between the selection device and job performance, and that if it did not use this procedure, the firm's training costs would become prohibitive. If the device has proved to be a predictor of job performance, business necessity has been established.

The second avenue available to employers should adverse impact be shown is the BFOQ defense. The BFOQ defense means that only one group can perform the job successfully. Courts have narrowly interpreted this defense because it almost always relates to sex discrimination. For instance, courts have rejected the concept that because most women cannot lift 100 pounds, all women should be eliminated from consideration for a job requiring heavy lifting.

The *Uniform Guidelines* adopted the bottom-line approach in assessing whether a firm's employment practices are discriminatory. For example, if a few separate procedures are used in selecting applicants, the enforcement agencies will focus on the result of these procedures to determine whether adverse impact has occurred. Essentially, the EEOC is more concerned with what is occurring than how it occurs. It admits that discriminatory employment practices that cannot be validated may exist; however, the net effect, or the bottom line, of the selection procedures is the focus of the EEOC's attention.

Affirmative Action

executive order (EO)
Directive issued by the president that has the force and effect of law enacted by Congress as it applies to federal agencies and federal contractors.

An **executive order (EO)** is a directive issued by the president and has the force and effect of a law enacted by Congress because it applies to federal agencies and federal contractors. An example of a contractor is a company that provides carpentry work in federal government buildings. In 1965, President Lyndon B. Johnson established EO 11246 has two provisions. First, it prohibits federal contractors and subcontractors from engaging in illegal employment discrimination based on race, color, religion, sex, or national origin. This requirement applies to contractors and subcontractors whose contracts with the federal government exceed $10,000. Second, contractors and sub contractors are required to take affirmative action to hire individuals from underrepresented groups. Contractors and subcontractors must prepare written affirmative action when their contracts exceed $50,000. The OFCCP is responsible for enforcing EO 11246. In 1968, EO 11375 changed the word *creed* to *religion* and added sex discrimination to the other prohibited items.

President Richard M. Nixon issued EO 11478 in 1969. It covers the federal civilian workforce. This EO prohibits discrimination in employment based on race, color, religion, sex, national origin, handicap, and age. And it requires all federal government departments and agencies to take affirmative steps to promote employment opportunities for those classes it covered. In 1998, President Bill Clinton amended EO 11478 with EO 13087, which adds sexual orientation to the list of protected classes. These EOs are enforced by the DOL through the OFCCP. Recently the VEVRAA and the Rehabilitation Act have received additional attention from the OFCCP.[25]

Affirmative action, stipulated by EO 11246, requires covered employers to take positive steps to ensure that employment of applicants and treatment of employees during employment are without regard to race, creed, color, or national origin.

Covered human resource practices relate to employment, upgrading, demotion, transfer, recruitment or recruitment advertising, layoffs or termination, rates of pay or other forms of compensation, and selection for training, including apprenticeships. Employers are required to post notices explaining these requirements in conspicuous places in the workplace. In the event of contractor noncompliance, contracts can be canceled, terminated, or suspended in whole or in part, and the contractor may be declared ineligible for future government contracts.

affirmative action program (AAP)
Approach developed by organizations with government contracts to demonstrate that workers are employed in proportion to their representation in the firm's relevant labor market.

An **affirmative action program (AAP)** is an approach developed by organizations with government contracts to demonstrate that workers are employed in proportion to their representation in the firm's relevant labor market.

An AAP may be voluntarily implemented by an organization. In such an event, goals are established and actions taken to hire and move minorities and women up in the organization. In other situations, an AAP may be mandated by the OFCCP. The degree of control the OFCCP will impose depends on the size of the contract, with contracts of $10,000 or less not covered. The first level of control involves contracts that exceed $10,000 but are less than $50,000. The second level of control occurs if the contractor (1) has 50 or more employees; (2) has a contract of $50,000 or more; (3) has contracts that, in any 12-month period, total $50,000 or more or reasonably may be expected to total $50,000 or more; or (4) is a financial institution that serves as a depository for government funds in any amount, acts as an issuing or redeeming agent for U.S. savings bonds and savings notes in any amount, or subscribes to federal deposit or share insurance. Contractors meeting these criteria must develop a written AAP for each of their establishments and file an annual EEO-1 report. Note that the threshold is 50 employees here, but it is 100 with regard to those covered by the Civil Rights Act of 1964.

The third level of control on contractors is in effect when contracts exceed $1 million. All previously stated requirements must be met, and in addition, the OFCCP is authorized to conduct pre-award compliance reviews. In determining whether to conduct a pre-award review, the OFCCP may consider, for example, the items presented in Table 3-1. Alcoa Mill Products Inc. paid $484,656.19 in back wages to 37 Hispanics and blacks as well as $35,516.88 to two women who were rejected for job positions at the company's plant in Lancaster, Pennsylvania. The OFCCP determined that the company had violated EO 11246 by failing to meet its obligations as a federal contractor. Alcoa holds contracts with the U.S. Army in excess of $50 million.

Recently every 25th supply and service federal contractor selected for a compliance evaluation by the OFCCP is subjected to a full compliance review that includes on-site visits by compliance officers, even though there are no indicators of potential discrimination or other violations. The "active case enforcement" directive also provides that the OFCCP will perform a full desk audit in every compliance evaluation to comprehensively analyze a contractor's written AAPs.[26] Before this decision, only 25 compliance reviews were made per year.[27]

If an investigation indicates a violation, the OFCCP first tries to secure compliance through persuasion. If persuasion fails to resolve the issue, the OFCCP serves a notice to show cause or a notice of violation. A show cause notice contains a list of the violations, a statement of how the OFCCP proposes that corrections be made, a request for a written response to the findings, and a suggested date for a conciliation conference. The firm usually has 30 days to respond. Successful conciliation results in a written contract between the OFCCP and the contractor. In a conciliation agreement, the contractor agrees to take specific steps to remedy noncompliance with an EO. Firms that do not correct violations can be passed over in the awarding of future contracts. The procedures for developing AAPs were published in the *Federal Register* of December 4, 1974. These regulations are referred to as Revised Order No. 4. Revised Order No. 4 is quite specific with regard to dissemination of a firm's EEO policy, both internally and externally. An executive should be appointed to manage the firm's EEO program. This person should be given the necessary support by top management to accomplish the assignment. Revised Order No. 4 specifies the minimum level of responsibility associated with the task of EEO manager. The OFCCP guide for compliance officers, outlining what to cover in a compliance review, is known as Order No. 14.

The OFCCP is specific about what should be included in an AAP. A policy statement must be developed that reflects the CEO's attitude regarding EEO, assigns overall responsibility for preparing and implementing the AAP, and provides for reporting and monitoring procedures. The policy should state that the firm intends to recruit, hire, train, and promote persons in all job titles without regard to race, color, religion, gender, or national origin, except where gender is a BFOQ. Recently protected military veterans and individuals with disabilities have been included in affirmative action. The policy should guarantee that all human resource actions involving areas such as compensation, benefits, transfers, layoffs, return from layoffs, company-sponsored training, education, tuition assistance, and social and recreational programs will be administered without regard to race, color, religion, gender, or national origin.

TABLE 3-1

Factors That the OFCCP May Consider in Conducting a Pre-award Review

1. The past EEO performance of the contractor, including its current EEO profile and indications of underutilization.
2. The volume and nature of complaints filed by employees or applicants against the contractor.
3. Whether the contractor is in a growth industry.
4. The level of employment or promotional opportunities resulting from the expansion of, or turnover in, the contractor's workforce.
5. The employment opportunities likely to result from the contract in issue.
6. Whether resources are available to conduct the review.

TABLE 3-2

Techniques to Improve Recruitment of Minorities and Women

- Identify referral organizations for minorities and women.
- Hold formal briefing sessions with representatives of referral organizations.
- Encourage minority and women employees to refer applicants to the firm.
- Include minorities and women on the personnel relations staff.
- Permit minorities and women to participate in career days, youth motivation programs, and related activities in their community.
- Actively participate in job fairs and give company representatives the authority to make on-the-spot commitments.
- Actively recruit at schools having predominant minority or female enrollments.
- Use special efforts to reach minorities and women during school recruitment drives.
- Undertake special employment programs whenever possible for women and minorities. These might include technical and nontechnical co-op programs, after-school or work-study jobs, summer jobs for underprivileged individuals, summer work-study programs, and motivation, training, and employment programs for the hardcore unemployed.
- Pictorially present minorities and women in recruiting brochures.
- Include the minority news media and women's interest media when expending help wanted advertising.

Source: Federal Register, 45, no. 251 (December 30, 2008): 86243.

An acceptable AAP must include an analysis of deficiencies in the utilization of minority groups and women. The first step in conducting a utilization analysis is to make a workforce analysis. The second step involves an analysis of all major job groups. An explanation of the situation is required if members of protected groups are currently being underutilized. A *job group* is defined as one or more jobs having similar content, wage rates, and opportunities.

Underutilization is defined as having fewer minorities or women in a particular job group than would reasonably be expected by their availability. The utilization analysis is important because the calculations determine whether underutilization exists. For example, if the utilization analysis shows that the availability of black employees for a certain job group is 30 percent, the organization should have at least 30 percent black employment in that group. If actual employment is less than 30 percent, underutilization exists, and the firm should set a goal of 30 percent black employment for that job group. The goal of affirmative action is for a contractor's workforce to generally reflect the gender, racial, and ethnic profile of the labor pools from which the contractor recruits and selects.

The primary focus of any AAP is on goals and timetables, with the issue being how many and by when. Goals and timetables developed by the firm should cover its entire AAP, including correction of deficiencies. These goals and timetables should be attainable; that is, they should be based on results that the firm, making good-faith efforts, could reasonably expect to achieve. Goals should be significant and measurable, as well as attainable. Two types of goals must be established regarding underutilization: annual and ultimate. The annual goal is to move toward elimination of underutilization, whereas the ultimate goal is to correct all underutilization. Goals should be specific in terms of planned results, with timetables for completion. However, goals should not establish inflexible quotas that must be met. Rather, they should be targets that are reasonably attainable. Some techniques that can be used to improve recruitment and increase the flow of minority and women applicants are shown in Table 3-2.

3.4 Explain the *Uniform Guidelines* related to various types of illegal employment discrimination, including sexual harassment, national origin, religion, and caregiver (family responsibility) discrimination.

Uniform Guidelines on Preventing Specific Illegal Employment Discrimination

Since the *Uniform Guidelines* were published in 1978, they have been modified several times. Some of these changes reflect Supreme Court decisions; others clarify implementation procedures. The five major changes discussed are the Guidelines on Sexual Harassment, Guidelines on Discrimination because of National Origin, Guidelines on Discrimination because of Religion, Guidelines on Caregiver (Family Responsibility) Discrimination, and Discrimination because of Disability.

Guidelines on Sexual Harassment

As previously mentioned, Title VII of the Civil Rights Act generally prohibits discrimination in employment based on gender. The EEOC has also issued guidelines that state that employers have a duty to maintain a workplace that is free from sexual harassment. The OFCCP has issued similar guidelines. Managers in both for-profit and not-for-profit organizations must be particularly alert to the issue of sexual harassment. The EEOC issued the guidelines because of the belief that sexual harassment was a widespread problem. Table 3-3 contains the EEOC's definition of sexual harassment. As you see, there are two distinct types of sexual harassment: (1) where a hostile work environment is created, and (2) when there is a quid pro quo, for example, an offer of promotion or pay raise in exchange for sex.

According to these guidelines, employers are totally liable for the acts of their supervisors, regardless of whether the employer is aware of the sexual harassment act. In *Faragher v. City of Boca Raton* and *Burlington Industries, Inc. v. Ellerth*, the Supreme Court held that an employer is strictly liable, meaning that it has absolutely no defense, when sexual harassment by a supervisor involves a tangible employment action. Courts expect employers to carefully train supervisors so they do not engage in any type of behavior that could be construed as sexual harassment. In addition, all employees should be trained to understand their rights and responsibilities.[28]

As is the case for the Civil Rights Act of 1964, retaliation is forbidden against an employee who has participated in an investigation, proceeding, or hearing. Recently Z Foods, Inc. entered into a consent judgment requiring it to pay more than $1.47 million to settle an employment discrimination lawsuit filed by EEOC. The EEOC had charged Z Foods with subjecting several female farmworkers to sexual harassment. The harassment took the form of basing promotions and employment on sexual favors, continuous sexual advances, stalking female employees and unwanted physical touching and leering. Several male and female employees who reported the exploitation were retaliated against and fired soon after airing their objections. Melissa Barrios, director of EEOC's Fresno Local Office, stated, "Workers have the right to voice their concerns about a sexually hostile work environment without fearing repercussions from their employer. With this ruling, the court sends the message that employers who ignore or punish employees for complaining of harassment leave themselves open to greater liability."[29]

Where coworkers are concerned, the employer is responsible for such acts if the employer knew, or should have known, about them. The employer is not responsible when it can show that it took immediate and appropriate corrective action on learning of the problem. Another important aspect of these guidelines is that employers may be liable for acts committed by nonemployees in the workplace if the employer knew, or should have known, of the conduct and failed to take appropriate action.

Firms are responsible for developing programs and policies to prevent sexual harassment in the workplace. Managers must be trained to know what to do when there is a complaint. They must investigate all formal and informal complaints alleging sexual harassment.[30] Failure to do so constitutes a violation of Title VII, as interpreted by the EEOC. To prevail in court, companies must have clear procedures for handling sexual harassment complaints. If the sexual harassment complaint appears legitimate, the company must take immediate and appropriate action.[31] However, this does not mean that everyone who is guilty of sexual harassment must be fired. A single incident does not mean that sexual harassment exists unless the employer ignores the incident and lets the situation worsen.[32]

TABLE 3-3

EEOC Definition of Sexual Harassment

Unwelcome sexual advances, requests for sexual favors, and verbal or physical conduct of a sexual nature that occur under any of the following situations:

1. When submission to such conduct is made either explicitly or implicitly a term or condition of an individual's employment.
2. When submission to or rejection of such contact by an individual is used as the basis for employment decisions affecting such individual.
3. When such conduct has the purpose or effect of unreasonably interfering with an individual's work performance or creating an intimidating, hostile, or offensive working environment.

The first sexual harassment case to reach the U.S. Supreme Court was the case of *Meritor Savings Bank v. Vinson* in 1986. In the *Vinson* decision, the Supreme Court recognized for the first time that Title VII could be used for offensive-environment claims. According to the EEOC, specific actions that could create a hostile workplace include a pattern of threatening, intimidating, or hostile acts and remarks, negative sexual stereotyping, or the display of written or graphic materials considered degrading. The 1993 Supreme Court decision in *Harris v. Forklift Systems, Inc.* expanded the hostile-workplace concept and made it easier to win sexual harassment claims. In a unanimous decision, the Supreme Court held that, "to be accountable as abusive work environment harassment, conduct need not seriously affect . . . the psychological well-being or lead the plaintiff to suffer injury." No longer does severe psychological injury have to be proved. Under this ruling, the plaintiff only needs to show that his or her employer allowed a hostile-to-abusive work environment to exist.

Duane Reade, the New York/New Jersey drug store chain, agreed to settle an EEOC lawsuit for $240,000 for allowing the work environment at one of its New York stores to become hostile. The store manager frequently made vulgar remarks about women's anatomy, sexually propositioned female employees, made lewd comments about them during pregnancies, assigned pregnant women the least desirable store tasks, and sometimes grabbed female employees' buttocks while they worked.[33] Unchecked sexual harassment can be financially crippling. In a recent case, a jury awarded the plaintiff $95 million, including $80 million in punitive damages.[34]

Males are not precluded from sexual harassment. In 2016, 16.6 percent of charges alleging sexual harassment were filed by men.[35] Recently, the Ninth U.S. Circuit Court of Appeals held that a female coworker's "relentless" pursuit of a male employee could form the basis of a sexually hostile environment claim, even without any physical conduct of a sexual nature. The Ninth Circuit pointed out that under Title VII of the Civil Rights Act of 1964, "[b]oth sexes are protected from discrimination."[36]

For a long time, an unresolved question in employment law has been whether same-sex harassment (for example, males harassing males) is unlawful under Title VII of the Civil Rights Act of 1964. The Supreme Court, in the case of *Oncale v. Sundowner Offshore Services*, held that same-sex sexual harassment may be unlawful under Title VII. The Supreme Court decided that a plaintiff could make a claim for sexual harassment if the harassing conduct was because of sex. The Court emphasized that Title VII does not prohibit all verbal or physical harassment in the workplace, only that which constitutes discrimination because of sex.

Guidelines on Discrimination Because of National Origin

Both EEOC and the courts have interpreted national origin protection under Title VII as extending far beyond discrimination against individuals who came from, or whose forebears came from, a particular country. National origin protection also covers (1) marriage or association with a person of a specific national origin; (2) membership in, or association with, an organization identified with, or seeking to promote the interests of national groups; (3) attendance at, or participation in, schools, churches, temples, or mosques generally used by persons of a national origin group; and (4) use of an individual's or spouse's name that is associated with a national origin group. As Table 3-4 shows, the EEOC has identified certain selection procedures that may be discriminatory.

Harassment on the basis of national origin is a violation of Title VII. Employers have a duty to maintain a working environment free from such harassment. Ethnic slurs and other verbal or physical conduct relating to an individual's national origin constitute harassment when this conduct (1) has the purpose or effect of creating an intimidating, hostile, or offensive working

TABLE 3-4

Selection Procedures That May Be Discriminatory with Regard to National Origin

1. Fluency in English requirements: One questionable practice involves denying employment opportunities because of an individual's foreign accent or inability to communicate well in English. When this practice is continually followed, the EEOC will presume that such a rule violates Title VII and will study it closely. However, a firm may require that employees speak only in English at certain times if business necessity can be shown.
2. Training or education requirements: Denying employment opportunities to an individual because of his or her foreign training or education, or practices that require an individual to be foreign trained or educated may be discriminatory.

environment; (2) has the purpose or effect of unreasonably interfering with an individual's work performance; or (3) otherwise adversely affects an individual's employment opportunity.

Of interest regarding national origin is the English-only rule. Courts have generally ruled in the employer's favor if the rule would promote safety and product quality and stop harassment. For example, suppose a company has a rule that only English must be spoken except during breaks. That rule must be justified by a compelling business necessity. In *Garcia v. Spun Steak*, the Ninth Circuit Court of Appeals (the Supreme Court refused to review) concluded that the rule did not necessarily violate Title VII. Spun Steak's management implemented the policy after some workers complained they were being harassed and insulted in a language they could not understand. The rule allowed workers to speak Spanish during breaks and lunch periods. A recent ruling supported the job-related aspect of the English-only rule. In *Montes v. Vail Clinic, Inc.*, the Tenth Circuit Court agreed with the English-only rule prohibiting housekeepers from speaking Spanish while working in the operating room. However, English-only policies that are not job related have been challenged and eliminated. The EEOC settled a Title VII lawsuit against a company that enforced an English-only rule solely against Hispanics. "What was strange was that the rule was only targeted at Hispanics. Tagalog, a Spanish language spoken in the Philippines, was openly spoken," said Anna Park, the EEOC's regional attorney in Los Angeles. "This was very troublesome."[37]

Guidelines on Discrimination Because of Religion

The number of religion-related discrimination complaints filed with the EEOC continues to increase. According to the Supreme Court's decision in *TWA v. Hardison*, employers have an obligation to accommodate sincerely held religious practices if the requested accommodation does not create more than a minimum cost to the employer.[38] Courts generally do not require employers to hire additional employees just to cover for another employee who needs a religious accommodation. Consideration is given to identifiable costs in relation to the size and operating costs of the employer and the number of individuals who need the accommodation. These guidelines recognize that regular payment of premium wages constitutes undue hardship, whereas these payments on an infrequent or temporary basis do not. Undue hardship would also exist if an accommodation required a firm to vary from its bona fide seniority system.

The most common claims filed under the religious accommodation provisions involve employees objecting to either Sabbath employment or membership in or financial support of labor unions. These guidelines identify several means of accommodating religious practices that prohibit working on certain days. Some of the methods suggested included voluntary substitutes, flexible scheduling, lateral transfer, and change of job assignments. Basically, employers that refuse to accommodate an employee's religious practice may need to provide evidence that doing so would constitute an undue burden.[39] However, if making an accommodation places a true hardship on the company, the accommodation does not have to be given.[40] That was not the case for clothing retailer Abercrombie & Fitch, which refused to hire a Muslim woman because of her religious practice of wearing a hijab. The company chose not to hire her because she did not conform to the company's "look policy." In *EEOC v. Abercrombie & Fitch*, the U.S. Supreme Court ruled that an employer may not refuse to hire an applicant if the employer was driven by sidestepping the need to accommodate a religious practice. In this case, the employer "failed to accommodate her religious beliefs by not making an exception to its "look policy" prohibiting head coverings."[41]

Some collective bargaining agreements include a provision that each employee must join the union or pay the union a sum equivalent to dues. When an employee's religious beliefs prevent compliance, the union should accommodate the employee by permitting that person to make an equivalent donation to a charitable organization.

☛ FYI

Almost everyone will assume a caregiver role at some point:

- Sixty percent of workers have or will provide unpaid care to an adult or child with special needs.
- Nearly 50 million employees have children under the age of 18.
- Fifty-three percent of individuals who are not working choose not to work because of family responsibilities.[42]

Guidelines on Caregiver (Family Responsibility) Discrimination

caregiver (family responsibility) discrimination
Discrimination against employees based on their obligations to care for family members.

Caregiver (family responsibility) discrimination is discrimination against employees based on their obligations to care for family members. The EEOC has issued a technical assistance document titled "Employer Best Practices for Workers with Caregiving Responsibilities" on how employers of workers with caregiving responsibilities can avoid violations of Title VII of the 1964 Civil Rights Act and other fair employment laws and reduce the likelihood of discrimination complaints. This form of discrimination makes an assumption based on what a person assumes to be true about a group, including people with family responsibilities.

According to the EEOC, the guidance is not binding on employers but rather offers best practices that are proactive measures that go beyond federal nondiscrimination requirements. Federal law does not prohibit discrimination based on "caregiver status," but rather it is concerned when workers with caregiving responsibilities are treated differently based on a characteristic that is protected by laws, such as gender, race, or association with an individual with a disability.

Caregiver discrimination has become the new battleground in employment claims.[43] Examples of possible caregiver discrimination violations include treating male caregivers more favorably than female caregivers; reassigning a woman to less desirable projects based on the assumption that, as a new mother, she will be less committed to her job; or lowering subjective evaluations of a female employee's work performance after she becomes the primary caregiver of her grandchildren, despite the absence of an actual decline in work performance.[44] Sometimes, it, "occurs when an employee suffers an adverse action that affects the terms and conditions of her employment based on unexamined biases about how women with family caregiving responsibilities will or should act."[45]

For instance, in *EEOC v. Denver Hotel Management Company, Inc.*, an employer supposedly told a female employee that she was denied consideration for a promotion because she "had a full-time job at home with her children."[46] According to the EEOC, the employee was never asked if she would be willing to relocate or work extended hours. Instead, the company's leadership assumed that the employee would be unwilling to relocate or work extended hours because the complainant was the mother and primary caregiver for small children. The EEOC concluded that the company discriminated against this female employee based on stereotypical views of a woman's caregiver status, calling it a form of sex discrimination prohibited by Title VII of the Civil Rights Act of 1964.

In recent years, employees have been filing more and more caregiver discrimination lawsuits. In the last decade alone, there has been a 267 percent increase.[47] Most cases share a common element—the employee alleges that the caregiving responsibilities cause the alleged discriminatory action by the employer. Employees win 67 percent of the cases that go to trial, which is higher than other federal discrimination cases combined.[48] The challenge for employers is to develop the right mix of flexibility and fairness in work scheduling, leave policies, dependent-care assistance, and benefits. This will promote positive employee relations, recruit and retain a diverse and well-qualified workforce, address and resolve job-related issues, and defend against claims of unfair or unlawful conduct. It will be ever more important for HR professionals to ensure flexibility in family responsibilities policies and educate line managers about policy guidelines. More and more employees will benefit from their employer's flexibility.

Discrimination Because of Disability

The ADA prohibits discrimination in employment because of one's disability and requires that employers provide an employee or job applicant with a reasonable accommodation unless doing so would cause significant difficulty or expense for the employer. For example, drug store chain Walgreens agreed to pay $180,000 to settle a disability discrimination lawsuit filed by the EEOC. The EEOC had charged that Walgreens unlawfully fired a qualified employee because of her disability after she ate a bag of chips prior to paying for it. The employee later explained that she was trying to stabilize her blood sugar during a hypoglycemic attack. Still, Walgreens denied a reasonable accommodation to a diabetic employee. EEOC San Francisco Regional Attorney William R. Tamayo said that, "People may think this case revolves around theft, but the real issue is how a company responded to a valued 18-year employee, whom it knew for 13 years to be diabetic, and who attempted to pay for the chips after she recovered from her hypoglycemic attack."[49]

The EEOC guidelines on pre-employment inquiries and tests regarding disabilities prohibit inquiries and medical examinations intended to gain information about applicants' disabilities before a conditional job offer. In the Supreme Court case of *Leonel v. American Airlines*, the Court ruled that the airline violated the ADA's required sequence for pre-hire medical inquiries/examinations by making medical inquiries and requiring individuals to take medical examinations before completing and making its hiring decisions.

The guiding principle is to ask only about potential employees' ability to do the job, and not about their disabilities. Lawful inquiries include those regarding performance of specific functions or possession of training appropriate to the job, whereas illegal inquiries include those that ask about previous medical conditions or extent of prior drug use. The ADA does not protect people currently using illegal drugs. It does protect those in rehabilitation programs who are not currently using illegal drugs, those who have been rehabilitated, and those erroneously labeled as drug users. Coverage under the ADA continues to evolve as evidenced with the passing of the American with Disabilities Act Amendments Act of 2008.

3.5 Describe the concept of diversity and diversity management.

Diversity and Diversity Management

In decades past, diversity was primarily concerned with race and gender.[50] Today, the definition is quite different. As we defined in the chapter introduction, diversity refers to *any* actual or perceived difference among people: age, race, religion, functional specialty, profession, sexual orientation, gender identity, geographic origin, lifestyle, tenure with the organization or position, and any other perceived difference. Further, as companies have become more global, the work group itself has become more diverse.[51] The challenge for managers is to recognize that people with characteristics that are common but are different from those in the mainstream, often think, act, learn, and communicate differently. Diversity is more than equal employment and affirmative action; the actual definition is constantly changing and expanding.

diversity management
Ensuring that factors are in place to provide for and encourage the continued development of a diverse workforce by melding actual and perceived differences among workers to achieve maximum productivity.

Diversity management is ensuring that factors are in place to provide for and encourage the continued development of a diverse workforce by combining these actual and perceived differences among workers to achieve maximum productivity. Because every person, culture, and business situation is unique, there are no simple rules for managing diversity; but diversity experts say that employers need to develop patience, open-mindedness, acceptance, and cultural awareness. Diversity management focuses on the principle that all workers regardless of any factor are entitled to the same privileges and opportunities.[52] According to R. Roosevelt Thomas Jr., former president of the American Institute for Managing Diversity, "diversity and diversity management are about managing and engaging people who are different and similar, all for the benefit of the organization and its goals."[53] In his book, *The Future and the Work Ahead of Us*, Harris Sussman writes, "Diversity is about our relatedness, our connectedness, our interactions, where the lines cross."[54]

If organizations want to remain competitive in the marketplace, diversity should be a part of the strategic goal. Credit card giant MasterCard employs more than 11,000. It has a complex diversity program that includes a diversity advisory board, diversity networks, diversity recruiting, accountability mechanisms, scorecards, mandatory training, and a diversity officer. Donna Johnson, chief diversity officer, maintains that, "The diversity in thoughts and experiences of our people drives real business impact and makes meaningful contributions to society."[55]

You will realize as you read the remainder of this chapter that diversity management and EEO are different. EEO focuses on laws, court decisions, and EOs. Diversity management is about pursuing an inclusive corporate culture in which newcomers feel welcome, and everyone sees the value of his or her job. It involves creating a supportive culture where all employees can be effective. In creating this culture, top management must strongly support workplace diversity as a company goal and include diversity initiatives in their companies' business strategies. It has grown out of the need for organizations to recognize the changing workforce and other social pressures that often result. Achieving diversity is more than being politically correct; it is about fostering a culture that values individuals and their wide array of needs and contributions.

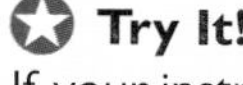

If your instructor has assigned this, go to **www.pearson.com/mylab/management** to complete the HR and Diversity simulation and test your application of these concepts when faced with real-world decisions.

3.6 Explain the various elements of a diverse workforce.

Elements of the Diverse Workforce

Several elements that combine to make up the diverse workforce will be discussed next.

Single Parents and Working Mothers

The number of single-parent households in the United States is growing. Although the divorce rate peaked in the early 1980s, the percentage of marriages ending in divorce remains around 50 percent. Often, children are involved. Of course, there are always widows and widowers who have children, and there are some men and women who choose to raise children outside of wedlock.

Managers need to be sensitive to the needs of working parents. Many women who formerly remained at home to care for children and the household now need and want to work outside the home. In fact, according to the U.S. Bureau of Labor Statistics data, just more than 70 percent of U.S. women with school-age children work.[56] If this valuable segment of the workforce is to be effectively used, organizations must fully recognize the importance of addressing work–family issues. Businesses are seeing that providing child-care services and workplace flexibility may influence workers' choice of employers. Companies that were chosen in *Working Mother* magazine's 100 best companies to work for placed greater emphasis on work–life balance, telecommuting, and flextime. The number of single-parent men has also increased, thus making the same work friendly issues important. According to the U.S. Bureau of the Census, in 2016 single fathers headed 7 percent of households with minor children, up from 1 percent in 1970.[57]

Women in Business

Numerous factors have contributed to the growth and development of the U.S. labor force. However, nothing has been more prominent than the rise in the number of women in the labor force. More and more women are entering the labor force in high-paying, professional jobs and women dominate the health-care sector, which is one of the fastest-growing categories. In 2010, for the first time ever, women made up the majority of the U.S. workforce. Women-owned businesses now account for 38 percent of all enterprises in the market today. The American Express Open State of Women-Owned Businesses Report shows the number of women-owned firms from 2007 to 2016 increased by 45 percent.[58] The report further indicates that among women of color, Latinas show the highest growth in the number of firms, Asian American women led in employment and revenue growth. Another study revealed that gender-diverse companies are 15 percent more likely to perform better than their peers and ethnically diverse companies are 35 percent more likely to do the same.[59]

Professional women are entering the workforce at the same rates as men. However, many opt out of the corporate life. Perhaps this is one of the reasons that women hold only 27 of the 500 CEO positions in Fortune's 2016 list of the largest U.S. companies.[60] But this does not mean that they are opting out of business careers. Instead, they are making their own career paths that allow them to combine work and life on their own terms. Thus, organizations are losing talented employees in whom they have made substantial investments. Numerous companies are working diligently keep professional women in the workforce although more work needs to be done.[61]

Women who chose to pursue advancement within corporations find it difficult to advance to the highest executive-level positions. A survey of 132 global companies revealed that women are underrepresented in senior management positions and C-level positions. Women accounted for 45 percent of entry-level professional jobs; however, only 32 percent were senior managers or directors, and fewer (17 percent) held positions in the C-suite.[62]

glass ceiling
Invisible barrier in organizations that impedes women and minorities from career advancement.

This phenomenon is often referred to as the glass ceiling. The **glass ceiling** is the invisible barrier in organizations that impedes women and minorities from career advancement. The Civil Rights Act of 1991 established a Glass Ceiling Commission to study the way businesses fill management and decision-making positions, the developmental and skill-enhancing practices used to foster the necessary qualifications for advancement to such positions, and the compensation programs and reward structures currently used in the workplace. It was also to study the limited progress made by minorities and women. One African-American female executive described the situation for minority females as more challenging than a glass ceiling. Annalisa Adams-Qualtiere said, "When I hear 'glass ceiling,' I think that's great, you can break through glass. When it is concrete, you need a door and there need to be people on the other side of that door."[63] As you will learn in the following Watch It video, the challenges women face are particularly noteworthy in male-dominated professions.

Watch It 3

If your instructor has assigned this, go to **www.pearson.com/mylab/management** to watch a video titled Woman on Track to Become First NFL Rep and to respond to questions.

Mothers Returning to the Workforce (on Ramping)

Today, many recruiters are focusing on educated women who have taken career breaks as a significant source of potential talent (on ramping).[64] To get them to return, companies are going beyond federal law and giving mothers a year or more for maternity leave. Other businesses are specifically trying to recruit them to return to the labor force.

Although some companies are recruiting these women, other employers have programs that help their employees leave and later return. IBM has a program that allows employees to take up to three years off. Typically, working mothers who use the program take a year or more off, and then they use the remainder of their leave to re-enter work on a part-time basis. After the three years are up, they have the option of returning either full- or part-time. IBM surveyed employees who had taken the leave and found that 59 percent would have left the company if the program had not been available. "We didn't want a situation where women had to opt out," says Maria Ferris, manager of work–life and women's initiatives at IBM. "We've invested in them, trained them. We want to retain them."[65]

A concept called *returnships* is being used to let organizations try-out professionals who are resuming their careers. It provides a vehicle for relaunching a career after a break (most often for full-time parenting). Essentially it is an internship for experienced workers who have been out of work for a while whose résumés might scare recruiters away.[66]

Dual-Career Families

dual-career family
A situation in which both spouses or partners have jobs and family responsibilities.

The increasing number of **dual-career families**—in which both spouses or partners have jobs and family responsibilities—presents both challenges and opportunities for organizations. Most children growing up today have both parents working outside the home. In the twenty-first century the proportion of U.S. households with only a male wage earner is less than 20 percent.[67] This fact stands in contrast to the 1950s when most households consisted of a male breadwinner married to a traditional housewife.

Today, employees have turned down relocations because of spouses' jobs and concerns about their children. Of the top three reasons employees turn down assignments, family or spouse's career is cited almost twice as often as concern with the employee's career or compensation.[68] Thus, firms are developing polices to assist the spouse of an employee who is transferred. Some are helping in finding a position for the spouse of a transferred employee. However, companies may need to learn more about how to handle dual-career couples in a global environment. If companies make the willingness to locate globally a requirement for promotion, many in this group will reject the offer, thereby reducing the size of the labor pool.

Ethnicity and Race

HR Web Wisdom
Bureau of Labor Statistics
www.bls.gov/
Principal fact-finding agency for the federal government in the broad field of labor economics and statistics.

According to the U.S. Bureau of Labor Statistics, the percentage of the U.S. labor force made up of white employees will decline while growth is expected for other racial groups.[69] These include Hispanics, African Americans, and Asians. Unfortunately, at times, these individuals may be subject to stereotyping. They may encounter misunderstandings and expectations based on ethnic or cultural differences. Members of ethnic or racial groups are socialized within their culture. People's attitudes are influenced by the ancestral and cultural experiences of their childhood. Many are socialized as members of two cultural groups—the dominant culture and their racial or ethnic culture. Ella Bell refers to this dual membership as *biculturalism*. In her study of black women, Bell identifies the stress of coping with membership in two cultures simultaneously as bicultural stress. She indicates that role conflict (competing roles from two cultures) and role overload (too many expectations to comfortably fulfill) are common characteristics of bicultural stress. Although these issues can be applied to other minority groups, they are particularly intense for women of color because this group experiences dynamics affecting both minorities and women.[70]

Socialization in one's culture of origin can lead to misunderstandings in the workplace. This is particularly true when the manager relies solely on the cultural norms of the majority group.

According to norms within U.S. culture it is acceptable, even considered positive, to publicly praise an individual for a job well done. However, in cultures that place primary value on group harmony and collective achievement, this method of rewarding an employee may cause emotional discomfort. Some employees feel that, if praised publicly, they will lose face within their group.

Try It!
If your instructor has assigned this, go to **www.pearson.com/mylab/management** to complete the Diversity simulation and test your application of these concepts when faced with real-world decisions.

Older Workers

Today, employees age 40 and older represent about 55 percent of the U.S. workforce.[71] In 2011, the first baby boomers turned 65, and approximately 10,000 more will continue to do so every day for the next 20 years. In recent years, many boomers deferred retirement because of a faltering economy and concerns about the viability of the Social Security retirement program.[72] As the economy improves, plans must be in place to handle a rapid departure of boomers from the workforce. Even so, many boomers will resist retirement, some because they feel healthy enough to continue work and others because their retirement income was hit hard by the economy. The U.S. Bureau of Labor Statistics estimates that nearly 13.5 million workers 65 and older will be working in 2024, up from about 8 million today.[73]

Many companies try to keep the worker older than 55. This may be the result, in part, of legal concerns based on the ADEA, discussed previously in this chapter, which protects workers 40 and older against discrimination. However, a large part of this movement is the desire to keep the experienced workers on board because they are often more productive than younger workers. Employing older workers may boost overall workplace productivity. In one study, researchers found that, "An older worker's experience increases not only his own productivity but also the productivity of working with him."[74] Other companies actively recruit older workers. For instance, Barclays Bank expanded its internship program to include workers older than age 50. Mike Thompson, head of apprenticeships at Barclays, said, "We see real benefit in employing a workforce that reflects the diversity of our customer base."[75] He went on to explain that, "individuals who have had previous careers and greater life experience can have empathy and are able to really understand and support our customers."

People with Disabilities

According to the U.S. Bureau of Labor Statistics, approximately 20 percent of the labor force possesses one or more disabilities.[76] Common disabilities include limited hearing or sight, limited mobility, mental or emotional deficiencies, and various nerve disorders. Such disabilities limit the amount or kind of work a person can do or make its achievement unusually difficult. In jobs for which they are qualified, however, disabled workers do as well as unimpaired workers in terms of productivity, attendance, and average tenure. In fact, in certain high-turnover occupations, disabled workers have lower turnover rates. A DOL survey found that many large businesses are hiring people with disabilities and discovering that costs for accommodations differ very little from those for the general employee population. In fact, the typical one-time expenditure is about $500, according the U.S. DOL's Office of Disability Employment Policy.[77] Further, once an employer hires one person with a disability, it is much more likely to hire other people with disabilities. Starbucks Coffee actively hires individuals with disabilities, providing a range of accommodations. For instance, the company makes iPads available in stores with deaf partners (employees) to provide immediate video remote interpreting as needed.[78]

Immigrants

Large numbers of immigrants from Asia and Latin America have settled in many parts of the United States. The U.S. Bureau of Labor Statistics estimates that 26.3 million foreign-born individuals are in the U.S. workforce, representing 24.1 percent of the total.[79] Some are highly skilled and well educated and others are only minimally qualified and have little education. Overall, the weekly earnings of foreign-born workers are substantially lower than for native-born workers—$681 versus $837. Despite these differences, they have one thing in common: an eagerness to work. For instance, the labor force participation rate of foreign-born men was recently 78.2 percent, which is higher than the 67.3 percent participation rate for native-born men. They have brought with them attitudes, values, and mores to their home country cultures.

After the end of hostilities in Vietnam, Vietnamese immigrants settled along the Mississippi and Texas Gulf Coast. At about the same time, thousands of Thais fleeing the upheaval in Thailand came to the Boston area to work and live. New York's Puerto Rican community has long been an economic and political force there. Cubans who fled Castro's regime congregated in southern Florida, especially Miami. A flood of Mexicans and other Hispanics continues across the southern border of the United States. The Irish, the Polish, the Italians, and others who came here in past decades have long since assimilated into, and indeed became, the culture. Newer immigrants require time to adapt. Meanwhile, they generally take low-paying and menial jobs, live in substandard housing, and form enclaves where they cling to some semblance of the cultures they left.

Wherever they settle, members of these ethnic groups soon begin to become part of the regular workforce in certain occupations and break out of their isolation. They begin to adopt the English language and U.S. customs. They learn new skills and adapt old skills to their new country. Managers can place these individuals in jobs appropriate to their skills, with excellent results for the organization. As corporations employ more foreign nationals in this country, managers must work to understand the different cultures of their employees.

Foreign Workers

In 2017, the H-1B employment visa brings in approximately 80,000 skilled foreign workers annually, including some 20,000 researchers and academicians not subject to the annual visa cap set by Congress. Of those 80,000, the majority are distributed to employers through a lottery system each April held by U.S. Citizenship and Immigration Services, an arm of the U.S. Department of Homeland Security. However, the exact number of H-1B visa holders is difficult to determine. A three-year initial visa can be renewed for another three years, and if a worker is on track for a green card, H-1B status can be renewed annually.

Until the recent recession, demand far outpaced supply, and companies constantly encouraged Congress to raise the cap. Many employers say the H-1B visa program provided the only practical avenue for finding high-tech workers with cutting-edge skills. Others do not agree, and there continues to be a debate regarding the hiring of foreign workers. Still, U.S. employers at both ends of the skills spectrum say they have no choice.

Young Persons, Some with Limited Education or Skills

A lower labor force participation rate for young people is being experienced for all those younger than 24 years of age and not merely young persons with limited education and skills, as was so often the case in the past. The recent recession denied many young workers the opportunity of entering the workforce, so a large number decided to gain additional education to be more competitive.[80]

The downturn was especially harsh for 16- to 24-year-olds when the unemployment rate was the highest recorded since the government began monitoring it in the 1940s. Even so, each year, thousands of young, unskilled workers are hired, especially during peak periods, such as holiday buying seasons. These workers generally have limited education, sometimes even less than a high school diploma. Those who have completed high school often find that their education hardly fits the work they are expected to do. Many of these young adults and teenagers have poor work habits; they tend to be tardy or absent more often than experienced or better-educated workers.

Although the negative attributes of these workers at times seem to outweigh the positive ones, they are a permanent part of the workforce. Certainly, when teenagers are hired, an organization is not hiring maturity or experience; but young people possess many qualities, such as energy, enthusiasm, excitement, and eagerness to prove themselves. There are many jobs they can do well. More jobs can be de-skilled, making it possible for lower-skilled workers to do them. A well-known example of de-skilling is McDonald's use of pictures on its cash register keys. Managers should also look for ways to train unskilled workers and to further their formal education.

Baby Boomers, Gen X, Gen Y, and Gen Z

Never in the history of the United States has so many different generations with such different views and attitudes been asked to work together. There have been tremendous changes since the boomers first entered the workplace. Each generation has its unique culture that has shaped its nature. Although generalizations about a group are risky, the following discussion may provide additional insight into each group. The discussion begins with baby boomers fully realizing that there remain some members of the *Silent Generation* in the workforce, those born during the Great Depression and World War II.[81]

baby boomers
People born just after World War II through the mid-1960s.

BABY BOOMERS **Baby boomers** were born just after World War II through the mid-1960s. Corporate downsizing in the 1980s and 1990s cast aside millions of baby boomers. Companies now want to keep the boomers. Employers seek out boomers because they bring a wealth of skills and experience to the workplace, as well as have low turnover rates and high engagement levels. Companies today place considerable value on their skill, experience, and a strong work ethic, characteristics that many boomers possess.[82]

Generation X
Label affixed to the approximately 41 million U.S. workers born between the mid-1960s and late 1970s.

GENERATION X **Generation X** is the label affixed to the approximately 41 million U.S. workers born between the mid-1960s and late 1970s. Many organizations have a growing cadre of Generation X employees who possess lots of energy and promise. Ranjan Dutta, a director at PwC Saratoga said, "Gen X workers will be the largest part of the workforce for years to come, and increasingly make up senior leadership ranks in organizations."[83] They are one of the most widely misunderstood phenomena facing management today. Generation Xers differ from previous generations in some significant ways, including their natural affinity for technology and their entrepreneurial spirit. Job instability and the breakdown of traditional employer–employee relationships brought a realization to Generation Xers that it is necessary to approach the world of work differently from past generations.

Generation Xers recognize that their careers cannot be founded securely on a relationship with any one employer. They are skeptical, particularly when it comes to the business world and job security. They worry about their jobs being outsourced and how they are going to pay for their children's education. They think of themselves more as free agents in a mobile workforce and expect to build career security, not job security, by acquiring marketable skills and expertise. Gen Xers are focused on gaining transferrable skills so that they can be ready should they no longer have a job.[84] They are not afraid of changing jobs quite often. The surest way to gain Gen Xers' loyalty is to help them develop career security. When a company helps them expand their knowledge and skills, it is preparing them for the job market. Gen Xers will often want to stay on board to learn those very skills.

HR BLOOPERS

Affirmative Action and Workforce Diversity

Anne Johnson is a newly hired human resources (HR) associate for Capitol Manufacturing Company. Her first assignment was to develop and propose a plan to increase the diversity of the company's workforce. Anne spent two weeks preparing her ideas and creating a presentation for the company's HR leadership team and department managers throughout the company. She started her presentation by saying that she is not a fan of jargon because it creates confusion. To that end, Anne told the audience, "Diversity is just Affirmative Action with a new coat of paint." And she made a similar statement about the relationship between diversity and EEO. About workforce diversity and affirmative action, Anne claimed that both are enforced by the Fair Labor Standards Board. She went on to state that affirmative action, equal opportunity, and workforce diversity are numbers oriented and have little to do with the company's culture. All are simply aimed at changing the demographic composition of the workforce. Anne continued by telling the audience that ensuring EEO is nothing more than a marketing ploy. Finally, she concluded her presentation by saying that only the leadership of the HR and marketing departments within the company is responsible for promoting diversity, affirmative action, and EEO.

If your professor has assigned this, go to **www.pearson.com/mylab/management** to complete the HR Bloopers exercise and test your application of these concepts when faced with real-world decisions.

Generation Y
Comprises people born between the late 1970s and mid-1990s.

GENERATION Y **Generation Y** comprises people born between the late 1970s and mid-1990s. Estimates are that Gen Yers (or Millennials) account for approximately half of all employees in the United States.[85] They have never wound a watch, dialed a rotary phone, or plunked the keys of a manual typewriter. But without a thought, they download music from the Internet and insert pictures of events on Facebook. Kevin C. Carlson, CEO of Brill Street + Company said, "They may not have lots of experience in the traditional sense, but they've grown up with technology and social media, which are skills many companies look for today."[86] They cannot imagine how the world ever got along without computers. These individuals are the leading edge of a generation that promises to be the richest, smartest, and savviest ever. They are well educated, well versed in technology, and bursting with confidence.[87] Generation Yers—often referred to as the echo boomers, Millennials, and Nexters—are the coddled, confident offspring of post–World War II baby boomers. Generation Y individuals are a most privileged generation, who came of age during the hottest domestic economy in memory.

Gen Yers tend to have a strong sense of morality and civic-mindedness.[88] They are more ethnically diverse than previous generations, and nearly one-third of them have been raised in single-parent households. They want a workplace that is both fun and rewarding. They want jobs where there is a balance between work and family. They want jobs that conform to their interests and do not accept the way things have been done in the past. Generation Y employees want flexible working hours, which is a benefit that they are very enthusiastic about. They also tend to have more of a sense of entitlement not found in other generation of workers. However, Gen Yers' childhoods have been short-lived because they have been exposed to some of the worst things in life: schoolyard shootings, drug use, terrorism, sex scandals, and war.

Generation Z or Digital Natives
Internet-assimilated children born between 1995 and 2009.

GENERATION Z OR DIGITAL NATIVES After Generation Y came **Generation Z or Digital Natives**, the Internet-assimilated children born between 1995 and 2009. Gen Zers are more worldly, high-tech, and confident in their ability to multitask; they tend to have short attention spans and desire speed over accuracy; and they enjoy media that provides live social interaction.[89] They tend to use social networks to avoid the complications of dealing with face-to-face situations. In a recent survey, almost 25 percent of respondents found their relationship with their significant other was over by first seeing it on Facebook.[90] Digital Natives do not trust politicians, social institutions, the media, or corporations. Rather, they rely largely on themselves and their peers to decide what to think, what to do, and what to buy. The main thrust of the book *2018: Digital Natives Grow Up and Rule the World* was that, "Digital natives are protagonists for massive technology adoption and a consequent adaption of human behavior."[91] Two Gen Z children sitting in the back seat of the family car may now be texting each other instead of speaking with each other.

GENERATION ALPHA Some have suggested that the next generation, born from 2010 forward, will be called Generation Alpha. Although Generation Z is often referred to as the twenty-first-century generation, Generation Alpha will be the first true millennial generation, as they will be the first born into the 21st century.

Multigenerational Diversity

Four generations are now participating in the workforce and each has different defining characteristics and nicknames. The concept of generational differences as a legitimate workplace diversity issue has gained increasing recognition. Baby boomers are remaining on the job longer because of the economy and often find themselves working with Generation Y employees. Traditionally, discussions of workplace diversity tended to focus on topics of race, ethnicity, gender, sexual orientation, and disability. Shirley A. Davis, SHRM's director of diversity and inclusion initiatives, said, "In all parts of the world, there is another category of diversity that cannot be overlooked: multigenerational diversity."[92] Today, there are greater numbers of workers from each segment that bring both new opportunities and challenges. At times, there are significant differences in communication style which has the potential to harm communication. Dana Brownlee, president of corporate training firm Professionalism Matters in Atlanta, Georgia said, "Typically the older generations prefer talking face-to-face or on the phone, and the younger generations tend toward text-based messages like email and instant message."[93] If organizations want to thrive in this competitive environment of global talent management, they need employees and managers who are aware of and skilled in dealing with the different generations that make up the workforce.

FYI

Eighty-four percent of employees who work for LGBT-inclusive companies say that:

- They are proud to work there.
- They are more likely to "go the extra" mile for company success.[94]

Lesbian, Gay, Bisexual, and Transgender Employees

There has been an increased focus in the political and workforce arena with regard to lesbian, gay, bisexual, and transgender (LGBT) employees. In addressing the United Nations General Assembly, President Barack Obama said, "No country should deny people their rights to freedom of speech and freedom of religion, but also no country should deny people their rights because of who they love, which is why we must stand up for the rights of gays and lesbians everywhere."[95] President Obama also decided that the 1996 Defense of Marriage Act that bars federal recognition of same-sex marriages was unconstitutional and told the Justice Department to stop defending the law in court, bringing harsh criticism from many congressional members.[96] This became a moot point because in 2013, the Supreme Court in its landmark decision (*United States vs. Windsor*) struck down Section 3 of the act, which prohibited federal recognition of state-sanctioned, same-sex marriages.[97] Then, in 2015, the Supreme Court ruled that same-sex marriage is protected under the Due Process and Equal Protection Clauses of the Fourteenth Amendment, which means that same-sex marriages performed out-of-state must be recognized in other states (*Obergefell v. Hodges*). In the same year, the Family and Medical Leave Act, (FMLA) was amended to recognize eligible employees in legal same-sex marriages, enabling them to take FMLA leave to care for their spouse or family member, regardless of where they live.

Many companies have policies supporting LGBT employees perhaps because of legal requirements. Other firms have policies to recruit and retain qualified employees no matter their sexual orientation.[98] Over the last decade, corporations have increasingly created a more-welcoming environment for LGBT employees. An estimated 89 percent of *Fortune 500* firms now ban discrimination on the basis of sexual orientation, up from 61 percent in 2002, and approximately 66 percent also ban discrimination against transsexuals, compared with 3 percent in 2002.[99] Nonetheless, surveys show that many LGBT employees still view their sexual orientation as a hindrance on the job, and approximately 48 percent of those surveyed remain "closeted" at work.[100] However, by 2013, 59 percent of gay workers reported they were "out" at work, a 7 point increase from the previous year.[101]

PREPARING FOR EXAM/QUIZZES

Chapter Summary by Learning Objectives

1. ***Explain the concept of equal employment opportunity (EEO) and identify the federal laws affecting EEO.*** Equal employment opportunity (EEO) refers to the principles and the set of laws and policies that requires all individuals' rights to equal opportunity in the workplace, regardless of race, color, sex, religion, national origin, age, or disability. Major laws include the Civil Rights Act of 1866; Equal Pay Act (EPA) of 1963, amended in 1972; Lilly Ledbetter Fair Pay Act of 2009; Title VII of the Civil Rights Act of 1964, amended in 1972; Pregnancy Discrimination Act of 1978; Civil Rights Act of 1991; Age Discrimination in Employment Act (ADEA) of 1967, amended in 1978, 1986, and 1990; Rehabilitation Act of 1973; Americans with Disabilities Act (ADA) of 1990; Americans with Disabilities Act Amendments Act (ADAAA) of 2008; Immigration Reform and Control Act (IRCA) of 1986; the Uniformed Services Employment and Reemployment Rights Act (USERRA) of 1994; the Vietnam Era Veterans' Readjustment Assistance Act (VEVRAA) of 1974, as amended, and the Genetic Information Nondiscrimination Act (GINA) of 2008.
2. ***Discuss who is responsible for ensuring equal employment opportunity.*** The government and employers are responsible for ensuring EEO in the workplace. Two government agencies are charged with this responsibility: Equal Employment Opportunity Commission (EEOC) and the Office of Federal Contract Compliance Programs (OFCCP).
3. ***Define the types of illegal employment discrimination and discuss affirmative action.*** With *disparate treatment,*

an employer treats some people less favorably than others because of race, religion, sex, national origin, or age. *Adverse impact* occurs if women and minorities are not hired at the rate of at least 80 percent of the best-achieving group. *Affirmative Action* creates the expectation and program requirements that companies make a positive effort to recruit, hire, train, and promote employees from groups who are underrepresented in the labor force. An *affirmative action program* is an approach that an organization with government contracts develops to demonstrate that women or minorities are employed in proportion to their representation in the firm's relevant labor market.

4. ***Explain the Uniform Guidelines related to various types of illegal employment discrimination, including sexual harassment, national origin, religion, and caregiver (family responsibility) discrimination.*** The *Uniform Guidelines* adopted a single set of principles that were designed to assist employers, labor organizations, employment agencies, and licensing and certification boards to comply with requirements of federal law prohibiting employment practices that discriminated on the basis of race, color, religion, sex, and national origin. Employers have an affirmative duty to maintain a workplace free from sexual harassment. Discrimination on the basis of national origin is the denial of EEO because of an individual's ancestors or place of birth or because an individual has the physical, cultural, or linguistic characteristics of a national origin group. Employers have an obligation to accommodate religious practices unless they can demonstrate a resulting hardship. Caregiver (family responsibility) discrimination is discrimination against employees based on their obligations to care for family members.
5. ***Describe the concept of diversity and diversity management.*** *Diversity* refers to any perceived difference among people: age, race, religion, functional specialty, profession, sexual orientation, geographic origin, lifestyle, tenure with the organization, or position, and any other perceived difference. *Diversity management* is ensuring that factors are in place to provide for and encourage the continued development of a diverse workforce by melding these actual and perceived differences among workers to achieve maximum productivity.
6. ***Explain the various elements of a diverse workforce.*** The workforce may include single parents and working mothers, women in business, mothers returning to the workforce, dual-career families, workers of color, older workers, people with disabilities, immigrants, foreign workers, young persons (some with limited education or skills), and multi-generational workers.

Key Terms

equal employment opportunity (EEO) 53
Affirmative Action 53
Diversity 53
Uniform Guidelines 68
disparate treatment 66
adverse impact 67
executive order (EO) 68
affirmative action program (AAP) 68
caregiver (family responsibility) discrimination 74
diversity management 75
glass ceiling 76
dual-career family 77
baby boomers 80
Generation X 80
Generation Y 81
Generation Z or Digital Natives 81

MyLab Management

If your instructor is using MyLab Management, go to **www.pearson.com/mylab/management** to complete the problems marked with this icon ✪.

Questions for Review

✪**3-1.** What are the components that combine to make up the present diverse workforce? Briefly describe each.

3-2. Briefly describe the following laws:
- (a) Civil Rights Act of 1866
- (b) Equal Pay Act of 1963
- (c) Lilly Ledbetter Fair Pay Act of 2009
- (d) Title VII of the Civil Rights Act of 1964, as amended in 1972
- (e) Pregnancy Discrimination Act of 1978
- (f) Civil Rights Act of 1991
- (g) Age Discrimination in Employment Act of 1967, as amended in 1978 and 1986
- (h) Rehabilitation Act of 1973
- (i) Americans with Disabilities Act of 1990
- (j) Americans with Disabilities Act Amendments Act of 2008
- (k) Immigration Reform and Control Act of 1986
- (l) Uniformed Services Employment and Reemployment Rights Act of 1994
- (m) Vietnam Era Veterans' Readjustment Assistance Act of 1974
- (n) Genetic Information Nondiscrimination Act of 2008

3-3. Briefly discuss who is responsible for ensuring equal employment opportunity.
3-4. What are the significant U.S. Supreme Court decisions that have had an impact on EEO? On Affirmative Action?
3-5. What are the steps that the EEOC uses once a charge is filed?
3-6. What is the purpose of the *Uniform Guidelines on Employee Selection Procedures*?
3-7. What is the difference between disparate treatment and adverse impact?
3-8. How does the EEOC define sexual harassment?
3-9. How does the EEOC interpret the national origin guidelines?
3-10. What are some guidelines to follow regarding religion-related discrimination?
3-11. What is meant by the term *caregiver discrimination*?
3-12. What is the purpose of the OFCCP?
3-13. Define what the four-fifths rule is.
3-14. What is an affirmative action program?
3-15. Define *diversity* and *diversity management*.

PREPARING FOR MY CAREER

P I A Personal Inventory Assessment

An additional Personal Inventory Assessment can be found on MyLab Management.

Intercultural Sensitivity Scale

The workforce is increasingly more diverse than ever before. As an employee, you will work with people who differ from you in a variety of ways that we discussed in this chapter. Cultural differences are among those factors. This PIA will assess your level of cultural sensitivity.

ETHICS DILEMMA

How About Me?

The number of older workers is expected to grow for many years to come. The Age Discrimination in Employment Act prohibits employment discrimination against individuals age 40 and older. Yet, age discrimination continues to be prevalent in the workplace. For example, Maria has a limited training budget. She wants to invest in management development seminars for her well-performing supervisors. Maria has six high potential supervisors, but can only afford to send five. Ultimately, she selected five supervisors who graduated from college six years ago at age 21. Maria excluded Jonathan from consideration even though he has been a stellar performer for the last 30 years. When Jonathan heard about the decision, he asked Maria, "How about me?" Maria was surprised by Jonathan's question, saying, "I thought you were planning to retire within the next couple of years."

3-16. What would you do?
3-17. What factor(s) in this ethics dilemma might influence a person to make a less-than-ethical decision?

HRM Is Everyone's Business

It is critical for HR professionals to have a working knowledge of legislative imperatives and organizational policies designed to oversee the development and implementation of HR practices. Together with the legal department, HR has the responsibility to educate managers and other decision makers in the organization as to what should and should not be done. While ultimately the administration of HR programs will be the responsibility of HR, managers must have enough awareness to make informed decisions which will both protect the company from certain liabilities as well as ensure the retention and engagement of employees critical to the success of the organization. The most successful managers are often quite adept at explaining these nuances and are respected by their employees for their concern with the factors that influence the employee experience.

Action checklist for managers and HR—understanding and applying the legal landscape

HR takes the lead

- ☑ Work with the legal department to conduct training sessions designed to educate managers on some of the most important legislation that will govern employee-related actions (e.g., Civil Rights Acts, ADEA, and ADA).
- ☑ Conduct an audit to identify potential for disparate impact; disparate impact training is conducted to ensure that managers and other decision makers are aware of the pitfalls.
- ☑ Consider private sector companies that hold government contracts to understand what additional standards may be placed on them because of their relationship with the federal government.
- ☑ Provide legal updates to managers because legislation is changing quickly (particularly in these times). Many law firms provide these services via pro bono teleconferences. In-house employment lawyers can also provide these updates. For instance, we learned in this chapter that the EEOC considers treating gay, lesbian, bisexual, and transgender employees less favorably than others as a form of sex discrimination under the Civil Rights Act of 1964.
- ☑ Make sure that the legislative necessities create a starting point for establishing company policy and not merely the justification for doing the bare minimum.

Managers take the lead

- ☑ Speak openly about the importance of mutual respect and lead by example.
- ☑ Identify employees who fall into a group addressed specifically by law or company policy (e.g., ADA) which may be a new experience for you to work with as a manager (e.g., in most jobs, you will have more experience working with minority employees than disabled employees or transgender employees).
- ☑ Encourage employees to discuss in confidence with managers and HR professionals any concerns they may have about instances of possible illegal discrimination whether it be about themselves or out of concern for their coworkers. It is important to provide a safe haven for employees who come forward.

HRM by the Numbers

Detecting Adverse Impact

✪ *An additional HRM by the Numbers exercise can be found on MyLab Management.*

Adverse impact *usually* takes place when an employment decision, practice, or policy has a disproportionately negative effect on a protected group. HR professionals rely on the "four-fifths" or "80 percent" rule to judge whether adverse impact may have occurred. Consider the situation for men and for women:

Sex	*Total Applicants*	*Selected Applicants*	*Selection Rate*
Female	750	375	
Male	1,050	450	
Total	1,800	825	

3-18. Calculate (a) the selection rate for females and (b) the selection rate for males.
3-19. What is the ratio of the female selection rate to the male selection rate?
3-20. Based on your answer to question 3-19, is there evidence of possible adverse impact?

Working Together: Team Exercise

In small groups of three or four, come up with specific answers to the following questions. Talk through your perspectives and come up with a brief team response. Be prepared to share your ideas with the class.

Most schools actively seek to admit a highly diversified student body. As a group, discuss student diversity at your school. Think about visible characteristics (e.g., race) and characteristics not visible (e.g., political party affiliation) that describe diversity. Besides your experiences, consider your school's registered student organizations.

3-21. What are some of the features that shape diversity at your school? Explain your reasoning.
3-22. How would your student experience be different if your school's student body was not diverse? Explain.

INCIDENT 1 You're Not a Good Employee

Ricardo Balart, director of the recruiting for Sabena Company, asked four employees to evaluate the effectiveness of its employee orientation program and make recommendations for improvement. Mr. Balart selected members from different departments: Committee chair Bill Jameson, director of the customer service department, Mary Hodge, manager of the accounts receivables department, Maria Diaz, newly hired staff member in the marketing department, and Enza Peroni, payroll clerk. (It just so happened that Ms. Hodge and Mr. Jameson were Baby Boomers, Ms. Diaz was a member of Generation X, and Ms. Peroni was a member of Generation Y.)

The committee got off to a rocky start, in part, because members disagreed about where and when to get the work done. Mr. Jameson called for a face-to-face meeting in the conference room and got the following reactions: Ms. Hodge asked for the time and place of the meeting as well as what she should prepare in advance of the meeting. Ms. Diaz and Ms. Peroni were of the same mind, disagreeing with the need to meet face-to-face. Ms. Diaz commented, "It's difficult to anticipate whether I will be working in the office or from home on a particular day because my child care arrangements are unpredictable." She went on to say, "Let's get this done over e-mail."

Mr. Jameson expressed frustration, saying, "The flexible approach to getting the work done is unacceptable! For years, we always completed our committee assignments together in the conference room." He went a step further by asserting, "Young mothers should never be considered for positions of significant responsibility because they are unreliable and not serious about their work." Ms. Diaz, visibly upset by Mr. Jameson's comment, instructed him to review the company's telecommuting policy. His response: "That policy does nothing other than permit young employees to work only when they feel like it and for women with children to work less than others."

Questions

3-23. Do you agree with Mr. Jameson's approach to addressing the situation? Discuss.

3-24. What actions should Mr. Jameson have taken to avoid his current predicament?

3-25. What might occur if Mr. Jameson tells Ms. Diaz's supervisor that she is an unreliable employee?

INCIDENT 2 So, What's Affirmative Action?

Supreme Construction Company began as a small commercial builder located in Baytown, Texas. Until the early 2000s, Alex Boyd, Supreme's founder, concentrated his efforts on small, freestanding shops and offices. Up to that time, Alex had never employed more than 15 people.

In 2008, Alex's son Michael graduated from college with a degree in construction management and immediately joined the company full-time. Michael had worked on a variety of Supreme jobs while in school, and Alex felt his son was cut out for the construction business. Michael was given increasing responsibility, and the company continued its success, although with a few more projects and a few more employees than before. In 2012, Michael approached his father with a proposition: "Let's get into some of the bigger projects now. We have the capital to expand and I really believe we can do it." Alex approved, and Supreme began doing small shopping centers and multistory office buildings in addition to work in its traditional area of specialization. Soon, the number of employees had grown to 75.

In 2013, the National Aeronautics and Space Administration (NASA) released construction specifications for two aircraft hangars to be built southeast of Houston. Although Supreme had never done any construction work for the government, Michael and Alex considered the job within the company's capabilities. Michael worked up the $1,982,000 bid and submitted it to the NASA procurement office.

Several weeks later the bids were opened. Supreme had the low bid. However, the acceptance letter was contingent on submission of a satisfactory affirmative action program.

Questions

3-26. Explain why Supreme must submit an affirmative action program.

3-27. Generally, what should the program be designed to accomplish?

3-28. In conducting a utilization analysis, Michael discovers that although 30 percent of the general population of construction workers are black, only 10 percent of Supreme's employees are black. According to affirmative action, what is Supreme Construction required to do?

MyLab Management

If your instructor is using MyLab Management, go to **www.pearson.com/mylab/management** for Auto-graded writing questions as well as the following Assisted-graded writing questions:

3-29. What is the purpose of the EEOC?

3-30. How do equal employment opportunity laws differ from diversity management?

Endnotes

1 "What You Should Know About EEOC and the Enforcement Protections for LGBT Workers," *Equal Employment Opportunity Commission.* Accessed January 24, 2017, at www.eeoc.gov/eeoc/newsroom/wysk/enforcement_protections_lgbt_workers.cfm.

2 "Target Corporation to Pay $2.8 Million to Resolve EEOC Discrimination Finding," *Equal Employment Opportunity* press release (August 24, 2015). Accessed January 26, 2017, at www.eeoc.gov/eeoc/newsroom/release/8-24-15.cfm.

3 Jean Sahadi, "6 Things to Know about the Gender Pay Gap," (April 12, 2016). *CNN.* Accessed December 20, 2016, at http://money.cnn.com.

4 Dick Weaver, "How Is Lilly Ledbetter Helping You Sell EPLI," *National Underwriter* / P&C 115 (March 28, 2011): 26.

5 Tyler M. Paetkau, "When Does a Foreign Law Compel a U.S. Employer to Discriminate Against U.S. Expatriates?" A Modest Proposal for Reform," *Labor Law Journal* 60 (Summer 2009): 92–103.

6 "Employment Status of the Civilian Noninstitutional Population by Age, Sex, and Race," *U.S. Bureau of Labor Statistics.* Accessed January 26, 2017, at www.bls.gov/cps/demographics.htm#age.

7 Mitra Toossi, "Labor Force Projections to 2024: The Labor Force Is Growing, but Slowly," *Monthly Labor Review* (December 2015): 1–33.

8 Reduction in Force Tainted by Willful Age Discrimination," *HR Magazine* 58 (August 2013): 8.

9 "OFCCP Issues Proposed Revision of Veterans' Affirmative Action Rules," *HR Focus* 88 (June 2011): 12.

10 U.S. Department of Labor, "Compliance Assistance—Vietnam Era Veterans' Readjustment Assistance Act of 1974, as amended," *U.S. Department of Labor*, Accessed May 12, 2014, at www.dol.gov/ofccp/regs/compliance/ca_vevraa.htm.

11 "Persons with a Disability: Labor Force Characteristics," U.S. Bureau of Labor Statistics (USDL-16-1248, June 21, 2016). Accessed January 24, 2017, at www.bls.gov; Give Employees with Disabilities an Assist," *HR Magazine* 58 (August 2013): 79–82.

12 "EEOC's Views on Accommodation under Amended ADA Discussed," *HR Focus* 89 (January 2012): 3–6.

13 Maggie Fox, "America's Obesity Epidemic Hits a New High," *CNBC* online (June 7, 2016). Accessed January 26, 2017, at www.cnbc.com/2016/06/07/americas-obesity-epidemic-hits-a-new-high.html.

14 "Resources for Human Development Settles EEOC Disability Suit for $125,000," *Equal Employment Opportunity Commission* (April 10, 2012). Accessed January 27, 2017, at www.eeoc.gov/eeoc/newsroom/release/4-10-12a.cfm.

15 Common Pitfalls: The Devil Is in the Details," *HR Magazine* 58 (February 2013): 26.

16 "FY 2015 Annual Report to Congress," *U.S. Department of Labor, Office of the Assistant Secretary for Veterans' Employment and Training* (July 2016). Accessed January 27, 2017, at www.dol.gov/vets/programs/userra/USERRA_Annual_FY2015.pdf.

17 New York City Outlaws Discrimination Against Unemployed Job Hunters," *HR Magazine* 58 (August 2013): 14.

18 David P. Twomey, "Employee Retaliation Claims under the Supreme Court's Burlington, Crawford and Thompson Decisions: Important Implications for Employers," *Labor Law Journal* 62 (Summer 2011): 57–66.

19 "Charge Statistics: FY 1997 Through FY 2016," *Equal Employment Opportunity Commission.* Accessed January 23, 2017, at www.eeoc.gov/eeoc/statistics/enforcement/charges.cfm.

20 "Charge Statistics: FY 1997 Through FY 2016," *Equal Employment Opportunity Commission.* Accessed January 23, 2017, at www.eeoc.gov/eeoc/statistics/enforcement/charges.cfm.

21 U.S. Department of Labor, "Office of Federal Contract Compliance Programs," *U.S. Department of Labor.* Accessed January 23, 2017, at www.dol.gov/ofccp/aboutof.html.

22 Todd H. Girshon, "Jury or Nonjury Trials," *HR Magazine* 57 (February 2012): 79–85.

23 Effective Responses to EEOC Charges," *HR Magazine* 58 (October 2013): 73–75.

24 "Equal Employment Opportunity Commission. Part 1607—Uniform Guidelines on Employee Selection Procedures," *Code of Federal Regulations 29 C.F.R. §1607.16* (1978). Accessed January 26, 2017, at www.gpo.gov/fdsys/pkg/CFR-2006-title29-vol4/xml/CFR-2006-title29-vol4-sec1607-16.xml.

25 Alissa A. Horvitz and Lance E. Gibbons, "Federal Contractors Get New Scrutiny," *HR Magazine* 56 (November 2011): 71–82.

26 "New Directive Calls for More Full Compliance Evaluations," *HR Focus* 88 (April 2011): 4–5.

27 Nadine Vogel, "The OFCCP Ramps Up Enforcement," *Profiles in Diversity Journal* 13 (January/February 2011): 18.

28 "Andrew Slobodien and Elizabeth Peters, "Beyond Harassment Prohibitions," *HR Magazine* 57 (November 2012): 75–78.

29 "Federal Judge Awards $1,470,000 in EEOC Sexual Harassment and Retaliation Case Against Z Foods," (July 22, 2016). Accessed January 27, 2017, at www.eeoc.gov/eeoc/newsroom/release/7-22-16a.cfm.

30 "Preventing Workplace Sexual Harassment Should Be HR Priority, Attorney Tells Webinar," *HR Focus* 89 (March 2012): 16.

31 David B. Ritter and Mari Kaluza, "Lesson from Walmart: How to Cut Risk when a Co-worker Harasses," *HR Specialist: Illinois Employment Law* 5 (May 2011): 6.

32 "Delete Your Liability: Copy Xerox Response to Harassment Complaint," *HR Specialist: Employment Law* 40 (May 2011): 3.

33 "Duane Reade Settles Sex Harassment Lawsuit," *HR Specialist: New York Employment Law* 4 (August 2009): 5.

34 "Price of Supervisor Pleasuring Himself Over an Employee: $95 Million," *Legal Alert for Supervisors* 6 (June 24, 2011): 4.

35 Equal Employment Opportunity Commission, "Charges Alleging Sex-Based Harassment: FY 2010—FY 2016, " *Equal Employment Opportunity Commission.* Accessed January 27, 2017, at www.eeoc.gov/eeoc/statistics/enforcement/sexual_harassment_new.cfm.

36 Maria Greco Danaher, "Men Entitled to Title VII Protection," *HR Magazine* 55 (December 2010): 93.

37 Allen Smith, "EEOC Settlement Reflects Challenges of English-Only Policies," *HR Magazine* 54 (June 2009): 26.

38 Tanya Marcum and Sandra J. Perry, "Dressed for Success: Can a Claim of Religious Discrimination Be Successful?" *Labor Law Journal* 61 (Winter 2010): 184–191.

39 Orthopedic Manufacturer Settles Religious Bias Suit," *HR Specialist: North Carolina Employment Law* 7 (January 2013): 5.

40 Does Boss Have to Excuse Key Worker from Crucial Job Duty so Man Can Go to Church?" *Alert for Supervisors* 8 (March 1, 2013): 1–2.

41 "Abercrombie Resolves Religious Discrimination Case Following Supreme Court Ruling in Favor of EEOC," *Equal Employment Opportunity Commission* (July 28, 2015). Accessed January 27, 2017, at www.eeoc.gov/eeoc/newsroom/release/7-28-15.cfm.

42 "Employment Characteristics of Families Summary," *U.S. Bureau of Labor Statistics* (April 22, 2016). Accessed January 20, 2017, at www.bls.gov; Cynthia Thomas Calvert, "Caregivers in the Workplace," *The Center for WorkLife Law* (2016). Accessed January 28, 2017, at www.worklifelaw.org/pubs/FRDupdate2016.pdf.

43 Abigail Crouse, "Be Careful! Caregiver Discrimination Claims Are on the Rise," *HR Specialist: Minnesota Employment Law* 3 (April 2010): 6.

44 Gerald E. Calvasina, Richard V. Calvasina, and Eugene J. Calvasina, "Caregiver Responsibility Discrimination and the Equal Employment Opportunity Commission (EEOC) Guidelines: Policy Issues for Employers," *Journal of Legal, Ethical & Regulatory Issues* 13 (June 2010): 1–10.

45 Cynthia Thomas Calvert, "The New Sex Discrimination: Family Responsibilities," *University of Maryland Law Journal of Race, Religion, and Class* (Vol. 9, No. 1): 33-44.

46 "Denver Hotel Management Company to Pay $105,000 to Settle EEOC Sex Discrimination Suit," *Equal Employment Opportunity Commission* (December 8, 2010). Accessed January 28, 2017, at www.eeoc.gov/eeoc/newsroom/release/12-8-10.cfm.

47 Cynthia Thomas Calvert, "Caregivers in the Workplace." *The Center for WorkLife Law* (2016). Accessed January 28, 2017, at www.worklifelaw.org/pubs/FRDupdate2016.pdf.

48 Ibid.

49 "America's Largest Drug Store Chain to Pay $180,000 to Settle EEOC Disability Discrimination Suit," *Equal Employment Opportunity Commission* (July 12, 2014), Accessed January 28, 2017, at www.eeoc.gov/eeoc/newsroom/release/7-2-14b.cfm.

50 Marie Y. Philippe, "Corporate Diversity Training: Is Yours Meeting 21st Century Needs?" *Profiles in Diversity Journal* 12 (January/February 2010): 60.

51 Andrew L. Molinsky, Thomas H. Davenport, Bala Iyer, and Cathy Davidson, "3 Skills Every 21-Century Manager Needs," *Harvard Business Review* 90 (January/February 2012): 139–143.

52 Mike Brennan, "The Measuring Stick," *Chief Learning Officer* 10 (August 2011): 22–25.

53 "R. Roosevelt Thomas," T+D (May 2011): 66–67.

54 Pamela Arnold, "The Role of Diversity Management in the Global Talent Retention Race," *Profiles in Diversity Journal* 13 (May/June 2011): 16.

55 "No. 7 | MasterCard | DiversityInc Top 50," *DiversityInc online*. Accessed January 25, 2017, at www.diversityinc.com/masterrcard/.

56 U.S. Bureau of Labor Statistics, "Women in the Labor Force: A Databook," *BLS Reports* (Report 1059, December 2015). Accessed January 21, 2017, at www.bls.gov.

57 "Families by Presence of Own Children Under 18: 1950 to Present," *U.S. Bureau of the Census* (Table FM-1). Accessed January 28, 2017, at www.census.gov/hhes/families/data/families.html.

58 "The 2016 State of Women-Owned Businesses Report," American Express OPEN (2016). Accessed January 23, 2017, at http://www.womenable.com/content/userfiles/2016_State_of_Women-Owned_Businesses_Executive_Report.pdf.

59 Josh Bersin, "Why Diversity and Inclusion Will Be a Top Priority for 2016," *Forbes* (December 6, 2015). Access January 4, 2017, at www.forbes.com.

60 "Female CEO's Are at Record Level in 2016, But It's Still Only 5%," *CNN Money* (September 29, 2016). Accessed January 3, 2017, at money.cnn.com/2016/09/29/investing/female-ceos-record-high/.

61 Saundra Stroope and Bonnie Hagemann, "Women, Water, + Leadership: Are We Making Progress?" *T+D* 65 (March 2011): 50–53.

62 "Women in the Workplace," *McKinsey & Company* (September 2015). Accessed January 28, 2017, at www.mckinsey.com/business-functions/organization/our-insights/women-in-the-workplace.

63 Jo Piazza, "Women of Color Hit a 'Concrete Ceiling' in Business," *The Wall Street Journal* online (September 27, 2016). Accessed December 2, 2016, at www.wsj.com.

64 Jennifer Schramm, "On-Ramps Lead Back to Work," *HR Magazine* 57 (September 2012): 120.

65 Kelley M. Butler, "Today's Working Women Seek Mentors, Motherhood Transition," *Employee Benefit News* 20 (April 2006): 17–19.

66 The 40-Year-Old Intern," *Harvard Business Review* 90 (November 2012): 21–23.

67 U.S. Bureau of Labor Statistics, "Women in the Labor Force: A Databook," *BLS Reports* (Report 1059, December 2015). Accessed January 30, 2017, at www.bls.gov.

68 Lorraine Bello and Galen Tinder, "Dual Career Implications on Workforce Mobility: The Evolution of the Relocating Spouse/Partner," *Benefits & Compensation Digest* 46 (September 2009): 36–39.

69 Mitra Toossi, "Labor Force Projections to 2020: A More Slowly Growing Workforce," *Monthly Labor Review* (January 2012): 43–64.

70 Ella Bell, "The Bicultural Life Experience of Career Oriented Black Women," *Journal of Organizational Behavior* 11 (November 1990): 459–478.

71 "Employment Status of the Civilian Noninstitutional Population by Age, Sex, and Race," *U.S. Bureau of Labor Statistics*. Accessed January 26, 2017, at www.bls.gov/cps/demographics.htm#age.

72 Companies Tweaking Policies and Practices for Older Workers," *HR Focus* 90 (May 2013): 4–6.

73 U.S. Bureau of Labor Statistics, "Labor Force Projections to 2024: The Labor Force Participation Rate Continues to Fall," *Monthly Labor Review* (December 2015). Accessed January 26, 2017, at www.bls.gov.

74 Greg Ip, "For Economy, Aging Population Poses Double Whammy," *The Wall Street Journal* online (August 3, 2016). Accessed January 5, 2017, at www.wsj.com.

75 Hunter Ruthven, "Barclays Shifts Perception by Rolling Out Apprenticeship Scheme for Those Over 50," *Real Business* online (February 9, 2015). Accessed January 4, 2017, at http://realbusiness.co.uk/current-affairs/2015/02/09/barclays-shifts-perception-by-rolling-out-apprenticeship-scheme-for-those-over-50/.

76 U.S. Bureau of Labor Statistics, "*Persons with a Disability: Labor Force Characteristics—2012*," (USDL 13-1141, June 12, 2013). Accessed May 12, 2014 at www.bls.gov.

77 Dori Meinert, "Opening Doors," *HR Magazine* 57 (June 2012): 55–57.

78 Sarah Blahoveck, "Why Disabled Workers? 4 Powerful (and Inclusive) Companies Answer," *Huffington Post* online (February 24, 2016). Accessed January 28, 2017, at www.huffingtonpost.com; "Starbucks Recognized as a "Best Place to Work"," *Starbucks Newsroom* (July 13, 2016). Accessed January 28, 2017, at https://news.starbucks.com/starbucks-is-recognized-as-a-best-oace-to-work-for-disability.

79 "Foreign-Born Workers: Labor Force Characteristics – 2015," *U.S. Bureau of Labor Statistics* (USDL-16-0989, May 19, 2016). Accessed January 29, 2017, at www.bls.com.

80 Jennifer Schramm, "Planning for Population Shifts," *HR Magazine* 56 (February 2011): 80.

81 Beverly Kaye, "Four Generations," *Leadership Excellence* 29 (January 2012): 20.

82 Amy Bladen Shatto, "In Practice Two Sides of the Retention Dilemma," *Chief Learning Officer* 10 (August 2011): 34.

83 "Turnover, Globalization Among Emerging Challenges Facing HR," *HR Focus* 88 (September 2011): 10–11.

84 Adrienne Fox, "Talkin' Bout My Generation," *HR Magazine* 56 (May 2011): 26–27.

85 "Employment Status of The Civilian Noninstitutional Population by Age, Sex, And Race," *U.S. Bureau of Labor Statistics*. Accessed January 28, 2017, at www.bls.gov/cps/cpsaat03.pdf.

86 Engaging Young Workers with Tailor Made Programs," *Employee Benefit News* 27 (June 2013): 19–21.

87 "How 'Recession-Proof' Will Millennial Workers Be?" *HR Focus* 86 (March 2009): 6–7.

88 "Winning Over the Next Generation of Leaders," *The 2016 Deloitte Millennial Survey*. Accessed January 15, 2017, at www2.deloitte.com/content/dam/Deloitte/global/Documents/About-Deloitte/gx-millenial-survey-2016-exec-summary.pdf.

89 Sharon Williams, "Welcome to Generation Z," *B&T Magazine* 60 (December 10, 2010): 12.

90 Eric Lauzon, "Paradox: The Anti-Social Generation," *Enterprise Innovation* 7 (February/March 2011): 44.

91 Jerry Selitto, "Anyone Up for Some Time Travel?" *Mortgage Banking* 71 (March 2011): 22–23.

92 "The Multigenerational Workforce: Opportunity for Competitive Success," *HR Magazine* 54 (March 2009): Special section 1–9.

93 How to Communicate in the New Multigenerational Office," Forbes.com (February 14, 2013): 26.

94 Sylvia Ann Hewlett and Kenji Yoshino, "LGBT-Inclusive Companies Are Better at 3 Big Things," *Harvard Business Review* online, (February 2, 2016). Accessed December 20, 2016 at www.hbr.org.

95 Samantha Power, "We Must Stand Up for the Rights of Gays and Lesbians Everywhere," *Press Release* (September 22, 2011). Accessed May 12, 2014 at www.whitehouse.gov.

96 Todd A. Solomon, Joseph S. Adams, and Brett R. Johnson, "How Conflicting Same-Sex Union Laws Are Impacting Employee Benefits," *Benefits Magazine* 49 (January 2012): 14–21.

97 In Strongly Worded Decision, Supreme Court Finds Defense of Marriage Act Unconstitutional," Forbes.com (July 26, 2013): 30.

98 Nadine Vogel, "Disability & LGBT—Similarities and Difference and How to Support Them in the Workplace," *Profiles in Diversity Journal* 13 (March/April 2011): 124.

99 "LGBTQ Equality at the Fortune 500," *Human Rights Campaign*, Accessed January 4, 2017, at www.hrc.org/resources/lgbt-equality-at-the-fortune-500; "Of Companies and Closets," *Economist* 402 (February 11, 2012): 70.

100 Sylvia Ann Hewlett and Karen Sumberg, "For LGBT Workers, Being 'Out' Brings Advantages," *Harvard Business Review* 89 (July/August 2011): 28.

101 "'Out' Is In: Gay Workers Find Workplaces More Welcoming," *BusinessWeek.com* (February 13, 2013): 3.

Part Two
Staffing

Chapter 4
Strategic Planning, Human Resource Planning, and Job Analysis

Chapter 5
Recruitment

Chapter 6
Selection

4

Strategic Planning, Human Resource Planning, and Job Analysis

LEARNING OBJECTIVES After completing this chapter, students should be able to:

4.1 Describe the HR strategic planning process.

4.2 Explain the human resource planning process.

4.3 Describe the job analysis process and methods.

4.4 Summarize the components of a job description.

4.5 Explain what competencies and competency modeling are.

4.6 Summarize job design concepts.

MyLab Management

Improve Your Grade!

If your professor is using MyLab Management, visit **www.pearson.com/mylab/management** for videos, simulations, and writing exercises.

Learn It

If your professor has chosen to assign this, go to **www.pearson.com/mylab/management** to see what you should particularly focus on and to take the Chapter 4 Warm-Up.

The tools we describe in this chapter and in Chapters 5 and 6 provide human resources (HR) professionals with a foundation to harness the capability of a company's human capital to its competitive advantage. Let's consider a metaphor to bring the opening sentence to life. Take, for example, your favorite hit movie or television show. Many factors contribute to the show's success, which we might measure as the size of enduring viewership and awards recognizing excellent talent. Among the most important are the story line, character development and scripts, and casting actors into roles.

From an HR standpoint, the story line can be thought of as a strategy to create a distinctive narrative that is unique from others, character development and scripts as job analysis and work flow, and casting requirements as HR planning. We take up these topics in this chapter.

4.1 Describe the HR strategic planning process.

HR Strategic Planning Process

strategic planning
Process by which top management determines overall organizational purposes and objectives and how they are achieved.

As discussed in Chapter 1, HR executives are now focusing their attention on how HR can help the organization achieve its business objectives through **strategic planning**, which is the process by which top management determines overall organizational purposes and objectives and how they are achieved. More specifically, strategic planning entails a series of judgments under uncertainty that companies direct toward achieving specific goals.[1] Companies base strategy formulation on environmental scanning activities, which we discuss later. HR executives are increasingly highly involved in the strategic planning process. In the past they often waited until the strategic plan was formulated before becoming a part of the conversation.[2]

Strategic planning is an ongoing process that is constantly changing to find a competitive advantage. At times an organization may see the need to diversify and increase the variety of the goods that are made or sold. At other times, downsizing may be required in response to the external environment. Or the strategic plan may see integration, the unified control of many successive or similar operations, as their driving force. Strategic planning attempts to position the organization in terms of the external environment. For example, the so-called Great Recession in 2007-2009 showed weakness in the marketplace for some firms, which led to lower company

FIGURE 4-1
Strategic Planning Process

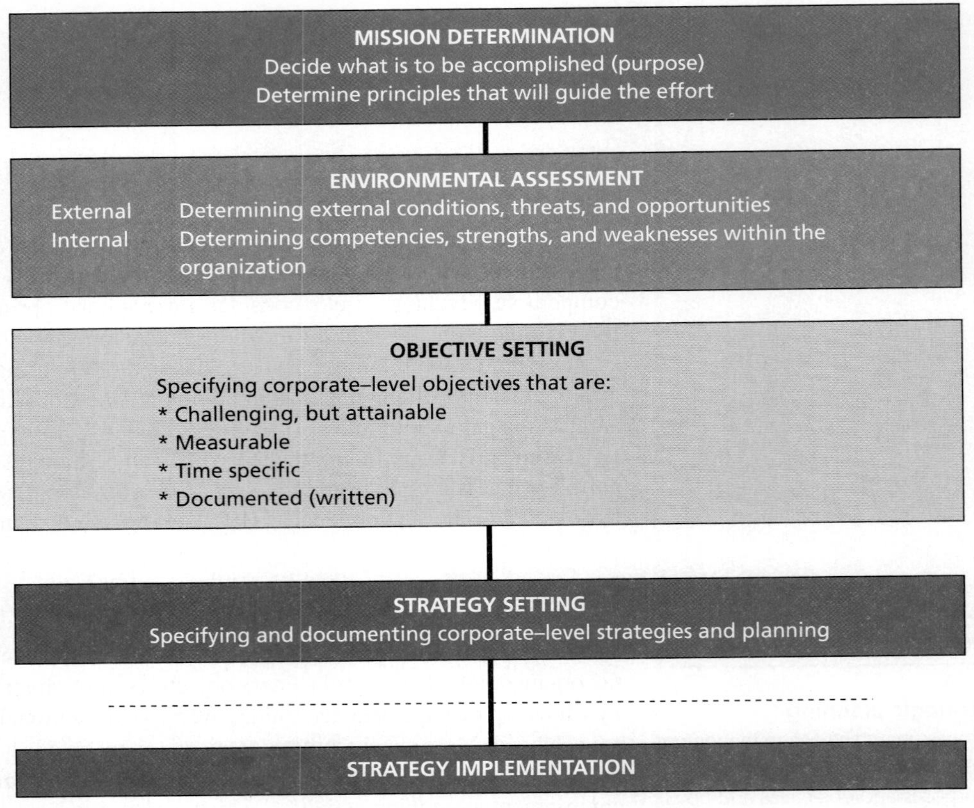

valuations, increased business failures, and selling off their noncore business units. Forward-thinking companies found opportunities that were not available when business was booming, such as expanding their company through acquisition.[3] Companies always need to look for ways to stay competitive, gain market share, and be the first to innovate a new product or service. For instance, automobile manufacturers have set their sights on building and selling affordable all-electric cars of similar or better quality than Tesla Motors' vehicles.

Strategic planning at all levels of the organization can be divided into four steps: (1) determination of the organizational mission; (2) assessment of the organization and its environment; (3) setting of specific objectives or direction; and (4) determination of strategies to accomplish those objectives (see Figure 4-1). The strategic planning process described here is basically a derivative of the strengths, weaknesses, opportunities, and threats (SWOT) framework that affects organizational performance, but it is less structured.

In strategic planning discussions, HR professionals' primary focus must be on talent. We define human resource management (HRM) as the use of *individuals* to achieve organizational objectives. According to HRM expert Edward E. Lawler III, "Positioning the HR function and talent management to contribute to the overall effectiveness and financial performance of the organization is the best way the HR function can add value to corporations."[4] Focusing on recruiting, developing, and retaining talent provides the rationale for choosing various HR strategies and practices.

Mission Determination

mission
Company's continuing purpose or reason for being.

The first step in the strategic planning process is to determine the corporate mission. The **mission** is a company's continuing purpose or reason for being. The corporate mission is the sum of the organization's ongoing purpose. Arriving at a mission statement should involve answering questions such as: What are we in management attempting to do for whom? Should we maximize profit so shareholders will receive higher dividends or so share price will increase? Or should we emphasize stability of earnings so employees will remain secure? In the case of not-for-profit companies, is the focus on extending its humanitarian reach from tragic events in the United States to tragic events in other countries? Certainly, HR can provide valuable assistance in answering these questions.

There are many other mission possibilities. Mission determination also requires deciding on the principles on which management decisions will be based. Will the corporation be socially responsible and environmentally friendly (sustainability)? Will the company be forthright in dealing with its various constituents such as its customers? The answers to these questions tend to become embedded in a corporate culture and help determine the organizational mission. Top management expects HR activities to be closely aligned to this mission and add value toward achieving these goals. The following is a part of General Mills' corporate mission:

We serve the world by making food people love.[5]

General Mills also includes two additional objectives: environmental sustainability (Nourishing the Future) and community enhancement (Nourishing Communities). For instance, General Mills employees helped prepare and serve food, renovated buildings, and participated in activities to benefit impoverished children and teenagers in Brazil.

ENVIRONMENTAL ASSESSMENT Once the mission has been determined, the organization should assess its *strengths* and *weaknesses* in the internal environment and the *threats* and *opportunities* from the external environment (often referred as a SWOT analysis). Making strategic plans involves information flows from both the internal and the external environments. From inside comes information about organizational competencies, strengths, and weaknesses. Scanning the external environment allows organizational strategists to identify threats and opportunities, as well as constraints. In brief, the strategy would be to take advantage of the company's strengths and minimize its weaknesses to grasp opportunities and avoid threats. For example, social networking company LinkedIn can capitalize on the following opportunities, which include the growing adoption of LinkedIn's recruitment services among corporations, growing urbanization, changing attitudes toward employment, and increasing premium subscriptions.[6]

HR professionals can take advantage of LinkedIn technology and services by connecting to more candidates who subscribe to LinkedIn than would typically otherwise be the case for traditional recruitment methods such as career portals on corporate Web sites, campus hiring, recruitment agencies, and job boards. Also, HR professionals are in the best position to identify workforce strengths and weaknesses. Should the company be considering, for instance, a merger or acquisition, HR would be able to work with top management to determine whether the present workforce can be effectively integrated into the workforce of the merged company. For example, does the workforce of the merged company improve the overall value of the company, or is there only duplication of talent? Any reorganization affects people and HR professionals must be in the forefront of people-related matters.

There are always threats that counterbalance opportunities. For example, LinkedIn faces at least two significant future threats.[7] Competitors such as Google and Facebook could challenge LinkedIn's success by offering similar services to customers such as mixing social networking with recruitment services. In addition, although LinkedIn has established a presence in Latin America, South America, and Asia-Pacific regions, the growth in average revenue per customer will be much lower than in the United States because of lower purchasing power of countries in these international regions.

LinkedIn's revenue challenges are relevant to the work of its HR professionals. Research and development (R&D) costs and sales and marketing costs are likely to rise. R&D costs increase when a company is enhancing current services or developing new ones. In addition, sales and marketing costs stand to increase when a company is expanding its reach to prospective customers. These activities are likely to translate into stepped up recruitment efforts for software engineers and sales professionals. As well, establishing competitive compensation and benefits programs stand to represent a significant challenge.

In the following Watch It video, learn about iRobot, which is best known for the iRobot Roomba® vacuum cleaning robot. This product helped to change how people view robots. iRobot continues to develop robotic products to change the way customers include robots in their daily life. This video will provide an appreciation of SWOT analysis.

Watch It I

If your instructor has assigned this, go to **www.pearson.com/mylab/management** to watch a video titled iRobot: Competitive Strategy of Home Robots and respond to questions.

OBJECTIVE SETTING *Objectives* are the desired end results of any activity. Objectives should have four basic characteristics: (1) They should be expressed in writing; (2) they should be measurable; (3) they should be specific as to time; and (4) they should be challenging but attainable. Strategic objectives might be directed at factors such as profitability, customer satisfaction, financial returns, technological leadership, and operating efficiency. Objectives should be developed only after a cost–benefit analysis of each alternative is considered. Because HR professionals are in the people business, it is difficult to imagine any strategic objective that would not involve them in some manner, and the LinkedIn example illustrates this point.

STRATEGY SETTING Strategies can now be developed for accomplishing those objectives. Strategies should be developed to take advantage of the company's strengths and minimize its weaknesses to grasp opportunities and avoid threats. HR professionals should be highly involved in these activities because the composition of the workforce will certainly influence the strategies chosen. For the sake of illustration, let's consider two fundamental strategies: lowest cost and differentiation.

Lowest-cost strategy focuses on gaining competitive advantage by being the lowest-cost producer of a product or service within the marketplace, while selling the product or service at a price advantage relative to the industry average. Lowest-cost strategies require aggressive construction of efficient-scale facilities and vigorous pursuit of cost minimization in such areas as operations, marketing, and HR. For example, you won't find many extras in clothes retailer Ross Stores. "We believe in "no frills"—no window displays, mannequins, fancy fixtures or decorations in our stores so we can pass more savings on to our customers."[8] Low overhead costs allow Ross to sell quality apparel and home items at 20 to 60 percent less than most department store prices, and the company is profitable.[9]

Companies adopt differentiation strategies to develop products or services that are unique from those of their competitors. Differentiation strategies lead to competitive advantage through building brand loyalty among devoted consumers. Brand-loyal consumers are less sensitive to price increases, which enables companies to invest in R&D initiatives to further differentiate themselves from competing companies. Differentiation strategy can take many forms, including design or brand image, technology, features, customer service, and price. Take retailer L.L. Bean for instance. The company allows customers to return merchandise at any time if not completely satisfied: "We make pieces that last, and if they don't, we want to know about it. So, if it's not working or fitting or standing up to its task, we'll take it back. L.L. himself always said that he didn't consider a sale complete 'until goods are worn out and the customer still satisfied.'"[10] Similarly, the Ritz-Carlton hotel established its Customer Loyalty Anticipation Satisfaction System, which is designed to fulfill, "even the unexpressed wishes and needs of our guests."[11] In addition, most Ritz-Carlton employees have the authority to spend up to $2,000 each day, per guest, to resolve any complaint.

In the following Watch It video, learn about the online retailer Zappos' competitive strategy. In many retail sectors, the goal is product differentiation to create brand-loyal customers and generate pricing power. Companies achieve differentiation through formulating and implementing competitive strategies that define how organizations will compete in their businesses. Zappo's strategy is to "be about the very best customer service."

 **Watch It 2**

If your instructor has assigned this, go to **www.pearson.com/mylab/management** to watch a video titled Zappos: Competitive Strategy and respond to questions.

FYI

- HR expert Edward E. Lawler III stated: "HR professionals are well positioned to facilitate the implementation of business strategies by ensuring that employees are working consistently with the mandates of strategic planning."[12]

EMPLOYEE ROLES ASSOCIATED WITH COMPETITIVE STRATEGIES Common wisdom and experience tell us that HR professionals must decide which employee roles are instrumental to the attainment of competitive strategies. Knowledge of these required roles should enable HR professionals to implement HR practices that encourage enactment of these roles. For instance, HR professionals are responsible for designing and implementing practices that elicit strategy-consistent employee roles. As we've noted in the introduction, job analysis is a critical tool used by HR professionals to define employee jobs; thus, the role behavior that is expected of them.

For the lowest-cost strategy, the imperative is to reduce output costs per employee. The desired employee roles for attaining a lowest-cost strategy include repetitive and predictable behaviors, a relatively short-term focus, primarily autonomous or individual activity, high concern for quantity of output, and a primary concern for results.

The key employees' roles for differentiation strategies include highly creative behavior, a relatively long-term focus, cooperative and interdependent behavior, and more risk taking. Compared with lowest-cost strategies, successful attainment of differentiation strategies depends on employee creativity, openness to novel work approaches, and willingness to take risks. In addition, differentiation strategies require longer time frames to provide sufficient opportunity to yield the benefits of these behaviors.

STRATEGY IMPLEMENTATION Once the strategic planning process is complete, the strategy must be implemented. Some people argue that strategy implementation is the most difficult and important part of strategic management. No matter how creative and well formulated the strategic plan, the organization will not benefit if it is incorrectly implemented. Strategy implementation requires changes in the organization's behavior, which can be brought about by changing one or more organizational dimensions, including management's leadership style, organizational structure, information and control systems, production technology, and HR.[13]

LEADERSHIP A leader can get others to do what he or she wants them to do. Managers must influence organization members to adopt the behaviors needed for strategy implementation. Top-level managers seeking to implement a new strategy may find it useful to build coalitions and persuade others to go along with the strategic plan and its implementation. HR must take the leadership role in dealing with HR matters. Basically, leadership is used to encourage employees to adopt supportive behaviors, and when necessary, to accept the required new values and attitudes.

ORGANIZATIONAL STRUCTURE A company's organizational structure is typically illustrated by its organizational chart. The form of structure needed is determined by the needs of the firm. It may be informal and highly changeable in small, uncomplicated businesses. By contrast, large, diverse, and complex organizations usually have a highly-formalized structure. But that should not mean the structure is so rigid that it does not change, perhaps even frequently. Newly formed high-tech companies are most likely to restructure or reorganize frequently, but even some of the largest *Fortune 500* firms, such as General Motors and Chrysler, have experienced major reorganizations. Many variations of organizational structures are available for use today. HR should be in a good position to recommend the most effective structure needed by the organization.

INFORMATION AND CONTROL SYSTEMS Among the information and control systems are reward systems; incentives; objectives-oriented systems; budgets for allocating resources; information systems; and the organization's rules, policies, and implementations. Certainly, HR should be a asset in developing and working with these systems. A proper mix of information and control systems must be developed to support the implementation of the strategic plan.

TECHNOLOGY The knowledge, tools, and equipment used to accomplish an organization's assignments comprise its technology. The appropriate level of technology must be found for proper implementation of the strategic plan. Certainly, technology is revolutionizing how organizations operate today. This is the case for HR professionals.

HUMAN RESOURCES The HR functions must be properly aligned to successfully implement the strategic plan. HR will be central to understanding the future of an asset that is increasingly important to the organization—the intellectual and productive capacity of its workforce. A proper balance of HR must be developed to support strategy implementation. Once strategic planning has taken place, HR planning may be developed to help implement the strategic plan.

FYI

According to the U.S. Bureau of Labor Statistics, in 2016:

- 74.7 percent of all jobs required on-the-job training.
- 47.8 percent required prior work experience.
- 21.8 percent required a professional certification, license, or other pre-employment training.[14]

4.2 Explain the human resource planning process.

human resource planning
Systematic process of matching the internal and external supply of people with job openings anticipated in the organization over a specified period.

requirements forecast
Determining the number, skill, and location of employees the organization will need at future dates to meet its goals.

availability forecast
Determination of whether the firm will be able to secure employees with the necessary skills, and from what sources.

Human Resource Planning

Human resource planning (workforce planning) is the systematic process of matching the internal and external supply of people with job openings anticipated in the organization over a specific period. Workforce planning has evolved from a knee-jerk planning undertaking to a fundamental strategic function. It includes business plan, HR data, and statistical analyses of those data. It is also incorporated into the business and financial planning process, so it provides a foundation for a plan that is aligned with the business strategy. As we discussed in Chapter 1, analyzing employment data and business outcomes has empowered HR professionals to quantify its influence, and more HR professionals have gotten on board. In 2016, 51 percent of companies correlated business outcomes with HR programs, which is up from 38 percent just one year earlier.[15]

The HR planning process is illustrated in Figure 4-2. Note that strategic planning precedes HR planning. HR planning has two components: *requirements* and *availability*. A **requirements forecast** involves determining the number, skill, and location of employees the organization will need at future dates to meet its goals. For example, discount retailer Dollar General launched a campaign to hire 10,000 workers in one month because it was planning to open more than 900 stores.[16] Since 2008, the company increased its staff by more than 70 percent.[17] Requirement forecasts also focus on seasonal hiring. For instance, UPS hired approximately 95,000 temporary workers for the holiday season when package delivery activity is at its peak.[18]

The determination of whether the firm will be able to secure employees with the necessary skills, and from what sources, is called an **availability forecast**. We can look to the manufacturing sector of the economy as an illustration. It's true that many manufacturing jobs in the United States were eliminated because so many companies moved their operations to other countries where the cost of doing business is often lower. This shift in operations effectively increased the supply of available workers relative to job openings (demand for workers), leaving scores of workers unemployed.

FIGURE 4-2
The Human Resource Planning Process

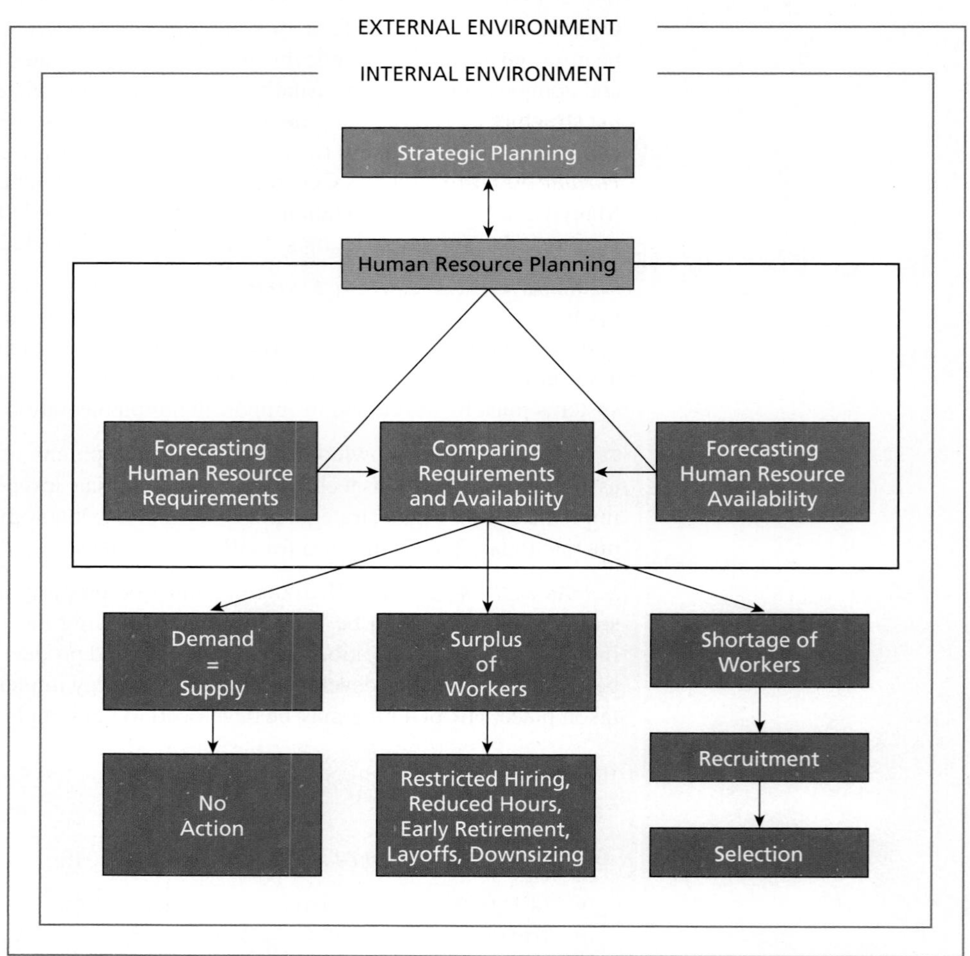

Ironically, companies in the manufacturing sector are experiencing a shortage of qualified workers because the use of complex robotic and automated equipment has risen more quickly than the supply of individuals who possess the necessary skills to function in such environments.[19]

When employee requirements and availability have been analyzed, the firm can determine whether it will have a surplus or shortage of employees. Ways must be found to reduce the number of employees if a surplus is projected. If a worker shortage is forecast, the firm must obtain the proper quantity and quality of workers from outside the organization. In this case, external recruitment and selection are required.

Because conditions in the external and internal environments can change quickly, the HR planning process must be continuous. Changing conditions could affect the entire organization, thereby requiring extensive modification to the forecasts. For instance, companies laid off millions of workers as business demand dropped precipitously. And, as the economy improved, plans were made to increase the size of the workforce.

Forecasting Human Resource Requirements

HR Web Wisdom

HR Planning Organization

www.hrps.org

This is the Web site for the Human Resource People and Strategy organization.

Before HR requirements can be projected, demand for the firm's goods or services must be forecasted. This forecast is then converted into people requirements for the activities necessary to meet this demand. For a firm that manufactures personal computers, activities might be stated in terms of the number of units to be produced, number of sales calls to be made, number of vouchers to be processed, or a variety of other activities. For example, manufacturing 1,000 laptop computers each week might require 10,000 hours of work by assemblers during a 40-hour week. Dividing the 10,000 hours by the 40 hours in the workweek gives 250 assembly workers needed. Similar calculations are performed for the other jobs needed to produce and market the computers.

Several techniques for forecasting HR requirements are currently used. Some of the techniques are qualitative in nature, and others are quantitative.

zero-base forecast
Forecasting method that uses the organization's current level of employment as the starting point for determining future staffing needs.

ZERO-BASE FORECAST The **zero-base forecast** uses the organization's current level of employment as the starting point for determining future staffing needs. Essentially, the same procedure is used for HR planning as for zero-base budgeting, whereby each budget must be justified again each year. If an employee retires, is fired, or leaves the firm for any reason, the position is not automatically filled. Instead, an analysis is made to determine whether the firm can justify filling it. Equal concern is shown for creating new positions when they appear to be needed. The key to zero-base forecasting is a thorough analysis of HR needs. Frequently, the position is not filled and the work is spread out among remaining employees, as often is the case with firms that downsize. Plans may also involve outsourcing or other approaches as an alternative to hiring.

HR BLOOPERS

Workforce Planning at Master Cleaners

Master Cleaners provides residential cleaning services through more than 100 cleaning employees throughout their geographic area. As the HR manager hired just more than a year ago, Jack Potts has worked hard to establish many of their HR practices. As the company's first HR manager, Jack believes his primary responsibility is to make sure administrative processes are in place. He has been attending senior leadership meetings regarding the organization's strategy and knows there are some plans to expand into the commercial market. However, he hasn't paid much attention to those discussions because there is just too much work to do to get HR processes established. Now he's received a request from one of the cleaning managers about hiring 25 new commercial cleaners and he's worried about finding these new hires. The problem is that because the commercial cleaners must work at night after the office buildings are closed for the day, his current recruiting strategy won't necessarily work. Jack now must find experienced cleaners willing to work in the evening and that is a challenging task. Further, turnover is already high in the residential cleaning business. Exit interviews with employees who have quit suggest that they find the work tedious. Jack expresses his concerns about these staffing challenges to the cleaning manager. But the cleaning manager reminds him they have been talking about this expansion for a while and suggests that Jack should have been planning for this.

If your professor has assigned this, go to **www.pearson.com/mylab/management** to complete the HR Bloopers exercise and test your application of these concepts when faced with real-world decisions.

bottom-up forecast
Forecasting method in which each successive level in the organization, starting with the lowest, forecasts its requirements, ultimately providing an aggregate forecast of employees needed.

BOTTOM-UP FORECAST In the **bottom-up forecast**, each successive level in the organization, starting with the lowest, forecasts its requirements, ultimately providing an aggregate forecast of employees needed.

It is based on the reasoning that the manager in each unit is most knowledgeable about employment requirements. Beginning with the lowest-level work units in the organization, each unit manager makes an estimate of personnel needs for the period encompassed by the planning cycle. As the process moves upward in the company, each successively higher level of management in turn makes its own estimates of needs, incorporating the input from each of the immediately preceding levels. The result, ultimately, is an aggregate forecast of needs for the entire organization. This process is often highly interactive in that estimated requirements from the previous level are discussed, negotiated, and re-estimated with the next level of management as the forecast moves upward through the organization. The interactive aspect of managerial estimating is one of the advantages of this procedure because it forces managers to justify their anticipated staffing needs.

RELATIONSHIP BETWEEN VOLUME OF SALES AND NUMBER OF WORKERS REQUIRED Historically, one of the most useful predictors of employment levels is sales volume. The relationship between demand and the number of employees needed is a positive one. As you can see in Figure 4-3, a firm's sales volume is depicted on the horizontal axis and the number of employees required is shown on the vertical axis. In this illustration, as sales decrease, so does the number of employees. Using such a method, managers can approximate the number of employees required at different demand levels. Quantitative methods such as regression analysis can be helpful in determining the number of workers needed.

Forecasting Human Resource Availability

To forecast availability, the HR manager looks to both internal sources (current employees) and external sources (the labor market). The determination of whether the firm will be able to secure employees with the necessary skills, and from what sources, is an *availability forecast*. It helps to show whether the needed employees may be obtained from within the company, from outside the organization, or from a combination of the two sources. Another possibility is that the required skills are not immediately available from any feasible source. Consider the following example:

> *A large manufacturing firm on the West Coast was preparing to begin operations in a new plant. Analysts had already determined there was a large long-term demand for the new product. Financing was available and equipment was in place, but production did not begin for two years! Management had made a critical mistake: it had studied the demand side of HR, but not the supply side. There were not enough qualified workers in the local labor market to operate the new plant. New workers had to receive extensive training before they could move into the newly created jobs.*

This illustration provides one more instance of the importance of HR involvement in strategic planning.

Shortage or Surplus of Workers Forecasted

When firms are faced with a shortage of workers, organizations should intensify their efforts to recruit the necessary people to meet the needs of the firm. Some possible actions will be discussed next.

FIGURE 4-3
Relationship of Sales Volume to Number of Employees

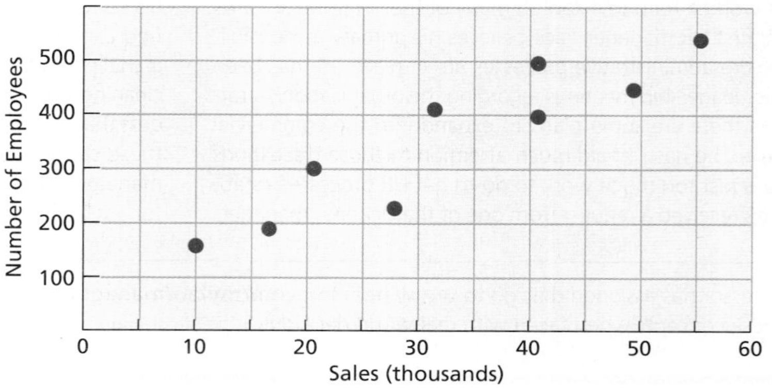

Information technology occupations are expected to grow rapidly from 2014 to 2024. The employment of information security analysts is expected to increase 18 percent during this period, which is faster than average for all occupations. According the U.S. Labor of Bureau of Statistics, multiple factors are contributing to increased demand for information security analysts:

> *Information security analysts plan and carry out security measures to protect an organization's computer networks and systems. Their responsibilities are continually expanding as the number of cyberattacks increases. Demand for information security analysts is expected to be very high, as these analysts will be needed to create innovative solutions to prevent hackers from stealing critical information or causing problems for computer networks.*[20]

Job openings by major occupational group are expected to vary widely from 2012 to 2022. Two factors contribute to the expected values: growth in a profession given demand (such as in the case of information security analysts) and company replacement needs, likely as employees retire or choose to work elsewhere. Figure 4-4 shows these projections for several occupational groups. The greatest growth in job openings is predicted to be in office and administrative support followed by food preparation and related services. The lowest growth is expected in the legal profession as well as in farming, fishing, and forestry.

INNOVATIVE RECRUITING A shortage of personnel often means that new approaches to recruiting must be used. The organization may have to recruit different kinds of candidates, search in different geographic areas than in the past, and explore new recruitment methods. For instance, Ikea launched an innovative, cost-effective recruitment campaign in Australia. The company advertised job opportunities to its customers with a "Careers Instructions" sheet packed inside

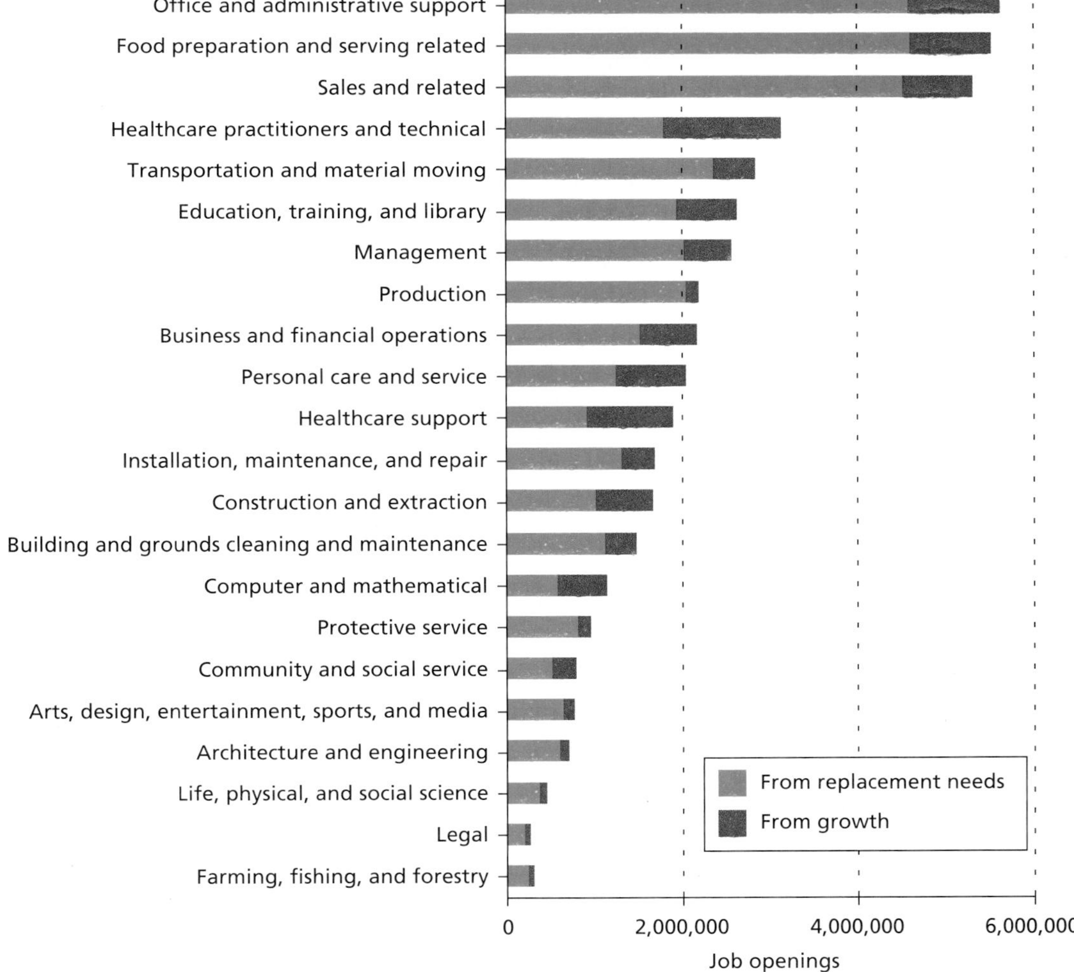

FIGURE 4-4

Job openings by major occupational group, projected 2014–2024, in thousands of openings

Source: Career Outlook (December 2015). Accessed February 17, 2017, at https://www.bls.gov/careeroutlook/2015/article/projections-occupation.htm.

product boxes. Customers were *instructed* to apply for a job. The campaign was highly successful for generating nearly 4,300 quality applicants that yielded 280 new hires.[21]

In using innovative recruiting, businesses must attempt to determine who their prospective employees are and what motivates them. For example, given the physical and emotional demands of the nursing profession, many organizations offer flexible work schedules, child care, and educational benefits. Other practices for other occupational groups may be required to attract employees to a firm, such as four-day workweeks (compressed workweeks), telecommuting, and part-time employment.

COMPENSATION INCENTIVES Firms competing for workers in a high-demand situation may have to rely on pay incentives. Premium pay is one obvious method, however, this approach may trigger a bidding war that the organization cannot sustain for an extended period. To offset the bidding war, some organizations use signing bonuses to entice individuals to join the firm. In 2016, 76 percent of companies surveyed use signing bonuses.[22] Even the military uses signing bonuses. For example, the U.S. Army Corps offers a signing bonus up to $40,000 for translators who speak certain Middle-Eastern languages and enlist as translator aides in the U.S. Army.[23]

As more people shop online, places such as Amazon.com, Inc. and Ikea have added additional warehousing facilities to handle rising demand. The limited supply of candidates for warehouse jobs has led to significant pay increases as these companies compete for talent. Sometimes, higher hourly pay alone is not sufficient to staff these facilities. Radial, an operations management company that manages the operations of retailer warehouses and fulfillment centers, awards additional compensation incentives, including attendance bonuses during the peak holiday season, gift cards, and monetary incentives for exceeding performance targets.[24] The company pays individuals an extra dollar for every hour an employee meets or exceeds the performance target of picking items off the shelves.

ALTERNATIVES TO LAYOFFS Special training programs may be needed to prepare previously unemployable individuals for positions with a firm. Remedial skills and training are two types of programs that may enable companies to reassign employees to other positions within the company. For example, a small firm in Los Angeles expanded its market by hiring people with few, if any, qualifications. The firm was willing to spend the necessary time and money needed to provide even basic training.

When a comparison of requirements and availability indicates that a worker surplus will result, most companies look to alternatives to layoffs but downsizing may ultimately be required. At times, layoffs can be a necessary cost-cutting measure. However, there are counterproductive problems associated with layoffs, such as increased turnover, especially among the best, most productive workers, and the creation of anxiety among remaining staff, resulting in lower morale, reduced worker engagement, and decreased productivity. Therefore, whenever financially feasible, firms need to look for alternatives to layoff and retain as many workers as possible. We consider four of these alternatives.

First, some companies choose to implement a restricted hiring policy that reduces the workforce by not replacing employees who leave. There are basically three forms of freezes. A *hard freeze* means that no new workers are hired to replace a vacated position. A *soft freeze* means that the company is only hiring to fill critical positions. New workers are hired only when the overall performance of the organization may be affected. For instance, President Donald J. Trump ordered a soft hiring freeze in most federal government agencies in 2017, excluding the military. A goal of this freeze was to save millions of dollars for working individuals whose income taxes fund much of federal government employment.[25] At the same time, he authorized that the head of any executive department or agency may fill vacant jobs that are deemed necessary to promote national security or public safety. Still, many concerns have been raised about the soft freeze. For example, Bill Valdez, President of the Senior Executives Association, expressed concerns, "that the freeze, coupled with negative views of federal workers in recent years in Congress and the press, will have a chilling effect on the ability of the federal government to attract and recruit talent it needs . . . "[26] A new term, *smart freeze* has entered HR vocabulary. HR and managers evaluate every position to determine the ones the company could not survive without and those that are difficult to fill and continue to hire them. Some critics of the federal government's hiring freeze argued for the need to adopt a smart freeze approach. Renee M. Johnson, President of the Federal Managers Association, said, "The American taxpayer would be better served with improvements to the workforce, not blind cuts. All federal agencies should be allowed to match hiring actions that align with essential mission and funding."[27]

Second, many companies are considering the use of voluntary severance packages to reduce workforce size and operating costs. **Severance packages**, also known as buyouts, refer to pay and benefits awarded to employees for a period after they leave the company. Oftentimes, buyouts include bonus payments that vary in amount based on salary and years of service. Recently, *The Wall Street Journal* offered an "enhanced voluntary severance benefit" to all news employees worldwide as an alternative to layoffs.[28] Several newspaper companies have experienced precipitous drops in advertising revenue, subscription fees, and profits because many reputable news sources are available free of charge on the internet.[29] As readership drops, advertisers choose to spend their money elsewhere to capitalize on larger audiences. Poor business performance is not the only trigger for buyouts. For instance, online shoe and apparel retailer Zappos transformed its organization from one with multiple layers of management and individual decision making to a self-managed arrangement where there were no formal titles or reporting relationships.[30] Instead, the company gave decision making power to flexible teams. Zappos CEO Tony Hsieh recognized that this change would not be a good fit for all employees. He decided to offer a voluntary buyout to anyone who wanted to leave the company. Nearly 20 percent of the workforce accepted the buyout.[31]

Third, early retirement is another way to reduce the number of workers. Some employees will be delighted to retire, but others will be somewhat reluctant. However, the latter may be willing to accept early retirement if the total retirement package is made sufficiently attractive. A tactic that is popular in the construction market is swapping employees. Some companies loan out staff to partner companies during slow times, while promising to hire back the workers when conditions improve. While the workers were away, they learned new skills and those left behind learned the skills to replace them.

Fourth, some companies permit an employee to go from full-time to 30 hours a week without losing health benefits.[32] Some companies may offer job-sharing arrangements. This arrangement can enable organizations to retain top talent in lieu of layoffs while having minimal impact on the overall labor budget. For example, employee benefits can be fairly managed on a per-employee basis, as two 20-hour-a-week part timers may have comparably pro-rated, scaled back benefits. Other companies may reduce the workweek from five days to four thereby having a 20 percent reduction in wages. Some companies may offer an unpaid holiday option where instead of taking two weeks off, employees are being asked to take five, with three being unpaid.

The classic case of a firm that believes a no-layoff policy is best for continuous well-being of the firm is Cleveland's Lincoln Electric, a manufacturer of arc welding equipment. Lincoln Electric offers its Guaranteed Continuous Employment Plan, which provides covered employees with security against layoffs because of lack of work.[33] The company has faithfully honored its commitment through the past 68 years (as of 2016, which was the latest available data) even through difficult economic climates.[34] Since the 1930s, this $3 billion company has kept its promise to its U.S. employees to never lay them off for economic reasons. For decades, wages were 20 to 30 percent above industry averages. The firm believes that a stable workforce provides a long-term competitive advantage. In difficult times, hours are reduced, people are reassigned, and white-collar salaries are cut. If workers meet the firm's performance standards, no one is laid off.

FYI

One survey of organizations revealed that only 21 percent had identified their workforce needs six to 10 years into the future.[35]

Succession Planning: A Component of Strategic Planning

succession planning
Process of ensuring that qualified persons are available to assume key managerial positions once the positions are vacant.

Succession planning is the process of ensuring that qualified persons are available to assume key managerial positions once the positions are vacant. Nothing could be as important to the strategic well-being of a company as ensuring that a qualified person is in place to lead the company both now and in the future. This succession planning definition includes untimely deaths, resignations, terminations, or the orderly retirements of key managerial personnel. The goal is to help ensure a smooth transition and operational efficiency, but the transition is often difficult. The Institute for Corporate Productivity (i4cp) paper "Succession Planning Highlight Report" found that succession planning will be among the top five challenges executives face in the future.[36] However, in another survey, more than half of United States and Canadian companies surveyed could not immediately name a successor to their organization's chief executive officer.

General Electric (GE) provides an example of a company with an excellent succession plan. At GE, the goal is same-day succession. When senior vice president Larry Johnston quit to become the CEO at Albertsons, the position was filled the same day. Bill Conaty, former senior vice president of HR at General Electric said, "We had candidates with two or three backups for all key positions—including the C-suite and all business units. And the board already knew who was lined up thanks to six-month reviews."[37] This process is in sharp contrast to the difficulty that Hewlett-Packard has experienced in the selection of a new CEO. HP has its third CEO in slightly more than a year[38] and its eighth CEO since 1999.[39] None of the former CEOs at HP had implemented a succession plan that would have at least identified internal candidates who were qualified to take over should the need arise.[40] This form of disruption can be a serious drain on both morale and the financial well-being of the firm.

Should companies focus exclusively on internal or external candidates? Joseph L. Bower, author of *The CEO Within*, found that CEOs who were promoted from within the company are generally more successful than CEOs recruited from other companies. Still, the succession plan needs to consider both external and internal candidates. One approach for increasing the success of external hires is to have them serve in an executive role for a short period before promoting them to the CEO position.[41]

Because of the tremendous changes that will confront management this century, succession planning is taking on more importance than ever before. Deaths are not the only challenges that have created an increased focus on succession planning. For example, the premature firing of CEOs is no longer a rare event. CEOs are being terminated more quickly than in the past.

In recent years, succession planning is going much deeper into the workforce. A firm might have a good succession plan for top-level positions but few plans for the levels where all the work is performed. There is a movement away from traditional succession planning, which was focused only on top executives of the company. Succession management is now involving middle managers, where they are developed to help ensure that key roles below the C-suite have ready replacements.[42]

Companies that do not engage in succession planning now will eventually be forced to do it in the future. Members of the baby boom generation—born between 1946 and 1964—are mostly in their 50s and 60s. In 2024, this cohort will be ages 60 to 78.[43] Although more people are working longer than ever before, companies will lose employees in leadership positions at an alarming rate. How can companies address this problem? It is in a company's best interests to ensure that there is a transfer of knowledge from older employees to younger employees. Establishing mentoring programs may help. Also, companies should not abruptly lay off older workers, but rather to ensure that there is a smooth transition of leadership as they retire.[44] Oftentimes, this goal can be accomplished with phased in retirement programs that permit full-time employees to gradually reduce their work hours over a few years.

Succession planning is often neglected in small businesses because it is generally thought of in terms of replacing CEOs and key executives within larger businesses. But, succession planning is just as, or more, important for small businesses. A problem, however, is that only 31 percent of small business owners say their businesses are extremely or very prepared for such an event.[45] Without proper succession planning, the company could face economic and tax disasters. Often the small business owner's argument against succession planning may be "we're too small," "we're too new," "we have good people in place," or "I'm not going anywhere soon."[46] Many of today's small businesses will not survive to the next generation of same family ownership. In fact, it is estimated that only 30 percent of businesses make it to the second generation, and just 10 percent survive to the third generation.[47] Peter Handal, president, CEO, and chairman of Dale Carnegie Training, said, "The failure to establish a comprehensive succession plan is a leading cause of this phenomenon."[48]

4.3 Describe the job analysis process and methods.

Job Analysis: Process and Methods

job analysis
Systematic process of determining the skills, duties, and knowledge required for performing jobs in an organization.

Job analysis is the systematic process of determining the skills, duties, and knowledge required for performing jobs in an organization. With job analysis, the tasks needed to perform the job are identified. Traditionally, it is an essential and pervasive HR technique and the starting point for other HR activities. In today's rapidly changing work environment, the need for a sound job analysis system is critical. New jobs are being created, and old jobs are being redesigned or eliminated. A job analysis that was conducted only a few years ago may now be obsolete and must be redone. Some have even suggested that changes are occurring too fast to maintain an effective job analysis system.

job
Group of tasks that must be performed for an organization to achieve its goals.

position
Collection of tasks and responsibilities performed by one person.

A **job** consists of a group of tasks that must be performed for an organization to achieve its goals. A job may require the services of one person, such as that of the president, or the services of 75, as might be the case with machine operators in a large manufacturing firm. A **position** is the collection of tasks and responsibilities performed by *one* person; there is a position for every individual in an organization.

In a work group consisting of a supervisor, two senior analysts, and four analysts, there are three jobs and seven positions. A small company might have 25 jobs for its 75 employees, whereas in a large company 2,000 jobs may exist for 50,000 employees. In some firms, as few as 10 jobs may make up 90 percent of the workforce.

The purpose of job analysis is to obtain answers to six important questions:

1. What physical and mental tasks does the worker accomplish?
2. When is the job to be completed?
3. Where is the job to be accomplished?
4. How does the worker do the job?
5. Why is the job done?
6. What qualifications are needed to perform the job?

Job analysis provides a summary of a job's duties and responsibilities, its relationship to other jobs, the knowledge and skills required, and working conditions under which it is performed. Job facts are gathered, analyzed, and recorded, as the job exists, not as the job should exist. Determining how the job should exist is most often assigned to industrial engineers, methods analysts, or others. Job analysis is conducted after the job has been designed, the worker has been trained, and the job is being performed.

job description
Document that provides information regarding the essential tasks, duties, and responsibilities of a job.

job specification
A document that outlines the minimum acceptable qualifications a person should possess to perform a job.

Job analysis is performed on three occasions: (1) when the organization is founded and a job analysis program is initiated for the first time; (2) when new jobs are created; and (3) when jobs are changed significantly because of new technologies, methods, procedures, or systems. Jobs also change when there is increased emphasis on teamwork in organizations, empowerment of employees, or other managerial interventions such as quality management systems. Job analysis is most often performed because of changes jobs. From job analysis information, both job descriptions and job specifications can be prepared.

The **job description** is a document that provides information regarding the essential tasks, duties, and responsibilities of the job. The minimum acceptable qualifications a person should possess to perform a job are contained in the **job specification.**[49] Both types of documents will be discussed in greater detail later in this chapter.

Reasons for Conducting Job Analysis

As Figure 4-5 shows, data derived from job analysis in the form of the job description/specification can have an impact on virtually every aspect of HR management. In practice, both the job description and job specification are combined into one document with the job specification presented after the job description.

FIGURE 4-5
Job Analysis: A Basic Human Resource Management Tool

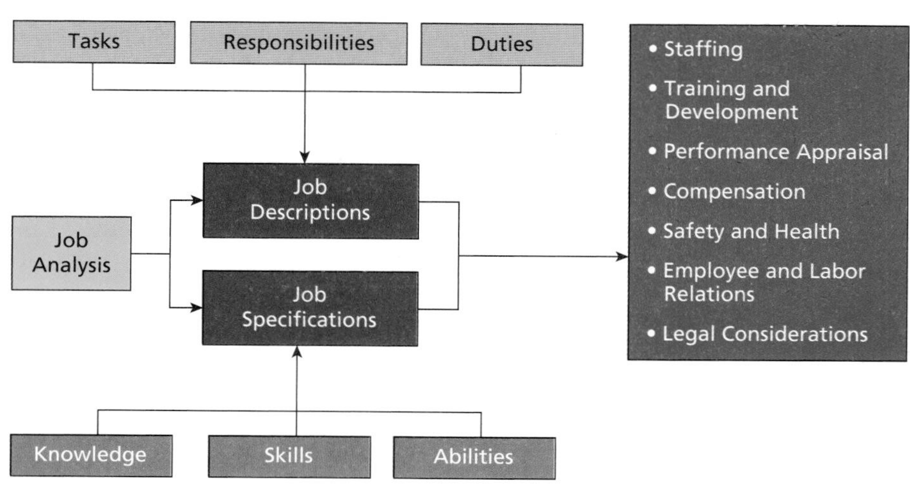

STAFFING All areas of staffing would be haphazard if the organization did not know the qualifications needed to perform the various jobs. A major use of job analysis data is found in HR planning (as discussed earlier in this chapter). Merely knowing that the firm will need 1,000 new employees to produce goods or services to satisfy sales demand is insufficient. Each job requires different knowledge, skills, and ability levels. Obviously, effective HR planning must take these job requirements into consideration. Also, lacking up-to-date job descriptions and specifications, a firm would have to recruit and select employees for jobs without having clear guidelines, a practice that could have disastrous consequences.

TRAINING AND DEVELOPMENT Job description information often proves beneficial in identifying training and development needs. If it suggests that the job requires a knowledge, skill, or ability, and the person filling the position does not possess all the qualifications required, training or development are probably in order. Training should be directed at assisting workers in performing duties specified in their present job descriptions or at developing skills for broader responsibilities.

PERFORMANCE APPRAISAL Most workers want to know what they are supposed to accomplish and good job descriptions provide that. Then, employees should be evaluated in terms of how well they accomplish the duties specified in their job descriptions and any other specific goals that may have been established. A manager who evaluates an employee on factors not clearly predetermined is left open to allegations of discrimination.

COMPENSATION In the area of compensation, it is helpful to know the relative value of a job to the company before a dollar value is placed on it. Jobs that require greater knowledge, skills, and abilities should be worth more to the firm. For example, the relative value of a job calling for a master's degree normally would be higher than that of a job that requires a high school diploma. This might not be the case if the market value of the job requiring only a high school diploma was higher, however. Such a situation occurred in a major West Coast city many years ago. It came to light that city sanitation engineers (garbage collectors) were paid more than better-educated public schoolteachers.

SAFETY AND HEALTH Information derived from job analysis is also valuable in identifying safety and health considerations. For example, employers are required to inform workers when a job is hazardous. The job description/specification should reflect this condition. In addition, in certain hazardous jobs, workers may need specific information about the hazards to perform their jobs safely.

EMPLOYEE AND LABOR RELATIONS Job analysis information is also important in employee and labor relations. When employees are considered for promotion, transfer, or demotion, the job description provides a standard for evaluation and comparison of talent. Information obtained through job analysis can often lead to more objective human resource decisions.

LEGAL CONSIDERATIONS A properly prepared job analysis is particularly important for supporting the legality of employment practices. Before the equal employment opportunity movement in the early 1960s and 1970s, few firms had effective job analysis systems.[50] But the need to validate basic job requirements hastened the growth in the use of job analysis to prepare job descriptions/specifications. The importance of job analysis is well documented in the *Uniform Guidelines on Employee Selection Procedures*.[51] Job analysis data are needed to defend decisions involving termination, promotion, transfers, and demotions. Job analysis provides the basis for tying the HR functions together and the foundation for developing a sound HR program. Although the law does not require that companies use job analysis, a successful defense against claims of alleged violations of the following laws may depend on the appropriate use of job analysis:

- *Fair Labor Standards Act:* Jobs are categorized as exempt or nonexempt, and job analysis is basic to this determination. Workers in nonexempt jobs must be paid time and a half when they work more than 40 hours per week. Overtime pay is not required for exempt employees.
- *Equal Pay Act:* If jobs are not substantially different, employees performing them must receive similar pay. When pay differences exist, job descriptions can be used to show whether jobs are substantially equal in terms of skill, effort, responsibility, and working conditions.

- *Civil Rights Act:* HR management has focused on job analysis because selection methods need to be clearly job related. Job descriptions may provide the basis for an equitable compensation system and an adequate defense against unfair discrimination charges in initial selection, promotion, and all other areas of HR administration. When job analysis is not performed, defending certain qualifications established for the job is usually difficult. In the *Griggs v. Duke Power Company* case, the company stated that supervisors must have a high school diploma. However, the company could show no business necessity for this standard. Placing a selection standard in the job specification without having determined its necessity through job analysis makes the firm vulnerable in discrimination suits.
- *Occupational Safety and Health Act:* Job descriptions are required to specify elements of the job that endanger health or are considered unsatisfactory or distasteful by much of the population. Showing the job description to the employee in advance is a good defense.
- *Americans with Disabilities Act (ADA)/ADA Amendments Act:* Employers are required to make reasonable accommodations for workers with disabilities who can perform the *essential functions* of a job and job analysis is needed to obtain this information. Key elements used to determine essential functions include physical skills, mental skills, job duties, and behavioral skills.[52] The EEOC defines *reasonable accommodation* as any modification or adjustment to a job, an employment practice, or the work environment that makes it possible for an individual with a disability to enjoy an equal employment opportunity. The ADA Amendments Act expands the definition of "disability" and many more applicants and employees are eligible for reasonable accommodations. Certainly, stating that every task in a job is essential sends a red flag to the EEOC.[53]

Job Analysis Methods

Considerable information is needed for the successful accomplishment of job analysis. The job analyst identifies the job's actual duties and responsibilities and gathers the other types of data such as work activities; worker-oriented activities; machines, tools, equipment, and work aids used; and personal requirements. This information is used to help determine the job skills needed. In addition, the job analyst looks at job-related tangibles and intangibles, such as the knowledge needed, the materials processed, and the goods made or services performed. Essential functions of the job are determined in this process.

Some job analysis systems identify job standards. Work measurement studies may be needed to determine how long it takes to perform a task. Regarding job content, the analyst studies the work schedule, financial and nonfinancial incentives, and physical working conditions. Education, training, and work experience pertinent to the job are identified. Because many jobs are often performed in conjunction with others, organizational and social contexts are also noted. Subjective skills required, such as strong interpersonal skills, should be identified if the job requires the jobholder to be personable.

Job analysis has traditionally been conducted in several different ways because organizational needs and resources for conducting job analysis differ. Selection of a specific method should be based on the purposes for which the information is to be used (job evaluation, pay increases, development, and so on) and the approach that is most feasible for a organization. The historically most common methods of job analysis are discussed in the following sections.

QUESTIONNAIRES Questionnaires are typically quick and economical to use. The job analyst may administer a structured questionnaire to employees, who identify the tasks they perform. However, in some cases, employees may lack verbal skills, a condition that makes this method less useful. Also, some employees may tend to exaggerate the significance of their tasks, suggesting more responsibility than exists.

OBSERVATION When using the observation method, the job analyst watches the worker perform job tasks and records his or her observations. This method is used primarily to gather information on jobs emphasizing manual skills, such as those of a machine operator. It can also help the analyst identify interrelationships between physical and mental tasks. Observation alone is usually an insufficient means of conducting job analysis, however, particularly when mental skills are dominant in a job. Observing a financial analyst at work would not reveal much about the requirements of the job.

INTERVIEWS An understanding of the job may also be gained through interviewing both the employee and the supervisor. Usually, the analyst interviews the employee first, helping him or her describe the duties performed. Then, the analyst normally contacts the supervisor for additional information, to check the accuracy of the information obtained from the employee, and to clarify certain points.

EMPLOYEE RECORDING In some instances, job analysis information is gathered by having employees describe their daily work activities in a diary or log. With this method, the problem of employees exaggerating job importance may have to be overcome. Even so, valuable understanding of highly specialized jobs, such as recreational therapist, may be obtained in this way.

COMBINATION OF METHODS Usually an analyst does not use one job analysis method exclusively. A combination of methods is often more appropriate. In analyzing clerical and administrative jobs, the analyst might use questionnaires supported by interviews and limited observation. In studying production jobs, interviews supplemented by extensive work observations may provide the necessary data. Basically, the analyst should use the combination of techniques needed for accurate job descriptions/specifications.

Over the years, attempts have been made to provide more systematic methods of conducting job analysis. Several of these approaches are discussed in Table 4-1.

The person who conducts job analysis is interested in gathering data on what is involved in performing a job. The people who participate in job analysis should include, at a minimum, the employee and the employee's immediate supervisor. Large organizations may have one or more job analysts, but in small organizations line supervisors may be responsible for the task. Organizations that lack the technical expertise may use outside consultants to perform job analysis.

Regardless of the approach taken, before conducting job analysis, the analyst should learn as much as possible about the job by reviewing organizational charts and talking with individuals acquainted with the jobs to be studied. Before beginning, the supervisor should introduce the analyst to the employees and explain the purpose of the job analysis. Upon completion of the job

TABLE 4-1

Other Methods Available for Conducting Job Analysis

Functional Job Analysis

Functional job analysis (FJA) is a comprehensive job analysis approach that concentrates on the interactions among the work, the worker, and the organization. This approach is a modification of the job analysis schedule. It assesses specific job outputs and identifies job tasks in terms of task statements.

Position Analysis Questionnaire

The position analysis questionnaire (PAQ) is a structured job analysis questionnaire that uses a checklist approach to identify job elements. It focuses on general worker behaviors instead of tasks. Some 194 job descriptors relate to job-oriented elements. Advocates of the PAQ believe that its ability to identify job elements, behaviors required of job incumbents, and other job characteristics makes this procedure applicable to the analysis of virtually any type of job. Each job descriptor is evaluated on a specified scale such as extent of use, amount of time, importance of job, possibility of occurrence, and applicability.

Each job being studied is scored relative to the 32 job dimensions. The score derived represents a profile of the job; this can be compared with standard profiles to group jobs into known job families, that is, job of a similar nature. In essence, the PAQ identifies significant job behaviors and classifies jobs. Using the PAQ, job descriptions can be based on the relative importance and emphasis placed on various job elements. The PAQ has been called one of the most useful job analysis methods.

Management Position Description Questionnaire

The management position description questionnaire (MPDQ) is a method of job analysis designed for management positions; it uses a checklist to analyze jobs. The MPDQ has been used to determine the training needs of individuals who are slated to move into managerial positions. It has also been used to evaluate and set compensation rates for managerial jobs and to assign the jobs to job families.

Guidelines-Oriented Job Analysis

The guidelines-oriented job analysis (GOJA) responds to the legislation affecting staffing and involves a step-by-step procedure to define the work of a job classification. It is also used for developing selection tools, such as application forms, and for documenting compliance with various legal requirements. The GOJA obtains the following types of information: (1) machines, tools, and equipment; (2) supervision; (3) contacts; (4) duties; (5) knowledge, skills, and abilities; (6) physical and other requirements; and (7) differentiating requirements.

analysis, two basic HR documents—job descriptions and job specifications—can be prepared. As previously mentioned, in practice, both the job description and job specification are combined into one document with the job specification presented after the job description.

4.4 Summarize the components of a job description.

Job Descriptions

Information obtained through job analysis is crucial to the development of job descriptions. It is vitally important that job descriptions are both relevant and accurate.[54] They should provide concise statements of what employees are expected to do on the job, how they do it, and the conditions under which the duties are performed. Concise job descriptions put an end to the possibility of hearing, "That's not my job." Among the items frequently included in a job description are these:

- Major duties performed
- Percentage of time devoted to each duty
- Performance standards to be achieved
- Working conditions and possible hazards
- Number of employees performing the job, and to whom they report
- The machines and equipment used on the job

Having accurate job descriptions is the starting point for most HR tasks. Table 4-2 provides some suggestions for the proper language to be used in job descriptions.

The contents of the job description vary somewhat with the purpose for which it will be used. The next sections address the parts of a job description.

Job Identification

The job identification section includes the job title, the department, the reporting relationship, and a job number or code. A good title will closely approximate the nature of the work content and will distinguish that job from others. Unfortunately, job titles are often misleading. An executive assistant in one organization may be little more than a highly paid clerk, whereas a person with the same title in another firm may practically run the company. For instance, one former student's first job after graduation was with a major tire and rubber company as an *assistant district service manager*. Because the primary duties of the job were to unload tires from trucks, check tread wear, and stack tires in boxcars, a more appropriate title would probably have been *tire checker and stacker*.

Date of the Job Analysis

The job analysis date is placed on the job description to aid in identifying job changes that would make the description obsolete. Some firms have found it useful to place an expiration date on the document. This practice ensures periodic review of job content and minimizes the number of obsolete job descriptions.

TABLE 4-2

Proper Language in the Job Description

Keep each statement in the job description crisp and clear:

- Structure your sentences in classic verb/object and explanatory phrases. Since the occupant of the job is your sentences' implied subject, it may be eliminated. For example, a sentence pertaining to the description of a receptionist position might read, "Greets office visitors and personnel in a friendly and sincere manner."
- Always use the present tense of verbs.
- If necessary, use explanatory phrases telling why, how, where, or how often to add meaning and clarity. For example, "Collects all employee time sheets on a biweekly basis for payroll purposes."
- Omit any unnecessary articles such as "a," "an," "the," or other words for an easy-to-understand description. Using the above example, the statement could have read, "Greets all visitors and the office personnel to the building in a friendly and a sincere manner."
- Use unbiased terminology. For example, use the 'he/she' approach or construct sentences in such a way that gender pronouns are not required.
- Avoid using words which are subject to differing interpretations. Try not to use words such as "frequently," "some," "complex," "occasional," and "several."

Source: www.sba.gov/content/writing-effective-job-descriptions

Job Summary

The job summary provides a concise overview of the job. It is generally a short paragraph that states job content.

Duties Performed

The body of the job description delineates the major duties to be performed. Usually, one sentence beginning with an action verb (such as *receives, performs, establishes*, or *assembles*) adequately explains each duty. Essential functions may be shown in a separate section to aid in complying with the Americans with Disabilities Act. An example of a job description/specification of a records clerk is shown in Figure 4-6.

Job Specification

Job specifications should always reflect the minimum, not the ideal qualifications for a job. Several problems may result if specifications are inflated. First, if specifications are set too high, they might systematically eliminate minorities or women from consideration for jobs. Therefore, the organization runs the risk of being charged with discrimination. Second, compensation costs will increase because ideal candidates should be compensated more than candidates with lesser skills. Third, job vacancies will be harder to fill because ideal candidates are more difficult to find than minimally qualified candidates. Finally, including an unnecessary requirement in the job specification may keep qualified applicants out of the selection pool.[55]

Determining the appropriate qualifications for a job is undoubtedly the most difficult part of job analysis. It requires a great deal of probing on the part of the job analyst as well as a broad

FIGURE 4-6
Job Description/ Specification Example

Administrative Information
Job Title: Records Clerk
Department: Loan Operations
eports To: Loan Operation Manager
Job Number: 11

Date of Job Analysis
January 3, 2018

Expiration Date
January 2021

Job Summary
Returns all consumer paid loan documents to customers. Supervises the daily activities of two clerks.

Essential Functions Performed
Receives monthly files for accounts that have been paid in full and require the return of contracts, mortgage documents, auto titles, and other documents.
Answers telephone and e-mail inquiries from customers or loan officers concerning documents.
Maintains file on temporary automobile titles until permanent title is received.
Files permanent automobile titles, contracts, mortgage documents, and other documents in customer files daily.
Supervises two file clerks who maintain correspondence and other general files.
Performs file clerk duties as needed.
Performs other duties, as required, on a temporary basis, to maintain section or departmental operations and services.

Job Specifications

Education
High school diploma preferred, but not required

Experience
Six months or more in a financial institution and familiarity with various loan documents

Skills Required
Working knowledge of Microsoft Word and Excel
Ability to enter data at a rate of 35 words per minute

understanding of the skills needed to perform varieties of work. Items typically included in the job specification are factors that are job related, such as educational requirements, experience, and job-related personality traits and physical abilities. As previously mentioned, in practice, job specifications are often included as a major section of job descriptions.

After jobs have been analyzed and the descriptions written, the results should be reviewed with the supervisor and the worker to ensure that they are accurate, clear, and understandable. The courtesy of reviewing results with employees also helps to gain their acceptance.

The Standard Occupational Classification:

- Classifies all workers into one of 840 detailed occupations according to their occupational definition.
- Detailed occupations are combined to form 461 broad occupations, 97 minor groups, and 23 major groups.[56]

HR Web Wisdom

Standard Occupational Classification (SOC)

www.bls.gov/soc/2010/soc_alph.htm

Provides an alphabetical list of SOC occupations.

Standard Occupational Classification (SOC)

The U.S. Bureau of Labor Statistics created and updates the Standard Occupational Classification (SOC) system, which is used by federal statistical agencies to classify workers into occupational categories for the purpose of collecting, calculating, or disseminating data. Detailed occupations in the SOC with similar job duties, and in some cases skills, education, or training, are grouped together. The federal government updates job descriptions for all U.S. workers every 10 years. The SOC's substantive structural changes are based on actual changes in the nature or organization of work activities being performed in the economy. The update also provides an opportunity for professional organizations and labor groups to seek recognition or a higher profile for their members' occupations by gaining a separate listing or reclassification. Most current occupations will be unaffected, except perhaps for a change in the description's wording. Some representative SOC descriptions for HR professionals may be seen in Table 4-3.[57]

TABLE 4-3

Representative SOC Descriptions for HR Professionals

13-1071 Human Resources Specialists

Perform activities in the human resource area. Includes employment specialists who screen, recruit, interview, and place workers. Excludes "Compensation, Benefits, and Job Analysis Specialists" (13-1141) and "Training and Development Specialists" (13-1151).

Illustrative examples: *Staffing Coordinator, Personnel Recruiter, Human Resources Generalist*

11-3111 Compensation and Benefits Managers

Plan, direct, or coordinate compensation and benefits activities of an organization. Job analysis and position description managers are included in "Human Resource Managers" (11-3121).

Illustrative examples: *Wage and Salary Administrator, Employee Benefits Director, Compensation Director*

13-1141 Compensation, Benefits, and Job Analysis Specialists

Conduct programs of compensation and benefits and job analysis for employer. May specialize in specific areas, such as position classification and pension programs.

Illustrative examples: *Employee Benefits Specialist, Retirement Plan Specialist, Job Analyst*

11-3131 Training and Development Managers

Plan, direct, or coordinate the training and development activities and staff of an organization.

Illustrative examples: *Labor Training Manager, Employee Development Director, E-Learning Manager*

17-2111 Health and Safety Engineers, Except Mining Safety Engineers and Inspectors

Promote worksite or product safety by applying knowledge of industrial processes, mechanics, chemistry, psychology, and industrial health and safety laws. Includes industrial product safety engineers.

Illustrative examples: *Product Safety Engineer, Fire Protection Engineer, Industrial Safety Engineer*

Source: www.bls.gov/soc.

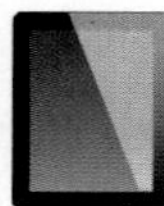

HR Web Wisdom

*O*NET OnLine*

www.onetonline.org/

O*NET OnLine has detailed descriptions of the world of work for use by job seekers, workforce development and HR professionals, students, researchers, and more!

The Occupational Information Network (O*NET)

The Occupational Information Network (O*NET) is a comprehensive database of worker attributes and job characteristics, which is administered by the U.S. Department of Labor's Employment and Training Administration and developed in collaboration with a variety of private and public companies. O*NET is comprehensive because it incorporates information about both jobs and workers. The *O*NET Content Model* lists six categories of job and worker information. Job information contains the components that relate to the actual work activities of a job (i.e., information that HR professionals should include in the summary and duties sections of job descriptions). Worker information represents characteristics of employees that contribute to successful job performance. Figure 4-7 shows the six categories of the O*NET Content Model. According to the creators of O*NET, the Content Model was developed using research on job and organizational analysis. It embodies a view that reflects the character of occupations (via job-oriented descriptors) and people (via worker-oriented descriptors). The Content Model also allows occupational information to be applied across jobs, sectors, or industries and within occupations.

O*NET is a flexible, easy-to-use database system that provides a common language for defining and describing occupations. Its flexible design also captures rapidly changing job requirements. It provides the essential foundation for facilitating career counseling, education, employment, and training activities by providing information about knowledge, skills, abilities, interests, general work activities, and work context.[58] Portions of the information included in an O*NET description for a Human Resources Specialist may be seen in Table 4-4. A particularly useful tool, available on the U.S. Department of Labor's Career One Stop web site, enables you to prepare job descriptions using O*NET data (https://www.careeronestop.org/BusinessCenter/JDW/GettingStarted.aspx).

4.5 Explain what competencies and competency modeling are.

Competencies and Competency Modeling

competencies
An individual's capability to orchestrate and apply combinations of knowledge, skills, and abilities consistently over time to perform work successfully in the required work situations.

The term *competency* has become an increasingly important topic in HR practice because of the changing nature of work. Competencies build on the use of knowledge, skills, and abilities, which we describe with job analysis, to describe work. **Competencies** refer to an individual's capability to orchestrate and apply *combinations* of knowledge, skills, and abilities consistently over time to perform work successfully in the required work situations. Traditionally, as we have seen, work has been described by many dimensions including knowledge, skills, and abilities; and, this information is reported in job descriptions. Indeed, although this is largely still the case, HR professionals have embraced the ideas of competencies as the field has increasingly taken on strategic importance.

FIGURE 4-7
O*NET Content Model

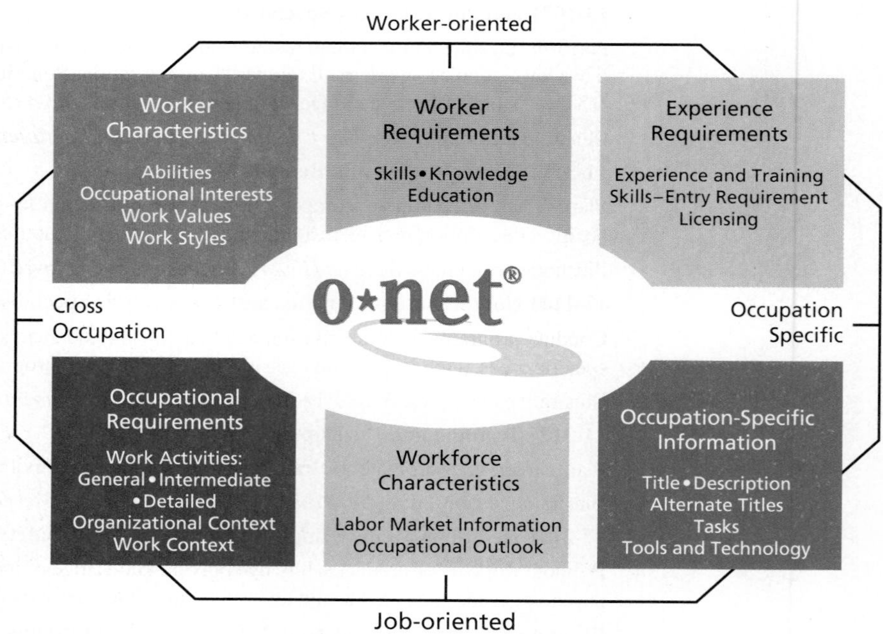

TABLE 4-4

Human Resources Specialist

Tasks

Prepare or maintain employment records related to events such as hiring, termination, leaves, transfers, or promotions, using human resources management system software.

Interpret and explain human resources policies, procedures, laws, standards, or regulations.

Hire employees and process hiring-related paperwork.

Inform job applicants of details such as duties and responsibilities, compensation, benefits, schedules, working conditions, or promotion opportunities.

Address employee relations issues, such as harassment allegations, work complaints, or other employee concerns.

Maintain current knowledge of Equal Employment Opportunity (EEO) and affirmative action guidelines and laws, such as the Americans with Disabilities Act (ADA).

Knowledge

Personnel and Human Resources—Knowledge of principles and procedures for personnel recruitment, selection, training, compensation and benefits, labor relations and negotiation, and personnel information systems.

English Language—Knowledge of the structure and content of the English language including the meaning and spelling of words, rules of composition, and grammar.

Clerical—Knowledge of administrative and clerical procedures and systems such as word processing, managing files and records, stenography and transcription, designing forms, and other office procedures and terminology.

Administration and Management—Knowledge of business and management principles involved in strategic planning, resource allocation, human resources modeling, leadership technique, production methods, and coordination of people and resources.

Skills

Active Listening—Giving full attention to what other people are saying, taking time to understand the points being made, asking questions as appropriate, and not interrupting at inappropriate times.

Speaking—Talking to others to convey information effectively.

Reading Comprehension—Understanding written sentences and paragraphs in work related documents.

Oral Comprehension—The ability to listen to and understand information and ideas presented through spoken words and sentences.

Oral Expression—The ability to communicate information and ideas in speaking so others will understand.

Written Comprehension—The ability to read and understand information and ideas presented in writing.

Source: http://online.onetcenter.org/

Oftentimes, HR professionals' identification of competencies is derived from an analysis of the overall strategic statements of companies. For example, GE emphasizes three strategic goals for corporate growth: Globalization, Product Services, and Six Sigma (quality improvement). GE's top management relies on four core competencies to drive business success, which they call the four "Es": high Energy, the ability to Energize others, Edge (i.e., the ability to make tough calls), and Execute (i.e., the ability to turn vision into results).

competency modeling Specifies and defines all the competencies necessary for success in a group of jobs that are set within an industry context.

Apart from the work of many private consulting firms, the U.S. Department of Labor's Employment and Training Administration developed a framework for describing competencies and for building competency models. **Competency modeling** specifies and defines all the competencies necessary for success in a group of jobs that are set within an industry context. Figure 4-8 shows the basic framework for the Department of Labor's competency model structure. According to the U.S. Department of Labor:

FIGURE 4-8

U.S. Department of Labor Competency Model

Source: U.S. Department of Labor Employment and Training Administration, "Competency Model General Instructions," *CareerOneStop*. Accessed February 10, 2017, at http://www.careeronestop.org/CompetencyModel/CareerPathway/CPWGenInstructions.aspx.

Occupation-Related Competencies

Tier 9 – Management Competencies
Tier 8 – Occupation-Specific Requirements
Tier 7 – Occupation-Specific Technical Competencies
Tier 6 – Occupation-Specific Knowledge Competencies

Industry-Related Competencies

Tier 5 – Industry-Sector Technical Competencies
Tier 4 – Industry-Wide Technical Competencies

Foundational Competencies

Tier 3 – Workplace Competencies
Tier 2 – Academic Competencies
Tier 1 – Personal Effectiveness Competencies

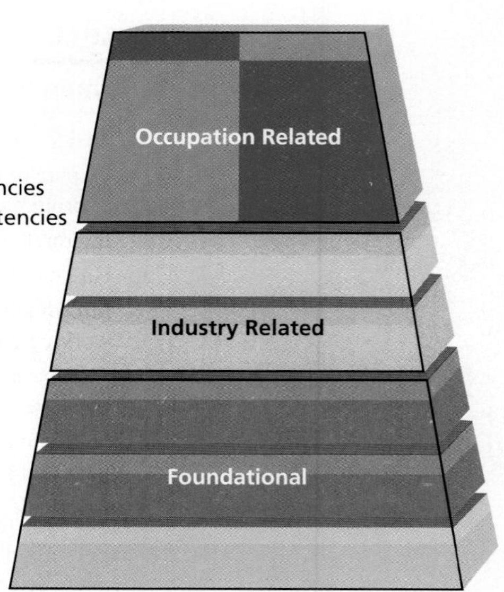

Foundational Competencies

At the base of the model, Tiers 1 through 3 represent competencies that provide the foundation for success in school and in the world of work. Foundational competencies are essential to a large number of occupations and industries. Employers have identified a link between foundational competencies and job performance and have also discovered that foundational competencies are a prerequisite for workers to learn industry-specific skills.

Industry-Related Competencies

The competencies shown on Tiers 4 and 5 are referred to as Industry Competencies and are specific to an industry or industry sector. Industry-wide technical competencies cut across industry subsectors making it possible to create career lattices where a worker can move easily across industry subsectors. Rather than narrowly following a single occupational career ladder, this model supports the development of an agile workforce.

Occupation-Related Competencies

The competencies on Tiers 6, 7, 8, and 9 are referred to as Occupational Competencies. Occupational competency models are frequently developed to define performance in a workplace, to design competency-based curriculum, or to articulate the requirements for an occupational credential such as a license or certification.[59]

Figure 4-9 illustrates an example of a competency model for Solar Photovoltaic Installers who work in the renewable energy industry. The lower tiers, from personal effectiveness competencies through industry-sector technical competencies, apply to most jobs within the renewable energy industry. Hydroelectric production managers and wind engineers are examples of jobs within this industry. The top tiers, in this case, management competencies and occupation-specific competencies, apply to one or more, but not all, jobs within this industry. Figure 4-9 lists sample management competencies and occupation-specific competencies for the solar photovoltaic installer job. The U.S. Department of Labor's *Career One Stop* Web site contains interactive tools for building competency models and career ladders (https://www.careeronestop.org/competencymodel/).

4.6 Summarize job design concepts.

Job Design Concepts

job design
Process of determining the specific tasks to be performed, the methods used in performing these tasks, and how the job relates to other work in an organization.

We previously said that new jobs were being created at a rapid pace. If this is so, jobs should be designed. **Job design** is the process of determining the specific tasks to be performed, the methods used in performing these tasks, and how the job relates to other work in the organization. Several concepts related to job design will be discussed next. First, consider how Blackbird Guitars gets work done. Blackbird Guitars is a very small firm that requires employees to combine the tasks of multiple jobs. It is an excellent illustration of the importance of careful job design.

FIGURE 4-9

Renewable Energy Industry Competency Model

Source: U.S. Department of Labor Employment and Training Administration, "Renewable Energy," *CareerOneStop*. Accessed February 10, 2017, at www.careeronestop.org/CompetencyModel/pyramid.aspx?RE=Y.

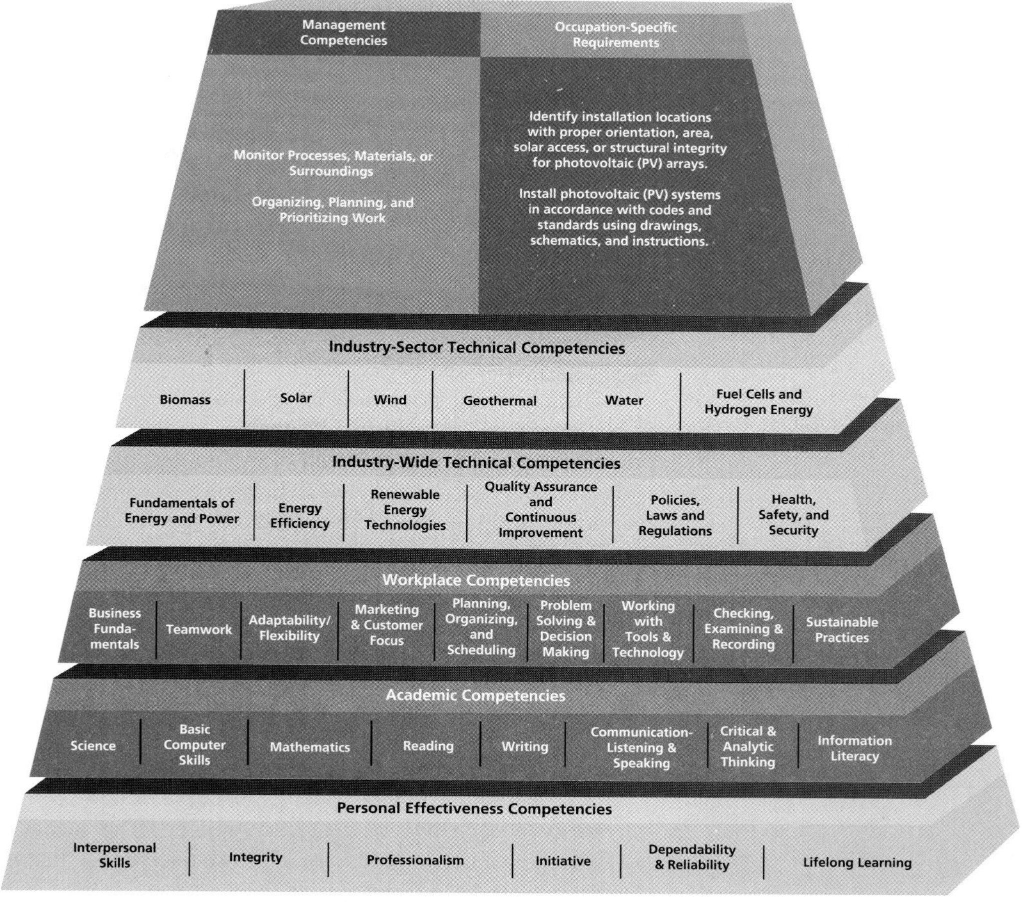

Watch It 3

If your instructor has assigned this, go to **www.pearson.com/mylab/management** to watch a video titled Blackbird Guitars: Managing HR Entrepreneurial Firms and respond to questions.

job enrichment
Changes in the content and level of responsibility of a job to provide greater challenges to the worker.

JOB ENRICHMENT Strongly advocated by Frederick Herzberg, **job enrichment** consists of basic changes in the content and level of responsibility of a job to provide greater challenges to the worker. Job enrichment provides a vertical expansion of responsibilities.

The worker can derive a feeling of achievement, recognition, responsibility, and personal growth in performing the job. Although job enrichment programs do not always achieve positive results, they have often brought about improvements in job performance and in the level of worker satisfaction in many organizations. Today, job enrichment is moving toward the team level, as more teams become autonomous, or self-managed.

job enlargement
Increasing the number of tasks a worker performs, with all the tasks at the same level of responsibility.

JOB ENLARGEMENT There is a clear distinction between job enrichment and job enlargement. **Job enlargement** is defined as increasing the number of tasks a worker performs, with all the tasks at the same level of responsibility.

Job enlargement, sometimes called cross-training, involves providing greater variety to the worker. For example, instead of knowing how to operate only one machine, a person is taught to operate two or even three, but no higher level of responsibility is required. Workers with broad skills may become increasingly important as fewer workers are needed because of tight budgets. Some employers have found that providing job enlargement opportunities improves employee engagement and prevents stagnation.[60]

job rotation
Moves workers from one job to another to broaden their experience.

JOB ROTATION **Job rotation** (cross-training) moves employees from one job to another to broaden their experience. Higher-level tasks often require this breadth of knowledge. Rotational training programs help employees understand a variety of jobs and their interrelationships, thereby improving productivity. Job rotation is often used by organizations to relieve boredom, stimulate better performance, reduce absenteeism, and provide additional flexibility in job assignments. Also, if the task to be accomplished is boring or distasteful, job rotation means that one person will not be stuck with it for all times.[61] Individuals who know how to accomplish more than one task are more valuable both to themselves and to the firm. Staffing then becomes more flexible and these multiskilled workers are then more insulated from layoffs.[62] If job rotation is to be effective, management must be sure to provide sufficient training so that everyone in the rotation can perform the task in a similar manner.[63]

reengineering
Fundamental rethinking and radical redesign of business processes to achieve dramatic improvements in critical, contemporary measures of performance such as cost, quality, service, and speed.

REENGINEERING **Reengineering** is "the fundamental rethinking and radical redesign of business processes to achieve dramatic improvements in critical contemporary measures of performance, such as cost, quality, service, and speed."[64]

Reengineering essentially involves the firm rethinking and redesigning its business system to become more competitive. It emphasizes the radical redesign of work in which companies organizes around process instead of by functional departments. Incremental change is not what is desired; instead, deep-seated changes are wanted that will alter entire operations at one time. Essentially, the firm must rethink and redesign its business system from the ground up.

Reengineering focuses on the overall aspects of job designs, organizational structures, and management systems. It stresses that work should be organized around outcomes as opposed to tasks or functions. Reengineering should never be confused with downsizing even though a workforce reduction often results from this strategy. Naturally, job design considerations are of paramount concern because as the process changes, so do essential elements of jobs. Through an initiative called Project Accelerate, Family Dollar reengineered its merchandising and supply chain processes to enable better performance by store teams. In doing so, it produced a new store layout that is easier and more convenient to shop.[65]

LG Electronics provides another example of how reengineering can work. LG management previously let each division deal with suppliers. That meant a procurement manager in Seoul did not know how much his counterpart at a flat-screen TV factory in Mexico paid for chips from the same company. Then Chief Executive Nam Yong decided to reengineer and rethink the company where managers seldom shared information. Today no one at LG can issue a purchase order without clearance from procurement engineering. By centralizing purchases, LG has cut more than $2 billion from its annual $30 billion purchases.[66]

PREPARING FOR EXAM/QUIZZES

Chapter Summary by Learning Objectives

1. ***Describe the HR strategic planning process.*** If HR is to be a strategic partner, HR executives must work with top management in achieving concrete plans and results. *Strategic planning* is the process by which top management determines overall organizational purposes and objectives and how they will be achieved. Strategic planning at all levels of the organization can be divided into four steps: (1) determination of the organizational mission; (2) assessment of the organization and its environment; (3) setting of specific objectives or direction; and (4) determination of strategies to accomplish those objectives.
2. ***Explain the human resource planning process.*** *Human resource planning* (sometimes called workforce planning) is the systematic process of matching the internal and external supply of people with job openings anticipated in the organization over a specified period.
3. ***Describe the job analysis process and methods.*** *Job analysis* is the systematic process of determining the skills, duties, and knowledge required for performing jobs in an organization. It is an essential and pervasive HR technique. Without a properly conducted job analysis, it would be difficult, if not impossible, to satisfactorily perform the other HR-related functions.

   Work activities, worker-oriented activities, and the types of machines, tools, equipment, and work aids used in the job are important. This information is used to help determine the job skills needed. In addition, the job analyst looks at job-related tangibles and intangibles.

   The job analyst may administer a structured questionnaire or witness the work being performed, or he or she may interview both the employee and the supervisor or ask them to describe their daily work activities in a diary or log. A combination of methods is often used.

4. ***Summarize the components of a job description.*** Components include the job identification section, which includes the job title, department, reporting relationship, and a job number or code; the job analysis date; the job summary; and the body of the job description that delineates the major duties to be performed.

5. ***Explain what competencies and competency modeling are.*** The term *competency* has become an increasingly important topic in HR practice because of the changing nature of work. Competencies build on the use of knowledge, skills, and abilities, which we describe with job analysis, to describe work. Competencies refer to an individual's capability to orchestrate and apply combinations of knowledge, skills, and abilities consistently over time to perform work successfully in the required work situation. A competency model specifies and defines all the competencies necessary for success in a group of jobs that are set within an industry context.

6. ***Summarize job design concepts.*** *Job design* is the process of determining the specific tasks to be performed, the methods used in performing the tasks, and how the job relates to other work in the organization. *Job enrichment* consists of basic changes in the content and level of responsibility of a job to provide greater challenge to the worker. *Job enlargement* is increasing the number of tasks a worker performs, with all the tasks at the same level of responsibility. *Job rotation* (sometimes called cross-training) moves employees from one job to another to broaden their experience. *Reengineering* is the fundamental rethinking and radical redesign of business processes to achieve dramatic improvements in critical contemporary measures of performance, such as cost, quality, service, and speed.

Key Terms

strategic planning 91
mission 92
human resource planning 96
requirements forecast 96
availability forecast 96
zero-base forecast 97
bottom-up forecast 98
severance packages 101
succession planning 101
job analysis 102
job 103
position 103
job description 103
job specification 103
competencies 110
competency modeling 111
job design 112
job enrichment 113
job enlargement 113
job rotation 113
reengineering 114

MyLab Management

If your instructor is using MyLab Management, go to **www.pearson.com/mylab/management** to complete the problems marked with this icon ✪.

Questions for Review

4-1. What are the steps involved in the strategic planning process?
4-2. What are the steps involved in the HR planning process?
4-3. What are the HR forecasting techniques?
4-4. Distinguish between forecasting HR requirements and availability.
4-5. What are the purposes of strategic planning?
✪**4-6.** What actions could a firm take if it forecasted a shortage of workers?
✪**4-7.** What are some alternatives to layoffs?
4-8. Define succession planning. Why is it important?
4-9. What is the distinction between a job and a position? Define job analysis.
4-10. When is job analysis performed?
4-11. What are the types of information required for job analysis?
4-12. What are the methods used to conduct job analysis? Describe each type.
✪**4-13.** What are the basic components of a job description? Briefly describe each.
4-14. What is the purpose of the Standard Occupational Classification (SOC)?
4-15. What is the purpose of the Occupational Information Network (O*NET)?
✪**4-16.** What is meant by the statement "With team design, there are no narrow jobs"?
4-17. Describe how effective job analysis can be used to satisfy each of the following statutes:
(a) Fair Labor Standards Act
(b) Equal Pay Act
(c) Civil Rights Act
(d) Occupational Safety and Health Act
(e) Americans with Disabilities Act (ADA)/ADA Amendments Act
4-18. Why is competency modeling an important practice?
4-19. Define each of the following:
(a) job design
(b) job enrichment
(c) job enlargement
(d) job rotation
(e) reengineering

PREPARING FOR MY CAREER

P I A Personal Inventory Assessment

An additional Personal Inventory Assessment can be found on MyLab Management.

Problem Solving, Creativity, and Innovation

As you saw in this chapter, strategic decision making is conducted under conditions of uncertainty and requires the skills and ability to find solutions amidst the uncertainty. This PIA will assess your decision making approach under these circumstances.

ETHICS DILEMMA

Which "Thinker" Should Go?

Your company is a leading producer of advanced microchips. You are the chief researcher in your firm's *think tank*, which consists of eight people with various specialties. Your group has generated most of the ideas and product innovations that have kept the company an industry leader for 10 years. In fact, the think tank has been so successful that another one has been organized to support the company's newest manufacturing operation on the West Coast. The individuals included in the new think tank have already been selected, but your boss has just assigned you the task of deciding who from your group of thinkers will head the new organization.

The person best qualified for the job is Tim Matherson. Tim is an MIT graduate, the informal team leader, and the individual who personally spearheaded three of the team's five most successful product advancements. However, if Tim receives the promotion, the void created by his leaving will be difficult to fill. On the other hand, the boss forced his nephew, Robert Jones, into your group. He is a sharp graduate of the local state university, but he is not a team player and he is always trying to push you around. You can either recommend Tim, illustrating that those who produce the most benefit, or you can recommend Robert, making the boss happy, getting rid of a problem, and, most important of all, keeping your best performer.

4-20. What would you do?

4-21. What factor(s) in this ethics dilemma might influence a person to make a less than ethical decision?

HRM Is Everyone's Business

HR professionals should always stay abreast of current and anticipated changes in the labor market. These include knowing about the current and anticipated supply of well qualified individuals in pertinent occupations relative to business demand for them. Additional important information includes changes in skill requirements and compensation trends. HR possesses the responsibility to work with managers and other decision makers to ensure that they maintain appropriate staffing levels. While HR planning is ultimately the responsibility of the company's HR leadership, managers must have enough awareness to participate in the planning process by making well-informed, proactive decisions about current and future departmental staffing requirements.

Action checklist for managers and HR—understanding and engaging in effective HR planning

HR takes the lead

- ☑ Work with managers to learn about their current and anticipated staffing needs.
- ☑ Understand the particulars of education, prior work experience, and unique skill sets required of new hires to perform their jobs effectively. Learn about the strengths and weaknesses of employees' preparation to perform well.
- ☑ HR planning should not be limited to considering the availability of qualified job candidates, it should also be about retention. HR professionals use information to develop actionable plans for designing and implementing onboarding programs, performance plans, and training opportunities to promote employee engagement and commitment.

Managers take the lead

- ☑ Based on current staffing levels and the mix of skill sets represented in the current workforce, consider additional anticipated staffing needs, including the time frame, number of employees, and job-relevant requirements such as prior work experience. Particularly communicate changes in job requirements and where there may currently be skills mismatches for current employees based on anticipated job modifications and changing technology.
- ☑ Provide HR with draft job descriptions to communicate details about job duties, responsibilities for new hires and job specifications.
- ☑ Discuss the department's budgetary resources available to provide competitive pay and benefits, and indicate where shortfalls may occur.

HRM by the Numbers

Severance Pay at Miller Furniture

An additional HRM by the Numbers exercise can be found on MyLab Management.

Since its establishment in 1940, Miller Furniture, a family owned furniture retailer, has successfully honored its no layoff policy. Founders Robert and Frances Miller believed that the company's success depended, in large part, on its dedicated workforce. In recent years, small family-owned furniture retailers have struggled to survive because large retail chains sell furniture at much lower prices. Recognizing this reality, the Miller family realizes that maintaining full staffing will lead to bankruptcy. Determined not to lay off employees, the Miller's decided to offer buyouts to its workforce of 500 employees.

4-22. How many employees would remain if 30 percent of the total workforce accepted the buyout offer?

4-23. Employees who accept the buyout offer will receive 2 weeks of severance pay for each year of service. Of the total who accepted the buyout (carefully consider your answer to Question 4-22), 20 percent completed 5 years of service, 40 percent completed 7 years of service, 20 percent completed 10 years of service, and 20 percent completed 15 years of service. How many total weeks of severance will Miller Furniture pay?

4-24. As part of the buyout package, the company will continue to pay its share of health insurance during the severance period. If Miller Furniture pays $100 per week for each employee to have health insurance, what is the total cost of health insurance based on the number of employees who have taken the buyout offer?

Working Together: Team Exercise

In small groups of three or four, come up with specific answers to the following questions. Talk through your perspectives and come up with a brief team response. Be prepared to share your ideas with the class.

As noted earlier in the chapter, a SWOT analysis assesses an organization's strengths, weaknesses, opportunities, and threats. As a group, select a company with which members are familiar. Conduct a brief SWOT analysis of this company.

4-25. Based on your analysis, which strengths, weaknesses, opportunities, and threats that you identified do you judge most important? Explain.

4-26. How might HR professionals help build upon the company's strengths and capitalize on its opportunities? How might they help address some of the weaknesses and threats? Explain.

INCIDENT 1 Competitive Strategy at Buddy Dog Foods

Buddy Dog Foods makes and sells dog food for puppies and adults. It has been a leader in the industry for more than 25 years. Until recently, the company has successfully pursued a low-cost strategy by selling a limited number of food recipes and holding down manufacturing costs. However, Buddy Dog has lately been struggling to maintain profitability because many new competitors offer low-cost food choices. Thus, the leadership team has decided it is time to change its strategic focus.

Buddy Dog's extensive market research shows that niche dog food markets have emerged where pet owners are willing to pay more for hypoallergenic food made only with all-natural ingredients. There are only a few competitors in this market space, and most do not have Buddy Dog's excellent reputation. The company's leadership believes they can manufacture hypoallergenic dog food to dominate niche markets. By distinguishing itself from the competition, Buddy Dog's leadership believes they can create a sustainable competitive advantage.

Having considered market factors and its manufacturing capacity, Buddy Dog will shift from a current low-cost strategy to a differentiation strategy by manufacturing hypoallergenic dog food. Buddy Dog must now make many tactical decisions in various functional areas of the company to support its new strategic approach. Its priority is to restructure the product development function. They will hire and retain talented veterinary nutritionists and food allergists. The company will also hire operations specialists. Finally, the leadership recognizes that job redesign will be needed and they must consider how to bring current employees up to speed. Clearly, Buddy Dog has a lot of work to do to ensure a successful implementation of its new strategic approach.

Questions

4-27. Strategic planning at all levels of the organization can be divided into four steps. Which step in the strategic planning process led Buddy Dog Food's management to change its focus?

4-28. Following Buddy Dog's shift in competitive strategy, what must the company's HR professionals consider?

4-29. What kinds of challenges could Buddy Dog face in the areas of recruitment, training, and compensation?

INCIDENT 2 Who's Flying the Plane?

Many industries face a shortage of individuals to fill essential jobs. Among them is the commercial airline industry where a pilot shortage is expected to swell to 20,000 by 2022[67] and more than 30,000 by 2034.[68] This trend weighs heavily on most airlines. Greg Muccio, a senior manager at Southwest Airlines Company lamented, "That is one of the things in my job I get to worry about every day and when I got to bed at night."[69] He sees an overall lack of interest in becoming a commercial pilot as a key problem; "That's what puts us in the most jeopardy."[70]

There are many factors that may be contributing to this lack of interest. Most commercial pilots spend the first several years working for regional airlines where annual pay has been traditionally quite low—in the $20,000 range. Eventually, many of these airlines doubled starting pay. Still, raising pay has done little to move the needle. The cost of flight-training is quite high, surpassing the $100,000 mark after factoring in the cost of tuition and living expenses. And, recent tighter government regulation requires substantially more flight hours and other experience, typically, at lower paying jobs, before they are eligible for co-pilot positions at commercial airlines. Undoubtedly, tightening regulations will make preparation for becoming a commercial pilot even more expensive.

Questions

4-30. What are some of the challenges facing the commercial airline industry? Discuss.

4-31. Given the changing landscape for staffing commercial airlines with qualified pilots, what are some considerations for the airlines' human resource management practices?

4-32. What role has recent government regulation played in this situation? Discuss.

MyLab Management

If your instructor is using MyLab Management, go to **www.pearson.com/mylab/management** for Auto-graded writing questions as well as the following Assisted-graded writing questions:

4-30. Why is job analysis considered to be a basic HR tool?

4-33. Why does the HR manager need to be a strategic partner with top management?

Endnotes

1 Cynthia A. Lengnick-Hall and Mark L. Lengnick-Hall, M. L, *Interactive Human Resource Management and Strategic Planning* (1990). New York: Quorum Books.

2 Juan Pablo Gonzalez and Dane Tyson, "How to Develop and HR Strategic Plan," *Workspan* (May 2016): 25– 28.

3 Rory Cooper, "Smart HR Strategies in an Unpredictable Economy," *Maryland Banker* (Third Quarter 2009): 8.

4 Edward E. Lawler III, "What Should HR Leaders Focus On In 2016?" *Forbes* (February 4, 2016). Accessed February 7, 2017, at www.forbes.com.

5 General Mills, *Purpose*, General Mills' Corporate Mission Statement (2017). Accessed February 7, 2017, at www.generalmills.com/en/Company/purpose.

6 Trefis Team, "LinkedIn: Opportunities & Threats (Part 1), *Forbes* (December 12, 2013). Accessed January 1, 2014, at www.forbes.com.

7 Trefis Team, "LinkedIn: Opportunities & Threats (Part 2), *Forbes* (December 18, 2013). Accessed January 1, 2014, at www.forbes.com.

8 From the Ross Stores website, "About Us," www.rossstores.com/about-us, accessed February 6, 2017.

9 J. Bennett, "Ross Stores: Rare Winer Amid the Retail Rubble," *Barrons* online, www.barrons.com, February 6, 2017.

10 From the L.L. Bean website, "100% Satisfaction Guarantee." Accessed February 7, 2017, at www.llbean.com/llb/shop/513705?nav=sr&term=guarantee.

11 Micah Solomon, "What Steve Jobs Stole from Ritz-Carlton (and You Should Steal from Apple," *Inc.* online (June 16, 2015). Accessed February 7, 2017, at www.inc.com.

12 Edward E. Lawler III, "HR Should Own Organizational Effectiveness," *Forbes* online (February 11, 2014). Accessed December 29, 2016, at www.forbes.com.

13 J. R. Gallbraith and Robert K. Kazannian, Strategy Implementation: *Structure, Systems, and Process*, 2nd ed. (St. Paul, MN: West Publishing, 1986), 115.

14 U.S. Bureau of Labor Statistics, "Prior Work Experience Required for 47.8 Percent of All Civilian Jobs in 2016," *The Economics Daily* online (February 3, 2017). Accessed February 10, 2017, at www.bls.gov.

15 "The New Organization: Different by Design," *Global Human Capital Trends 2016* (2016). Accessed December 20, 2016, www2.deloitte.com/us/en/pages/human-capital/articles/introduction-human-capital-trends.html.

16 Tess Stynes, "Dollar General Seeks to Hire 10,000 Workers Within the Next Month," *The Wall Street Journal* online (September 15, 2016). Accessed December 30, 2016, at www.wsj.com.

17 "Dollar General Will Add 10,000 Jobs This Year," *Times Free Press* online (February 7, 2017). Accessed February 7, 2017, at www.timesfreepress.com/news/business/aroundregion/story/2017/feb/07/dollar-general-will-add-10000-jobs-year/411521/.

18 "UPS to Hire 95,000 Seasonal Workers for Upcoming Holidays," *The Wall Street Journal* online (September 14, 2016). Accessed January 15, 2017, at www.wsj.com.

19 Anna Louie Sussman, "As Skill Requirements Increase, More Manufacturing Jobs Go Unfilled," *The Wall Street Journal* online (September 1, 2016). Accessed January 6, 2017, at www.wsj.com.

20 U.S. Bureau of Labor Statistics, "Information Security Analysts," *Occupational Outlook Handbook* (2016-17 Edition). Accessed February 7, 2017, www.bls.gov/ooh/computer-and-information-technology/information-security-analysts.htm.

21 Y. Bahgat, "The Top 10 Most Innovative Recruitment Campaigns," Zoomforth Blog, www.blog.zoomforth.com, May 18, 2015.

22 WorldatWork, "Bonus Programs and Practices," A Report by WorldatWork (July 2016). Accessed January 31, 2017, at www.worldatwork.org/waw/adimLink?id=80398.

23 U.S. Army, "Bonuses," (February 2017). Accessed February 7, 2017, at http://myarmybenefits.us.army.mil/Home/Benefit_Library/Federal_Benefits_Page/Bonuses.html?serv=147.

24 Jennifer Smith, "Online Retailers' New Warehouses Heat Up Local Job Markets," *The Wall Street Journal* online (April 9, 2017). Accessed May 25, 2017, at www.wsj.com.

25 Juliet Eilperin, "Trump Freezes Hiring of Many Federal Workers," *The Washington Post* online (January 23, 2017). Accessed February 10, 2017, at www.washingtonpost.com.

26 Joe Davidson, "Federal Managers Say Trump's Hiring Freeze Hurts Government,"

The Washington Post online (February 10, 2017). Accessed February 10, 2017, at www.washingtonpost.com.

27 Ibid.

28 Tom Kludt, "Wall Street Journal Seeks 'Substantial Number' of Buyouts," *CNN Money* online (October 21, 2016). Accessed February 10, 2017, at http://money.cnn.com.

29 Anne Steele, "The Wall Street Journal Offers Buyouts to News Employees," *The Wall Street Journal* online (October 21, 2016). Accessed February 10, 2017, at www.wsj.com.

30 Ethan Bernstein, John Bunch, Niko Canner, and Michael Lee, "Beyond the Holocracy Hype," *Harvard Business Review* online (July-August 2016). Accessed February 11, 2017, at www.hbr.org.

31 Bourree Lam, "What Are So Many Zappos Employees Leaving?" *The Atlantic* online (January 15, 2016). Accessed February 11, 2017, at https://www.theatlantic.com.

32 Darryl Demos, "Flexible Staffing Meets Branch Needs," *CU360* 35 (July 7, 2009): 4–5.

33 Lincoln Electric, "*Why Lincoln Electric*," Accessed February 22, 2014, at http://www.lincolnelectric.com/en-us/company/careers/Pages/lincoln-tradition.aspx.

34 Frank Koller, "2016 Ends at Lincoln Electric, No Layoffs for, Now, 68 Years and 83 Years of Amazing Profit-Sharing Bonuses," *Frank Koller's* Blog (December 9, 2016). Accessed February 10, 2017, at www.frankkoller.com/2016/12/2016-ends-at-lincoln-electric-no-layoffs-for-now-68-years-and-83-years-of-amazing-profit-sharing-bonuses/.

35 Heather Tinsley-Fix, "Succession Planning: Why It's Critical Now," *Workspan* (February 2017): 23–26.

36 Robert Kleinsorge, "Expanding the Role of Succession Planning," *T+D* 64 (April 2010): 66–69.

37 Robert J. Grossman, "Rough Road to Succession," *HR Magazine* 56 (June 2011): 46–51.

38 Jeffrey Burt, "IBM, Apple, HP: Stark Contrasts in CEO Succession," *eWeek* 28 (November 7, 2011): 10.

39 "'HP Matters' Says Incoming CEO Meg Whitman," *Channel Insider* (September 23, 2011): 1–2.

40 A. G. Lafley and Noel M. Tichy, "The Art and Science of Finding the Right CEO," *Harvard Business Review* 89 (October 2011): 66–74.

41 Joseph L. Bower, "More Insiders Are Becoming CEOs, and That's a Good Thing," *Harvard Business Review* online (March 18, 2016). Accessed February 10, 2017, at www.hbr.org.

42 Victoria Luby and Jane Stevenson, "7 Tenets of a Good CEO Succession Process," *Harvard Business Review* online (December 7, 2016). Accessed February 10, 2017, at www.hbr.org; Joe Shaheen, "Talent Acquisition as a Potent Tool of Succession Management," *Journal of Corporate Recruiting Leadership* 5 (November 2010): 9–12.

43 Mitra Toossi, "Labor Force Projections to 2024: The Labor Force Is Growing, but Slowly," *Monthly Labor Review* online (December 2015). Accessed February 15, 2017, at www.bls.gov/opub/mlr/2015/article/labor-force-projections-to-2024-1.htm.

44 Heather Tinsley-Fix, "Succession Planning: Why It's Critical Now," *Workspan* (February 2017): 23–26.

45 "Business Owners Fall Short on Contingency Planning," *North Western Financial Review* 196 (September 15, 2011): 22.

46 Sara LaForest and Tony Kubiac, "Understanding the Role of Succession Planning for Small Business Success," *Alaska Business Monthly* 27 (June 2011): 26–28.

47 David Harvey, "A Family Affair," *Commercial Motor* 216 (September 22, 2011): 48–49.

48 Joanne L. Stewart, "Train for the Future," *T+D* 65 (July 2011): 54–57.

49 Jonathan A. Segal, "Hiring Days Are Here Again," *HR Magazine* 56 (July 2011): 58–60.

50 Thomas A. Stetz, Scott B. Button, and W. Benjamin Poor, "New Tricks for an Old Dog: Visualizing Job Analysis Results," *Public Personnel Management* 38 (Spring 2009): 91–100.

51 *Uniform Guidelines on Employee Selection Procedures, Federal Register*, Friday, August 25, 1978, Part IV.

52 "Get It in Writing: Creating Effective and Legal Job Descriptions," *HR Specialist: California Employment Law* 4 (November 2010): 4.

53 "Is Every Function Really Essential? Be Flexible about Disabled Employees' Duties," *HR Specialist: Illinois Employment Law* 6 (January 2012): 3.

54 Laurie Burkhard, "Define Employees' Roles and Responsibilities," *Advisor Today* 104 (January 2009): 59–60.

55 Liz Ryan, "10 Ways to Fix Broken Corporate Recruiting Systems," BusinessWeek.com (July 13, 2011): 3.

56 U.S. Bureau of Labor Statistics, "Alphabetical List of SOC Occupations," *Standard Occupational Classification*. Accessed February 10, 2017, at www.bls.gov/soc/home.htm.

57 U.S. Bureau of Labor Statistics, "Alphabetical List of SOC Occupations," *Standard Occupational Classification*. Accessed February 10, 2017, at www.bls.gov/soc/2010/soc_alph.htm.

58 National Center for O*NET Development, *O*Net OnLine*. Accessed February 10, 2017, at http://online.onetcenter.org/.

59 U.S. Department of Labor, Employment and Training Administration, "Competency Model General Instructions." *CareerOneStop.Org*. Accessed February 10, 2017, at www.careeronestop.org/CompetencyModel/CareerPathway/CPWGenInstructions.aspx.

60 Yvette Lee, Shari Lau, and Patricia Graves, "Job Swapping, I-9 Forms, Travel Pay," *HR Magazine* 56 (April 2011): 24–25.

61 Wendi Everton, "Keeping Your Best & Brightest Workers," *Nonprofit World* 28 (November/December 2010): 12–13.

62 "Training Budgets Bounce Back: Where to Spend," *HR Specialist* 9 (March 2011): 1–5.

63 Jill Jusko, "When One Job Becomes Three," *Industry Week* 260 (July 2011): 16–17.

64 Michael Hammer and James Champy, *Reengineering the Corporation: A Manifesto for Business Revolution* (New York: Harper Collins Publishers, 1993), 32.

65 "Initiatives Pay Dividends for Family Dollar," *MMR* 28 (May 16, 2011): 94.

66 Moon Ihlaw and Kevin Cho, "Creative When No One's Looking," *BusinessWeek* (April 25, 2010): 37.

67 "The Coming U.S. Pilot Shortage Is Real," *Aviation Week* online (February 16, 2015). Accessed February 11, 2017, at www.aviationweek.com.

68 Brian Prentice and Philippe Gouel, "Pilot Shortage Threatens to Slow U.S. Airline Growth," *Forbes* online (January 28, 2016). Accessed February 11, 2017, at www.forbes.com.

69 Mary Schlangenstein and Michael Sasso, "Shrinking Pool of Future Pilots Keeps Major Airlines on Edge," *Bloomberg News* online (June 29, 2016). Accessed February 11, 2017, at www.bloomberg.com.

70 Ibid.

5 Recruitment

LEARNING OBJECTIVES After completing this chapter, students should be able to:

5.1 Define *recruitment* and describe the recruitment process.

5.2 Summarize the environment of recruitment.

5.3 Explain internal recruitment methods.

5.4 Identify external recruitment sources.

5.5 Summarize external recruitment methods.

5.6 Describe alternatives to recruitment.

MyLab Management®

Improve Your Grade!

If your professor is using MyLab Management, visit **www.pearson.com/mylab/management** for videos, simulations, and writing exercises.

Learn It

If your professor has chosen to assign this, go to **www.pearson.com/mylab/management** to see what you should particularly focus on and to take the Chapter 5 Warm-Up.

5.1 Define *recruitment* and describe the recruitment process.

recruitment
Process of attracting individuals on a timely basis, in sufficient numbers, and with appropriate qualifications to apply for jobs with an organization.

employee requisition
Document that specifies job title, department, the date the employee is needed for work, and other details.

Recruitment and the Recruitment Process

Recruitment is the process of attracting individuals on a timely basis, in sufficient numbers, and with appropriate qualifications to apply for jobs with an organization. The firm may then select those applicants with qualifications most closely related to job descriptions. Finding the appropriate way of encouraging qualified candidates to apply for employment is extremely important, however, because recruiting costs can be expensive. Thus, a properly functioning recruiting program can have a major impact on the bottom line of a company.

The recruitment process is critical because employees quickly become either assets or liabilities based on how they contribute to the value of the company.[1] How many times have we heard CEOs state, "Our employees are our most important asset"? Instead they should be saying, "The right employees are our most important asset." Hiring the best people available has never been more critical than it is today because of the economy and global competition. A company's ability to recruit and manage talent has become the measure for the overall health and longevity of the organization.[2] It is estimated that just the cost of replacing an employee alone when a bad decision is made is two to three times the employee's annual salary.[3] Therefore, it is crucial to have a finely tuned recruitment process if the selection process is to function properly.

When human resource planning indicates a need for employees, the firm may evaluate alternatives to hiring (see Figure 5-1). Frequently, recruitment begins when a manager initiates an **employee requisition**, a document that specifies job title, department, the date the employee is needed for work, and other details. With this information, managers can refer to the appropriate job description to determine the qualifications the recruited person needs.

The next step in the recruitment process is to determine whether qualified employees are available within the firm (the internal source) or if it is necessary to look to external sources, such as colleges, universities, and other organizations. Because of the high cost of recruitment, organizations need to use the most productive recruitment sources and methods available.

FIGURE 5-1
The Recruitment Process

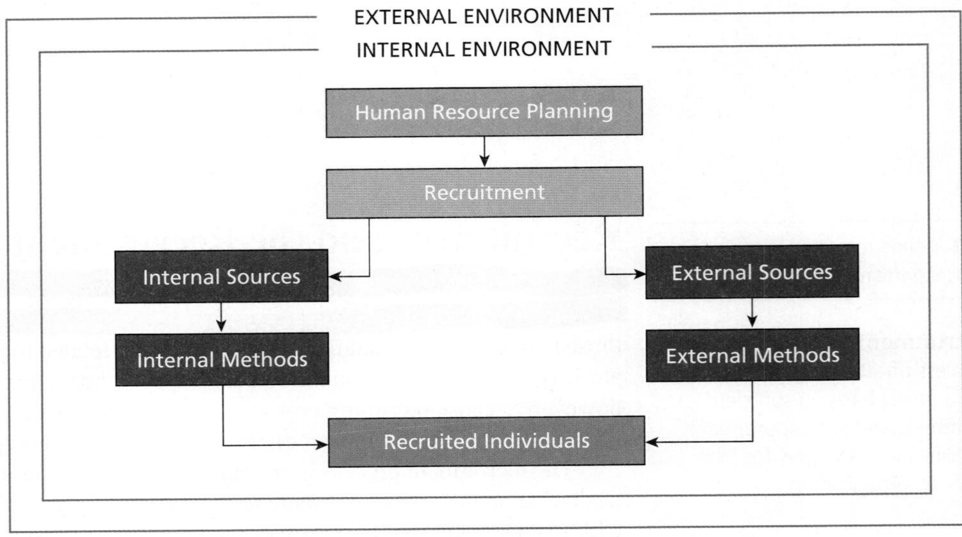

recruitment sources
Where qualified candidates are located.

recruitment methods
Specific means used to attract potential employees to the firm.

HR Web Wisdom
Social Network Recruiting
www.linkedin.com
LinkedIn is an online social network Web site.

Recruitment sources are where qualified candidates are located, such as colleges or competitors. **Recruitment methods** are the specific means used to attract potential employees to the firm, such as online recruiting.

Identifying productive sources of applicants and using suitable recruitment methods are essential to maximizing recruiting efficiency and effectiveness. When a firm identifies the sources of candidates, it uses appropriate methods for either internal or external recruitment to accomplish recruitment objectives. A candidate responds to the firm's recruitment efforts by submitting professional and personal data on either an application for employment or a résumé, depending on the company's policy.

Companies may discover that some recruitment sources and methods are superior to others for locating and attracting potential talent. Smart recruiters want to post their job where the best prospects are likely to be. For instance, one large, heavy-equipment manufacturer determined that medium-sized, state-supported colleges and universities located in rural areas were good sources of potential managers. Far fewer companies advertise job openings in newspapers. Instead, recruiters are now placing their recruiting money in areas that are most productive, such as with the use of social media. To maximize recruiting effectiveness, using recruitment sources and methods tailored to specific needs is vitally important (a topic discussed later in this chapter).

5.2 Summarize the environment of recruitment.

Environment of Recruitment

Like other human resource functions, the recruitment process does not occur in a vacuum. Factors external to the firm can significantly affect its recruitment efforts.

Labor Market Conditions

Of importance to the success of recruitment is the demand for and supply of specific skills in the labor market. In general, a firm's recruitment process is often simplified when the unemployment rate in an organization's labor market is high. The number of unsolicited applicants is usually greater, and the increased size of the labor pool provides a better opportunity for attracting qualified applicants. However, if demand for a certain skill is high relative to supply, an extraordinary recruiting effort may be required. Further, the area where recruitment takes place often impacts the labor market conditions. Today, the labor market for many professional and technical positions is much broader and truly global particularly as new technologies take hold. For example, wind turbine technicians are in considerably high demand.[4]

Possessing a college degree used to be the passport to secure a good job.[5] This largely remains to be the case when we consider unemployment rates and average weekly earnings by educational attainment. Figure 5-2 shows lower unemployment rates and higher average weekly earnings for progressively highly educational attainment. However, the type of degree

FIGURE 5-2

Earnings and Unemployment Rates by Educational Attainment

Source: Bureau of Labor Statistics, Current Population Survey

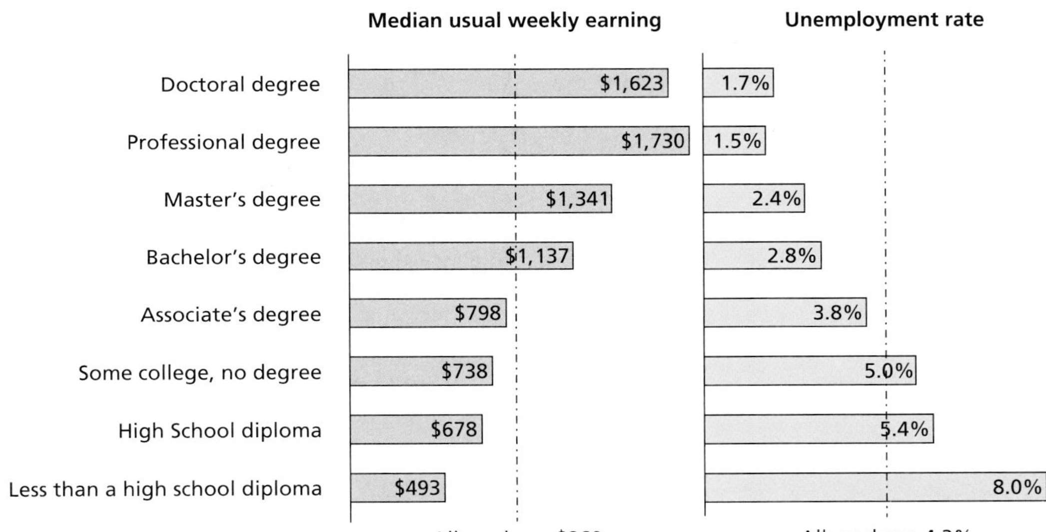

awarded may mean the difference between getting a job that does not require a college degree and obtaining a professional well-paying position.[6] Also, many of the jobs available today do not require a college degree. Rather, skills to perform crafts such as welders, pipe fitters, painters, and machinists are needed. In fact, today there is a critical shortage of such skills, particularly in the construction industry.[7]

According to a recent McKinsey Global Institute report, 40 percent of full-time job openings in companies planning to hire remain unfilled for six months or longer because they cannot find qualified applicants.[8] New technology may require that workers have a specialized degree even though one was unnecessary 10 years ago.[9] There has been a "skill-based technology" change in the job market. According to CareerBuilder's Brent Rasmussen, "Two in five employers (41 percent) reported that they continuously recruit throughout the year so that they have candidates in their pipeline in case a position opens up down the road. The skills gap that exists for high-growth, specialized occupations will become even more pronounced in the years to come, prompting the need to place a greater emphasis on reskilling workers through formal education and on-the-job training."[10] Computers have automated many of the repetitive physical and mental tasks. Workers are now being recruited who can perform tasks that cannot be automated and are nonrepetitive and more sophisticated.[11]

Active or Passive Job Seekers

active job seekers
Individuals committed to finding another job whether presently employed or not.

passive job seekers
Potential job candidates, who are typically employed, satisfied with their employer, and content in their current role but if the right opportunity came along, they might like to learn more.

The recruitment method that proves to be most successful will depend to an extent on whether the recruited individual is an active or passive job seeker. **Active job seekers** are individuals who are committed to finding another job whether presently employed or not. These individuals are usually easier to identify because their names have been placed in the job market. Their résumés are on job boards and friends, associates, or companies have been contacted directly to learn about job opportunities. **Passive job seekers**, on the other hand, are potential job candidates who are typically employed, satisfied with their employer, and content in their current role. But if the right opportunity came along, they might like to learn more. These individuals want to move slower and will ask a lot of questions before making a job change. They are more hesitant to risk leaving a good job for a new challenge and increased risk. Inevitably, opinions differ regarding whether one type of job seeker turned out to be a better employee than the other. A prevalent view favors active job seekers. B/E Aerospace routinely considered both active and passive job seekers. Over time, they concluded that active job seekers were better employees and stayed longer than passive job seekers. B/E Aerospace HR Director Jonathan Turner reasoned, "Active candidates are already looking and fundamentally prepared to switch companies, locations, or careers."[12] He went on to say that passive candidates are, "more difficult to find, engage with, and motivate to make major life changes, which leads to longer times to fill."

This chapter identifies numerous recruitment methods. Some are more useful in identifying active job seekers and others are better used in recruiting passive job seekers. Naturally, some will be directed at both groups.

FYI

A recent study revealed that 90 percent of recent hires were actively searching for a new job. Of these, 44 percent relied on online job alerts.[13]

Legal Considerations

Legal matters also play a significant role in recruitment practices in the United States. This is not surprising because the candidate and the employer first make contact during the recruitment process. A poorly conceived recruiting process can do much to create problems in the selection process. Therefore, it is essential for organizations to emphasize nondiscriminatory practices at this stage.

The Office of Federal Contract Compliance Programs (OFCCP) has issued guidelines concerning the online recruiting policies of federal contractors and subcontractors. Companies must keep detailed records of each online job search. They must also identify what selection criteria were used and can explain why a person with protected status was not hired. Equal Employment Opportunity Commission (EEOC) guidelines suggest that companies with more than 100 employees keep staffing records for a minimum of two years. The threshold coverage is 50 employees if dealing with the OFCCP.

A dramatic increase in firms using the Internet for recruiting has added to management's challenge to comply with the OFCCP. Under the rule, there are four criteria to determine whether an individual is an Internet applicant:

- The job seeker has expressed interest through the Internet. Applicants have gone to the corporate career Web site and applied for a job that is listed.
- The employer considers the job seeker for employment in an open position. If the applicant does not meet specific qualifications spelled out in the job-specification section of the job description, the résumé does not have to be considered.
- The job seeker has indicated that he or she meets the position's basic qualifications. If the position description calls for three years of work experience, and the individual has three years of experience in previous jobs, he or she would believe they meet the basic qualifications.
- The applicant has not indicated he or she is no longer interested in the position.[14]

Employers must keep records of all expressions of interest through the Internet, including online résumés and internal databases. Employers are also expected to obtain the gender, race, and ethnicity of each applicant, when possible. This information enables a compilation of demographic data, such as age, race, and gender, based on that applicant pool. This data is used to determine whether a company's hiring practices are discriminatory.

5.3 Explain internal recruitment methods.

Internal Recruitment Methods

Management should be able to identify current employees who are capable of filling positions as they become available. Helpful tools used for internal recruitment include human resource databases, job postings and job bidding, and employee referrals.

Human Resource Databases

Human resource databases permit organizations to determine whether current employees possess the qualifications for filling open positions. As a recruitment device, these databases have proven to be extremely valuable to organizations. Databases can be valuable in locating talent internally and supporting the concept of promotion from within.

job bidding
Procedure that permits employees who believe that they possess the required qualifications to apply for a posted position.

job posting
Procedure for informing employees that job openings exist.

Job Posting and Job Bidding

Job posting is a procedure for informing employees that job openings exist. **Job bidding** is a procedure that permits employees who believe that they possess the required qualifications to apply for a posted job.

Hiring managers usually want to give internal candidates priority to improve employees' attitudes and stimulate their interest in the company. The job posting and bidding procedures can

HR BLOOPERS

Recruiting Skilled Machinists

Two months into her new position as Lead Recruiter at New World Manufacturing, Emily Lang is starting to feel frustrated. Emily was promoted to the Lead Recruiter position after three years as a recruiter for the company's management training program. In that position, Emily impressed upper management with her ability to fill the trainee positions quickly and cost-effectively. Emily's expertise in using social media helped her develop an impressive pipeline of talented candidates. Thus, she was promoted to a Lead Recruiter in the manufacturing division to help address their challenging staffing issues. The unemployment rate in the area is high and the company is having problems finding skilled machinists to staff their manufacturing positions. Emily immediately put her expertise to work to attempt to build a solid pipeline of candidates for the multitude of entry level positions in the factory. She started an online recruiting campaign including a LinkedIn and a Facebook page specifically for the division. She also started using the company Twitter account to spread the word about the open positions. Knowing that many of the applicants for these entry-level positions didn't have résumés, she also created an easy to use online application on the company Web site. But her recruiting savvy doesn't seem to be paying off. The manufacturing manager has informed her that there are still a dozen open positions and she doesn't have any new applicants to share.

If your professor has assigned this, go to **www.pearson.com/mylab/management** to complete the HR Bloopers exercise and test your application of these concepts when faced with real-world decisions.

help minimize the commonly heard complaint that insiders never hear of a job opening until it is filled. Typically, vacant jobs are posted to internal candidates before external recruiting takes place. Several forums are available today to advise employees that a vacancy exists. In years past, jobs were literally posted on a bulletin board. Today, companies use the intranet, the Internet, or post the job on the company Web site or company Facebook page. Some companies send out e-mails and voice mail to selected managers and employees advising them that a vacancy exists.

Many organizations, including Whirlpool, BMW, Kellogg, Hyatt, and Hewlett-Packard, manage internal candidates with Web-based applications. Employees create profiles that detail their skills and interests for their next ideal position and are notified when such a position exists. FedEx's philosophy is that employees should be doing the kind of work they want to do. Its Web site helps candidates identify their ideal job. Using drop-down lists, it prompts them to enter data about desires, location, type of work, and so forth; it also asks them to describe their skills. When jobs open, managers have instant access to these electronic résumés in which the candidates have specified what they can and want to do.

Today, if a worker does not know about a vacancy, it is usually because he or she did not check the internal posting system regularly. Yet, even with an online system, a job posting and bidding system has some potential negative features. For one thing, an effective system requires the expenditure of time, effort, and money. Organizations need to be sure to treat internal candidates properly so they will not be discouraged or prompted to leave if they do not get the job. When bidders are unsuccessful, someone must explain to them why they were not selected. Management must choose the most qualified applicant or else the system will lack credibility. Still, complaints may occur, even in a well-designed and well-implemented system.

Employee Referrals

employee referral
An employee of the company recommends a friend or associate as a possible member of the company; this continues to be the way that top performers are identified.

Employee referrals involve an employee of the company recommending a friend or associate as a possible member of the company; this continues to be the way that top performers are identified. In many organizations, the use of employee referrals produces the most and best-qualified applicants. Organizations such as Southwest Airlines, Microsoft, Disney, and Ritz-Carlton typically employ many of their new hires exclusively through employee referrals. It is just human nature that employees do not want to recommend a person unless they believe they are going to fit in and be productive. Thus, it is a powerful recruiting tool. Because of this, many companies have strengthened their employee referral program. These organizations have found that their employees can serve an important role in the recruitment process by actively soliciting applications from among their friends and associates.

Some firms give incentives to their employees for successful referrals. A WorldatWork Bonus Program Practices survey found that 63 percent of companies offer referral bonuses and an additional 15 percent are considering one.[15] Typically, the types of positions that a company would pay referral bonuses include professionals, technical, IT staff, and sales.[16] Most often, bonuses range from $1,000 to $2,500 per successful referral, but, it is not unheard of to find substantially larger bonuses. For instance, Intel offers bonuses amounts as high as $4,000 for job candidate referrals that help the company meet its diversity objectives.[17] Intel, like many technology companies, has come under criticism for not taking extra measures to recruit qualified women and minority candidates. In addition, it should be noted that employee referral practices have also proven valuable for other professions.

FYI

The percentage of companies that use employee referral bonuses pay them after the new employee completes:

- At least 45 days: 23 percent
- Between 1.5 and 3 months: 44 percent
- Between 3 and 6 months: 28 percent
- More than 6 months: 5 percent[18]

Typically, those who are referred by a present employee are more productive. Costs can be much lower than using advertising or agencies. Using referrals also reduces turnover among both new and existing employees because applicants come prescreened for culture fit. Small companies especially prefer to find candidates through referrals and networks of people they trust. Groupon, the online discounter, grew from 37 to 7,100 employees in 21 months. It acquires about 40 percent of new hires through employee referrals.[19] A recent study found that referrals are twice as more likely to be interviewed than those who are not referred.[20] Also, referrals are 40 percent more likely to be hired than those who are not referred.

Employee enlistment is a unique form of employee referral in which every employee becomes a company recruiter. This is different from merely asking employees to refer friends to the company. The firm supplies employees with simple business cards that do not contain names or positions. Instead, these cards have a message like, "We are always looking for great. For additional information, log on to our Web site." Employees then distribute the cards wherever they go, at parties, sports events, family gatherings, picnics, or the park. The purpose is to let people know that the company does want people to apply. An interesting way of using e-mail in the recruitment process is to ask employees to put a footer in their e-mails reminding people that their company is hiring. It might say something like the following: "Note: We're hiring amazing engineers, BD people, and a star Ops person. Refer a friend and get a fully paid trip to Hawaii for two."[21]

Recruiters can often obtain referrals from new employees when they first join the firm. These new hires may provide leads regarding other candidates that have the skills and competences that the organization needs. Information from such candidates is often easy to obtain because the new hire is excited about joining the company and would like to have their friends and associates join them. Recruiters may simply ask, "Do you know anyone in your field who might like to work here?" A capable recruiter can then develop a list of good candidates with special skills who can be recruited.

A note of caution should be observed about the extensive use of employee referrals. The *EEOC Compliance Manual* explicitly warns that recruiting only at select colleges or relying on word-of-mouth recruiting, which includes employee referral programs, may generate applicant pools that do not reflect diversity in the labor market.

5.4 Identify external recruitment sources.

External Recruitment Sources

At times, a firm must look beyond its own borders to find employees, particularly when expanding its workforce. External recruitment is needed to (1) fill entry-level jobs; (2) acquire skills not possessed by current employees; and (3) obtain employees with different backgrounds to provide a diversity of ideas. As Figure 5-3 shows, even with internal promotions, firms still must

FIGURE 5-3
Internal Promotion and External Recruitment

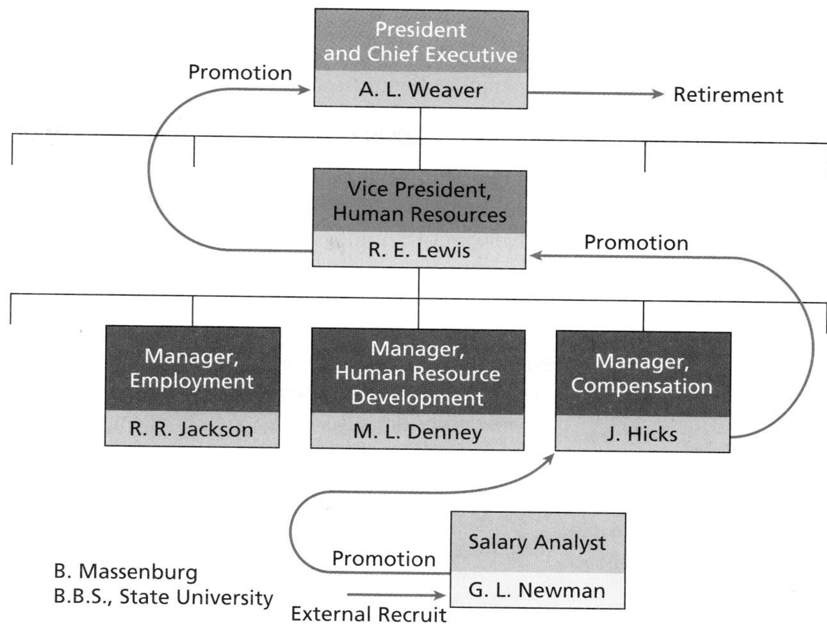

fill entry-level jobs from the outside. Thus, after the president of a firm retires, a series of internal promotions follows. Ultimately, however, the firm must recruit externally for the entry-level position of salary analyst. If an outside candidate was selected for the president's position, the chain reaction of promotions from within would not have occurred. If no current employee has the desired qualifications, candidates may be attracted from many outside sources.

HR Web Wisdom

HR Internet Guides

www.hr-guide.com

This Web site contains links to other Internet-based resources for topics such as recruitment, selection, and equal employment opportunity.

High Schools and Vocational Schools

High schools and vocational schools play an important role in preparing individuals for the workforce. Approximately 39 percent of the jobs in the U.S. labor force require a high school diploma or equivalent.[22] Understandably, organizations concerned with recruiting clerical and other entry-level employees often depend on high schools and vocational schools. Many of these institutions have outstanding training programs for specific occupational skills, such as home appliance repair and small engine mechanics. Some companies work with schools to ensure a constant supply of trained individuals with specific job skills. In some areas, companies even loan employees to schools to assist in the training programs.

Community Colleges

Many community colleges are sensitive to the specific employment needs in their local labor markets and graduate highly sought-after students with marketable skills. Typically, community colleges have two-year programs designed for both a terminal education and preparation for a four-year university degree program. Many community colleges also have excellent mid-management programs combined with training for specific trades. For example, San Juan College located in Farmington, New Mexico, has a well-respected veterinary technology program that is known nationwide. Career centers often provide a place for employers to contact students, thereby facilitating the recruitment process.

Colleges and Universities

Colleges and universities represent a major recruitment source for potential professional, technical, and management employees. Placement directors, faculty, and administrators can be helpful to organizations in their search for recruits. Establishing a relationship with faculty members is important because most professors are aware of their students' academic performance and abilities. Because on-campus recruitment is mutually beneficial, both employers and universities should take steps to develop and maintain close relationships. It is important that the firm knows the school and the school knows the firm.

Competitors in the Labor Market

When recent experience is required, competitors and other firms in the same industry or geographic area may be the most important source of recruits. Another name for actively recruiting employees from competitors is called *poaching*. It has been estimated that poaching may account for 30 percent of the movement in labor.[23] In fact, the most highly qualified applicants often come directly from competitors in the same labor market. Competitors and other firms serve as external sources of recruitment for high-quality talent. Even organizations that have policies of promotion from within actively recruit employees from competitors' most productive workers. For example, tech companies are aggressively recruiting engineers, designers, computer scientists, and executives who could compete and adapt to the rapid changes that are occurring in the industry.[24] This competition for specific skills has driven up pay for certain job skills. The competition for qualified applicants has been especially aggressive among workers involved in social media, mobile technology, and e-commerce even when the unemployment rate remained relatively high. With an improved economy, more organizations are susceptible to having employees lured away by competitors. In addition, managers are likely to be facing even more challenges than ever before because of business, demographic trends, and poor leadership development practices within firms.[25] John Sullivan, author of *1000 Ways to Recruit Top Talent*, states two problems when competitors "steal" employees; "One, you have to replace the talent, and in a time of tight labor markets, that's a very hard—and very expensive—endeavor." He goes on to say, "And two, the talent is taking ideas with them to a competitor."[26]

Smaller firms look for employees trained by larger organizations that have greater developmental resources. For instance, one optical firm believes that its own operation is not large enough to provide extensive training and development programs. Therefore, a person recruited by this firm for a significant management role is likely to have held at least two previous positions with a competitor. In the following Watch It video, Hanno Holm, Chief Operating Office of Rudi's Organic Bakery, discusses how his small, dynamic, and fast-growing company searches for the right employees and how the process differs from large companies.

Watch It I

If your instructor has assigned this, go to **www.pearson.com/mylab/management** to watch a video titled Rudi's Bakery: Human Resource Management and respond to questions.

Former Employees

At one time, when employees quit, their managers and peers tended to view them as being disloyal and ungrateful, and they were "punished" with no-return policies. A common attitude was that if you left your firm, you did not appreciate what the company had done for you. Those days are gone and often "goodbye" may not be forever. In fact, according to a recent survey, only 11 percent of human resources (HR) professionals said that they would not rehire departing workers if they wished to return.[27] Today's young workers are more likely to change jobs and later return to a former employer than their counterparts who entered the workforce 20 or 30 years ago, and smart employers try to get their best ex-employees to come back. The *boomerang* effect might happen because there was a strong bond with previous coworkers or the new job was not what the employee envisioned. Van Alstyne, HR manager for Staffing Plus, based in Haverford, Pennsylvania, said, "If employees depart on good terms, contact should be maintained through proactive networking efforts by the company. It keeps the door open for good employees to return."[28]

The advantage of tracking former employees is that the firm knows their strengths and weaknesses and the ex-employees know the company. Tracking, recruiting, and hiring a former employee can be a tremendous benefit and can encourage others to stay with the firm. It sends the message that things are not always greener on the other side of the fence. The large number of people who will change jobs during their lifetime means businesses would be foolish to lose touch with them.

Unemployed

The unemployed often provide a valuable source of recruits. Qualified applicants join the unemployment rolls every day for various reasons. Companies may downsize their operations, go out of business, or merge with other firms, leaving qualified workers without jobs. Employees are also fired sometimes merely because of personality differences with their bosses. Frequently, employees become frustrated with their jobs and quit. Even individuals who have been out of work for extended periods should not be overlooked. According to the U.S. Bureau of Labor Statistics, the total number of job openings in 2016 was 5.5 million,[29] with more than 7.5 million unemployed workers.[30] In January 2017, the unemployment rate was 4.9 percent. However, if discouraged workers and marginally attached workers are counted, the total unemployment rate rose to about 6.2 percent.[31] Who are discouraged and marginally attached workers? *Discouraged workers* have given up looking for jobs, and *marginally attached workers* wanted and were available for work, and had looked for a job sometime in the prior 12 months. It should be noted that the unemployment rate has dropped steadily from more than 10 percent since the Great Recession ended in 2009. While the unemployed represents a source of potential employees, the improved economy will leave companies with fewer choices.

Military Personnel

Hiring former service members makes sense to a lot of employers because many of these individuals have a proven work history, are flexible and highly motivated. General Electric (GE) recognizes the value of military veterans as employees; "Your service made you a leader and a disciplined, strategic thinker with a level of loyalty that is unmatched."[32] Many other companies have discovered the benefits of recruiting military talent. For instance, Starbucks launched an initiative in 2003 to hire 10,000 veterans and their spouses by 2018. By early 2017, the company made great strides toward meeting its goal by having already hired 8,000 new employees.[33] AT&T pledged to hire 20,000 veterans by 2020.[34] These statistics show that many companies successfully recruit veterans; however, they do not remain for very long. A 2016 U.S. Chamber of Commerce Foundation survey revealed that 44 percent of veteran hires left their first post-military jobs within a year.[35] According to Brian Stann, a former captain in the Marines and head of Hire Heroes USA, a nonprofit that helps veterans find jobs and prepare for the corporate world, "One of the biggest mistakes employers can make is not understanding how to take advantage of veterans' skills" despite wanting to hire them."[36] Some companies are working diligently to retain veteran hires. For example, J.P. Morgan Chase & Co. instituted Pathfinder, an experimental project that pairs newly recruited veterans with a more established veteran to help them set goals, understand the differences between civilian and military cultures, and offer support. Besides active company campaigns, service members nationwide looking for jobs can consider visiting the HirePatriots.com web site. "We help citizens and businesses to thank our current military, veterans, and their spouses by posting their job opportunities on our free military job posting and search Web site," said Mark Baird, president of Patriotic Hearts.[37]

Self-Employed Workers

The self-employed worker may also be a good potential source. These individuals may be true entrepreneurs who are ingenious and creative. For many firms, these qualities are essential for continued competitiveness. Such individuals may constitute a source of applicants for any number of jobs requiring technical, professional, administrative, or entrepreneurial expertise within a firm.

Ex-Offenders

Some organizations have found it beneficial to hire ex-offenders. A recent analysis by the National Employment Law Project shows that more than one in four U.S. adults has an arrest or conviction that would appear in a routine criminal background check.[38] Studies estimate that as many as 60 to 75 percent of ex-offenders are unemployed.[39] Many are nonviolent substance abusers who were locked up because of federal and state drug laws. This statistic is not surprising because of an increase in the use of criminal background checks in the employment process, and most employers indicate that they would "probably" or "definitely" not be willing to hire an applicant with a criminal record.[40]

As of this writing, 25 states and several U.S. cities and counties have *Ban the Box* laws or policies that reduce unfair barriers to employment of people with criminal records.[41] The *box* refers to the job application question that asks whether the person has a criminal history. Most of these laws ban including questions about an applicant's criminal history. The ban the box laws require companies to do more than simply eliminate the question. Variations in the law are evident across the states, however, most include additional requirements such as placing limits on the scope or type of criminal record that can be considered. Angela Preston, vice president of compliance and general counsel at background screening firm EmployeeScreenIQ said, "No two versions of ban the box are the same, and they often conflict or overlap with existing anti-discrimination laws, the Fair Credit Reporting Act (FCRA), and others requiring or relating to background screening,"[42] These differences are creating challenges for HR professionals, particularly for ones that have facilities in multiple states.

According to Multicultural Foodservice & Hospitality Alliance President Gerry Fernandez, "I'm aware of several chains that have programs to hire ex-offenders, though they do not want publicity. Who do you think works third shift, where they don't come in contact with customers?"[43] In another example, supermarket retail consultant and restaurateur Howard Solganik has launched a program that puts ex-offenders to work helping area farmers increase the supply of local, seasonal produce to consumers. Solganik said, "My experience in the restaurant business exposed me to ex-offenders. I saw that most were hard workers and were grateful for the jobs they were given."[44]

5.5 Summarize external recruitment methods.

External Recruitment Methods

The use of online and mobile recruiting methods has revolutionized the way companies recruit employees and job seekers search and apply for jobs. Using technology for recruitment provides HR professionals with additional choices besides traditional methods, which we review shortly.

Online and Mobile Recruiting

Owen Williams, executive recruiting director at Macys Inc., provides an example of the power of mobile recruiting. During the three-block walk to his office, Owen regularly uses his mobile device and the mobile version of LinkedIn to post job listings and connect to potential candidates. Time is money for Owen because he personally fills more than 80 store manager and regional buyer positions a year. "It's amazing what work I can get done in that walk," he says.[45]

The world of recruiting via mobile technology is moving at lightning speed. When LinkedIn was new, recruiters saw mobile technology as a complement to the time-honored paper résumés and face-to-face interviews.[46] As mobile apps have improved, many organizations are successfully using mobile devices in the recruiting process. Recruiters use mobile apps to post jobs, run text message–based recruiting campaigns, create online communities for potential new hires to learn about their companies, monitor social networks for news about industries they hire for, and keep in touch with staff and outside agencies. Their efforts have been paying off. One survey found that approximately 14.4 million U.S. workers have used social media to find employment, and 73 percent of companies surveyed have successfully hired job candidates using social media.[47]

The number of mobile apps for conducting job searches is on the rise. And, many of the newer apps are setting themselves apart from the pack. For instance, one innovative app follows the model of many dating sites where people are matched based on compatible interests and personality. For job searches, of course, the matches are based on work experience and other job-related qualifications. The following Watch It video describes a job search app that oftentimes is compared to dating sites such as Tinder where users swipe right if they "like" the potential match.

Watch It 2

If your instructor has assigned this, go to **www.pearson.com/mylab/management** to watch a video titled Swipe Right for Employment: New App is Tinder for Job Seekers and respond to questions.

Internet recruiter
Person whose primary responsibility is to use the Internet in the recruitment process (also called cyber recruiter).

INTERNET RECRUITER The **Internet recruiter**, also called a cyber recruiter, is a person whose primary responsibility is to use the Internet in the recruitment process.

Most companies currently post jobs on their corporate career Web site. Individuals must be in place to monitor and coordinate these activities. The more companies recruit on the Internet, the greater the need for Internet recruiters. Currently, high-tech firms have the greatest needs.

virtual job fair
Online recruiting method engaged in by a single employer or group of employers to attract a large number of applicants.

VIRTUAL JOB FAIR A **virtual job fair** is an online recruiting method engaged in by a single employer or group of employers to attract many applicants. They are designed to be a first step in the recruitment process. Many recruiters have found that traditional job fairs where applicants and recruiters go to a physical location are ineffective. In addition to the time and expense of attending them in person, recruiters often find them wasteful because many people who stop by their booth do not possess the right skills.

At virtual job fairs, recruiters prescreen résumés, contact candidates who are a potential fit, and store e-mail addresses. If applicants pass the initial screening, they typically must complete a questionnaire, take a behavioral test, and do a telephone interview before meeting a recruiter in person. Virtual fairs usually last about five hours, though recruiters can receive résumés online for as long as a week after the event. In their virtual "booth," recruiters often provide links to their online career site, obtained résumés from candidates, and interact with applicants in a live chat room.

corporate career Web sites
Job sites accessible from a company home page that list available company positions and provide a way for applicants to apply for specific jobs.

CORPORATE CAREER WEB SITES **Corporate career Web sites** are job sites accessible from a company home page that list the company positions available and provide a way for applicants to apply for specific jobs. They have become a major resource for both job seekers and companies seeking new employees.

A career Web site should be relevant and engaging, informing the reader about the company and the specific position being advertised. It should be used as a selling device that promotes the company to prospective job candidates. Writing effective recruitment ads on the Internet is different from the short, one-inch-column ads in the Sunday newspaper. The Internet provides enough space to fully describe the job, location, and company. It provides an opportunity to convert consumers into great employees. A good Web site should provide a feeling of the kind of corporate culture that exists within the company.

WEBLOGS (BLOGS FOR SHORT) Weblogs, or *blogs*, have changed the ways in which individuals access information. Google or a blog search engine such as Technorati.com can be used. All a person must do is type in a key phrase like *marketing jobs*. The blogs themselves make it easy to find, with names like HRJobs.com and SalesJobs.com. Some employers and employment agencies have also discovered that blogging is a way to do detailed and stealthy background checks.

GENERAL-PURPOSE JOB BOARDS Firms use general-purpose job boards by typing in key job criteria, skills, and experience, and indicating their geographic location. Job seekers can search for jobs by category, experience, education, location, or any combination of categories. Many believe that the general-purpose big job boards are best for job seekers in professions that experience high turnover like sales but often are less effective for highly qualified applicants or those looking for work in smaller industries. We review some of the more visible services here.

CareerBuilder offers a vast online network to help job seekers connect with employers. CareerBuilder.com powers the career sites for more than 1,000 Web sites, including 300 newspapers and various other online portals.[48]

Facebook started out exclusively as a social media website. More recently, Facebook recognized an opportunity to extend its services to more subscribers. The company learned that many small businesses are struggling to hire as well as many people are willing to consider a better, higher paying job.[49]

Glassdoor is a job posting site and more. Subscribers have access to millions of employees' reviews of their companies, CEO approval ratings, salary reports, interview reviews, and employee benefits reviews, office photos, and more.[50] The company distinguishes itself from other sites by relying exclusively on employees' input.

LinkedIn connects individuals who want to build their professional networks and stay abreast of the latest trends in business. This service also permits job postings. The company reported that it has more than 450 million subscribers from approximately 200 countries.[51] Its success may be attributed in part to publishing the site in a multitude of languages including traditional Chinese, German, and Malay.

Monster Worldwide, Inc. is the parent company of *Monster*. It is a premier global online employment solution for people seeking jobs and the employers who need people. Information helpful to job seekers such as résumé tips, interview tips, salary information, and networking information is available on the site.

Twitter is a well-known social media site. Increasingly, companies are taking to Twitter to post job openings.[52] Examples include package delivery service UPS, Google, Ernst & Young, Disney Parks, and PepsiCo.[53]

NACElink Network
The result of an alliance among the National Association of Colleges and Employers, DirectEmployers Association, and Symplicity Corporation, it is a national recruiting network and suite of Web-based recruiting and career services automation tools serving the needs of colleges, employers, and job candidates.

NACELINK NETWORK The **NACElink Network**, the result of an alliance among the National Association of Colleges and Employers, DirectEmployers Association, and Symplicity Corporation, is a national recruiting network and suite of Web-based recruiting and career services automation tools serving the needs of colleges, employers, and job candidates. Currently more than 900 colleges use the NACElink system. The system includes three components: job posting, résumé database, and interview scheduling. It is available to employers to post jobs and search for students and new graduates. DirectEmployers Association has also created an employment Web site for returning veterans that uses military codes to help veterans identify jobs in their fields.

.jobs
Network of employment Web sites where any company can list job openings for free.

.JOBS **.Jobs** is a network of employment Web sites where any company can list job openings for free. There are 40,000 sites, with all Web addresses ending in ".jobs." The initiative is being backed by nearly 600 hundred companies such as Whirlpool and Disney Parks. Finding jobs on the sites is simple. Possible searches might include Nurse.jobs and Sales.jobs. For someone looking for a job in the Washington, D.C. area, there's districtofcolumbia.jobs. It works for many professions and is available in every state and any U.S. city with more than 5,000 people.

AllianceQ
Group of *Fortune 500* companies, along with more than 3,000 small and medium-sized companies, that have collaborated to create a pool of job candidates.

ALLIANCEQ **AllianceQ** is a group of *Fortune 500* companies, along with more than 3,000 small and medium-sized companies, that have collaborated to create a pool of job candidates. AllianceQ provides a way for candidates to be found by top employers.[54] Those passed over by one company are invited to submit their résumés to the AllianceQ database. "It's a no-brainer," says Phil Hendrickson, a recruiting manager at member company Starbucks.[55]

niche sites
Web sites that cater to highly specialized job markets such as a profession, industry, education, location, or any combination of these specialties.

NICHE SITES **Niche sites** are Web sites that cater to highly specialized job markets, such as a profession, industry, education, location, or any combination of these specialties. They continue to grow in popularity and are giving general-purpose job boards major competition.[56] There seems to be a site for virtually everyone. A few catchy ones include:

- cfo.com (a comprehensive online resource center for senior finance executives)
- dice.com (a leading provider of online recruiting services for technology professionals)
- internships.com (employers who are exclusively looking for interns)
- justtechjobs.com (focuses on the recruiting needs of the technology companies)
- coolworks.com (find seasonal job or career in places such as Yellowstone, Yosemite, or other national parks)
- college.monster.com (job listings and résumé service that targets college students and alumni)
- Job.com (maintains sites specialized by geography)
- HirePatriots.com (job listings for service members)

A niche site is also available for professors who desire to change jobs. Formerly, college and university professors went to the campus library and thumbed through the many pages of *The Chronicle of Higher Education* to hunt for a job. Now all they need to do is enter www.chronicle.com, *The Chronicle of Higher Education* Web site. All the jobs listed with the *Chronicle* are available to view for free. Each position announcement has a hot link to a university home page where additional information can be obtained. The universities pay the fees.

CONTINGENT WORKERS' SITES Contract workers are a part of the contingent workforce. Recruiting technology also serves the benefit of these workers. Sites are available to assist contingent workers. Specialized Web sites let workers advertise their skills, set their price, and pick an employer. Two such sites are:

contingent workers
Described as the "disposable American workforce" by a former secretary of labor, they have a nontraditional relationship with the worksite employer, and work as part-timers, temporaries, or independent contractors.

- Freelance.com (a company that offers to clients the services of talented freelancers)
- Guru.com (an online marketplace for freelance talent)

But who are contingent workers? According to the U.S. Bureau of Labor Statistics, **contingent workers**[57] are those who do not have an implicit or explicit contract for ongoing employment. Persons who do not expect to continue in their jobs for such personal reasons as retirement or returning to school are not considered contingent workers, if they would have the option of continuing in the job were it not for these reasons. These individuals account for 40.2 percent of the U.S. labor force, which is up from 30.6 percent in 2005.[58] Figure 5-4 details questions that determine whether workers expect their employment to continue, that is, whether their work arrangement is considered to be contingent.

Contingent workers are the human equivalents of just-in-time inventory. These workers permit maximum flexibility for the employer and lower labor costs. Historically, contingent workers have been called the bookends of recessions. They are the first to go when a recession begins and the last to be recalled when the economy gets better. However, toward the end of the recent recession, many companies were reversing this trend and following the strategy of holding off on the hiring of regular full-time employees and choosing instead to use contingent workers. Companies are now using contingent workers as a continuing strategy in both good and bad times.[59]

After the recession ended in 2009, companies rethinking about the way work gets done. This brought a refocus on the use of contingent workers, who can be added or cut as demand requires. In fact, the pace of contingent job growth suggests a shift toward more use of temporary labor at the expense of permanent jobs.[60] Garry Mathiason, vice chairman of Littler Mendelson in San Francisco, said, "In the future companies will likely make wider use of staffing methods like those practiced by the film industry. There, entire crews of contingent production workers are assembled for a movie then disbanded once it is finished."[61] A study by the Institute for Corporate Productivity (i4cp) found that high-performing organizations have increased their use

FIGURE 5-4

Questions that Determine Whether Workers Expect Their Employment to Continue

Source: Polivka, A. E. (1996). Contingent and alternative work arrangements, defined. *Monthly Labor Review, 119*(10), p. 5.

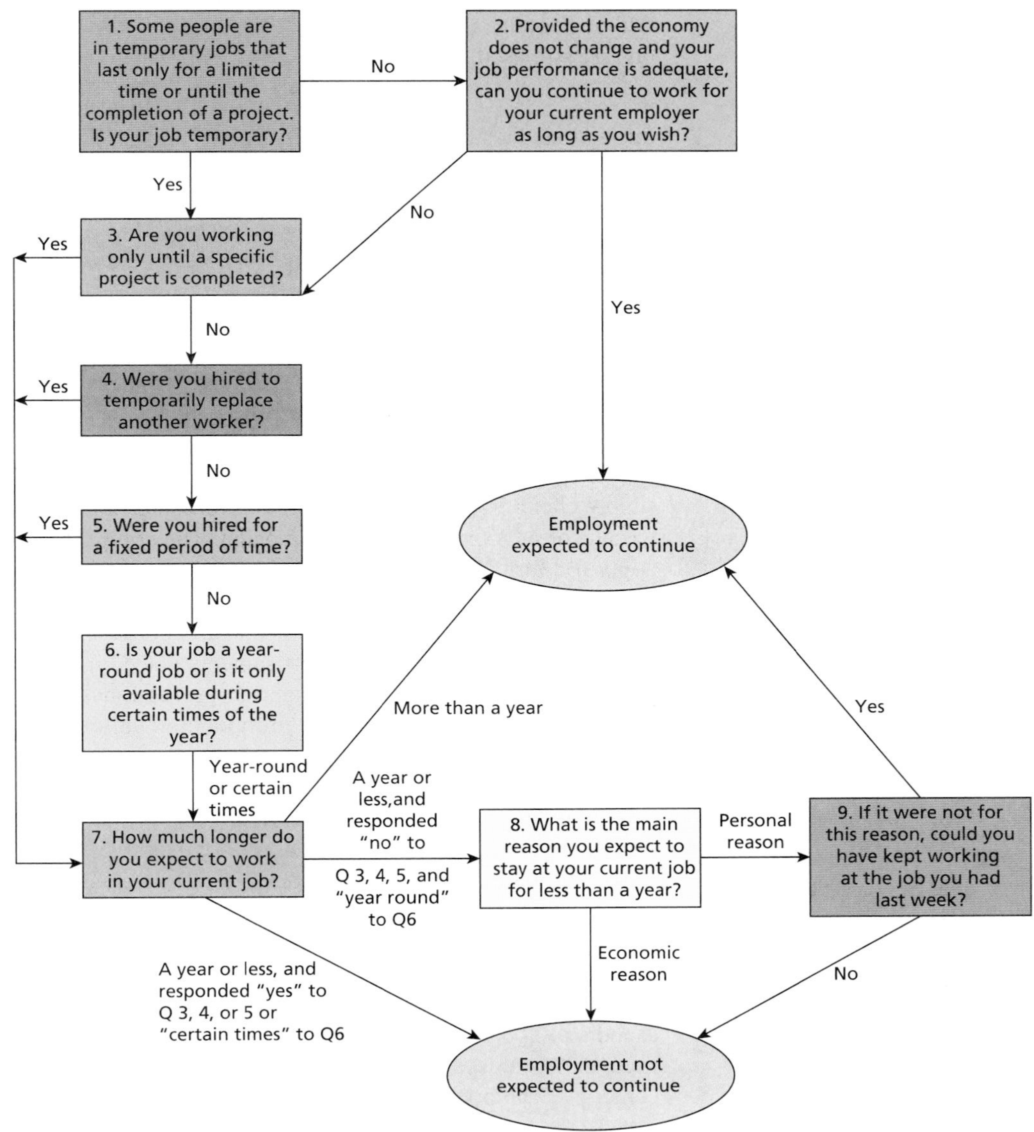

of contingent workers from traditional administrative positions to technical support, operations, and high-skilled professional positions, including engineering, legal, and finance.[62] If the use of contingent workers is indeed the trend, the manner that human resource is practiced will experience considerable change.

FYI

The U.S. General Accountability Office estimates that 40.2 of the U.S. labor force are contingent workers. Some of the more common categories of contingent workers are:

- Temporary employees: 1.3 percent
- On-call workers: 3.5 percent
- Contract company workers: 3.0 percent
- Independent contractors: 12.9 percent
- Self-employed workers: 3.3 percent
- Standard part-time workers: 5 percent[63]

Traditional Methods

Although online recruiting has greatly impacted how recruiting is accomplished, traditional methods are still used.

MEDIA ADVERTISING *Advertising* communicates the firm's employment needs to the public through media such as newspapers, trade journals, radio, television, and billboards found along highways. The firm's previous experience with various media should suggest the most effective approach for specific types of jobs. Although few individuals base their decision to change jobs on advertising, ads create awareness, generate interest, and encourage a prospect to seek more information about the firm and the job opportunities that it provides. A traditional common form of advertising that provides broad coverage at a relatively low cost is the newspaper ad. Firms using the newspaper ad attempt to appeal to the self-interest of prospective employees, emphasizing the job's unique qualities. Recently, the use of newspaper advertising has declined because other recruiting methods are more effective and less expensive.

Television media has sometimes been considered a way to broadcast information other than products and services. For instance, Super Bowl games often attract more than 100 million viewers and is a good way to promote products and services. In 2017, 84 Lumber Company, a building supply chain, purchased a 90-second advertising slot not only to advertise its products, but also to launch a national recruiting campaign. The company hoped that qualified individuals would apply for various jobs, including 400 management trainee positions to support the company's planned growth.[64]

Certain media attract audiences that are more homogeneous in terms of employment skills, education, and orientation. Advertisements placed in publications such as the *The Wall Street Journal* relate primarily to managerial, professional, and technical positions. The readers of these publications are generally individuals qualified for many of the positions advertised. Focusing on a specific labor market minimizes the likelihood of receiving marginally qualified or even totally unqualified applicants. Like most professional publications, jobs that are advertised in the paper copy of the *Journal* are also available on the publication's Web site. Journals specific to trades are also widely used. For example, *Automotive News* might have jobs related to the automobile industry and *American Drycleaner* likely will list jobs in the dry-cleaning business.

Qualified prospects who read job ads in newspapers and professional and trade journals may not be so dissatisfied with their present jobs that they will pursue opportunities advertised. Therefore, in high-demand situations, a firm needs to consider all available media resources such as radio, billboards, and television. These methods are likely more expensive than newspapers or journals, but in specific situations, they may prove successful. For instance, a regional medical center used billboards effectively to attract registered nurses. One large manufacturing firm had considerable success in advertising for production trainees by means of spot advertisements on the radio. A large electronics firm used television to attract experienced engineers when it opened a new facility and needed more engineers immediately. Thus, in situations where hiring needs are urgent, television and radio may provide good results. Broadcast messages can let people know that an organization is seeking recruits. A primary limitation is the amount of information they can transmit.

PRIVATE EMPLOYMENT AGENCIES *Private employment agencies*, often called "headhunters," are best known for recruiting white-collar employees and offer an important service in bringing qualified applicants and open positions together.[65] Firms and job hunters use private employment agencies for virtually every type position. Job seekers should carefully select the employment agency to use because there are both good and bad recruiters. Today, private employment agencies often specialize in filling a niche in the job market. Agencies should be selected based on knowledge of the industry and the specific position being sought.

Private employment agencies fees can range up to 35 percent of a person's first year salary. The one-time fees that some agencies charge often turn off candidates, although many private employment agencies also deal with firms that pay the fees. Either way, the headhunter does not get paid until a person is placed. The recent recession has significantly impacted the use of private employment agencies, which has resulted in a general retrenchment of the industry.

PUBLIC EMPLOYMENT AGENCIES Public employment agencies are operated by each state but receive overall policy direction from the U.S. Employment Service. Public employment agencies have become increasingly involved in matching people with technical, professional, and managerial positions. They typically use computerized job-matching systems to aid in the recruitment process, and they provide their services without charge to either the employer or the prospective employee.

EXECUTIVE SEARCH FIRMS *Executive search firms* are used by some firms to locate experienced professionals and executives when other sources prove inadequate. The key benefit of executive search firms is the targeting of ideal candidates. In addition, the executive search firm can often find passive candidates, those not actively looking for a job.

An executive search firm's representatives often visit the client's offices and interview the company's management. This enables them to gain a clear understanding of the company's goals and the job qualifications required. After obtaining this information, they contact and interview potential candidates, check references, and refer the best-qualified person to the client for the selection decision. Search firms maintain databases of résumés for this process. Other sources used include networking contacts, files from previous searches, specialized directories, personal calls, previous clients, colleagues, and unsolicited résumés. The search firm's task is to present candidates who are eminently qualified to do the job; it is the company's decision whom to hire.

There are two types of executive search firms: contingency and retained. *Contingency search firms* receive fees only on successful placement of a candidate in a job opening. The search firm's fee is generally a percentage of the individual's compensation for the first year. The client pays expenses, as well as the fee. A contingency recruiter goes to work when there is an urgent need to fill a position, when an opening exists for a difficult position, or when a hiring executive wants to know about top-notch talent as those people surface, regardless of whether there is an opening.

Retained search firms are considered consultants to their client organizations, serving on an exclusive contractual basis, and typically recruit top business executives. With a retained search firm, the company typically gets a firmer commitment from their search firm, as well as more personalized attention, dedicated time, and customized searches.[66]

RECRUITERS Recruiters most commonly focus on technical and vocational schools, community colleges, colleges, and universities. The key contact for recruiters on college and university campuses is often the student placement director. This administrator is in an excellent position to arrange interviews with students possessing the qualifications desired by the firm. Placement services help organizations use their recruiters efficiently. They identify qualified candidates, schedule interviews, and provide suitable rooms for interviews.

The company recruiter plays a vital role in attracting applicants. The interviewee often perceives the recruiter's actions as a reflection of the character of the firm. If the recruiter is dull, the interviewee may think the company is dull; if the recruiter is apathetic, discourteous, or vulgar, the interviewee may well attribute these negative characteristics to the firm. Recruiters must always be aware of the image they present because it makes a lasting impression. Recruitment success comes down to good personal selling, appealing to the candidate's priorities, and addressing his or her concerns. The recruiter should underscore the job's opportunities and keep the lines of communication open.

A recent trend is the use of videoconferencing with equipment at both corporate headquarters and on college campuses. Recruiters can communicate with college career counselors and interview students through a videoconferencing system without leaving the office.

job fair
Recruiting method engaged in by a single employer or group of employers to attract many applicants to one location for interviews.

JOB FAIRS A **job fair** is a recruiting method engaged in by a single employer or group of employers to attract many applicants to one location for interviews.

From an employer's viewpoint, a primary advantage of job fairs is the opportunity to meet many candidates in a short time. Conversely, applicants may have convenient access to several employers. As a recruitment method, job fairs offer the potential for a much lower cost per hire than traditional approaches. Job fairs are often organized by universities to assist their students in obtaining jobs. Here, employers from many organizations meet at a single point on the campus. The job fair is available from disciplines from across the university. Students and employers can meet here to ask and answer questions.

At times job fairs are tailored to recruit specific types of individuals. At a job fair in Tucson, Arizona, the event was designed to bring together senior citizens and companies looking to hire them, as well as offer assistance to those seeking to improve their job skills as a first step toward employment. The job fair attracted two dozen companies seeking to fill positions for everything from teachers' aides to bank tellers to tour bus drivers and call-center staff.[67] Job fairs are also held to bring together military service members and companies with openings to fill. Recently the Veterans Career Fair and Expo was held in Washington, D.C. Employers representing companies across the private sector, as well as several government agencies, were on site to discuss career and job opportunities to thousands of veterans from the mid-Atlantic region.[68]

internship
Special form of recruitment that involves placing a student in a temporary job with no obligation either by the company to hire the student permanently or by the student to accept a permanent position with the firm following graduation.

INTERNSHIPS An **internship** is a special form of recruitment that involves placing a student in a temporary job with no obligation either by the company to hire the student permanently or by the student to accept a permanent position with the firm following graduation.

An internship typically involves a temporary job for the summer months or a part-time job during the school year. It may also take the form of working full-time one semester and going to school full-time the next. Recently nontraditional virtual internships are being used by businesses for students who would be required to commute long distances with Skype, e-mail, and conference calls.[69] Employers can *try out* future employees prior to making a job offer. If the trial period proves unsuccessful, there is no obligation on either side. Google has long been known for using the internship as a recruiting method. Google offers interns competitive pay and on-site perks that include free gourmet food, a gym, fitness classes, massage therapy, bike repair, dry cleaning, a hair stylist, oil changes, and car washes.[70]

During the internship, the student gets to view business practices firsthand. At the same time, the intern contributes to the firm by performing needed tasks. In addition to other benefits, internships provide opportunities for students to bridge the gap from business theory to practice. Through this relationship, a student can determine whether a company would be a desirable employer. Similarly, having a relatively lengthy time to observe the student's job performance, the firm can make a better judgment regarding the person's qualifications.

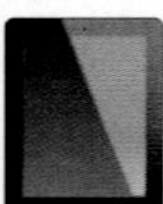

HR Web Wisdom
Internship Web Site
www.internships.com
The world's largest internship marketplace.

In today's job market, just having a degree is often not enough to get a job offer; internships are often the deciding factor in getting a good job or not. Students with internship and co-op experience are often able to find jobs easier, and they progress much further and faster in the business world than those without. Paid internships for college students have become even more valuable in recent years for both new graduates and companies. In a NACE 2015

Student Survey, more than half of the interns were paid, and 72 percent of students with a paid summer internship received at least one full-time job offer after graduation; the median starting salary for subsequent full-time jobs was about 55 percent higher than students with unpaid or no internship experience.[71] Steve Canale, manager, global recruiting and staffing services, at General Electric Co., based in Fairfield, Connecticut, said, "If I had my budget slashed and only had $100 to spend, I'd spend it all on my internship program. They become my brand ambassadors."[72]

PROFESSIONAL ASSOCIATIONS Virtually every professional group publishes a journal and has a Web site that is widely used by its members. Many professional associations in business areas including finance, marketing, accounting, and human resources provide recruitment and placement services for their members. Jobs advertised are placed in the journal in hard copy and advertised on the professional group's Web site. The Society for Human Resource Management (SHRM), for example, operates a job referral service for members seeking new positions and employers with positions to fill.

UNSOLICITED APPLICANTS A company must have a positive image or employer brand to attract unsolicited applicants. If an organization has the reputation of being a good place to work, it may be able to attract qualified prospects even without extensive recruitment efforts. Acting on their own initiative, well-qualified workers may seek out a specific company to apply for a job. Unsolicited applicants who apply because they are favorably impressed with the firm's reputation often prove to be valuable employees. In the Internet age, applicants can go to the firm's corporate career Web site and *walk in* by making an application online.

OPEN HOUSES Open houses pair potential hires and recruiters in a warm, casual environment that encourages on-the-spot job offers. Open houses are cheaper and faster than hiring through recruitment agencies, and they are also more popular than job fairs. There are pros and cons to holding a truly *open* house. If the event is open, it may draw a large turnout, but it also may attract many unqualified candidates. Some companies prefer to control the types of candidates they host, and so they conduct invitation-only sessions. In this scenario, someone screens résumés in response to ads, then invites only preselected candidates. Open house advertising may be through both conventional media and the Internet, where a firm might feature its open house on its home page.

event recruiting
Recruiters going to events being attended by individuals the company is seeking.

EVENT RECRUITING **Event recruiting** involves having recruiters go to events being attended by individuals the company is seeking. Cisco Systems pioneered event recruiting as a recruitment approach. In the case of programmers in the Silicon Valley, the choice spots have been marathons and bike races. Companies that participate in these events become involved in some way that promotes their name and cause. For example, they might sponsor or cosponsor an event, pass out refreshments, and give away prizes. Individuals get to know that the company is recruiting and the types of workers it is seeking. Event recruiting gives a company the opportunity to reflect its image.

SIGN-ON BONUSES Employers use sign-on bonuses to attract top talent, particularly in high-demand fields such as health care, sales, marketing, and accounting. Bonuses allow a firm to pay a premium to attract individuals without dramatically upsetting its salary scale. Even as Wall Street continued to lay off workers, some firms were offering sign-on bonuses for top management talent. NACE's *Job Outlook 2016* survey revealed that 51.8 percent of employers planned to offer signing bonuses to college graduates. Signing bonuses are most commonly found in the utilities, food and beverage manufacturing, finance, insurance and real estate, and pharmaceutical manufacturing industries.[73]

COMPETITIVE GAMES Many companies in the software industry use public competitions to identify talented prospects.[74] For instance, Google established Code Jam, which is an international programming competition. The competition began in 2003 as a means to identify top engineering talent for potential employment at Google. The competition consists of a set of algorithmic problems that must be solved in a fixed amount of time. Competitors may use any programming language and development environment to obtain their solutions.

Tailoring Recruitment Methods to Sources

Because each organization is unique, so are the needed types and qualifications of workers to fill positions. Thus, to be successful, a firm must tailor its recruitment sources and methods to its specific needs.

Suppose, for example, that a large firm has an immediate need for an experienced information technology manager and no one within the firm has these qualifications. Figure 5-5 shows a matrix that depicts sources and methods of recruitment for such a manager. Managers must first identify the *source* (where prospective employees are located) before choosing the *methods* (how to attract them). It is likely that other firms, possibly competitors, employ such individuals. After considering the recruitment source, the recruiter must then choose the method (or methods) of recruitment that offers the best prospects for attracting qualified candidates. Perhaps it would be appropriate to advertise the job in the classified section of *The Wall Street Journal* and use online recruiting. Alternatively, an executive search firm, such as Korn Ferry International, may serve as a viable option. In addition, the recruiter may attend meetings of professional information technology associations, such as the Association of Information Technology Professionals. One or more of these methods will likely yield a pool of qualified applicants.

In another scenario, consider a firm's need for 20 entry-level machine operators, whom the firm is willing to train. High schools and vocational schools would probably be good recruitment sources. Methods of recruitment might include newspaper ads, public employment agencies, recruiters, visiting vocational schools, and employee referrals.

5.6 Describe alternatives to recruitment.

Alternatives to Recruitment

Even when HR planning indicates a need for additional employees, a firm may decide against increasing the size of its workforce. Recruitment and selection costs are significant when you consider all the related expenses. Estimates vary. For instance, the cost of replacing a person making $50,000 per year can easily reach $75,000.[75] Therefore, a firm should consider alternatives carefully before engaging in recruitment.

FIGURE 5-5

Methods and Sources of Recruitment for an Information Technology Manager

External Sources \ External Methods	Online recruiting	Advertising	Employment agencies	Recruiters	Job fairs	Internships	Executive search firms	Professional associations	Walk-in applicants	Open houses	Event recruiting	Sign-on bonuses	High tech competition
High/Vocational schools													
Community colleges													
Colleges and universities													
Competitors in the labor market	X	X	X				X	X					
Unemployed													
Self-employed													
Former employees													
Military personnel													
Ex-offenders													

Promotion Policies

promotion from within (PFW)
Policy of filling vacancies above entry-level positions with current employees.

Promotion from within (PFW) is the policy of filling vacancies above entry-level positions with current employees. An organization's promotion policy can have a significant impact on recruitment. A firm can stress a policy of promoting from within its own ranks or one in which positions are generally filled from outside the organization. Depending on specific circumstances, either approach may have merit, but usually a combination of the two approaches proves best.

When an organization emphasizes PFW, its workers have an incentive to strive for advancement. When employees see coworkers promoted, they become more aware of their own opportunities. General Motors and Cisco fill approximately 60 to 80 percent of their senior management positions internally.[76] As another example, employees with Royal Caribbean Cruises can progress over time based on performance from an entry-level position such as assistant cabin steward to an officer position. Motivation provided by PFW often improves employee morale. PFW also communicates to the workers that the firm wants them to succeed.

Another advantage of internal recruitment is that the organization is usually aware of its employees' capabilities. Internal candidates have knowledge of the firm, its policies, and its people.[77] An employee's present job performance, by itself, may not be a reliable criterion for promotion. Nevertheless, management will know many of the employee's personal and job-related qualities. The employee has a track record, as opposed to being an unknown entity. Also, the company's investment in the individual may yield a higher return.

It is unlikely, however, that a firm can, or would even desire to, adhere rigidly to a practice of PFW. A strictly applied PFW policy eventually leads to inbreeding, a lack of cross-fertilization, and a lack of creativity. Although seldom achieved, a good goal would be to fill 80 percent of openings above entry-level positions from within. Frequently, new blood provides new ideas and innovation that must take place for firms to remain competitive. In such cases, even organizations with PFW policies may opt to look outside the organization for new talent. In any event, a promotion policy that first considers insiders is great for employee morale and motivation, which is beneficial to the organization.

In the following Watch It video, learn about the online fashion retailer Hautelook, which is growing quickly and needs to recruit new employees at a rapid rate. Hautelook prefers most of all to promote internal job candidates, but also to employ applicants who are most familiar with the company: ideally, previous customers. The company's methods for recruiting job applicants as well as finding the best potential employees from among its applicants are discussed.

Watch It 3

If your instructor has assigned this, go to **www.pearson.com/mylab/management** to watch a video titled Hautelook: Recruiting and respond to questions.

Overtime

Perhaps the most commonly used alternative to recruitment, especially in meeting short-term fluctuations in work volume, is overtime. Overtime may help both employer and employee. The employer benefits by avoiding recruitment, selection, and training costs. The employees gain from increased income during the overtime period.

There are potential problems with overtime, however. Some managers believe that when employees work for unusually long periods, the company pays more and receives less in return. Employees may become fatigued and lack the energy to perform at a normal rate. Two additional possible problems relate to the use of prolonged overtime. Consciously or not, employees may pace themselves to ensure overtime. They may also become accustomed to the added income resulting from overtime pay. Employees may even elevate their standard of living to the level permitted by this additional income. Then, when a firm tightens its belt and overtime is limited, employee morale may deteriorate along with the pay.

onshoring
Moving jobs not to another country but to lower-cost U.S. cities.

Onshoring

Onshoring involves moving jobs not to another country but to lower-cost U.S. cities. Some companies might like to offshore their jobs but the government may require onshore handling of certain financial, health, and defense data. This requirement often represents more than 15 percent of all IT service work. As an example, one global company opened a midwestern U.S. facility with more than 1,000 IT service employees. Wages at the facility were 35 percent lower than at headquarters, and the company also received $50 million in government incentives.[78]

PREPARING FOR EXAM/QUIZZES

Chapter Summary By Learning Objectives

1. ***Define* recruitment *and describe the recruitment process.*** *Recruitment* is the process of attracting individuals on a timely basis, in sufficient numbers, and with appropriate qualifications to apply for jobs with an organization. Recruitment frequently begins when a manager initiates an employee requisition. Next, the firm determines whether qualified employees are available from within (the internal source) or must be recruited externally from sources such as colleges, universities, and other firms. Sources and methods are then identified.
2. ***Summarize the environment of recruitment.*** Of importance to the success of recruitment is the demand for and supply of specific skills in the labor market. The recruitment method that proves to be most successful will depend to an extent on whether the recruited individual is an active or passive job seeker. Legal matters also play a significant role in recruitment practices in the United States. This is not surprising because the candidate and the employer first make contact during the recruitment process. A poorly conceived recruiting process can do much to create problems in the selection process. Therefore, it is essential for organizations to emphasize nondiscriminatory practices at this stage. The Office of Federal Contract Compliance Programs (OFCCP) has issued guidelines concerning the online recruiting policies of federal contractors and subcontractors.
3. ***Explain internal recruitment methods.*** Human resource databases permit organizations to determine whether current employees possess the qualifications for filling open positions. *Job posting* is a method of internal recruitment that is used to communicate the fact that job openings exist. *Job bidding* is a system that permits individuals in an organization to apply for a specific job within the organization. *Employee referrals* involves an employee of the company recommending to management a friend or associate as a possible member of the company and continues to be the way that top performers are identified.
4. ***Identify external recruitment sources.*** External sources of recruitment include high schools and vocational schools, community colleges, colleges and universities, competitors and other firms, the unemployed, older individuals, military personnel, self-employed workers, and ex-offenders.
5. ***Summarize external recruitment methods.*** The world of recruiting via mobile technology is moving at lightning speed. More and more people are adopting mobile technology, and many organizations are trying to figure out how to start using mobile devices in the recruiting process. Some online methods include Internet recruiter, virtual job fairs, corporate career Web sites, blogs, general-purpose job boards, NACElink Network, .jobs, AllianceQ, niche sites, and contract workers' sites. Traditional external recruitment methods include media advertising, private employment agencies, public employment agencies, recruiters, job fairs, internships, executive search firms, professional associations, unsolicited applicants, open houses, event recruiting, sign-on bonuses, and high-tech competition. Recruitment must be tailored to the needs of each firm. In addition, recruitment sources and methods often vary according to the type of position being filled.
6. ***Describe alternatives to recruitment.*** Even when HR planning indicates a need for additional employees, a firm may decide against increasing the size of its workforce. Recruitment and selection costs are significant when you consider all the related expenses. Alternatives include promotion policies, overtime, and onshoring.

Key Terms

recruitment 121
employee requisition 121
recruitment sources 122
recruitment methods 140
active job seekers 123
passive job seekers 123
job posting 124
job bidding 124
employee referral 125
Internet recruiter 130
virtual job fair 131
corporate career Web sites 131
NACElink Network 132
.jobs 132
AllianceQ 132
niche sites 132
contingent workers 132
job fair 136
internship 136
event recruiting 137
promotion from within (PFW) 139
onshoring 140

MyLab Management

If your instructor is using MyLab Management, go to **www.pearson.com/mylab/management** to complete the problems marked with this icon ✪.

Questions for Review

5-1. Define *recruitment*.

✪**5-2.** What are factors external to the organization that can significantly affect the firm's recruitment efforts?

5-3. How has social media emerged as an important force in recruiting?

5-4. What are the steps involved in the recruitment process?

5-5. Distinguish between recruitment sources and recruitment methods.

5-6. What are some internal recruitment methods?

5-7. Why is employee referral so important in the recruitment process?

5-8. What external methods of recruitment are available?

5-9. What external sources of recruitment are available?

5-10. What might be some advantages of using mobile recruiting?

5-11. What online recruitment methods are available?

✪**5-12.** What are the typical alternatives to recruitment that a firm may use?

5-13. What is meant by the policy of *promotion from within*?

PREPARING FOR MY CAREER

ETHICS DILEMMA

Unfair Advantage?

You are the vice-president of human resources for a high-tech company that is competing for a major government project. You believe that one of your key competitors is ahead of you in project development and you would like to recruit some of its engineers who are knowledgeable about the project. You receive an anonymous e-mail that includes the names and phone numbers of key people involved in your competitor's project. If you use the information and can hire some of the competitor's key people, your company has a chance to beat the competitor and you will become a hero. If you do not use the information, your company may lose a great deal of money.

5-14. What would you do?

5-15. What factor(s) in this ethics dilemma might influence a person to make a less than ethical decision?

HRM Is Everyone's Business

One of the goals of how HR professionals and managers conduct HR planning is to identify current and future staffing needs. HR professionals and managers use that information to formulate recruitment plans that will help generate a pool of qualified external and internal candidates. Recruitment must be tailored to the needs of each firm and the types of positions being filled. Successful recruitment requires collaboration between HR professionals and managers who bring different perspectives to completing the task.

Action checklist for managers and HR—understanding and applying recruitment sources and methods

HR takes the lead

- ☑ Write new or modify existing job descriptions to ensure that the job duties and applicant requirements match and are clearly stated.
- ☑ Discuss whether it makes sense to recruit internally or externally and the pros and cons of each approach.

- ☑ Ask managers to identify external sources of potential employees such as professional associations, college or universities with excellent reputations for preparing prospective employees, and job search websites; and, suggest additional methods to round out a comprehensive recruitment plan.
- ☑ Discuss the relevant legal requirements that must be taken into consideration when recruiting prospective employees.

Managers take the lead

- ☑ Inform HR about staffing needs and prepare employee requisitions.
- ☑ Emphasize job-relevant skills and abilities of importance such as software knowledge, project management skills, or leadership.
- ☑ Share with HR whether the company already employs qualified individuals for the new job and consider possible external sources.

HRM by the Numbers

Recruitment Source Cost Effectiveness

An additional HRM by the Numbers exercise can be found on MyLab Management.

HR professionals regularly stay abreast of recruitment costs and the number of new hires associated with each recruitment source. Below is a listing of this information.

Recruitment Source	Cost	Number of New Hires
Employment Agency Fees	$250,000	30
Employee Referral Bonuses	5,000	5
Career Website Subscription Fees	10,000	15
Newspaper Advertising (online and print)	125,000	45

Questions

5-16. How much did recruitment cost based on all the sources listed in the table?
5-17. Calculate the cost per hire for each recruitment source.
5-18. Which of the sources is most cost effective?

Working Together: Team Exercise

In small groups of three or four, come up with specific answers to the following questions. Talk through your perspectives and come up with a brief team response. Be prepared to share your ideas with the class.

As a group, think about a job you could imagine getting five years after graduation. Also, think about the main objectives of the job and the kinds of knowledge and skills you believe are necessary to perform the job well.

5-19. What is the most likely recruitment source of candidates for this job? Explain.
5-20. What is the most likely recruitment method for identifying qualified applicants for this job? Explain.

INCIDENT 1 A Problem Ad?

Dorothy Bryant was the new recruiting supervisor for International Manufacturing Company in Salt Lake City, Utah. One of Dorothy's first assignments was to recruit two software design engineers for International. Design engineers are hard to recruit because of the difficulty of their training and the high demand for them. After considering various recruitment alternatives, Dorothy placed the following ad in a local newspaper with a circulation more than 1,000,000:

Employment Opportunity for Software Design Engineers

2 positions available for engineers desiring career in growth industry.

Prefer recent college graduates with good appearance.

Good credit rating

Apply Today! Send your résumé,

in confidence, to: D. A. Bryant

International Manufacturing Co., P.O. Box 1515

Salt Lake City, UT 84115

More than 300 applications arrived in the first week, and Dorothy was elated. When she reviewed the applicants, however, it appeared that few people possessed the desired qualifications for the job.

Questions

5-21. Dorothy overlooked some of the proper recruiting practices, which resulted in an excessive number of unqualified people applying. What are they?

5-22. Are there any hiring standards that should be avoided? Identify them and explain why they should be avoided.

5-23. What recruitment sources and methods might have been used to have generated a better applicant pool for the two software design engineer positions for International Manufacturing? Defend your recommendations.

INCIDENT 2 I Am Qualified, Why Not Me?

Five years ago, when Bobby Bret joined Crystal Productions as a junior accountant, he felt that he was on his way up. He had just graduated with a B+ average from college where he was well liked by his peers and by the faculty, and had been an officer in several student organizations. Bobby had shown a natural ability to get along with people as well as to get things done. He remembered what Roger Friedman, the controller at Crystal, had told him when he was hired, "I think you will do well here, Bobby. You've come highly recommended. You are the kind of guy that can expect to move right on up the ladder."

Bobby felt that he had done a good job at Crystal, and everybody seemed to like him. In addition, his performance appraisals had been excellent. However, after five years he was still a junior accountant. He had applied for two senior accountant positions that had opened, but they were both filled by people hired from outside the firm. When the accounting supervisor's job came open two years ago, Bobby had not applied. He was surprised when his new boss turned out to be a hotshot graduate of State University whose only experience was three years with a large accounting firm. Bobby had hoped that Ron Greene, a senior accountant he particularly respected, would get the job.

On the fifth anniversary of his employment at Crystal, Bobby decided it was time to do something. He made an appointment with the controller. At that meeting, Bobby explained to Mr. Friedman that he had worked hard to obtain a promotion and shared his frustration about having been in the same job for so long. "Well," said Mr. Friedman, "you don't think that you were all that much better qualified than the people that we have hired, do you?" "No," said Bobby, "but I think I could have handled the senior accountant job. Of course, the people you have hired are doing a great job too." The controller responded, "We just look at the qualifications of all the applicants for each job, and considering everything, try to make a reasonable decision."

Questions

5-24. Do you believe that Bobby has a legitimate complaint? Explain.

5-25. Explain the benefits of a promotion from within policy. Would such a policy be appropriate for Crystal?

MyLab Management

If your instructor is using MyLab Management, go to **www.pearson.com/mylab/management** for Auto-graded writing questions as well as the following Assisted-graded writing questions:

5-26. Why might a firm want to use contingent workers as opposed to full-time employees?

5-27. Why is it important to match sources and methods of recruitment?

Endnotes

1 Matthew Beecher, "Only Assets Need Apply," *HR Magazine* 56 (November 2011): 84–85.

2 Anonymous, "For Incoming Executives: Defining and Delivering Your Talent Agenda," *Risk & Compliance Journal* (January 13, 2014). Accessed February 1, 2014, at http://deloitte.wsj.com/riskandcompliance/2014/01/13/for-incoming-executives-defining-and-delivering-your-talent-agenda.

3 Julie Kantor, "High Turnover Costs Way More Than You Think," *Huffington Post* online (February 11, 2016). Accessed February 13, 2017, at www.huffingtonpost.com.

4 U.S. Bureau of Labor Statistics, "Wind Turbine Technicians," *Occupational Outlook Handbook 2016-17*. Accessed February 13, 2017, at www.bls.gov.

5 Dylan Matthews, "The Tuition is too Damn High Part II: Why College is Still Worth It," *Washington Post* (August 27, 2013). Accessed February 5, 2014, at www.washingtonpost.com.

6 Elka Torpey and Audrey Watson, "Education Level and Jobs: Opportunities by State," *Career Outlook* online (September 2014), U.S. Bureau of Labor Statistics. Accessed January 10, 2017, at www.bls.gov; Hope Yen, "New Study Shows the Value of a College Education," *Boston Globe* (February 11, 2014). Accessed February 12, 2014, at www.bostonglobe.com.

7 Alexia Elejalde-Ruiz, "Construction Contractors Warn of a Labor Shortage as Building Booms," *Chicago Tribune* online (May 31, 2016). Accessed January 31, 2017, at www.chicagotribune.com.

8 James E. Leemann, "The Jobs Are Out There," *Industrial Safety & Hygiene News* 46 (January 2012): 18–20.

9 Stephen Whitaker and Mary Zenker, "Are Underemployed Graduates Displacing Non-graduates?" *Economic Trends* (July 2011): 21–23.

10 Constantine Von Hoffman, "Many Jobs Go Unfilled for over 3 Months," *CBS News Money-Watch* (July 18, 2013). Accessed February 18, 2014, at www.cbsnews.com.

11 Anthony P. Carnevale, "Old Jobs, New Jobs: Here's the Difference," *HR Magazine* 57 (January 2012): 25.

12 Rachel Emma Silverman, "Companies Are Chasing the Wrong Hires," *The Wall Street Journal* online (June 10, 2015). Accessed February 5, 2017, at http://blogs.wsj.com.

13 Rachel Emma Silverman, "Companies Are Chasing the Wrong Hires," *The Wall Street Journal* online (June 10, 2015). Accessed February 5, 2017, at http://blogs.wsj.com.

14 U.S. Department of Labor, Office of Federal Contract Compliance Programs "Internet Applicant Recordkeeping Rule." Accessed February 13, 2017, at www.dol.gov/ofccp/regs/compliance/faqs/iappfaqs.htm\#Q1GI.

15 WorldatWork, *Bonus Programs and Practices* (July 2016). Accessed May 22, 2017, at www.worldatwork.org/adimLink?id=80398.

16 "Study Finds Bonus Pay Geared to Attract, Not Retain, Talent," *Report on Salary Surveys* 9 (March 2009): 1–7.

17 Cat Zakrzewski, "Intel Doubles Up on Hiring Women and Minorities," *The Wall Street Journal* online (August 3, 2015). Accessed February 3, 2017, at www.wsj.com.

18 "Bonus Programs and Practices," *Worldat-Work report*, July 2016. Accessed January 5, 2017, at www.worldatwork.org/waw/adimLink?id=80398.

19 Vickie Elmer, "Hiring without a Net: Groupon's Recruiter Speaks," *Fortune* 164 (July 25, 2011): 34.

20 Nelson D. Schwartz, "In Hiring a Friend in Need is a Prospect, Indeed. *New York Times* (January 27, 2013). Accessed February 3, 2014, at www.nytimes.com.

21 Auren Hoffman, "Seeking Great Candidates Online," *BusinessWeek Online* (December 10, 2009): 1.

22 Elka Torpey and Audrey Watson, "Education Level and Jobs: Opportunities by State," *Career Outlook* online (September 2014), U.S. Bureau of Labor Statistics. Accessed January 10, 2017, at www.bls.gov.

23 Alice Andore, "The Value of Poaching," *HR Magazine* 57 (April 2012): 36–37.

24 John Helyar and Douglas MacMillan, "In Tech, Poaching Is the Sincerest Form of Flattery," *Bloomberg Businessweek* (March 7, 2011): 17–18.

25 Rebecca Knight, "When the Competition Is Trying to Poach Your Top Employee," *Harvard Business Review* online (September 29, 2015). Accessed February 3, 2017, at www.hbr.org.

26 Ibid.

27 "Technology Talent Poaching to Get More Aggressive in 2011," *Channel Insider* (March 3, 2011): 1.

28 Michael A. Tucker, "Don't Say Goodbye," *HR Magazine* 56 (August 2011): 71–73.

29 U.S. Bureau of Labor Statistics, *"Job Openings and Labor Turnover–December 2016"* (USDL 17-0179, February 7, 2017). Accessed February 14, 2017, at www.bls.gov.

30 U.S. Bureau of Labor Statistics, *"The Employment Situation–January 2017"* (USDL 17-0141, February 3, 2017). Accessed February 14, 2017, at www.bls.gov.

31 Ibid.

32 "Careers for Veterans," *General Electric Careers* Web site. Accessed February 14, 2017, at www.ge.com/careers/culture/us-veterans.

33 "Starbucks Hiring Efforts for Military, Youth and Refugees," *Starbucks' New Room* online (January 31, 2017). Accessed February 14, 2017, at https://news.starbucks.com/news/starbucks-hiring-initiatives.

34 "Careers for Veterans," AT&T Careers Web site. Accessed February 14, 2017, at http://att.jobs/doing-great-things/military.

35 "Veterans in the Workplace," U.S. Chamber of Commerce Foundation (November 2016). Accessed May 25, 2017, at www.uschamber-foundation.org.

36 Vanessa Fuhrmans, "Hiring Veterans Is Easy, Keeping Them Is Hard," *The Wall Street Journal* online (March 29, 2017). Accessed May 25, 2017, at www.wsj.com.

37 Agency Group 09, "America Supports You: Group Helps Troops, Families Find Jobs," FDCH Regulatory Intelligence Database (January 30, 2008): Department of Defense, 703-695-0192.

38 Eric Krell, "Criminal Background," *HR Magazine* 57 (February 2012): 45–54.

39 National Institute of Justice, *Research on Re-Entry and Employment*, April 3, 2013. Accessed January 15, 2014, at www.nij.gov.

40 U.S. Equal Employment Opportunity Commission, "Arrest and Conviction Records as a Barrier to Employment," (July 26, 2011). Written Statement for Amy Solomon. Accessed February 18, 2014, at www.eeoc.gov.

41 Michelle Natividad Rodriguez and Beth Avery, "Ban the Box: U.S. Cities, Counties, and States Adopt Fair Hiring Policies," National Employment Law Project (February 1, 2017). Accessed February 14, 2017, at www.nelp.org/publication/ban-the-box-fair-chance-hiring-state-and-local-guide/.

42 Roy Mauer, "Ban-the-Box Movement Goes Viral," *Society for Human Resource Management* online. Accessed February 14, 2017, at www.shrm.org/resourcesandtools/hr-topics/risk-management/pages/ban-the-box-movement-viral.aspx.

43 David Farkas, "Employee Search," *Chain Leader* 13 (June 2008): 44–45.

44 Roseanne Harper, "CSA Offers Second Chance," *Supermarket News* 57 (September 14, 2009): 30.

45 Michelle V. Rafter, "Goin' Mobile In," *Workforce Management* 90 (February 2011): 26–28.

46 Nicole Fallon Taylor, "Hiring in the Digital Age: What's Next for Recruiting?" *Business News Daily* online (January 11, 2016). Accessed January 31, 2017, at www.businessnewsdaily.com/6975-future-of-recruiting.html.

47 Abha Bhattarai, "Facebook Wants to Help You Find a Job—Even If You're Not Looking for One," *The Washington Post* online (February 16, 2017). Accessed February 17, 2017, at www.washingtonpost.com.

48 CareerBuilder.com, "About Us." Accessed February 17, 2017, at www.careerbuilder.com/share/AboutUs/.

49 Jack Constine, "Facebook's New Job Opening Posts Poach Business from LinkedIn," *TechCrunch* Web site. Accessed February 17, 2017, at https://techcrunch.com/2017/02/15/facebook-jobs/.

50 Glassdoor.com, "About Us." Accessed February 17, 2017, at www.glassdoor.com/about/index_input.htm.

51 LinkedIn.com, "About LinkedIn." Accessed February 17, 2017, at https://press.linkedin.com/about-linkedin.

52 Marci Reynolds, "Twitter: The Newest Job Board?" Accessed February 15, 2017, at www.job-hunt.org/social-networking/twitter-job-board.shtml.

53 "How Disney and 5 Other Top Employers Use Twitter to Recruit," *The Under Cover Recruiter* Web site. Accessed February 5, 2017, at http://theundercoverrecruiter.com/how-disney-and-5-other-top-employers-use-twitter-to-recruit/.

54 "AllianceQ Fortune 500 Company Recruiting: A Different Recruiting Model." (July 13, 2011). Accessed May 20, 2014 at http://jobsearch.about.com/od/jobsdatabases/a/allianceq.htm.

55 "This Résumé Pool Is Deepening Fast," *BusinessWeek* (July 13, 2009): 72.

56 Deborah Silver, "Niche Sites Gain Monster-Sized Following," *Workforce Management* 90 (March 2011): 10–11.

57 U.S. Bureau of Labor Statistics. (2005). *Workers on Flexible and Shift Schedules, May 2004.* USDL: 05-1198. Accessed January 19, 2014, at www.bls.gov.

58 U.S. Government Accountability Office, "Contingent Workforce: Size, Characteristics, Earnings, and Benefits," *Report: GAO-15-168R* (April 20, 2015). Accessed February 1, 2017, at www.gao.gov/assets/670/669766.pdf.

59 Robert J. Grossman, "Strategic Temptations," *HR Magazine* 57 (March 2012): 24–31.

60 Daniel N. Janich, "Without Proper Planning, Contingent Workers Pose Serious Legal Risks to Employer Benefit Plans," *Employee Benefit Plan Review* 66 (July 2011): 8–11.

61 Irwin Speizer, "An On-Demand Workforce," *Workforce Management* 88 (October 19, 2009): 45–49.

62 "Temporary Workforce Stronger Than Ever," *T+D* 65 (May 2011): 21.

63 U.S. Government Accountability Office, "Contingent Workforce: Size, Characteristics, Earnings, and Benefits," *Report: GAO-15-168R* (April 20, 2015). Accessed February 1, 2017, at www.gao.gov/assets/670/669766.pdf.

64 Joshua Jamerson, "Super Bowl Ad to Kick Off Hiring Spree," *The Wall Street Journal* online (January 31, 2017). Accessed February 1, 2017, at www.wsj.com.

65 Chris McCarthy, "The Art of Headhunting," *Accountancy* 147 (June 2011): 60.

66 Lin Grensing-Pophal, "Executive Search," *Credit Union Management* 35 (January 2012): 32–35.

67 Philip S. Moore, "Seniors Flood Older Worker Fair," *Inside Tucson Business* 14 (March 3, 2005): 15–17.

68 "Vets Descend on Washington for Career Fair and Expo," Agency Group 09, *FDCH Regulatory Intelligence Database* (January 19, 2012).

69 Alison Damast, "Virtual Internships in Rising Demand," *BusinessWeek.com* (January 19, 2012): 2.

70 "Employers Are Being Creative with Perks & Pay for Internships," *HR Focus* 87 (March 2010): 9.

71 National Associate for Colleges and Employers, *Paid Interns/Co-ops See Greater Offer Rates and Salary Offers Than Their Unpaid Classmates* (press release, March 23, 2016). Accessed February 15, 2017, at www.naceweb.org/s03232016/paid-unpaid-interns-offer-rates-salary-offers.aspx.

72 Rita Pyrillis, "Companies, Again, Are Giving It the Old College Try," *Workforce Management* 90 (February 2011): 16–17.

73 National Association of Colleges and Employers, *Percentage of Employers Planning to Offer Signing Bonuses Climbs for Class of 2016* (February 10, 2016). Accessed February 20, 2017, at www.naceweb.org/s02102016/signing-bonuses-for-class-of-2016.aspx.

74 Dennis Carey and Matt Smith, "How Companies Are Using Simulations, Competitions, and Analytics to Hire," *Harvard Business Review* online (April 22, 2016). Accessed February 3, 2017, at www.hbr.org.

75 Lisa V. Gillespie, "Climbing the Corporate Lattice?" *Employee Benefit News* 26 (January 2012): 17–18.

76 George Anders, "HP Thinks Its Talent Strategy: Promote More, Go Outside Less," *Forbes* (May 23, 2013). Accessed January 15, 2014, at www.forbes.com.

77 Suzanne Lucas, "I Keep Losing Out to Job Candidates," CBS News *MoneyWatch* (August 16, 2013). Accessed February 2, 2014, at www.cbsnews.com.

78 Aditya Pande, "How to Make Onshoring Work," *Harvard Business Review* 89 (March 2011): 30.

6 Selection

LEARNING OBJECTIVES After completing this chapter, students should be able to:

6.1 Explain employee selection and environmental factors that affect the selection process.

6.2 Explain the importance of preliminary screening as well as reviewing applications and résumés.

6.3 Describe the use of tests in the selection process.

6.4 Explain the use of the employment interview.

6.5 Describe the use of pre-employment screening and background checks.

6.6 Explain the selection decision and the metrics for evaluating recruitment/selection effectiveness.

MyLab Management

Improve Your Grade!

If your professor is using MyLab Management, visit **www.pearson.com/mylab/management** for videos, simulations, and writing exercises.

Learn It

If your professor has chosen to assign this, go to **www.pearson.com/mylab/management** to see what you should particularly focus on and to take the Chapter 6 Warm-Up.

6.1 Explain employee selection and environmental factors that affect the selection process.

selection
Process of choosing from a group of applicants the individual best suited for a particular position and the organization.

Selection and Environmental Factors Affecting the Selection Process

Selection is the process of choosing from a group of applicants the individual best suited for a position and the organization (optimal types and levels of human capital). Properly matching people with jobs and the organization is the goal of the selection process. If individuals are overqualified, underqualified, or for any reason do not fit either the job or the organization's culture, they will be ineffective and probably leave the firm, voluntarily or otherwise. There are many ways to improve productivity, but none is more powerful than making the right hiring decision. A firm that selects high-quality employees reaps substantial benefits, which recur every year the employee is on the payroll. On the other hand, poor selection decisions can cause irreparable damage. A bad hire can negatively affect the morale of the entire staff, especially in a position where teamwork is critical.

Many companies would rather go short and work overtime than hire one bad apple. If a firm hires many bad apples, it cannot be successful for long even if it has perfect plans, a sound organizational structure, and finely tuned control systems. Competent people must be available to ensure the attainment of organizational goals. Today, with many firms having access to the same technology, *people* make the real difference.

The Selection Process

Companies make selection decisions to determine whether individuals who were identified through the recruitment process will be offered employment. Figure 6-1 illustrates a generalized selection process, but it may vary from company to company and according to the type of job being filled. This process typically begins with preliminary screening. Next, applicants complete

FIGURE 6-1
Selection Process

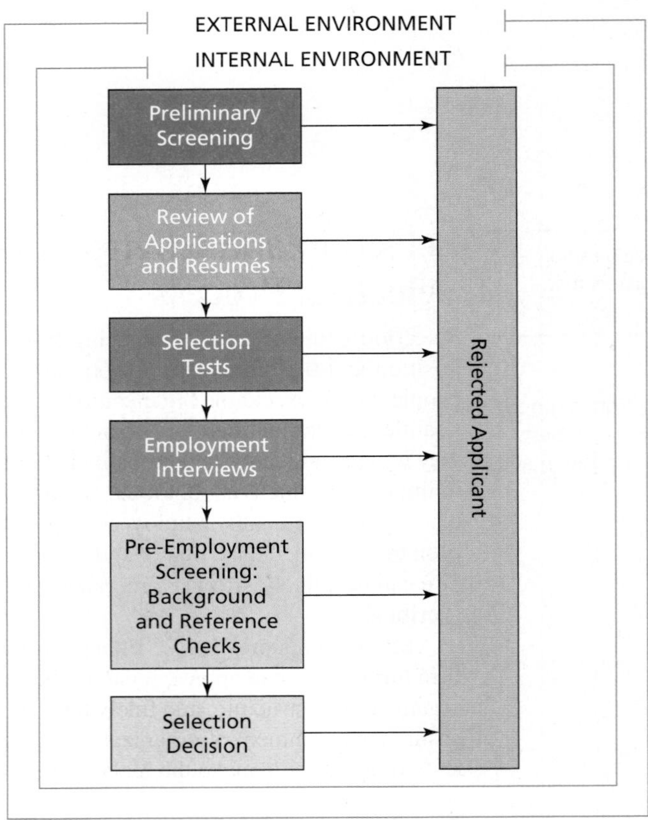

the firm's application for employment or provide a résumé. Then they progress through a series of selection tests, one or more employment interviews, and pre-employment screening, including background and reference checks. The hiring manager then offers the successful applicant a job, subject to successful completion of a medical examination. Notice that an applicant may be rejected or opt out at any time during the selection process. To a point, the more screening tools used to assess an applicant, the greater the chance of making a good selection decision. A good selection decision results in either one of two outcomes. First, job candidates who fail to meet the standard for employment are not offered employment. Second, job candidates who do meet the standard for employment are offered employment.

The Environment of Selection

A standardized selection process followed consistently would greatly simplify the selection process. However, circumstances may require making exceptions. The following sections describe environmental factors that affect the selection process.

OTHER HR FUNCTIONS The selection process affects, and is affected by, virtually every other HR function. For example, if the compensation package is inferior to those provided by competitors, hiring the best-qualified applicants will be difficult or impossible to achieve. The same situation applies if the firm's safety and health record is substandard or if the firm has a reputation for providing minimal training. Certainly, if marginal workers are hired, additional training will be needed to get them qualified.

LEGAL CONSIDERATIONS Legal matters play a significant role in HR management because of EEOC legislation, executive orders, and court decisions. Although the basic purpose of selection is to determine candidates' eligibility for employment, it is also essential for organizations to maintain non-discriminatory practices. The guiding principles in determining what information to get from an applicant are: Why am I asking this question and why do I want to know this information? If the information is job-related, usually asking for the information is appropriate. We will take up some of the particulars of legal matters later in the chapter after we examine selection testing.

SPEED OF DECISION MAKING The time available to make the selection decision can also have a major effect on the selection process. Conditions also can impact the needed speed of decision making. Suppose, for instance, that the only two quality-control inspectors on a production line just had a fight and both resigned, and the firm cannot operate until the positions are filled. In this situation, speed is crucial, and a few phone calls, two brief interviews, and a prayer may constitute the entire selection procedure. On the other hand, conducting a national search to select a CEO may take months or even a year. In bureaucracies, it is common for the selection process to take a considerable amount of time.

ORGANIZATIONAL HIERARCHY Organizations usually take different approaches to filling positions at varying levels. For instance, consider the differences in hiring a CEO versus filling a clerical position. Extensive background investigations and multiple interviews would most likely apply for the executive position. On the other hand, an applicant for a clerical position would probably take a word-processing test and perhaps have a short employment interview.

applicant pool
Number of qualified applicants recruited for a particular job.

APPLICANT POOL The number of qualified applicants recruited for a particular job makes up the **applicant pool**. The process can be truly selective only if there are several qualified applicants. Yet, only one or two applicants with the required skills may be available, and companies report a shortage of skilled individuals available for employment, particularly in the science, technology, engineering, and mathematics fields.[1] The expansion and contraction of the labor market also affects the size of the applicant pool. According to the U.S. Bureau of Labor Statistics, the total number of job openings in May 2017 was 5.7 million,[2] with nearly 7 million unemployed workers.[3]

TYPE OF ORGANIZATION The type of organization employing individuals, such as private, governmental, or not-for-profit, can also affect the selection process. Most private-sector businesses are heavily profit oriented. Prospective employees who can help achieve profit goals are the preferred candidates. Consideration of the total individual, including job-related personality factors, is involved in the selection of employees for this sector.

Government civil service systems typically identify qualified applicants through competitive examinations. Often a manager may select only the top three applicants for a position. Rules such as this one may result in overlooking a strong candidate.

Individuals considered for positions in not-for-profit organizations (e.g., the Boy Scouts and Girl Scouts, YMCA, or YWCA) confront still a different situation. The salary level in these organizations may not be competitive with those of private and governmental organizations.[4] Therefore, a person who fills one of these positions must be not only qualified but also dedicated to this type of work.

PROBATIONARY PERIOD Many firms use a probationary or introductory period that permits them to evaluate an employee's ability based on established performance. The purpose of a probationary period is to establish the suitability of a new employee for the position and to resolve any issues there might be in the new employee's performance over the first three months or so. This practice may be either a substitute for certain phases of the selection process or a check on the validity of the process. The rationale is that if an individual can successfully perform the job during the probationary period, the process does not require other selection tools. From a legal viewpoint, the use of a probationary period in the selection process is certainly job-related.

Even in unionized firms, the labor–management agreement typically does not protect a new employee until after a certain probationary period. This period is typically from 60 to 90 days. During that time, an employee can be terminated with little or no justification. On the other hand, firing a marginal employee in a union environment may prove to be quite difficult after the probationary period.

organizational fit
Management's perception of the degree to which the prospective employee will fit in with the firm's culture or value system.

ORGANIZATIONAL FIT **Organizational fit** refers to management's perception of the degree to which the prospective employee will fit in with the firm's culture or value system. There are numerous reasons that a new hire does not work out but none is as important as cultural fit. Knowledge and skill are important but the most lasting component of the employment relationship is cultural match.[5] The commonly heard statement, "the chemistry was just not right" may describe a poor fit. This was supported by Steven Rice, executive vice president of HR Juniper Networks Inc., who said, "If the customer sees you as team-oriented and such and the customer service guy is different, you have a problem. You have to hire against the brand.[6] A poor fit harms organizational effectiveness, hurts morale, and drains creativity." Nina Brody, head of talent for Take Care Health Systems in Conshohocken, Pennsylvania, said, "If we have 10 qualified clinical people in front of us, we want to know who will fit best with our culture, because that's where we tend to experience trouble, not necessarily with someone's ability to do the job technically."[7]

Using *fit* as a criterion may raise legal and diversity questions, and perhaps this explains the low profile of its use.[8] Lauren Rivera, an associate professor of management and organizations at Northwestern University, warns, "In many organizations, it is this catchall for, 'I don't feel right about this person.'"[9] In the process, a company possibly compromises diversity goals. Nevertheless, there is considerable evidence that managers use *fit* in making selection decisions and that it is not a minor consideration. Complicating the situation further is the fact that the same employee may be a poor fit with one firm and a perfect fit with another. Applicants also should consider organizational fit when assessing whether to accept a job offer.

SELECTION TECHNOLOGY The application of technology to employee selection practices has increased dramatically in recent years.[10] Two tools that are invaluable to the selection process in the technology boom that is sweeping HR today are applicant-tracking systems (ATSs) and candidate relationship management (CRM). "ATS and CRM are really your backbone," says Jim McCoy, vice-president of solutions for ManpowerGroup Solutions, the RPO software division of Milwaukee-based ManpowerGroup.[11]

An *ATS*, also called a talent management system, is a software application designed to help an enterprise select employees more efficiently. Current ATSs permit human resource and line managers to oversee the entire selection process. They often involve screening résumés and spotting qualified candidates, conducting personality and skills tests, and handling background investigations. They allow companies to compile job applications electronically, to gather candidates more quickly, set up interviews, and get new hires on board. An ATS can be used to post job openings on a corporate Web site or job board and generate interview requests to potential candidates by e-mail. Other features may include individual applicant tracking, requisition tracking, automated résumé ranking, customized input forms, prescreening questions and response tracking, and multilingual capabilities. ATSs are used extensively to help ease the labor-intensive process of sorting résumés from online job boards. In most cases, the goal is not merely to reduce costs but also to speed up the hiring process and find people who fit an organization's success profile. ATSs are not flawless. Some ATSs sort out résumés exclusively based on formatting, insufficient use of keywords, and other criteria that are unrelated to an applicant's qualifications.[12] Fortunately, ATSs continue to be enhanced to make recruiters more efficient and extend sourcing into the global market. Developers of ATSs are now focusing efforts on developing quality-of-hire metrics.

Helene Richter, director of talent operations for Liz Claiborne, New York City, said, "People choose an applicant-tracking tool to streamline process. But you have EEO and compliance issues that you need to streamline as well." The applicant-tracking function does both.[13] Hiring information is tracked to comply with Office of Federal Contract Compliance Programs.

The purpose of *candidate relationship management (CRM)* is to help manage potential and actual applicants in an organized manner. It is useful in managing the relationship between the company and prospective applicants.[14] CRM can be used to send job postings and job descriptions to job boards and other sites. It has the capability to search the Internet, including social media sites, for résumés, and then adds and catalogues them and other information to the database. CRM systems can link with other ATSs and any Web site. CRM systems permit candidates to get to know more about the company and allow the company to get to know more about the candidate.

CRM systems are used to communicate with those who have applied or appear qualified for jobs with the firm. Once the CRM system identifies an individual who might be appropriate for an open position, the system can e-mail that person asking them to respond. Gerry Crispin, a principal at the consulting firm CareerXroads in Kendall Park, New Jersey, said, "Candidate relationship management systems can provide information that helps a candidate recognize himself as an employee of the company, creating an 'I'd fit there' attitude."[15]

The Internet has created a situation in which many résumés can be received. Often, candidates send an application and never get a reply. Whether because of arrogance, ignorance, or incompetence, companies sometime fail to inform applicants after they have been rejected. To overcome this situation, organizations use CRM software to help job seekers have good experiences with the companies' Web sites and to bolster efforts to build talent pools. Companies truly dedicated to CRM do not stop after sending an auto reply; they also let them know when the position has been filled.

6.2 Explain the importance of preliminary screening as well as reviewing applications and résumés.

preliminary screening
In employee selection, a review to eliminate those who obviously do not meet the position's requirements.

Preliminary Screening and Review of Applications and Résumés

The selection process often begins with preliminary screening. The basic purpose of **preliminary screening** is to eliminate those who obviously do not meet the position's requirements. Preliminary screening may take the form of reviewing for obviously unqualified applicants with a brief interview, test, or only a review of the application or résumé for clear mismatches. In addition to eliminating clearly unqualified job applicants quickly, preliminary screening may produce other positive benefits for the firm. It is possible that the position for which the applicant applied is not the only one available. If the person doing the screening knows about other vacancies in the firm, he or she may be able to steer the prospective employee to another position. For instance, the assessor may decide that although an applicant is not a good fit for the applications-engineering job, she is an excellent candidate for an internal research-and-development position. This type of assessment not only builds goodwill for the firm but also can maximize recruitment and selection effectiveness.

At times, a short test may be administered to determine if a person should proceed in the selection process. For example, in the recruitment of sales representatives, a brief sales aptitude test may be given to determine if the applicant has a talent or interest in sales. Then, the company knows that the people they interview are already more likely to succeed in the role. By conducting a quick assessment before scheduling interviews, the company is more likely to hire people who will add value to the organization.

Having the candidate complete an application for employment is another early step in the selection process. This step may either precede or follow preliminary screening. The employer then evaluates it to see whether there is an apparent match between the individual and the position. A well-designed and properly used application form can be helpful because essential information is included and presented in a standardized format. Completion of an application may not be initially required for many management and professional positions. In these cases, a résumé may suffice. A complete application usually is obtained later—often for job candidates who have successfully passed the initial screening process and for whom the company intends to further consider for employment.

The specific information requested on an application form may vary from firm to firm, and even by job type within an organization. An application typically contains sections for name, address, telephone number, e-mail address, military service, education, and work history. Managers compare the information contained in a completed application to the job description to determine whether a potential match exists between the firm's requirements and the applicant's qualifications. As you might expect, this judgment is often difficult.

Several pre-printed statements are usually included on the application form. First, by signing the form, the applicant certifies that information provided on the form is accurate and true. Employers will likely reject candidates who make false claims for key issues. Candidates may be terminated after employment if they made any representation or statement that was not accurate or if they did not disclose matters that might significantly prejudice the employer's hiring decision. Second, when not prohibited by state law, the form should also state that a condition of employment is employment-at-will. *Employment-at-will* is a policy that either the employer or the employee can terminate employment at any time for any reason. Finally, the form should contain a statement whereby the candidate gives permission to have his or her background and references checked.

An employment application form must reflect not only the firm's informational needs but also legal requirements. Potentially discriminatory questions inquiring about such factors as gender, race, age, convictions, national origin, citizenship, birthplace, dependents, disabilities, religion, color, and marital status should be avoided.

Applicants sometimes deliberately leave out information on the application that may present them in a negative light. To combat this problem, many employers are requiring applicants to use online applications that force a person to complete a required field before the application is successfully submitted. In fact, corporations have increasingly declined to accept a printed résumé, and applicants are directed to company Web sites for employment application and résumé submission.

résumé
Goal-directed summary of a person's experience, education, and training developed for use in the selection process.

A **résumé** is a goal-directed summary of a person's experience, education, and training developed for use in the selection process. Professional and managerial applicants often begin the selection process by submitting a résumé. Figure 6-2 illustrates a traditional résumé. Note that the résumé includes the career objective for the specific position the applicant is seeking. Some human resources (HR) professionals suggest that a professional summary at the beginning of the résumé is more useful to the recruiter. However, young job seekers with little work experience may be best served by using a career objective statement. The remainder of the résumé should be directed toward showing how a person has the skills and competencies necessary to accomplish the position identified in the career objective statement.[16] Using keywords from the job description or employment ad will help an applicant get past the résumé-scanning programs many firms use.[17] Only information necessary to show a relationship to the objective should be included. The all-important concept of relevancy is crucial in selling the applicant to the company. A new trend that has evolved over time is that the content of the résumé is more important than fitting an applicant's entire career onto one page. Historically, a one-page résumé was the standard that applicants were told to use.

FIGURE 6-2
Example of a Traditional Résumé

Marianne Sanders

Current Address
1234 Main Street
Anytown, MA 02176
Phone: 555.555.5151
E-mail: MSanders@internet.com

Objective:	To obtain an entry level position in accounting.
Education:	Southern State University **Bachelor of Science, Accounting,** **Expected date of graduation, May 2019** **GPA: 3.5/4.0**
Experience:	January 2017 – Present Accounting Internship with McElroy, Quirk, & Burch, APC (Accounting firm) Lake Charles, LA January 2015 – December 2012 McNeese State University Student worker (Financial Aid) Lake Charles, LA • Assist full-time worker with office work • Help students complete financial aid question/forms
Honors:	Beta Gamma Sigma Honor Fraternity Beta Alpha Psi Honor Fraternity Pi Beta Lambda – Business Professionals President Honor Role (Six times)
Personal:	Hard working, goal-oriented, conscientious, positive thinker, work well in teams, excellent people skills
Interests:	Accounting, physical fitness, traveling, tennis
Software Proficiency:	Microsoft Office 2010, Excel, Word, PowerPoint, Windows 7, Drop Office 2010, Social Networking (Facebook, Twitter, LinkedIn)

In developing a résumé, the sender should be careful not to misrepresent the truth. An applicant who has three credit hours to meet graduation requirements has not graduated, and therefore, does not possess the degree for which she or he is studying. Certainly, the résumé should be designed to present the applicant in a positive light, but without exaggeration. Regarding job history, dates of employment should be accurate. It goes without saying that résumés should not contain grammar and spelling errors. The résumé should show that the applicant understands the job and how his or her work history can assist in accomplishing the job.

When sending a résumé via the Internet, applicants should realize that most large companies now use applicant-tracking systems. These systems assume a certain résumé style. Résumés that deviate from the assumed style are ignored or deleted. These systems scan résumés into databases, search the databases on command, and rank the résumés according to the number of resulting "hits" they receive. At times, such searches use multiple (10–20) criteria. Some systems flag résumés that appear to misrepresent the truth, present misleading information, or are in other ways suspicious.

The use of applicant-tracking systems coupled with the downsizing of HR departments has resulted in a situation in which many résumés are never seen by human eyes once they enter the system. Therefore, a job applicant should make his or her résumé as computer/scanner friendly as possible so that its life in a database will be extended. Even if you are a perfect match for the job, your résumé may never get to someone who could decipher your potential value. To make the process work, a keyword résumé style should be used. **Keywords** refer to those words or phrases that are used to search databases for résumés that match. A **keyword résumé** contains an adequate description of the job seeker's characteristics and industry-specific experience presented in keyword terms to accommodate the computer search process. The keywords are often job titles, skills, or areas of expertise related to the position. Keywords tend to be more of the noun or noun-phrase type (Office 2016, Windows 10, Biochemist) as opposed to power action verbs often found in traditional résumés (developed, coordinated, empowered, organized). Another way to look at keyword phrases is to think in terms of job duties. The terms employers search for most often are problem solving and decision making, oral and written communication, customer service or retention, performance and productivity improvement, leadership, technology, team building, project management, and bilingual.

keywords
Words or phrases that are used to search databases for résumés that match.

keyword résumé
Résumé that contains an adequate description of the job seeker's characteristics and industry-specific experience presented in keyword terms to accommodate the computer search process.

Applicants should study the job posting and industry ads to get an overview of the phrases that keep reappearing. Detailing an individual's job duties may require a change in mind-set away from traditional résumé writing. Recruiters should be mindful that applicants have gotten smarter in résumé preparation and at times include words that hardly resemble their past accomplishment.

6.3 Describe the use of tests in the selection process.

Selection Tests

Tests are essential components of employee selection. There are many considerations, including advantages and disadvantages, property of tests, validation approaches, and test type. We also conclude this section with a review of important legal matters that pertain to selection tests.

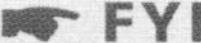

FYI

The use of selection tests is on the rise. In 2015, 57 percent of large U.S. employers used selection testing, up from 26 percent in 2013.[18]

Preliminary Considerations

Recognizing the shortcomings of other selection tools, many firms have added selection tests to their hiring process. These tests rate factors such as aptitude, personality, abilities, and motivation of potential employees, allowing managers to choose candidates according to how they will fit into the open positions and corporate culture. However, tests alone are not enough to make a sufficient evaluation of a candidate because they are not fool proof. Firms need to use them in conjunction with other selection tools such as reference checks and interviews.

Advantages and Disadvantages of Selection Tests

Research indicates that customized tests can be a reliable and accurate means to predict on-the-job performance.[19] Organizations use tests to identify attitudes and job-related skills that interviews cannot recognize. Also, the cost of employment testing is small in comparison to ultimate hiring costs. They are a more efficient way to get at information that results in better-qualified people being hired.

Job performance depends on an individual's ability and motivation to do the work. Selection tests may accurately predict an applicant's ability to perform the job, the *can do*, but they are less successful in indicating the extent to which the individual will be motivated to perform it, the *will do*. The most successful employees are likely to have two things in common: they identify with their firm's goals, and they are highly motivated. For one reason or another, some employees with high potential never seem to reach it. The factors related to success on the job are so numerous and complex that selection may always be more of an art than a science.

Employers should be aware that tests might be unintentionally discriminatory. Office of Federal Contract Compliance Programs (OFCCP) former director Charles E. James Sr. said, "Testing is a 'necessary business tool' to help employers select qualified candidates. Hiring the wrong person puts your company at risk. The key is to make the test fit the job you're using it for."[20] When a test excludes a protected class at a significant rate, the test should be avoided unless the employer can show that the test is job related for the position in question and consistent with business necessity. Using selection tests carries with it legal liabilities of two types. One is a lawsuit from rejected applicants who claim a test was not job related or that it unfairly discriminated against a protected group, violating federal employment laws. The second potential legal problem relates to *negligent hiring* lawsuits filed by victims of employee misbehavior or incompetence (a topic discussed later in this chapter).

Test anxiety can also be a problem. Applicants often become quite anxious when confronting yet another hurdle that might eliminate them from consideration. The test administrator's reassuring manner and a well-organized testing operation should serve to reduce this threat. Although a great deal of anxiety is detrimental to test performance, a slight degree is helpful.

The problems of hiring unqualified or less-qualified candidates and rejecting qualified candidates will continue regardless of the procedures followed. Well-developed tests administered by competent professionals help organizations minimize such consequences.

Characteristics of Properly Designed Selection Tests

Properly designed selection tests are standardized, objective, based on sound norms, reliable, and of utmost importance, valid. These concepts and the application of these concepts are discussed next.

standardization
Uniformity of the procedures and conditions related to administering tests.

STANDARDIZATION The uniformity of the procedures and conditions related to administering tests is **standardization**. To compare the performance of several applicants taking the same test, it is necessary for all to take the same test under conditions that are as identical as possible. For example, the content of instructions provided and the time allowed must be the same, and the physical environment must be similar. If one person takes a test in a room with jackhammers operating just outside and another takes it in a more tranquil environment, differences in test results are likely.

objectivity
Condition that is achieved when everyone scoring a given test obtains the same results.

OBJECTIVITY In testing, **objectivity** occurs when everyone scoring a test obtains the same results. Multiple-choice and true/false tests are objective. The person taking the test either chooses the correct answer or does not.

norm
Frame of reference for comparing an applicant's performance with that of others.

NORMS A frame of reference for comparing an applicant's performance with that of others is a **norm**. Specifically, a norm reflects the distribution of many scores obtained by people similar to the applicant being tested. A score by itself is insignificant. It becomes meaningful only when compared with other applicants' scores. To better understand this important concept, think about one of the standardized tests required for college admission such as the ACT or SAT. For example, scores of 400 and 700 have limited usefulness. At best, they indicate that the applicant who scored 700 answered more questions correctly than the applicant who scored 400, and this conclusion might favor admission for the higher score. However, a comparison of raw test scores does not inform college admissions committees about how well these individuals performed relative to everyone who took this test. A more useful metric is to convert the raw scores into percentile rankings. For example, a percentile ranking of 90 tells admissions committees that the raw scores earned by those in this percentile ranking exceed 90 percent of the scores of other test takers.

When enough employees are performing the same or similar work, employers can standardize their own tests. Typically, this is not the case, and a national norm for a test is used. A prospective employee takes the test, the score obtained is compared to the norm, and the significance of the test score is then determined.

reliability
Extent to which a selection test provides consistent results.

RELIABILITY The extent to which a selection test provides consistent results is **reliability**. For example, if a person were to take the same test of personality several times and received highly similar scores (consistent results), this personality test would be judged to be reliable. Reliability data reveal the degree of confidence placed in a test. For example, if a person scores 130 on a certain test of conscientiousness this week and retakes the test next week and scores 80, the test reliability would likely be low. Tests with low reliability have implications for validity. For example, if a test has low reliability, its validity (accuracy) as a predictor (for example, of job performance) will also be low. If after scoring 130 the first week a person scores another 130 the second week, the test is reliable. However, the existence of reliability alone does not guarantee the test's validity.

Reliability is expressed as a correlation coefficient. A correlation coefficient shows the strength and direction of the relationship between two variables, for example, personality measured at time 1 (say, on February 1, 2018) and the same personality test measured later, time 2 (say, on December 1, 2018). Correlation coefficients can range between −1.0 and +1.0. In the cases of −1.0 and +1.0, there is evidence of perfect correlation. For example, when the correlation coefficient is +1.0, for every 1-unit change in personality test score at time 1, we see a corresponding 1-unit *increase* in personality score at time 2. When the correlation coefficient is −1.0, for every 1-unit change in personality score assessed at time 1, we see a corresponding 1-unit *decrease* in personality measured at time 2. When the correlation coefficient equals 0, then there is no correspondence between changes in scores on the personality test at times 1 and 2. In the selection context, we hope to obtain correlations equal to +1.0. Realistically, correlation coefficients fall somewhere between these scores, which allows us to talk about the reliability of the test in terms of *degrees* of reliability. The goal is to obtain positive correlations that are as close to 1.0 as possible. Correlations equal to zero or thereabouts have no utility as a selection tool. That is, such tests do not aid in the selection process.

validity
Extent to which a test measures what it claims to measure.

VALIDITY The basic requirement for a selection test is that it be valid. **Validity** is the extent to which a test measures what it claims to measure. If a test cannot indicate ability to perform the job, it has no value. And if used, it will result in poor hiring decisions and a potential legal liability for the employer.

Title VII requires the test to work without having an adverse impact on minorities, females, and individuals with backgrounds or characteristics protected under the law. If using the test results in an adverse impact on certain members of protected groups, the firm must have a compelling reason why it is used; that is, it must validate the test. Employers are not required to validate their selection tests automatically.

Test Validation Approaches

The *Uniform Guidelines on Employee Selection Procedures* established three approaches to validating selection tests: criterion-related validity, content validity, and construct validity.

criterion-related validity
Test validation method that compares the scores on selection tests to some aspect of job performance determined, for example, by performance appraisal.

CRITERION-RELATED VALIDITY A test validation method that compares the scores on selection tests to some aspect of job performance determined, for example, by performance appraisal is **criterion-related validity**. Performance measures might include quantity and quality of work, turnover, and absenteeism. A close relationship between the score on the test and job performance suggests that the test is valid. The two basic forms of criterion-related validity are concurrent and predictive validity.

Concurrent validity is determined when the firm obtains test scores and the criterion data at essentially the same time. For instance, it administers the test to all currently employed telemarketers and compares the results with company records that contain current information about each employee's job performance. If the test can identify productive and less productive workers, one could say that it is valid. A potential problem in using this validation procedure results from changes that may have occurred within the work group. For example, firms may have fired the less productive workers, and promoted the more productive employees out of the group.

Predictive validity involves administering a test and later obtaining the criterion information. For instance, all applicants take the test but the firm uses other selection criteria, not the test results, to make the selection decision. After observing employee performance over time, the company analyzes test results to determine whether they differentiate the successful and less successful employees.

content validity
Test validation method whereby a person performs certain tasks that are required by the job or completes a paper-and-pencil test that measures relevant job knowledge.

CONTENT VALIDITY A test validation method whereby a person performs certain tasks that are required by the job or completes a paper-and-pencil test that measures relevant job knowledge is **content validity**. Although statistical concepts are not involved, many practitioners believe that content validity provides a sensible approach to validating a selection test. This form of validation requires thorough job analysis and carefully prepared job descriptions. An example of the use of content validity is giving a word-processing test to an applicant whose primary job would be word processing. Court decisions have supported the concept of content validity.

construct validity
Test validation method that determines whether a test measures certain constructs, or traits, that job analysis finds to be important in performing a job.

CONSTRUCT VALIDITY A test validation method that determines whether a test measures certain constructs, or traits, that job analysis finds to be important in performing a job is **construct validity**. For instance, a sales representative position may require the applicant to be extroverted and assertive. The goal in construct validation studies is to observe correlations between the test under study and a grouping of related variables such as positive correlations between extroversion and sales performance as well as between assertiveness and sales performance. It is equally important to establish statistically insignificant correlations between the measures of constructs for which there is no reason to expect a relationship—for instance, birth month and job performance. Construct validity in and of itself is not a primary method for validating selection tests.

Employment Tests

aptitude tests
A test of how well a person can learn or acquire skills or abilities.

achievement tests
A test of current knowledge and skills.

cognitive ability tests
Tests that determine general reasoning ability, memory, vocabulary, verbal fluency, and numerical ability.

Individuals differ in characteristics related to job performance. Broadly, tests fall into one of two categories: aptitude tests and achievement tests. **Aptitude tests** measure how well a person can learn or acquire skills or abilities. **Achievement tests** assess a person's current knowledge and skills. These differences, which are measurable, relate to cognitive abilities, psychomotor abilities, job knowledge, work samples, and personality.

COGNITIVE ABILITY TESTS Tests that determine general reasoning ability, memory, vocabulary, verbal fluency, and numerical ability are **cognitive ability tests**.

Cognitive ability tests are a form of IQ tests and these measure the capacity of an individual to learn at higher levels of difficulty (for example, learning to write at the fifth-grade level and learning to write at the college level). As the content of jobs becomes broader and more fluid, employees must be able to adapt quickly to job changes and rapid technological advances. It is likely that testing will be necessary to match the broader range of characteristics required for successful performance of these flexible jobs. The NFL uses the Wonderlic Personnel Test, which is designed to measure cognitive ability, the applicant's natural aptitude for learning new information.

PSYCHOMOTOR ABILITIES TESTS Psychomotor abilities refer to the capacity to connect brain or cognitive functions and functions of the body such as physical strength. An example of a psychomotor ability is reaction time, which is defined as, "the ability to quickly respond (with the hand, finger, or foot) to a signal (sound, light, picture) when it appears."[21]

personality
Individual differences in characteristic patterns of thinking, feeling, and behaving.

personality tests
Self-reported measures of traits, temperaments, or dispositions.

PERSONALITY TESTS According to the American Psychological Association, "**personality** refers to individual differences in characteristic patterns of thinking, feeling and behaving. The study of personality focuses on two broad areas: one is understanding individual differences in particular personality characteristics, such as sociability or irritability. The other is understanding how the various parts of a person come together as a whole."[22] Self-reported measures of temperaments, or dispositions, are **personality tests**. For example, health-care social workers, "Job requires being reliable, responsible, and dependable, and fulfilling obligations."[23] Personality tests, unlike ability tests, are not time constrained and do not measure specific problem-solving skills. These questionnaires tap into areas, such as leadership, teamwork, and personal assertiveness. Vacation planning company Delaware North found that they hired better fitting employees after including personality testing in their selection process. The company used personality testing to identify individuals who demonstrated traits such as friendliness, curiosity, and ability to multitask.[24] With careful planning, a properly designed personality profile can measure and match the appropriate personality dimensions to the requirements of the job.

Most large companies now use psychometric testing to identify future managers. These individuals are being assessed for their ability to bring about long-term change and their ability to handle day-to-day management tasks. Generally, fire departments and law enforcement agencies use the Minnesota Multiphasic Personality Inventory (MMPI) test, which consists of 567 statements that help to determine a subject's degree of paranoia, depression, mania, or anxiety. In police departments, the MMPI is used to detect the inclination toward substance abuse. These types of tests are typically used in the early stage of the selection process.

Integrity tests represent a specific type of personality attribute. Integrity refers to, "being honest and ethical."[25] Employers have used them to measure candidates' attitudes toward theft, dishonesty, absenteeism, violence, drug use, alcohol abuse, and other counterproductive behaviors. Retail stores, nuclear plants, law enforcement agencies, and child-care facilities typically use integrity tests. Research has shown that integrity tests have high validity for predicting undesirable behaviors at work.[26] Because the polygraph test (discussed later) has been effectively banned in the private sector as a hiring tool, integrity tests have often been used to detect dishonesty in candidates.

As the previous discussion indicates, many companies consider a variety of factors before offering employment. Rudi's Organic Bakery discusses the elements and dimensions they look for in potential employees. In addition to looking at a candidate's "ability" (mental horsepower to understand and process information and find solutions to problems), which comes from experience, they are also looking at "personality" (how motivated a person is and how they will interact as part of a team). Besides "technical fit"—a background in food science—the company is looking for how an individual will fit into the company's organizational culture and wants individuals who are reliable, positive, team players, and proactive. The following Watch It video describes Rudi Bakery's employee selection considerations.

 **Watch It 1**

If your instructor has assigned this, go to **www.pearson.com/mylab/management** to watch a video titled Rudi's Bakery: Ability and Testing and respond to questions.

CH2M Hill is another example of a company that considers both ability and personality in their selection process. An employee from CH2M Hill, an industry-leading and global project delivery engineering firm, discusses key indicators that they look for in potential employees—from ability (technical fit) to personality (organizational fit) and why these indicators are essential to finding the right candidate for the job.

 **Watch It 2**

If your instructor has assigned this, go to **www.pearson.com/mylab/management** to watch a video titled CH2M Hill's and respond to questions.

job-knowledge tests
Tests designed to measure a candidate's knowledge of the duties of the job for which he or she is applying.

JOB-KNOWLEDGE TESTS Tests that measure a candidate's knowledge of the duties of the job for which he or she is applying are **job-knowledge tests**. For example, lawyers must have knowledge of law and government, which is defined as, "Knowledge of laws, legal codes, court procedures, precedents, government regulations, executive orders, agency rules, and the democratic political process."[27] Such tests are commercially available but individual firms may also design them specifically for any job, based on data derived from job analysis.

work-sample tests
Tests that require an applicant to perform a task or set of tasks representative of the job.

JOB PERFORMANCE AND WORK-SAMPLES Tests that require an applicant to perform a task or set of tasks representative of the job are **work-sample tests**. For positions that require heavy use of spreadsheets, having the applicant construct a sample spreadsheet, with data the firm provides, will be useful in assessing a required ability. Electrical and electronic equipment assemblers, "position, align, or adjust work pieces or electrical parts to facilitate wiring or assembly."[28] Such tests, by their nature, are job related. A real test of validity, in the opinion of some experts, should be a performance assessment: take individuals to a job and give them the opportunity to perform it.

assessment center
Selection technique that requires individuals to perform activities similar to those they might encounter in an actual job.

An **assessment center** is a selection approach that requires individuals to perform activities similar to those they might encounter in an actual job. The assessment center is one of the most powerful tools for assessing managerial talent because it is designed to determine if they will be effective in performing a specific job. Research has established the validity of the assessment center approach to predicting performance. Many of the top companies in the United States have set up assessment centers where they can first interview potential employees and then evaluate them in real work situations. It provides an excellent way to determine an individual's capabilities to perform an entry-level management job.

In an assessment center, candidates perform several exercises that simulate the tasks they will carry out in the job they seek. Typical assessment center tests include having applicants complete *in-basket exercises* and perform in *management games*, *leaderless discussion groups*, *mock interviews*, and other simulations. The traditional in-basket exercise has received a technological boost by replacing the paper memos with e-mail messages, faxes, tweets, or voice mail. Assessment centers measure candidates' skills in prioritizing, delegating, and decision making. The professional assessors who evaluate the candidates' performance usually observe them away from the workplace over a certain period, perhaps a single day. The assessors selected are typically experienced managers who may not only evaluate performance but also participate in the exercises.

HR Web Wisdom
Genetic Testing
http://ghr.nlm.nih.gov/
A guide to understanding genetic conditions.

An advantage of the assessment center approach is the increased reliability and validity of the information provided. Research has shown that the in-basket exercise, a typical component of assessment centers, is a good predictor of management performance. Its validity provides an alternative to paper-and-pencil tests.

Unique Forms of Testing

genetic tests
Tests given to identify predisposition to inherited diseases, including cancer, heart disease, neurological disorders, and congenital diseases.

GENETIC TESTING Tests performed to identify predisposition to inherited diseases, including cancer, heart disease, neurological disorders, and congenital diseases are **genetic tests**. DNA-testing companies can tell us our potential risk for breast cancer, cystic fibrosis, Alzheimer's disease, and other common chronic conditions. Scientists have assembled the entire set of genetic instructions for building a human body, and world leaders likened this achievement to putting a human being on the moon. This brings both hope and concerns to the forefront in employment testing.

Genetic tests may predict a predisposition to having a disease. However, such tests cannot tell whether a person is certain to get the disease or when he or she would become ill. In addition, everyone has some disposition to genetic disease and a genetic predisposition is different from a preexisting condition.

The Equal Employment Opportunity Commission (EEOC) has issued guidelines stating that healthy individuals with a genetic predisposition to a disease, and thus perceived as disabled, are protected by the Americans with Disabilities Act (ADA). The Genetic Information Nondiscrimination Act (GINA) of 2008 is designed to prohibit the improper use of genetic information in health insurance and employment. Recently the EEOC issued a final regulation, which generally bars employers, unions, employment agencies, and joint apprenticeship programs from requesting, requiring, or purchasing an individual's genetic information and making employment decisions based on such data.[29]

graphoanalysis
Use of handwriting analysis as a selection factor.

GRAPHOANALYSIS (HANDWRITING ANALYSIS) The use of handwriting analysis as a selection factor is **graphoanalysis**. Many in the United States view handwriting analysis in the same context as psychic readings or astrology. In Europe, however, many employers use graphoanalysis to help screen and place job applicants. It is not unusual for European companies to have full-time handwriting analysts on staff. With graphoanalysis, every stroke of handwriting has a meaning that can be understood only within the context of the other strokes present in the handwriting.

Although no definitive study exists on the extent of its use in the United States, according to some handwriting experts, graphoanalysis is becoming more common. A basic reason for the reluctance of U.S. employers to use this approach appears to be a concern over the ability to validate such tests. And there is little research demonstrating the effectiveness of graphology in employee selection. This and the worry about possible legal action seem to make many U.S. employers wary of the process.

POLYGRAPH TESTS For many years, another means used to verify background information was the polygraph, or lie-detector test. One purpose of the polygraph was to confirm or refute the information contained in a candidate's application. However, the *Employee Polygraph Protection Act* of 1988 prohibited the use of polygraph tests in the private sector. However, the act does not apply to governmental employers, and there are other limited exceptions. Even here, the technology has been found to be flawed. Effective techniques for beating lie detectors, which only measure stress and anxiety, have been developed and are available for use.

The act permits use of polygraph tests in the private sector in screening certain prospective employees for security service firms and pharmaceutical manufacturers, distributors, and dispensers. The act also permits, with certain restrictions, polygraph testing of certain employees reasonably suspected of involvement in a workplace incident, such as theft or embezzlement. Persons who take polygraph tests have a few specific rights. For example, they have the right to a written notice before testing, the right to refuse or discontinue a test, and the right not to have test results disclosed to unauthorized persons.

Legal Considerations

Earlier, we recognized the law an important environmental factor in the selection process. Now that we have studied selection testing, we will address some important examples of EEOC litigation and settlements illustrating basic EEO principles that focus on testing:[30]

- **Title VII and Cognitive Ability Tests:** Less Discriminatory Alternative for Cognitive Ability Test with Disparate Impact. *EEOC v. Ford Motor Co. and United Automobile Workers of America*, involved a court-approved settlement agreement on behalf of a nationwide class of African Americans who were rejected for an apprenticeship program after taking a cognitive ability test known as the Apprenticeship Training Selection System (ATSS). The ATSS was a written cognitive ability test that measured verbal, numerical, and spatial reasoning to evaluate mechanical aptitude. Although it had been validated in 1991, the ATSS continued to have a statistically significant disparate impact by excluding African American applicants. Less discriminatory selection procedures were subsequently developed that would have served Ford's needs, but Ford did not modify its procedures. In the settlement agreement, Ford agreed to replace the ATSS with a selection procedure, to be designed by a jointly-selected industrial psychologist, that would predict job success and reduce adverse impact. Additionally, Ford paid $8.55 million in monetary relief.
- **Title VII and Physical Strength Tests:** Strength test must be job-related and consistent with business necessity if it disproportionately excludes women. In *EEOC v. Dial Corp.*, women were disproportionately rejected for entry-level production jobs because of a strength test. The test had a significant adverse impact on women; prior to the use of the test, 46 percent of hires were women, and after use of the test, only 15 percent of hires were women. Dial defended the test by noting that it looked like the job and use of the test had resulted in fewer injuries to hired workers. The EEOC established through expert testimony, however, that the test was considerably more difficult than the job and that the reduction in injuries occurred two years before the test was implemented, most likely because of improved training and better job rotation procedures. On appeal, the Eighth Circuit upheld the trial court's finding that Dial's use of the test violated Title VII under the disparate impact theory of discrimination. *See* www.eeoc.gov/press/11-20-06.html.
- **ADA and Test Accommodation:** Employer must provide reasonable accommodation on pre-employment test for hourly, unskilled manufacturing jobs. The EEOC settled *EEOC v. Daimler Chrysler Corp.*, a case brought on behalf of applicants with learning disabilities who needed reading accommodations during a pre-employment test given for hourly unskilled manufacturing jobs. The resulting settlement agreement provided monetary relief for 12 identified individuals and the opportunity to take the hiring test with the assistance

of a reader. The settlement agreement also required that the employer provide a reasonable accommodation on this test to each applicant who requested a reader and provided documentation establishing an ADA disability. The accommodation consisted of either a reader for all instructions and all written parts of the test, or an audiotape providing the same information.

6.4 Explain the use of the employment interview.

Employment Interview

employment interview
Goal-oriented conversation in which an interviewer and an applicant exchange information.

The **employment interview** is a goal-oriented conversation in which the interviewer and applicant exchange information. Traditionally, interviews have not been valid predictors of success on the job.[31] In fact, courts are often suspicious of hiring decisions based primarily on interview results because of their inherently subjective nature. For more than 500 years, Leonardo da Vinci's *Mona Lisa* has confounded viewers who try to read her expression. Like the *Mona Lisa*, every job applicant presents a mysterious façade. Nevertheless, interviews continue to be the primary method companies use to evaluate applicants. The employment interview is especially important because the applicants who reach this stage are the survivors. They have endured preliminary screening, had their applications reviewed, and scored satisfactorily on selection tests. At this point, the candidates appear to be qualified, at least on paper. Every seasoned manager knows, however, that appearances can be quite misleading. Additional information is needed to indicate whether the individual is willing to work and can adapt to that organization (organizational fit).

Interview Planning

Interview planning is essential to effective employment interviews. A primary consideration should be the speed in which the process occurs. Many studies have demonstrated that the top candidates for nearly any job are hired and off the job market within anywhere from 1 to 10 days.

The physical location of the interview should be both pleasant and private, providing for a minimum of interruptions. The interviewer should possess a pleasant personality, empathy, and the ability to listen and communicate effectively. He or she should become familiar with the applicant's qualifications by reviewing the data collected from other selection tools. As preparation for the interview, the interviewer should develop a job profile based on the job description/specification. After listing job requirements, it is helpful to have an interview checklist that involves comparing an applicant's application and résumé with the job description. Also, questions should be prepared that relate to the qualities needed in a person being sought. In doing so, it is helpful to ask for examples of past job-related applicant behavior.

HR BLOOPERS

The First Interview

As Henry Davidson heads to the conference room for his first interview, he starts to think about what he is going to ask the candidate. As a new Human Resources Assistant at Samson Corporation, Henry is conducting interviews of candidates being considered for an administrative assistant position. Although he has a degree in HR and has worked in the field for more than a year now, this is his first opportunity to conduct an interview. His manager directed him to the company's interview training program, but Henry believes that an interview is just a conversation so he didn't bother with the training. He has great interpersonal skills and can't wait to tell the candidate all about the company. As Henry enters the room and shakes the candidate's hand, he realizes that he forgot to bring her résumé and the job description he had sitting on his desk. He's not worried though, as he is good at engaging people in conversation and should do just fine without them. After greeting the candidate, Henry spends the first 20 minutes telling her about the job and the company. Once finished he asks her to, "tell me about yourself." The first thing Henry learns is that she attended the same college as he did, so he knows she is a good candidate. Although he is unsure on what to ask next, he doesn't think it matters as he already knows he is going to recommend her for the job.

If your professor has assigned this, go to **www.pearson.com/mylab/management** to complete the HR Bloopers exercise and test your application of these concepts when faced with real-world decisions.

Content of the Interview

Both the interviewer and the candidate have agendas for the interview. After establishing rapport with the applicant, the interviewer seeks additional job-related information to complement data provided by other selection tools. The interview permits clarification of certain points, the uncovering of additional information, and the elaboration of data needed to make a sound selection decision. The interviewer should provide information about the company, the job, and expectations of the candidate. Other areas typically included in the interview are discussed next.

OCCUPATIONAL EXPERIENCE The interviewer will explore the candidate's knowledge, skills, abilities, and willingness to handle responsibility. Although successful performance in one job does not guarantee success in another, it does provide an indication of the person's ability and willingness to work.

ACADEMIC ACHIEVEMENT In the absence of significant work experience, a person's academic record takes on greater importance. Managers should, however, consider grade point average in the light of other factors. For example, involvement in work, extracurricular activities, or other responsibilities may have affected an applicant's academic performance.

INTERPERSONAL SKILLS An individual may possess important technical skills significant to accomplishing a job. However, if the person cannot work well with others, chances for success are slim. This is especially true in today's world, with the increasing use of teams. The biggest mistake an interviewee can make is thinking that firms hire people only for their technical skills. Indeed, more and more companies are competing for people who have both technical skills and "soft" skills such as the ability to get along with coworkers. For instance, a CEO of a financial investment company said, "You can't just be the general of your own army."[32]

PERSONAL QUALITIES Personal qualities normally observed during the interview include physical appearance, speaking ability, vocabulary, poise, adaptability, assertiveness, leadership ability, and cooperative spirit. As with all selection criteria, these attributes should be considered only if they are relevant to job performance.

Candidate's Role and Expectations

Although the interviewer will provide information about the company, it is still important for candidates to do their homework, including studying the job description and checking the Internet (including the firm's Web site) before the interview. Employees are also conducting background checks on companies to check out potential employers on such things as financial stability, whether the company would be a good place to work, and career opportunities. Most company sites include information tailored to job seekers. They often provide a history of the company and a description of its products and customers. Applicants can often find out the culture of the firm by doing a thorough search of the Internet and the news media. WetFeet.com provides insightful profiles of companies, careers, and industries to guide job seekers toward finding the right career, the right industry, the right company, and the right job for them. A person applying for a management position, especially, should have a thorough understanding of the firm's business priorities, its strengths and weaknesses, and its major competitors. Applicants should consider how they would address some of the issues facing the company. They need to be able to show how their experiences can help in addressing these issues.

HR Web Wisdom
www.wetfeet.com/

Helps equip job seekers with the advice, research, and inspiration needed to plan and achieve a successful career

Recruiters need to remember that interviewees also have objectives for the interview. One might be to determine what the firm is willing to pay as a starting salary. Job seekers have other goals that may include the following:

- To be listened to and understood
- To have ample opportunity to present their qualifications
- To be treated fairly and with respect
- To gather information about the job and the company
- To make an informed decision concerning the desirability of the job

Candidates can learn what interviewing skills they need to improve by undergoing a mock interview or two. Having a colleague or friend interview them and afterward critically reviewing their own responses can be beneficial. This mock interview allows candidates to analyze the strengths and interests that they would bring to a job. The process would also help them prioritize the points they want to make in the real interview.

General Types of Interviews

Types of interviews are often broadly classified as unstructured, structured, behavioral, and situational. A discussion of the differences follows.

unstructured interview
Interview in which the job applicant is asked probing, open-ended questions.

UNSTRUCTURED INTERVIEW An **unstructured interview** is one in which the interviewer asks probing, open-ended questions. This type of interview is comprehensive, and the interviewer encourages the applicant to do much of the talking. Questions such as, "What professional accomplishments are you most proud of and why?"; "What is your greatest professional strength, and how have you used it to overcome a challenge in your career?"; and "What specifically attracted you to our organization?" might be asked. The unstructured interview is often more time consuming than the structured interview and results in obtaining different information from different candidates. This adds to the potential legal woes of organizations using this approach. Compounding the problem is the likelihood of discussing ill-advised, potentially discriminatory information. Applicants who are being encouraged to pour their heart out may volunteer facts that the interviewer does not need or want to know. Unsuccessful applicants subjected to this interviewing approach may later claim in court that the reason for their failure to get the job was the employer's use of this information.

structured interview
Interview in which the interviewer asks each applicant for a particular job the same series of job-related questions.

STRUCTURED INTERVIEW In the **structured interview**, the interviewer asks each applicant for a job the same series of job-related questions. Although interviews have historically been very poor predictors of job success, use of structured interviews increases reliability and accuracy by reducing the subjectivity and inconsistency of unstructured interviews. With the structured interview, questions are developed and asked in the same order of all applicants applying for the vacant position. This makes it easier to compare candidates fairly. There is a better chance that the best candidate will be selected using this technique. Often benchmark answers are determined beforehand.

Certainly, job-knowledge questions would be asked to probe the applicant's job-related knowledge; these questions may relate to basic educational skills or complex scientific or managerial skills. Worker requirements questions might also be asked of each applicant to determine the applicant's willingness to conform to the requirements of the job. For example, the interviewer may ask whether the applicant is willing to perform repetitive work or move to another city. Determining what questions to ask involves a thorough analysis of the position including a detailed analysis of the job description. Questions related to major job requirements in the job description make the process extremely job related.

behavioral interview
Structured interview in which applicants are asked to relate actual incidents from their past relevant to the target job.

BEHAVIORAL INTERVIEW Traditional interviewing has a reputation of being a poor predictor of job success. Because of the low success rate of traditional interviews, the behavioral interview is often used. The **behavioral interview** is a structured interview in which applicants are asked to relate actual incidents from their past relevant to the target job. Once used exclusively for senior executive positions, behavioral interviewing is now a popular technique for lower-level positions also. The assumption is that past behavior is the best predictor of future behavior.

Behavioral interviewers look for three main things: a description of a challenging situation, what the candidate did about it, and measurable results. In the behavioral interview, the questions are selected for their relevance to job success in a job. Questions are formed from the behaviors by asking applicants how they performed in the described situation. For example, when probing to determine how creative an applicant is, the candidate might be requested to, "Describe an experience when you were faced with a new problem and how you handled it."[33] Or if seeking to determine the applicant's enthusiasm, the request might be, "Relate a scenario during which you were responsible for motivating others." Behavioral interviewers ask each candidate the same open-ended questions, and then score responses on a scale. Interviewing is based on the principle that what you did previously in your life is a good predictor of what you will do in the future. Interviewees are asked to give an example of a situation when they faced a dilemma, a problem, or a situation.

In behavioral interviews, candidates may unwittingly reveal information about their attitudes, intelligence, and truthfulness. Arrogance, lack of cooperation with team members, and anger can all spill out during such an interview. Although some candidates may think the interview is all about technical skills, it is as much about them as a person as anything.

Questions asked during behavioral interviews are legally safe because they are job related. Equally important, because both questions and answers are related to successful job performance, they are more accurate in predicting whether applicants will be successful in the job they are hired to perform. It answers the one question both the hiring manager and the candidate want to know most: Is this a good fit?

situational interview Gives interviewers better insight into how candidates would perform in the work environment by creating hypothetical situations candidates would be likely to encounter on the job and asking them how they would handle them.

SITUATIONAL INTERVIEW Whereas the behavioral interview focuses on how an individual handled circumstances in the past, the **situational interview** creates hypothetical situations candidates would likely encounter on the job and asks how they would handle them. For example, the question might be asked, "One of your employees has experienced a significant decline in productivity. How would you handle it?" As another example, "You completely disagree with the way that your boss has told you to handle a project. What would you do?" Basically, a situational interview provides a preview of the "how" a candidate might handle situations in a simulated work environment. Most often, interviewers are looking to hear the best course of action. However, some companies have expanded their expectations by seeking "practical intelligence," which refers to knowing how to avoid pitfalls and potential predicaments.[34]

Methods of Interviewing

Organizations conduct interviews in several ways. The level of the open position and the appropriate labor market determine the most fitting approach. A discussion of these methods follows.

ONE-ON-ONE INTERVIEW In a typical employment interview, the applicant meets one-on-one with an interviewer. As the interview may be a highly emotional occasion for the applicant, meeting alone with the interviewer is often less threatening. This method provides a better opportunity for an effective exchange of information to take place.

group interview Meeting in which several job applicants interact in the presence of one or more company representatives.

GROUP INTERVIEW In a **group interview**, several applicants interact in the presence of one or more company representatives. This approach, although not mutually exclusive of other interview types, may provide useful insights into the candidates' interpersonal competence as they engage in a group discussion. Another advantage of this technique is that it saves time for busy professionals and executives.

board interview An interview approach in which several of the firm's representatives interview a candidate at the same time.

BOARD (OR PANEL) INTERVIEW In a **board interview**, several of the firm's representatives interview a candidate at the same time. Companies use the board interview to gain multiple viewpoints because there are many cross-functional workplace relationships in business these days. Once the interview is complete, the board members pool their evaluation of the candidate. Most Ph.D. recipients are quite familiar with the board interview because they were required to defend their dissertation as their professors asked questions. At times, some candidates claimed that professors having opposing views were deliberately placed on the board and the candidate had to tiptoe through the session, hoping not to offend anyone.

MULTIPLE INTERVIEWS At times, applicants are interviewed by peers, subordinates, and potential superiors. This approach permits the firm to get a more encompassing view of the candidate. It also gives the candidate a chance to learn more about the company from a variety of perspectives. The result of this type of interview is a stronger, more cohesive team that shares the company's culture and helps ensure organizational fit.

stress interview Form of interview in which the interviewer intentionally creates anxiety.

STRESS INTERVIEW What would you do if you were in an interview that was going quite well and all at once the interviewer said, "I think your answer is totally inadequate: it doesn't deal with my concerns at all, can't you do better than that?" You may not realize it, but you have just been exposed to a stress interview. In the **stress interview**, the interviewer intentionally creates anxiety.

Most interviewers strive to minimize stress for the candidate. However, in the stress interview, the interviewer deliberately makes the candidate uncomfortable by asking blunt and often discourteous questions. The purpose is to determine the applicant's tolerance for stress that may accompany the job. Knowledge of this factor may be important if the job requires the ability to deal with a high level of stress.

Amazon.com interviewers have been known to ask job candidates to guess how many gas stations there are in the United States or to estimate the cost to wash all of Seattle's windows. Google interviewers have also been known to ask, "You are shrunk to the height of a nickel and your mass is proportionally reduced so as to maintain your original density. You are then thrown into an empty glass blender. The blades will start moving in 60 seconds. What do you do?"[35] The answer is not as important as your logic in approaching an answer.

Stress interviews are not new. The late Admiral Hyman G. Rickover, father of the U.S. Navy's nuclear submarine program, was known to offer interviewees a chair that had one or two legs shorter than the other. The candidates' problems were compounded by the chair's polished seat. The admiral once stated that, "they had to maintain their wits about them as they answered questions while sliding off the chair."[36]

realistic job preview (RJP) Method of conveying both positive and negative job information to an applicant in an unbiased manner.

REALISTIC JOB PREVIEW A **realistic job preview (RJP)** conveys both positive and negative job information to the applicant in an unbiased manner. Many applicants have unrealistic expectations about the prospective job they are seeking. They may have been told the exciting part of the job, but the less glamorous areas are not mentioned. RJPs have become increasingly common in certain fields because of the high turnover rates and the constant cost of replacing those individuals who do not work out.[37] For instance, when conducting an interview in the fast-food restaurant industry, an applicant might be taken behind the counter to see what it is like to work in a hot, greasy environment, smell food cooking all day, and scramble around other bodies in close quarters. An inaccurate perception may occur when interviewers paint false, rosy pictures of the job and the company. This practice leads to mismatches of people and positions. What compounds the problem is when candidates exaggerate their own qualifications. The RJP should typically be done early in the selection process, and before a job offer is made.

An RJP conveys information about tasks the person would perform and the behavior required to fit into the culture of the organization. This approach helps applicants develop a more accurate perception of the job and the firm. Employers who give detailed RJPs get two results: fewer employees accept the job offer, and applicants who do accept the offer are less likely to leave the firm. Given an RJP, some candidates will take themselves out of the selection process, minimizing the number of unqualified candidates. Another reason to use RJPs is the benefit a firm receives from being an up-front, ethical employer.

As the previous discussion indicates, interviews play a crucial role in the employee selection process. Zipcar is a car-sharing business. When interviewing, they recommend not speaking negatively about past employers, being genuine but respectful, showing interest in the organization with which you are interviewing, and being prepared. The interview process helps Zipcar to identify prospective employees who are passionate about the brand, professional, courteous, and presentable. The following Watch It video describes Zipcar's perspectives on employee selection.

Watch It 3

If your instructor has assigned this, go to **www.pearson.com/mylab/management** to watch a video titled Zipcar: Interviewing Candidates and respond to questions.

Potential Interviewing Problems

Potential interviewing problems that can threaten the success of employment interviews are discussed next.

INAPPROPRIATE QUESTIONS Many questions are clearly hiring standards to avoid. When they are asked, the responses generated create a legal liability for the employer. The most basic interviewing rule is this: Ask only job-related questions. The definition of a test in the *Uniform Guidelines* includes, "physical, education, and work experience requirements *informal or casual interviews*." Because the interview is a test, if adverse impact is shown, it is subject to the same validity requirements as any other step in the selection process. For unstructured interviews, this constraint presents special difficulties. Historically, the interview has been more vulnerable to charges of discrimination than any other tool used in the selection process.

The ADA also provides a warning for interviewers. Interviewers should inquire about the need for reasonable accommodations in only a few situations. For example, the topic is appropriate if the applicant is in a wheelchair or has an obvious disability that will require accommodation. Also, the applicant may voluntarily disclose a disability or even ask for some reasonable accommodation. Otherwise, employers should refrain from broaching the subject. Instead, interviewers should frame questions in terms of whether applicants can perform the essential functions of the jobs for which they are applying.

PERMITTING NON–JOB-RELATED INFORMATION If a candidate begins volunteering personal information that is not job-related, the interviewer should steer the conversation back on course. The interviewer might do well to begin the interview by tactfully stating something like, "This selection decision will be based strictly on qualifications. Let's not discuss topics such as religion, social activities, national origin, gender, or family situations. We are definitely interested in you, personally. However, these factors are not job related and will not be considered in our decision." This enables better decisions to be made while decreasing the likelihood of discrimination charges.[38]

To elicit needed information in any type of interview, the interviewer must create a climate that encourages the applicant to speak freely. However, the conversation should not become too casual. Whereas engaging in friendly chitchat with candidates might be pleasant, in our litigious society, it may be the most dangerous thing an interviewer can do. Asking a woman a question about her children that has nothing to do with the job would not be appropriate.

INTERVIEWER BIAS Often a problem that may arise in an interview is interviewer bias where the interviewer makes assumptions about the interviewee that may be incorrect and lets these biases influence the selection decision. Various forms of biases will next be discussed.

Stereotyping bias occurs when the interviewer assumes that the applicant has certain traits because they are members of a certain class. The classic case of stereotyping bias is when an interviewer assumes that a woman applicant cannot meet a certain physical requirement such as being able to lift 50 pounds.

A *positive halo bias* occurs when the interviewer generalizes one positive first impression feature of the candidate. Such might be the case with discovering that you have something in common with the applicant. The opposite could occur with negative *horn bias* where the interviewer's first negative impression of the candidate generalizes throughout the interview.

Contrast errors may occur when, for example, an interviewer meets with several poorly qualified applicants and then confronts a mediocre candidate. By comparison, the last applicant may appear to be better qualified than he or she is. The opposite can also occur. Suppose that a clearly outstanding candidate is followed by a very good candidate. The second candidate may not be considered even if the first candidate turns down the job offer.

Premature judgment bias suggests that interviewers often make a judgment about candidates in the first few minutes of the interview.[39] Apparently, these interviewers believe that they can determine immediately whether a candidate will be successful or not. When this occurs, a great deal of potentially valuable information is not considered. Even if an interviewer spent a week with an applicant, the sample of behavior might be too small to judge the candidate's qualifications properly. In addition, the candidate's behavior during an interview is seldom typical or natural, thereby making a quick judgment difficult.

Interview illusion bias is closely related to premature judgment but not the same. Managers may say something to the effect, "Give me just five minutes with an applicant and I can tell if they will be successful with our company." Their belief in their interview ability was likely exaggerated. Recruiters are often overconfident about their ability to judge others in general. Interviewers should be careful about placing excessive weight on interviews and thinking, "I just feel good about this applicant" when making the hiring decision.[40]

INTERVIEWER DOMINATION In successful interviews, relevant information must flow both ways. Sometimes, interviewers begin the interview by telling candidates what they are looking for, and then are excited to hear candidates parrot back their own words. Other interviewers are delighted to talk through virtually the entire interview, either to take pride in their organization's accomplishments or to express frustrations over their own difficulties. After dominating the meeting for an hour or so, these interviewers feel good about the candidate. Therefore, interviewers must learn to be good listeners as well as suppliers of information.

LACK OF TRAINING Anyone who has ever conducted an interview realizes that it is much more than carrying on a conversation with another person. The interviewer is attempting to gain insight into how the applicant answers job-related questions. There should be a reason for asking each question. For instance, suppose the applicant is told, "Tell me about yourself." A trained interviewer asks this question to determine whether the applicant's life experiences qualify the applicant for the job, not the fact that he or she had a little dog named Moe as a child. Interviewers should be trained to have a job-related purpose for asking each question. When the cost of making poor selection decisions is considered, the expense of training employees in interviewing skills can be easily justified.

NONVERBAL COMMUNICATION *Body language* is the nonverbal communication method in which physical actions such as motions, gestures, and facial expressions convey thoughts and emotions. The interviewer is attempting to view the nonverbal signals from the applicant. Applicants are also reading the nonverbal signals of the interviewer. Therefore, interviewers should make a conscious effort to view themselves as applicants do to avoid sending inappropriate or unintended nonverbal signals.

Concluding the Interview

When the interviewer has obtained the necessary information and answered the applicant's questions, he or she should conclude the interview. Management must then determine whether the candidate is suitable for the open position and organization. If the conclusion is positive, the process continues; if there appears to be no match, the candidate is no longer considered. Also in concluding the interview, the interviewer should tell the applicant that he or she will be notified of the selection decision shortly. Keeping this promise helps maintain a positive relationship with the applicant. The Watch It video illustrates the process from the application and planning phases through concluding the interview.

Watch It 4

If your instructor has assigned this, go to **www.pearson.com/mylab/management** to watch a video titled Applying and Interviewing for Employment and respond to questions.

6.5 Describe the use of pre-employment screening and background checks.

Pre-Employment Screening and Background Checks

Pre-employment screening and background investigations are more important than ever before because of the rise in negligent hiring (to be discussed later in this chapter) lawsuits, recent corporate scandals, and national security concerns. At this stage of the selection process, an applicant has normally completed an application form or submitted a résumé, taken the necessary selection tests, and undergone an employment interview. On the surface the candidate looks qualified. It is now time to determine the accuracy of the information submitted or to determine whether vital information was not submitted.

Background investigations involve obtaining data from various sources, including previous employers, business associates, credit bureaus, government agencies, and academic institutions. Fingerprinting also is becoming a more common part of checks, especially for companies that employ workers in charge of securing a worksite—for example, airports, the financial services industry, hospitals, schools, the gaming industry, and hazardous materials services. Reasons for leaving jobs or gaps in employment may be cleverly disguised to present a work history that does not provide an accurate or complete picture. Letters of recommendation from companies that are no longer in existence and differences between their résumé and completed job application may raise a red flag.

HR Web Wisdom

HR Advice for Small Businesses

http://hradviceforsmallbusinesses.blogspot.com/

Offers advice for the small business owner to hire, manage, and retain employees.

FYI

A survey of companies revealed that pre-employment screening is conducted to ensure:

- Higher quality of hires: 74%
- Government compliance: 56%
- Enhanced company reputation: 49%
- Greater safety and security: 43%
- Increased company reputation: 37%[41]

The intensity of background investigations depends on the nature of the open position's tasks and its relationship to customers or clients. To be legally safe, employers should ask applicants to sign a liability waiver permitting a background investigation. The waiver is typically a statement on the application form that releases former employers, business references, and others from liability. It also authorizes checks of court records and the verification of the applicant's educational history and other credentials.

Employment Eligibility Verification (Form I-9)

The employment eligibility verification form I-9 must be filled out by U.S. job applicants, but it allows any number of documents to be used to demonstrate their legal right to work in the United States. Every employee hired since 1986 must have a completed Form I-9 on file. In an audit, federal immigration agents review the Form I-9 that employers are required to keep on file. The law provides for penalties from $100 to $1,000 for each incorrect or missing I-9. For example, Hartmann Studios, an event design and production company, was fined $605,250 for improper completion of I-9 forms. The total fine was based on a $700 rate for each violation.[42]

An additional level of verification involves the use of E-Verify to check out new hires, and its use is required for federal contractors and subcontractors with contracts of $100,000 or more. Recently, the U.S. Supreme Court granted states the right to require employers to use the federal E-Verify system to check on the eligibility of employees to work in the United States. E-Verify is a Web-based system that lets employers check Social Security and visa numbers submitted by workers against government databases. The system is not checking for citizenship, but for eligibility to be lawfully employed in the United States. The E-Verify system is not flawless because a recent report found that 6 percent passed the E-Verify checks because they had used fraudulent or stolen identities.[43]

FYI

According to the U.S. Citizenship and Immigration Services, more than 600,000 employers of all sizes use *E-Verify*.[44]

Continuous Background Investigation

Background investigations are not just for pre-employment any more. Some employers are screening their employees on an ongoing basis. In certain industries, such as banking and health care, employers are required by regulation to routinely research the criminal records of employees. People and events are ever-changing. For example, financial devastation, marital collapse, or a medical crisis can send a person with the cleanest record over the edge. It has been estimated that every year one or two of every 1,000 existing employees acquire a new criminal record. Because only a small percent of convictions lead to jail time, the employer may never know of a conviction unless there is an ongoing background investigation.

Background Investigation with Social Media

An increasing number of employers are using social media to conduct background investigations. Employers use an applicant's Facebook page, LinkedIn profile, and postings made on an industry blog to find out about individuals they are considering hiring. One study revealed that 4 in 10 organizations use social media or online searches to screen candidates.[45] According to another study, more than 8 out of 10 employers say that a positive online reputation influences their hiring decisions at least to some extent, and nearly half say a strong online reputation influences their decisions to a great extent.[46] Still, many companies have expressed concerns about using social media profiles to screen job candidates. In 2015, a study by the Society for Human Resource Management (SHRM) revealed that 76 percent of surveyed organizations were concerned about legal risks, and 60 percent maintained that information from social media sites do not provide job-related information.[47]

Employers reported that they have found content on social networking sites that caused them not to hire the candidate. Some examples include posting provocative or inappropriate photographs or information, posting content about alcohol or drug use, and posting negative comments about their previous employer, coworkers, or clients. Other information found on these sites supported their decision to hire the candidate. For example, the profile provided a good feel for the candidate's personality and fit within the organization, the profile supported candidate's professional qualifications, and other people posted good references about the candidate.

As the cost of background checking has dropped and technology has improved, background checking has entered new dating relationships. Prior to accepting an invitation for a date with a new person, that individual can be "checked out" to determine if what was said was fact or fiction. Apps are now available to conduct a background check before entering into any relationship. Through these new apps, one can quickly determine if a person is telling the truth about factors such as age, relatives, addresses, criminal history, bankruptcies, judgments, liens, aliases, and current contact information.

Remembering Hiring Standards to Avoid

Some of the standards used in the background investigation have the potential to violate a hiring standard to avoid. A word of caution is advised in situations when an applicant *acknowledges* that he or she has been convicted of a crime. A major implication of the *Griggs v. Duke Power Company* Supreme Court case was that when HR management practices eliminate substantial numbers of minority or female applicants (prima facie evidence), the burden of proof is on the employer to show that the practice is job related. If a criminal record automatically eliminates a candidate that means that approximately 65 million people who have been convicted of felonies and misdemeanors may struggle to find employment.[48] Some states and cities have done away with asking about criminal convictions on applications, and there is a push to do it also on the national level. Therefore, caution should be taken using criminal conviction as a hiring criterion if it cannot be shown to be job related.

The same rationale can be said for conducting credit checks. If a disproportionate number of members of a protected group are rejected through the use of the credit check, the company would need to validate its use. Certainly, if a company does a credit check on all applicants, it is difficult to say that the credit check is job related. Presently 11 states have laws on their books banning credit check uses, and other states are considering credit check proposals.

Congress created somewhat of an obstacle for employers when it amended the federal Fair Credit Reporting Act (FCRA). Employers' obligations are triggered under the act when they use consumer reports that contain information about an individual's personal and credit characteristics, character, general reputation, and lifestyle. To avoid legal problems, employers need to allow sufficient time between notifying an applicant or employee of a less than favorable consumer report and taking adverse action. If an unfavorable credit check surfaces, the potential employee should be given time to dispute and correct the errors.[49] Making mistakes can prove costly to companies. In 2015, several companies—BMW, Calvin Klein, Chuck E. Cheese, Food Lion, Home Depot, and Whole Foods—paid exorbitant settlements ranging from $716,400 to $3 million.[50]

The EEOC has recently conducted hearings claiming there are employers that hire only individuals who are presently employed.[51] Paul C. Evans, a partner with law firm Morgan Lewis & Bockius LLP in Philadelphia, said, "I do think the EEOC will look to see whether or not employers are de facto, even without an explicit policy, precluding or eliminating from consideration those who have been out of work for long periods of time."[52]

Much of the social media content contains information regarding possible hiring standards to avoid. The typical Facebook page will reveal race, sex, age, ethnic background, and more by just looking at the pictures and profile. Religion, especially if it is a strong part of the member's belief system, is often easy to detect. None of these factors should be considered in the selection process. However, information is usually available that is legal to consider. In fact, according to a survey by Microsoft Corporation, 7 out of 10 U.S. hiring managers reject candidates based on information they have posted online even though 90 percent of these managers are concerned that the information they find can be inaccurate and unreliable.[53]

reference checks
Validations from individuals who know the applicant that provide additional insight into the information furnished by the applicant and verification of its accuracy.

Reference checks are validations from those who know the applicant that provide additional insight into the information furnished by the applicant and allow verification of its accuracy. They are a valuable source of information to supplement the background investigation. Applicants are often required to submit the names of several references who can provide additional information about them. A possible flaw with reference checking is that virtually everyone can name three or four individuals willing to make favorable statements about him or her. Even so, there is anecdotal evidence that personal references do not always provide favorable information. They may not necessarily be committed to shading the truth for the applicant.

A related problem in obtaining information from previous employers is their general reluctance to reveal such data and this trend continues to grow. In 2010, a SHRM poll on background investigations, 98 percent of respondents said their organizations would verify dates of employment for current or former employees, 68 percent said they would not discuss work performance, and 82 percent said they would not discuss character or personality.[54]

There are two schools of thought about supplying information about former employees. One is, "Don't tell them anything." The other is, "Honesty is the best policy." In the more conservative approach, the employer typically provides only basic data such as name, job title, and dates of employment. The honesty approach is based on the reality that facts honestly given or opinions honestly held constitute a solid legal defense. It is helpful to know why the person left that job. If the response differs from that given by the applicant, it is a red flag. Although protective laws regarding reference checking do exist, apparently, there is a wait-and-see attitude among some employers. It will likely take litigation and court rulings before employers fully understand, and have confidence in, the statutes.

Traditional reference checking has been heavily labor-intense. *Automated reference checking (ARC)* has been a boon in this area. With ARC, references are anonymous and more efficient and a more comprehensive report can be provided. ARC automates one of the last elements of recruiting that used to be heavily manual. Because it is confidential, people are more forthcoming. And because it is online, the process goes faster. Reference checking requires an e-mail link to the job candidate. It is the candidate, not the recruiter, who contacts references to fill out the questionnaire. The system collects the surveys and prepares a report for the recruiter. Referencing is much faster, going from an average of 4 days to an average of 1.2 days. ARC can help reduce the legal risks for the company seeking the reference because the request comes from the candidate, not the organization. The company does not run the risk of a recruiter asking an inappropriate question, because the applicant has preapproved the questions.

negligent hiring
Liability a company incurs when it fails to conduct a reasonable investigation of an applicant's background, and then assigns a potentially dangerous person to a position in which he or she can inflict harm.

Negligent hiring is the liability an employer incurs when it fails to conduct a reasonable investigation of an applicant's background, and then assigns a potentially dangerous person to a position in which he or she can inflict harm. The typical negligent hiring case involves a deliberate inflicting of harm committed by an employee including fraud, assault, or battery. Reasonable investigation varies according to the nature of the job. The risk of harm to third parties, for example, requires a higher standard of care when hiring a taxi driver as opposed to a machinist. The taxi cab driver is alone and has control of his or her customer during the time the customer is in the car. California law has strengthened background check requirements that directly influence riding sharing services, such as Uber and Lyft. These companies are banned from employing drivers who are confirmed sex offenders or had a violent felony conviction at any time in their past. In addition, hiring drivers with misdemeanors, including domestic violence or driving while under the influence of drugs or alcohol during the previous seven years, is prohibited.[55] This would not be the case for the machinist. Employers who operate home-service businesses, day-care centers, and home health-care operations are particularly at risk, as are those with employees who drive company vehicles, visit customer locations, handle money, or work with children, the elderly, or the impaired.[56] The primary consideration in negligent hiring is whether the risk of harm from a dangerous employee was reasonably foreseeable. Accusers will argue that employers knew, or should have known, about a hire's potential threat to others.[57] In one negligent hiring case, a hospital nursing assistant was hired without a background investigation and the medical center did not ask former employers why the worker had left. If it had, the medical center would have discovered that the worker had previously sexually harassed, assaulted, and inappropriately touched female patients. Once hired, the worker was left alone in rooms with vulnerable female patients and sexually abused them.[58]

6.6 Explain the selection decision and the metrics for evaluating recruitment/selection effectiveness.

Selection Decision and Evaluating the Effectiveness of Selection Decisions

At this point, the focus is on the manager who must take the most critical step of all: the actual hiring decision. If a firm is going to invest thousands of dollars to recruit, select, and train an employee, it is important for the manager to hire the most qualified available candidate, according to the firm's criteria. The final choice is made from among those still in the running after selection tests, interviews, background investigations, and reference checks have been evaluated. Usually, the person selected has qualifications that most closely conform to the requirements of the open position and the organization.

Making the Selection Decision

The person who normally makes the final selection is the manager who will be responsible for the new employee's performance. In making this decision, the manager will review results of the selection methods used. Everything will not likely be weighted the same. The question then becomes, "Which data are most predictive of job success?" For each firm or group of jobs, the optimal selection method may be different.

MEDICAL EXAMINATION The ADA does not prohibit pre-employment medical examinations. However, it does determine the point at which they may be administered during the selection process. The ADA explicitly states that all exams must be directly relevant to the job requirements and that a firm cannot order a medical exam until the applicant is offered employment. Typically, a job offer is contingent on the applicant's passing this examination. The basic purpose of the medical examination is to determine whether an applicant is physically capable of performing the work. The *Uniform Guidelines* state that these examinations can be used to reject applicants only when the results show that job performance would be adversely affected.

At this stage, some companies may also require drug testing to determine whether applicants are using chemical substances or alcohol. There are a variety of reasons for choosing to test applicants for drug use. Primarily, the use of illegal drugs, which impairs judgment and psychomotor coordination, and may create workplace hazards. Pre-empting drug-related accidents through systematic drug testing may reduce the cost to provide employees with disability insurance. In addition, health-care claims may be higher for drug users than for those who do not use illegal substances. Ultimately, employers bear the cost of higher health insurance premiums. Finally, wherever called for by industry standards or government regulation, drug testing help companies to maintain compliance.

NOTIFICATION OF CANDIDATES Management should notify both successful and unsuccessful candidates of selection decisions as soon as possible. This action is a matter of courtesy and good public relations. Any delay may also result in the firm losing a prime candidate because top prospects often have other employment options.

Employers may reject applicants at any time during the selection process. Most people can accept losing if they lose fairly. Problems occur when the selection process appears to be less than objective. It is therefore important for firms to develop and use rational selection tools. Time constraints prevent firms from spending much time explaining a decision to an unsuccessful candidate. If the person rejected was an internal candidate, managers may visit or make a personal phone call to the rejected applicant. A rejection letter is a more likely method if the candidate was not an internal candidate. However, a letter with a personal touch may reduce the stigma of rejection and avoid the applicant's having a negative feeling about the company. An impersonal letter is likely to have the opposite effect. The best an organization can do is to make selection decisions objectively. Hopefully, most unsuccessful individuals can, with time, accept the fact that they were not chosen.

Evaluating Selection Decisions

There is, however, no one-size-fits-all metric that employers can adopt to achieve greater hiring efficiency. The metrics that best suit each company depends on a variety of factors, including its business goals. The recent recession heightened the need to have metrics regarding the productivity of employees. When employee cost-cutting decisions must be made, it is important that the most productive employees are retained. One survey revealed that companies with best-in-class talent acquisition programs were most successful at measuring the following four performance criteria: time to hire, quality of hire, new-hire retention, and hiring managers' overall satisfaction with the program.[59] Possible metrics for evaluating the effectiveness of recruitment/selection are described next. Metrics for evaluating other functions are discussed at the appropriate time.

QUALITY OF HIRE Many recruiters believe that quality of hire is the most important metric to use in the selection process. Some possible measures to determine the quality of hire might be communication effectiveness, ability to motivate others, leadership ability, and cultural fit.[60] Even though the question of how to measure quality of hire and set standards for new-hire performance is difficult to determine, it is an important decision that HR professionals are constantly striving to determine. Realistically, the answer depends on the system and the company involved. For quality of hire to be usable, one needs to have performance assessment for two or three years before the real capabilities of a new hire will be understood.

TIME REQUIRED TO HIRE The shorter the time to hire, the more efficient the HR department is in finding the replacement for the job. The top candidates for nearly any job are hired and off the job market within anywhere from 1 to 10 days. It then becomes crucial that the time required to hire be as low as possible while still ensuring quality of hire. Otherwise your best prospect will have already signed on to work for a competitor.

NEW-HIRE RETENTION It is important to measure new-hire retention because costs go up dramatically if a position must be filled again in a short period. New-hire retention is calculated by determining the percentage of the new hires that remain with the company at selected intervals, typically one or two years. If this situation is happening excessively, HR should analyze the selection process to determine if there are flaws in the system that cause new hires to terminate prematurely. Perhaps, as was mentioned previously, an RJP needs to be instituted.

HIRING MANAGER OVERALL SATISFACTION The manager is largely responsible for the success of his or her department. It is the quality of the employees in the workgroup that have a major impact on success of the department. A manager's belief that employees being hired through the recruitment and selection system do not perform as well as expected casts doubt on the entire selection process. Some measure manager satisfaction based on the survey of hiring managers, compared to previous period. Other firms provide a rating scale for the manager to evaluate how a new hire is performing after the employee's first 90 or 120 days.

TURNOVER RATE *Turnover rate* is the number of times on average that employees must be replaced during a year. For example, if a company has 200 employees and 200 workers had been hired during the year, a 100 percent turnover rate would be experienced. As one might expect, a 100 percent rate is quite costly to the organization, and ways need to be found to reduce the rate. Employees who are hired and then quit within 120 days are called "False Starts" and are especially expensive because the company spends money on their hire but then quickly must spend even more to replace them. Across all industries, the average turnover rate based on quitting in 2016 was approximately 25 percent with the highest rates in services industries—for example, nearly 54 percent in the accommodation and food services industry.[61]

As the previous discussion indicates, there are a variety of measures to judge whether recruitment and selection decisions are effective. Among them is turnover. Patagonia, maker of outdoor gear, strives to select employees whose values are consistent with the philosophies and values of the company. They boast a high employee retention rate, which they attribute, in part, to their approach to employee selection. The following Watch It video describes Patagonia's approach to employee selection.

Watch It 5

If your instructor has assigned this, go to **www.pearson.com/mylab/management** to watch a video titled Patagonia: Employee Testing and Selection and respond to questions.

COST PER HIRE In determining the recruiting cost per hire, the total recruiting expense must first be calculated. Then, the cost per hire may be determined by dividing the recruiting expenses (calculation of advertising, agency fees, employee referrals, relocation, recruiter pay, and benefits costs) by the number of recruits hired. Naturally, the difficulty associated with this measure is in determining the exact costs to include as recruiting expenses. It may be beneficial for a firm to use a benchmark cost per hire to compare to the specific cost for the company.

YIELD RATE A *yield rate* is the percentage of applicants from a particular source and method that make it to the next stage of the selection process. HR professionals calculate yield rates for each recruitment source, which they compare to judge relative effectiveness. For example, if 100 applicants submitted their résumés through the firm's corporate career Web site and 25 were asked in for an interview, the yield rate for the corporate career Web site would be 25 percent (that is, 25 asked for an interview/100 who applied through the corporate career Web site). Each recruitment method would be analyzed in a similar manner. Continuing this example, assume that 10 of the 25 applicants who were interviewed received job offers. The yield rate at this stage would be 40 percent. Finally, assume that 5 of the 10 applicants who received job offers accepted them. The yield rate would be 50 percent. As previously noted, the yield rates would be calculated for each recruitment source and comparisons would be made at each stage. The goal is to compare the yield rates between each recruitment source at each stage. Larger yield rates generally signal higher effectiveness.

PREPARING FOR EXAM/QUIZZES

Chapter Summary by Learning Objectives

1. ***Explain employee selection and environmental factors that affect the selection process.*** *Selection* is the process of choosing from a group of applicants the individual best suited for a particular position. There are many ways to improve productivity, but none is more powerful than making the right hiring decision.

   The selection process typically begins with preliminary screening. Next, applicants complete the firm's application form, and this is followed by the administration of selection tests and a series of employment interviews with reference and background investigations. Once the selection decision has been made, the prospective employee may be given a company medical examination.

   The environmental factors that affect the selection process include other HR functions, legal considerations, speed of decision making, organizational hierarchy, applicant pool, type of organization, probationary period, organizational fit, and selection technology.
2. ***Explain the importance of preliminary screening as well as reviewing applications and résumés.*** Preliminary screening is important because it identifies those who obviously do not meet the position's requirements. Preliminary screening may take the form of reviewing for obviously unqualified applicants with a brief interview, test, or only a review of the application or résumé for clear mismatches.

   Having the applicant complete an application for employment is another early step in the selection process. The employer evaluates this application to see whether there is an apparent match between the individual and the position.

   When writing their résumés, applicants should realize that most companies now use automated résumé systems. These systems assume a certain résumé style. Résumés that deviate from the assumed style are ignored or deleted.
3. ***Describe the use of tests in the selection process.*** Recognizing the shortcomings of other selection tools, many firms have added pre-employment tests to their hiring process. Selection tests may accurately predict an applicant's ability to perform the job, the "can do," but they are less successful in indicating the extent to which the individual will be motivated to perform it, the "will do." Employers should also be aware that tests might be unintentionally discriminatory. Test anxiety can also be a problem.
4. ***Explain the use of the employment interview.*** The interview permits clarification of certain points, the uncovering of additional information, and the elaboration of data needed to make a sound selection decision. The interviewer should provide information about the company, the job, and expectations of the candidate.

   The general types of interviews are the unstructured interview and the structured interview, including the behavioral interview and the situational interview.
5. ***Describe the use of pre-employment screening and background checks.*** Pre-employment screening has experienced tremendous growth. It went from a possible step in the selection process to that of a necessary step. Background investigation is more important than ever because of the rise in negligent hiring, lawsuits, recent corporate scandals, and national security concerns. Background investigations involve obtaining data from various sources, including previous employers, business associates, credit bureaus, government agencies, and academic institutions.
6. ***Explain the selection decision and the metrics for evaluating recruitment/selection effectiveness.*** The selection decision is when the final choice is made from among those still in the running after reference checks, selection tests, background investigations, and interview information are evaluated.

   Metrics available to assess HR efficiency are numerous, and a comprehensive set of metrics can be produced to evaluate recruitment and selection. Possible metrics include quality of hire, time required to hire, new-hire retention, hiring manager overall satisfaction, turnover rate, costs per hire, and yield rate.

Key Terms

selection 147
applicant pool 149
organizational fit 149
preliminary screening 151
résumé 152
keywords 153
keyword résumé 153
standardization 154
objectivity 154
norm 154
reliability 155
validity 155
criterion-related validity 155
content validity 156
construct validity 156
aptitude tests 156
achievement tests 156
cognitive ability tests 156
personality 156
personality tests 156
job-knowledge tests 157
work-sample tests 158
assessment center 158
genetic tests 158
graphoanalysis 158
employment interview 160
unstructured interview 162
structured interview 162
behavioral interview 162
situational interview 163
group interview 163
board interview 163
stress interview 163
realistic job preview (RJP) 164
reference checks 168
negligent hiring 169

MyLab Management

If your instructor is using MyLab Management, go to **www.pearson.com/mylab/management** to complete the problems marked with this icon ✪.

Questions for Review

6-1. What are the typical steps in the selection process?
6-2. What is the general purpose of preliminary screening?
6-3. What is the purpose of the application form?
6-4. What types of questions should be asked on an application form?
✪ **6-5.** What are the advantages and potential problems in the use of selection tests?
6-6. What are the basic characteristics of a properly designed selection test?
6-7. What are the test validation approaches? Define each.
6-8. Identify and describe the various types of employment tests.
6-9. What is the purpose of an assessment center?
6-10. Describe genetic testing, graphoanalysis, and polygraph tests.
6-11. What are the general types of interviews? Explain each.
6-12. What types of questions would make up a behavioral interview?
6-13. What are the various methods of interviewing? Define each.
6-14. What are some potential interview problems?
6-15. What are some of the hiring standards to avoid?
✪ **6-16.** Why should an employer be concerned about negligent hiring?
6-17. Why should the selection decision be made before conducting a medical examination?
6-18. What are some metrics for evaluating recruitment and selection?
6-19. What environmental factors could affect the selection process? Discuss each.
✪ **6-20.** In terms of employee selection, what is the significance of organizational fit?
6-21. Distinguish between an applicant-tracking system and candidate relationship management.

PREPARING FOR MY CAREER

P I A Personal Inventory Assessment

✪ *Additional Personal Inventory Assessments can be found on MyLab Management.*

Are You a Type A Personality?

As you saw in this chapter, many companies consider applicants' personality characteristics an important criterion in the selection process. Type A personality is defined as a person who is seen by their coworkers as a hard worker and extremely focused on details. This PIA will assess the extent to which you exhibit the characteristics of a Type A personality.

ETHICS DILEMMA

Hiring with Incomplete Information

Roberta Blythe recently opened a new business named "Assisting You." The company is a referral agency, matching service providers with customers who have home projects. Roberta's strategy is to build a large clientele quickly by offering lower prices and shorter wait times than the competing agencies. Before long, clients' requests began coming in faster than she could meet them on a timely basis. Also, the recruiting and selection process from start to finish increased from 30 days to 50 days. Desperate to meet demand, Roberta decided to streamline the process. Dropping background checks would reduce the wait time by 15 days. Feeling intense pressure to succeed, Roberta began hiring providers without first conducting background checks. Roberta feels confident in her decision because she has heard about many of the service providers, but certainly not all.

6-22. What would you do?

6-23. What factor(s) in this ethics dilemma might influence a person to make a less-than-ethical decision?

HRM Is Everyone's Business

In Chapter 5, we explained the role of HR professionals and managers in the recruitment process. Together, identified the best approaches to building a pool of qualified candidates. Now, it's time to make selection (hiring) decisions. Successful selection decisions are based on the collaboration between HR professionals and hiring managers who bring complementary expertise and perspectives to the task. HR professionals are experts on every aspect of the selection process (e.g., reliability and validity), and hiring managers are most well-acquainted with their staffing needs.

Action checklist for managers and HR—understanding and applying selection concepts and methods

HR takes the lead

- ☑ Review the appropriate guidelines for evaluating applications and résumés. Communicate what should and should not be considered. For example, some people list birthdate or marital status on their résumés and this information should never be considered when formulating interview questions or making the selection decision.
- ☑ Discuss whether testing will add useful information for making more accurate selection decisions.
- ☑ Review the guidelines for conducting effective interviews and coordinate the types of interview questions that will be asked by HR and the questions that will be asked by managers.
- ☑ HR professionals conduct background checks.
- ☑ HR professionals share their evaluations of the job candidates, and inform managers whether the results of the background check warrant further consideration.

Managers take the lead

- ☑ Review the top candidates with HR after prescreening applications and résumés.
- ☑ If testing is considered relevant, explain the minimum performance standards expected of successful employees.
- ☑ Share interview questions with HR to ensure job-relatedness.
- ☑ Consider all the job-related information and discuss whether a job offer should be made.

HRM by the Numbers

Measuring Selection Outcomes

An additional HRM by the Numbers exercise can be found on MyLab Management.

You were hired to develop a new recruitment and selection system to fill marketing assistant jobs. The Vice President of HR asked you to calculate various metrics to judge the effectiveness of the system using data from the previous calendar year. You have the following data to judge the effectiveness of the selection system:

Number of Qualified Applicants	
Employee Referrals	10
Job Fairs	335
Job Web sites	4,000
Number of Applicants Interviewed	
Employee Referrals	5
Job Fairs	30
Job Web sites	210
Number of Job Offers	
Employee Referrals	3
Job Fairs	11
Job Web sites	45
Number of Job Offer Acceptances	
Employee Referrals	3
Job Fairs	4
Job Web sites	15

Questions

6-24. Calculate the yield rate for each recruitment source (based on the number interviewed relative to the number of qualified applicants): (a) employee referrals, (b) job fairs, and (c) job Web sites. Which source is most effective?

6-25. Calculate the yield rate for each recruitment source (based on the number of job offers relative to the number of applicants interviewed): (a) employee referrals, (b) job fairs, and (c) job Web sites. Which source is most effective?

6-26. Calculate the yield rate for each recruitment source (based on the number of job offer acceptances to the number of job offers): (a) employee referrals, (b) job fairs, and (c) job Web sites. Which source is most effective?

Working Together: Team Exercise

In small groups of three or four, come up with specific answers to the following questions. Talk through your perspectives and come up with a team response. Be prepared to share your ideas with the class.

As a group, identify a job with which you are familiar. Perhaps it is a job that a group member currently holds or once held. Or, it could be a job currently or previously held by a family member or friend. Briefly describe some of the job duties.

6-27. Assuming the interviewer's role, what are three questions that you would ask job candidates? Explain.

6-28. Assuming the interviewer's role again, what are two questions that you would not ask job candidates? Explain.

INCIDENT 1 A Matter of Priorities

As production manager for Thompson Manufacturing, Sheila Stephens has the final authority to approve the hiring of any new supervisors who work for her. The human resource manager performs the initial screening of all prospective supervisors and then sends the most likely candidates to Sheila for interviews.

One day recently, Sheila received a call from Pete Peterson, the human resource manager; "Sheila, I've just spoken to a young man who may be just who you're looking for to fill the final line supervisor position. He has some good work experience and appears to have his head screwed on straight. He's here right now and available if you could possibly see him."

Sheila hesitated a moment before answering. "Gee, Pete," she said, "I'm certainly busy today, but I'll try to squeeze him in. Send him on down."

A moment later Allen Guthrie, the applicant, arrived at Sheila's office and she introduced herself. "Come on in, Allen," said Sheila. "I'll be right with you after I make a few phone calls." Fifteen minutes later Sheila finished the calls and began talking with Allen. Sheila was quite impressed. After a few minutes Sheila's door opened and a supervisor yelled, "We have a small problem on line one and need your help." Sheila stood up and said, "Excuse me a minute, Allen." Ten minutes later Sheila returned, and the conversation continued for 10 more minutes before a series of phone calls again interrupted the pair.

The same pattern of interruptions continued for the next hour. Finally, Allen looked at his watch and said, "I'm sorry, Mrs. Stephens, but I have to pick up my wife."

"Sure thing, Allen," Sheila said as the phone rang again. "Call me later today."

Questions

6-29. What should Sheila have done to avoid interviews like this one?

6-30. Explain why Sheila, not Pete, should make the selection decision.

6-31. What steps in the selection process were missed, if any? What problems might occur because of these omissions?

INCIDENT 2 National Career Day

Chipotle Mexican Grill launched an initiative in 2015—National Career Day—to hire 4,000 workers in just one day. The company deemed the initiative a success and repeated the event a year later in search of 5,000 additional workers. More than 60,000 individuals registered online and each store manager selected 100 candidates for interviews. Store managers set aside six to eight hours to conduct interviews.

Questions

6-32. Based on a highly compressed time frame, what are some of the pre-employment activities Chipotle might have set aside?

6-33. What are some of the pros and cons of undertaking a massive hiring spree in one day?

MyLab Management

If your instructor is using MyLab Management, go to **www.pearson.com/mylab/management** for Auto-graded writing questions as well as the following Assisted-graded writing questions:

6-34. What is the significance of employee selection?

6-35. Why is background investigation important to the selection process?

Endnotes

1 Saranja Kapur, "Lack of Skilled Workers Hinders Hiring by Private Firms," *CFO Journal* (February 4, 2014). Accessed February 16, 2014, at www.wsj.com.

2 U.S. Bureau of Labor Statistics, "Job Openings and Labor Turnover—May 2017" (USDL 17-0959, July 11, 2017). Accessed July 28, 2017, at www.bls.gov.

3 U.S. Bureau of Labor Statistics, "The Employment Situation—June 2017" (USDL 17-0934, July 7, 2017). Accessed July 28, 2017, at www.bls.gov.

4 "Nonprofits in America: New Research Data on Employment, Wages, and Establishments," *Monthly Labor Review* online (February 2016). Accessed February 17, 2017, at www.bls.gov/opub/mlr/2016/article/nonprofits-in-america.htm.

5 Anita Weyland, "How to Recruit People Who Fit," *Training Journal* (July 2011): 41–45.

6 Bill Roberts, "Values-Driven HR," *HR Magazine* 57 (March 2012): 44–48.

7 Dave Zielinski, "Effective Assessments," *HR Magazine* 56 (January 2011): 61–64.

8 Jonathan A. Segal, "Hiring Days Are Here Again," *HR Magazine* 56 (July 2011): 58–60.

9 Rachel Feintzeig, "'Culture Fit' May Be the Key to Your Next Job," *The Wall Street Journal* online (October 12, 2016). Accessed January 31, 2017, at www.wsj.com.

10 Ryan and Ployhart, "A Century of Selection."

11 Susan G. Hauser, "Tech Turbo Boosters on Hyperdrive," *Workforce Management* 90 (August 2011): 24–26.

12 Lynda Spiegel, "How Job Seekers Can Get Around Flaws in the Hiring Software," *The Wall Street Journal* online (May 24, 2016). Accessed February 17, 2017, at www.wsj.com.

13 "Automate Recruiting and Onboarding," *Chain Store Age* 85 (April 2009): 19.

14 Sue Weeks, "Putting CRM at the Heart of Recruiting," *Recruiter* (April 14, 2010): 32–34.

15 Bill Roberts, "Manage Candidates Right from the Start," *HR Magazine* 53 (October 2008): 73–76.

16 Peter Vogt, "Avoid the Top 10 Résumé Mistakes," *Monster.com* (2014). Accessed February 15, 2014, at http://career-advice.monster.com/résumés-cover-letters/resume-writing-tips/avoid-the-top-10-resume-mistakes/article.aspx.

17 Jim Boulden, "Software Weeds Out Weak Résumés," *CNN.Com*, international edition (January 8, 2013). Accessed February 15, 2014, at: http://edition.cnn.com/2013/01/08/business/resume-software-scanning/index.html.

18 Lauren Weber, "Today's Personality Tests Raise the Bar for Job Seekers," *The Wall Street Journal* online (April 14, 2015). Accessed January 7, 2017, at www.wsj.com.

19 Ann Marie Ryan and Robert E. Ployhart, "A Century of Selection, *Annual Review of Psychology*, 65 (2014): 693–717

20 "Validate Hiring Tests to Withstand EEO Scrutiny: DOL & EEOC Officials," *HR Focus* 85 (May 2008): 8–9.

21 O*NET, "Psychomotor Abilities," *Occupational Information Network*. Accessed February 16, 2014, at www.onetonline.org/find/descriptor/browse/Abilities/1.A.2/.

22 American Psychological Association, "*Personality*". Accessed February 16, 2014, at www.apa.org/topics/personality/.

23 O*NET, "Healthcare Social Workers," *Occupational Information Network*. Accessed February 16, 2014, at www.onetonline.org/link/summary/21-1022.00#WorkStyles.

24 Lauren Weber, "Today's Personality Tests Raise the Bar for Job Seekers," *The Wall Street Journal* online (April 14, 2015). Accessed January 7, 2017, at www.wsj.com.

25 O*NET, "Integrity," *Occupational Information Network Content Model*. Accessed February 16, 2014, at www.onetcenter.org/dl_files/Content-Model_DetailedDesc.pdf.

26 Bill Roberts, "Your Cheating Heart," *HR Magazine* 56 (June 2011): 54–60.

27 O*NET, "Lawyers," *Occupational Information Network*. Accessed February 16, 2014, at www.onetonline.org/link/summary/23-1011.00#Knowledge.

28 O*NET, "Electrical and Electronic Equipment Assemblers," *Occupational Information Network*. Accessed February 16, 2014, at www.onetonline.org/link/summary/51-2022.00.

29 "EEOC Issues Final Rule Interpreting Federal Law on Genetic Information," *HR Focus* 88 (January 2011): 1–5.

30 U.S. Equal Employment Opportunity Commission, "Employment Tests and Selection Procedures," *Fact Sheet on Employment Tests and Selection Procedures* (September 23, 2010). Accessed February 16, 2014, at www.eeoc.gov.

31 Ryan and Ployhart, "A Century of Selection."

32 Kate Davidson, "Employers Find 'Soft Skills' Like Critical Thinking in Short Supply," *The Wall Street Journal* online (August 30, 2016). Accessed January 13, 2017, at www.wsj.com.

33 "How to: Hire for Creativity," *Inc.* 32 (October 2010): 53–56.

34 Lauren Weber, "Hiring Tip: Find the Person Who Knows What Not to Do," *The Wall Street Journal* online (October 4, 2016). Accessed February 18, 2017, at www.wsj.com.

35 Michael Kaplan, "Job Interview Brainteasers," *Business 2.0* 8 (September 2007): 35–37.

36 Martha Frase-Blunt, "Games Interviewers Play," *HR Magazine* 46 (January 2001): 107–108.

37 Michael A. Tucker, "Show and Tell," *HR Magazine* 57 (January 2012): 51–53.

38 "Job Interviews: How to Pose Risky Questions the Legal Way," *HR Specialist: New Jersey Employment Law* 5 (April 2010): 6.

39 AR Mazzotta, "*Just Like Me: Tips for Reducing Perception-Driven Biases in CT Hiring,*" (July 16, 2013). Accessed January 10, 2014, at www.armazzotta.com/

tips-for-reducing-perception-driven-biases-in-ct-hiring/.

40 "The Hidden Risks of Hiring Based on 'Chemistry,'" *HR Specialist* 8 (February 2010): 1–2.

41 "Background Screening Trends & Best Practices Report: 2015-2016," Sterling Backcheck report. Accessed January 15, 2017, at www.sterling-backcheck.com.

42 Bruce Buchanan, "Company Fined $600,000 for I-9 Violations," *LawLogix.com* blog (January 22, 2016). Accessed February 1, 2017, at www.lawlogix.com/company-fined-600000-9-violations/.

43 "Evaluation of the Accuracy of E-Verify Findings,"] *Report submitted to the U.S. Department of Homeland Security* (July 2012). Accessed February 15, 2017, at www.uscis.gov; Bill Leonard, "Researchers: Stolen Identities Often Slip Through E-Verify," *HR Magazine* 55 (April 2010): 11.

44 "What is E-Verify?" *U.S. Citizenship and Immigration Services, February 26, 2016*. Accessed January 27, 2017, at www.uscis.gov/e-verify/what-e-verify.

45 Roy Mauer, "Know Before You Hire: 2016 Employment Screening Trends," *Society for Human Resource Management* online (January 20, 2016). Accessed February 18, 2017, at www.shrm.org/resourcesandtools/hr-topics/talent-acquisition/pages/2016-employment-screening-trends.aspx.

46 Sherrie A. Madia, "Why Shifting Efforts to Social Media Is Smart Strategy for 2011," *Journal of Corporate Recruiting Leadership* 5 (December 2010): 12–13.

47 "SHRM Survey Findings: Using Social Media for Talent Acquisition—Recruitment and Screening," *Society for Human Resource Management* (January 7, 2016). Accessed January 31, 2017, (available for download) at www.shrm.org/hr-today/trends-and-forecasting/research-and-surveys/pages/social-media-recruiting-screening-2015.aspx.

48 "Vast Majority of Large Employers Screen Applicants for Criminal Records, Survey Says," *HR Focus* 88 (May 2011): 11–12.

49 Juliette Fairley, "Employers Face Challenges in Screening Candidates," *Work force Management* 89 (November 2010): 7–9.

50 Roy Mauer, "Know Before You Hire: 2016 Employment Screening Trends," *Society for Human Resource Management* online (January 20, 2016). Accessed February 18, 2017, at www.shrm.org/resourcesandtools/hr-topics/talent-acquisition/pages/2016-employment-screening-trends.aspx.

51 Kathryn M. Nash, "Get Ready for a New Federally Protected Class: The Unemployed," *HR Specialist: Minnesota Employment Law* 5 (January 2012): 6.

52 Judy Greenwald, "New Type of Hiring Discrimination Claim in Works," *Business Insurance* 45 (February 28, 2011): 1–20.

53 Andrea Siedsma, "Are Background Checks on Web Posts Too Much Information?" *Workforce Management* 91 (January 2012): 10.

54 Dori Meiert, "Seeing Behind the Mask," *HR Magazine* 56 (February 2011): 30–37.

55 Greg Bensinger, "California Law Strengthens Background Checks for Uber and Lyft," *The Wall Street Journal* online (September 28, 2016). Accessed January 28, 2017, at www.wsj.com.

56 Michael L. Forte, "Sexual Assaults at Work: When Can the Employer Be Held Liable?" *Florida Underwriter* 28 (2011): 10.

57 Bill Roberts, "Backgrounds to the Foreground," *HR Magazine* 55 (December 2010): 46–51.

58 "Stakes Rise for Preventing Sexual Harassment and Age Discrimination," *Security Director's Report* 9 (March 2009): 8.

59 Theresa Minton-Eversole, "Quality Measurement: Key to Best-in-Class Talent Acquisition," *HR Magazine* 53 (December 2008): 64–66.

60 "Quality of Hires Is Vital," *Recruiter* (June 9, 2010): 6.

61 U.S. Bureau of Labor Statistics. "Job Openings and Labor Turnover Survey (JOLTS) Data Query System." *United States Department of Labor*. Accessed February 18, 2017, at www.bls.gov/jlt/data.htm.

Part Three
Performance Management and Training

7 Performance Management and Appraisal

LEARNING OBJECTIVES After completing this chapter, students should be able to:

7.1 Describe performance management, performance appraisal, and the performance appraisal process.

7.2 Explain the uses of performance appraisal and performance criteria.

7.3 Describe the choice of various performance appraisal methods.

7.4 Assess the effectiveness and limitations of performance appraisal practices.

7.5 Explain how to conduct the appraisal interview.

7.6 Summarize key trends in performance appraisal practice.

MyLab Management

Improve Your Grade!

If your professor is using MyLab Management, visit **www.pearson.com/mylab/management** for videos, simulations, and writing exercises.

Learn It

If your professor has chosen to assign this, go to **www.pearson.com/mylab/management** to see what you should particularly focus on and to take the Chapter 7 Warm-Up.

The tools we describe in this chapter and in Chapter 8 provide human resources (HR) professionals with a foundation to evaluate and improve employees (human capital) to promote competitive advantage. Let's consider a metaphor to bring the opening sentence to life. Think about, for example, a delivery vehicle. Many factors contribute to fuel efficiency, one of which is tire pressure. Insufficient tire pressure creates greater drag on the vehicle, which raises fuel consumption.

Companies prefer fuel-efficient vehicles to maintain lower operating costs because they want to maximize profitability. Mechanics can use an air gauge to determine whether tire pressure falls within standard limits specified by the automobile manufacturer.

Delivery vehicles represent physical capital, and we have learned that employees are human capital. Both help add value to companies. In this example, fuel efficiency is a measure of performance. Lower-than-standard or expected fuel efficiency equates with (lower) job performance. Air gauges can be thought of as a performance appraisal technique that helps mechanics (managers or supervisors) judge a vehicle's fuel efficiency (an employee's job performance). We take up the topics of performance management and performance appraisal in this chapter.

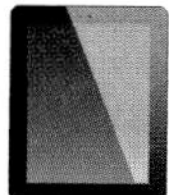

HR Web Wisdom

Performance Management

www.opm.gov/perform/overview.asp

Office of Personnel Management Web site on performance management.

7.1 Describe performance management, performance appraisal, and the performance appraisal process.

Performance Management, Performance Appraisal, and the Performance Appraisal Process

Performance management and performance appraisal are tools that organizations use to judge whether employees are meeting expectations. Beyond this common purpose, performance management addresses organizational processes and performance appraisal focuses on individual or group performance. Following a review of these practices, we will examine the performance appraisal process.

Performance Management

performance management (PM) Goal-oriented process directed toward ensuring that organizational processes are in place to maximize the productivity of employees, teams, and ultimately, the organization.

Performance management (PM) is a goal-oriented process directed toward ensuring that organizational processes are in place to maximize the productivity of employees, teams, and ultimately, the organization. It is a major player in accomplishing organizational strategy in that it involves measuring and improving the value of the workforce. PM includes incentive goals and the corresponding incentive values so that the relationship can be clearly understood and communicated. There is a close relationship between incentives and performance.

PM systems are one of the major focuses in business today. Although every HR function contributes to PM, training, performance appraisal, and compensation play a more significant role. Whereas performance appraisal occurs at a specific time, PM is a dynamic, continuous process. Every individual in the organization is a part of the PM system. Every component of the system is integrated to ensure continuous organizational effectiveness. With PM, every worker's efforts should focus on achieving strategic goals. A well-developed job description is needed to determine whether performance expectations have been achieved. If workers' skills need improvement, additional training should be provided. In PM systems, training has a direct tie-in to achieving organizational effectiveness, as does pay and performance. A good PM system ensures that people make good, effective use of their time.

PM may be the single largest contributor to organizational effectiveness in recent years. An effective PM system should be the responsibility of everyone in the organization starting with the CEO and moving throughout the entire organization because companies that disregard PM do not prosper.[1]

Performance Appraisal

performance appraisal (PA) Formal system of review and evaluation of individual or team task performance.

Performance appraisal (PA) is a formal system of review and evaluation of individual or team task performance. A critical point in the definition is the word *formal* because managers should be reviewing an individual's performance on a continuing basis.

PA is especially critical to the success of PM. Although PA is but one component of PM, it is a vital one, in that it directly reflects the organization's strategic plan. Although evaluation of team performance is critical when teams exist in an organization, the focus of PA in most firms remains on the individual employee. Regardless of the emphasis, an effective appraisal system evaluates accomplishments and initiates plans for development, goals, and objectives.

Most managers rely on PA techniques as a basis to provide feedback, encourage performance improvement, make valid decisions, justify terminations, identify training and development needs, and defend personnel decisions such as why one employee received a higher pay increase than another employee. PA serves many purposes, and improved results and efficiency are increasingly critical in today's globally competitive marketplace. Therefore, abandoning the only program with *performance* in its name and *employees* as its focus would seem to be an ill-advised overreaction. Additionally, managers must be concerned about legal issues, which we consider later in this chapter. Developing an effective PA system has been and will continue to be a high priority for management.

Performance Appraisal Process

As shown in Figure 7-1, the starting point for the PA process is identifying specific performance goals. An appraisal system probably cannot effectively serve every desired purpose, so management should select the specific goals it believes to be most important and realistically achievable. For example, some firms may want to stress employee development, whereas other organizations may want to focus on pay adjustments. Many firms rely on PA results to help inform decisions to terminate employment, particularly after a regular pattern of inadequate job performance. In any case, PA serves a developmental purpose, evaluative purpose, or both.

The next step in this ongoing cycle continues with establishing performance criteria (standards) and communicating these performance expectations to those concerned. Then the work is performed and the supervisor appraises the performance. At the end of the appraisal period, the appraiser reviews work performance and evaluates it against established performance standards. This review helps determine how well employees have met these standards, determines reasons for deficiencies, and develops a plan to correct the problems. At this meeting, goals are set for the next evaluation period, and the cycle repeats.

FIGURE 7-1
Performance Appraisal Process

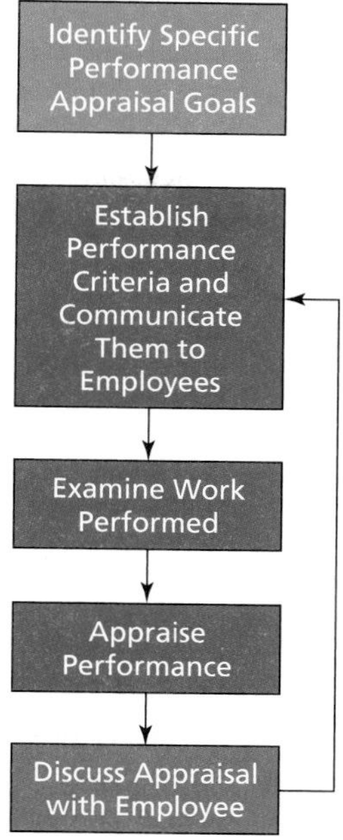

7.2 Explain the uses of performance appraisal and performance criteria.

The Uses of Performance Appraisal and Performance Criteria

Management must carefully plan for how it will use the results of performance appraisal and select performance criteria as it pertains to achieving corporate goals.[2] For instance, performance appraisal can help inform managers whether a low performing employee would benefit from remedial training. The most common appraisal criteria are traits, behaviors, competencies, goal achievement, and improvement potential. Once these considerations are well understood, HR professionals should educate managers about who should be involved in the appraisal process.

Uses of Performance Appraisal

For many organizations, the primary goal of an appraisal system is to improve individual and organizational performance. There may be other goals, however. A potential problem with PA, and a possible cause of much dissatisfaction, is expecting too much from one appraisal plan. For example, a plan that is effective for developing employees may not be the best for determining pay increases. Yet a properly designed system can help achieve organizational objectives and enhance employee performance. In fact, PA data are potentially valuable for virtually every human resource functional area.

HUMAN RESOURCE PLANNING In assessing a firm's HR, data must be available to identify those who have the potential to be promoted or for any area of internal employee relations. Through PA it may be discovered that there is an insufficient number of workers who are prepared to enter management. Plans can then be made for greater emphasis on management development, which we will discuss in Chapter 8. Succession planning is a key concern for all firms. A well-designed appraisal system provides a profile of the organization's human resource strengths and weaknesses to support this effort.

TRAINING AND DEVELOPMENT Performance appraisal should point out an employee's specific needs for training and development. For instance, if Pat Compton's job requires skill in technical writing and her evaluation reveals a deficiency in this factor, she may need additional training to overcome this shortcoming. If a firm finds that many first-line supervisors are having difficulty in administering disciplinary action, training sessions addressing this problem may be appropriate. By identifying deficiencies that adversely affect performance, training and development (T&D) programs can be developed that permit individuals to build on their strengths and minimize their deficiencies. An appraisal system does not guarantee properly trained and developed employees. However, determining T&D needs is more precise when appraisal data are available.

CAREER PLANNING AND DEVELOPMENT *Career planning* is an ongoing process whereby *an individual* sets career goals and identifies the means to achieve them. On the other hand, *career development* is a formal approach used by the organization to ensure that people with the proper qualifications and experiences are available when needed. PA data is essential in assessing an employee's strengths and weaknesses and in determining the person's potential. Managers may use such information to counsel employees and assist them in developing and implementing their career plans.[3]

COMPENSATION PROGRAMS PA results provide a basis for rational decisions regarding pay adjustments. Most managers believe that you should reward outstanding job performance tangibly with pay increases. They believe that *the behaviors you reward are the behaviors you get*. Rewarding behaviors necessary for accomplishing organizational objectives is at the heart of a PM system. To encourage good performance, a firm should design and implement a reliable PA system and then reward the most productive workers and teams accordingly. Substantial evidence substantiates the expectation that better performance ratings lead to higher pay increases and bonuses.[4] Creators of total rewards systems want to ensure that individual performance supports organizational objectives.

INTERNAL EMPLOYEE RELATIONS PA data are also used for decisions in several areas of internal employee relations, including promotion, demotion, termination, layoff, and transfer. For example, an employee's performance in one job may be useful in determining his or her ability to perform another job on the same level, as is required in the consideration of transfers. Certainly, PA data is vital when promotions are considered or layoffs must be made. However, when the performance level is unacceptable, demotion, or even termination, may be appropriate.

ASSESSMENT OF EMPLOYEE POTENTIAL Some organizations attempt to assess an employee's potential as they appraise his or her job performance. Although past behaviors may be a good predictor of future behaviors in some jobs, an employee's past performance may not accurately indicate future performance in other jobs. The best salesperson in the company may not have what it takes to become a successful district sales manager, where the tasks are distinctly different. Similarly, the best systems analyst may, if promoted, be a disaster as an information technology manager. Overemphasizing technical skills and ignoring other equally important skills is a common error in promoting employees into management jobs. Recognition of this problem has led some firms to separate the appraisal of performance, which focuses on past behavior, from the assessment of potential, which is future oriented.

Performance Criteria

Traits, behaviors, and competencies are often used as PA standards. Other standards include goal attainment and improvement potential.

TRAITS, BEHAVIORS, AND COMPETENCIES *Traits* represent an individual's predisposition to think, feel, and behave, and many traits are usually thought of as being biologically created. A personality trait is more ingrained with an individual as with a person being introverted or extroverted, or less conscientious or more conscientious.

Behaviors are typically viewed as resulting from a variety of sources including traits and situational context. For example, a highly conscientious person is more likely to engage in behaviors that lead to timely task completion than someone who is less conscientious because conscientiousness is associated with dutifulness. Employees who tend to be less conscientious may step up their game in situations where they could earn substantial performance-based bonuses than in situations where pay is the same regardless of performance differences.

A behavior may have been learned from parents, from significant friends, or from a certain work environment. A behavior can be changed, but traits are usually more established. Often a young person who joins the military will have many behavioral changes take place prior to returning to civilian life. An appropriate behavior to evaluate for a manager might be leadership style. For individuals working in teams, developing others, teamwork and cooperation, or customer service orientation might be appropriate. Desired behaviors may be appropriate as evaluation criteria because if they are recognized and rewarded, employees tend to repeat them. If certain behaviors result in desired outcomes, there is merit in using them in the evaluation process.

Competencies, as we discussed in Chapter 4, refer to an individual's capability to orchestrate and apply combinations of knowledge, skills, and abilities consistently over time to perform work successfully in the required work situations. Competencies may be technical in nature, relate to interpersonal skills, or are business oriented. For example, analytical thinking and achievement orientation might be essential in professional jobs. In leadership jobs, relevant competencies might include developing talent, delegating authority, and people management skills. The competencies selected for evaluation purposes should be those that are closely associated with job success.

Many of these commonly used traits, behaviors, and competencies are subjective and may be either unrelated to job performance or difficult to define. In such cases, inaccurate evaluations may occur and create legal problems for the organization as well. This was the case in *Wade v. Mississippi Cooperative Extension Service* where the circuit court ruled:

> *In a performance appraisal system, general characteristics such as leadership, public acceptance, attitude toward people, appearance and grooming, personal conduct, outlook on life, ethical habits, resourcefulness, capacity for growth, mental alertness, and loyalty to organization are susceptible to partiality and to the personal taste, whim, or fancy of the evaluator as well as patently subjective in form and obviously susceptible to completely subjective treatment by those conducting the appraisals.*

At the same time, certain traits, behaviors, and competencies may relate to job performance and, if this connection is established, using them may be appropriate.

GOAL ACHIEVEMENT If organizations consider *ends* more important than *means*, goal achievement outcomes become an appropriate factor to evaluate. The outcomes established should be within the control of the individual or team and should be results that lead to the firm's success. At upper levels, the goals might deal with financial aspects of the firm such as profit or cash flow, and market considerations such as market share or position in the market. At lower organizational levels, the outcomes might be meeting the customer's quality requirements and delivering according to the promised schedule.

To assist the process, the manager needs to provide specific examples of how the employee can further his or her development and achieve specific goals. Both parties should reach an agreement as to the employee's goals for the next evaluation period and the assistance and resources the manager needs to provide. This aspect of employee appraisal should be the most positive element in the entire process and help the employee focus on behavior that will produce positive results for all concerned.

IMPROVEMENT POTENTIAL When organizations evaluate employees' performance, many of the criteria used focus on the past. From a PM viewpoint, the problem is that you cannot change the past. Unless a firm takes further steps, the evaluation data become merely historical documents. Therefore, firms should emphasize the future, including the behaviors and outcomes needed to develop the employee, and in the process, achieve the firm's goals. This involves an assessment of the employee's potential. Including *potential* in the evaluation process helps to ensure more effective career planning and development.

The HR Director of the California Health Foundation explains the nature of the company's PM system. The system is open-ended and includes just a few general categories, covering the employee's past performance with respect to their objectives set at the previous year's appraisal, and their future goals in the company. The following Watch It video describes the California Health Foundation's PA system, including a review of the criteria for an employee receiving a good PA, and HR's methods of dealing with both positive and negative PAs and efforts to maintain a positive work culture that emphasizes a culture of personal responsibility, flexibility, and development.

Watch It 1

If your instructor has assigned this, go to **www.pearson.com/mylab/management** to watch a video titled The California Health Foundation: Performance Management and respond to questions.

Responsibility for Performance Appraisal

Often, the human resource department is responsible for coordinating the design and implementation of PA programs. However, it is essential that line managers play a key role from beginning to end. These individuals usually conduct the appraisals, and they must directly participate in developing the program if it is to succeed. In a recent survey of 1,143 U.S. employees, 53 percent get feedback about their performance from their managers. But many would like to get an expanded view of their performance and receive input from others such as from peers, project leaders, and even clients.[5] Several possibilities exist regarding the person(s) who will rate the employee.

IMMEDIATE SUPERVISOR An employee's immediate supervisor has traditionally been the most logical choice for evaluating performance, and this continues to be the case. The supervisor is usually in an excellent position to observe the employee's job performance, and the supervisor has the responsibility for managing a unit. When someone else has the task of evaluating employees, the supervisor's authority may be undermined. Also, employee T&D is an important element in every manager's job, and as previously mentioned, appraisal programs and employee development are usually closely related.

On the negative side, the immediate supervisor may emphasize certain aspects of employee performance and neglect others. Also, managers have been known to manipulate evaluations to justify pay increases and promotions and vice versa.

In most instances, the immediate supervisor will probably continue to be involved in evaluating performance. Organizations will seek alternatives, however, because of technological advances and a desire to broaden the perspective of the appraisal.

EMPLOYEES Historically, our culture has viewed evaluation by employees negatively. However, this thinking has changed somewhat. Some firms conclude that evaluations of managers by employees are both feasible and needed. They reason that employees are in an excellent position to view managers' effectiveness. Advocates believe that this approach leads supervisors to become especially conscious of the work group's needs and to do a better job of managing. In the higher education environment, it is a common practice for instructors to be evaluated by students. Critics are concerned that managers (and instructors) will be caught up in a popularity contest or that employees will be fearful of reprisal. If this approach has a chance for success, one thing is clear: the evaluators must be guaranteed anonymity. Ensuring anonymity might be particularly difficult in a small department and especially if demographic data on the appraisal form could identify raters.

PEERS AND TEAM MEMBERS A major strength of using peers to appraise performance is that they work closely with the evaluated employee and probably have an undistorted perspective on typical performance, especially in team assignments. Problems with peer evaluations include the reluctance of some people who work closely together, especially on teams, to criticize each other. On the other hand, if an employee has been at odds with another worker, he or she might really "unload on the enemy," which results in an unfair evaluation. Another problem concerns peers who interact infrequently and lack the information needed to make an accurate assessment.

Organizations are increasingly using teams, including those that are self-directed. Team members know each other's performance better than anyone and can, therefore, evaluate performance more accurately. Also, peer pressure is a powerful motivator for team members, and members who recognize that peers within the team will be evaluating their work show increased commitment and productivity. When employees work in teams and their appraisal system focuses entirely on individual results, it is not surprising that they show little interest in their teams. But this problem can be corrected. If teamwork is essential, make it a criterion for evaluating employees; rewarding collaboration will encourage teamwork.

SELF-APPRAISAL If employees understand their objectives and the criteria used for evaluation, they are in a good position to appraise their own performance. Many people know what they do well on the job and what they need to improve. If they have the opportunity, they will criticize their own performance objectively and act to improve it. Many times, employees are tougher on themselves than the supervisor will be. Also, because employee development is self-development, employees who appraise their own performance may become more highly motivated. Self-appraisal provides employees with a means of keeping the supervisor informed about everything they have done during the appraisal period.[6]

Even if a self-appraisal is not a part of the system, the employee should at least provide the manager a list of his or her most important accomplishments and contributions over the appraisal period. This will prevent the manager from being blindsided when the employee complains, perhaps justifiably, "You didn't even mention the Bandy contract I landed last December!"

As a complement to other approaches, self-appraisal has great appeal to managers who are primarily concerned with employee participation and development. For compensation purposes, however, its value is considerably less. Some individuals are masters at attributing good performance to their own efforts and poor performance to someone else's.

CUSTOMER APPRAISAL Customer behavior determines a firm's degree of success. Therefore, some organizations believe it is important to obtain performance input from this critical source. Organizations use this approach because it demonstrates a commitment to the customer, holds employees accountable, and fosters change. Customer-related goals for executives generally are of a broad, strategic nature, whereas targets for lower-level employees tend to be more specific. For example, an objective might be to improve the rating for accurate delivery or reduce the number of dissatisfied customers by half. It is important to have employees participate in setting their goals and to include only factors that are within the employees' control.

HR Web Wisdom

360-Degree Evaluation

www.custominsight.com/360-degree-feedback/what-is-360-degree-feedback.asp

360-Degree Evaluation—Delivering Feedback

360-DEGREE FEEDBACK People all around the employee whose performance is being judged may provide input. Those sources, as we have already discussed, include senior managers, the employee himself or herself, a supervisor, employees, peers, team members, and internal or external customers. By shifting the responsibility for evaluation to more than one person, many of the common appraisal errors can be reduced or eliminated. Software is available to permit managers to give the ratings quickly and conveniently. Furthermore, including the perspective of multiple sources results in a more comprehensive and fair view of the employee's performance and minimizes biases resulting from limited views of performance.

Having multiple raters also makes the process more legally defensible. However, it is important for all parties to know the evaluation criteria, the methods for gathering and summarizing the feedback, and the use to which the feedback will be put. An appraisal system involving numerous evaluators will naturally take more time and, therefore, be costlier. Nevertheless, the way firms are being organized and managed may require innovative alternatives to traditional top-down appraisals.

In a survey of training participants, 84 percent said their 360-degree experience was useful.[7] However, some managers believe that the 360-degree feedback method has problems. General Electric's (GE's) former CEO Jack Welch maintains that the 360-degree system in his firm had been "gamed" and that people were saying nice things about one another, resulting in all good ratings.[8] Another critical view with an opposite twist is that input from peers, who may be competitors for raises and promotions, might intentionally distort the data and sabotage the colleague. Yet because so many firms use 360-degree feedback evaluation, it seems that many firms have found ways to avoid the pitfalls.

Significant risks with 360-degree feedback are confidentiality and possible legal ramifications. Many firms outsource the process to make participants feel comfortable that the information they share and receive is completely anonymous. Information is very sensitive, and in the wrong hands, could impact careers. In addition, Nesheba Kittling, an attorney at labor law firm Fisher & Phillips, states that, "Employees' performance reviews are an employers' first line of defense against discrimination claims."[9] Detailed documentation of job performance, "provides support for an employer's contention that it had legitimate, non-discriminatory reasons," for adverse action against an employee such as a demotion or termination.[10]

360-degree feedback evaluation method
Popular performance appraisal method that involves evaluation input from multiple levels within the firm as well as external sources.

As an important aside, the **360-degree feedback evaluation method** is based on the reliance of multiple sources to provide information about an employee's performance.

The 360-degree method is unlike traditional performance reviews, which provide employees with feedback only from supervisors. The 360-degree feedback approach provides an all-inclusive view of each employee. As many as 90 percent of *Fortune* 500 companies use some form of 360-degree feedback for either employee evaluation or development. Many companies use results from 360-degree programs not only for conventional applications but also for succession planning, training, and professional development.[11]

Performance Appraisal Period

Formal performance evaluations are usually prepared at specific intervals. Although there is nothing magical about the period for formal appraisal reviews, in most organizations they occur either annually or semiannually. Even more significant, however, is the continuous interaction (primarily informal), including coaching and other developmental activities, that continues throughout the appraisal period. Managers should be conditioned to understand that managing performance is a continuous process that is built into their job every day.

In the current business climate, firms may want to consider monitoring performance more often. Changes occur so fast that employees need to look at objectives and their own roles throughout the year to see whether changes are in order. Southwest Airlines has asked its managers to have monthly check-ins with staff rather than semiannual ones.[12] Employees with Royal Caribbean Cruises are evaluated approximately three weeks prior to the completion of their contract, which is typically six months. Some even consider these relatively shorter intervals to be too long; "Think of a sports team: A coach doesn't wait until the end of a season to give his players feedback."[13]

Some organizations use the employee's date of hire to determine the rating period. At times an employee's first appraisal may occur at the end of a probationary period, anywhere from 30 to 90 days after his or her start date. However, in the interest of consistency, it may be advisable to perform evaluations on a calendar basis rather than on anniversaries. If firms do not conduct all appraisals at the same time, it may be impossible to make needed comparisons between employees.

The frequency of providing employees with performance feedback is important. The following Watch It video describes The Weather Channel PA process in which appraisals are recommended to be done on an ongoing, continual basis so that an employee always knows where he or she stands as far as what is expected and how well he or she is doing. This way, the employee can look forward to performance reviews instead of dreading them; performance reviews will be an official confirmation of all the progress that the employee has been making under the ongoing relationship of appraisal and feedback with the employee's manager.

Watch It 2

If your instructor has assigned this, go to **www.pearson.com/mylab/management** to watch a video titled Weather Channel: Performance Appraisal and respond to questions.

7.3 Describe the choice of various performance appraisal methods.

Choosing a Performance Appraisal Method

The various methods are next presented as if they are separate and distinct when each may be used in conjunction with another method. For instance, the 360-degree feedback method may incorporate portions of the ranking scale. There are multiple approaches to appraising employee performance. It is instructive to group them into categories according to what they are designed to measure. PA methods fall into four broad categories:

- Trait systems
- Comparison systems
- Behavioral systems
- Results-based systems

Trait Systems

trait systems
Type of performance-appraisal method, requiring raters (e.g., supervisors or customers) to evaluate each employee's traits or characteristics (e.g., quality of work and leadership).

Trait systems ask raters to evaluate each employee's traits or characteristics (e.g., quality of work, quantity of work, appearance, dependability, cooperation, initiative, judgment, leadership responsibility, decision-making ability, or creativity). Appraisals are typically scored using descriptors ranging from unsatisfactory to outstanding. Figure 7-2 contains an illustration of a trait method of performance appraisal.

The trait approach does have limitations. First, trait systems are highly subjective[14] because they assume that every supervisor's perception of a given trait is the same. For example, the trait "quality of work" may be defined by one supervisor as, "The extent to which an employee's performance is free of errors." To another supervisor, quality of work might mean, "The extent to which an employee's performance is timely." Human resource professionals and supervisors can avoid this problem by working together in advance to specify the definition of traits clearly.

FIGURE 7-2
Trait-Oriented Performance Appraisal Rating Form

Employee's Name:			***Employee's Position:***	
Supervisor's Name:			***Review Period:***	
Instructions: For each trait, circle the phrase that best represents the employee.				
1. Diligence				
a. Outstanding	b. Above average	c. Average	d. Below average	e. Poor
2. Cooperation with others				
a. Outstanding	b. Above average	c. Average	d. Below average	e. Poor
3. Communication skills				
a. Outstanding	b. Above average	c. Average	d. Below average	e. Poor
4. Leadership				
a. Outstanding	b. Above average	c. Average	d. Below average	e. Poor
5. Decisiveness				
a. Outstanding	b. Above average	c. Average	d. Below average	e. Poor

Another drawback is that systems rate individuals on subjective personality factors rather than on objective job performance data. Essentially, trait assessment focuses attention on employees rather than on job performance. Employees may simply become defensive rather than trying to understand the role that the trait plays in shaping their job performance and then taking corrective actions. Moreover, traits represent a predisposition to behave, think, or feel. Although traits do influence behavior, these do not fully account for behavior.[15] For example, highly conscientious individuals tend to be dutiful and complete assignments on a regular basis. However, other factors, including illness or ongoing distractions, could interfere with the productivity that one might expect to be associated with a trait.

Comparison Systems

comparison systems
A type of performance-appraisal method, require that raters (e.g., supervisors) evaluate a given employee's performance against other employees' performance attainments. Employees are ranked from the best performer to the poorest performer.

forced distribution method
Performance appraisal method in which the rater is required to assign individuals in a work group to a limited number of categories, like a normal frequency distribution.

Comparison systems evaluate one employee's performance against that of other employees. Employees are ranked from the best performer to the poorest performer. In simplest form, supervisors rank each employee and establish a performance hierarchy such that the employee with the best performance receives the highest ranking. Employees may be ranked on overall performance or on various traits.

An alternative approach, called a **forced distribution method** PA and sometimes referred to as a stacked ranking system, assigns employees to groups that represent the entire range of performance. For example, three categories that might be used are best performers, moderate performers, and poor performers. A forced distribution approach, in which the rater must place a specific number of employees into each of the performance groups, can be used with this method. Figure 7-3 displays a forced distribution rating form for an animal keeper job with five performance categories.

Many companies use forced distribution approaches to minimize the tendency for supervisors to rate most employees as excellent performers. This tendency usually arises out of supervisors' self-promotion motives. Also, supervisors often provide positive performance ratings to most employees because they do not want to alienate them. After all, supervisory performance depends largely on how well employees perform their jobs.

Although used by some prestigious firms, the forced distribution system appears to be unpopular with many managers.[16] Some believe it fosters cutthroat competition, paranoia, and general ill will, and destroys employee loyalty.[17] For example, David Auerback, a former Microsoft employee, stated that this type of appraisal system had employees feeling helpless and, "encouraged people to backstab their co-workers."[18] Many believe that a "rank-and-yank" system such as forced distribution is not compatible when a company encourages teamwork. In addition, critics of forced distribution contend that they compel managers to penalize a good, although not a great, employee who is part of a superstar team. Another reason employees are opposed to forced ranking is that they suspect that the rankings are a way for companies to rationalize firings

FIGURE 7-3
A Forced Distribution Performance Appraisal Rating Form

Instructions: You are required to rate the performance for the previous 3 months of the 15 workers employed as animal keepers to conform with the following performance distribution:

- *15 percent* of the animal keepers will be rated as having exhibited poor performance.
- *20 percent* of the animal keepers will be rated as having exhibited below-average performance.
- *35 percent* of the animal keepers will be rated as having exhibited average performance.
- *20 percent* of the animal keepers will be rated as having exhibited above-average performance.
- *10 percent* of the animal keepers will be rated as having exhibited superior performance.

Use the following guidelines for rating performance. Based on the five duties listed in the job description for animal keeper, the employee's performance is characterized as:

- *Poor* if the incumbent performs only one of the duties well.
- *Below average* if the incumbent performs only two of the duties well.
- *Average* if the incumbent performs only three of the duties well.
- *Above average* if the incumbent performs only four of the duties well.
- *Superior* if the incumbent performs all five of the duties well.

more easily. Yahoo's employee-ranking system was challenged in court for this very reason. Allegedly, Yahoo executives required managers to give poor rankings to a designated percentage of employees regardless of actual performance, and high-level executives subjectively changed managers' ratings.[19]

Forced distribution approaches have drawbacks. The forced distribution approach can distort ratings because employee performance may not fall into these predetermined distributions. Let's assume that a supervisor must use the following forced distribution to rate her employees' performance:

- 15 percent well below average
- 25 percent below average
- 40 percent average
- 15 percent above average
- 5 percent well above average

This distribution is problematic to the extent that the actual distribution of employee performance is substantially different from this forced distribution. If 35 percent of the employees' performance were either above average or well above average, then the supervisor would be required to underrate the performance of 15 percent of the employees. Based on this forced distribution, the supervisor can rate only 20 percent of the employees as having demonstrated above-average or well-above-average job performance. Management–employee relationships ultimately suffer because workers feel that ratings are dictated by unreal models rather than by individual performance. Perhaps extensive training and development interventions enabled many more employees than anticipated to perform well above average (12 percent versus 5 percent). The "forced" nature of this system results in 7 percent of employees being placed in an undeservedly lower rating category. Also, under a pay-for-performance plan, those 7 percent would receive a lower than earned pay increase award.

paired comparisons
Supervisors compare each employee to every other employee, identifying the better performer in each pair.

Another comparative technique for ranking employees is the **paired comparisons method**. Supervisors compare each employee to every other employee, identifying the better performer in each pair. Figure 7-4 displays a paired comparison form. Following the comparison, the employees are ranked according to the number of times they were identified as being the better performer. In this example, Allen Jones is the best performer because he was identified most often as the better performer, followed by Bob Brown (identified twice as the better performer) and Mary Green (identified once as the better performer).

FIGURE 7-4

A Paired Comparison Performance Appraisal Rating Form

Instructions: Please indicate by placing an X which employee of each pair has performed most effectively during the past year.

X	*Bob Brown*	X	*Mary Green*
	Mary Green		Jim Smith
X	*Bob Brown*		Mary Green
	Jim Smith	X	*Allen Jones*
	Bob Brown		Jim Smith
X	*Allen Jones*	X	*Allen Jones*

Comparative methods are best suited for small groups of employees who perform the same or similar jobs. They are cumbersome for large groups of employees or for employees who perform different jobs. For example, it would be difficult to judge whether a production worker's performance is better than a secretary's performance because the jobs are substantively different. The assessment of a production worker's performance is based on the number of units he or she produces during each work shift; a secretary's performance is based on the accuracy with which he or she types memos and letters.

As do trait systems, comparison approaches have limitations. They tend to encourage subjective judgments, which increase the chance for rater errors and biases. In addition, small differences in performance between employees may become exaggerated by using such a method if supervisors feel compelled to distinguish among levels of employee performance.

Behavioral Systems

behavioral systems
Performance appraisal methods that focus on distinguishing between successful and unsuccessful behaviors.

critical incident technique (CIT)
Performance appraisal method that requires keeping written records of highly favorable and unfavorable employee work actions.

Behavioral systems rate employees on the extent to which they display successful job performance behaviors. In contrast to trait and comparison methods, behavioral methods rate objective job behaviors. When correctly developed and applied, behavioral models provide results that are relatively free of rater errors and biases. The three main types of behavioral systems are the critical incident technique (CIT), behaviorally anchored rating scales (BARS), and behavioral observation scales (BOS).

The **critical incident technique (CIT)**[20] requires job incumbents and their supervisors to identify performance incidents (e.g., on-the-job behaviors and behavioral outcomes) that distinguish successful performances from unsuccessful ones. The supervisor then observes the employees and records their performance on these critical job aspects. Supervisors usually rate employees on how often they display the behaviors described in each critical incident. Figure 7-5 illustrates a CIT form for an animal keeper job. Two statements represent examples of ineffective

FIGURE 7-5

A Critical Incidents Performance Appraisal Rating Form

Instructions: For each description of work behavior, circle the number that best describes how frequently the employee engages in that behavior.

1. The incumbent removes manure and unconsumed food from the animal enclosures.

1	2	3	4	5
Never	Almost never	Sometimes	Fairly often	Very often

2. The incumbent haphazardly measures the feed items when placing them in the animal enclosures.

1	2	3	4	5
Never	Almost never	Sometimes	Fairly often	Very often

3. The incumbent leaves refuse dropped by visitors on and around the public walkways.

1	2	3	4	5
Never	Almost never	Sometimes	Fairly often	Very often

4. The incumbent skillfully identifies instances of abnormal behavior among the animals, which represent signs of illness.

1	2	3	4	5
Never	Almost never	Sometimes	Fairly often	Very often

job performance (numbers 2 and 3), and two statements represent examples of effective job performance (numbers 1 and 4).

The CIT tends to be useful because this procedure requires extensive documentation that identifies successful and unsuccessful job performance behaviors by both the employee and the supervisor. The CIT's strength, however, is also its weakness: implementation of the CIT demands continuous and close observation of the employee. Supervisors may find the record keeping to be overly burdensome.

behaviorally anchored rating scale (BARS)
Performance appraisal method that combines elements of the traditional rating scale and critical incident methods; various performance levels are shown along a scale with each described in terms of an employee's specific job behavior.

Behaviorally anchored rating scales (BARS)[21] are based on the CIT, and these scales are developed in the same fashion with one exception. For the CIT, a critical incident would be written as "the incumbent completed the task in a timely fashion." For the BARS format, this incident would be written as "the incumbent is expected to complete the task in a timely fashion." The designers of BARS write the incidents as expectations to emphasize the fact that the employee does not have to demonstrate the exact behavior that is used as an anchor to be rated at that level. Because a complete array of behaviors that characterize a job would take many pages of description, it is not feasible to place examples of all job behaviors on the scale. Experts therefore list only those behaviors that they believe are most representative of the job the employee must perform. A typical job might have 8–10 dimensions under BARS, each with a separate rating scale.

Table 7-1 illustrates a portion of a BARS system that was developed to evaluate college recruiters. Suppose the factor chosen for evaluation is *Ability to Present Positive Company Image*. On the *very positive* end of this factor would be, "Makes excellent impression on college recruits. Carefully explains positive aspects of the company. Listens to applicant and answers questions in a very positive manner." On the *very negative* end of this factor would be, "Even with repeated instructions continues to make a poor impression. This interviewer could be expected to turn off college applicant from wanting to join the firm." As may be noted, there are several levels in between the very negative and the very positive. The rater can determine more objectively how frequently the employee performs in each defined level.

As with all PA techniques, BARS has its advantages and disadvantages.[22] Among the various PA techniques, BARS is the most defensible in court because it is based on actual observable job behaviors. In addition, BARS encourages all raters to make evaluations in the same way. Perhaps the main disadvantage of BARS is the difficulty of developing and maintaining the volume of

TABLE 7-1

BARS for Factor: Ability to Present Positive Company Image

Clearly Outstanding Performance	Makes excellent impression on college recruits. Carefully explains positive aspects of the company. Listens to applicant and answers questions in a very positive manner.
Excellent Performance	Makes good impression on college recruits. Answers all questions and explains positive aspects of the company. Answers questions in a positive manner.
Good Performance	Makes a reasonable impression on college recruits. Listens to applicant and answers questions in knowledgeable manner.
Average Performance	Makes a fair impression on college recruits. Listens to applicant and answers most questions in a knowledgeable manner.
Slightly Below Average Performance	Attempts to make a good impression on college recruits. Listens to applicants but at times could be expected to have to go to other sources to get answers to questions.
Poor Performance	At times makes poor impression on college recruits. Sometimes provides incorrect information to applicant or goes down blind avenues before realizing mistake.
Very Poor Performance	Even with repeated instructions continues to make a poor impression. This interviewer could be expected to turn off college applicant from wanting to join the firm.

data necessary to make it effective. The BARS method requires companies to maintain distinct appraisal documents for each job. As jobs change over time, the documentation must be updated for each job.

behavioral observation scale (BOS)
A specific kind of behavioral system for evaluating job performance by illustrating positive incidents (or behaviors) of job performance for various job dimensions.

Another kind of behavior system, a **behavioral observation scale (BOS)**,[23] displays illustrations of positive incidents (or behaviors) of job performance for various job dimensions. The evaluator rates the employee on each behavior according to the extent to which the employee performs in a manner consistent with each behavioral description. Scores from each job dimension are averaged to provide an overall rating of performance. BOS is developed in the same way as a BARS instrument, except that it incorporates only positive performance behaviors. The BOS method tends to be difficult and time-consuming to develop and maintain. Moreover, to ensure accurate appraisal, raters must be able to observe employees closely and regularly. However, observing employees on a regular basis may not be feasible where supervisors are responsible for several people.

Results-Based Systems

results-based performance appraisal
Performance appraisal method in which the manager and employee jointly agree on objectives for the next appraisal period; in the past a form of management by objectives.

Results-based performance appraisal methods focus on measurable outcomes such as an individual's or team's sales, customer service ratings, productivity, reduced incidence of workplace injuries, and so forth. The selection of results largely depends on three factors. The first factor is the relevance of the results that may be used to judge a company's progress toward meeting its strategic goals. The second factor is the reliability with which results can be measured. The third factor is the extent to which the results measure is truly a measure of performance over which an employee has the resources and latitude to achieve the designated results.

Management by objectives (MBO) could possibly be the most effective PA technique because supervisors and employees determine objectives for employees to meet during the rating period and employees appraise how well they have achieved their objectives. MBO is used mainly for managerial and professional employees and typically evaluates employees' progress toward strategic planning objectives.

Employees and supervisors together determine objectives tied to corporate strategies. Employees are expected to attain these objectives during the rating period. The crucial phase of the MBO process requires that challenging but attainable objectives and standards be established through interaction between managers and employees. Individuals jointly established objectives with their managers, who then give them some latitude in how to achieve the objectives. Action plans require clear delineation of what specifically is to be accomplished and when it is to be completed. For example, if a sales manager has a performance objective of increasing sales in his

HR BLOOPERS

Appraising Performance at Global Insurance

As Devin Franklin hung up from a call with yet another unhappy employee, he realized there was a problem with the new PA system. Devin, the HR Manager at Global Insurance, rolled out a new performance rating form about a month ago and has since heard from several frustrated employees. Devin met his goal to get the new system in place before the end of the year, but may have rushed the process too much. He created a basic form using rating scales that asked supervisors to rate all employees on the same common factors such as quality and quantity of work, customer service skills, and general attitude. The easy to use form allowed supervisors to just check the right boxes and give it to the employees. But, there have been a variety of complaints suggesting the appraisals aren't effectively evaluating the employees' performance. Many complaints have argued different definitions of the factors being evaluated such as attitude. Some of the field insurance agents who work outside of the office on their own have even suggested that their direct supervisors shouldn't evaluate their customer service skills because the supervisors never actually observe their customer interactions. The supervisors have asked him a lot of questions about the form as well. Devin considered organizing a training program for the supervisors, but he decided there just wasn't enough time. Now, he's not sure if a training program would even fix the problems.

If your professor has assigned this, go to **www.pearson.com/mylab/management** to complete the HR Bloopers exercise and test your application of these concepts when faced with real-world decisions.

or her area by 38 percent next year, the action plan might include the employment of three experienced salespersons, six calls a week by the sales manager on major customers, and assignment of appropriate sales quotas to all the salespeople.

At the end of the rating period, the employee writes a report explaining his or her progress toward accomplishing the objectives, and the employee's supervisor appraises the employee's performance based on accomplishment of the objectives. Despite the importance of managerial employees to company success, it is often difficult to establish appropriate performance goals because many companies simply do not fully describe the scope of these positions. MBO can promote effective communication between employees and their supervisors.

With MBO, performance is evaluated based on progress toward objective attainment. Having specific performance objectives provides management with a basis for comparison. When objectives are agreed on by the manager and the employee, self-evaluation and controls become possible. In fact, with MBO, PA can be a joint effort, based on agreement.

With MBO, it is left up to the managers to take corrective action when results are not as planned. Such action may take the form of changes in personnel, changes in the organization, or even changes in the objectives. Other forms of corrective action may include providing additional training and development of individual managers or employees to enable them to better achieve the desired results. Corrective action should not necessarily have negative connotations. Under MBO, objectives can be renegotiated downward without penalty or fear of job loss. Various segments of the MBO process can easily be integrated into an effective *goal-oriented system*. Goal-oriented systems are often a component of broader development programs that help employees achieve career goals.

On the downside, MBO is time-consuming and requires a constant flow of information between employees and employers. Moreover, its focus is only on the attainment of goals, often to the exclusion of other important outcomes. This drawback is known as a "results at any cost" mentality.[24] The role of automobile sales professionals historically was literally limited to making sales. Once these professionals and customers agreed on the price of a car, the sales professionals' work with customers was completed. Automobile salespeople today remain in contact with clients for several months following the completion of the sale. The purpose is to ensure customer satisfaction and build loyalty to the product and dealership by addressing questions about the vehicle's features and reminding clients about scheduled service checks.

work standards method
Performance appraisal method that compares each employee's performance to a predetermined standard or expected level of output.

Another results-oriented practice is the work standards method. The **work standards method** is a PA method that compares each employee's performance to a predetermined standard or expected level of output. Standards reflect the normal output of an average worker operating at a normal pace. Firms may apply work standards to virtually all types of jobs, but production jobs generally receive the most attention. An obvious advantage of using work standards as appraisal criteria is objectivity. However, for employees to perceive that the standards are objective, they should understand clearly how the standards were set. Management must also explain the rationale for any changes to the standards.

The work standards method is often coupled with an incentive pay plan known as the piecework plan. *Piecework plans* typically found in manufacturing settings, rewards employees based on their individual hourly production against an objective output standard and is determined by the pace at which manufacturing equipment operates. For each hour, workers receive piecework incentives for every item produced over the designated production standard. Workers also receive a guaranteed hourly pay rate regardless of whether they meet the designated production standard. Companies use piecework plans when the time to produce a unit is relatively short, usually less than 15 minutes, and the cycle repeats continuously.

Figure 7-6 illustrates the calculation of a piecework incentive.

FYI

In a survey commissioned by the Society for Human Resource Management:

- Nine out of ten companies reported using annual or semi-annual performance reviews.
- Only three out of ten expressed that they conducted them well.[25]

FIGURE 7-6
Calculation of a Piecework Award for a Garment Worker

Piecework standard: 15 stitched garments per hour
Hourly base pay rate awarded to employees when the standard is not met: $4.50 per hour
That is, workers receive $4.50 per hour worked regardless of whether they meet the piecework standard of 15 stitched garments per hour.
Piecework incentive award: $0.75 per garment stitched per hour above the piecework standard

	Guaranteed Hourly Base Pay ($)	Piecework Award (No. of Garments Stitched above the Piecework Standard × Piecework Incentive Award)	Total Hourly Earnings ($)
First hour	4.50	10 garments × $0.75/garment = $7.50	12.00
Second hour	4.50	Fewer than 15 stitched garments, thus piecework award equals $0	4.50

7.4 Assess the effectiveness and limitations of performance appraisal practices.

Assessing the Effectiveness and Limitations of Performance Appraisal Practices

It is important to understand how to distinguish between effective and ineffective performance appraisal practices. Also, as noted earlier, there are potentially legal consequences for the firm when ineffective practices are not remedied. We review these issues next.

Characteristics of an Effective Appraisal System

The basic purpose of a PA system is to improve the performance of individuals, teams, and the entire organization. The system may also serve to assist in making administrative decisions concerning pay increases, promotions, transfers, or terminations. In addition, the appraisal system must be legally defensible. Although a perfect system does not exist, every system should possess certain characteristics. The following factors assist in accomplishing these purposes.

RELIABILITY AND VALIDITY We discussed the reliability and validity of selection practices in Chapter 6. These issues equally apply to performance appraisal methods. Applied to performance appraisal, reliability refers to the extent to which a method provides consistent results. For example, let's assume that two managers are similarly familiar with an employee's job performance, and they independently rate performance using the same method at the same time. If the supervisors' judgements were in alignment, we could say that the performance appraisal method is reliable (normally, we talk about degrees of reliability).

Validity is the extent to which a test measures what it claims to measure. If a performance appraisal method measures something other than job performance, it has no value. For instance, if a sales professional is judged on monthly sales revenue, then, measuring anything else leads to the conclusion that the method is not valid. An illustration would be measuring motivation to perform well rather than sales revenue.

JOB-RELATED CRITERIA Job-relatedness is perhaps the most basic criterion needed in employee performance appraisals. The evaluation instrument should tie in closely to the accomplishment of organizational goals.[26] The *Uniform Guidelines on Employee Selection Procedures* and court decisions are quite clear on this point. More specifically, evaluation criteria should be determined through job analysis. Subjective factors, such as initiative, enthusiasm, loyalty, and cooperation may be important; however, unless clearly shown to be job related, they should not be used.

PERFORMANCE EXPECTATIONS Employees must understand in advance what is expected of them. How can employees function effectively if they do not know what they are being measured against? On the other hand, if employees clearly understand the expectations, they can evaluate their own performance and make timely adjustments as they perform their jobs, without having to wait for the formal evaluation review. The establishment of highly objective work standards is relatively simple in many areas, such as manufacturing, assembly, and sales. For numerous other types of jobs, however, this task is more difficult. Still, evaluation must take place based on clearly understood performance expectations.

FYI

- Only about half of employees strongly agree that they know what is expected of them at work.[27]

STANDARDIZATION Firms should use the same evaluation instrument for all employees in the same job category who work for the same supervisor. Supervisors should also conduct appraisals covering similar periods for these employees. Regularly scheduled feedback sessions and appraisal interviews for all employees are essential. Most large companies require groups of supervisors to come together to standardize employee performance reviews. They hash out the rationale behind each employee's performance rating and adjust them to ensure that they reflect similar standards and expectations.[28]

Formal documentation of appraisal data serves several purposes, including protection against possible legal action. Employees should sign their evaluations. If the employee refuses to sign, the manager should document this behavior. Records should also include a description of employee responsibilities, expected performance results, and the role these data play in making appraisal decisions. Although PA is important for small firms, they are not expected to maintain PA systems that are as formal as those used by large organizations. Courts have reasoned that objective criteria are not as important in firms with only a few employees because in smaller firms, top managers are more intimately acquainted with employees' work.

TRAINED APPRAISERS A common deficiency in appraisal systems is that the evaluators seldom receive training on how to conduct effective evaluations. Unless everyone evaluating performance receives training in the art of giving and receiving feedback, the process can lead to uncertainty and conflict. The training should be an ongoing process to ensure accuracy and consistency. It should cover how to rate employees and how to conduct appraisal interviews. Instructions should be rather detailed and the importance of making objective and unbiased ratings should be emphasized.

CONTINUOUS OPEN COMMUNICATION Most employees have a strong need to know how well they are performing. A good appraisal system provides highly desired feedback on a continuing basis. There should be few surprises in the performance review. However, in one survey, only 45 percent of individuals felt their managers consistently communicated their performance concerns throughout the year.[29] Managers should handle daily performance problems as they occur and not allow them to pile up for six months or a year and then address them during the PA interview. When something new surfaces during the appraisal interview, the manager probably did not do a good enough job communicating with the employee throughout the appraisal process. Even though the interview presents an excellent opportunity for both parties to exchange ideas, it should never serve as a substitute for the day-to-day communication and coaching required by performance management.

CONDUCT PERFORMANCE REVIEWS In addition to the need for continuous communication between managers and employees, a special time should be set for a formal discussion of an employee's performance. Because improved performance is a common goal of appraisal systems, withholding appraisal results is absurd. Employees are severely handicapped in their developmental efforts if denied access to this information. A performance review allows them to detect any errors or omissions in the appraisal, or an employee may disagree with the evaluation and want to challenge it.

Constant employee performance documentation is vitally important for accurate PAs. Although the task can be tedious and boring for managers, maintaining a continuous record of observed and reported incidents is essential in building a useful appraisal. The appraisal interview will be discussed in a later section.

DUE PROCESS Ensuring due process is vital. If the company does not have a formal grievance procedure, it should develop one to provide employees an opportunity to appeal appraisal results that they consider inaccurate or unfair. They must have a procedure for pursuing their grievances and having them addressed objectively.

Limitations of Performance Appraisal

PA is constantly under a barrage of criticism. The rating scales method seems to be the most vulnerable target. Yet in all fairness, many of the problems commonly mentioned are not exclusive to this method but rather, reflect improper implementation. The following section highlights some of the more common problem areas.

APPRAISER DISCOMFORT Conducting PAs is often a frustrating task for managers. If a PA system has a faulty design, or improper administration, employees will dread receiving appraisals and the managers will despise giving them. In fact, some managers have always loathed the time, paperwork, difficult choices, and discomfort that often accompanies the appraisal process. Going through the procedure cuts into a manager's high-priority workload and the experience can be especially unpleasant when the employee in question has not performed well.

SUBJECTIVITY OF PERFORMANCE EVALUATIONS A potential weakness of many PA methods is that they lack objectivity. For example, commonly used factors such as traits, behaviors, and competencies are virtually impossible to measure with objective measures. In addition, these factors may have little to do with an employee's job performance. Although subjectivity will always exist in appraisal methods, employee appraisal based primarily on personal characteristics may place the evaluator and the company in untenable positions with the employee and equal employment opportunity guidelines. The firm may be hard-pressed to show that some of these factors are job related.

rating errors
In performance appraisals, differences between human judgment processes versus objective, accurate assessments uncolored by bias, prejudice, or other subjective, extraneous influences.

Almost all people make **rating errors**. Rating errors reflect differences between human judgment processes versus objective, accurate assessments uncolored by bias, prejudice, or other subjective, extraneous influences.[30] Human resource departments can help raters to minimize errors by carefully choosing rating systems and to recognize and avoid common errors. Major types of rater errors include:

- Bias errors
- Contrast errors
- Errors of central tendency
- Errors of leniency or strictness

bias errors
Evaluation errors that occur when the rater evaluates the employee based on a personal negative or positive opinion of the employee rather than on the employee's actual performance.

first-impression effect
An initial favorable or unfavorable judgment about an employee's which is ignored or distorted.

positive halo effect (or halo effect)
Evaluation error that occurs when a manager generalizes one positive performance feature or incident to all aspects of employee performance, resulting in a higher rating.

negative halo effect (or horn error)
Evaluation error that occurs when a manager generalizes one negative performance feature or incident to all aspects of employee performance, resulting in a lower rating.

BIAS ERRORS **Bias errors** happen when the rater evaluates the employee based on a personal negative or positive opinion of the employee, rather than on the employee's actual performance. Four ways supervisors may bias evaluation results are first-impression effects, positive and negative halo effects, similar-to-me effects, and illegal discriminatory biases.

A manager biased by a **first-impression effect** might make an initial favorable or unfavorable judgment about an employee and then ignore or distort the employee's actual performance to fit this impression. For instance, a manager expects that a newly hired graduate of a prestigious university will be an exemplary performer. After one year on the job, this employee fails to meet many of the work objectives, nevertheless, the manager rates the job performance more highly because of the initial impression.

A **positive halo effect** (oftentimes, referred to simply as a **halo effect**) or **negative halo effect** (also known as a **horn error**) occurs when a rater generalizes an employee's good or bad behavior on one aspect of the job to all aspects of the job. For example, Rodney Pirkle, accounting supervisor, placed a high value on neatness, a factor used in the company's PA system. As Rodney was evaluating the performance of his senior accounting clerk, Jack Hicks, he noted that Jack was a very neat individual and gave him a high ranking on this factor. Also, consciously or unconsciously, Rodney permitted the high ranking on neatness to carry over to other factors, giving Jack undeserved high ratings on some other performance criteria even though his actual performance was low. This phenomenon is known as the *positive halo effect*, an evaluation error that occurs when a manager generalizes one positive performance feature or incident to all aspects of employee performance, resulting in a higher rating. Of course, if Jack had not been neat, yet, performed well on every other dimension, the opposite, the *horn error* would have occurred.

FYI

- Researchers maintain that 61 percent of an employee's rating is based on the manager's judgment of him/herself rather than on the employee.[31]

A **similar-to-me effect** refers to the tendency on the part of raters to judge favorably employees whom they perceive as like themselves. Supervisors biased by this effect rate more favorably employees who have attitudes, values, backgrounds, or interests like theirs. For example, employees whose children attend the same elementary school as their manager's children receive higher PA ratings than do employees who do not have children. Similar-to-me errors or biases easily can lead to charges of **illegal discriminatory bias**, wherein a supervisor rates members of his or her race, gender, nationality, or religion more favorably than members of other classes.

illegal discriminatory bias
A bias error for which a supervisor rates members of his or her race, gender, nationality, or religion more favorably than members of other classes.

This pitfall occurs when managers allow individual differences to affect the ratings they give. If there are factors to avoid such as gender, race, or age, not only is this problem detrimental to employee morale, but it is obviously illegal and can result in costly lawsuits. The effects of cultural bias, or stereotyping, can influence appraisals.[32] Managers establish mental pictures of what are considered ideal typical workers, and employees who do not match this picture may be unfairly judged. Although all people have biases of some type that can affect the appraisal process, a successful evaluator will manage these biases.[33]

contrast errors
A rating error in which a rater (e.g., a supervisor) compares an employee to other employees rather than to specific explicit performance standards.

CONTRAST ERRORS Supervisors make **contrast errors** when they compare an employee with other employees rather than to specific, explicit performance standards. Such comparisons qualify as errors because other employees are required to perform only at minimum acceptable standards. Employees performing at minimally acceptable levels should receive satisfactory ratings, even if every other employee doing the job is performing at outstanding or above-average levels.

central tendency error
Evaluation appraisal error that occurs when employees are incorrectly rated near the average or middle of a scale.

ERRORS OF CENTRAL TENDENCY When supervisors rate all employees as average or close to average, they commit **errors of central tendency**. Such errors are most often committed when raters are forced to justify only extreme behavior (i.e., high or low ratings) with written explanations, therefore, HR professionals should require justification for ratings at every level of the scale and not just at the extremes. With such a system, the rater may avoid possible controversy or criticism by giving only average ratings.[34] However, because these ratings tend to cluster in the *fully satisfactory* range, employees do not often complain. Nevertheless, this error does exist and it influences the accuracy of evaluations. Typically, when pay raises are given, they will be based on an employee's rated performance. When a manager gives an underachiever or overachiever an average rating, it undermines the compensation system.[35]

leniency error
Giving an undeserved high performance appraisal rating to an employee.

ERRORS OF LENIENCY OR STRICTNESS Raters sometimes place every employee at the high or low end of the scale, regardless of actual performance. With a **leniency error**, managers tend to appraise employees' performance more highly than they rate compared with objective criteria. This behavior is often motivated by a desire to avoid controversy over the appraisal. However, leniency provides a false sense of confidence to the employee and diminishes exceptional performance by other workers. It is most prevalent when highly subjective (and difficult to defend) performance criteria are used, and the rater is required to discuss evaluation results with employees. When managers know they are evaluating employees for administrative purposes, such as pay increases, they are likely to be more lenient than when evaluating performance to achieve employee development. Leniency, however, may result in failure to recognize correctable deficiencies. The practice may also deplete the merit budget and reduce the rewards available for superior employees. Rather than confronting employees whose performance is not acceptable, managers may avoid the situation by giving false-positive performance evaluations. An organization may find itself in a difficult situation when after firing a problem employee, the recent excellent performance evaluation shows up as part of a lawsuit.[36] Rating an employee as outstanding and then firing him or her because of poor performance will make a supervisor look foolish if taken to court. On the other hand, **strictness errors** occur when a supervisor rates an employee's performance lower than it would be if compared against objective criteria.

strictness errors
Being unduly critical of an employee's work performance.

EMPLOYEE ANXIETY The evaluation process may also create anxiety for the appraised employee.[37] This may take the form of discontent, apathy, and turnover. In a worst-case scenario, a lawsuit is filed based on real or perceived unfairness. Opportunities for promotion, better work assignments, and increased compensation may hinge on the results. This could cause not only apprehension but also outright resistance. One opinion is that if you surveyed typical employees, they would tell you PA is management's way of highlighting all the bad things they did all year.

Legal Considerations

Employee lawsuits may result from negative evaluations. Employees often win these cases, thanks in part to the firm's own PA procedures. A review of court cases makes it clear that legally defensible PA systems should be in place. Perfect systems are not expected, and the law does not preclude supervisory discretion in the process. However, the courts normally require an absence of adverse impact on members of protected classes or validation of the process. It also expects a system that keeps one manager from directing or controlling an employee's career. There should also be a system whereby the appraisal is reviewed and approved by someone or some group in the organization. Another requirement is that the evaluator must have personal knowledge of the employee's job performance. In addition, the system uses predetermined norms that limit the manager's discretion.

Mistakes in appraising performance and decisions based on invalid results can have serious repercussions. For example, discriminatory merit pay increases have resulted in costly legal action. In settling cases, courts have held employers liable for back pay, court costs, and other costs related to training and promoting certain employees in protected classes. Further, giving higher-than-earned evaluations and then firing an employee may set the stage for a suit, especially if the individual is a member of a protected group. The apparent inconsistency may give the employee a basis for claiming discrimination.[38]

Legislation that prohibits illegal discrimination in employment practices (e.g., the Age Discrimination in Employment Act) certainly applies to PA practices. In the case of *Mistretta v. Sandia Corporation* (a subsidiary of Western Electric Company, Inc.), a federal district court judge ruled against the company, stating, "There is sufficient circumstantial evidence to indicate that age bias and age based policies appear throughout the performance rating process to the detriment of the protected age group." The *Albemarle Paper v. Moody* case also supported validation requirements for PAs, as well as for selection tests. Organizations should avoid using any appraisal method that results in a disproportionately negative impact on a protected group.

An employer may also be vulnerable to a *negligent retention* claim if an employee who continually receives unsatisfactory ratings in safety practices, for example, is kept on the payroll and he or she causes injury to a third party. In these instances, firms might reduce their liability if they provide substandard performers with training designed to overcome the deficiencies.

It is unlikely that any appraisal system will be immune to legal challenge. However, systems that possess the characteristics discussed are more legally defensible. At the same time, they can provide a more effective means for achieving PM goals.

7.5 Explain how to conduct the appraisal interview.

Performance Appraisal Interview

The appraisal interview is the Achilles' heel of the entire evaluation process. In fact, appraisal review sessions often create hostility and can do more harm than good to the employee-manager relationship. To minimize the possibility of hard feelings, the face-to-face meeting and the written review must have performance improvement, not criticism, as their goal. The reviewing manager must use all the tact he or she can muster in discussing areas needing improvement. Managers should help employees understand that they are not the only ones under the gun. Rating managers should emphasize their own responsibility for the employee's development and commitment for support.

The appraisal interview has the potential for confrontation and undermining the goal of motivating employees. Still, some employees who receive negative feedback respond by yelling or getting defensive; others may cry. As disarming as these reactions may be, managers must avoid responding to reactive employees in the same manner.[39] The situation improves considerably when several sources provide input, including perhaps the employee's own self-appraisal. Regardless of the system used, employees will not trust a system they do not understand.

Scheduling the Interview

Supervisors usually conduct a formal appraisal interview at the end of an employee's appraisal period. It should be made clear to the employee as to what the meeting is about.[40] Employees typically know when their interview should take place, and their anxiety tends to increase if their supervisor delays the meeting. Interviews with top performers are often pleasant experiences for all concerned. However, supervisors may be reluctant to meet face-to-face with poor performers. They tend to postpone these anxiety-provoking interviews.

Interview Structure

A successful appraisal interview should be structured in a way that allows both the supervisor and the employee to view it as a problem-solving rather than a fault-finding session. The manager has several purposes when planning an appraisal interview. Certainly, the employee's performance should be discussed, focusing on specific accomplishments.[41] Also, the employee should be assisted in setting goals and personal development plans for the next appraisal period. The manager should suggest means for achieving established goals, including support from the manager and firm. For instance, a worker may receive an average rating on a factor such as *quality of production*. In the interview, both parties should agree to the specific improvement needed during the next appraisal period and specific actions that each should take.[42]

During performance reviews, managers might ask employees whether their current duties and roles are effective in achieving their goals. In addition to reviewing job-related performance, they might also discuss subjective topics, such as career ambitions. For example, in working on a project, perhaps an employee discovered an unrealized aptitude. This awareness could result in a new goal or serve as a springboard to an expanded role in the organization.

The amount of time devoted to an appraisal interview varies considerably with company policy and the position of the evaluated employee. Although costs are a consideration, there is merit in conducting separate interviews for discussing: (1) employee performance and development; and (2) pay. Many managers have learned that as soon as the topic of pay emerges in an interview, it tends to dominate the conversation, with performance improvement taking a back seat. For this reason, if pay increases or bonuses are involved in the appraisal, it might be advisable to defer those discussions for one to several weeks after the appraisal interview.

Use of Praise and Criticism

Some managers believe that they should focus only on negative items. However, focusing only on weaknesses has the potential to damage relationships with employees.[43] No one wants a lengthy interview where they are constantly bombarded with criticism. A person might reason that, "If I am this bad, I had better find another job."

As suggested previously, conducting an appraisal interview requires tact and patience on the part of the evaluator. Praise is appropriate when warranted, but it can have limited value if not clearly deserved. If an employee must eventually be terminated because of poor performance, a manager's false praise could bring into question the "real" reason for being fired. In addition, giving praise should be a positive experience for both the manager and employee. However, the message sometimes is lost when the manager displays inconsistent body language. Other factors may also undermine the intended message. Tone of voice, facial expressions, nonverbal, and emotion may be as important as the spoken word.[44] For instance, frequently looking at the clock on the wall rather than making direct eye contact sends mixed signals.

Criticism, even if warranted, is especially difficult to give. The employee may not perceive it as being constructive. It is important that discussions of these sensitive issues focus on the deficiency, not the person. Effective managers minimize threats to the employee's self-esteem whenever possible. When giving criticism, managers should emphasize the positive aspects of performance; criticize actions, not the person; and ask the employee how he or she would change things to improve the situation. Also, the manager should avoid supplying all the answers and try to turn the interview into a win-win situation so that all concerned gain.

Employees' Role

From the employees' side, two weeks or so before the review, they should go through their diaries or files and make a note of all projects worked on, regardless whether they were successful.[45] The best recourse for employees in preparing for an appraisal review is to prepare a list of creative ways they have solved problems with limited resources. They will look especially good if they can show how their work contributes to the value of the company. This information should be on the appraising manager's desk well before the review. Reminding managers of information, they may have missed should help in developing a more objective and accurate appraisal.

Concluding the Interview

Ideally, employees will leave the interview with positive feelings about management, the company, the job, and themselves. If the meeting results in a deflated ego, the prospects for improved performance will be bleak. Although you cannot change past behavior, future performance is another matter. The interview should end with specific and mutually agreed-on plans for the employee's development. Managers should assure employees who require additional training that it will be forthcoming and that they will have the full support of their supervisor. When management does its part in employee development, it is up to the individual to perform in an acceptable manner.

7.6 Summarize key trends in performance appraisal practice.

Trends in Performance Appraisal Practice

In recent years, many HR professionals, business executives, and employees have questioned the value of traditional annual performance appraisal methods. A survey by Deloitte University revealed that 78 percent of HR professionals said that performance management is important or very important.[46] However, only eight percent of the respondents stated that that their performance management process drove business results.[47] Some firms have transitioned to ongoing reviews that entail more frequent, developmental feedback, often making pay raise and promotion decisions separately. For instance, Kris Duggan, CEO of information technology company BetterWorks, maintains, "When evaluating who gets promotions, raises and bonuses, it has to be done in a more subjective manner, taking into account the competitive rate for the market, the amount of time since the last raise, what sorts of customer or internal relationships have been developed, and how well the employee is executing on his or her objectives."[48]

By September 2015, 51 large firms were changing to a system without ratings.[49] Many more are contemplating the same. Several other firms have modified their performance appraisal methods. General Electric (GE), once known for using forced ranking systems, stopped using them. At GE, employees who were rated in the bottom 10 percent of the performance distribution were either encouraged to leave or fired. Instead, the company now expects 200,000 salaried employees and managers to share frequent feedback via a mobile app called PD@GE.[50] Janice Semper, a GE human resource executive, maintained that eliminating ratings, "led to more meaningful, richer conversations that were not getting distracted by . . . a label."[51]

Adobe Systems had used a forced ranking system for many years until 2012. The company estimated that managers spent a total of 80,000 hours to conduct annual reviews.[52] Nowadays, the company provides extensive training to educate employees and managers about how to conduct more frequent "check-in" meetings. Donna Morris, senior vice president of human resources, described check-ins as, " . . . a 180 [-degree turn] in terms of giving people the material they need to improve their performance and change course."[53] Morris added, "It completely changes how employees feel about their jobs and opportunities. Feedback is now viewed as a gift." Adobe also deemed the new approach as successful based on an analysis of involuntary and voluntary turnover. The voluntary turnover rate has decreased by 30 percent and involuntary turnover increased by 50 percent.[54]

Some companies recognize the value of frequent feedback and elements of a rating system. For instance, IBM uses technology to facilitate more frequent performance reviews. IBM uses the Checkpoint app to set short-term goals and managers provide quarterly feedback on their progress. For the ratings portion, managers evaluate every employee on five criteria—business results, impact on client success, innovation, personal responsibility to others, and skills. Diane Gherson, chief human resource officer at IBM, said, "In the old system, there was one score. People [got] sort of obsessed by that."[55] In addition, she spoke highly of the five-factor rating, "It leads to a much richer, more balanced discussion." The following Watch It video describes online retailer Hautelook's PA system. The system blends the use of traditional ratings and frequent discussions between managers and employees.

Watch It 3

If your instructor has assigned this, go to **www.pearson.com/mylab/management** to watch a video titled Hautelook: Appraising and respond to questions.

Despite some companies' shifts away from traditional performance appraisal methods, these practices are far from extinction. One survey revealed that roughly 90 percent of firms worldwide use performance ratings. In addition, these firms rely on ratings as a factor in pay raise decisions.[56]

There are many reasons that companies maintain the status quo. Perhaps most noteworthy is the lack of executive-level support for change. For example, Intel Corporation executives were worried that sacrificing ratings would draw healthy tension out of a workplace.[57] In addition, others were concerned that managers may not possess sufficient skills to use performance discussions effectively. There is some merit to this concern. In some cases, managers displayed difficulties explaining job performance to employees as well as clearly describing specific steps for improvement.[58] Perhaps managers have become accustomed to using traditional ratings. Without them, they may be having difficulty framing the discussion.[59]

In summary, traditional performance appraisal methods have come under greater scrutiny in recent years. Some firms have changed their approach and others remain somewhat skeptical about moving away from traditional methods. HR professionals have had decades to analyze the effectiveness of traditional methods. The alternatives discussed in this section may well prove to be superior; however, sufficient time has not passed to complete rigorous evaluations in much the same way that HR professionals and researchers have done for traditional methods.

Try It!

If your instructor has assigned this, go to **www.pearson.com/mylab/management** to complete the Individual Behavior simulation and test your application of these concepts when faced with real-world decisions.

PREPARING FOR EXAMS/QUIZZES

Chapter Summary by Learning Objectives

1. ***Describe performance management, performance appraisal, and the performance appraisal process.*** *Performance management (PM)* is a goal-oriented process that is directed toward ensuring that organizational processes are in place to maximize productivity of employees, teams, and ultimately, the organization. PM systems are one of the major focuses in business today. With PM, the effort of each worker should be directed toward achieving strategic goals. *Performance appraisal (PA)* is a system of review and evaluation of individual or team task performance.

   The identification of specific goals is the starting point for the PA process and the beginning of a continuous cycle. Then job expectations are established with the help of job analysis. The next step involves examining the actual work performed. Performance is then appraised. The final step involves discussing the appraisal with the employee.

2. ***Explain the uses of performance appraisal and performance criteria.*** The most common appraisal criteria are traits, behaviors, competencies, goal achievement, and improvement potential.

   PA data are potentially valuable for use in numerous human resource functional areas, including human resource planning, recruitment and selection, training and development, career planning and development, compensation programs, internal employee relations, and assessment of employee potential.

   People who are usually responsible for PA include immediate supervisors, employees, peers and team members, self-appraisal, and customer appraisal.

   Formal performance evaluations are usually prepared at specific intervals. Although there is nothing magical about the period for formal appraisal reviews, in most organizations they occur either annually or semi-annually.

3. ***Describe the choice of various performance appraisal methods.*** PA methods include 360-degree feedback evaluation, rating scales, critical incidents, work standards, ranking, forced distribution, behaviorally anchored rating scales, and results-based approaches.

4. ***Assess the effectiveness and limitations of performance appraisal practices.*** Characteristics of effective performance appraisal practices include reliable and valid methods, job-related criteria, setting performance expectations, standardization, trained appraisers, continuous open communication, conducting performance reviews, and ensuring due process.

   The problems associated with PAs include appraiser discomfort, lack of objectivity, halo/horn errors, leniency/strictness, central tendency, recent behavior bias, personal bias (stereotyping), and employee anxiety.

A review of court cases makes it clear that legally defensible PA systems should be in place. Perfect systems are not expected, and the law does not preclude supervisory discretion in the process. However, systems that possess certain characteristics are more legally defensible.

5. ***Explain how to conduct the appraisal interview.*** A successful appraisal interview should be structured in a way that allows both the supervisor and the employee to view it as a problem-solving rather than a fault-finding session. Activities include scheduling the interview, structuring the interview, appropriate use of praise and criticism, clarifying employees' role and concluding the interview by setting plans for effective performance.
6. ***Summarize key trends in performance appraisal practice.*** Traditional performance appraisal methods have come under scrutiny for a variety of reasons. Five reasons include limiting performance appraisal to one-year intervals, ratings do not fully capture the scope and depth of performance, supervisors and managers may find it difficult to accurately recall employees' performance over an extended period, companies coordinate performance appraisals with pay increase decisions, and traditional methods most often focus on past rather than future performance.

    Many companies have set aside traditional performance appraisal approaches for continuous performance discussions; others have introduced hybrid methods that combine features of ratings and continuous discussions.

    Criticisms of traditional methods do not signal the extinction of this approach. While new approaches show promise, they are not without limitations, including crafting clear discussions about performance. Over time, evaluation studies will shed light on the effectiveness of newer approaches.

Key Terms

MyLab Management

If your instructor is using MyLab Management, go to **www.pearson.com/mylab/management** to complete the problems marked with this icon ✪.

Questions for Review

7-1. Define performance management and performance appraisal.

7-2. What are the uses of performance appraisal?

✪**7-3.** What are some reasons that people give for getting rid of performance appraisal?

7-4. What are the steps in the performance appraisal process?

7-5. What aspects of a person's performance might an organization evaluate?

7-6. Many different people can conduct performance appraisals. What are the various alternatives?

7-7. What appraisal intervals are often used in appraisal reviews?

7-8. Briefly describe each of the following methods of performance appraisal:

(a) 360-degree feedback evaluation
(b) rating scales
(c) critical incidents
(d) work standards
(e) ranking
(f) forced distribution
(g) behaviorally anchored rating scales
(h) results-based systems

7-9. What are the various problems associated with performance appraisal? Briefly describe each.

✪**7-10.** What are the legal considerations associated with performance appraisal?

✪**7-11.** Explain why the following statement is often true: "The *Achilles' heel* of the entire evaluation process is the appraisal interview itself."

✪**7-12.** What are some of the considerations associated with changing from the use of employee ratings to continuous discussions?

PREPARING FOR MY CAREER

P I A Personal Inventory Assessment

An additional Personal Inventory Assessment can be found on MyLab Management.

Work Performance Assessment

This self-assessment helps you identify obstacles you are experiencing (or have experienced) that prevent you from achieving a high level of performance in a work setting. Provide responses regarding work performance based on a current (or a recent) work situation.

ETHICS DILEMMA

Abdication of Responsibility

You are the new vice president for HR of a company that has not been performing well, and everyone, including yourself, has a mandate to deliver results. The pressure has never been greater. Shareholders are angry after 3 years of a tough market that has left their company stock losing value every day. Many shareholders desperately need stock performance to pay for their retirement. Working for you is a 52-year-old manager with two kids in college. In previous evaluations, executives told him he was doing fine, when he clearly was not, and his performance is still far below par.

If you are to show others in the company that you are willing to make tough decisions, you feel you must fire this individual. The question is who's going to suffer: the firm and ultimately shareholders whose retirements are in jeopardy, or a nice guy who's been lied to for 20 years?

7-13. What would you do?

7-14. What factor(s) in this ethics dilemma might influence a person to make a less than ethical decision?

HRM Is Everyone's Business

Employee performance appraisals will ultimately be a managerial decision. As a manager, your focus will be on the broader issues of production, revenue, customer service, and competition. Managing and appraising employees' performance will be an important factor in sustaining high levels of production, revenue, and competitive advantage. Making effective decisions requires managers and HR to work together to determine the most appropriate method for appraising performance and effectively communicating the result to employees.

Action checklist for managers and HR—planning and conducting effective performance appraisals

HR takes the lead

- ☑ Work with line managers to design the performance appraisal plan that best fits the specific duties and responsibilities of roles.
- ☑ Consider implementing a training program wherein managers are trained in two areas: (1) accurately assessing performance; and (2) recording the assessment in a way that is lawful and easily understood by both the employer and employee.
- ☑ Set in motion the discussions between managers and employees where performance will be discussed and action plans based on the particular circumstances (e.g., discussing training opportunities to remedy performance deficiencies, or career planning for advancing high performing employees).

Managers take the lead

- ☑ Determine performance criteria and accurate measurements to ensure that a specific output is the expectation of both the employee and employer.
- ☑ Work with HR to become educated on the limitations of different performance appraisal methods, particularly methods that require subjective evaluations of employee performance. Certain roles have objective standards (e.g., sales numbers), but most require a subjective evaluation, introducing the possibility of rating errors.
- ☑ Following company policy, use appraisals to accurately compensate employees, set training plans to help turnaround poor performance, or develop a plan for career advancement based on past excellent performance. Review these plans with HR professionals.

HRM by the Numbers

Performance Appraisal: Forced Distribution

An additional HRM by the Numbers exercise can be found on MyLab Management.

Despite the limitations of forced distribution performance appraisal methods, many companies continue to use them. The forced distribution method follows the principles of forced distribution grading systems found in some colleges and universities where professors award grades that fit a prescribed distribution. It is the HR professional's responsibility to review the performance evaluations submitted by each department and determine whether the ratings conform to the company's prescribed performance distribution.

Prescribed Performance Distribution

1. Outstanding	2. Above average	3. Average	4. Below average	5. Poor
10%	20%	40%	20%	10%

You just received the following sets of performance ratings from the customer service department and warehouse:

Customer Service Department (300 employees)

1. Outstanding	2. Above average	3. Average	4. Below average	5. Poor
30 employees	60 employees	120 employees	60 employees	30 employees

Warehouse (500 employees)

1. Outstanding	2. Above average	3. Average	4. Below average	5. Poor
75 employees	75 employees	200 employees	50 employees	100 employees

Questions

7-15. State the distribution (in percentage terms) for the (a) customer service department and (b) warehouse. Starting with the customer service department, list the percentages in order from outstanding through poor. Then, do the same for the warehouse.

7-16. One or both of the performance distributions calculated in question 17-15 does not match the prescribed performance distribution. Compare each distribution to the prescribed performance distribution. Does the customer service department meet the prescribed distribution? Does the warehouse distribution meet the prescribed distribution?

7-17. Focus on the mismatched distribution(s) identified in question 7-16. Correct the mismatched distribution(s) to match the prescribed standard distribution by indicating the number of employees expected to fall in each performance category.

Working Together: Team Exercise

In small groups of three or four, come up with specific answers to the following questions. Talk through your perspectives and come up with a team response. Be prepared to share your ideas with the class.

As a group, use O*NET (which we reviewed in Chapter 4) to select a job for further study. Start by browsing jobs in different occupations (www.onetonline.org/find/). Next, from the *find occupations* drop down list, select *job family*. There, you will see 23 unique job families (occupations). Then, select a job family (click on the link for the chosen job family). Finally, select a job from the chosen job family (click on the link for the chosen job) and review the information contained in the detailed report.

7-18. Among the broad performance appraisal methods categories reviewed in this chapter, which one would you choose for the selected job? Explain.

7-19. What are some of the limitations of the selected approach for appraising job performance? Be sure to answer this question using your selected job as a frame of reference.

INCIDENT 1 These Things Are a Pain

"There, at last it's finished," thought Rajiv Chaudhry, as he laid aside the last of 12 PA forms. It had been a busy week for Rajiv, who supervises a road maintenance crew for the Georgia Department of Highways.

In passing through Rajiv's district a few days previously, the governor had complained to the area superintendent that repairs were needed on several of the highways. Because of this, the superintendent assigned Rajiv's crew an unusually heavy workload. In addition, Rajiv received a call from the HR office that week reminding him that the PAs were late. Rajiv explained his predicament, but the HR specialist insisted that the forms be completed right away.

Looking over the appraisals again, Rajiv thought about several of the workers. The PA form had places for marking *quantity of work*, *quality of work*, and *cooperativeness*. For each characteristic, the worker could be graded *outstanding*, *good*, *average*, *below average*, or *unsatisfactory*. As Rajiv's crew had completed all the extra work assigned for that week, he marked every worker *outstanding* in *quantity of work*. He marked Joe Blum *average* in *cooperativeness* because Joe had questioned one of his decisions that week. Rajiv had decided to patch a pothole in one of the roads, and Joe thought the small section of road surface ought to be broken out and replaced. Rajiv didn't include this in the remarks section of the form, though. As a matter of fact, he wrote no remarks on any of the forms.

Rajiv felt a twinge of guilt as he thought about Roger Short. He knew that Roger had been goofing off, and the other workers had been carrying him for quite some time. He also knew that Roger would be upset if he found that he had been marked lower than the other workers. Consequently, he marked Roger the same to avoid a confrontation. "Anyway," Rajiv thought, "these things are a pain, and I really shouldn't have to bother with them."

As Rajiv folded up the PAs and put them in the envelope for mailing, he smiled. He was glad he would not have to think about PAs for another six months.

Questions

7-20. What weaknesses do you see in Rajiv's performance appraisals?

7-21. Should HR have the ability to "insist that the forms be completed right away?" Discuss.

7-22. Many managers would agree with Rajiv in saying that, "these things are a pain, and I really shouldn't have to bother with them." What are the disadvantages in doing away with performance appraisal?

INCIDENT 2 Good Job!

Chandra LaMar just celebrated her 20th-year anniversary at Westfield Farm Implement Company, a large retailer of farm equipment ranging from small riding lawn mowers to gigantic combines. She started her career as an office clerk and received excellent performance reviews, which led to many promotions through the years. Chandra worked the longest in the customer service department as a product specialist.

Chandra was well liked by her peers. She was an easygoing individual who tried to help in any way possible. For instance, when a coworker did not understand details about new products, Chandra always took the time to answer their questions. When a coworker needed to leave early or come in late, Chandra answered his or her calls as well as her own. All the while, she never took credit for helping others.

Chandra was thrilled when the company promoted her to manager of the customer service department. First unsure about whether to accept the promotion, she asked her peers for their opinions. Everybody expressed excitement and support for Chandra's promotion.

Everything had been going easily for Chandra, at least until she completed performance appraisals of her staff members. One employee, Janine Melton, has been distracted during most of the past year while she was caring for an ill parent. Her performance was suffering. For instance, Janine routinely failed to return customer phone calls and e-mails, and she missed important product introduction meetings.

When it was time for Janine's annual PA, Chandra felt conflicted about what to do. Chandra and Janine were peers and they are close friends. Chandra did not want to add more stress to Janine's life. After much thought, she decided to overlook Janine's performance deficits, focusing instead on a couple of examples of good performance. Although Janine could not be considered more than an average worker, Chandra rated her outstanding overall. Janine was relieved when she got her review from Chandra. She had been concerned about performing poorly given all of the distractions in her life, but concluded that she simply must have been too hard on herself.

Questions

7-23. From Westfield Farm Implement's standpoint, what difficulties might Chandra's evaluation of Janine create?

7-24. What are the possible long-term consequences for Janine's employment status?

7-25. What can Chandra do to correct her mistake?

MyLab Management

If your instructor is using MyLab Management, go to **www.pearson.com/mylab/management** for Auto-graded writing questions as well as the following Assisted-graded writing questions:

7-26. Why are performance management and performance appraisal practices so important to a firm?

7-27. What are the characteristics of an effective appraisal system?

Endnotes

1 Ann Pace, "The Performance Management Dilemma," *T+D* 65 (July 2011): 22.

2 Hugh J. Watson and Jim Hill, "What Gets Watched Gets Done: How Metrics Can Motivate," *Business Intelligence Journal* 14 (2009): 4–7.

3 Chris Cancialosi, "The Future of Performance Management Is Not One-Size-Fits-All," *Forbes* online (February 22, 2016). Accessed February 27, 2017, at www.forbes.com.

4 Peter Cappelli and Martin Conyon, "What Do Performance Appraisals Do?" *National Bureau of Economic Research*. Working Paper Series (Working Paper 22400). Accessed February 5, 2017, at www.nber.org/papers/w22400.

5 "U.S. Employees Desire More Sources of Feedback for Performance Reviews," Piecework Award (No. of Garments Stitched above the Piecework *T+D* Incentive Award) 66 (February 2012): 18.

6 Joan Lloyd, "Performance Reviews Never Easy," *Receivables Report for America's Health Care Financial Managers* 24 (March 2009): 8–10.

7 "Full-Circle Assessments," *Training* 47 (November/December 2010): 7.

8 John F. Welch Jr., *Jack: Straight from the Gut* (New York: Warner Business Books, 2001): 157–158.

9 Anne Fisher, "Should performance reviews be crowdsourced?" *CNNMoney* (October 8, 2013). Accessed February 10, 2014, at www.management.fortune.cnn.com.

10 Ibid.

11 G. N. Salunke, "Colleagues, Managers, Customers and Competitors Keys to Development: 360 Degree Approach to Development," *Advances in Management* 3 (August 2010): 32–35.

12 Jena McGregor, "The Midyear Review's Sudden Impact," *BusinessWeek* (July 6, 2009): 50–52.

13 Claire Suddath, "Performance Reviews: Why Bother?" *Bloomberg Businessweek* (November 7, 2013). Accessed March 10, 2014, at www.businessweek.com.

14 Bernardin, H. J., and Beatty, R. W. (1984). *Performance Appraisal: Assessing Human Behavior at Work*. Boston, MA: Kent.

15 M.R. Barrick and M.K. Mount, "The Big Five Personality Dimensions and Job Performance: A Meta-Analysis," *Personnel Psychology* 44 (1991): 1–26.

16 Joshua Brustein, "Microsoft Kills Its Hated Stack Rankings. Does Anyone Do Employee Reviews Right?" *Bloomberg Businessweek* (November 13, 2013). Accessed January 25, 2014, at www.businessweek.com.

17 Liz Ryan, "Ten Management Practices to Throw Overboard in 2012," *BusinessWeek.com* (January 23, 2012): 1.

18 Joshua Brustein, "Microsoft Kills Its Hated Stack Rankings. Does Anyone Do Employee Reviews Right?" *Bloomberg Businessweek* (November 13, 2013). Accessed January 25, 2014, at www.businessweek.com.

19 Vindu Goel, "A Yahoo Employee-Ranking System Favored by Marissa Mayer Is Challenged in Court," *The New York Times* online (February 1, 2016). Accessed February 27, 2017, at www.nytimes.com.

20 Fivars, G. (1975). The critical incident technique: A bibliography. *JSAS Catalog of Selected Documents in Psychology*, *5*, p. 210.

21 Smith, P., and Kendall, L. M. (1963). Retranslation of expectation: An approach to the construction of unambiguous anchors for rating scales. *Journal of Applied Psychology*, 47, 149–155.

22 Latham and Wexley (1981), *Increasing Productivity Through Performance Appraisal,* Reading, MA: Addison-Wesley Publishing Company.

23 Latham, G. P., and Wexley, K. N. (1977). Behavioral observation scales for performance appraisal purposes. *Personnel Psychology*, *30*, pp. 255–268.

24 Ibid.

25 Stephanie Taylor Christensen, "3 Ways Companies Are Changing the Dreaded Performance Review," *Fast Company* online (October 2, 2015). Accessed February 27, 2017, at www.fastcompany.com.

26 Nishchae Suri, "Career Journal: Making Performance Appraisals More Effective," *Wall Street Journal Online* (April 29, 2011).

27 Marco Nink, "Many Employees Don't Know What's Expected of Them at Work," *Gallup Business Journal* (October 13, 2015). Accessed February 1, 2017, at www.gallup.com.

28 Rebecca R. Hastings, "Most Large Companies Calibrate Performance, Poll Finds," *HR Magazine* 57 (February 2012): 87.

29 Alexandra Bradley, "Taking the Formality Out of Performance Reviews," *T+D* 64 (June 2010): 18.

30 Blum, M. L., and Naylor, J. C. (1968). *Industrial Psychology: Its Theoretical and Social Foundations*. New York: Harper & Row.

31 Steffen Maier, "4 Unconscious Biases that Distort Performance Reviews," *Entrepreneur.com* (September 22, 2016). Accessed January 5, 2017, at www.entrepreneur.com/article/281919.

32 Jeffrey Pfeffer, "Low Grades for Performance Reviews," *BusinessWeek* (August 8, 2009): 68.

33 Eric Krell, "An Impartial Review," *HR Magazine* 56 (October 2011): 97–99.

34 Peter C. Fisk, "Appraising the Performance of Performance Appraisals," *Monthly Labor Review* online (December 2016). Accessed February 3, 2017, at www.bls.gov/opub/mlr/2016/beyond-bls/pdf/appraising-the-performance-of-performance-appraisals.pdf.

35 Tom Krattenmaker, "Appraising Employee Performance in a Downsized Organization," *Harvard Management Update* 14 (May 2009): 3–5.

36 "10 HR Mistakes Your Employee's Lawyer Will Try to Exploit," *HR Specialist: Texas Employment Law* 7 (January 2012): 4.

37 Sarah Raj, "How to Impress at Appraisals," *Enterprise Innovation* 6 (December 2010/January 2011): 40–41.

38 Jonathan A. Segal, "The Dirty Dozen Performance Appraisal Errors," *BusinessWeek.com* (January 17, 2011): 2.

39 Amy Jen Su, "How to Give Feedback to People Who Cry, Yell, or Get Defensive," *Harvard Business Review* online (September 21, 2016). Accessed February 3, 2017, at www.hbr.org.

40 "Addressing Performance Problems: 7 Steps to Success," *HR Specialist* 7 (October 2009): 6.

41 "Cite Specifics," *Communication Briefings* 29 (April 2010): 6.

42 "Performance Prep," *Communication Briefings* 29 (March 2010): 9.

43 Rick Wartzman, "Yes, You Can Make Performance Reviews Worthwhile," *BusinessWeek.com* (April 11, 2011): 4.

44 Ben Dattner, "The Key to Performance Reviews is Preparation," *Harvard Business Review* online (June 21, 2016). Accessed January 31, 2017, at www.hbr.org.

45 Charlene Kesee, "Toot Your Horn . . . Loudly," *OfficePro* 70 (March/April 2010): 14–17.

46 Jeff Schwartz, Laurence Collins, Heather Stockton, Darryl Wagner, and Brett Walsh, "Rewriting the Rules for the Digital Age: 2017 Deloitte Global Human Capital Trends," Deloitte University Press (2017). Accessed March 3, 2017, at www2.deloitte.com/us/en/pages/human-capital/articles/introduction-human-capital-trends.html.

47 David Schatsky and Jeff Schwartz, "Leading in the New World of Work: Global Human Capital Trends," Deloitte University Press (2015). Accessed February 27, 2017, at www2.deloitte.com/au/en/pages/human-capital/articles/global-human-capital-trends-2015-leading-new-world-work.html.

48 Dana Wilke, "If the Annual Performance Review Is on the Way Out, What Can Replace It?" *Society for Human Resource Management* online (December 7, 2015). Accessed February 15, 2017, at www.shrm.org/resourcesandtools/hr-topics/employee-relations/pages/performance-reviews-dead.aspx.

49 David Rock and Beth Jones, "Why More and More Companies Are Ditching Performance Ratings," *Harvard Business Review* online (September 8, 2015). Accessed February 15, 2017, at www.hbr.org.

50 Rachel Emma Silverman, "GE Does Away with Employee Ratings," *The Wall Street Journal* online (July 26, 2016). Accessed March 9, 2017, at www.wsj.com.

51 Ibid.

52 Graham Kenny, "Fixing Performance Appraisal Is About More Than Ditching Annual Review," *Harvard Business Review* online (February 2, 2016). Accessed March 2, 2017, at www.hbr.org.

53 David Burkus, "How Adobe Scrapped Its Performance Review System and Why It Worked," *Forbes* online (June 1, 2016). Accessed March 13, 2017, at www.forbes.com.

54 Ibid.

55 Claire Zillman, "IBM Is Blowing Up Its Annual Performance Review," *Fortune* online (February 1, 2016). Accessed February 28, 2017, at www.fortune.com.

56 "The Measure of a Man," *The Economist* online (February 20, 2016). Accessed March 13, 2017, at www.economist.com.

57 Rachel Feintzeig, "The Trouble With Grading Employees," *The Wall Street Journal* online (April 21, 2015). Accessed March 1, 2017, at www.wsj.com.

58 Rachel Emma Silverman, "GE Does Away with Employee Ratings," *The Wall Street Journal* online (July 26, 2016). Accessed March 13, 2017, at www.wsj.com.

59 Jenna McGregor, "This Big Change Was Supposed to Make Performance Reviews Better. Could It Be Making Them Worse?" *The Washington Post* online (June 7, 2016). Accessed March 9, 2017, at www.washingtonpost.com.

8 Training and Development

LEARNING OBJECTIVES After completing this chapter, students should be able to:

8.1 Define *training and development (T&D)* and summarize related practices.

8.2 Describe the training and development process.

8.3 Summarize some human resource management training initiatives.

8.4 Explain the concept of careers and career planning approaches and methods.

8.5 Describe management development.

8.6 Define organization development (OD) and the learning organization.

MyLab Management

Improve Your Grade!

If your professor is using MyLab Management, visit **www.pearson.com/mylab/management** for videos, simulations, and writing exercises.

Learn It

If your professor has chosen to assign this, go to **www.pearson.com/mylab/management** to see what you should particularly focus on and to take the Chapter 8 Warm-Up.

training and development (T&D)
Heart of a continuous effort designed to improve employee competency and organizational performance.

No other human resources (HR) practice set is most squarely designed to develop a company's employees than training and development. **Training and development (T&D)** is the heart of a continuous effort designed to improve employee competency and organizational performance. There are many elements that fit within a T&D umbrella. The most common elements include training, career development, organizational development, and organizational learning. For the sake of organization, we can distinguish between these four elements based on two dimensions—focus on the individual employee or groups of employees and time frame, short and long term. Time frames do not come with a set number of years. Short time frames are based on the specific learning objectives and expected period for employees to learn and apply those skills. Long time frames are based on the period a company sets to achieve its strategic objectives. Figure 8-1 shows the organization of T&D elements.

8.1 Define *training and development (T&D)* and summarize related practices.

Training and Development and Related Practices

training
Activities designed to provide learners with the knowledge and skills needed for their present jobs.

development
Learning that goes beyond today's job and has a more long-term focus.

Our focus in this chapter is on related practices aimed at building human capital and overall organizational capabilities. These practices are training and development, organizational development, and the learning organization.

Training provides learners with the knowledge and skills needed for their present jobs. Showing a worker how to operate a lathe or a supervisor how to schedule daily production are examples of training. On the other hand, **development** involves learning that goes beyond today's job and has a more long-term focus. It prepares employees to keep pace with the organization as it changes and grows. We often associate development with the concept of careers and career development, management development, and mentoring and coaching practices, which we discuss later in this chapter.

T&D activities have the potential to align a firm's employees with its corporate strategies. Some possible strategic benefits of T&D include employee satisfaction, improved morale, higher retention, lower turnover, improved hiring, a better bottom line, and the fact that satisfied employees produce satisfied customers. Individuals and groups receive the bulk of T&D efforts. However,

FIGURE 8-1
Organization of Training and Development Elements

	Short Term	Long Term
Groups/Organization	Organizational Development	Organizational Learning
Individuals	Training	Career Management

organization development (OD)
Planned and systematic attempts to change the organization, typically to a more behavioral environment.

learning organization
Firm that recognizes the critical importance of continuous performance-related T&D and takes appropriate action.

some firms believe that to achieve needed change, they must move the entire organization in a different direction. Efforts to achieve this goal are the focus of **organization development (OD)**.

Improved performance, the bottom-line purpose of T&D, is a strategic goal for organizations. Toward this end, many firms have become or are striving to become learning organizations. A **learning organization** is a firm that recognizes the critical importance of continuous performance-related T&D and takes appropriate action.

As previously noted, many companies embrace these philosophies and rely on a variety of training and development approaches to align workforce capabilities with their strategic mission. The following Watch It video describes how the use of various methods helps PTC, a product development company, maintain its competitive edge.

Watch It I
If your professor has assigned this, sign into **www.pearson.com/mylab/management** to watch a video titled PTC Employee Engagement and to respond to questions.

8.2 Describe the training and development process.

Training and Development Process

Major adjustments in the external and internal environments necessitate corporate change. The general T&D process that anticipates or responds to change may be seen in Figure 8-2. First, an organization must determine its specific needs for training. As we will see, needs are considered at the levels of the organization, task, and persons. From that information, HR professionals judge whether training is essential, and if so, what the training should be, why training should be conducted, who should be trained, and where training should occur. Then specific objectives need to be established. The objectives might be quite narrow if limited to the supervisory ability of a manager, or they might be broad enough to include improving the management skills of all

FIGURE 8-2
Training and Development Process

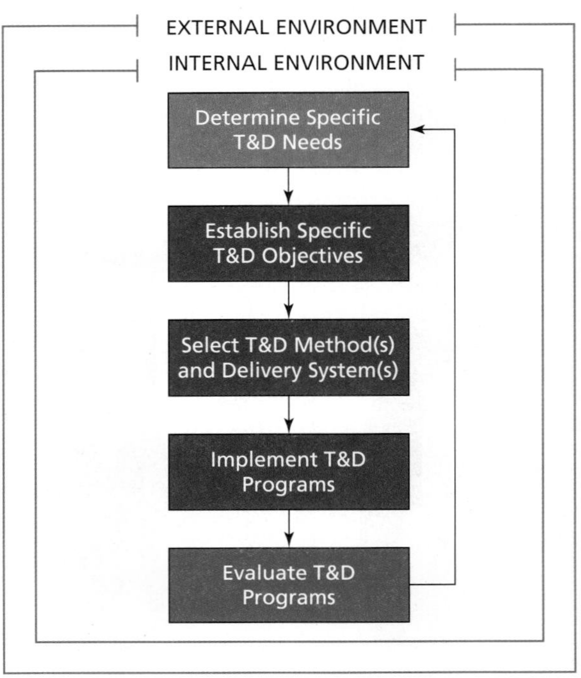

first-line supervisors. In exemplary organizations, there is a close link between the firm's strategic mission and the objectives of the T&D program. Review and periodic updating of these objectives is necessary to ensure that they support the firm's changing strategic needs. After setting the T&D objectives, management can determine the appropriate methods and the delivery system to be used. Naturally, management must continuously evaluate T&D to ensure its value in achieving organizational objectives and the HR department should lead the charge. Unfortunately, more companies need to do a better job of this. One survey found that, "only one in four HR organizations have effectively integrated their talent management practices . . . with the company's strategic objectives."[1]

FYI

Companies spent an average $814 per employee for training in 2016. The amount varied by company size:

- Small (100 to 999 employees): $1,052
- Midsize (1,000 to 9,999 employees): $870
- Large (10,000 or more employees): $379[2]

Determine Specific Training and Development Needs

The first step in the T&D process is to determine specific T&D needs. In today's highly competitive business environment, undertaking a program because other firms are doing it is asking for trouble. A systematic approach to addressing bona fide needs must be undertaken and must be done taking into consideration the mission of the organization.

training and development needs assessment
Heart of a continuous effort designed to improve employee competency and organizational performance.

A **training and development needs assessment** helps companies determine whether training is necessary. It may be determined by conducting analyses on three levels, which include organization, task, and person.

organizational analysis
Training needs assessment activity, which focuses on the firm's strategic mission, goals, and corporate plans are studied, along with the results of strategic HR planning.

ORGANIZATIONAL ANALYSIS **Organizational analysis** focuses on the firm's strategic mission, goals and corporate plans are studied, along with the results of strategic human resource planning. Let's consider a brief example of AT&T Corp. to illustrate an organizational analysis. AT&T Corp. is a subsidiary of AT&T (formerly American Telephone & Telegraph) and its headquarters are in Dallas, Texas. The company offers voice, video, data, and Internet telecommunications and professional services to businesses, consumers, and government agencies. The company operates the second-largest wireless network in the United States behind Verizon Wireless with 134.8 million subscribers compared to Verizon Wireless' base of 145.7 million.[3]

AT&T led the revolution in landline telephone service in the nineteenth century and had long been the leader for decades in technology based on cables and hardware (telephone handsets). Although AT&T Corp. successfully made the transition to wireless service, the technology continues to change at breakneck speeds. Like other companies in the industry, AT&T needs to adapt to the internet and the cloud. This change entails transitioning from cable networks to fiber network technology. That's easier said than done. AT&T's average employee job tenure is 22 years with most of its 280,000 employees trained decades ago in "old" technology that no longer provides the company with a competitive advantage.[4] AT&T Corp. recognized investments in employee development are essential to competitive advantage. Marty Richter, corporate communications manager, stated, "We're focused on aligning company leaders to strategic business innovation and results, skilling and reskilling our 280,000 employees and inspiring a culture of continuous learning."[5] Since 2013, the company invested more than $250 million in employee development and approximately $30 million in tuition reimbursement.[6]

task analysis
A training needs assessment activity, which focuses on the tasks required to achieve the firm's purposes.

TASK ANALYSIS **Task analysis** focuses on the *tasks* required to achieve the firm's purposes. In this case, working with fiber-optic technology is one of AT&T's goals. Job descriptions are important data sources for this analysis level, and it is logical that customer service employees who serve in the role of sales and those who serve in post-sales service are most relevant to the CEO's objective because they not only specify the tasks of these jobs, but also indicate the knowledge, skills, and abilities (KSAs) required to perform these jobs adequately. The following are some of the Customer Service Representative job tasks that are specified in the Occupational Information Network (O*NET).[7]

- Confer with customers by telephone or in person to provide information about products or services, take or enter orders, cancel accounts, or obtain details of complaints.
- Check to ensure that appropriate changes were made to resolve customers' problems.
- Keep records of customer interactions or transactions, recording details of inquiries, complaints, or comments, as well as actions taken.
- Resolve customers' service or billing complaints by performing activities such as exchanging merchandise, refunding money, or adjusting bills.
- Complete contract forms, prepare change of address records, or issue service discontinuance orders, using computers.

These tasks can help HR professionals determine training content and how best to design training to impart knowledge and skills. In addition, specifying the tasks better enable HR professionals to select evaluation measures of training effectiveness, including learning of knowledge and skills to perform these jobs more effectively as well as indicators of job performance changes (hopefully improvements) following the completion of training over time.

person analysis
A training needs assessment activity that focuses on finding answers to questions such as Who needs to be trained? What do they need to do differently from what they're doing today? What kind of knowledge, skills, and abilities (KSAs) do employees need?

PERSON ANALYSIS **Person analysis** focuses on obtaining answers to the questions: Who needs to be trained? What do employees need to do differently from what they're doing today? And what kind of KSAs do employees need?

Specifying the KSAs necessary for task performance is essential information that will help in the selection of training methods. For example, a simple classroom lecture could be an effective vehicle for imparting basic knowledge about customer service principles and product knowledge. Role plays could be an effective approach to having trainees demonstrate whether they have learned basic knowledge and can effectively combine knowledge with skills to effectively complete customer service representative tasks. Among many, O*NET lists the following most important KSAs, respectively, to the customer service representative job:[8]

- *Customer and Personal Service*—Knowledge of principles and processes for providing customer and personal services. This includes customer needs assessment, meeting quality standards for services, and evaluation of customer satisfaction.
- *Active Listening*—Giving full attention to what other people are saying, taking time to understand the points being made, asking questions as appropriate, and not interrupting at inappropriate times.
- *Oral Comprehension*—The ability to listen to and understand information and ideas presented through spoken words and sentences.

Establish Training and Development Program Objectives

T&D must have clear and concise objectives and be developed to achieve organizational goals. Without them, designing meaningful T&D programs would not be possible. Worthwhile evaluation of a program's effectiveness would also be difficult, at best. As we discussed in the previous section, AT&T might pursue training in various aspects of fiber-optics technology to support its goal of continual reinvention and competitiveness among its major competitors.[9] Consider these purposes and objectives for a training program involving employment compliance:

TRAINING AREA: EMPLOYMENT COMPLIANCE

Purpose: To provide the supervisor with

1. Knowledge and value of consistent human resource practices
2. The intent of Equal Employment Opportunity Commission (EEOC) legal requirements
3. The skills to apply them

Objectives: To be able to

1. Cite the supervisory areas affected by employment laws on discrimination
2. Identify acceptable and unacceptable actions
3. State how to get help on EEOC matters
4. Describe why we have disciplinary action and grievance procedures
5. Describe our disciplinary action and grievance procedures, including who is covered

As you see, the *purpose* is established first. The specific *learning objectives* that follow leave little doubt about what the training should accomplish. With these objectives, managers can determine whether training has been effective. For instance, in the example, a trainee either can or cannot state how to get help on equal employment opportunity matters.

Training Methods

When a person is working in a garden, some tools are more helpful in performing certain tasks than others. The same logic applies when considering T&D methods, and these methods are changing continuously and improving. Regardless of whether programs are in-house or outsourced, firms use many methods for imparting knowledge and skills to the workforce and usually more than one method, called *blended training*, is used to deliver T&D. As part of the blended training process, e-learning is enhancing or replacing some traditional training methods. T&D methods are discussed next. Each of these training methods should be evaluated and selected for what it does best.

CLASSROOM METHOD The classroom method, in which the instructor physically stands in front of students, continues to be effective for many types of training. One advantage of instructor-led training is that the instructor may convey a great deal of information in a relatively brief time. The effectiveness of instructor-led programs improves when groups are small enough to permit discussion, and when the instructor can capture the imagination of the class and use new technology to provide a better classroom learning experience. Also, the charisma or personality that the instructor brings to class may excite the students to want to learn. The classroom setting allows for real-time discussion that is not easily replicated, even with the most advanced technology.

e-learning
The T&D method for online instruction using technology-based methods such as the DVDs, company intranets, and the Internet.

E-LEARNING The tradition of instructors physically lecturing in front of live corporate students has diminished somewhat in recent years. **E-learning** is the T&D method for online instruction using technology based methods such as DVDs, company intranets, and the Internet. The Internet offers many opportunities for learning. For example, companies such as Coursera and Udacity partner with universities to offer *massive open online courses* (*MOOCs*) that enable thousands of students who are located anywhere in the world at any time of the day to take university-level courses. Initially, the audience for MOOCs was mainly college-level students. Increasingly, companies are adopting MOOCs as an e-learning tool. Altogether, more than 35 million people have enrolled in MOOCs since 2011.[10] Partnering with highly recognized universities that offer MOOCs could increase the value of training in a variety of ways, including through learning leading-edge information and techniques from world-famous professors and assessments by current and prospective clients that training is state-of-the art. "There's a lot of potential for how MOOCs can be used for corporate training and development," said Julia Stiglitz, head of business development and strategic partnerships for Coursera, which also partners with universities such as Stanford and UC Berkeley to offer online college courses.[11] "The companies are looking for new ways to train their employees and get them up to speed on skills that may not have been relevant five years ago."

FYI

- In a survey of individuals who completed at least one MOOC, 52 percent stated a primary goal of improving their current job or finding a new job.[12]

The benefits of e-learning are numerous and include decreased costs, greater convenience and flexibility, improved retention rates, and a positive environmental impact.[13] It can be self-paced, can often be individualized, and can be done while at work or off-shift. A concept can be viewed as often as needed. Individuals using e-learning can be working on different parts of a program, at varying speeds, and in different languages.

Luxottica is an Italian eyewear and optical company whose chain stores include LensCrafters, Pearle Vision, and Sunglass Hut, with 38,000 employees worldwide. Angi Willis, Luxottica's learning technology project manager said, "We just didn't have the manpower, technology or budget to efficiently and effectively manage and execute our various training programs." Luxottica put training online so employees could have instant access to information they needed to do their jobs, including details on new products and regulations as well as continuing education.[14]

The advantages of using e-learning are numerous, however, the biggest advantage is cost savings. According to Gordon Johnson, vice president of marketing for infrastructure provider Expertus, "Online meetings are one-third the cost of face-to-face meetings, so the question becomes not which is best, but whether face-to-face training is three times better. Usually not."[15]

For Union Pacific, the largest railroad company in North America, both distance and time have been hurdles to learning. About 19,000 of its 48,000 widely disbursed employees work on the railroad's locomotives and freight cars, many on different schedules. So, the company uses a blend of traditional learning and e-learning that provides the kind of training far-flung employees require, at a time when they can use it.

Firms that consistently have a high turnover rate have turned to e-learning because classroom learning is not cost-effective. Nike faced a challenge that many retailers today are confronting. Nike designed an online training program that the company could offer to employees in its own stores as well as at other retailers that sell Nike products. The program conveys a lot of information quickly, but it is also easy to learn. This is important because the training is directed at 16- to 22-year-olds.[16]

A takeoff on e-learning is the *live virtual classroom*, often referred to as *virtual instructor led*, that uses a Web-based platform to deliver live, instructor-led training to geographically dispersed learners. Organizations can bring together entire teams for just an hour or two per week. They can also bring content specialists into the classroom for only the necessary time required from two minutes to two hours. Virtual instructor led training is ideal for organizations that have many technicians needing frequent training while they continue to do their job in the field.[17] The need to have large blocks of time that takes workers away from their jobs is thus eliminated. Training can now be provided in blocks of time as opposed to several days. For example, a two-day live training session might be provided in five 75-minute modules delivered over time. These provide both cost savings and convenience.[18]

case study
T&D method in which trainees are expected to study the information provided in the case and make decisions based on it.

CASE STUDY The **case study** is a T&D method in which trainees study the information provided in the case and make decisions based on it. The goal of the case study method is to provide trainees with the opportunity to sharpen critical thinking skills. Often, the case study method occurs with an instructor who serves as a facilitator. It is also quite common for trainees to analyze the case in teams because problem solving typically involves consultation with others.

If an actual company is involved, the student would be expected to research the firm to gain a better appreciation of its financial condition and environment. Research on companies has been significantly enhanced through the availability of case studies of a variety of business functions. There are many sources of business case studies, including Harvard Business School Publishing.

behavior modeling
T&D method that permits a person to learn by copying or replicating behaviors of others to show managers how to handle various situations.

BEHAVIOR MODELING AND TWEETING **Behavior modeling** is a T&D method that permits a person to learn by copying or replicating behaviors of others. Behavior modeling has been used to train supervisors in such tasks as conducting performance reviews, correcting unacceptable performance, delegating work, improving safety habits, handling discrimination complaints, overcoming resistance to change, orienting new employees, and mediating individuals or groups in conflict.

Social networking, such as Twitter, has been used as a learning tool involving behavior modeling. "In a corporation, micro-blogging can be a way to augment behavior modeling," says Sarah Millstein, author of the *O'Reilly Radar Report*. This works by having a person who excels at a task send out frequent updates about what he or she is doing. The company might even formalize the process to the extent that it would select exemplary performers to post on a regular basis and determine those employees who should follow their posts.[19]

role-playing
T&D method in which participants are required to respond to specific problems they may encounter in their jobs by acting out real-world situations.

ROLE-PLAYING **Role-playing** is a T&D method in which participants are required to respond to specific problems they may encounter in their jobs by acting out real-world situations. Rather than hearing an instructor talk about how to handle a problem or by discussing it, they learn by doing. Role-playing is often used to teach such skills as administering disciplinary action, interviewing, grievance handling, conducting performance appraisal reviews, team problem solving, effective communication, and leadership-style analysis. A successful role-playing activity occurs if the activity mirrors real-life situations. It has also been used successfully to teach workers how to deal with individuals who are angry, irate, or out of control. Some restaurant chains use role-playing to train servers how to deal with difficult situations such as a couple having an argument at the dinner table. The classic case of using role-playing is when a manager must take disciplinary action against a worker for something they did improperly. Managers never know how an employee will react when being reprimanded. When acting out the role of the worker, he or she may randomly choose from a variety of roles such as being stoic, starting to cry, promising never to do it again, or take this job and shove it.

TRAINING GAMES Games can be quite useful learning tools to aid in the group dynamic process. Games are a cost-effective means to encourage learner involvement and stimulate interest in the topic, thereby enhancing employees' knowledge and performance.[20] According to Elizabeth Treher, founder, president, and CEO of The Learning Key Inc., "Team-based business games result in better knowledge retention, provide focused, memorable learning and a more enjoyable learning atmosphere than traditional methods."[21] A major benefit of games is that learners retain 75 percent of the knowledge they acquire when playing games, according to research by the National Training Laboratories. McDonald's in Japan estimates new employee training time to prepare burgers has been cut in half because of a video game created in conjunction with Nintendo.[22] Microsoft Xbox support agents use the Xbox Customer Care Framework (CCF) Assessment simulator training game. The game simulates real-life circumstances caused by generating the stress and anxiety of receiving difficult customer relations calls.[23] Even the U.S. Marine Corps uses a game-based training program called Mission Impact, which places learners in a simulated battalion to improve their environmental performance.

business games
T&D method that permits participants to assume roles such as president, controller, or marketing vice president of two or more similar hypothetical organizations and compete against each other by manipulating selected factors in a business situation.

Business games are a T&D method that permits participants to assume roles such as president, controller, or marketing vice president of two or more similar hypothetical organizations and compete against each other by manipulating selected factors in a business situation. Participants make decisions affecting such factors as price levels, production volumes, and inventory levels. Typically, a computer program manipulates their decisions, with the results simulating those of an actual business situation. Participants can see how their decisions affect other groups and vice versa. The best thing about this type of learning is that if a poor decision costs the company $1 million, no one gets fired, yet the business lesson is learned.

in-basket training
T&D method in which the participant is asked to establish priorities for and then handle several business papers, e-mail messages, memoranda, reports, and telephone messages that would typically cross a manager's desk.

IN-BASKET TRAINING **In-basket training** is a T&D method in which the participant is asked to establish priorities for and then handle many business papers, e-mails, texts, memoranda, reports, and telephone messages that would typically cross a manager's desk. The messages, presented in no order, call for anything from urgent action to routine handling. The participant is required to act on the information contained in these messages. In this method, the trainee assigns a priority to each situation before making any decisions. This form of training has been quite beneficial to help predict performance success in management jobs. Assessment centers commonly make use of this method in the selection process.

on-the-job training (OJT)
An informal T&D method that permits an employee to learn job tasks by performing them.

ON-THE-JOB TRAINING **On-the-job-training (OJT)** is an informal T&D method that permits an employee to learn job tasks by performing them. Often OJT will also have a significant impact on personal development. The key to this training is to transfer knowledge from a highly skilled and experienced worker to a new employee, while maintaining the productivity of both workers. OJT is used to pass on critical "how to" information to the trainee. Individuals may also be more highly motivated to learn because it is clear to them that they are acquiring the knowledge needed to perform the job. At times, however, the trainee may feel so much pressure to produce that learning is negatively affected. Firms should be selective about who provides OJT. Regardless of who does the training, that person must have a good work ethic and correctly model the desired behavior.

apprenticeship training
Training method that combines classroom instruction with on-the-job training.

APPRENTICESHIP TRAINING **Apprenticeship training** is a training method that combines classroom instruction with OJT. While in training, the employee earns less than the master craftsperson, who is the instructor. The National Association of Manufacturers projects that by 2020 some 10 million skilled workers will be needed and apprenticeships remain one of the most vital sources for securing skilled labor. The Manufacturing Institute projects that there will be approximately 3.5 million manufacturing job vacancies through 2025 and more than half are expected to go unfilled because of a significant shortage of skilled workers.[24] Apprenticeship training is common with craft jobs, such as those of plumber, carpenter, machinist, welder, fabricator, laser operator, electrician, and press brake operator. As baby boomers continue to leave the workforce, they must be replaced by competent operators, and apprenticeship programs provide an effective way of accomplishing this. Many organizations are partnering with high schools, vocational schools, and universities as they search for new skilled workers. Organizations often donate look-alike equipment to the schools so students can be trained on the system.

The U.S. Department of Labor has implemented regulations governing apprenticeships. Historically apprenticeships were defined by the amount of instruction time—typically 10,000 hours over four years. The new regulations offer provisions for competency-based apprenticeships, electronic and distance training, and the issuance of interim credentials. These credentials can be used toward college credits. "It's nice because a person isn't waiting until the end of the program to get some kind of reward," says Steve Mandes, executive director at National Institute for Metalworking Skills (NIMS).[25] For instance, Scot Forge, a metals manufacturer, pays apprentices' tuition and wages while they complete a three-year apprenticeship program. Upon completion, apprentices earn an associate degree and a guaranteed job at the company for two years.[26]

The concept of apprenticeships has been expanding beyond the skilled trades. The U.S. Bureau of Labor Statistics predicts that the demand for software jobs is on the rise relative to the supply of qualified individuals. Some private companies have anticipated this need for software professionals by creating "code" schools. Code schools offer short-term education on software development basics.[27] The goal is to prepare individuals to take entry-level jobs in the information technology field.

FYI

- Individuals who complete an apprenticeship have substantially higher annual earnings—$50,000 compared to those who do not complete an apprenticeship ($44,720).[28]

team training
Training focused on teaching knowledge and skills to individuals who are expected to work collectively toward meeting a common objective.

TEAM TRAINING **Team training** focuses on imparting knowledge and skills on individuals who are expected to work collectively toward meeting a common objective. For example, many automobile manufacturers organize teams to focus on the completion of car assembly. One such team installs the interior components, including dashboard, seats, carpeting, headliner, and trim. Many individuals work together to complete these tasks in an ordered sequence within a designated period to ensure that the factory meets its daily production quota. Other examples include teams of sales representatives and post-sales representatives to ensure that the customer receives a product configuration that meets its business needs and has subsequent support to ensure that employees of the client firm can properly use the product, such as inventory software.

team coordination training
Team training focused on educating team members how to orchestrate the individual work that they do to complete the task.

The nature of the work and business needs determines whether coordination training or cross-training is necessary. **Team coordination training** educates team members how to orchestrate the work that they do to complete the task such as in the previous examples. All team training initiatives involve information sharing and procedures for ensuring that the work is conducted in proper order. For example, in the automobile assembly example, team members must ensure that all the electrical wires that run across the floor are properly connected to their appropriate components (such as power window motors) before door trim is installed.

The success of team coordination training can mean the difference between life and death. The U.S. Coast Guard (USCG) regularly conducts a program for its rescue and recovery mission teams, which it calls Team Coordination Training (TCT).

> *Team Coordination Training (TCT) is a program that focuses on reducing the probability for human error by increasing individual and team effectiveness. Safety has long been the Commanding Officer's responsibility and, until recently, was assumed to be the logical result of finely tuned technical skills. USCG mishap data suggests that while technical skills are an essential component of any job, they alone will not ensure safety.*[29]

cross-training
Type of training for educating team members about the other members' jobs so that they may perform them when a team member is absent, is assigned to another job in the company, or has left the company altogether.

Cross-training educates team members about the other members' jobs so that they may perform them when a team member is absent, is assigned to another job in the company, or has left the company altogether. Ideally, effective cross-training initiatives will raise flexibility, communication, morale, and interdepartmental relations. Cross-training is also prevalent in a variety of employment settings because pressures to manage labor costs have often led to fewer employees who are hired to perform the same job. Restaurants are a common setting where cross-training is important. For example, it may be necessary for servers to step in to assist the kitchen staff prepare meals when one or more kitchen staff members are absent.

Training and Development Delivery Systems

The previous section focused on the various T&D methods available to organizations, and the list is constantly changing. In this section, our attention is devoted to how training may be delivered to participants.

corporate university
T&D delivery system provided under the umbrella of the organization.

CORPORATE UNIVERSITIES A T&D delivery system provided under the umbrella of the organization is referred to as a **corporate university**. The corporate T&D institution's focus is on creating organizational change that involves areas such as company training, employee development, and adult learning. It aims to achieve its goals by conducting activities that foster individual and organizational learning and knowledge. It is proactive and strategic rather than reactive and tactical and can be closely aligned to corporate goals. Even though they are called universities, they are not so in the straightest sense because degrees in specific subjects are not granted. General Electric (GE) has its Crotonville campus and McDonald's has its Hamburger University.

Recent years have seen the decline of corporate universities as companies such as Xerox, Ford, Pfizer, Aetna, and Merrill Lynch moved away from them largely because of the significant overhead costs associated with maintaining learning facilities and dedicated staff. However, in New York City, North Shore-Long Island Jewish Health System's corporate university serves 42,000 employees across 15 hospitals.[30] Deloitte LLP has recently built a $300 million corporate university in Westlake, Texas. Its 750,000 square feet will house state-of-the-art learning technology, 800 sleeping rooms, and even a ballroom. Marc Rosenberg, a learning consultant, says, "There's only so much you can do with social networking on the Internet, especially in services firms where you rely so much on your colleagues for help."[31] Also, firms are better able to control the quality of training and to ensure that all employees receive the same messages.

COLLEGES AND UNIVERSITIES For decades, colleges and universities have been the primary delivery system for training professional, technical, and management employees. Many public and private colleges and universities are taking similar approaches to training and education as have the corporate universities. Corporate T&D programs often partner with colleges and universities or other organizations, such as the American Management Association, to deliver both training and development. As we discussed, the advent of MOOCs has created greater opportunities for partnerships between educational institutions and companies.

COMMUNITY COLLEGES Community colleges are publicly funded higher education establishments that deliver vocational training and associate degree programs. Also, labor unions partner with some community colleges to sponsor formal courses as part of apprenticeship programs in the skilled trades such as carpentry and plumbing. For example, a course on electrical wiring principles and practices would be found in the curriculum for apprentices preparing to become master electricians. Some employers have discovered that community colleges can provide certain types of training better and more cost effectively than the company can. Rapid technological changes and corporate restructuring have created a new demand by industry for community college training resources.

online higher education
Educational opportunities including degree and training programs that are delivered, either entirely or partially, via the Internet.

ONLINE HIGHER EDUCATION A form of online e-learning that has increased substantially in recent years is the use of online higher education. **Online higher education** is defined as formal educational opportunities including degree and training programs that are delivered, either entirely or partially, via the Internet. One reason for the growth of online higher education is that it allows employees to attend class at lunchtime, during the day, or in the evening. It also saves employees time because it reduces their need to commute to school. It increases the range of learning opportunities for employees and increases employee satisfaction. Another point that needs to be made is that skepticism regarding the quality of online degrees appears to be fading. John Challenger, chief executive of outplacement firm Challenger, Gray & Christmas, agrees. "We did once have a clear line between online and brick-and-mortar degrees, but that's changing," he says. "Hiring managers are catching up."[32]

Enrollment in online universities continues to grow.[33] The University of Phoenix has the largest student body in North America. The university has more than 200 campuses worldwide and confers degrees in more than 100 degree programs at the bachelor's, master's, and doctoral levels. Clemson University's Master of Human Resource Development is a fully online course designed for in-career practitioners. The 36-credit program follows a cohort structure, with approximately 40 students in each unit. Class sessions are offered several times a week, to allow for an average of 10 students in each class. Students are assigned a "home group" within the cohort, but can choose another class to attend when work/life demands such as schedule conflicts or travel arise.[34]

In recent years, programs have been introduced that provide students with more and more autonomy and control of their programs of study. There are basically three categories of online higher education programs available: hybrid, synchronous, and asynchronous. *Hybrid programs* permit students to take some classes online and some in a traditional university setting. *Online synchronized study* offers students the choice of studying through an online portal system, however, the student is expected to appear for most classes on a real-time schedule. With this approach, students interact with a real professor and obtain real-time support for the learning material. With *asynchronous learning*, students have a series of assignments that need to be completed in a certain time frame. A system is available that allows students to communicate with the professor and classmates. For instance, the University of Phoenix gives the option of completing an MBA entirely online or completing a portion on campus. All courses were six weeks in length and each assignment had to be completed in a fixed time frame. Online higher education is not for everyone and the key to success is discipline. Jeff Seaman of Babson Survey Research Group, which studies online education, said, "You need discipline. Otherwise, the 'anytime, anywhere' aspect frees you to put off the work."[35]

vestibule system
T&D delivery system that takes place away from the production area on equipment that closely resembles equipment used on the job.

VESTIBULE SYSTEM **Vestibule system** is a T&D delivery system that takes place away from the production area on equipment that closely resembles equipment used on the job. For example, a group of lathes may be in a training center where the trainees receive instruction in their use. A primary advantage of the vestibule system is that it removes the employee from the pressure of having to produce while learning. The emphasis is focused on learning the skills required by the job.

VIDEO MEDIA The use of video media such as DVDs continues to be a popular T&D delivery system. These media are especially appealing to small businesses that cannot afford more expensive training methods and are often incorporated in e-learning and instructor-led instruction. In addition, they provide the flexibility desired by any firm. Behavior modeling, previously mentioned, has long been a successful training method that uses video media.

simulators
T&D delivery system comprised of devices or programs that replicate actual job demands.

SIMULATORS **Simulators** are a T&D delivery system comprised of devices or programs that replicate actual job demands. The devices range from simple paper mock-ups of mechanical devices to computerized simulations of total environments. T&D specialists may use simulated sales counters, automobiles, and airplanes. A prime example is the use of simulators to train pilots. Simulated crashes do not cost lives or deplete the firm's fleet of jets. John Deere uses an Excavator Training Simulator to train new operators in a risk-free environment. The simulator provides specific realistic lessons on proper operator techniques, machine controls, and safe operation at a virtual job site.[36] Crane operator trainees use a software simulator based on actual crane functions. Trainees sit in an authentic crane cab, with real control options while the simulation offers a realistic experience.[37]

SOCIAL NETWORKING Today's employees interact, learn, and work in much different ways and styles than in the not-so-distant past. Increasingly mobile and geographically dispersed workforces are becoming the norm. At the same time, dwindling or stagnant travel budgets are creating a need for different training methods. Thus, some organizations are using social networking and collaborative tools to enable informal learning. In a recent study, 55 percent of respondents also expect an increase in informal learning usage, which includes social media, blogs, wikis, and discussion groups.[38] Informal learning often takes place outside the corporate training departments. It does not necessarily follow a specified curriculum. The absence of formal curricula requires employers to embrace informal learning. By embracing informal learning, learners may be more motivated to gain knowledge. Thus, informal learning has surfaced as an important part of employee development.

The premise behind the educational success of social networking is the learning approach referred to as *constructivism*. A constructivist learning environment differs from the traditional model. In this setting, the teacher guides the learner toward multiple learning sources, rather than acting as the sole source of knowledge.[39] With more workers around the world using social media, they are getting and trusting information from their peer group more than in the past.[40] Communities of practice are usually a good source of informal learning. Before joining one, the learner should conduct due diligence by gaining an understanding the kinds of knowledge and skills that are important to them. Smaller, invitation-only communities are usually beneficial, particularly when the learner knows at least one member.[41] Often organizations are using communication meetings called huddles, which are usually called daily for a short period such as seven minutes, as informal learning opportunities.[42] Many believe that using shared, social learning solutions will grow.

Implementing Training and Development Programs

A perfectly conceived training program will fail if management cannot convince the participants of its merits. Participants must believe that the program has value and will help them achieve their personal and professional goals. A long string of successful programs certainly enhances the credibility of T&D.

Implementing T&D programs is often difficult. One reason is that managers are typically action-oriented and feel that they are too busy for T&D. According to one management development executive, "Most busy executives are too involved chopping down the proverbial tree to stop for the purpose of sharpening their axes." Another difficulty in program implementation is that qualified trainers must be available. In addition to possessing communication skills, the trainers must know the company's philosophy, its objectives, its formal and informal organization, and the goals of the training program. T&D requires more creativity than perhaps any other human resource function.

Implementing training programs presents unique problems. Training implies change, which employees may vigorously resist. It may also be difficult to schedule the training around present work requirements. Unless the employee is new to the firm, he or she undoubtedly has specific full-time duties to perform. Another difficulty in implementing T&D programs is record keeping. It is important to maintain training records, including how well employees perform during training and later on the job. This information helps measure program effectiveness and charts the employees' progress in the company.

Metrics for Evaluating Training and Development

Managers should strive to develop and use T&D metrics because such information can smooth the way to budget approval and executive buy-in. Most managers agree that training does not cost, it pays, and that training is an investment, not an expense. However, the actual value of the training must be determined if top management will be ready to invest in it.

The traditional framework for evaluation of training is based on four criteria.[43] Although this framework was developed decades ago, HR professionals call on it to organize evaluation efforts.

reactions
Training evaluation criterion focused on the extent to which trainees liked the training program related to its usefulness, and quality of conduct.

REACTIONS The first criterion, trainee **reactions**, refers to the extent to which trainees liked the training program related to its usefulness, and quality of conduct. Trainee reactions, when assessed, are measured upon completion of the training session by survey. The survey questions can be specific or general ("how satisfied were you with the presentation of sales skill strategies?" versus "how satisfied were you with the overall training program?"). This information may help training designers pinpoint potential problem aspects of the training as well as possible reasons for the shortcomings.

Evaluating a T&D program by asking the participants' opinions of it is an approach that provides a response and suggestions for improvements, essentially a level of customer satisfaction. You cannot always rely on such responses, however. The training may have taken place in an exotic location with time for golfing and other fun activities, and the overall experience may bias some reports. Nevertheless, this approach is a good way to obtain feedback and to get it quickly and inexpensively.

learning
The extent to which an employee understands and retains principles, facts, and techniques.

LEARNING The second criterion, **learning**, refers to the extent to which principles, facts, and techniques were understood and retained in memory by the employee. As with trainee reactions, learning is often assessed on completion of the training program (and sometimes, throughout the training course) by the appropriate tests (typing speed or recall of concepts from memory). Both evaluation criteria are important because positive trainee reactions and learning are expected to lead to more job-related and concrete ways of assessing training.

Some organizations administer tests to determine what the participants in a T&D program have learned. The pre-test/post-test control group design is one evaluation procedure that may be used. In this procedure, both groups receive the same test before and after training. The experimental group receives the training but the control group does not. Each group receives randomly assigned trainees. Differences in pretest and posttest results between the groups are attributed to the training provided. A potential problem with this approach is controlling for variables other than training that might affect the outcome. Personality differences should be considered. In many cases, highly conscientious individuals tend to perform better in training than less conscientious individuals. The training environment also matters. For instance, loud noises such as jackhammering just outside the classroom window will inevitably interfere with trainees' ability to concentrate.

behavior change
Change in job-related behaviors or performance that can be attributed to training.

transfer of training
Training evaluation method focusing on the extent to which an employee generalizes knowledge and skill learned in training to the work place, as well as maintains the level of skill proficiency or knowledge learned in training.

BEHAVIOR The third criterion, **behavior change**, refers to the changes in job-related behaviors or performance that can be attributed to training. Specifically, this criterion assesses transfer of training. **Transfer of training** refers to the extent to which an employee generalizes knowledge and skill learned in training to the work place, as well as maintains the level of skill proficiency or knowledge learned in training. The necessity of generalization may be more evident in highly complex, changing environments; maintenance is typically sought after in more straightforward settings. At AT&T, an example of generalization may be taking the principles of cybersecurity and applying them in a highly virtualized environment.[44] An example of skill maintenance is whether a typing speed of 90 words per minute demonstrated during training is sustained over time when the employee is back on the job.

Tests may accurately indicate what trainees learn, but they give little insight into whether the training leads participants to change their behavior. For example, it is one thing for a manager to learn about motivational techniques but quite another matter for this person to apply the new knowledge. A manager may sit in the front row of a training session dealing with empowerment of subordinates, absorb every bit of the message, understand it totally, make a grade of 100 on a test on the material, and then return the next week to the workplace and continue behaving in the same old autocratic way. The best demonstration of value occurs when learning translates into lasting behavioral change. Michael Allen, winner of the Distinguished Contribution to Workplace Learning and Performance Award, said, "We don't care about what people know. We care about what they can do . . . with what they know. Our challenge, as effective instructional designers, is to get people to make the leap from knowing to doing and that's where we often fail."[45]

organizational results
Typically, training outcomes such as enhanced productivity, lower costs, and higher product or service quality.

ORGANIZATIONAL RESULTS The fourth criterion, results, refers to the extent to which tangible outcomes that can be attributed to training are realized by the organization. **Organizational results** refer to such outcomes as enhanced productivity, lower costs, and higher product or service quality. Results in the context of training indicate whether (and how well or poorly) an organization has attained competitive advantage. Likewise, assessment of results over time can inform whether (and how well or poorly) competitive advantage has been sustained over time. Whereas much research on trainee reactions, learning, and behavior has amassed over the last several decades, relatively few gains have been made for results.

Here metrics address the business's bottom line, such as productivity data, rather than numbers of training sessions completed or the satisfaction employees gained from a training session. For instance, if the objective of an accident-prevention program is to reduce the number and severity of accidents by 15 percent, comparing accident rates before and after training provides a useful metric of success. Leslie Joyce, vice president of global talent management at Novelis and former CLO at Home Depot, said, "If there is change in behavior or improvement in performance, most CEOs I've worked with will agree that training has had an impact."[46]

HR Web Wisdom
Benchmarking
www.benchnet.com
The Benchmarking Exchange and Best Practices homepage is provided

Return on investment (ROI) is an important results criterion. CEOs want to see training in terms that they can appreciate such as business impact, business alignment, and ROI, that is, the extent to which benefits of training outweigh the costs to provide it. However, a recent study from the ROI Institute showed that although 96 percent of executives want to see the business effects of learning, only 8 percent receive it.[47] Nevertheless, in today's global competitive environment, training will not be rewarded with continued investment unless training results in improved performance that impacts the bottom line. Today, organizations can only justify investing in training that is clearly essential to business success and that delivers results that enable the company to compete effectively.

benchmarking
Process of monitoring and measuring a firm's internal processes, such as operations, and then comparing the data with information from companies that excel in those areas.

Benchmarking is the process of monitoring and measuring a firm's internal processes, such as operations, and then comparing the data with information from companies that excel in those areas. Because training programs for different firms are unique, the training measures are necessarily broad. Common benchmarking questions focus on metrics such as training costs, the ratio of training staff to employees, and whether new or more traditional delivery systems are used. Information derived from these questions probably lacks the detail to permit specific improvements of the training curricula. However, a firm may recognize, for example, that another organization can deliver a lot of training for relatively little cost. This information could then trigger the firm to follow up with interviews or site visits to determine whether that phenomenon represents a "best practice."

Quality standards are another important results measure. A well-recognized standard is the ISO 9001 quality assurance standard, which states, "Employees should receive the training and have the knowledge necessary to do their jobs." To comply with the standard, companies must maintain written records of their employee training to show that employees have been properly trained. Think of possible questions that a compliance auditor might ask when auditing a firm. Some might be, "How does your firm assess the need for the types and amounts of training and education received by all categories of employees? What percentage of employees receives training annually? What is the average number of hours of training and education per employee?" Under ISO 9001, monitoring the quality of training is important.

We have considered a variety of training methods, delivery systems, and training evaluation criteria. Careful planning and orchestration of these methods and systems is essential to achieving effective training. The Watch It video describes Wilson Learning's approach and philosophy.

 **Watch It 2**
If your professor has assigned this, sign into **www.pearson.com/mylab/management** to watch a video titled Wilson Learning: Training and to respond to questions.

HR Web Wisdom
Association for Talent Development
www.td.org
The homepage for the Association for Talent Development is presented.

Factors Influencing Training and Development

There are numerous factors that both impact and are impacted by T&D.

TOP MANAGEMENT SUPPORT For T&D programs to be successful, top management support is required; without it, a T&D program will not succeed. The most effective way to achieve success is for executives to provide the needed resources to support the T&D effort. The comments by Carol Freeland, principal/owner of ACTS+ in Hot Springs Village, Arizona, best described the importance of support from the CEO when she said, "If the CEO does not believe in the inherent value of training, any training effort on the part of the company will be fruitless and languish."[48]

SHORTAGE OF SKILLED WORKERS Shortage of future skilled workers was first projected in the 1980s but has recently received additional attention. Mark Tomlinson, executive director and general manager of the Society of Manufacturing Engineers, compares the shortage of skilled workers to viewing an iceberg in stormy seas. "We're just approaching it; we haven't hit it yet but we know it's there. People are starting to see it. They just don't know how to deal with it."[49] It took Cianbro Corporation, a heavy construction company in the Northeast, 18 months to hire 80 experienced welders.[50] JetBlue Airways, like most commercial airlines, are feeling the pinch of a pilot shortage. The substantial expense to meet the lengthy period over which they qualify to fly passenger jets has contributed to this shortage. JetBlue has developed an innovative trial training program to prepare pilots for flight duties over a much shorter period. JetBlue spokesman Doug McGraw said that the trial program is designed to build, "the complex skills required of airline pilots from the first day."[51] Though shorter, McGraw emphasized that the quality of preparation will not be compromised, by emphasizing the goal, "to ensure the quality of our current cadre of pilots is maintained."[52] These examples point to the problems of finding qualified employees and providing them with essential training.

Unemployment figures are misleading because they do not show employers who are begging for skilled workers. Worldwide many companies are struggling to find skilled workers. Baby boomers—the best-educated and most-skilled workforce in U.S. history—are preparing to retire. Labor experts are concerned that workers in the United States lack the critical skills needed to replace baby boomers. Silicon Valley companies are having difficulty finding software engineers; Union Health Service and the Harvard hospital system find it hard to find nurses and technicians; and manufacturers such as Caterpillar and Westinghouse cannot hire enough welders and machinists to operate their state-of-the-art lathes.[53]

Part of the problem in finding qualified people for manufacturing jobs is that there is a generation of young people for which manufacturing has not been an attractive job prospect because they have seen many jobs outsourced and they question the long-term future in these jobs. In addition, training needs are changing and the old skill requirements of reading, writing, and arithmetic have been expanded. Executives are increasingly demanding additional skills of their new hires such as critical thinking and problem solving, communication, collaboration, and creativity.[54]

TECHNOLOGICAL ADVANCES Change is occurring at an amazing speed, with knowledge doubling every year. Perhaps no factor has influenced T&D more than technology. As technology becomes capable of handling more and more tasks, employers combine jobs and confer broader responsibilities on remaining workers. For example, the technology of advanced automated manufacturing, such as that in the automobile industry, is today doing the jobs of other employees, including the laborer, the materials handler, the operator-assembler, and the maintenance person. In fact, it is now commonplace for a single employee to perform all those tasks in a position called "manufacturing technician." The expanding range of tasks and responsibilities in almost all jobs demand higher levels of reading, writing, and problem-solving skills. Employees must possess higher levels of reading skills than before because they must now be able to read the operating and troubleshooting manuals (when problems arise) of automated manufacturing equipment that is based on computer technology. Previously, the design of manufacturing equipment was relatively simple and easy to operate, based on simple mechanical principles such as pulleys.

Technological innovation also has fostered increased autonomy and team-oriented work places, which also demand different job-related skills than employees once needed. For example, the manufacturing technician's job mentioned previously, is generally more autonomous than its predecessor. Thus, technicians must be able to manage themselves and their time. Employers now rely on working teams' technical and interpersonal skills to drive efficiency and to improve quality. Today's consumers often expect customized products and applications, which require that employees possess sufficient technical skill to tailor products and services to customers' needs, as well as the interpersonal skills necessary to determine client needs and customer service.

GLOBAL COMPLEXITY The world is simply getting more complex, and this has had an impact on how an organization operates. No longer does a firm just compete against other firms in the United States. Now more than ever, to sustain competitive advantage companies must provide their employees with leading-edge skills, and encourage employees to apply their skills proficiently. Increasing customer expectations also mean the standards for success are constantly rising. To compete in the more complex global environment, companies must be able to simultaneously integrate global operations, respond to diverse local/national needs within subsidiary operations, and implement innovation rapidly around the world.

There is reason to suspect that many U.S. firms are already behind in this regard. Employers in both the European Common Market and some Pacific Rim economies have long emphasized learning as a proactive tool for responding to strategic change. For example, in Ireland, the private sector offers graduate employment programs in skill areas such as science, marketing, and technology. In short, global competition necessitates that companies in the United States become more productive and there is growing consensus that training must be at the forefront of their attempts to do so.

LEARNING STYLES Although much remains unknown about the learning process, what is known affects the way firms conduct training. It is known that adults retain approximately 20 percent of what they read and hear, 40 percent of what they see, 50 percent of what they say, 60 percent of what they do, and 90 percent of what they see, hear, say, and do.[55] Because of these differences, it is important to use a wide range of T&D methods. Learning style supports the concept that people have a natural preference, based on their dominant sense, in how they choose to learn and process information. It may be visual, hearing, or touching.[56] Some learn best from working in a group whereas others prefer studying on an individual basis. Still others absorb best by seeing how the material provides a practical application, and others want to know the theoretical basis. Some learners can readily absorb information by reading written words whereas others learn best through hearing the words spoken.

In studying the information in this text, the different learning styles will become apparent. There are exercises at the end of each chapter to provide hands-on application of the material. Being able to read the words in the text will appeal to some whereas others will learn best through hearing the instructor's lecture. Each chapter's PowerPoint slides provide a visual representation of the material. The incidents at the end of each chapter require extending your newfound knowledge in a practical manner.

blended training
The use of multiple training methods to deliver T&D.

To cope with the different learning styles, firms use multiple methods, called **blended training** (also referred to as blended learning), to deliver T&D. This involves using a combination of training methods that are strategically combined to best achieve a training program's objectives.[57] John Leutner, head of global learning services for Xerox corporate HR, said, "The new blended learning is about creating a richer, more meaningful development experience that relates to a person's work and performance."[58] Starbucks Coffee uses a blended learning approach to certify its baristas. Trainees receive 70 percent of their training through on-the-job experiences and hands-on training, 20 percent from peer feedback and peer mentorship, and 10 percent from online training modules.[59]

Another learning principle is that learners progress in an area of learning only as far as they need to achieve their purposes. Professors have long known that telling students which concepts are important motivates them to study the material, especially if the information is prime test material. Research indicates that unless there is relevance, meaning, and emotion attached to the material taught, trainees will not learn.

just-in-time training (on-demand training)
Training provided anytime, anywhere in the world when it is needed.

Another learning principle is that the best time to learn is when the learning can be useful. One way this impacts T&D is the need for training on a timely basis. **Just-in-time training (on-demand training)** is training provided anytime, anywhere in the world when it is needed. For example, transport and logistics company AP Moller Maersk, capitalizes on team-based learning that begins with finding solutions to significant market threats and opportunities. The company assembles global teams to tackle business problems. Team members benefit from each other's unique expertise and perspectives. In just a few years, AP Moller Maersk deemed this program a success based on financial outcomes and growth of new business opportunities.[60] In addition to working alongside team members, computer technology, the Internet, intranets, smartphones, and similar devices have made these approaches economically feasible to a degree never possible before. The ability to deliver knowledge to employees on an as-needed basis, anywhere on the globe, and at a pace consistent with their learning styles greatly enhances the value of T&D.

OTHER HUMAN RESOURCE FUNCTIONS Successful accomplishment of other human resource functions can also have a crucial impact on T&D. For instance, if recruitment-and-selection efforts or its compensation package attract only marginally qualified workers, a firm will need extensive T&D programs. Hiring marginally qualified workers will likely have a significant impact on the firm's safety and health programs. Therefore, additional training will be required.

8.3 Summarize some human resource management training initiatives.

Human Resource Management Training Initiatives

HR is responsible for many company-wide training initiatives on HR-related matters. Among these initiatives are orientation (onboarding), ethics, compliance (equal employment opportunity, Occupational Safety and Health), and diversity. We will limit our discussion to orientation (onboarding) here and safety training is discussed in Chapter 13. Resources for other types of compliance training are available online on the government agency responsible for the compliance issue. For example, the Office of Federal Contract Compliance Programs Web site addresses affirmative action requirements, and the U.S. Department of Labor provides learning resources for determining whether jobs are exempt from the overtime pay provision of the Fair Labor Standards Act.

orientation
Initial T&D effort for new employees that informs them about the company, the job, and the

Orientation is the initial T&D effort to inform new employees about the company, the job, and the work group. It becomes a way to engage new employees and reinforce the fact that they made the proper career choice. It also familiarizes them with the corporate culture and helps them to quickly become productive. A good orientation program is quite important because first impressions are often the most lasting and need to start the minute an applicant accepts an offer of employment. One of the orientation goals at Booz Allen is to make a positive first impression and create excitement before the new hire's first day on the job, using their online new-hire portal.[61]

New employees usually decide whether to stay at a company within their first six months of employment, and orientation programs give organizations an opportunity to get the relationship off to a good start. Therefore, new-hire orientation programs are particularly crucial for the rapid transition from new hires to contributing members of the organization. Orientation formats are unique to each firm. However, some basic purposes are listed here.

- *The Employment Situation.* At an early point in time, it is helpful for the new employee to know how his or her job fits into the firm's organizational structure and goals.
- *Company Policies and Rules.* Every job within an organization must be performed within the guidelines and constraints provided by policies and rules. Employees must understand these to ensure a smooth transition into the workplace.
- *Compensation.* Employees have a special interest in obtaining information about the reward system. Management normally provides this information during the recruitment-and-selection process and often reviews it during orientation.
- *Corporate Culture.* The firm's culture reflects, in effect, "How we do things around here." This relates to everything from the way employees dress to the way they talk.
- *Team Membership.* A new employee's ability and willingness to work in teams was likely determined before he or she was hired. In orientation, the program may again emphasize the importance of becoming a valued member of the company team.
- *Employee Development.* An individual's employment security is increasingly becoming dependent on his or her ability to acquire needed knowledge and skills that are constantly changing. Thus, firms should keep employees aware not only of company-sponsored developmental programs, but also of those available externally.
- *Socialization.* To reduce the anxiety that new employees may experience, the firm should take steps to integrate them into the informal organization. Some organizations have found that employees subjected to socialization programs, including the topics of politics and career management, perform better than those who have not undergone such training.

To this list, add the fact that there are numerous forms and documents a new employee must complete or read and acknowledge.

Supervisors represent the front line of orientation. Roger Chevalier, California-based management consultant and author of *A Manager's Guide to Improving Workplace Performance,* said, "If employees are selected properly, 85 percent of whether they will succeed is based on the environment created by a supervisor."[62] Peers also often serve as excellent information agents. There are several reasons for using peers in performing this function. For one thing, they are accessible to newcomers, often more so than the boss. Peers also tend to have a high degree of empathy for new people. In addition, they have the organizational experience and technical expertise to which new employees need access. Some organizations assign a mentor or "buddy" to new hires to work with them until they are settled in.

Although orientation can occupy a new employee's first few days on the job, some firms believe that learning is more effective if spread out over time. A company may deliver a program in a system of 20 one-hour sessions over a period of several weeks, or extend the program over a much longer period. For example, IBM developed Succeeding@IBM, which is a two-year program that delivers new information covering corporate values, strategy, tools, and the resources needed to be successful. IBM distinguishes its orientation program from others, in part, by incorporating personalized learning plans.

Some firms are sensitive to information overload and make information available to employees on an as-needed basis. For example, a new supervisor may eventually have the responsibility for evaluating his or her subordinates. But knowledge of how to do this may not be needed for six months. A training segment on performance evaluation may be placed on the Internet or a firm's intranet and be available when the need arises. This approach is consistent with *just-in-time training*, mentioned previously.

8.4 Explain the concept of careers and career planning approaches and methods.

Careers and Career Planning Approaches and Methods

career
General course that a person chooses to pursue throughout his or her working life.

career path
A flexible line of movement through which a person may travel during his or her work life.

In the sections that follow, we will address a series of interrelated topics—careers, career paths, and career planning. A **career** is a general course that a person chooses to pursue throughout his or her working life. Historically, a *career* was a sequence of work-related positions an individual occupied during a lifetime, although not always with the same company. However, today there are few relatively static jobs. A **career path** is a flexible line of movement through which a person may travel during his or her work life. Following an established career path, the employee can undertake career development with the firm's assistance. From a worker's perspective, following a career path may involve weaving from company to company and from position to position as he or she obtains greater knowledge and experience. Career paths have historically focused on upward mobility within an occupation, which was a choice not nearly as available as in the past. The days of the cradle to the grave job have largely disappeared. Other career paths include the network, lateral skill, dual-career paths, adding value to your career, demotion, and being your own boss as a free agent. Most careers are no longer a straight ascent up the corporate ladder. By selecting an alternative career path, a person may transfer current skills into a new career, one that was only dreamed about in the past. Typically, these career paths are used in combination and may be more popular at various stages of a person's career.

In the following Watch It video, you will learn that Verizon provides employees with the opportunity to develop a career path that fits their interests and the company's needs. Verizon also provides a variety of training programs to help facilitate the attainment of career goals.

 **Watch It 3**

If your professor has assigned this, sign into **www.pearson.com/mylab/management** to watch a video titled Verizon: Career Planning and to respond to questions.

Traditional Career Path

traditional career path
Employee progresses vertically upward in the organization from one specific job to the next.

Although the traditional career path is not as viable a career path option as it previously was, understanding it furthers one's comprehension of the other career path alternatives. The **traditional career path** is one in which an employee progresses vertically upward in the organization from one specific job to the next. The assumption is that each preceding job is essential preparation for the next-higher-level job. Therefore, an employee must move, step-by-step, from one job to the next to gain needed experience and preparation. One of the biggest advantages of the traditional career path is that it was straightforward and very predictable.[63] The path was clearly laid out, and the employee knew the specific sequence of jobs through which he or she must progress.

Today, the old model of a career in which an employee worked his or her way up the ladder in a single company is becoming somewhat rare. The up-or-out approach, in which employees must keep getting promoted quickly or get lost, is becoming outmoded. The certainties of yesterday's business methods and growth have disappeared in most industries. However, the one certainty that remains is that there will always be top-level managers and individuals who strive to achieve these positions. The way these positions are obtained may be different.

Network Career Path

network career path
Method of career progression that contains both a vertical sequence of jobs and a series of horizontal opportunities.

The **network career path** contains both a vertical sequence of jobs and a series of horizontal opportunities. The network career path recognizes the interchangeability of experience at certain levels and the need to broaden experience at one level before promotion to a higher level. Often, this approach provides more realistic opportunities for employee development in an organization than does the traditional career path. For instance, a person may work as an inventory manager for a few years and then move to a lateral position of shift manager before being considered for a promotion. The vertical and horizontal options lessen the probability of blockage in one job. Royal Caribbean crew members are often given several different work assignments prior to a promotion. One major disadvantage of this type of career path is that it is more difficult to explain to employees the specific route their careers may take for a given line of work.

The benefits of a network career path are not limited to lower-level positions in the organizational job structure. An interesting research study provides evidence that following a network career path may be the best route to becoming a high-ranking executive, including CEO. Data from LinkedIn revealed that experience in one additional functional area improved the odds of becoming an executive as much as gaining three years of additional experience.[64] Also, taking assignments in four functions was nearly as helpful as earning an MBA from a highly-ranked program.

Lateral Skill Path

lateral skill path
Career path that allows for lateral moves within the firm, taken to permit an employee to become revitalized and find new challenges.

The **lateral skill path** allows for lateral moves within the firm, taken to permit an employee to become revitalized and find new challenges. Neither pay nor promotion may be involved, but by learning a different job, an employee can increase his or her value to the organization and become rejuvenated and reenergized. Firms that want to encourage lateral movement may choose to use a skill-based pay system that rewards individuals for the type and number of skills they possess. Another approach is job enrichment. This approach rewards (without promotion) an employee by increasing the challenge of the job, giving the job more meaning, and giving the employee a greater sense of accomplishment.

Dual-Career Path

dual-career path
Career path that recognizes that technical specialists can and should be allowed to contribute their expertise to a company without having to become managers.

The dual-career path was originally developed to deal with the problem of technically trained employees who had no desire to move into management through the normal upward mobility procedure. The **dual-career path** recognizes that technical specialists can and should be allowed to contribute their expertise to a company without having to become managers. A dual-career approach is often established to encourage and motivate professionals in fields such as engineering, sales, marketing, finance, and HR. Individuals in these fields can increase their specialized knowledge, make contributions to their firms, and be rewarded without entering management. Whether on the management or technical path, compensation would be comparable at each level. The dual system has been a trademark in higher education, where individuals can move through the ranks of instructor, assistant professor, associate professor, and professor without having to go into administration.

Adding Value to Your Career

Adding value to your career may appear to be totally self-serving, but nevertheless, it is a logical and realistic career path. In the rapidly changing world today, professional obsolescence can creep up on a person. What makes a person valuable in today's work environment is the knowledge and experience he or she brings to a job. An individual's knowledge must be ever expanding, and continual personal development is a necessity. The better an employee's qualifications, the greater the opportunities he or she has with the present firm and in the job market. A person must discover what companies need, then develop the skills necessary to meet these needs as defined by the marketplace. Individuals should always be doing something that contributes significant, positive change to the organization. If any vestige of job security exists, this is it. Basically, the primary tie that binds a worker to the company, and vice versa, is mutual success resulting in performance that adds value to the organization.

Demotion

demotion
Process of moving a worker to a lower level of duties and responsibilities, which typically involves a reduction in pay.

Demotion is the process of moving a worker to a lower level of duties and responsibilities, which typically involves a reduction in pay. Demotions have long been associated with failure, but limited promotional opportunities in the future and the fast pace of technological change may make demotion a legitimate career option. If the stigma of demotion can be removed, more employees, especially older workers, might choose to make such a move. Some people get into a position only to find their skills were better suited to their old job. Sometimes they decide they do not want to have as much responsibility because of things going on in their personal lives. Working long hours for limited promotional opportunity loses its appeal to some after a while, especially if the worker can financially afford the demotion. In certain instances, this approach might open a clogged promotional path and at the same time permit a senior employee to escape unwanted stress without being viewed as a failure.

free agents
People who take charge of all or part of their careers by being their own bosses or by working for others in ways that fit their needs or wants.

Free Agents (Being Your Own Boss)

Free agents are people who take charge of all or part of their careers by being their own bosses or by working for others in ways that fit their needs or wants. Many became free agents because of company downsizing and have no desire or would have difficulty reentering the corporate world.[65] Free agents are said to work in the *gig economy*, which simply refers to working as an independent contractor to complete projects for one or more clients. Free agents most often get projects (or gigs) using a Web site or mobile app that helps to match them with customers.[66]

Some free agents work full-time, others work part-time. Still, others work full-time and run a small business in the hope of converting it into their primary work. Free agents come in many shapes and sizes, but what distinguishes them is a commitment to controlling part or all their careers. They have a variety of talents and are used to dealing with a wide range of audiences and changing their approach on the spot in response to new information or reactions. Free agents most commonly work in one or more of the following industries (and a common job title): arts and design (graphic designers), computer and information technology (Web developers), construction and extraction (painters), media and communications (photographers), and transportation and material moving (delivery drivers).[67] They also tend to love challenges and spontaneity.[68]

career planning
Ongoing process whereby an individual sets career goals and identifies the means to achieve them.

Career Planning Approaches

Career planning is an ongoing process whereby *an individual* sets career goals and identifies the means to achieve them. Individuals in today's job market must truly manage their careers. Career planning should not concentrate only on advancement opportunities because the present work environment has reduced many of these opportunities. At some point, career planning should focus on achieving successes that do not necessarily entail promotions, even if it means taking a lower-paying job in an industry, such as health care, where growth opportunities are plentiful.[69] Or, it may mean staying put under the right circumstances. A *Glassdoor* survey revealed that a positive workplace culture, often established by good working relationships, is associated with higher retention.[70] The survey also found that a negative workplace culture is associated with significantly higher turnover. Altogether, these findings may suggest that employees are satisfied with their current career status.

"If you don't know where you're going, any road will get you there," is certainly true in career planning. Career planning must now accommodate several objectives and enable us to prepare for each on a contingency basis. It will need updating to accommodate changes in our own interests as well as in the work environment. Historically, it was thought that career planning was logical, linear, and indeed, planned. Today, a new job assignment often is thought of as being paid to learn a new task and increase your experience level in case you must leave your job. Because of the many changes that are occurring, career planning is essential for survival for individuals and organizations. Individuals should have a strategy or plan for unexpected career events that begins while they are still employed.

self-assessment
Process of learning about oneself.

SELF-ASSESSMENT **Self-assessment** is the process of learning about oneself. Anything that could affect one's performance in a future job should be considered. It is one of the first things that a person should do in planning a career. A self-assessment can help a person target career choices and goals. Conducting a realistic self-assessment may help a person avoid mistakes that could affect his or her entire career progression. A person should take time to analyze his or her past successes and failures. A thorough self-assessment will go a long way toward helping match an individual's specific qualities and goals with the right job or profession. Remember, you cannot get what you want until you know what you want. The self-assessment is not something that is done once and forgotten. It is something that spans a career and into retirement. The self-assessment may show that you do not want to retire at 65. Some enjoy working well past what traditionally has been thought of as the retirement age. As a 95-year-old former mentor said, "work is what keeps me alive and going. Everyone I know who retired died young, and certainly much younger than me."[71]

strength/weakness balance sheet
A self-evaluation procedure, developed originally by Benjamin Franklin, that assists people in becoming aware of their strengths and weaknesses.

A self-evaluation procedure, developed originally by Benjamin Franklin that assists people in becoming aware of their strengths and weaknesses is the **strength/weakness balance sheet**. Employees who understand their strengths can use them to maximum advantage. By recognizing their weaknesses, they are in a better position to overcome them. This statement sums up that attitude; "If you have a weakness, understand it and make it work for you as a strength; if you have a strength, do not abuse it to the point at which it becomes a weakness."

To use a strength/weakness balance sheet, the individual lists strengths and weaknesses as he or she perceives them. This is quite important, because believing, for example, that a weakness exists even when it does not can equate to a real weakness. Thus, if you believe that you make a poor first impression when meeting someone, you will probably make a poor impression. The perception of a weakness often becomes a self-fulfilling prophecy.

Table 8-1 shows an example of a strength/weakness balance sheet. Typically, a person's weaknesses will outnumber strengths after the first few attempts. However, as the individual repeats the process, some items that first appeared to be weaknesses may eventually be strengths and should then be moved from one column to the other. A person should devote sufficient time to the project to obtain a clear understanding of his or her strengths and weaknesses. Typically, the process should take at least several days during which the list is drafted and subsequently modified. People change, and every few years the process should again be undertaken again.

likes and dislikes survey
Procedure that helps individuals in recognizing restrictions they place on themselves.

A **likes and dislikes survey** assists individuals in recognizing restrictions they place on themselves. Connecticut-based career counselor Julie Jansen said, "It's important in identifying what you want to do, what your skills are, and what you don't—and do—like about your current occupation."[72] You are looking for qualities you want in a job and attributes of a job you do not want. For instance, some people are not willing to live in certain parts of the country, and such feelings should be noted as a constraint. Some positions require a person to spend considerable amount of time traveling. Thus, an estimate of the amount of time a person is willing to travel would also be helpful. Recognition of such self-imposed restrictions may reduce future career problems.

The size of the firm might also be important. Some like a major organization whose products or services are well known; others prefer a smaller organization, believing that the opportunities for advancement may be greater or that the environment is better suited to their tastes. All factors that could affect an individual's work performance should be listed in the likes and dislikes survey. An example of this type of survey is shown in Table 8-2.

formal assessment
The use of established external approaches to facilitate evaluation of an issue at hand.

FORMAL ASSESSMENT Combining self-assessment with formal assessment tools designed to inform career planning considerations provides a more comprehensive approach. **Formal assessment** refers to the use of established external approaches to facilitate evaluation of an issue at hand. There are many tools, including the use of performance appraisal, which we already addressed in Chapter 7. An example is the 360-degree feedback method. In this chapter, we will focus on another approach. In the career planning domain, testing tools to identify career interests

TABLE 8-1

Strength/Weakness Balance Sheet

Strengths	Weaknesses
Work well with people.	Do not like constant supervision.
Good manager of people.	Often say things without realizing consequences.
Hard worker.	Cannot sit at a desk all the time.
Lead by example.	A rebel at heart but have portrayed myself as just the opposite. My conservatism has gotten me jobs that I emotionally did not want.
People respect me as being fair and impartial.	Am sometimes nervous in an unfamiliar environment.
Tremendous amount of energy.	Interest level hits peaks and valleys.
Get the job done when it is defined.	Many people look on me as being unstable.
Excellent at organizing other people's time.	Not a tremendous planner for short range.
Can get the most out of people who are working for me.	Exclusively better at long-range planning.
Have a great amount of empathy.	Impatient—want to have things happen fast.

TABLE 8-2

Likes and Dislikes Survey

Likes	Dislikes
Enjoy traveling	Do not want to work for a large firm
Would like to live in the Southeast United States	Would not want to work in a large city
Enjoy being my own boss	Would not like to work behind a desk all day
Would like to live in a medium-sized city	Would not like to wear suits all the time
Enjoy watching football and baseball	
Enjoy playing racquetball	

based on values and personality represent one approach. Although individuals may complete these tests on their own and read the report that is generated based on their responses, it often makes sense to work with a career counselor who can answer questions and make further recommendations.

Perhaps the most well-known example is the Myers-Briggs Type Indicator (MBTI). This assessment tool contains dozens of questions that elicit an individual's preferences for how they would behave in different situations. The MBTI describes the following four preferences: *Energy* measures an individuals' degree of extraversion or introversion to determine whether a person gains energy through interpersonal relationships (extraversion) or through self-reflection (introversion). *Information-Gathering* measures a preference for gathering information about facts to consider before deciding (Sensing) or a preference for gathering information about possibilities before deciding. *Decision making* measures a preference for consideration a person gives to their own or others' feelings and values relative to facts and details. Preferences to consider the effect of a decision on personal feelings as well as on others (Feeling) stand in contrast to a preference to make objective decisions (Thinking). *Lifestyle* refers to an individual's inclination to be either flexible or structured. A preference to establish goals, strategies for goal attainment, and deadlines for meeting them (Judging) stands in contrast to a preference for embracing the unexpected, modifying decisions, and working without definitive timelines and deadlines (Perceiving).

An example of a formal test is the Career Key, which is based on Holland's Theory of Career Choice. This theory is premised on the idea that people are more likely to thrive in situations that match their personalities. It specifies six personality and corresponding situational types. For example, according to Holland's theory:[73]

> *Persons having an Investigative personality type "dominate" this environment. There are more of them than there are people of other personality types. For example, in a scientific laboratory there will be more persons having an "Investigative" personality than there will be people who have an "Enterprising" type. "Investigative" people create an "Investigative" environment. For example, they particularly value people who are precise, scientific, and intellectual—who are good at understanding and solving science and math problems.*

Examples of jobs that fit this description include architects and physicians.

As you can see, both informal and formal career assessments provide you with useful information. The sheer volume of information can be overwhelming. Still, it is important to sort through this information and think strategically about the next steps. Marketing strategist Dorie Clark suggests preparing a résumé of how you envision yourself five years into the future.[74] Specifically, state your desired job title and responsibilities. This exercise not only provides a vision for the foreseeable future, but also should serve as a prompt to figure out the next steps toward getting there.

Try It!

If your professor has assigned this, sign onto **www.pearson.com/mylab/management** to complete the Managing Your Career simulation and test your application of these concepts when faced with real-world decisions.

Career Development Methods

career development
Formal approach used by the organization to ensure that people with the proper qualifications and experiences are available when needed.

Career development is a formal approach used by the organization to ensure that people with the proper qualifications and experiences are available when needed. Beverly Kaye, coauthor of *Love 'Em or Lose 'Em: Getting Good People to Stay*, studied the top 20 reasons employees remain with their company and discovered that career development opportunities were number one on the list. It was even more important than receiving greater pay.[75] With career development, the organization identifies paths and activities for individual employees as they develop.

Career planning rests with the employee. However, career development must closely parallel individual career planning if a firm is to retain its best and brightest workers. Employees must see that the firm's career development effort is directed toward furthering their specific career objectives. Companies must therefore help their employees obtain their career objectives and most notably, career security. They must provide them with opportunities to learn and do different things. Performing the same or a similar task over and over provides little development. Through effective career development, a pool of men and women can be developed who can thrive in any number of organizational structures in the future.

Properly designed and implemented career development programs can aid in recruiting and hiring and ensure that the best employees are in the pipeline for future leadership positions. Formal career development is important to maintain a motivated and committed workforce. In fact, Gen Y workers tend to favor personalized career guidance as opposed to big salaries and retirement packages. Further, high-potential employees are more likely to remain with organizations that are willing to invest in their development.

Career development should begin with a person's job placement and initial orientation. Management then observes the employee's job performance and compares it to job standards. At this stage, strengths and weaknesses will be noted, enabling management to assist the employee in making a tentative career decision. Naturally, this decision can be altered later as the process continues. This tentative career decision is based on several factors, including personal needs, abilities, and aspirations, and the organization's needs. Management can then schedule development programs that relate to the employee's specific needs.

Career development programs are expected to achieve one or more of the following objectives:

- *Effective development of available talent.* Individuals are more likely to be committed to career development that is part of a specific career plan. This way, they can better understand the purpose of development. Career development consistently ranks high on employees' *want lists*, and they can often be a less expensive option than pay raises and bonuses.
- *Self-appraisal opportunities for employees considering new or nontraditional career paths.* Some excellent workers do not view traditional upward mobility as a career option because firms today have fewer promotion options available. Other workers see themselves in dead-end jobs and seek relief. Rather than lose these workers, a firm can offer career planning to help them identify new and different career paths.
- *Development of career paths that cut across divisions and geographic locations.* The development should not be limited to a narrow spectrum of one part of a company.
- *A demonstration of a tangible commitment to developing a diverse work environment.* Individuals who recognize a company as desiring a diverse environment often have greater recruiting and retention opportunities.
- *Satisfaction of employees' specific development needs.* Individuals who see their personal development needs being met tend to be more satisfied with their jobs and the organization. They tend to remain with the organization.
- *Improvement of performance.* The job itself is the most important influence on career development. Each job can provide different challenges and experiences.
- *Increased employee loyalty and motivation, leading to decreased turnover.* Individuals who believe that the firm is interested in their career planning are more likely to remain with the organization.
- *A method of determining training and development needs.* If a person desires a certain career path and does not currently have the proper qualifications, this identifies a training and development need.

There are numerous methods for career development. Some currently used methods, most of which are used in various combinations, are discussed next.

MANAGER/EMPLOYEE SELF-SERVICE Manager and employee self-service have proven to be useful in career development. Many companies are providing managers with the online ability to assist employees in planning their career paths and developing required competencies. Through employee self-service, employees are provided with the ability to update performance goals online and to enroll in training courses.

DISCUSSIONS WITH KNOWLEDGEABLE INDIVIDUALS In a formal discussion, the superior and subordinate employees may jointly agree on what career development activities are best. The resources made available to achieve these objectives may also include developmental programs. In some organizations, human resource professionals are the focal point for helping on the topic. In other instances, psychologists and guidance counselors provide this service. In an academic setting, colleges and universities often provide career planning and development information to students. Students often go to their professors for career advice.

COMPANY MATERIAL Some firms provide material specifically developed to assist in career development. Such material is tailored to the firm's special needs. In addition, job descriptions provide valuable insight for individuals to personally determine whether a match exists between their strengths and weaknesses and specific positions.

PERFORMANCE APPRAISAL SYSTEM The firm's performance appraisal system can also be a valuable tool in career development. Discussing an employee's strengths and weaknesses with his or her supervisor can uncover developmental needs. If overcoming a weakness seems difficult or even impossible, an alternative career path may be the solution.

WORKSHOPS Some organizations conduct workshops lasting two or three days for helping workers develop careers within the company. Employees define and match their specific career objectives with the needs of the company. At other times, the company may send workers to workshops available in the community or workers may initiate the visit themselves. Consider just two of the developmental activities available for HR professionals:

- *Society for Human Resource Management Seminar Series.* Many HR seminars are available to SHRM members.
- *American Management Association, Human Resource Seminars.* There are numerous human resource seminars offered through the AMA.

8.5 Describe management development.

management development
Consists of all learning experiences provided by an organization resulting in upgrading skills and knowledge required in current and future managerial positions.

Management Development

Management development consists of all learning experiences provided by an organization resulting in upgrading skills and knowledge required in current and future managers. Although leadership is often depicted as an exciting and glamorous endeavor, there is another side; failure can quickly result in losing one's position. The risks are especially high because of today's rapid changes. This situation magnifies the importance of providing development opportunities for a firm's management group. A recent study found that almost 70 percent of companies believe that senior executives also need to improve their leadership skills. More than half of companies reported that their top leaders also needed to improve their strategic planning skills. Several other skills teamwork, motivating people, and creativity.[76] Increasingly, organizations recognize the importance of leader empathy. Empathy refers to the ability to understand and share the feelings of other people. Companies such as Cisco Systems and Ford Motor Company provide empathy training to improve management effectiveness, employee retention, and product design. For instance, the Ford design team shows empathy toward pregnant women who need more room and other accommodations in vehicles. Designers wear the weighty "empathy belly," which is a garment that simulates some of the feelings of a pregnant woman. Empathy training is paying off for many companies.[77] The 2015 Global Empathy Index revealed that the top 10 organizations (of 160 in total) generated 50 percent more net income per employee than the bottom 10 organizations.[78] In addition, overall, the DDI's *Global Leadership Forecast 2014–2015* found that organizations with the highest-quality leaders were nine times more likely to outperform their competition in metrics such as financial accomplishment, product quality and services, employee engagement, and customer approval.[79]

A firm's future lies largely in the hands of its managers. This group performs certain functions essential to the organization's survival and prosperity. Managers must make the right choices in most of their decisions; otherwise, the firm will not grow and may even fail. Therefore, it is imperative that managers keep up with the latest developments in their respective fields and, at the same time, manage an ever-changing workforce operating in a dynamic environment. Also, note that as managers reach higher levels in the organization, it is not so much their technical skills that they need, but their interpersonal skills and their business knowledge. In the extreme, unethical senior leaders whose behavior is counterproductive comes with consequences. For instance, turnover is likely to increase. And, by one estimate, a poor leader can cost a company up to $2.7 million dollars.[80]

First-line supervisors, middle managers, and executives may all participate in management development programs. These programs are available in-house, by professional organizations, and at colleges and universities. T&D specialists often plan and present in-house programs, at times using line managers. Organizations such as the SHRM and AMA conduct conferences and seminars in many specialties. Numerous colleges and universities also provide management development programs. Colleges and universities may possess expertise not available within business organizations. In these cases, academicians and management practitioners can advantageously present T&D programs jointly.

Mentoring and Coaching

Mentoring and coaching have become important means of management development. Because the purposes of mentoring and coaching are similar in concept and the terms are often used interchangeably in the literature, they are discussed together. Coaching and mentoring activities, which may occur either formally or informally, are primarily development approaches emphasizing one-on-one learning.

mentoring
Approach to advising, coaching, and nurturing for creating a practical relationship to enhance individual career, personal, and professional growth and development.

Mentoring is an approach to advising, coaching, and nurturing for creating a practical relationship to enhance individual career, personal, and professional growth and development. The concept of a mentor is believed to have its origins in Greek mythology when Odysseus set out for the Trojan War and placed the running of his palace in the hands of his trusted friend, Mentor.[81] Mentors may be anywhere in the organization or even in another firm. For years, mentoring has repeatedly been shown to be the most important factor influencing careers. In a study done by Gartner Research, having a mentor helps a person get promoted five times more often than his or her peers who do not have mentors. They are also promoted six times more than the competition.[82]

FYI

- Having a mentor matters to the millennial generation. Those who intend to stay with their firm for more than five years are twice as likely to have a mentor (68 percent) than those who do not intend to stay as long (32 percent).[83]

Most *Fortune 500* companies have a mentoring program. Mentors equip protégés to learn for themselves by sharing experiences, asking demanding questions, challenging decision making, and expanding problem-solving skills. It focuses on skills to develop protégés to perform to their highest potential, leading to career advancement. Mentors have the potential to help mentees discover their strengths and weaknesses, formulate a career path, set goals, manage stress, and balance work and personal obligations. Mentors can also help protégés learn to stand up to their superiors when circumstances dictate. For example, United Airlines encourages experienced captains to mentor co-pilots, and to help them be more insistent with veteran captains if they detect problems or hazards.[84] Technology can be used to match up mentors and mentees; however, the best algorithms are destined to fail if mentors and protégés do not find common ground as people.[85] Successful mentoring relationships do not necessarily last forever. These relationships may be quite fluid and form and dissolve around specific issues, such as helping younger people to build their professional networks.

E-mentoring, or open mentoring, is being used more and more today as opposed to face-to-face interaction with positive results. Many keep in touch with their mentors via e-mail, Facebook, and Twitter, but they may get together for lunch if they happen to be in the same location.

Most believe that women can truly benefit from a female mentor who has knowledge and experience and can show them "the ropes." For various reasons, mentors tend to seek out their mirror images. Because women and minorities are not equally represented at the firm's top levels, they sometimes are left without a female mentor. For instance, only 20 women were CEOs of *Fortune 500* companies in 2016.[86] Women who are mentored, particularly by other women, are more likely to enhance and expand career skills, advance in their careers, receive higher salaries, and enjoy their work more. Women want and need to have advice provided by mentors to use their talents and realize their potential, not only for their personal benefit but also to assist their firms.[87]

Discussions about the importance of mentoring and structuring mentoring practices has almost exclusively focused on developing younger or less experienced individuals. Very little has been said about mentoring high ranking executives, including the CEO. Most of us probably assume that executives have successfully climbed the corporate ladder and do not need mentoring. Still, many CEOs could benefit from the wise counsel of their peers—other CEOs or retired CEOs. Companies do not establish mentoring programs for CEOs. Rather, it is up to the CEO to reach out to trusted members of their networks. There is evidence to support payoffs of such mentoring relationships for the company. In a survey of CEOs who have mentoring relationships, 71 percent expressed confidence that company performance improved, 69 percent stated that they were making better decisions, and 76 percent said that they were more ably meeting stakeholder expectations.[88] In addition, employees within the organization also stand to benefit indirectly from their CEO's mentoring experiences. For instance, David Nish, now former CEO of Scottish insurance company Standard Life, stated, "The storytelling my mentor gave me was way beyond expectations. It's about believing I'm unlimited . . . and I try to give my people the same—belief that they can do anything."[89]

coaching
Often considered a responsibility of the immediate boss, who provides assistance, much like a mentor.

Coaching is often considered a responsibility of the immediate boss, who helps, much like a mentor, but the primary focus is about performance. Coaching involves helping workers see why they have been selected to perform the task or why they have been selected for the team. The coach has greater experience or expertise than the protégé and is in the position to offer wise advice. It is employee development that is customized to each individual and is therefore immediately applicable and does not require stepping away from work for extended periods of time.

Reverse Mentoring

reverse mentoring
A process in which older employees learn from younger ones.

Reverse mentoring is a process in which older employees learn from younger ones. There are people in organizations who are approaching retirement who do not want to retire and who have tremendous knowledge that should not go to waste. There are young people who know things

HR BLOOPERS

Management Development at Trends Apparel

As the HR Director at Trends Apparel, Laura Kent finds it challenging to support management development for the retail chain's local store managers. Turnover of the managers is high and exit interviews indicate lack of training as a concern. After reading an article about other organizations using a new e-learning training program on management skills, she thinks she has found a solution to the dilemma. She contacted the company that developed the training program and learned that the training helps managers develop skills in inventory management and marketing products. Laura thought it sounded perfect for Trends Apparel managers and immediately purchased the training. However, after a month, only 2 of the 40 managers have enrolled in the training, and those two did not finish the training. In frustration, Laura organized a conference call with a group of managers to discuss the problem. She is surprised to learn that the managers don't see the training as relevant. They said what they need is training in managing employees. For example, they need to learn how to better deal with employee problems and how to motivate employees. In addition, the managers told Laura that the e-learning program was just hard to work into their schedules. They felt coaching from other managers would be more helpful to them. Laura now realizes that even though the e-learning training program is already paid for, it is likely not going to be used.

If your professor has assigned this, go to **www.pearson.com/mylab/management** to complete the HR Bloopers exercise and test your application of these concepts when faced with real-world decisions.

HR Web Wisdom

CareerOneStop

www.careeronestop.org/

Career One Stop Pathways to Career Success.

others do not know and who are anxious to expand their horizons. The existence of these two diverse, but potentially mutually helpful, populations has led to reverse mentoring. At Procter & Gamble, the reverse mentoring program allows senior management to be mentored in areas such as biotechnology. It pairs scientists and top managers to explore the potential impact of biotechnology on P&G's customers, suppliers, and overall business. Time Warner has a Digital Reverse Mentoring Program between their executives and technology savvy college students.[90] Phil McKinney, a vice president at Hewlett-Packard, uses reverse mentoring by spending time with his company's college interns to understand what motivates them and how they work.[91]

8.6 Define organization development (OD) and the learning organization.

Organization Development and the Learning Organization

Individuals and groups receive the bulk of T&D effort. However, some firms believe that to achieve needed change, they must move the entire organization in a different direction. As noted earlier in the chapter, efforts to achieve this goal are the focus of OD—planned and systematic attempts to change the organization, typically to a more behavioral environment. OD education and training strategies are designed to develop a more open, productive, and compatible workplace despite differences in personalities, culture, or technologies. The OD movement has been strongly advocated by researchers such as Chris Argyris and Warren Bennis.[92] OD applies to an entire system, such as a company or a plant, and is a major means of achieving change in the corporate culture. Various factors in the firm's corporate culture affect employees' behavior on the job. To bring about desired changes in these factors and behavior, organizations must be transformed into market-driven, innovative, and adaptive systems if they are to survive and prosper in today's highly competitive global environment. This type of development is increasingly important as both work and the workforce diversify and change.

OD Interventions

Numerous OD interventions are available to the practitioner. Interventions covered in the following sections include survey feedback, a technique often combined with other interventions such as quality circles and team building.

survey feedback
Organization development method of basing change efforts on the systematic collection and measurement of subordinate's attitudes through anonymous questionnaires.

SURVEY FEEDBACK The organization development method of basing change efforts on the systematic collection and measurement of subordinate's attitudes through anonymous questionnaires is **survey feedback**. It enables management teams to help organizations create working environments that lead to better working relationships, greater productivity, and increased profitability. Survey feedback generally involves the following steps:

1. Members of the organization, including top management, are involved in planning the survey.
2. All members of the organizational unit participate in the survey.
3. The OD consultant usually analyzes the data, tabulates results, suggests approaches to diagnosis, and trains participants in the feedback process.
4. Data feedback usually begins at the top level of the organization and flows downward to groups reporting at successively lower levels.
5. Feedback meetings provide an opportunity to discuss and interpret data, diagnose problem areas, and develop action plans.

quality circles
Groups of employees who voluntarily meet regularly with their supervisors to discuss problems, investigate causes, recommend solutions, and take corrective action when authorized to do so.

QUALITY CIRCLES The United States received the concept of quality circles from Japan several decades ago. This version of employee involvement is still in use today, improving quality, increasing motivation, boosting productivity, and adding to the bottom line. **Quality circles** are groups of employees who voluntarily meet regularly with their supervisors to discuss their problems, investigate causes, recommend solutions, and take corrective action when authorized to do so. The team's recommendations are presented to higher-level management for review, and the approved actions are implemented with employee participation.

Toyota North America Inc. uses quality circles to develop a competitive workforce spirit. Approximately 37 percent of the automaker's assemblers participate in Toyota's global "Quality Circles" competition that pits worker against worker in a friendly competition to develop more efficient manufacturing methods. The ultimate target is 100 percent. Quality circles are one way that Toyota sees as providing an edge over the competition. Toyota holds competitions twice a year to identify the best ideas.[93]

team building
Conscious effort to develop effective work groups and cooperative skills throughout the organization.

TEAM BUILDING **Team building** is a conscious effort to develop effective work groups and cooperative skills throughout the organization. It helps members diagnose group processes and devise solutions to problems. Effective team building can be the most efficient way to boost morale, employee retention, and company profitability. Whether it's a lieutenant leading troops into battle or executives working with their managers, the same principles apply. An important by-product of team building is that it is one of the most effective interventions for improving employee satisfaction and work-related attitudes. Individualism has deep roots in U.S. culture. This trait has been a virtue and will continue to be an asset in our society. However, there are work situations that make it imperative to subordinate individual autonomy in favor of cooperation with a group. It seems apparent that teams are clearly superior in performing many of the tasks required by organizations. The building of effective teams, therefore, has become a business necessity.

Team building uses self-directed teams, each composed of a small group of employees responsible for an entire work process or segment. Team members work together to improve their operation or product, to plan and control their work, and to handle day-to-day problems. They may even become involved in broader, company-wide issues, such as vendor quality, safety, and business planning. There are basically two types of team-building exercises. In the first, there is an attempt to break down barriers to understanding that workers have built. In the second, participants "place their lives" in the hand of others such as falling backward, believing that the team will catch you.[94] Team-building exercises run the spectrum from a paint-ball battle[95] to the raw egg exercise that Southwest Airlines creates. At Southwest Airlines, the firm divides new employees into teams and gives them a raw egg in the shell, a handful of straws, and some masking tape. Their task is, in a limited amount of time, to protect that delicate cargo from an eight-foot drop. The exercise prepares teams of employees for creative problem solving in a fast-paced environment.[96]

In one team-building exercise, participants were instructed to untangle a 60-foot yellow rope. At first participants tried to untangle the rope on an individual basis, which resulted in failure. Ultimately, they began to share their ideas on how to untangle the rope, and within minutes it was untangled.[97] A classic team-building exercise is called "blind man's bluff" where a blindfolded person who is "it" must chase others with only the verbal assistance of team members to guide him or her.[98]

Pump It Up sells inflatable playgrounds throughout the United States and uses the playgrounds and childlike activities to create team-building exercises. The head office worked with team-building experts to devise a handbook of business-related team-building activities, including "Leading the Crowd Playfully" (to break the ice) and "Tag Team Climbing" (to improve cooperation). However, just bouncing around—in socks, in full view of the boss—may improve team morale.[99]

A classic team-building exercise is called "Team Banquets," where workers with different knowledge, skills, and experience are brought together to accomplish a single goal: create a banquet. The Team Banquet brings together 25 to 30 employees and challenges them to prepare a gourmet banquet within two hours. Only the raw ingredients and equipment are provided.[100] Through team building, management and participants discover that the exercises provide an excellent analogy to the workplace and provide an outstanding means for developing teamwork.

Learning Organization

A learning organization needs to provide a supportive learning environment and it provides specific learning processes and practices. Also, it is vital that management supports and reinforces learning. A learning organization moves beyond delivering tactical training projects to initiating learning programs aligned with strategic corporate goals. Once undervalued in the corporate world, training programs are now credited with strengthening customer satisfaction, contributing to partnership development, enhancing research and development activities, and finally, reinforcing the bottom line. Being recognized as a company that encourages its employees to continue to grow and learn can be a major asset in recruiting. Learning organizations view learning and development opportunities in all facets of their business and try to constantly look ahead and ensure that all employees are taking full advantage of their learning opportunities.[101] In a learning organization employees are rewarded for learning and are provided enriched jobs, promotions, and compensation. Organizations with a reputation for having a culture of being a learning leader tend to attract more and better-qualified employees.

In the competition to become listed in the "100 Best Companies to Work for in America," learning and growth opportunities were a high priority. On nearly every survey, T&D ranks in the top three benefits that employees want from their employers, and they search for firms that will give them the tools to advance in their profession. T&D is not merely a nice thing to provide, it is a strategic resource—one that firms must tap to energize their organizations in the twenty-first century.

PREPARING FOR EXAMS/QUIZZES

Chapter Summary by Learning Objectives

1. ***Define training and development (T&D) and summarize related practices.*** *Training* is designed to permit learners to acquire knowledge and skills needed for their present jobs. *Development* involves l earning that goes beyond today's job. Related to training and development practices is *organization development,* is planned and systematic attempts to change the organization, typically to a more behavioral environment. Also, a *learning organization* is a firm that recognizes the critical importance of continuous performance-related T&D and takes appropriate action.
2. ***Describe the training and development process.*** The process begins with the organization's determination of its specific training needs. Then specific objectives need to be established. After setting the T&D objectives, management can determine the appropriate methods and the delivery system to be used. Management must continuously evaluate T&D to ensure its value in achieving organizational objectives.

   Training professionals rely on three analytic approaches to determine *training needs*—organizational analysis, task analysis, and person analysis. *Training methods* include instructor-led training, e-learning, case study, behavior modeling, role-playing, training games, in-basket training, on-the-job training, and apprenticeship training. *Delivery systems* include corporate universities, colleges and universities, community colleges, online higher education, vestibule system, video media, and simulators. Some possible metrics for *evaluating training and development* include participants' opinion, extent of learning, behavioral change, accomplishment of T&D objectives, return on investment from training, and benchmarking. There are numerous factors that both impact and are impacted by T&D, including top management support, shortage of skilled workers, technological advances, learning styles, and other human resource functions.
3. ***Summarize some human resource management training initiatives.*** *Orientation* is the guided adjustment of new employees to the company, the job, and the work group. HR typically takes the lead on a variety of other training programs including ethics, compliance (for example, safety and health), and diversity training.
4. ***Explain the concept of a careers and career planning approaches and methods.*** A *career* is the general course that a person chooses to pursue throughout his or her working life. A *career path* is a flexible line of movement through which a person may travel during his or her work life. Career paths include traditional career path, network career path, lateral skill path, dual-career path, adding value to your career, demotion, and free agents.

   Career planning is an ongoing process whereby an individual sets career goals and identifies the means to achieve them. Self-assessment (for example, a likes and dislikes survey) and formal assessment approaches (for example, surveys that measure how an individual would behave situations) help organizations and employees with career planning.

   Career development is a formal approach used by the organization to ensure that people with the proper qualifications and experiences are available when needed. Career development methods include manager/employee self-service, discussions with knowledgeable individuals, company material, performance appraisal system, and workshops.
5. ***Describe management development.*** *Management development* consists of all learning experiences provided by an organization for providing and upgrading skills and knowledge required in current and future managers.
6. ***Define organization development (OD) and the learning organization.*** As noted earlier, *organization development* is planned and systematic attempts to change the organization, typically to a more behavioral environment. OD techniques include survey feedback, a technique often combined with other interventions such as quality circles and team building. Also, as noted earlier, a *learning organization* is a firm that recognizes the critical importance of continuous performance-related T&D and takes appropriate action. Learning organizations view learning and development opportunities in all facets of their business and try to constantly look ahead and ensure that all employees are taking full advantage of their learning opportunities.

Key Terms

training and development (T&D) 209
training 209
development 209
organization development (OD) 210
learning organization 210
training and development needs assessment 211
organizational analysis 211
task analysis 211
person analysis 212
e-learning 213
case study 214
behavior modeling 214
role-playing 214
business games 215
in-basket training 215
on-the-job training (OJT) 215
apprenticeship training 215
team training 216
team coordination training 216
cross-training 216
corporate university 217
online higher education 217
vestibule system 218
simulators 218
reactions 219
learning 219
behavior change 220
transfer of training 220
organizational results 220
benchmarking 221
blended training 223
just-in-time training (on-demand training) 223
orientation 224
career 225
career path 225
traditional career path 225
network career path 225
lateral skill path 226
dual-career path 226
demotion 226
free agents 227
career planning 227
self-assessment 227
strength/weakness balance sheet 227
likes and dislikes survey 228
formal assessment 228
career development 230
management development 231
mentoring 232
coaching 233
reverse mentoring 233
survey feedback 234
quality circles 234
team building 235

MyLab Management

If your instructor is using MyLab Management, go to **www.pearson.com/mylab/management** to complete the problems marked with this icon ✪.

Questions for Review

8-1. Define *training* and *development*.
8-2. What is a learning organization?
8-3. What are the steps in the T&D process?
8-4. What are the various training and development methods? Briefly describe each.
8-5. What are the various training and development delivery systems? Briefly describe each.
8-6. How is social networking used in informal training?
8-7. Define *orientation*, and explain the purposes of orientation.
8-8. What are some metrics for evaluating training and development?
8-9. Define *career*. Why is it important for individuals to conduct career planning?
8-10. What is the process of developing a strength/weakness balance sheet?
✪**8-11.** Why is it important for a firm to conduct career development?
8-12. What are some career development methods?
8-13. What are the various career paths that individuals may use?
8-14. Define *management development*. Why is it important?
8-15. Distinguish between mentoring and coaching. What is reverse mentoring?
✪**8-16.** Define each of the following:
(a) organization development
(b) survey feedback
(c) quality circles
(d) team building

PREPARING FOR MY CAREER

P I A Personal Inventory Assessment

✪ *An additional Personal Inventory Assessment can be found on MyLab Management.*

Core Evaluation Scale

This instrument assesses one's core self-evaluation. Core evaluation describes how a respondent views his or her current life and abilities. In this PIA, you'll see how you view yourself and your confidence in specific situations.

ETHICS DILEMMA

Consequences of Inadequate Training Design

You are the HR manager for a hospital that is updating its online system for patient registration, billing, and medical records management. The current system has been in place for the past several years and most employees are proficient users. In anticipation of transitioning to the new system, you contacted area hospitals that adopted the same new system. Your goal is to understand the training protocol and how well employees are applying what they learned to performing their jobs. Some hospitals surveyed used a blended learning approach that included a three-hour traditional classroom lecture, one-hour video instruction, and three hours of hands-on experience following the lecture segments. Those hospitals reported successful learning and transfer. Other hospitals limited training exclusively to either the three-hour lecture or one-hour online learning module. Administrators in these hospitals admitted that employees were generally not well prepared to use the system, and ill preparation led to service delays and countless customer complaints. Based on the result of your inquiry, you decided to adopt the blended approach.

Excited about your decision, you met with your HR director to review the training plan. The HR Director asked you about the cost differences between each approach. Naturally, the blended learning approach is the costliest option because it requires the most time away from work (employees are paid while taking training) and the hands-on module requires the purchase of expensive software to run simulations. Without hesitation, the HR Director instructed you to adopt the less expensive method.

Worried about this decision, you emphasized the superiority of the blended learning approach as well as the shortcomings of the least costly approach, including ill preparation, lower job performance, substantially more customer complaints, excessive work stress, and possible dissemination of confidential medical information to unauthorized individuals. Nevertheless, she responded by shrugging her shoulders and motioned you out of her office.

8-17. What would you do?

8-18. What factor(s) in this ethics dilemma might influence a person to make a less than ethical decision?

HRM Is Everyone's Business

Skills requirements are changing rapidly, creating gaps between what it takes to perform a job at a high level of proficiency and employees' readiness to do the work. Companies have two broad options for addressing these situations. One option is to select better qualified individuals in anticipation of these changes. Another is to invest in training current employees. Both options have pros and cons. Realistically most organizations will address these gaps by using a combination of both. The decision often comes down to cost effectiveness and whether there are qualified individuals in the labor market who are available for work. Where training current employees best suits an organization's objectives, both HR professionals and managers play a role in documenting a need for training (e.g., task and person analyses).

Action checklist for managers and HR—anticipating training needs

HR takes the lead

- ☑ HR professionals are responsible for pinpointing how training and development, management development, career development, and organizational development will propel organizational success.
- ☑ Ensure managers see the connection between organizational success and talent development, and hold managers accountable for making it happen.
- ☑ Guide managers through the process of recognizing current and anticipating possible future skill gaps.
- ☑ Work with managers to select, implement, and evaluate training to ensure positive learning and training transfer.

Managers take the lead

- ☑ Discuss with HR professionals changing skill requirements by educating them about how current or anticipated new technology changes the way work gets done.
- ☑ Provide examples where current employees' performance is declining by pointing out skills gaps, and offer how they may be brought up to speed. This kind of information will help HR professionals identify the appropriate training design.
- ☑ Describe examples of desired performance attainments that you anticipate from successful training initiatives. In doing so, you are helping HR professionals identify relevant metrics of training success.

HRM by the Numbers

Estimating Training Expenses

✪ *An additional HRM by the Numbers exercise can be found on MyLab Management.*

Training and development programs can create value for companies. In the short-term, at least, training programs represent a monetary cost. Consider the following example of training costs:

- Program development (e.g., salaries and benefits [health insurance] of personnel, equipment): $30,000
- Direct training program implementation (e.g., training materials, technology costs, facilities, travel, instructor's salary and benefits): $12,500
- Indirect (e.g., overhead [cost of utilities], general and administrative [e.g., staff time to schedule training facilities, registering employees for training sessions]): $95,000
- Hourly pay for all employees who are participating in training activities: $240,000
- Lost productivity while employees are participating in the training activities: $200,000

Questions

8-19. What is the total cost of training based on the current expenses?

8-20. Let's assume that 100 employees will participate in this training program. What is the average training cost per employee? (For simplicity, assume that each employee makes the same hourly pay rate.)

8-21. Employees' hourly rate is $20, and 100 employees receive training. Based on total hourly pay for employees who are participating in training activities, how many hours does each employee spend in training?

Working Together: Team Exercise

In small groups of three or four, come up with specific answers to the following questions. Talk through your perspectives with team members. Be prepared to share your ideas with the class.

As a group, identify an activity that you understand and perform well. Perhaps the task could come from a hobby, chores at home, or a previous or current job. Write a summary of how you (would) perform this activity and specify the knowledge, skills, and abilities that (would) enable you to do well.

8-22. How would you train others to perform the task? Explain.

8-23. In which ways would you measure training success? Explain.

INCIDENT 1 Career Development at Meyers and Brown

Regina Passalaqua joined Meyers and Brown, a management consulting firm, three years ago after she earned an MBA from Prestige University. During her short tenure, Regina received excellent performance reviews. Pleased with her accomplishments, Regina eventually became bored because her assignments were always similar—developing employee attitude surveys, analyzing the data, and preparing recommendations for clients. Regina was yearning for new challenges and professional growth, but was unsure about how to go about getting them. Over time, she became frustrated with the situation and began interviewing for jobs in other management consulting firms.

Bill Meyers, senior partner in the firm, heard from a colleague outside the firm that Regina was interviewing for jobs. Bill also noticed that Regina demonstrated less enthusiasm in meetings. Concerned about Regina, Bill called her in for a meeting. He said, "Regina, thank you for taking the time to meet with me. I asked for this meeting to tell you that you are a highly-valued member of this firm."

"Thank you, Mr. Meyers. Your opinion means a lot to me," Regina replied. Then, she shrugged her shoulders and seemed a bit uneasy. Bill was not assured by Regina's body language.

"Are you happy here, Regina?" he asked. Regina replied, "Yes, but . . . well, I'm not feeling very challenged these days and I am having a difficult time figuring out how I can advance to more challenging assignments. Frankly, I am looking for another job where I hope to find greater challenges."

Bill replied, "Regina, I had no idea that you felt this way." Then, he reflected on his 30-year career in management consulting, and how he advanced to a partnership role in the firm. Bill recalled that his managers and successful management consultants from other firms were instrumental in shaping a career plan and figuring out the logical steps to fulfill the milestones in the plan.

"Regina, now, I understand how you are feeling. I felt the same way when I was at your career stage," Bill said.

Regina replied, "Mr. Meyers, I had no idea that someone of your professional stature ever felt this way." He reacted, "Of course, most everyone does. I attribute much of my success to the people who took an interest in my career . . . people in whom I felt comfortable confiding."

Enthusiastically, Regina exclaimed, "Yes, that's it! That's it!"

In a concerned tone, "Underutilizing your talents or losing you altogether would be a disservice to all concerned. I want to work with you to find your path at Meyers and Brown. Please, let me help guide you," Bill said. Regina smiled in response to Bill's offer.

Bill stated, "I want to meet with you monthly to discuss your career. And, I am also going to ask Margaret and Samuel to meet with you as well. You see . . . they are successful management consultants who followed very different paths to achieving success in this firm. And, they are very supportive of others who are trying to find their way."

"Thank you so much, Mr. Meyers! Yes, thank you. I will look forward to our meetings," Regina stated in a gleeful manner.

Questions

8-24. Evaluate Meyers and Brown's approach to career development.

8-25. How might the firm change its approach to mentoring high potential employees?

INCIDENT 2 There's No Future Here!

"Could you come to my office for a minute, Bob?" asked Terry Geech, the plant manager.

"Sure, be right there," said Bob Glemson. Bob was the plant's quality control director. He had been with the company for four years. After completing his degree in mechanical engineering, he worked as a production supervisor and then as a maintenance supervisor prior to moving to his present job. Bob thought he knew what the call was about.

"Your letter of resignation catches me by surprise," began Terry.

"I know that Wilson Products will be getting a good person, but we sure need you here, too."

"I thought about it a lot," said Bob, "but there just doesn't seem to be a future for me here."

"Why do you say that?" asked Terry.

"Well," replied Bob, "the next position above mine is yours. Since you're only 39, I don't think it's likely that you'll be leaving soon."

"The fact is that I *am* leaving soon," said Terry. "That's why it's even more of a shock to learn that you're resigning. I think I'll be moving to the corporate office in June of next year. Besides, the company has several plants that are larger than this one, and we need good people in those plants from time to time, both in quality control and in general management."

"Well, I heard about an opening in the Cincinnati plant last year," said Bob, "but by the time I checked, the job had already been filled. We never know about opportunities in the other plants until we read about the incumbent in the company paper."

"All this is beside the point now. What would it take to get you to change your mind?" asked Terry.

"I don't think I will change my mind now," replied Bob, "because I've given Wilson Products my word that I'm going to join them."

Questions

8-26. Evaluate the career planning and development program at this company.

8-27. What actions might have prevented Bob's resignation?

MyLab Management

If your instructor is using MyLab Management, go to **www.pearson.com/mylab/management** for Auto-graded writing questions as well as the following Assisted-graded writing questions:

8-28. Why is executive onboarding for external hires so difficult?

8-29. What are some factors that influence T&D?

Endnotes

1 Ron Ashkenas, "You Can't Delegate Talent Management to the HR Department," *Harvard Business Review* online (September 23, 2016). Accessed March 7, 2017, at www.hbr.org.

2 "2016 Training Industry Report," *Training* (November/December 2016): 28–41.

3 Mike Dano, "How Verizon, AT&T, T-Mobile, Sprint and More Stacked Up in Q4 2016: The Top 7 Carriers," *Fiercewireless* online (March 8, 2017). Accessed March 9, 2017, at www.fiercewireless.com/wireless/how-verizon-at-t-t-mobile-sprint-and-more-stacked-up-q4-2016-top-7-carriers.

4 Quentin Hardy, "Gearing Up for the Cloud, AT T Tells Its Workers: Adapt, or Else," *The New York Times* online (February 13, 2016). Accessed February 27, 2017, at www.nytimes.com.

5 Isabel Thottam, "10 Companies with Awesome Training and Development Programs," *Monster.com*. Accessed March 2, 2017, at www.monster.com/career-advice/article/companies-with-awesome-training-development-programs.

6 John Donovan and Cathy Benko, "AT T's Talent Overhaul," *Harvard Business Review* online (October 2016). Accessed March 1, 2017, at www.hbr.org.

7 Summary Report For: 43-4051.00 - Customer Service Representatives. *Occupational Information Network*. Accessed March 3, 2017, at www.onetonline.org/link/summary/43-4051.00.

8 Ibid.

9 Eben Harrell, "The Solution to the Skills Gap Could Already Be Inside Your Company," *Harvard Business Review* online (September 27, 2016). Accessed February 15, 2017, at www.hbr.org.

10 Josh Bersin, "Use of MOOCs and Online Education Is Exploding: Here's Why," *Forbes* online (January 5, 2016). Accessed March 3, 2017, at www.forbes.com.

11 Ellen Lee, "Online Courses Trim Billions in Personnel Training," *CNBC* (February 14, 2014). Accessed April 5, 2014, at www.cnbc.com.

12 Chen Zhenghao, Brandon Alcorn, Gayle Christensen, Nicholas Eriksson, Daphne Koller, and Ezekiel J. Emanuel, "Who's Benefiting from MOOCs and Why," *Harvard Business Review* online (September 22, 2015). Accessed February 28, 2017, www.hbr.org.

13 "A Closer Look at E-learning: Expert Advice on Why Technology-based Training Works," *Industrial Safety & Hygiene News* 46 (January 2012): 56.

14 Greg Wright, "Retailers Buy Into E-Learning," *HR Magazine* 55 (December 2010): 87–90.

15 Gail Dutton, "Tech Check," *Training* 46 (January 2009): 24–26.

16 Michael A. Tucker, "E-Learning Evolves," *HR Magazine* 50 (October 2005): 74–78.

17 Margery Weinstein, "Is Technology Fulfilling Its Promise?" *Training* 48 (September/October 2011): 32–34.

18 Martyn Lewis, "Moving into the Live Virtual Classroom," *T+D* 65 (July 2011): 76–77.

19 Pat Galagan, "Twitter as a Learning Tool, Really," *T+D* 63 (March 2009): 28–31.

20 Dave Zielinski, "Gaming for Engagement," *HR Magazine* 57 (January 2012): 16.

21 "Companies Are Using Team-Based Business Games to Increase Productivity, Expert Says," *CPA Practice Management Forum* 6 (2010): 22.

22 "Training Budgets Bounce Back: Where to Spend," *HR Specialist* 9 (March 2011): 1–5.

23 Brandon Hall, "Learning at Play," *Chief Learning Officer* 10 (May 2011): 18.

24 Jeremy Diebel, "Remedy the Skills Gap with Apprenticeship Programs," *Industry Week* online (October 26, 2016). Accessed March 3, 2017, at www.industryweek.com/manufacturing-day/remedy-skills-gap-apprenticeship-programs.

25 Peter B. Alpern, "Need Skilled Workers? Try Growing Your Own," *American Machinist* 153 (May 2009): 40–43.

26 Elizabeth Schulze, "U.S. Companies Turn to German Training Model to Fill Jobs Gap," *The Wall Street Journal* online (September 26, 2016). Accessed February 19, 2017, at www.wsj.com.

27 Christopher Mims, "A New Kind of Jobs Program for Middle America," *The Wall Street Journal* online (February 26, 2017). Accessed March 2, 2017, at www.wsj.com.

28 Elizabeth Schulze, "U.S. Companies Turn to German Training Model to Fill Jobs Gap," *The Wall Street Journal* online (September 26, 2016). Accessed January 18, 2017, at www.wsj.com.

29 United States Coast Guard, "Introduction," (Chapter 1), *Team Coordination Training (TCT)*. Accessed March 3, 2017, at https://www.uscg.mil/auxiliary/training/tct/.

30 Kathryn Tyler, "A New U," *HR Magazine* 57 (April 1, 2012): 27–34.

31 Pat Galagan, "Back to Bricks and Mortar," *T+D* 65 (March 2011): 30–31.

32 Laura Cohn, "Grad Degrees from a Distance," *Kiplinger's Personal Finance* 64 (August 2010): 49.

33 "Distance Education Enrollment Continues to Grow," *Babson Survey Research Group* (February 9, 2016). Accessed March 7, 2017, at https://onlinelearningconsortium.org//news_item/babson-study-distance-education-enrollment-growth-continues-2

34 Ann Pace, "Higher Education: Paves the Way for New Career Opportunities," *T+D* 65 (September 2011): 74–77.

35 Elaine Pofeldt, "Make a Digital Degree Pay Off," *Money* 40 (June 2011): 32.

36 Jeff Griffin, "Simulator Provides Effective—And Fun—Training," *Underground Construction* 64 (August 2009): 16–18.

37 Euan Youdale, "Open View," *International Cranes & Specialized Transport* 19 (May 2011): 23–24.

38 Ladan Nikravan, "Back to Class," *Chief Learning Officer* 11 (January 2012): 18–21.

39 Daniel W. Bixby, "To Be Continued: Using Social Media for Training Conversations," *T+D* 64 (July 2010): 30–33.

40 Dave Zielinski, "Group Learning," *HR Magazine* 57 (May 2012): 49–52.

41 Alexandra Samuel, "Using Social Media to Build Professional Skills," *Harvard Business Review* online (August 4, 2016). Accessed March 1, 2017, at www.hbr.org.

42 "Four Ways to Facilitate Informal Learning," *T+D* 66 (February 2012): 18.

43 Donald L. Kirkpatrick, "Evaluation of Training," In R. L. Craig (Ed.). *Training and Development Handbook* (pp. 18-1–18-27). New York: McGraw-Hill.

44 Rachel King, "AT T's Ambitious Effort to Retrain More Than 100,000 Workers," *The Wall Street Journal* online (March 17, 2016). Accessed March 11, 2017, at www.wsj.com.

45 Paula Ketter, "Creative Instructional Design Equals Successful Learning Transfer," *T+D* 65 (July 2011): 10.

46 Pat Galagan, "Measure for Measure," *T+D* 65 (May 2011): 28–30.

47 Edward Trolley, "Lies About Learning," *Chief Learning Officer* 10 (June 2011): 82.

48 Emily Johnson, "Maximize Your Training Investment," *Collector* 77 (February 2012): 42–43.

49 Dennis Seeds, "Scouting for Talent: What the Shortage in Skilled Manufacturing Workers Means to a Hungry Industry," *Smart Business Indianapolis* 8 (July 2011): 9–13.

50 Joanne L. Stewart, "Train for the Future," *T+D* 65 (July 2011): 54–57.

51 Andy Pasztor, "JetBlue Eyes Flying Time Rules with New Pilot-Training Program," *The Wall Street Journal* online (November 26, 2015). Accessed January 31, 2017, at www.wsj.com.

52 Ibid.

53 Drake Bennett, "Do the Unemployed Get a Second Act?" *Bloomberg Businessweek* (September 9, 2011): 64–70.

54 "The 21st Century Requires More Skilled Workers," *MWorld* 10 (Summer 2011): 17–19.

55 Fred E. Fanning, "Engaging Learners: Techniques to Make Training Stick," *Professional Safety* 56 (August 2011): 42–48.

56 "Using Your Clients' Learning Style to Close Sales," *Kitchen & Bath Design News* 30 (February 2012): 20.

57 Armin Hopp, "Soft Steps Towards Digital Learning," *Training Journal* (January 2012): 51–54.

58 Lance Dublin, "Finding the Right Learning Mix," *Chief Learning Officer* 10 (August 2011): 36–39.

59 Joseph Michelli, "Starbucks' Partnership Approach," *Training* online (March 4, 2014). Accessed March 1, 2017, at https://trainingmag.com/starbucks%E2%80%99-partnership-approach.

60 Jon Younger, "How Are Learning and Development Are Becoming More Agile," *Harvard Business Review* online (October 11, 2016). Accessed February 5, 2017, at www.hbr.org.

61 David Milliken, "Poised for Discovery," *T+D* 65 (August 2011): 70–71.

62 Angelia Chapin, "How to Get Your New Hires from Zero to 100 in Weeks," *Canadian Business* 83 (November 23, 2010): 72.

63 Beverly Kaye and C. Patrick Smith, "Career Development: Shifting from Nicety to Necessity," *T+D* 66 (January 2012): 52–55.

64 Neil Irwin, "How to Become a C.E.O.? The Quickest Path Is a Winding One," *The New York Times* online (September 9, 2016). Accessed March 7, 2017, at www.nytimes.com.

65 Diane Mulcahy, "Why I Tell My MBA Students to Stop Looking for a Job and Join the Gig Economy," *Harvard Business Review* online (October 20, 2016). Accessed March 7, 2017, at www.hbr.org.

66 Elka Torpey and Andrew Hogan, "Working in a Gig Economy," U.S. Bureau of Labor Statistics, *Career Outlook* online (May 2016). Accessed March 2, 2017, at www.bls.gov/careeroutlook/2016/article/what-is-the-gig-economy.htm.

67 Ibid.

68 Thomas Lawrence, "Integrating Contingent Workers," *Baseline* 114 (January/February 2012): 3.

69 Kate Davidson, "To Switch or Not to Switch? How Workers' Career Choices Could Help the Economy," *The Wall Street Journal* online (August 11, 2016). Accessed February 27, 2017, at www.wsj.com.

70 Andrew Chamberlain, "Why Do Employees Stay? A Clear Career Path and Good Pay, for Starters," *Harvard Business Review* online (March 6, 2017). Accessed March 7, 2017, at www.hbr.org.

71 Rebecca Weingarten, "Thinking of Retiring? Not So Fast," *BusinessWeek Online* (March 26, 2009): 20.

72 John Mullins, "Career Planning the Second Time Around," *Occupational Outlook Quarterly* 53 (Summer 2009): 12–15.

73 The Career Key, "Investigative Type Work Environment," Accessed April 5, 2014, at www.careerkey.org/choose-a-career/investigative-work-environment.html.

74 Dorie Clark, "Think Strategically About Your Career Development," *Harvard Business Review* online (December 6, 2016). Accessed March 1, 2017, at www.hbr.org.

75 Ann Field, "Do Your Stars See a Reason to Stay?" *Harvard Management Update* 13 (June 2008): 3–5.

76 Aparna Nancherla, "C-Level Boot Camp," *T+D* 64 (January 2010): 24.

77 Joann S. Lublin, "Companies Try a New Strategy: Empathy," *The Wall Street Journal* online (June 21, 2016). Accessed February 21, 2017, at www.wsj.com.

78 Belinda Parmar, "The Most Empathetic Companies, 2016," *Harvard Business Review* online (December 1, 2016). Accessed February 28, 2017, at www.hbr.org.

79 The Conference Board and DDI, "Ready-Now Leaders: 25 Findings to Meet Tomorrow's Business Challenges," *Global Leadership Forecast 2014|2015*. Accessed February 28, 2017, at www.ddiworld.com/DDI/media/trend-research/global-leadership-forecast-2014-2015_tr_ddi.pdf.

80 Tomas Chamorro-Premuzic, "What Science Tells Us about Leadership Potential," *Harvard Business Review* online (September 21, 2016). Accessed February 1, 2017, at www.hbr.org.

81 Kristy Allen, "Mentoring Builds a Stronger Profession," *Charter* 81 (February 2010): 54.

82 Amy Alexander, "Mentoring Give-and-Take," *Investor's Business Daily* (January 24, 2012): 3.

83 "The 2016 Deloitte Millennial Survey," Deloitte (2016). Accessed December 29, 2016, at www2.

deloitte.com/content/dam/Deloitte/global/Documents/About-Deloitte/gx-millenial-survey-2016-exec-summary.pdf.

84 Andy Pasztor and Susan Carey, "United Calls in Pilots for Extra Training," *The Wall Street Journal* online (January 29, 2016). Accessed February 27, 2017, at www.wsj.com.

85 Anthony K. Tjan, "What the Best Mentors Do," *Harvard Business Review* online (February 27, 2017). Accessed March 3, 2017, at www.hbr.org.

86 Wendy Murphy, "How Women (and Men) Can Find Role Models When None Are Obvious," *Harvard Business Review* online (June 1, 2016). Accessed January 31, 2017, at www.hbr.org.

87 Michael Laff, "The Guiding Hand: Mentoring Women," *T+D* 63 (September 2009): 32–35.

88 Suzanne de Janasz and Maury Peiperl, "CEOs Need Mentors Too," *Harvard Business Review* online (April 2015). Accessed March 7, 2017, at www.hbr.org.

89 Ibid.

90 Christian Hamaker, "An Example in Their Youth," *Rural Telecom* 28 (September/October 2009): 9.

91 Richard R. Reilly and Karen Sobel Lojeski, "Leading the Dispersed Workforce," *Mechanical Engineering* 131 (November 2009): 30–34.

92 R. Wayne Mondy and Shane R. Premeaux, *Management: Concepts, Practices, and Skills,* 7th ed. (Englewood Cliffs, NJ, Prentice Hall, 1995): 497.

93 Byron Pope, "Toyota Says Quality Circles Still Paying Dividends," *Ward's Auto World* 44 (June 2008): 20.

94 Mike Donlin, "Take One for the Team," *Corporate Meetings & Incentives* 28 (August 2009): 26.

95 "Team Building Treachery," *Accountancy* 143 (March 2009): 20.

96 Kathryn Tyler, "Take New Employee Orientation off the Back Burner," *HR Magazine* 43 (May 1998): 49.

97 René Street, "We Move Forward as a Team," *Women in Business* 61 (December 2009/January 2010): 6.

98 Swati Karve, "Facilitation Skills: Using Training Games," *T+D* 65 (July 2011): 30–31.

99 Belinda Luscombe, "Getting Jumpy at Work," *Time International (South Pacific Edition)* 173 (May 25, 2009): 30.

100 Howard Prager, "Cooking Up Effective Team Building," *Training & Development* 53 (December 1999): 14–15.

101 Rich Cordivari, "From Training Company to Learning Organization," *T+D* 64 (January 2010): 60–63.

Part Four
Compensation

9 Direct Financial Compensation (Monetary Compensation)

LEARNING OBJECTIVES After completing this chapter, you should be able to:

9.1 Summarize the usual components of a total compensation plan and the environment of compensation practice.

9.2 Explain the direct financial compensation practices.

9.3 Discuss job structures and how they are established.

9.4 Summarize competitive pay policies: pay level and pay mix.

9.5 Explain what pay structures are and how they are created.

9.6 Review exceptions to the rules: compensation for sales representatives, contingent workers, and executives.

MyLab Management

Improve Your Grade!

If your professor is using MyLab Management, visit **www.pearson.com/mylab/management** for videos, simulations, and writing exercises.

Learn It

If your professor has chosen to assign this, go to **www.pearson.com/mylab/management** to see what you should particularly focus on and to take the Chapter 9 Warm-Up.

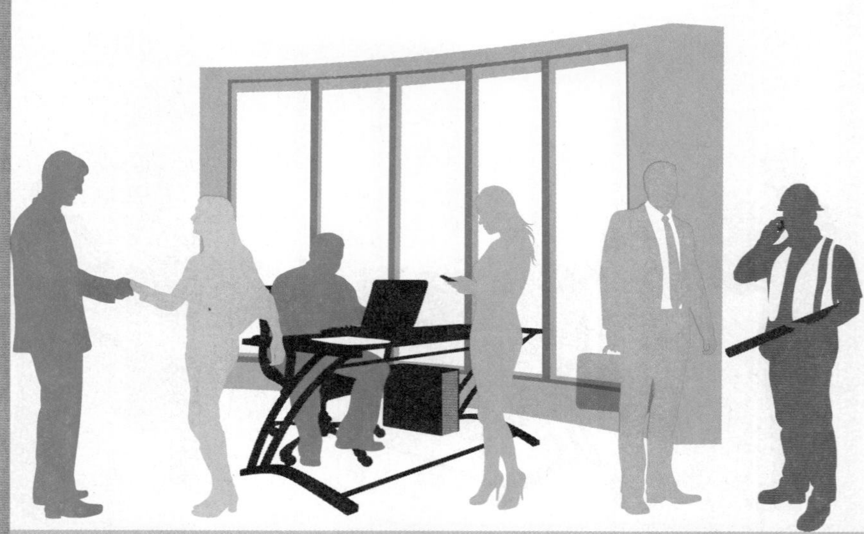

A Society of Human Resource Management (SHRM) survey of human resource (HR) executives identified recruiting and retaining top talent in a competitive labor market as their number one challenge.[1] Compensation is an important HR practice that helps firms address this and other challenges. There are two mechanisms by which compensation contributes to recruitment and retention. First, pay helps define a person's standard of living and sense of security. All else equal, higher pay enables people to meet their most basic needs such as food and shelter as well as save money for retirement more easily than those who earn less. Also, higher pay enables people to enjoy the finer things in life such as frequenting gourmet restaurants, driving a luxury car, and taking exotic vacations. Second, in most cases, employees and firms alike strive to maximize their earnings. The use of incentive compensation practices serves this common interest by aligning the interests of employees with a company's mission. For instance, sales employees have the potential to earn greater amounts of incentive pay for the attainment of progressively higher sales goals. From the company's perspective, higher sales contribute to increased earnings. In addition, highly successful companies, such as management consulting company Boston Consulting Group, provide highly competitive compensation packages that consist of lucrative pay amounts and employee benefits (e.g., paid family leave). In fact, Boston Consulting Group is among the top 25 companies known for offering extremely generous compensation amounts.[2]

9.1 Summarize the usual components of a total compensation plan and the environment of compensation practice.

Total Compensation and the Environment of Compensation Practice

total compensation
Both the intrinsic and extrinsic rewards employees receive for performing their jobs.

At the broadest level, **total compensation** represents both the intrinsic and extrinsic rewards employees receive for performing their jobs. The components of a total compensation program are shown in Figure 9-1. These building blocks are embedded within a system of three structural elements: job structures, competitive compensation policies, and pay structures.

FIGURE 9-1
Components of a Total Compensation Program

Compensation

Financial		Nonfinancial	
Direct	**Indirect (Benefits)**	**The Job**	**Job Environment**
Wages	***Legally Required Benefits***	Meaningful	Sound Policies
Salary	Health Care	Appreciated	Capable Managers
Commissions	Social Security	Satisfying	Competent Employees
Bonuses	Unemployment Compensation	Learning	Congenial Coworkers
	Workers' Compensation	Enjoyable	Appropriate Status Symbols
	Family & Medical Leave	Challenging	Working Conditions
	Discretionary Benefits		**Workplace Flexibility**
	Paid Time Off		Flextime
	Life Insurance		Compressed Workweek
	Retirement Plans		Job Sharing
	Employee Stock Option Plans		Telecommuting
	Employee Services		Part-Time Work
	Premium Pay		

Direct and Indirect Financial Compensation

direct financial compensation (monetary compensation)
Pay that a person receives in the form of wages, salary, commissions, and bonuses.

indirect financial compensation (employee benefits)
All financial rewards that are not included in direct financial compensation.

nonfinancial compensation
Satisfaction that a person receives from the job itself or from the psychological and/or physical environment in which the person works.

Extrinsic compensation refers to rewards that come from outside the person. There are two kinds. The first, **direct financial compensation (monetary compensation)** consists of the pay that a person receives in the form of wages, salaries, commissions, and bonuses. The second, **indirect financial compensation (employee benefits)**, refers to extrinsic compensation other than hourly wages or annual salary. This form of compensation includes a wide variety of rewards of monetary value such as paid vacation and medical care. For instance, companies spend money to purchase medical care coverage for employees. HR professionals often refer to intrinsic rewards as nonfinancial compensation. **Nonfinancial compensation** derives from within an employee's self. For example, nonfinancial compensation can come from the satisfaction that a person receives from the job itself or from the psychological or physical environment in which the person works. For instance, it is easy to imagine that a teacher derives great satisfaction from seeing his students excel. Although our focus will be on financial compensation, it is worth briefly considering nonfinancial compensation. Employers may choose to award nonfinancial compensation to complement an employee's paycheck, especially when financial compensation budgets make it difficult to award higher pay. Some examples of simple nonfinancial compensation practices include recognition awards, team leadership opportunities, prizes, and gift cards. Other examples include training for employees who value professional development and flexible work scheduling for those who give high priority to work/life balance. As you will learn in the following Watch It video, the effectiveness of nonfinancial compensation practices significantly depends on knowing each employee as an individual to provide options of interest and value to them.

Watch It 1
If your professor has assigned this, sign into **www.pearson.com/mylab/management** to watch a video titled Motivation (TWZ Role Play) and to respond to questions.

Managers tend to view financial compensation as both an expense and an asset. It is an expense in the sense that it reflects the cost of labor. For example, on average, companies spent $35.28 per hour worked per employee in March 2017. Of this total, companies spent $24.10 on wages and $11.18 on all employee benefits.[3] The costs of labor continually rise. For example, the cost of wages rose, on average, 9.7 percent between March 2014 and March 2017. The increase in the cost of employee benefits was greater, equaling 12.1 percent.[4]

Financial compensation is instrumental in recruiting and hiring good people and in encouraging them to put forth their best efforts and remain in their jobs. A firm that pays well attracts many applicants, enabling management to pick and choose the skills and traits it values. It holds on to these quality hires by equitably sharing the fruits of its financial success, not only among the management team but also with the rank and file. Compensation programs have top management's attention because they have the potential to influence employee work attitudes and behavior that lead to improved organizational performance and achieving the firm's strategic plan. We can find evidence for top management's interest in identifying the right type of employees by reviewing the "About Careers" sections of company Web sites. For example, software developer and manufacturer Adobe describes the role of their engineering professionals:

> *You could work at a unicorn, a startup with a $1 billion valuation. Or you could work at Adobe, a 30-year-old company that's home to a number of unicorns. Our size and trajectory mean exciting opportunities for you to feed your curiosity, stretch your creativity, and work with a diverse group of whip-smart people on the vanguard of technology engineering, research, and development. Define a rewarding career path while creating beautiful, usable products that touch millions of people.*[5]

Structure of Direct Financial Compensation Plans

Now that we have defined the components of direct financial compensation, it is important to consider how companies structure monetary compensation plans. There are many factors to consider, which are shown in Figure 9-2, starting with the environment of compensation practice. But, first, we briefly summarize the three structural elements of compensation plans here to round out the introduction of total compensation. These elements include job structures, competitive compensation policies, and pay structures, which are also shown in Figure 9-2 and will be examined in detail later in this chapter.

JOB STRUCTURES Management techniques used for determining a job's relative worth include job analysis, job descriptions, and job evaluation, and together, these lead to the creation of *job structures*. As we discussed in Chapter 4, an organization must first define and describe job content. HR professionals use job analysis for this purpose. The primary by-product of job analysis is the job description. Job descriptions serve many different purposes, including data for evaluating jobs. With job descriptions, HR professionals can use job evaluation to judge the relative worth of all jobs within the company. The primary basis for making value judgments is consideration of skill, knowledge, ability, and working conditions.

COMPETITIVE COMPENSATION POLICIES After companies have clearly written job descriptions and they have specified job structures that show the relative worth of jobs, they move on to the next step, which is to decide on *competitive compensation policies*. HR professionals must consider the compensation policies that it will pursue, and these focus on pay level (for example, paying higher salaries, on average, than the competition for similar jobs) and pay mix (percentage of money that goes toward salary, employee benefits [Chapter 10], and adjustments such as incentive pay).

PAY STRUCTURES Coupled closely with these choices is job pricing, which leads to the construction of *pay structures*. HR professionals conduct compensation surveys to identify what and how the competition is paying its employees. Once armed with information about market pay rates, HR professionals develop pay structures features that facilitate administration of pay policies. These include pay range and pay grades.

FIGURE 9-2
Determinants of Direct Financial Compensation

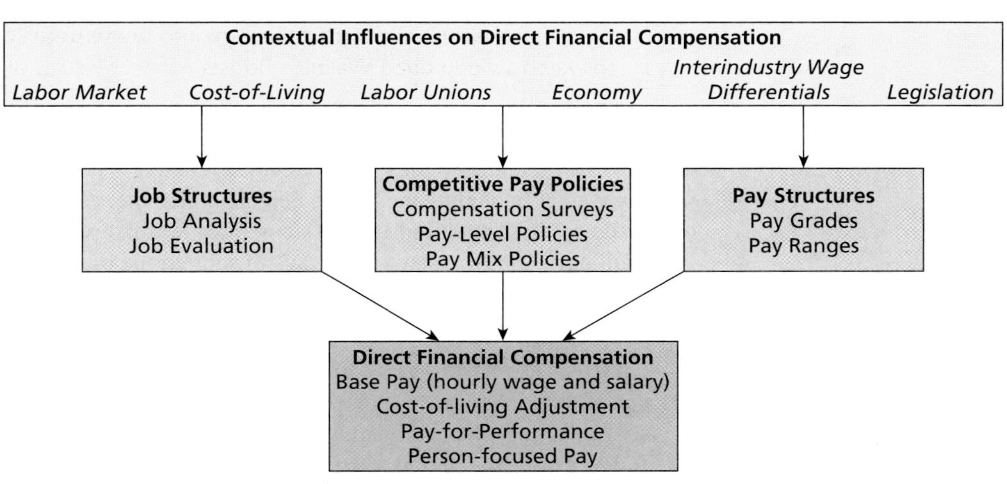

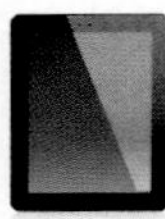

HR Web Wisdom

Calculate Salary Differences from City to City

www.salary.com

Web site to determine numerous costs of a move to another city.

labor market
Potential employees located within the geographic area from which employees are recruited.

Contextual Influences

HR professionals build the compensation system in a dynamic environment. There are many contextual influences that must be considered. Among the most prominent considerations are labor market, cost-of-living differences between geographic locations, labor unions, the economy, interindustry wage differentials, and legislation.

LABOR MARKET Potential employees located within the geographic area from which employees are recruited constitute the **labor market**. Labor markets for some jobs extend far beyond the location of a firm's operations. An aerospace firm in St. Louis, for example, may be concerned about the labor market for engineers in Fort Worth or Orlando, where competitive firms are located. Managerial and professional employees are often recruited from a wide geographic area. As global economics increasingly sets the cost of labor, the global labor market grows in importance as a determinant of financial compensation for individuals.

Companies' demand for qualified individuals relative to supply often influences compensation decisions. There are upward pressures to raise starting pay when the demand for qualified workers is greater than supply. These market dynamics require that companies compete for limited qualified workers for skilled jobs. Oftentimes, base pay exceeds the national annual median pay—and pay levels are fastest growing.[6] Many of these jobs are found in the healthcare and computer fields. This appears to be the case for information security analysts. According to the *Occupational Outlook Handbook*,[7] demand for information security analysts is expected to be very high through at least the next 10 years. Annual median pay for information security analysts is approximately 2.5 times higher than the national median for all jobs. Cyberattacks have grown in frequency and sophistication over the last few years, and many organizations are behind in their ability to detect these attacks. For example, Eddie Bauer and Target experienced breaches of their databases that contained customers' credit card numbers. Analysts will be needed to come up with innovative solutions to prevent hackers from stealing critical information or creating havoc on computer networks. Also, the federal government is expected to greatly increase its use of information security analysts to protect the nation's critical information technology (IT) systems, particularly as it has recently experienced breaches that could compromise national security. Finally, as the healthcare industry expands its use of electronic medical records, ensuring patients' privacy and protecting personal data are becoming more important. More information security analysts will be employed to create essential safeguards.

The previous example focused on one of many highly skilled jobs in the computer profession. A common assumption is that high demand for workers applies only to highly skilled jobs. That assumption is incorrect. Recently, Starbucks raised base pay as much as 15 percent and awards company stock for most employees with at least two years of continuous employment.[8] (We will review stock awards later in this chapter.) Starbucks made this decision, in part, because it has been more difficult to hire well-qualified workers at lower pay rates, particularly since the unemployment rate has declined in recent years. Other retailers have made similar moves. The following Watch It video describes Walmart's rationale behind the decision to raise its starting hourly wage to $9.

 **Watch It 2**

If your professor has assigned this, sign into **www.pearson.com/mylab/management** to watch a video titled Walmart Boosts Entry-Level Pay and to respond to questions.

Higher base pay has become increasingly more common in industries where business activity peaks around the holiday season. Online retailers such as Amazon.com Inc. and package delivery companies, including the United Parcel Service Inc. vigorously compete for seasonal workers. For instance, Amazon hired 120,000 temporary warehouse workers for whom they provide extensive training.[9] Amazon also found ways to shorten the training time without sacrificing quality, thus, reducing costs. In turn, the company offered higher pay in hopes of attracting the best qualified candidates.

COST-OF-LIVING DIFFERENCES Cost-of-living differences between geographic locations may account for variations in compensation for similar jobs, and HR professionals sometimes consider cost-of-living when competing for talent in a competitive labor market. For example, let's assume that a firm offers equal starting pay to two equally qualified individuals who have been hired to perform the same job. The only difference is their placement—Jackson, Mississippi, and Washington, D.C. The cost-of-living difference between these cities is staggering. An individual earning $100,000 annually in Jackson would need to earn approximately $175,000 in D.C. to maintain a similar standard of living. If a differential was to be considered, it might be based on housing costs. Housing costs—rent or mortgage—are among the largest financial obligations most individuals assume. In D.C., average housing prices are about 230 percent higher than in Jackson.[10] The company may consider offering the D.C.-based employee a higher salary to help offset cost-of-living differences.

LABOR UNIONS The National Labor Relations Act declared legislative support, on a broad scale, for the right of employees to organize and engage in collective bargaining. Unions normally prefer to determine compensation through the process of collective bargaining, which describes the negotiations between the labor union that represents employee interests and company management. An excerpt from the National Labor Relations Act prescribes the areas of mandatory collective bargaining between management and unions as, "wages, hours, and other terms and conditions of employment." These broad bargaining areas obviously have great potential to impact compensation decisions. When a union uses comparable pay as a standard in making compensation demands, the employer needs accurate labor market data. For example, unions often rely on the Consumer Price Index (CPI) as the criterion for awarding cost-of-living adjustments. The U.S. Bureau of Labor Statistics publishes the CPI monthly.[11]

Unions' gains also influenced compensation practices in non-union companies. Many non-union companies offered similar compensation to their employees. This phenomenon is known as a **spillover effect**. Non-union companies' motivation is to minimize employees' interests in seeking union representation.[12]

spillover effect
Non-union companies' offer of similar compensation unionized companies with the goal of reducing the likelihood that nonunion workforces will seek union representation.

ECONOMY The economy affects compensation decisions. For example, a depressed economy generally increases the labor supply, and this condition serves to lower the market rate. In addition, companies often choose not to award pay raises to contribute to cost containment objectives in a slow economic environment where business activity is likely to suffer. A booming economy, on the other hand, results in greater competition for workers and the price of labor is driven upward.

FYI

Average weekly compensation varies by industry:

- Mining: $1,434
- Construction: $1,109
- Manufacturing: $1,075
- Retail: $557
- Leisure and Hospitality: $395[13]

INTERINDUSTRY WAGE DIFFERENTIALS In competitive labor markets, companies attempt to attract and retain the best individuals for employment partly by offering lucrative wage and benefits packages. Some companies, unfortunately, find it difficult to compete based on wage and benefits. Indeed, there are noteworthy wage differences among industries. These differences are known as **interindustry wage differentials** or **compensation differentials**.

interindustry wage or compensation differentials
Pattern of pay and benefits associated with characteristics of industries.

Interindustry differentials can be attributed to many factors, including the industry's product market, degree of capital intensity, profitability of the industry, unionization, and gender mix of the workforce.[14] Companies that operate in product markets in which there is relatively little competition from other companies tend to pay higher wages because these companies exhibit substantial profits. This phenomenon can be attributed to such factors as higher barriers to entry into the product market and an insignificant influence of foreign competition. Government regulation and extremely expensive equipment represent entry barriers in such industries as mining. The U.S. defense industry and the public utilities industry have high entry barriers and no threats from foreign competitors.

Capital intensity also explains pay differentials between industries. The average pay amount varies with the degree of capital intensity. On average, capital-intensive industries such as construction pay more than industries that are less capital intensive such as retail. Capital-intensive businesses require highly capable employees who have the aptitude to learn how to use complex technology. Service such as retail industries are not capital intensive, and most have the reputation of paying low wages. The operation of service industries depends almost exclusively on employees with relatively common skills rather than on employees with specialized skills to operate such physical equipment as casting machines or robotics.

The discussion of environmental factors, thus far, concisely conveys various dynamics in the pay setting process. However, the picture has become somewhat more complicated. Increasingly, technologies and market demand have led to the formation of (very small) niche industries. Many of these industries rely on newly created jobs that did not exist in the recent past.[15] Take, for instance, remote control vehicle and drone operators. In addition, cost-of-living differentials extend beyond the comparison of two geographic locations as described earlier because members of work teams are distributed across the globe.

LEGISLATION Federal and state laws can also affect the amount of compensation a person receives and how that amount is determined. For example, prevailing wage laws specify how pay rates should be calculated. The Equal Pay Act prohibits an employer from paying a female employee less money than a male employee if both employees do work that is substantially the same. As we discussed in Chapter 3, equal employment legislation, including the Civil Rights Act, the Age Discrimination in Employment Act, and the Americans with Disabilities Act, prohibits discrimination against specified groups in employment matters, including compensation. The same is true for federal government contractors or subcontractors covered by Executive Order 11246 and the Rehabilitation Act. States and municipal governments also have laws that affect compensation practices. Our focus in the next section, however, is on the federal legislation that provides broad coverage and specifically deals with compensation issues. These laws appear in chronological order of their passage.

DAVIS-BACON ACT OF 1931 The Davis-Bacon Act of 1931 was the first national law to deal with minimum wages. It mandates a *prevailing wage* for all federally financed or assisted construction projects exceeding $2,000. Contractors must pay wages at least equal to the prevailing wage in the local area. The U.S. Secretary of Labor determines prevailing wage rates based on compensation surveys of different areas. In this context, "local" area refers to the general location where work is performed. Cities and counties represent local areas. The prevailing wage is the typical hourly wage paid to more than 50 percent of all laborers and mechanics employed in the local area. The act also requires that contractors offer employee benefits that are equal in scope and value to employee benefits that prevail in the local area.

WALSH-HEALY ACT OF 1936 The Walsh-Healy Act covers contractors and manufacturers who sell supplies, materials, and equipment to the federal government. Its coverage is more extensive than the Davis-Bacon Act. This act applies to both construction and non-construction activities. In addition, this act covers all the contractors' employees except office, supervisory, custodial, and maintenance workers who do any work in preparation for the performance of the contract. The minimum contract amount that qualifies for coverage is $10,000 rather than the $2,000 amount under the Davis-Bacon Act of 1931. This legislation also requires paying one-and-a-half times the regular pay rate for hours more than 8 per day or 40 per week.

FAIR LABOR STANDARDS ACT OF 1938, AS AMENDED The most significant law affecting compensation is the Fair Labor Standards Act (FLSA) of 1938. The purpose of the FLSA is to establish minimum labor standards on a national basis and to eliminate low wages and excessive working hours. The FLSA attempts to eliminate low wages by setting a minimum wage and to make long hours expensive by requiring a higher overtime pay rate for excessive hours. It also requires record keeping and provides standards for child labor. The Wage and Hour Division of the U.S. Department of Labor administers this act. The amount of the federal minimum wage has changed several times since it was first introduced in 1938 and continues to do so; however, the increases are relatively small and implemented infrequently. For instance, the federal minimum wage rose from $6.55 to $7.25 per hour in 2009.

Many of the federal laws have counterparts in state and local legislation, and minimum wage is a good example. In general, state and local legislation may be concurrent with federal law or may exist in the absence of similar federal legislation. Wherever inconsistencies in federal, state, or local laws exist, the law that provides individuals the greatest benefit generally prevails.

According to the U.S. Department of Labor, in January 2017, 45 states had minimum wage requirements.[16] Two states with minimum wage rates set lower than the federal minimum wage. There were 29 states plus the District of Columbia with minimum wage rates set higher than the federal minimum wage. Fourteen states that have a minimum wage requirement equal the federal minimum wage amount. The remaining five states do not have an established minimum wage requirement. In January 2017, the District of Columbia had the highest minimum wage at $11.50 per hour while Georgia and Wyoming had the lowest minimum wage ($5.15 per hour) of the 45 states that have a minimum wage requirement. Some state laws include provisions for increasing the minimum wage rate over time. The increases are often tied to rises in the cost of living or legislated amounts. For instance, California's minimum wage rate is rising incrementally until it reaches $15 in 2022. Altogether, 4.4 million low-wage workers will receive pay raises because pay would otherwise fall below higher rates.[17]

Even though the federal and some state and local governments raise the minimum wage from time to time, most workers who earn the minimum wage argue that it is insufficient to afford the necessities. In the summer of 2013, fast food workers across the United States walked off their jobs to protest what they believe is insufficient pay. The following Watch It video captures workers' concerns about the minimum wage level and the collective response of restaurant owners to their concerns.

Watch It 3

If your professor has assigned this, sign into **www.pearson.com/mylab/management** to watch a video titled Fast Food Workers Walk Out, Demanding Higher Pay and to respond to questions.

The FLSA distinguishes between exempt and nonexempt jobs for the purposes of determining which employees are required to be paid an overtime rate of one-and-one-half times the employee's regular rate after 40 hours of work in a consecutive 7-day period. Companies are not required to pay overtime to exempt employees, but they are required to do so for nonexempt employees. **Exempt employees** are categorized as executive, administrative, professional, or outside salespersons. All others are **nonexempt employees**. Aggressive action is being taken against companies that fail to pay the overtime requirement.[18] Although the act covers most organizations and employees, certain classes of employees are specifically exempt from overtime provisions.

exempt employees
Employees categorized as executive, administrative, professional, or outside salespersons, and not required to be paid at an overtime rate for work beyond the completion of standard work hours.

nonexempt employees
Employees not categorized as executive, administrative, professional, or outside salespersons, and required to receive overtime pay for work beyond the completion of standard work hours.

An executive employee is essentially a manager (such as a production manager) with broad authority over subordinates. An administrative employee, although not a manager, occupies an important staff position in an organization and might have a title such as account executive or market researcher. A professional employee performs work requiring advanced knowledge in a field of learning, normally acquired through a prolonged course of specialized instruction.[19] This type of employee might have a title such as company physician, legal counsel, or senior statistician. Outside salespeople who sell tangible or intangible items away from the employer's place of business are exempted from the overtime pay requirement.

EQUAL PAY ACT OF 1963 Congress enacted the Equal Pay Act of 1963 to remedy a serious problem of employment discrimination in private industry; "Many segments of American industry [have] been based on an ancient but outmoded belief that a man, because of his role in society, should be paid more than a woman even though his duties are the same."[20] The Equal Pay Act of 1963 is based on a simple principle: Men and women should receive equal pay for performing equal work.

The Equal Pay Act of 1963 pertains explicitly to jobs of equal worth. Companies assign pay rates to jobs according to the skill, effort, responsibility, and working conditions required to perform them.

Pay differentials for equal work are not always illegal. Pay differentials between men and women who are performing equal work are acceptable only when made on a seniority system, merit system, incentive system, or on any factor other than sex. Valid performance appraisal practices are essential to determine whether pay differentials between men and women performing equal work are illegal.

Despite the goal of equal pay for equal work, various recent studies indicate that women make approximately 79 percent as much as men. Still, many researchers have cautioned that this statistic is possibly misleading because it does not focus explicitly on equal work or account for differences in the length of work history for men and women. Certainly, more research is necessary that measures these factors when estimating the gender wage gap.[21]

WALL STREET REFORM AND CONSUMER PROTECTION ACT (DODD-FRANK ACT) The Dodd-Frank Act was signed into law in 2010 and has provisions relating to executive compensation and corporate governance that impact the executives, directors, and shareholders of publicly traded companies. We will cover specific provisions of the act in the discussion about executive compensation, which follows later in this chapter.

9.2 Explain the direct financial compensation practices.

Direct Financial Compensation Components

There are five types of direct financial compensation. These include employee base pay, cost-of-living adjustments, seniority pay, pay-for-performance, and person-focused pay. An employee's direct financial compensation rarely consists of all five components. Most employees receive base pay, and companies choose which of the remaining four types of financial compensation to include. Companies choose one additional or combination of direct financial compensation components for employee groups based on how best to direct employee job performance (for example, sales employees versus clerical employees). Also, factors such as labor unions influence how direct employee compensation is structured.

base pay
The monetary compensation employees earn on a regular basis for performing their jobs. Hourly pay and salary are the main forms of base pay.

hourly pay
One type of base pay. Employees earn hourly pay for each hour worked.

salary
One type of base pay. Employees earn salaries for performing their jobs, regardless of the actual number of hours worked. Companies generally measure salary on an annual basis.

Base Pay

Employees receive **base pay**, or money, for performing their jobs. Base pay is recurring; that is, employees continue to receive base pay as long as they remain in their jobs. Companies disburse base pay to employees in one of two forms: **hourly pay** or **wage** or as **salary**. Employees earn hourly pay for each hour worked. They earn salaries for performing their jobs, regardless of the actual number of hours worked. Companies measure salary on an annual basis. As noted earlier, the Fair Labor Standards Act established criteria for determining whether employees should be paid hourly or by salary. In January 2017, the average weekly rate for workers was approximately $894.[22] On an annual basis, this figure translates to $46,488 (based on a 40-hour work week over 52 calendar weeks).

Over time, HR professionals work with managers and supervisors to adjust base pay. There are various methods for making these adjustments, which we review next. These include cost-of-living adjustments, seniority pay, pay-for-performance, and person-focused pay.

cost-of-living adjustment (COLA)
Escalator clause in a labor agreement that automatically increases wages as the U.S. Bureau of Labor Statistics' cost-of-living index rises.

real hourly compensation
Measure of the purchasing power of a dollar.

nominal hourly compensation
The face value of a dollar.

Cost-of-Living Adjustments

Cost-of-living adjustments (COLAs) represent periodic base pay increases that are founded on changes in prices as recorded by the CPI. In recent years, the typical COLA equaled approximately 2-3 percent annually. COLAs enable workers to maintain their purchasing power and standard of living by adjusting base pay for inflation. **Real hourly compensation** measures the purchasing power of a dollar, whereas **nominal hourly compensation** is the face value of a dollar. Increases in the costs of goods and services cause nominal pay to be less than real pay. Let's say that a $5 bill buys 50 pieces of candy (10 cents each). Next year, the price of candy doubles; a $5 bill buys just 25 pieces of candy.

COLAs are most common among workers represented by unions because one of the main goals of unionization is to protect the standard of living of its membership. When a union emphasizes cost of living, it may try to pressure management into including a COLA, which rarely is found outside unionized employment settings. Provisions for COLAs are contained in an escalator clause in the labor agreement that automatically increases wages as the CPI registers general price increases.

seniority
Length of time an employee has been associated with the company, division, department, or job.

seniority pay
Pay program in which pay increases are based on length of service.

Seniority Pay

Seniority is the length of time an employee has been associated with the company, division, department, or job. **Seniority pay** systems reward employees with periodic additions to base pay according to employees' length of service in performing their jobs. These pay plans assume that employees become more valuable to companies with time and that valued employees will leave if they do not have a clear idea that their salaries will progress over time.[23] This rationale comes from **human capital theory**,[24] which, as we discussed in earlier chapters, states that employees' knowledge and skills generate productive capital known as **human capital**. Employees can develop such knowledge and skills from formal education and training, including on-the-job experience. Over time, employees presumably refine existing skills or acquire new ones that enable them to work more productively. Thus, seniority pay rewards employees for acquiring and refining their skills as indexed by seniority.

human capital theory
A theory premised on the idea that employees' knowledge and skills generate productive capital known as human capital. Employees can develop knowledge and skills from formal education or on-the-job experiences.

human capital
As defined by economists, refers to sets of collective skills, knowledge, and ability that employees can apply to create economic value for their employers.

Historically, seniority pay programs were common methods for rewarding employee performance. However, most companies set aside the use of seniority plans in favor of pay-for-performance methods that explicitly measure performance such as merit pay and incentive pay methods. Increased competitive and economic pressures make it important that companies reward employees commensurately with their measurable contributions.

Still, we do find seniority pay programs commonly in use within government agencies and in a variety of other employment settings in which labor unions represent the interests of workers. We can look to the U.S. federal government for an example of a comprehensive seniority pay program that is known as the **General Schedule**. Figure 9-3 displays this arrangement. The General Schedule classifies federal government jobs into 15 classifications (GS-1 through GS-15) based on such factors as skill, education, and experience levels. Employees are eligible for 10 within-grade step pay increases. At present, it takes employees 18 years to progress from Step 1 to Step 10. Employees spend one year each in Steps 1 through 3, two years each in Steps 4-6, and three years each in Steps 7-9.

General Schedule (GS)
Classification of federal government jobs into 15 classifications (GS-1 through GS-15), based on such factors as skill, education, and experience levels. In addition, jobs that require high levels of specialized education (e.g., a physicist), significantly influence public policy (e.g., law judges), or require executive decision making are classified in three additional categories: Senior Level (SL), Scientific & Professional (SP) positions, and the Senior Executive Service (SES).

FYI

In a survey of companies, 70 percent revealed that base pay increases are mainly determined by performance relative to job performance standards rather than comparisons between employees.[25]

Performance-Based Pay

Performance-based pay is governed by how well one performs the job. To maximize company objectives of the firm, it is important to link employee compensation to performance. This basic rule applies to all within the organization, ranging from the company president to hourly employee. It recognizes that some workers are just better than other workers in performing the same job.

The objective of performance-based pay is to improve productivity by rewarding those who best assist in achieving this goal. It assumes that given the proper incentives, most employees will work

FIGURE 9-3

Salary Table: 2017 General Schedule

Annual Rates by Grade and Step ($)

Grade	Step 1	Step 2	Step 3	Step 4	Step 5	Step 6	Step 7	Step 8	Step 9	Step 10	WITHIN GRADE AMOUNTS
1	18,526	19,146	19,762	20,375	20,991	21,351	21,960	22,575	22,599	23,171	Varies
2	20,829	21,325	22,015	22,599	22,853	23,525	24,197	24,869	25,541	26,213	Varies
3	22,727	23,485	24,243	25,001	25,759	26,517	27,275	28,033	28,791	29,549	758
4	25,514	26,364	27,214	28,064	28,914	29,764	30,614	31,464	32,314	33,164	850
5	28,545	29,497	30,449	31,401	32,353	33,305	34,257	35,209	36,161	37,113	952
6	31,819	32,880	33,941	35,002	36,063	37,124	38,185	39,246	40,307	41,368	1,061
7	35,359	36,538	37,717	38,896	40,075	41,254	42,433	43,612	44,791	45,970	1,179
8	39,159	40,464	41,769	43,074	44,379	45,684	46,989	48,294	49,599	50,904	1,305
9	43,251	44,693	46,135	47,577	49,019	50,461	51,903	53,345	54,787	56,229	1,442
10	47,630	49,218	50,806	52,394	53,982	55,570	57,158	58,746	60,334	61,922	1,588
11	52,329	54,073	55,817	57,561	59,305	61,049	62,793	64,537	66,281	68,025	1,744
12	62,722	64,813	66,904	68,995	71,086	73,177	75,268	77,359	79,450	81,541	2,091
13	74,584	77,070	79,556	82,042	84,528	87,014	89,500	91,986	94,472	96,958	2,486
14	88,136	91,074	94,012	96,950	99,888	102,826	105,764	108,702	111,640	114,578	2,938
15	103,672	107,128	110,584	114,040	117,496	120,952	124,408	127,864	131,320	134,776	3,456

Source: U.S. Office of Personnel Management. http://www.opm.gov. Accessed March 9, 2017.

harder and smarter. In a survey, companies that reported the best results from their pay-for-performance programs used multiple rewards to recognize and reward performance, including base pay increases (91 percent), short-term incentives (71 percent), spot bonuses (49 percent), equity awards (33 percent), other long-term incentives (18 percent), and profit sharing (7 percent).[26] An effective performance appraisal program is a prerequisite for any pay system tied to performance. Using this approach, workers would need to first have a clear understanding of what goals the organization wanted them to achieve. Then, based on the result of performance appraisal, rewards would be forthcoming.

When Sprint's CEO Dan Hesse took over the wireless provider, he wanted employees to clearly understand what he thought was important and what they should focus on to achieve maximum rewards. He wanted compensation to be based on improving the customer experience, strengthening the brand, and generating cash to increase profits. The amount paid for performance extended from 5 percent for entry-level employees to 50 percent and higher at the vice-president level.[27] As another example, if it is important to improve safety in the workplace, this goal must be communicated to employees and included in their performance review. If worker behavior leads to fewer accidents, workers should be rewarded.[28] Rewards might be as simple as a pat on the back or additional money in their paychecks. Appraisal data provide input for such approaches as merit pay and incentive pay bonuses. Each of these approaches to compensation management will be discussed in the following sections. These include merit pay, merit bonuses; and, incentive pay, of which there are three categories: individual incentive pay, group incentive pay, and company-wide incentive pay.

merit pay
Pay increase added to employees' base pay based on their level of performance.

MERIT PAY **Merit pay** is a pay increase added to employees' base pay based on their level of performance. It assumes that employees' compensation over time should be determined, at least in part, by differences in job performance.[29] Employees earn permanent merit increases based on their performance. The pay increases reward excellent effort or results, motivate future performance, and help employers retain valued employees. Merit increases are usually expressed as a percentage of hourly wages for nonexempt employees and as a percentage of annual salaries for exempt employees. In 2016, employees earned average merit increases of 3.1 percent. The rate varied according to the level of employee performance. The highest performers earned 3.9 percent of base pay and average performers earned 2.7 percent.[30]

In practice, however, merit pay increases historically have been merely a cost-of-living increase in disguise.[31] This is the case because most companies do not offer cost-of-living increases as well as merit pay increases. For example, a 4 percent merit pay increase is misleading from the standpoint of recognizing employee performance when cost-of-living has increased by 3 percent. The pay increase amount attributed to performance is a mere 1 percent.

At times, companies provide automatic pay increases under the guise of merit pay, which defeats the purpose. As John Rubino, president of Rubino Consulting Services, an international HR consulting firm, said, "Companies with base-salary programs and automatic annual pay increases offer little to motivate employees."[32] Past studies by compensation professionals have determined that merit pay is *marginally successful* in influencing pay satisfaction and performance. From the employer's viewpoint, a distinct disadvantage to the typical merit pay increase is that it increases the employee's base pay. Therefore, employees receive the added amount each year they are on the payroll regardless of later performance levels.

It has become increasingly more difficult to justify merit pay increases based on a previous employment period but added perpetually to base pay. There are many long-term employees who are poor performers who have high salaries because of past automatic cost-of-living increases. Although numerous companies continue with traditional merit pay plans, some companies are starting to quietly freeze or cut pay for some to be able to reward others. According to Myrna Hellerman, senior vice-president at Sibson Consulting, "much can be learned from best-practices companies where base pay increases must be earned, based on demonstrated individual achievement. Pay raises are not an entitlement; the entitlement era is over."[33]

merit bonus
One-time annual financial award, based on productivity that is not added to base pay.

MERIT BONUSES Companies are increasingly placing a higher percentage of their compensation budget in **merit bonuses**, which is a one-time annual financial award, based on productivity that is not added to base pay. This approach better enables companies to control the cost of direct compensation by not adding pay increases to base pay on a permanent basis, which is the case for seniority and merit pay. Figure 9-4 shows the differences in cost between the use of merit pay and merit bonuses.

More and more companies embrace the concept of *pay for performance*. When the economy was slowing down and employers were holding down across-the-board pay raises, companies still put a large percentage of salary budgets toward bonuses.[34] A recent survey found that 87

FIGURE 9-4

Permanent Annual Merit Increases versus Bonus Awards: A Comparison

(At the end of 2017, John Smith earned an annual salary of $35,000.)

	Cost of Increase (Total Current Salary—2017 Annual Salary)			Total Salary under	
Year	Increase Amount (%)	Permanent Merit Increase ($)	Bonus Award ($)	Permanent Merit Increase (Merit Increase + Previous Annual Salary) ($)	Bonus Award Annual (Bonus Award + 2017 Salary) ($)
2018	3	1,050	1,050	36,050	36,050
2019	5	2,853	1,750	37,853	36,750
2020	4	4,367	1,400	39,367	36,400
2021	7	7,122	2,450	42,122	37,450
2022	6	9,649	2,100	44,649	37,100
2023	5	11,881	1,750	46,881	36,750
2024	3	13,287	1,050	48,287	36,050
2025	6	16,185	2,100	51,185	37,100
2026	8	20,279	2,800	55,279	37,800
2027	7	24,148	2,450	59,148	37,450

percent of employers offer at least two or more types bonuses as a reward to employees.[35] The use of bonuses helps managers control their cash outlay in a tough business environment while laying the foundation to share success with top producers.[36] Managers commonly contend that the use of bonuses is a win-win situation because it boosts production and efficiency and gives employees some control over their earning power. A positive side effect of using bonuses to reward high performance is that it may positively affect employee engagement, motivation, and satisfaction.[37]

spot bonus
Relatively small monetary gifts provided to employees for outstanding work or effort during a reasonably short period.

Approximately 60 percent of organizations today are providing *spot bonuses* for critical areas and talents.[38] **Spot bonuses** are relatively small monetary gifts provided to employees for outstanding work or effort during a reasonably short period. If an employee's performance has been exceptional, the employer may reward the worker with a one-time bonus of as low as $50 and $100 or $500. For certain professional jobs, it is not unheard of for a highly productive worker to receive $5,000 or more shortly after a noteworthy achievement.

incentive pay
Compensation, other than base wages or salaries, that fluctuates according to employees' attainment of some standard (e.g., a pre-established formula, individual or group goals, or company earnings).

INCENTIVE PAY **Incentive pay** rewards employees for partially or completely attaining a predetermined work objective. Incentive or variable pay is defined as compensation—other than base wages or salaries—that fluctuates according to employees' attainment of some standard, such as a pre-established formula, individual or group goals, or company earnings. Much like seniority and merit pay approaches, incentive pay augments employees' base pay, but incentive pay appears as one-time payments. Employees usually receive a combination of recurring base pay and incentive pay, with base pay representing the greater portion of direct financial compensation. More employees are presently eligible for incentive pay than ever before, as companies seek to control costs and motivate personnel continually to strive for exemplary performance. Companies increasingly recognize the importance of applying incentive pay programs to various kinds of employees as well, including production workers, technical employees, and service workers.

Companies generally institute incentive pay programs to control payroll costs or to motivate employee productivity. Companies can control costs by replacing annual merit or seniority increases or fixed salaries with incentive plans that award pay raises only when the company enjoys an offsetting rise in productivity, profits, or some other measure of business success. Well-developed incentive programs base pay on performance, so employees control their own compensation levels. Companies can choose incentives to further business objectives.

There are many kinds of incentive pay plan options. Companies use incentive pay to reward individual employees, groups of employees, or whole companies based on their performance. Management typically relies on business objectives to determine incentive pay levels.

INDIVIDUAL INCENTIVE PLANS In a recent survey, 52 percent of companies indicated that they use individual incentive pay plans.[39] We will review the four commonly used individual incentive pay plans: piecework, management incentives, behavioral encouragement plans, and referral plans. Then, we will briefly address the pros and cons of individual incentive plans.

piecework
Incentive pay plan in which employees are paid for each unit they produce.

Piecework is an incentive pay plan in which employees are paid for each unit they produce. For example, if a worker is paid $8 a unit and produces 10 units a day, the worker earns $80. Sometimes a guaranteed base is included in a piece-rate plan, meaning that a worker would receive this base amount no matter what the output. Historically, piecework is especially prevalent in the production/operations area. Requirements for the plan include developing output standards for the job and being able to measure the output of a single employee. Piecework pay plans have declined in use somewhat because the plan requires constant monitoring. For instance, if on day one the worker produced 8 units and on day two the worker produced 12 units, each day must be counted separately. Also, professionals such as industrial engineers are needed to maintain the system. Obviously, a piecework plan would not be feasible for many jobs.

management incentive plans
Bonuses to managers who meet or exceed objectives based on sales, profit, production, or other measures for their division, department, or unit.

Management incentive plans award bonuses to managers when they meet or exceed objectives based on sales, profit, production, or other measures for their division, department, or unit. Management incentive plans differ from piecework plans in that piecework plans base rewards on the attainment of one specific objective, and management incentive plans often require multiple complex objectives. For example, management incentive plans reward managers for increasing market share or reducing their budgets without compromising the quality and quantity of output. The best-known management incentive plan is management by objectives (MBO).[40] When used as part of incentive programs, superiors (that is, managers' managers) communicate the amount of incentive pay managers will receive based on the attainment of specific goals. As an aside, when MBO is used as part of merit pay systems, superiors make subjective assessments of managers' performance, and they use these assessments to determine permanent merit pay increases.

behavioral encouragement plans
Individual incentive pay plans that reward employees for specific such behavioral accomplishments as good attendance.

Under **behavioral encouragement plans**, employees receive payments for specific behavioral accomplishments (e.g., good attendance or safety records). For example, companies usually award monetary bonuses to employees who have exemplary attendance records for a specified period. When behavioral encouragement plans are applied to safety records, workers earn awards for lower personal injury or accident rates associated with the improper use of heavy equipment or hazardous chemicals. Behavioral encouragement plans have the potential to save companies substantially more money than the cost of these awards. For example, frequent absenteeism in a company's workforce could disrupt production goals and quality. Customers may respond by choosing to make purchases for better quality products from other companies. Loss of customer bases will have a negative impact on profitability and reputation that prompts prospective customers to choose alternate sources to purchase products.

referral plans
Individual incentive pay plans for rewarding the referral of new customers or recruiting successful job applicants.

As discussed in Chapter 5, approximately 74 percent of companies rely on **referral plans** to enhance recruitment of highly qualified employees.[41] Employees may receive monetary bonuses for referring new customers or recruiting successful job applicants. In the case of recruitment, employees can earn bonuses for making successful referrals for job openings. For example, there has been a tremendous shortage of nurses for the past several years and the shortage is expected to grow as the population ages. Because of the shortage, hospitals commonly offer sign-on bonuses and referral bonuses. In Florida, for instance, many signing bonuses top out at $20,000 and referral bonuses are as high as $2,500.[42] A successful referral usually means that companies award bonuses only if hired referrals remain employed with the company in good standing beyond a designated period, often at least 45 days. Referral plans rely on the idea that current employees' familiarity with company culture should enable them to identify viable candidates for job openings more efficiently than employment agencies could because agents are probably less familiar with client companies' cultures. Employees are likely to make only those referrals they truly believe are worthwhile because their personal reputations are at stake.

Individual incentive plans have advantages and disadvantages. On the positive side, individual incentive plans promote an equitable distribution of compensation within companies (i.e., the amount employees earn depends on their job performance). The better employees perform, the more they earn. Equitable pay ultimately enables companies to retain the best performers. Paying better performers more money sends a signal that the company appropriately values positive job performance. Another advantage of individual incentive plans is their compatibility with individualistic cultures, such as the United States. Because U.S. employees are socialized to make individual contributions and be recognized for them, the national culture of the United States probably enhances the motivational value of individual incentive programs.

A downside of individual incentive plans is that they may encourage undesirable workplace behavior when these plans reward only one or a subset of dimensions that constitute employees' total job performance. Let's assume that an incentive plan rewards employees for quantity of output. If employees' jobs address such various dimensions as quantity of output, quality, and customer satisfaction, employees may focus on the one dimension—in this case, quantity of output—that leads to incentive pay and thereby neglect the other dimensions.

GROUP INCENTIVE PLANS In baseball, as with other team sports, you do not judge the team based on its ace pitcher or great outfielder. The criterion for success is overall team performance, its win–loss record. In business, companywide plans offer a possible alternative to the incentive plans previously discussed. *Team-based incentives* are determined by how well the team performs in the accomplishment of the job. Because team performance consists of individual efforts, individual employees should be recognized and rewarded for their contributions. However, if a team is to function effectively, firms should also provide a reward based on the overall team performance as well. Changing a firm's compensation structure from an individual-based system to one that involves team-based pay can have powerful results. By so doing, a firm can improve efficiency, productivity, and profitability.

There are many kinds of team incentive programs. Most companies define these programs based on the type of team.[43] Work (process) teams refer to organizational units that perform the work of the organization on an ongoing basis. Membership is relatively permanent, and members work full time on the team. Customer service teams and assembly teams on production lines represent excellent examples of work teams. Work teams are effective when individuals are cross-trained to perform team members' work when they are absent. The goal is to maintain consistency in performance quality (e.g., addressing customer concerns promptly even when one or more team members are absent) and output (e.g., in the case of assembly teams). Team members ultimately engage in performance sharing rather than focusing exclusively on one set of tasks.

Project teams consist of a group of people assigned to complete a one-time project. Members usually have well-defined roles and may work on specific phases of the project, either full time or in addition to other work responsibilities of the team. Project teams usually work across such functions as engineering, product development, and marketing to ensure that the final product meets company specifications in terms of cost, quality, and responsiveness to market demands (e.g., Toyota's hybrid vehicles). Many individuals collaborated to ensure the production of cars that rely less on fossil fuels, demonstrate excellent gas mileage, and offer the same driving experience that people have come to expect of gasoline-powered automobiles.

Parallel teams, or task forces, include employees assigned to work on a specific task in addition to normal work duties. The modifier *parallel* indicates that an employee works on the team task while continuing to work on normal duties. Also, parallel teams or task forces operate on a temporary basis until their work culminates in a recommendation to top management. Task forces are used to evaluate existing systems and processes, to select new technology, and to improve existing products. People often serve on a voluntary basis or are appointed; in many cases, they are not compensated specifically for extra work or outcome of extra work.

Teams or groups may ultimately receive incentive pay based on such criteria as customer satisfaction (i.e., customer service quality), safety records, quality, and production records. Although these criteria apply to other categories of incentive programs as well (individual, company-wide, and group plans), companies allocate awards to each worker based on the group's attainment of predetermined performance standards.

Team incentives have both advantages and disadvantages. On the positive side, firms find it easier to develop performance standards for groups than for individuals. For one thing, there are fewer standards to determine. Also, the output of a team is more likely to reflect a complete product or service. Another advantage is that employees may be more inclined to assist others and work collaboratively if the organization bases rewards on the team's output. When teams perform highly, it is the interaction among team members, not the members themselves, that creates the high performance. If a team member is asked who was responsible for the high performance of the team, he or she would likely say, "We were," and mean it. A potential disadvantage for team incentives relates to exemplary performers. If individuals in this category perceive that they contribute more than other employees in the group, they may become disgruntled and leave. Christopher Avery, a Texas-based speaker and consultant who specializes in issues concerning individual and shared responsibility in the workplace and the author of *Teamwork Is an Individual Skill: Getting Your Work Done When Sharing Responsibility*, said, "If management wants to reward a high-performing team member, give that person a raise."[44]

gain sharing
Group incentive systems that provide participating employees with an incentive payment based on improved company performance for increased productivity, increased customer satisfaction, lower costs, or better safety records.

Gain sharing describes group incentive systems that reward employees with an incentive payment based on improved company performance for increased productivity, increased customer satisfaction, lower costs, or better safety records.[45] Gain sharing was developed so that all employees could benefit financially from productivity improvements resulting from a formal employee suggestion system. In addition to serving as a compensation tool, most gain sharing reflects a management philosophy that emphasizes employee involvement. The use of gain sharing is most appropriate where workplace technology does not constrain productivity improvements. For example, assembly line workers' abilities to improve productivity may be limited. Increasing the speed of the conveyor belts may compromise workers' safety. Gain sharing programs, such as the Scanlon, Rucker, and Improshare plans, are the most popular gain sharing plans that have been adopted by U.S. corporations. Gain sharing helps align an organization's people strategy with its business strategy. Gain sharing plans (also known as *productivity incentives*, *team incentives*, and *performance sharing incentives*) generally refer to incentive plans that involve many or all employees in a common effort to achieve a firm's performance objectives.

Joseph Scanlon, after whom the Scanlon plan was named, developed the first gain sharing plan during the Great Depression, and it continues to be a successful approach to awarding group incentives. The **Scanlon plan** provides a financial reward to employees for savings in labor costs resulting from their suggestions. Employee-management committees evaluate these suggestions. Participants in these plans calculate savings as a ratio of payroll costs to the sales value of what that payroll produces. If the company can reduce payroll costs through increased operating efficiency, it shares the savings with its employees. Scanlon plans are not only financial incentive systems, but also systems for participative management. The Scanlon plan embodies management-labor cooperation, collaborative problem solving, teamwork, trust, gain sharing, open-book management, and servant leadership.

Scanlon plan
Gain sharing plan that provides a financial reward to employees for savings in labor costs resulting from their suggestions.

HR Web Wisdom
Scanlon Leadership Network
www.scanlon.org/
A promoter of the Scanlon principles to advance their applications among organizations.

COMPANYWIDE INCENTIVE PLANS The use of companywide incentive plans can be traced to the nineteenth century. Companies instituted profit sharing programs to ease workers' dissatisfaction with low pay and to change their beliefs that company management paid workers substandard wages while earning substantial profits. Quite simply, management believed that workers would be less likely to challenge managerial practices if they received a share of company profits. Organizations normally base companywide plans on the firm's profitability or market value. Companywide plans include profit sharing and employee stock option plans.

HR BLOOPERS

Motivating Software Development Teams

As she gets ready to start her presentation, Jennifer Senders is excited about her new plan to improve performance of the software development teams at Creators Software. As a senior compensation analyst, she was charged with creating a new team-based pay plan to replace the company's current individual bonus system. All the software developers at Creators work in teams to design and deliver software solutions for a wide variety of clients. The workforce at Creators is very talented, but many of the developers would prefer to work alone. Thus, many of the teams were having problems meeting deadlines and other expected team outcomes. Jennifer knows that for the team to work well together, the incentives should focus on team goals instead of individual goals. However, a glance at her audience as she explains the new bonus structure suggests they may not share her enthusiasm. She gets a hint about their concerns as soon as she asks for questions. Several hands go up and the employees begin to ask about individual rewards. One developer states that he knows he works harder than others on his team and he doesn't want them affecting his pay. As Jennifer starts to respond, she is thinking fast about what she might need to change.

If your professor has assigned this, go to **www.pearson.com/mylab/management** to complete the HR Bloopers exercise and test your application of these concepts when faced with real-world decisions.

profit sharing
Compensation plans that result in the distribution of a predetermined percentage of the firm's profits to employees.

Profit sharing pays a portion of company profits to employees, separate from base pay, cost-of-living adjustments, or permanent merit pay increases. These plans award cash to employees, typically on a quarterly or annual basis. Many firms use this type of plan to integrate the employees' interests with those of the company. Profit-sharing plans can aid in recruiting, motivating, and retaining employees, which usually enhances productivity. For instance, General Motors' hourly workers received profit sharing awards based on the company's substantial $12 billion profit in 2016. UAW Vice President Cindy Estrada stated, "Today's performance bonus announcement of a maximum of $12,000 each rewards our members' dedication and commitment to building some of the most popular and high-quality vehicles in the world."[46]

The results of profit sharing include increased efficiency and lower costs. However, variations in profits may present a special problem. When employees have become accustomed to receiving added compensation from profit sharing, and then there is no profit to share, they may become disgruntled.

Another problem with a profit-sharing plan stems from the recipients' seldom knowing precisely how they helped generate the profits, beyond just doing their jobs. HR professionals refer to this as a line-of-sight problem. And, if employees continue to receive a payment, they will come to expect it and depend on it. If they do not know what they have done to deserve it, they may view it as an entitlement program and the intended ownership attitude may not materialize.

employee stock plans
The right to purchase shares of company stock.

stock options
Incentive plan in which employees can buy a specified amount of stock in their company in the future at or below the current market price.

company stock
The total equity or worth of the company.

company stock shares
Equity segments of equal value, which increase with the number of stock shares held.

Under **employee stock plans**, companies grant employees the right to purchase shares of company stock. **Company stock** represents total equity of a company. **Company stock shares** represent equity segments of equal value. Equity interest increases positively with the number of stock shares. **Stock options** describe an employee's right to purchase company stock. Employees do not actually own stock until they exercise the stock option rights. This is done by purchasing stock at a designated price after a company-chosen period lapses, usually no more than 5 years. Employee stock options provide an incentive to work productively, with the expectation that collective employee productivity will increase the value of company stock over time. Employees earn monetary compensation when they sell the stock at a higher price than they originally paid for it.

Person-Focused Pay

job-based pay
Employee compensation for jobs employees currently perform.

person-focused pay
Compensation for developing the flexibility, knowledge, and skills to perform a number of jobs effectively.

skill-based pay
System that compensates employees for their job-related skills and knowledge, not for their job titles.

Thus far, we have studied job-based pay practices. **Job-based pay** compensates employees for jobs they currently perform. HR professionals establish a minimum and maximum acceptable amount of pay for each job. In the case of merit pay, managers evaluate employees based on how well they fulfilled their designated roles as specified by their job descriptions and periodic objectives. Managers then award a permanent merit addition to base pay, based on employee performance. With incentive pay, managers award one-time additions to base pay. Pay raise amounts are based on the attainment of work goals, which managers communicate to employees in advance.

In contrast, **person-focused pay** compensates employees for developing the flexibility, knowledge, and skills to perform many jobs effectively. Moreover, these programs reward employees on their *potential* to make positive contributions to the workplace based on their successful acquisition of work-related skills or knowledge. Job-based pay plans reward employees for the work they have done as specified in their job descriptions or periodic goals (i.e., how well they have *fulfilled* their potential to make positive contributions in the workplace).

Skill-based pay is a system that compensates employees for their job-related *skills* and *knowledge*, rather than how well he or she performs on the present job. Skill-based pay is a method of recruiting and retaining highly skilled employees that enables employers to offer compensation based on the knowledge, skills, and abilities that employees bring to the company and that they develop over the course of their employment, rather than based solely on the duties associated with a position.[47] Essentially, job descriptions, job evaluation plans, and job-based salary surveys are replaced by skill profiles, skill evaluation plans, and skill-based salary surveys. The system assumes that employees who know more are more valuable to the firm and, therefore, they deserve a reward for their efforts in acquiring new skills. When employees obtain additional job-relevant skills, both individuals and the departments they serve benefit. For example, a department may have six different types of machines, each requiring different skills to operate. Under a skill-based pay system, the worker would increase his or her pay as additional machines are learned.

Although skill-based pay appears to have advantages for both employer and employee, there are some challenges for management. The firm must provide adequate training opportunities or else the system can become a demotivator. Also, because it takes an average of only three years for a worker to reach a maximum level in a skill-based pay system, what will keep employees motivated? Notwithstanding these concerns, there is evidence to suggest that companies with skill-based plans were more likely than other plans to have greater levels of workforce flexibility. That greater flexibility, in turn, led to greater productivity.[48]

As we discussed in Chapter 4, competencies refer to an individual's capability to orchestrate and apply combinations of knowledge, skills, and abilities consistently over time to perform work successfully in the required work situations. Traditionally, as we have seen, work has been described by many dimensions including knowledge, skills, and abilities. Another common person-focused plan is competency-based pay. **Competency-based pay** plans generally reward employees for acquiring job-related competencies, knowledge, or skills rather than for demonstrating successful job performance. There are times when companies combine competency-based pay programs with traditional job-based pay programs by awarding pay raises to employees according to how well they demonstrate competencies.

competency-based pay
Compensation plan that rewards employees for the capabilities they attain.

9.3 Discuss job structures and how they are established.

Building Job Structures

job structure
An ordered set of similar jobs based on worth.

job evaluation
Process that determines the relative value of one job in relation to another.

As noted earlier, a **job structure** is an ordered set of jobs that represents the job structure or hierarchy. That is, jobs that require higher qualifications, more responsibilities, and more complex job duties should be paid more than jobs that require lower qualifications, fewer responsibilities, and less-complex job duties. Internally consistent job structures formally recognize differences in job characteristics that enable compensation managers to set pay accordingly. HR professionals use **job evaluation** systematically to recognize differences in the relative worth among a set of jobs and to establish pay differentials accordingly.

When done properly, job evaluation helps to eliminate internal pay inequities that exist because of illogical pay structures. For example, pay inequity probably exists if the mailroom supervisor earns more than the chief accountant. For obvious reasons, organizations prefer internal pay equity. However, when a job's pay rate is ultimately determined to conflict with the market rate, the latter is almost sure to take precedence. Job evaluation measures job worth in an administrative rather than an economic sense. The latter can be determined only by the marketplace and made known through compensation surveys.[49] We will discuss compensation surveys later in this chapter.

The HR department may be responsible for administering job evaluation programs. However, committees made up of individuals familiar with the specific jobs to be evaluated often perform the actual evaluations. A typical committee might include the HR executive and representatives from other functional areas such as finance, production, information technology, and marketing. The composition of the committee usually depends on the type and level of the jobs being evaluated. In all instances, it is important for the committee to keep personalities out of the evaluation process and to remember that it is evaluating the job, not the person(s) performing the job. Some people have difficulty making this distinction. This is understandable because some job evaluation systems are similar to some performance appraisal methods. In addition, the duties of a job may, on an informal basis, expand, contract, or change depending on the person holding the job.

The four traditional job evaluation methods are the *ranking*, *classification*, *factor comparison*, and *point*. There are innumerable versions of these methods, and a firm may choose one and modify it to fit its purposes. Another option is to purchase a proprietary method such as the Hay Plan. The ranking and classification methods are nonquantitative, whereas the factor comparison and point methods are quantitative approaches.

Ranking Method

job evaluation ranking method
Job evaluation method in which the raters examine the description of each job being evaluated and arrange the jobs in order according to their value to the company.

The ranking method is the simplest of the four job evaluation methods. In the **job evaluation ranking method**, the raters examine the description of each job being evaluated and arrange the jobs in order according to their value to the company. The procedure is essentially the same as the ranking method for evaluating employee performance. The only difference is that you evaluate jobs, not people.

Classification Method

classification method
Job evaluation method in which classes or grades are defined to describe a group of jobs.

The **classification method** involves defining many classes or grades to describe a group of jobs. In evaluating jobs by this method, the raters compare the job description with the class description. Class descriptions reflect the differences between groups of jobs at various difficulty levels. The class description that most closely agrees with the job description determines the classification for that job. For example, in evaluating the job of receptionist, the description might include these duties:

- Greet and announce visitors
- Answer phone and route calls
- Receive and route mail

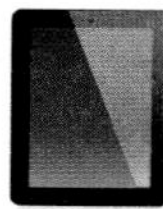

HR Web Wisdom

The Hay Group Guide Chart-Profile Method

www.haygroup.com

Homepage of the Hay Plan, the most widely used job measurement system in the world, is provided.

If the remainder of the job description includes similar routine work, this job would probably be placed in the lowest job class.

Each class is described in such a way that it captures sufficient work detail, yet is general enough to cause little difficulty in slotting a job description into its appropriate class.

Factor Comparison Method

factor comparison method
Job evaluation method that assumes there are five universal factors consisting of mental requirements, skills, physical requirements, responsibilities, and working conditions; the evaluator makes decisions on these factors independently.

The factor comparison method is somewhat more involved than the two previously discussed qualitative methods. The **factor comparison method** of job evaluation assumes that there are five universal factors consisting of mental requirements, skills, physical requirements, responsibilities, and working conditions; the evaluator makes decisions on these factors independently.

The five universal job factors are:

- *Mental requirements,* which reflect mental traits such as intelligence, reasoning, and imagination
- *Skills,* which pertain to facility in muscular coordination and training in the interpretation of sensory impressions
- *Physical requirements,* which involve sitting, standing, walking, lifting, and so on
- *Responsibilities,* which cover areas such as raw materials, money, records, and supervision
- *Working conditions,* which reflect the environmental influences of noise, illumination, ventilation, hazards, and hours

In this method, the evaluation committee creates a monetary scale, containing each of the five universal factors, and ranks jobs according to their value for each factor. Unlike most other job evaluation methods, which produce relative job worth only, the factor comparison method determines the absolute value as well.

Point Method

point method
Job evaluation method in which the raters assign numerical values to specific job factors, such as knowledge required, and the sum of these values provides a quantitative assessment of a job's relative worth.

In the **point method**, raters assign numerical values to specific job factors, such as knowledge required, and the sum of these values provides a quantitative assessment of a job's relative worth. Quantitative methods assign numerical values to compensable factors (e.g., knowledge and skills) that describe jobs, and these values are summed as an indicator of the overall value for the job. The point method evaluates jobs by comparing compensable factors. Each factor is defined and assigned a range of points based on the factor's relative value to the company. Compensable factors are weighted to represent the relative importance of each factor to the job.

Point plans require time and effort to design. A redeeming feature of the method has been that, once developed, the plan was useful over a long time. In today's environment, the shelf life may be considerably less because job requirements change frequently. In any event, as new jobs are created and old jobs substantially changed, job analysis must be conducted and job descriptions rewritten on an ongoing basis. The job evaluation committee then evaluates the jobs. Only when job factors change, or for some reason the weights assigned become inappropriate, does the plan become obsolete.

compensation policy
Policies that provide general guidelines for making compensation decisions.

pay level compensation policies
Determine whether the company will be a pay leader (market lead), a pay follower (market lag), or assume an average position (market match) in the labor market.

9.4 Summarize competitive pay policies: pay level and pay mix.

Establishing Competitive Compensation Policies

A **compensation policy** refers to choices that compensation professionals make to promote competitive advantage. Broadly, policy choices are made about pay level and pay mix. **Pay level compensation policies** determine whether the company will be a pay leader, be a pay follower, or strive for an average position in the labor market. Pay level policies have the greatest impact

pay mix compensation policies
Combination of direct (monetary compensation) and indirect financial compensation (employee benefits) components that make up an employee's total compensation package.

on attracting and retaining employees. **Pay mix compensation policies** refer to the combination of direct and indirect financial compensation and employee benefits components (see Figure 9-1) that make up an employee's compensation package. Pay mix policies have the greatest impact on motivating employees. The components of the compensation package help focus an employee's performance on what the employer expects, such as excellent customer service, sales, innovative use of technology, and so forth.

Pay Level Compensation Policies

We will review the three pay level policies followed by pay mix. Figure 9-5 illustrates the market lead, market match, and market lag pay level policies.

market lead policies
Pay policy that distinguishes companies from the competition by compensating employees more highly than most competitors. Leading the market denotes market levels above the market pay line.

MARKET LEAD Companies that pursue a **market lead policy** are organizations that pay higher wages and salaries than competing firms. In most companies, a lead policy translates to pay at the 75th percentile. That is, 75 percent of the market pay rates for comparable jobs are lower. Using this strategy, they feel that they will be able to attract high-quality, productive employees and thus achieve lower per-unit labor costs. Higher-paying firms usually attract more highly qualified applicants than lower-paying companies in the same labor market. The Mayo Clinic, headquartered in Rochester, Minnesota, is a pay leader.[50] The Mayo Clinic is known for its leading research and medical care, which requires it to hire and retain bright and talented researchers and medical practitioners.

market match policy
Average pay that most employers provide for a similar job in an area or industry.

MARKET MATCH The **market match policy** is usually the median pay that most employers provide for a similar job in an area or industry.[51] Median pay is expressed as the 50th percentile. That is, 50 percent of the market pay rates for similar jobs are lower. Many organizations have a policy that calls for paying the market rate. In such firms, management believes that it can still employ qualified people and remain competitive.

market lag policies
Pay policy that distinguishes companies from the competition by compensating employees less than most competitors. Lagging the market indicates that market levels fall below the market pay line.

MARKET LAG Companies may choose to pay below the market rate (**market lag policy**) because of poor financial conditions or because they are hiring employees whose skills and expected impact on the company's success are relatively lower than employees whose skills and expected impact are much greater. Market lag policies typically translate to pay at the 25th percentile, meaning that 25 percent of the market pay rates for similar jobs are lower. For example, in pharmaceutical companies that rely heavily on research and development, janitorial services workers might receive below-market pay rates compared to research scientists who are directly responsible for the firm's success through innovative product development.

FIGURE 9-5
Pay Level Policy

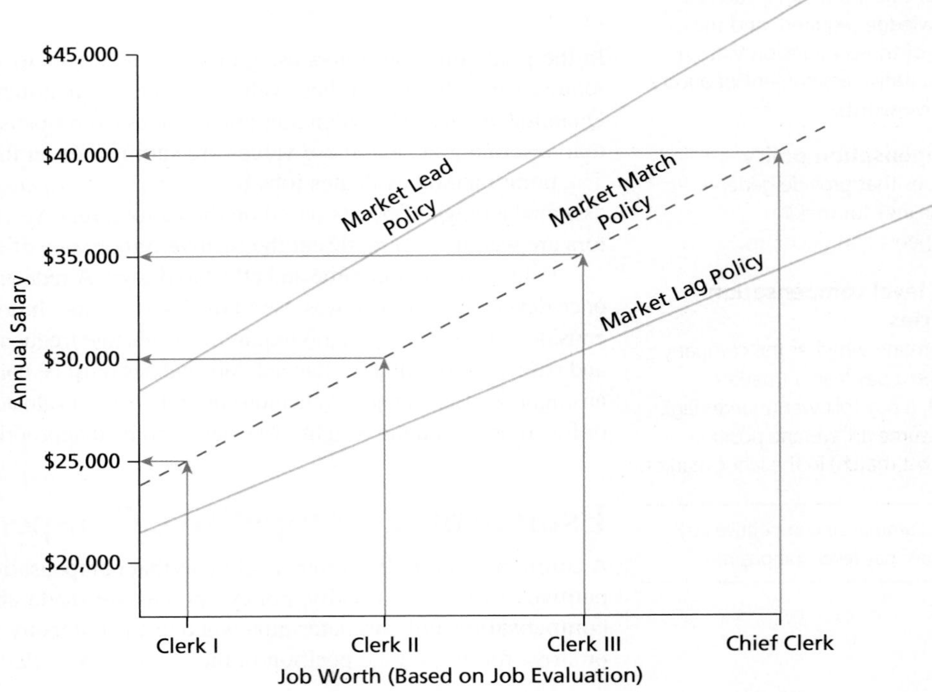

Besides the considerations already discussed, two additional issues bear mention. First, most companies do not pursue a single pay level policy. As emphasized in the market lag discussion, the relative importance of jobs to the company and the level of knowledge and skills required to perform the jobs influence pay policy level choices. Second, the principles of labor supply and demand factor into companies' decisions about which pay level policy to choose. For example, companies will likely choose the pay leader policy for jobs that are in high demand by companies, but for which jobs are in relatively low supply. Consider the case of biomedical engineers.

> *Employment of biomedical engineers is projected to grow 23 percent from 2014 to 2024, much faster than the average for all occupations. Growing technology and its application to medical equipment and devices, along with an aging population, will increase demand for the work of biomedical engineers.*[52]

Pay Mix

As noted earlier, pay mix compensation policies refer to the combination of direct and indirect financial compensation and employee benefits components (see Figure 9-1) that make up an employee's compensation package. Pay policy mix may be expressed in dollars (or other currency as relevant) or as a percentage of total dollars allocated for an employee's total compensation. Figure 9-6 illustrates an example of a pay policy mix.

This example indicates that base pay accounts for 57 percent of the money allocated to an employee's total compensation. Let's assume that the company spends $200,000 annually to fund an employee's total compensation package. Of the total, an employee receives base pay in the amount of $114,000 (that is, $200,000 × 57 percent).

What is an appropriate pay mix? For policy purposes, it makes sense to consider guidelines for jobs within a structure (for example, managerial, administrative, or sales) because of the common job content and worker requirements of jobs. For example, in a technology company, a greater portion of incentive compensation might be allocated to engineers than to administrative staff. Engineers possess crucial skills relating to the company's ability to find innovative applications of technology, and awarding bonuses throughout the year may promote innovation initiatives. On the other hand, the administrative staff, though important to the company, may not play a central role in determining the company's profitability or objectives. Therefore, less of their total compensation would likely be devoted to incentive awards. Also, some employees, such as sales representatives, may receive much of their compensation in the form of incentive pay. To motivate a sales force to continually exceed quarterly targets, quarterly bonuses equal to or exceeding their annual base salaries might be used.

pay structures
Pay rate differences for jobs of unequal worth and the framework for recognizing employee contributions.

compensation survey
A means of obtaining data regarding what other firms are paying for specific jobs or job classes within a given labor market.

9.5 Explain what pay structures are and how they are created.

Building Pay Structures

Pay structures represent pay rate differences for jobs of unequal worth and the framework for recognizing employee contributions. These structures result from an analysis based on compensation survey work. **Compensation surveys** involve the collection and subsequent analysis of

FIGURE 9-6
Pay Mix Policy

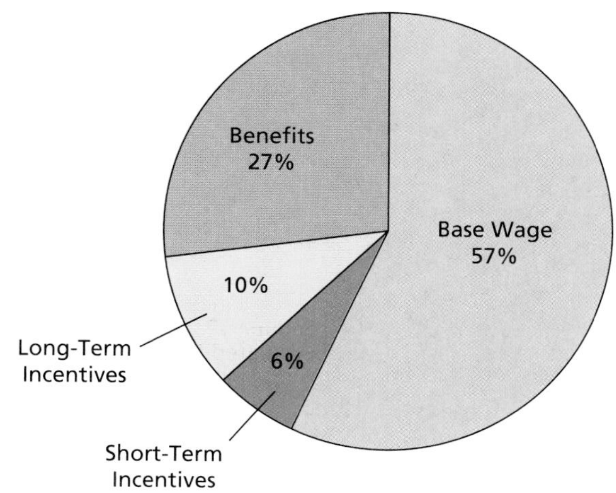

competitors' compensation data. Compensation surveys traditionally focused on competitors' wage and salary practices. Employee benefits have more recently also becomes a target of surveys because benefits are a key element of market-competitive pay systems. For instance, some individuals may accept an offer from one company rather than another because it provides generous paid family leave. Compensation surveys are important because they enable compensation professionals to obtain realistic views of competitors' pay practices. Companies recognize these differences by paying individuals according to their credentials, knowledge, or job performance. When completed, pay structures should define the boundaries for recognizing employee contributions. Well-designed structures should promote the retention of valued employees. Pay grades and pay ranges are structural features of pay structures.

FYI

Approximately 90 percent of companies rely on market pricing to determine the value of jobs.[53]

Pay Grades

pay grade
Grouping of similar jobs to simplify pricing jobs.

A **pay grade** is the grouping of similar jobs to simplify pricing jobs. For example, it is much more convenient for organizations to price 15 pay grades than 200 separate jobs. The simplicity of this approach is like a college or university's practice of grouping grades of 90-100 into an *A* category, grades of 80-89 into a *B*, and so on. In following this approach, you also avoid a false suggestion of preciseness. Although job evaluation plans may be systematic, none are scientific.

Plotting jobs on a scatter diagram is often useful to managers in determining the appropriate number of pay grades for a company. Looking at Figure 9-7 notice that each dot on the scatter diagram represents one job. The location of the dot reflects the job's relationship to pay and evaluated points, which reflects its worth. When this procedure is used, a certain point spread determines the width of the pay grade (100 points in this illustration). Although each dot represents one job, it may involve dozens of individuals who have positions in that one job. The large dot at the lower left represents the job of receptionist, evaluated at 75 points. The receptionist's hourly rate of $12.90 represents either the average wage currently paid for the job or its market rate. This decision depends on how management wants to price its jobs.

FIGURE 9-7
Scatter Diagram of Evaluated Jobs Illustrating the Wage Curve, Pay Grades, and Pay Ranges

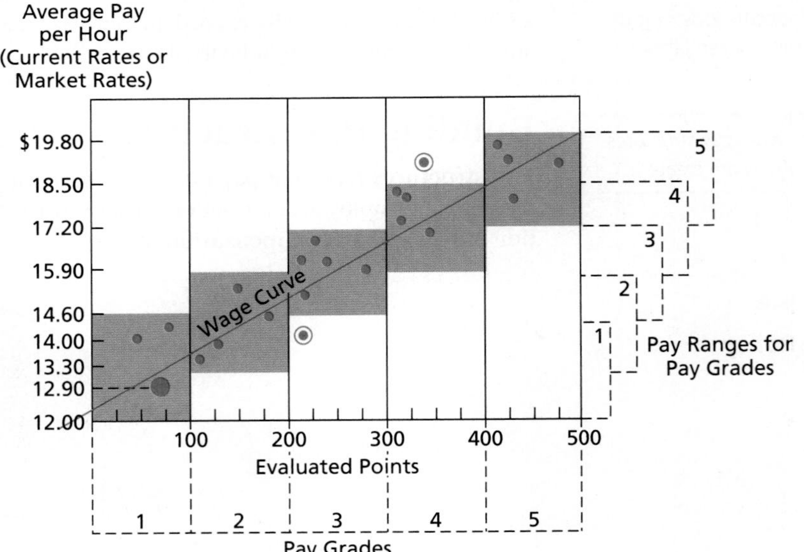

Summary Evaluated Points	Pay Grade	Minimum	Pay Range Midpoint	Maximum
0–99	1	$12.00	$13.30	$14.60
100–199	2	13.30	14.60	15.90
200–299	3	14.60	15.90	17.20
300–399	4	15.90	17.20	18.50
400–500	5	17.20	18.50	19.80

Pay Ranges

pay range
Minimum and maximum pay rate with enough variance between the two to allow for a significant pay difference.

After pay grades have been determined, the next decision is whether all individuals performing the same job will receive equal pay or whether pay ranges should be used. A **pay range** includes a minimum and maximum pay rate with enough variance between the two to allow for a significant pay difference. Pay ranges are generally preferred over single pay rates because they allow a firm to compensate employees according to performance and length of service. Pay then serves as a positive incentive. When pay ranges are used, a firm must develop a method to advance individuals through the range. Companies typically use larger range spreads for jobs that are more valuable to the company.

wage curve
Fitting of plotted points to create a smooth progression between pay grades (also known as the pay curve).

POINTS ALONG THE RANGE A **wage curve** (or pay curve) is the fitting of plotted points to create a smooth progression between pay grades. The curve often equates to the market match policy. The line drawn minimizes the distance between all dots and the line; a line of best fit may be straight or curved. However, when the point system is used, a straight line is often the result, as illustrated in Figure 9-7. The use of statistical methods to determine the line is essential given the sheer number of data points (pay rates) collected during the compensation survey process.

Pay ranges are centered along the wage curve. That is, the midpoint of each pay range equals the typical market pay rate for jobs within a pay grade. Referring again to Figure 9-7, note that anyone can readily determine the minimum, midpoint, and maximum pay rates per hour for each of the five pay grades. For example, for pay grade 5, the minimum rate is $17.20, the midpoint is $18.50, and the maximum is $19.80. The minimum rate may be the *hiring-in* rate that a person receives when joining the firm, although in practice, new employees often receive pay that starts above this level. The maximum pay rate represents the maximum that an employee can receive for that job regardless of how well he or she performs the job.

TOPPING OUT A person at the top of a pay grade should be promoted to a job in a higher pay grade to receive a pay increase unless: (1) an across-the-board adjustment is made; or (2) the job is re-evaluated and placed in a higher pay grade. This situation has caused numerous managers some anguish as they attempt to explain the pay system to an employee who is doing a tremendous job but is at the top of a pay grade. Consider this situation:

> *Everyone in the department realized that Beth Smithers was the best administrative assistant in the company. At times, she appeared to do the job of three people. Bob Marshall, Beth's supervisor, was especially impressed. Recently, he had a discussion with the human resource manager to see what he could do to get a raise for Beth. After Bob described the situation, the human resource manager's only reply was, "Sorry, Bob. Beth is already at the top of her pay grade. There is nothing you can do except have her job upgraded or promote her to another position.*

Situations like Beth's present managers with a perplexing problem. Many would be inclined to make an exception to the system and give Beth a salary increase. However, this action would violate a traditional principle, which holds that every job in the organization has a maximum value, regardless of how well an employee performs the job. The rationale is that making exceptions to the compensation plan would result in widespread pay inequities. Having stated this, today many organizations are challenging traditional concepts as they strive to retain top-performing employees.

RATE RANGES AT HIGHER LEVELS The rate ranges established should be large enough to provide an incentive to do a better job. At higher levels, pay differentials may need to be greater to be meaningful. There may be logic in having the rate range become increasingly wide at each consecutive level. Consider, for example, what a $200-per-month salary increase would mean to a file clerk earning $2,000 per month (a 10 percent increase) and to a senior cost accountant earning $5,000 per month (a 4 percent increase). Assuming an inflation rate of 4 percent, the accountant's *real pay* would remain unchanged.

broadbanding
Compensation technique that collapses many pay grades (salary grades) into a few wide bands to improve organizational effectiveness.

Broadbanding

Broadbanding is a technique that collapses many pay grades (salary grades) into a few wide bands to improve organizational effectiveness. Employees today perform more diverse tasks than they previously did. Broadbanding creates the basis for a simpler compensation system that de-emphasizes structure and control and places greater importance on judgment and flexible decision making. Bands may also promote lateral development of employees and direct attention away from vertical promotional opportunities. The decreased emphasis on job levels should encourage employees to make cross-functional moves to jobs that are on the same or an even lower level because their pay rate would remain unchanged. Broadbanding allows for more flexibility within ranges, allows more movement of employees within the ranges, and can reduce the need for promotions.[54]

The use of broadbanding has declined in recent years. According to a WorldatWork survey, the use of broadbanding steadily declined from 14 percent in 2010 to 6 percent in 2016. This shift may be in response to possible pitfalls.[55] Because each band consists of a broad range of jobs, the market value of these jobs may also vary considerably. Unless carefully monitored, employees in jobs at the lower end of the band could progress to the top of the range and become overpaid.[56]

Two-Tier Wage System

two-tier wage system
A wage structure where newly hired workers are paid less than current employees for performing the same or similar jobs.

Two-tier wage systems reward newly hired employees less than established employees. Companies may choose to keep newly hired workers in the lower tier on a temporary or permanent basis. Under the temporary basis, employees can progress from lower entry-level pay rates to the higher rates enjoyed by more senior employees. Permanent two-tier systems reinforce the pay-rate distinction by retaining separate pay scales; lower-paying scales apply to newly hired employees, and current employees enjoy higher-paying scales. Although pay progresses within each scale, the maximum rates to which newly hired employees can progress are always lower than more senior employees' pay scales.

Two-tier pay structures also enable companies to reward long-service employees while keeping costs down by paying lower rates to newly hired employees who do not have an established performance record. Higher-tier employees who leave the company are usually replaced with workers who are compensated on the lower-paying scale.

Two-tier wage systems are more prevalent in unionized companies, particularly in the manufacturing industry. During economic recessions, unions sometimes reluctantly agree to include two-tier wage structures in their contracts with management. A union's motivation to accept a two-tier wage structure is to help lower labor costs in exchange for greater job security. When economic conditions improve and companies return to profitability, unions resist the inclusion of two-tier wage structures in subsequent agreements. For example, at Ford Motor Company, a two-tier wage structure was eliminated even though management expressed concern about the impact of substantially higher labor costs on competitive pricing. Still, Ford recognizes some benefits coming from the elimination of the two-tier wage system, including reduced tension between upper- and lower-tier workers. Joe Hinrichs, Ford's president of the Americas, stated, "That's really good, because one of the things you really need in a manufacturing plant is there to be focus and discipline. Anxiety or distraction is the enemy of process discipline."[57]

Adjusting Pay Rates

When pay ranges have been determined and jobs assigned to pay grades, it may become obvious that some jobs are overpaid and others underpaid. Underpaid jobs are normally brought up to the minimum of the pay range as soon as possible. Referring again to Figure 9-7, you can see that a job evaluated at about 225 points and having a rate of $14.00 per hour is represented by a circled dot immediately below pay grade 3. The job was determined to be difficult enough to fall in pay grade 3 (200-299 points). However, employees working in the job are being paid 60 cents per hour less than the minimum for the pay grade ($14.60 per hour). If one or more female employees should be in this circled job, the employer might soon learn more than desired about the Equal Pay Act. Good management practice would be to correct this inequity as rapidly as possible by placing the job in the proper pay grade and increasing the pay of those in that job.

Overpaid jobs present a different problem. Figure 9-7 illustrates an overpaid job for pay grade 4 (note the circled dot above pay grade 4). Employees in this job earn $19.00 per hour, or 50 cents more than the maximum for the pay grade. An ideal solution to the problem of an overpaid job is to promote the employee to a job in a higher pay grade. This is a great idea if the employee is qualified for a higher-rated job and a job opening is available. Another possibility would be to bring the job rate and employee pay into line through a pay cut. Although this decision may appear logical, it is generally not a good management practice because this action would punish employees for a situation they did not create. Somewhere in between these two possible solutions is a third: to freeze the rate until across-the-board pay increases bring the job into line.

Pricing jobs is not an easy task. It requires effort that never ends. It is also one of those tasks that managers may dislike but must do anyway.

Pay Compression

pay compression
A company's pay spread between newly hired or less qualified employees and more qualified job incumbents is small.

Pay compression occurs whenever a company's pay spread between newly hired or less qualified employees and more qualified job incumbents is small. In extreme cases, less experienced employees are paid as much as or more than employees who have been with the organization a long time because of a gradual increase in starting salaries and limited salary adjustments for long-term employees.

As workers discover inequities in their pay, resentment and lower productivity may follow with the employees ultimately leaving the company when the economy improves. Further, from a risk management perspective, companies need to make sure that salary compression is not causing problems with such laws as the Equal Pay Act. Unfortunately, no easy solution is available, and it is projected that the gap between current and new employees is getting wider and will continue to do so.

In principle, the solution to salary compression is simple. Unfortunately, the solution usually requires money, which is limited for most organizations. A company can build in compression funding to any annual budget increases. Still yet another way to remedy salary compression is to focus a primary portion of raises to your best employees and not waste compensation on across-the-board adjustments.

9.6 Review exceptions to the rules: compensation for sales representatives, contingent workers, and executives.

Exceptions to the Rules: Sales Professionals, Contingent Workers, and Executives

The discussion of compensation components and structures, thus far, applies to most occupational groups in a variety of organizations. There are some exceptions to the rules: sales professionals, contingent workers, and executives. We briefly review each of them next.

Sales Professionals

Designing compensation programs for sales employees involves unique considerations. Bob Cartwright, SPHR, president and CEO of Texas-based Intelligent Compensation LLC, advises companies on sales strategies saying, "Understanding what the business needs are, where the gaps exist and what needs to be driven to get business from point A to point B—that's the key."[58] Proper ratio of base pay, commissions, and bonuses must be established. For this reason, this task may belong to the sales staff rather than to HR. Nevertheless, many general compensation practices apply to sales jobs. For example, job content, relative job worth, and job market value are all relevant factors.

The *straight salary* approach is one extreme in sales compensation. In this method, salespersons receive a fixed salary regardless of their sales levels. Organizations use straight salary primarily to emphasize product support after the sale. For instance, sales representatives who deal largely with the federal government on a continuous basis often receive this form of compensation.

At the other extreme is *straight commission*, in which the person's pay is totally determined as a percentage of sales. If the salesperson makes no sales, the individual receives no pay. On the other hand, highly productive sales representatives can earn a great deal of money under this plan.

Between these extremes are the endless varieties of *part-salary, part-commission* combinations. The possibilities increase when a firm adds various types of *bonuses* to the basic compensation package. The emphasis given to either commission or salary depends on several factors, including the organization's philosophy toward service, the nature of the product, and the amount of time required to close a sale.

Try It!
If your professor has assigned this, sign onto **www.pearson.com/mylab/management** to complete the Motivation simulation and test your application of these concepts when faced with real-world decisions.

Contingent Workers

As we discussed in Chapter 5, contingent workers are those who do not have an implicit or explicit contract for ongoing employment. Some contingent workers are employed through an employment agency or on an on-call basis and often earn approximately 10.6 percent less on an hourly basis than traditional employees.[59] The magnitude and direction of the gap differ by industry. For instance, contingent workers in professional/technical services earn 17 percent less than their noncontingent counterparts. On the other hand, contingent workers in the construction industry earn 0.8 percent more.[60] Other contingent workers provide services as independent contractors, which represents the most common type of contingent workers (Chapter 5). Flexibility and lower costs for the employer are key reasons for the growth in the use of contingent workers. An inherent compensation problem relates to internal equity. You may have two employees working side by side, one a contingent worker and the other a regular employee, performing the same or near identical tasks, and one makes more money than the other. In most cases, contingents earn less pay and are far less likely to receive health or retirement benefits.[61] In March 2017, 88 percent of full-time workers were offered participation in a health insurance plan whereas only 19 percent of part-time workers were offered the same.[62] Similarly, 81 percent of full-time workers had access to retirement plans whereas this was the case for only 38 percent of part-time workers.

Executive Compensation

Executive compensation amounts are on the rise. Median compensation (without perquisites such as country club memberships) rose nearly 15 percent to $7.4 million between 2013 and 2015.[63] Although there has been considerable discussion regarding what some say are excessive salaries by executives, one should remember that the skills possessed by company executives largely determine whether a firm will prosper, survive, or fail. A company's executive compensation program is a critical factor in attracting and retaining the best available talent. Thus, compensation programs need to be developed that motivate these executives to strive to achieve long-term success for the firm. The five main components of executive compensation packages include: base salary, bonuses and performance-based pay, stock option plans, perquisites (perks), and severance packages.

BASE SALARY Although it may not represent the largest portion of the executive's compensation package, base salary is obviously important. It is a factor in determining the executive's standard of living. Salary also provides the basis for other forms of compensation. For example, it may determine bonus amounts and certain benefits. The U.S. tax law does not allow companies to deduct more than $1 million of an executive's salary unless it is performance based and meets specified criteria.[64]

BONUSES AND PERFORMANCE-BASED PAY As shareholders become increasingly disenchanted with the high levels of executive compensation for less-than-stellar accomplishments, performance-based pay is gaining in popularity. Although the Dodd-Frank Act has influenced executive pay, it appears that the greater influence has been the initiative to link pay to performance.[65] If pay for performance is appropriate for lower-level employees, should top executives be exempt from the same practice? The true superstars can still have huge earnings if their targets are met.

Payment of bonuses reflects a managerial belief in their incentive value. Cash bonuses, paid periodically based on performance goals, often provide real incentives. In the past, bonuses could be quite large and often were not tied to "real" performance goals. Hopefully, million-dollar pay packages not tied to performance are becoming a thing of the past. It appears that some progress is being made. According to an Equilar survey, the median performance- versus time-based equity mix for S&P 500 CEOs was 51.6 percent performance- and 48.4 percent time-based in 2015, compared to 31.5 percent performance- and 68.5 percent time-based in 2011.[66]

Sometimes, executives miss their performance targets even though they have already received compensation in anticipation of meeting them. Many boards of directors and shareholders were displeased with this reality. This problem has been remedied, in part, by the Dodd-Frank Act, which established clawback policies. A **clawback policy** allows the company to recover compensation if a later review indicates that payments were not calculated accurately or performance goals were not met. For instance, the Wells Fargo board of directors took back cash bonuses for

clawback policy
Allows the company to recover compensation if subsequent review indicates that payments were not calculated accurately or performance goals were not met.

eight executives after the company fraudulently opened bank accounts in customers' names. The board said the move was intended, "to show their [executives'] accountability for the bank's overall performance and reputation risk as a result of the scandal."[67]

The Dodd-Frank Act also requires the Securities and Exchange Commission (SEC) and other government agencies to regulate incentive pay at financial institutions. The SEC requires that institutions with $1 billion or more in assets be required to discourage "inappropriate risk" and disclose bonus details. Firms with $50 billion in assets would have to defer at least half of the top executives' bonuses for three years. These mechanisms are designed to discourage short-term thinking.

STOCK OPTION PLANS Stock option plans give the executive the option to buy a specified amount of stock in the future at or below the current market price. The stock option is a long-term incentive designed to integrate the interests of management with those of the organization. To ensure this integration, some boards of directors require their top executives to hold some of the firm's stock. Stock options have lost some of their appeal because of accounting rule changes that require companies to value and book an appropriate expense for options as they are granted. Nevertheless, there are several bona fide reasons for including stock ownership in executive compensation plans. In addition to potentially aligning employees' interests with those of shareholders, retaining top executives is also a factor.

perquisites (perks)
Special benefits provided by a firm to a small group of key executives and designed to give the executives something extra.

PERQUISITES (PERKS) **Perquisites (perks)** are any special benefits provided by a firm to a small group of key executives and designed to give the executives "something extra." Possible perks include a company-provided car, limousine service, use of the company plane and yacht, and security services. A Willis Towers Watson survey found that 82 percent of S&P 500 companies awarded one or more types of perks, and 47 percent offered at least three different types of perks.[68] And, perks are costly. Overall, companies are spending more on perks than ever before. Between 2013 and 2015, perquisites grew 21.6 percent to a median value of $126,550.[69] The more expensive perks were personal use of corporate aircraft (median value of $103,799), home security ($28,505), and use of a company car ($20,618).[70] At the high end, Facebook's Chairman and CEO Mark Zuckerberg received aircraft perks equaling about $775,000, and Coca-Cola's Chairman and CEO Muhtar Kent received automobile perks totaling $198,217.[71]

golden parachute contract
Perquisite that protects executives if another company acquires their firm or the executive is forced to leave the firm for other reasons.

SEVERANCE PACKAGES What most people may not understand is that massive severance payments are not set up by a board of directors after a CEO has quit or been fired. These payments were negotiated prior to being hired and are referred to as golden parachute contracts. A **golden parachute contract** is a perk that protects executives if another company acquires their firm or if the executive is forced to leave the firm for other reasons. To hire and retain talented individuals, some corporations negotiate employment agreements that include golden parachutes.[72] At times, golden parachute contracts have been abused. For example, United Airlines (former) CEO Jeff Smisek resigned during a federal probe after allegedly engaging in many illegal dealings. One could say that Smisek was rewarded for wrongdoing. He received a severance package worth $28.6 million which includes a $5 million payment, stock and bonus awards, and expensive company perks (among them, free first class airfare for himself and a companion for life).[73] Not only should CEO pay be considered but CEO pay contracts should also be examined. But hopefully the environment is changing.

The SEC has adopted far-reaching executive compensation disclosure rules that apply to publicly traded companies. The new rules require companies to list all the agreements for each executive, to disclose the payment triggers, and, most importantly, to give an estimated dollar value of potential payments and benefits and the specific factors used to determine them. For the first time, investors will see the estimated total dollar value of the exit packages. No longer will these agreements become exposed only at the time of a merger and acquisition deal or when the board removes a CEO.

say on pay
Provision that gives shareholders in all but the smallest companies an advisory vote on executive pay.

WALL STREET REFORM AND CONSUMER PROTECTION ACT (DODD–FRANK ACT) We have referred to the clawback provision of the Dodd-Frank Act, which has increased the transparency of how executives are compensated. The Dodd-Frank Act contains several additional provisions. We review two of the more noteworthy ones here. The first provision, **say on pay**, gives shareholders in all but the smallest companies an advisory vote on executive pay. This is something that governance advocates have long wanted. Those who support the concept of say on pay believe that the vote will cause greater accountability on executive pay decisions.[74] The Dodd-Frank Act requires 5,000 companies to hold nonbinding shareholder say-on-pay votes at least every three years. Companies must also hold shareholder votes on the frequency of say on pay with the option of one, two, or three years, or to abstain. Frequency votes are required to be held every three years. Thus far, shareholder votes appear to be highly favorable in support of company pay plans. A survey by Semler Brossy revealed that 76 percent of companies have passed say on pay with more than 90 percent shareholder approval.[75] A recent study found that boards that give CEOs higher pay opportunities are more likely to receive lower levels of support in shareholder say-on-pay votes than those with lower CEO pay.[76] Also, shareholders appear to want their say on pay on an annual basis as opposed to every two or three years.[77] Institutional Shareholder Services (ISS), which recommends mutual funds and other large shareholders on how to vote in corporate elections, has recommended "no" votes on executive pay in about 13 percent of the proposals it has reviewed this proxy season.[78] All of the companies with a failed say-on-pay vote in 2012 had a negative recommendation from the proxy advisory firm ISS.[79] One major company to receive a negative vote on say on pay was Spectrum Pharmaceuticals. The negative vote may have been influenced by the high pay relative to shareholder return.[80]

The second provision requires that companies report the ratio of CEO compensation to the median compensation of its employees in SEC filings. This disclosure will help inform shareholders when taking a "say on pay" vote. The SEC adopted this rule in August 2015, with which companies must comply for their first fiscal year beginning on or after January 1, 2017. The rule provides companies with flexibility in calculating this pay ratio. For instance, a company may choose the methodology for identifying its median employee and that employee's compensation. The pay ratio rule has come with extensive criticism. Many companies have reported problems with meeting the compliance requirements. Other companies have strongly argued that disclosing this ratio has little to do with whether investors will buy or sell shares of company stock. These concerns have prompted the SEC to review the rule.[81]

PREPARING FOR EXAMS/QUIZZES

Chapter Summary by Learning Objectives

1. ***Summarize the usual components of a total compensation plan and the environment of compensation practice.*** *Total compensation* represents both the intrinsic and extrinsic rewards employees receive for performing their jobs. *Direct financial compensation (monetary compensation)* consists of the pay that a person receives in the form of wages, salaries, commissions, and bonuses. *Indirect financial compensation (employee benefits)* consists of all financial rewards that are not included in direct financial compensation. *Nonfinancial compensation* consists of the satisfaction that a person receives from the job itself or from the psychological or physical environment in which the person works. Direct financial compensation is set within a structure of three elements: job structures, competitive compensation policies, and pay structures. There are many factors that HR professionals must consider when building compensation programs. The most prominent considerations are labor markets, cost-of-living differences, labor unions, the economy, interindustry wage differentials, and a variety of legislation.
2. ***Explain the direct financial compensation practices.*** These practices include base pay (hourly wage and salary) and various adjustments to base pay over time. The categories are cost-of-living adjustments, seniority pay, performance-based pay (merit pay and various types of incentive pay practices), and person-focused pay (including competency-based pay).
3. ***Discuss job structures and how they are established.*** Job evaluation is a process that determines the relative value of one job in relation to another. In the job evaluation ranking method, the raters examine the description of each job being evaluated and arrange the jobs in order according to their value to the company. The *classification* method involves defining several classes or grades to describe a group of jobs. In the *factor comparison* method, raters need not keep the entire job in mind as they evaluate; instead, they make decisions on separate aspects or factors of the job. In the *point method*, raters assign numerical values to specific job factors, such as knowledge required, and the sum of these values provides a quantitative assessment of a job's relative worth.

4. ***Summarize competitive pay policies: pay level and pay mix.*** Broadly, competitive pay policies refer to pay level and pay mix. *Pay level* choices include whether to lag, match, or lead the market pay rates, on average. *Pay mix* refers to the composition of an employee's direct (monetary compensation) and indirect (employee benefits) financial compensation. Choices about how to structure pay (for example, base pay, short-term incentives, and employee benefits versus incentives and employee benefits) must be made.
5. ***Explain what pay structures are and how they are created.*** *Pay structures* represent pay rate differences for jobs of unequal worth and the framework for recognizing employee contributions. Pay structures result from an analysis based on compensation survey work. *Compensation surveys* enable HR professionals to know the pay level and pay mixes of its competitors. Assigning dollar values to the company's jobs is job pricing. Features of pay structures include pay grades and pay ranges. *Pay grades* refer to the grouping of similar jobs to simplify job pricing. *Pay ranges* specify a minimum and maximum pay rate with enough variance between the two to allow for a significant pay difference. *Broadbanding* and *two-tier wage structures* are alternative pay structure designs.
6. ***Review exceptions to the rules: compensation for sales representatives, contingent workers, and executives.*** Contingent workers are employed on the expectation of a defined term of employment. Most often, contingent workers receive less pay and employee benefits than workers who do not have an expectation of a defined term of employment. Designing compensation programs for sales employees involves unique considerations such as the formula for determining incentive payments. In determining executive compensation, firms typically prefer to relate salary growth for the highest-level managers to overall corporate performance. Executive compensation often has five basic elements: base salary, bonuses and performance-based pay, stock option plans, perquisites, and severance packages.

Key Terms

total compensation 245
direct financial compensation (monetary compensation) 246
indirect financial compensation (employee benefits) 246
nonfinancial compensation 246
labor market 248
spillover effect 249
interindustry wage or compensation differentials 249
exempt employees 251
nonexempt employees 251
base pay 252
hourly pay (wage) 252
salary 252
cost-of-living adjustment (COLA) 252
real hourly compensation 252
nominal hourly compensation 252
seniority 252
seniority pay 252
human capital theory 253
human capital 253
General Schedule 253
merit pay 254
merit bonuses 254
spot bonuses 255
incentive pay 255
piecework 256
management incentive plans 256
behavioral encouragement plans 256
referral plans 256
gain sharing 258
Scanlon plan 258
profit sharing 259
employee stock plans 259
company stock 259
company stock shares 259
stock options 259
job-based pay 259
person-focused pay 259
skill-based pay 259
competency-based pay 260
job evaluation 260
job evaluation ranking method 260
classification method 260
factor comparison method 261
point method 261
compensation policy 261
pay level compensation policies 261
Pay mix compensation policies 261
market lead policies 262
market match policies 262
market lag policies 262
pay mix compensation policies 262
pay structures 263
compensation survey 263
pay grade 264
pay range 265
wage curve 265
broadbanding 265
two-tier wage systems 266
pay compression 267
clawback policy 268
perquisites (perks) 269
golden parachute contract 269
say on pay 270

MyLab Management

If your instructor is using MyLab Management, go to **www.pearson.com/mylab/management** to complete the problems marked with this icon ✪.

Questions for Review

9-1. Define each of the following terms:
(a) compensation
(b) direct financial compensation
(c) indirect financial compensation
(d) nonfinancial compensation

9-2. What are the contextual influences on direct financial compensation?

9-3. Discuss the determinants of direct financial compensation.

9-4. Discuss the difference between pay-for-performance and person-focused pay.

✪**9-5.** What are the differences between pay level and pay mix compensation policies?

9-6. How has government legislation affected compensation?

9-7. What is the difference between an exempt and a nonexempt employee?

9-8. Distinguish between the following job evaluation methods:
(a) ranking
(b) classification
(c) factor comparison
(d) point method

9-9. Define *job pricing*. What is the purpose of job pricing?

9-10. Define *pay grades*. State the basic procedure for determining pay grades.

9-11. Define *pay ranges*. What is the purpose of establishing pay ranges?

9-12. Define *broadbanding*. What is the purpose of using broadbanding?

9-13. Distinguish between merit pay, bonus, spot bonuses, and piecework.

9-14. Discuss the key issues that are associated with compensating contingent workers.

9-15. What are some companywide pay plans? Briefly discuss each.

9-16. How is the compensation for sales representatives determined?

✪**9-17.** Describe each of the following:
(a) say on pay
(b) golden parachute contract
(c) clawback policies

9-18. What are the various types of executive compensation?

PREPARING FOR MY CAREER

ETHICS DILEMMA

Sales Tactics at Wells Fargo Bank[82]

In September 2016, news about Wells Fargo Bank's questionable sales practice made the headlines. It was estimated that more than 5,000 employees opened approximately 2 million bank accounts for customers who did not request them. The bank's leadership claimed that the employees acted on their own volition, and they were subsequently fired. Many current and past employees claimed that Wells Fargo raised daily sales goals to unrealistic levels, creating a high-pressure environment. Other employees talked about how managers regularly asked them about their progress, focusing exclusively on the number of accounts opened rather than discussing appropriate sales techniques that could help employees legitimately meet their quotas. When goals were not met, these individuals alleged that they were threatened with formal written warnings and termination.

Many employees used fraudulent sales tactics to meet their sales quotas out of fear of receiving a bad employment reference; others could not afford to be unemployed even for a brief time. Apparently, employees who called the company's ethics line to report their concerns were punished or fired. Even branch managers felt the pinch. Allegedly, high-ranking bank officials ordered employees to shred documents before auditor inspections.

9-19. What would you do?

9-20 What factor(s) in this ethics dilemma might influence a person to make a less than ethical decision?

HRM Is Everyone's Business

HR professionals and other managers share the responsibility for building and maintaining pay structures that are most suitable for recognizing employee contributions. They should follow some general guidelines for building effective pay structures. Over time, companies will likely benefit from higher retention of high-performing employees.

Action checklist for managers and HR—keeping the focus on employees as pay structures are built

HR takes the lead

- ☑ A single firm-wide pay structure is rarely sufficient to support differences in job functions. Relying on an understanding of the company's strategic objectives and the role of various job structures, recommend separate pay structures such as ones for hourly workers and salaried workers or for business and occupational functions such as ones for engineering professionals and marketing professionals.
- ☑ Partner with compensation specialists to group employees into pay grades that are determined by similarity in the work they produce; corresponding ranges will also be established for each grade.
- ☑ HR professionals work with compensation specialists to conduct market analyses and certify that current employees are compensated in line with the competition.

Managers take the lead

- ☑ Communicate with HR regarding desired job-related behaviors in the employee population—HR and other managers work together to ensure that the compensation and benefits incentives are continuing to encourage the correct behaviors.
- ☑ Employees will continue to progress within their pay grade, receiving pay increases (as determined by their managers in consultation with HR) commensurate with job performance attainments—compensation specialists will work with HR and managers to ensure that, with these pay increases, equity still exists in the grade and that the pay raise percentage increases correspond to levels of performance.

HRM by the Numbers

Pay Progression in a Job Classification Plan

An additional HRM by the Numbers exercise can be found on MyLab Management.

The federal government's General Schedule (GS) is an example of a job classification plan in which pay rates are based, in part, on compensable factors such as knowledge and skills. Jobs are grouped into 15 classifications, ranging from GS level 1 through GS level 15 as well as the level or degrees of compensable factors (e.g., follow procedures vs. establishing procedures). Over time, employees receive pay increases according to length of service (Steps 1-10) and progression through the steps assumes a minimum of acceptable performance. The pay increase from step to step equals the within-grade increase (WGI) amount. The waiting periods within steps are:

- Steps 1-3: 1 year in each step
- Steps 4-6: 2 years in each step
- Steps 7-9: 3 years in each step

2017 General Schedule

Annual Rates by Grade and Step ($)

Grade	Step 1	Step 2	Step 3	Step 4	Step 5	Step 6	Step 7	Step 8	Step 9	Step 10	WITHIN GRADE INCREASE (WGI)
1	18,526	19,146	19,762	20,375	20,991	21,351	21,960	22,575	22,599	23,171	VARIES
2	20,829	21,325	22,015	22,599	22,853	23,525	24,197	24,869	25,541	26,213	VARIES
3	22,727	23,485	24,243	25,001	25,759	26,517	27,275	28,033	28,791	29,549	758
4	25,514	26,364	27,214	28,064	28,914	29,764	30,614	31,464	32,314	33,164	850
5	28,545	29,497	30,449	31,401	32,353	33,305	34,257	35,209	36,161	37,113	952
6	31,819	32,880	33,941	35,002	36,063	37,124	38,185	39,246	40,307	41,368	1,061
7	35,359	36,538	37,717	38,896	40,075	41,254	42,433	43,612	44,791	45,970	1,179
8	39,159	40,464	41,769	43,074	44,379	45,684	46,989	48,294	49,599	50,904	1,305
9	43,251	44,693	46,135	47,577	49,019	50,461	51,903	53,345	54,787	56,229	1,442
10	47,630	49,218	50,806	52,394	53,982	55,570	57,158	58,746	60,334	61,922	1,588
11	52,329	54,073	55,817	57,561	59,305	61,049	62,793	64,537	66,281	68,025	1,744
12	62,722	64,813	66,904	68,995	71,086	73,177	75,268	77,359	79,450	81,541	2,091
13	74,584	77,070	79,556	82,042	84,528	87,014	89,500	91,986	94,472	96,958	2,486
14	88,136	91,074	94,012	96,950	99,888	102,826	105,764	108,702	111,640	114,578	2,938
15	103,672	107,128	110,584	114,040	117,496	120,952	124,408	127,864	131,320	134,776	3,456

Questions

9-21. Using the General Schedule, calculate the number of years it would take an employee to advance from her starting position in Grade 11 (Step 1) to Step 10 if she is demonstrating acceptable performance.

9-22. Another employee asked what his salary would likely be after completing two additional years of service. This employee just entered his first year in Grade 4 (Step 5). If he was to demonstrate acceptable performance, calculate the expected salary after completing two years of service.

9-23. All pay rates typically increase each year based on changes in the Consumer Price Index. Calculate the Grade 7 WGI amount based on an overall 3 percent increase.

Working Together: Team Exercise

In small groups of three or four, come up with specific answers to the following questions. Talk through your perspectives and come up with a team response. Be prepared to share your ideas with the class.

As a group, use O*NET (which we reviewed in Chapter 4) to select a job for further study. Start by browsing jobs in different occupations (www.onetonline.org/find/). Next, from the *find occupations* drop down list, select *job family*. There, you will see 23 unique job families (occupations). Then, select a job family (click on the link for the chosen job family). Finally, select a job from the chosen job family (click on the link for the chosen job) and review the information contained in the detailed report.

9-24. Based on your understanding of the various components of direct financial compensation (Learning Objective 9-2), which approach is most fitting for recognizing job incumbents' contributions? Explain.

9-25. Which approach is least fitting for the job? Explain.

INCIDENT 1 The Pay Gap at Barker Enterprise

Roger Babbit is an administrative assistant at Barker Enterprise. For the past 12 years, he has been working for Maria Mendoza, Director of Human Resources, and they have developed a good working rapport. Roger's current annual salary of $75,000 places him slightly higher than the midpoint of his salary range. His work has been consistently exemplary, earning the highest performance appraisal score every year. In addition, Roger regularly receives recognition rewards (a plaque and an Amazon.com gift certificate) for his willingness to go the extra mile. In fact, Roger is known for his trustworthiness, leading many coworkers to ask for career advice.

On a recent Monday morning, Maria introduced Roger to Bianca McCann, a newly hired administrative assistant in the marketing department. Roger offered to meet Bianca for lunch to share his positive experiences at Barker. During their conversation, Roger learned that Bianca earned her associate degree in administrative science from his alma mater where he earned the same degree 13 years ago. She graduated 2 years ago, and held a job as an administrative assistant at Madigan Manufacturing prior to joining Barker Enterprise. Bianca said that she enjoyed her work at Madigan, but was dissatisfied with the pay because of substantial student loan debt. Barker's pay scale is substantially higher than Madigan's, making it difficult to refuse a $70,000 salary offer.

Roger thought a lot about his conversation with Bianca, particularly, the relatively small pay difference of $5,000, considering his outstanding track record. He started to resent Bianca. Rather than letting his resentment get out of control, Roger made an appointment with Maria to discuss his concerns.

Maria listened carefully to Roger's concerns. He stated the salary difference and went on to explain that he is a proven quantity given his consistent track record of top notch performance and many more years of work experience than Bianca possesses. Maria assured Roger that he is a highly valued employee and that the department would suffer if he were ever to leave the company. She also understood and openly acknowledged Roger's perspective. Roger then asked Maria for a salary increase. Maria denied Roger's request, telling him that there are many other similar pay gaps within the company and the salary budget could not accommodate making pay adjustments for everyone else in this situation. Surprised by Maria's answer, Roger left her office pondering what his next steps should be.

Questions

9-26. Name and explain the issue underlying the pay gap between Roger and Bianca.

9-27. What might be problems associated with withholding a pay adjustment for Roger under these circumstances?

INCIDENT 2 The Controversial Job

David Rhine, compensation manager for Farrington Lingerie Company, was generally relaxed and good-natured. Although he was a no-nonsense, competent executive, David was one of the most popular managers in the company. This Friday morning, however, David was not his usual self. As chairperson of the company's job evaluation committee, he had called a late-morning meeting at which several jobs were to be considered for re-evaluation. The jobs had already been rated and assigned to pay grade 3. But the office manager, Ben Butler, was upset that one was not rated higher. To press the issue, Ben had taken his case to two executives who were also members of the job evaluation committee. The two executives (production manager Bill Nelson and general marketing manager Betty Anderson) then requested that the job ratings be reviewed. Bill and Betty supported Ben's side of the dispute, and David was not looking forward to the confrontation that was almost certain to occur.

The controversial job was that of receptionist. Only one receptionist position existed in the company, and Marianne Sanders held it. Marianne had been with the firm 12 years, longer than any of the committee members. She was extremely efficient, and virtually all the executives in the company, including the president, had noticed and commented on her outstanding work. Bill Nelson and Betty Anderson were particularly pleased with Marianne because of the cordial way she greeted and accommodated Farrington's customers and vendors, who frequently visited the plant. They felt that Marianne projected a positive image of the company.

When the meeting began, David said, "Good morning. I know that you're busy, so let's get the show on the road. We have several jobs to evaluate this morning and I suggest we begin . . . " Before he could finish his sentence, Bill interrupted, "I suggest we start with Marianne." Betty nodded in agreement. When David regained his composure, he quietly but firmly asserted, "Bill, we are not here today to evaluate Marianne. Her supervisor does that at performance appraisal time. We're meeting to evaluate jobs based on job content. To do this fairly, regarding other jobs in the company, we must leave personalities out of our evaluation." David then proceeded to pass out copies of the receptionist job description to Bill and Betty, who were obviously very irritated.

Questions

9-28. Do you feel that David was justified in insisting that the job, not the person, be evaluated? Discuss.

9-29. Do you believe that there is a maximum rate of pay for every job in an organization, regardless of how well the job is being performed? Justify your position.

9-30. Assume that Marianne is earning the maximum of the range for her pay grade. In what ways could she obtain a salary increase?

✪ MyLab Management

If your instructor is using MyLab Management, go to **www.pearson.com/mylab/management** for Auto-graded writing questions as well as the following Assisted-graded writing questions:

9-31. Why is it important for HR professionals to understand legislation, labor unions, and interindustry wage differentials when establishing compensation programs?

9-32. Why might a firm want to be a pay leader as opposed to paying market rate?

Endnotes

1 Jen Schramm, "The Big Issues Facing HR," *Society for Human Resource Management* online (March 1, 2016). Accessed March 9, 2017, at www.shrm.org/hr-today/news/hr-magazine/0316/pages/the-big-issues-facing-hr.aspx.

2 CNBC, "The 25 Highest-Paying Companies in America," *CNBC.com*. Accessed March 2, 2017, at www.cnbc.com/2016/08/03/the-25-highest-paying-companies-in-america.html.

3 U.S. Bureau of Labor Statistics, "Employer Costs for Employee Compensation—March 2017," (USDL 17-0770). Accessed August 1, 2017, at www.bls.gov.

4 Ibid.; and U.S. Bureau of Labor Statistics, "Employer Costs for Employee Compensation—March 2014," (USDL 14-1075). Accessed August 1, 2017, at www.bls.gov.

5 *Adobe, "Careers/Engineering." Accessed February 28, 2017, at www.adobe.com/careers/engineering.html.*

6 Jeffrey Sparshott, "The Short List of Jobs with High and Rising Pay," *The Wall Street Journal* online (July 26, 2016). Accessed March 1, 2017, at www.wsj.com.

7 U.S. Bureau of Labor Statistics. Information Security Analysts. *Occupational Outlook Handbook*, 2016-17 Edition. Accessed March 1, 2017, at www.bls.gov/ooh/computer-and-information-technology/information-security-analysts.htm.

8 Joshua Jamerson, "Starbucks to Raise Wages Up to 15%," *The Wall Street Journal* online (July 11, 2016). Accessed February 15, 2017, at www.wsj.com.

9 Laura Stevens, "How Amazon Gets Its Holiday Hires Up to Speed in Two Days," *The Wall Street Journal* online (November 28, 2016). Accessed January 31, 2017, at www.wsj.com.

10 "Cost of living: How Far Will My Salary Go in Another City?" *CNN Money* online. Accessed February 28, 2017, at http://money.cnn.com/calculator/pf/cost-of-living/.

11 U.S. Bureau of Labor Statistics, "Consumer Price Index," Accessed March 17, 2017, at www.bls.gov/cpi/.

12 Loren M. Solnick, "The Effect of the Blue Collar Unions on White Collar Wages and Benefits." *Industrial and Labor Relations Review*, *38* (1985): 23–35.

13 U.S. Bureau of Labor Statistics, "Employment and Earnings," (January 2017). Accessed February 28, 2017, at www.bls.gov/opub/ee/2017/ces/summarytable_201701.pdf.

14 Jane Osburn, "Interindustry Wage Differentials: Patterns and Possible Sources. *Monthly Labor Review*, February (2000): 34–46.

15 Tim Low, "Why It's So Hard to Figure Out What to Pay Top Talent," *Harvard Business Review* online (February 19, 2015). Accessed March 1, 2017, at www.hbr.org.

16 U.S. Department of Labor. *Minimum Wage Laws in the States—January 1, 2017*. Accessed February 28, 2017, at www.dol.gov/whd/minwage/america.htm.

17 Eric Morath, "Minimum Wages Set to Increase in Many States in 2017," *The Wall Street Journal* online (December 30, 2016). Accessed February 3, 2017, at www.wsj.com.

18 Denise Martin, Stephanie Plancich, and Janeen McIntosh, "Trends in Wage and Hour Settlements: 2012 Update," NERA Economic Consulting, *Insight in Economics*™ (March 12, 2013). Accessed September 4, 2013, at www.nera.com.

19 Roger S. Achille, "FLSA Requires Education for Professional Exemption," *HR Magazine* 55 (February 2010): 70.

20 S. Rep. No. 176, 88th Congress, 1st Session, 1 (1963).

21 Karin Agness, "Don't Buy into the Gender Pay Gap Myth," *Forbes* online (April 12, 2016). Accessed March 9, 2017, at www.forbes.com.

22 U.S. Bureau of Labor Statistics, "Employment and Earnings," (January 2017). Accessed February 28, 2017, at: www.bls.gov/opub/ee/2017/ces/summarytable_201701.pdf.

23 Joseph Cayer, *Public Personnel Administration in the United States*. New York: St. Martin Press.

24 Gary Becker, *Human Capital*. New York: St. Martin Press, 1975.

25 "Compensation Programs and Practices Survey," WorldatWork (August 2016). Accessed December 29, 2016, at www.worldatwork.org/adimLink?id=80656.

26 "Study Says Pay for Performance Linked to Positive Results," *Report on Salary Surveys* 11 (March 2011): 10–11.

27 Eric Krell, "All for Incentives, Incentives for All," *HR Magazine* 56 (January 2011): 34–38.

28 Kathryn Tyler, "Design an Effective Rewards Program," *HR Magazine* 56 (October 2011): 94.

29 Peck, C. (1984). *Pay and Performance: The Interaction of Compensation and Performance Appraisal* (Research Bulletin No. 155). New York: The Conference Board.

30 "Stuck Below," *Workspan* (September 2016): 20-25.

31 "Pay for Performance," *Controller's Report 2010* (January 2010): 6–8.

32 "Use Variable Pay to Promote Success in the Workplace," *HR Focus* 87 (July 2010): 5–6.

33 "Compensation & Incentives: The Entitlement Era Is Over," *HR Magazine* 57 (Special Supplement, SHRM 2012 HR Trend Book): 60.

34 "Raises Cut in '09, But Bonus Budgets Inch Up," *Treasury & Risk* (September 2009): 8.

35 "Bonus Programs and Practices," *A Report by WorldatWork* (July 2016). Accessed January 5, 2017, at www.worldatwork.org.

36 Angie Herbers, "Bonus Babies," *Investment Advisor* 30 (February 2010): 47–48.

37 "Bonus Programs and Practices," *A Report by WorldatWork* (July 2016). Accessed January 5, 2017, at www.worldatwork.org.

38 Ibid.

39 "Compensation Programs and Practices," *A Report by WorldatWork* (August 2016). Accessed February 1, 2017, at www.worldatwork.org.

40 Drucker, P. (1954). *The Practice of Management*. New York: Harper.

41 "Inventory of Total Rewards Programs & Practices," *A Report by WorldatWork* (January 2017). Accessed March 9, 2017, at www.worldatwork.org.

42 Frank Gluck "Nursing Demand Driving Hospital Hiring Spree, Bonuses," *News-Press* online (February 15, 2016). Accessed March 8, 2017, at www.news-press.com/story/news/local/2016/02/15/nursing-demand-driving-hospital-hiring-spree-bonuses/80007832/.

43 Greene, R. J. (2007). Team incentives. In D. Scott (Ed.), *Incentive Pay: Creating a Competitive Advantage*. Phoenix, AZ: Worldat-Work Press.

44 Matt Bloch, "Rewarding the Team," *HR Magazine* 52 (February 2007): 91–93.

45 Belcher, J. G., Jr. "Gain Sharing and Variable Pay: The State of the Art." *Compensation & Benefits Review* (May–June 1994): 50–60.

46 Joann Muller, "GM Factory Workers Take Home $12,000 Bonuses on Record 2016 North American Profits," *Forbes* online (February 7, 2017). Accessed March 8, 2017, at www.forbes.com.

47 "Demand for Highly Skilled Labor Requires Effective Pay Strategy," *HR Focus* 90 (March 2013): 8–9.

48 Mitra, Atul, Nina Gupta, N., and Jason D. Shaw, J. D. "A Comparative Examination of Traditional and Skill-Based Pay Plans." *Journal of Managerial Psychology 26* (April 2011): 278–296.

49 Nancy Hatch Woodward, "Matching Jobs with Pay," 57 *HR Magazine* (May 2012): 55–58.

50 Jean Christofferson, "The Mayo Way . . . With Pay," *Workspan* (February 2012): 19–23.

51 Lauren Weber, "What Is the Best Way to Pay Workers?" *The Wall Street Journal* online (August 2, 2016). Accessed January 31, 2017, at www.wsj.com.

52 "Biomedical Engineers," *Occupational Outlook Handbook (2016–2017 Edition). Accessed March 1, 2017, at www.bls.gov.*

53 "Compensation Programs and Practices Survey," *WorldatWork* (August 2016). Accessed December 29, 2016, at www.worldatwork.org/adimLink?id=80656.

54 "Strategic Use of Pay Ranges Can Maximize a Tight Budget," *Report on Salary Surveys* (May 2010): 8–9.

55 "Compensation Programs and Practices Survey," *WorldatWork* (August 2016). Accessed December 29, 2016, at www.worldatwork.org/adimLink?id=80656.

56 Frank L. Giancola, "A Framework for Understanding New Concepts in Compensation Management," *Benefits & Compensation Digest* 46 (September 2009): 1–16.

57 Nick Bunkley, "Ford Finds Mixed Blessing in End of Tiered Wages," *Automotive News* online (May 8, 2016). Accessed March 1, 2017, at www.autonews.com.

58 Scott Ladd, "May the Sales Force Be with You," *HR Magazine* 55 (September 2010): 105–107.

59 U.S. Government Accountability Office, "Contingent Workforce: Size, Characteristics, Earnings, and Benefits," Report: GAO-15-168R (April 20, 2015). Accessed February 1, 2017, at www.gao.gov/assets/670/669766.pdf.

60 Ibid.

61 Nancy Hatch Woodward, "Part-Time Benefits: A Moving Target," *HR Magazine* 57 (November 2012): 61–64.

62 U.S. Bureau of Labor Statistics, "Employee Benefits in the United States—March 2017," USDL: 17-1013. Accessed August 1, 2017, at www.bls.gov.

63 John Simons, "CEOs Enjoy Rich Perks," *The Wall Street Journal* online (December 6, 2016). Accessed March 10, 2017, at www.wsj.com.

64 Susan R. Holmberg and Lydia Austin, "Fixing a Hole: How the Tax Code for Executive Pay Distorts Economic Incentives and Burdens Taxpayers." Accessed September 4, 2013, at http://rooseveltinstitute.org/policy-and-ideas/big-ideas/fixing-hole-how-tax-code-executive-pay-distorts-economic-incentives.

65 "Executive Pay Recovers Heartily in 2010, Three Surveys Find," *Report on Salary Surveys* 11 (June 2011): 1–5.

66 "One in Nine CEOs Are Paid without Ties to Performance," Equilar Blog (January 6, 2017). Accessed March 1, 2017, at www.equilar.com/blogs/199-one-in-nine-ceos-are-paid-without-ties.html.

67 Emily Glazer and Austen Hufford, "Wells Fargo: Top Executives Won't Get Cash Bonus for 2016," *The Wall Street Journal* online (March 1, 2017). Accessed March 2, 2017, at www.wsj.com.

68 Mina Ahmed, "An Update on Executive Perquisite Trends in the S&P 500," *Executive Compensation Bulletin* (February 17, 2016). Accessed March 10, 2017, at www.towerswatson.com/en-US/Insights/Newsletters/Global/executive-pay-matters/2016/Executive-Compensation-Bulletin-Update-Executive-Perquisite-Trends-SP-500.

69 Emily Glazer and Austen Hufford, "Wells Fargo: Top Executives Won't Get Cash Bonus for 2016," *The Wall Street Journal* online (March 1, 2017). Accessed March 2, 2017, at www.wsj.com.

70 Mina Ahmed, "An Update on Executive Perquisite Trends in the S&P 500," *Executive Compensation Bulletin* (February 17, 2016). Accessed March 10, 2017, at www.towerswatson.com/en-US/Insights/Newsletters/Global/executive-pay-matters/2016/Executive-Compensation-Bulletin-Update-Executive-Perquisite-Trends-SP-500.

71 "Which S&P 500 Execs Received the Largest Aircraft and Auto Perks?" Equilar Blog (January 20, 2017). Accessed March 1, 2017, at www.equilar.com/blogs/205-500-execs-received-largest-aircraft-and-auto-perks.html.

72 William G. Ruffner, "The Golden Parachute Paradox," *Pennsylvania CPA Journal* 82 (Summer 2011): 1.

73 Brad Tuttle, "Why Disgraced CEOs Get Insanely Generous Payout Packages When They're Fired," *Money* online (September 11, 2015). Accessed March 2, 2017, at http://time.com/money/4031287/united-jeff-smisek-scandal-ceo-severance-package/.

74 David Lynn, "Implementing Say-On-Pay in 2011," *Corporate Board* 32 (July/August 2011): 17–20.

75 Semler Brossy, "*Say on Pay Results*," (July 17, 2013). Accessed September 4, 2013, at www.semlerbrossy.com/sayonpay.

76 Dori Meinert, "High CEO Pay Leads to Lower Shareholder Support," 57 *HR Magazine* (May 2012): 18.

77 Melissa Klein Aguilar, "Lack of Investor Support for Less-Frequent Say-on-Pay Votes," *Compliance Week* 8 (April 2011): 9–10.

78 Semler Brossy, "*Say on Pay Results*," (July 17, 2013). Accessed September 4, 2013, at www.semlerbrossy.com/sayonpay. "Company Dinged for Failure to Disclose CEO Perks," *Compliance Week* 8 (March 2011): 8–10.

79 John K. Wilson and Joshua A. Agen, "Say on Pay Best Practices for 2012," *Corporate Board* 33 (March/April 2012): 6–10.

80 Semler Brossy, "*Say on Pay Results*," (July 31, 2013). Accessed September 4, 2013, at www.semlerbrossy.com/sayonpay. Arielle Bikard, "Say-on-Pay Losses Catch HP, Others Off Guard," *Compliance Week* 8 (June 2011): 44–45.

81 Benjamin Bain, "Pay Ratio Rule That CEROs Hate is Getting a Fresh Look at the SEC," *Bloomberg* online (February 6, 2017). Accessed March 8, 2017, at www.bloomberg.com.

82 Sources Referenced: Emily Glazer, "Wells Fargo Fires Four Executives Following Probe of Sales-Practices Scandal," *The Wall Street Journal* online (February 21, 2017). Accessed March 10, 2017, at www.wsj.com; Ariel Zambelich, "Former Wells Fargo Employees Describe Toxic Sales Culture, Even at HQ," *National Public Radio* online (October 4, 2016). Accessed February 28, 2017, at www.npr.org; Geoff Colvin, "The Wells Fargo Scandal Is Now Reaching VW Proportions," *Fortune* online (January 26, 2017). Accessed March 10, 2017, at www.fortune.com; Michael Corkery and Stacy Cowley, "Wells Fargo Warned Workers Against Sham Accounts, but 'They Needed a Paycheck,'" *The New York Times* online (September 16, 2016). Accessed March 10, 2017, at www.nytimes.com.

10

Indirect Financial Compensation (Employee Benefits)

LEARNING OBJECTIVES After completing this chapter, students should be able to:

10.1 Define *indirect financial compensation (employee benefits)*.

10.2 Describe legally required benefits and the various kinds.

10.3 Define *discretionary benefits* and explain the various types.

10.4 Explain workplace flexibility (work–life balance).

10.5 Describe customized benefits plans.

10.6 Summarize the issues of communicating information about benefits plans.

MyLab Management

Improve Your Grade!

If your professor is using MyLab Management, visit **www.pearson.com/mylab/management** for videos, simulations, and writing exercises.

Learn It

If your professor has chosen to assign this, go to **www.pearson.com/mylab/management** to see what you should particularly focus on and to take the Chapter 10 Warm-Up.

In Chapter 9, we considered the importance of monetary compensation, which contributes to recruitment and retention of highly qualified employees. Assorted surveys reveal the same for employee benefits. For instance, an Employee Benefit Research Institute survey revealed that 77 percent of employees said that a company's benefits package is either very important or extremely important in their decision to accept or reject a job offer.[1] In a Society for Human Resource Management (SHRM) survey, human resource (HR) professionals reported changing benefits packages to promote retention. For example, 61 percent made changes to health care benefits, 31 percent modified flexible work arrangements, and 25 percent adjusted retirement savings and planning benefits.[2]

10.1 Define *indirect financial compensation (employee benefits).*

Indirect Financial Compensation (Employee Benefits)

indirect financial compensation (employee benefits)
All financial rewards that are not included in direct financial compensation.

Most organizations recognize that they have a responsibility to their employees to provide certain benefits such as insurance and other programs for their health, safety, security, and general welfare (see Figure 10-1). **Indirect financial compensation (employee benefits)** consists of all financial rewards not included in direct financial compensation. These rewards typically account for about 30 percent of a firm's financial compensation costs. As stated in Chapter 9, in March 2017, companies spent on average, $35.28 per hour worked per employee for wages and employee benefits for all civilian workers. Of this total, companies spent $24.10 on wages and $11.18 on all employee benefits.[3] Benefits accounted for 31.6 percent of total compensation costs. The increase in the cost of employee benefits was greater, equalling 12.6 percent.[4] The most expensive benefit was health insurance, which cost $2.94 per hour worked for each employee.[5]

As a rule, employees receive benefits because of their membership in the organization. Benefits are typically unrelated to employee productivity; therefore, although they may be valuable

FIGURE 10-1
Indirect Financial Compensation (Employee Benefits)

EXTERNAL ENVIRONMENT

INTERNAL ENVIRONMENT

Compensation

Financial		Nonfinancial	
Direct	**Indirect (Benefits)**	**The Job**	**Job Environment**
	Legally Required Benefits	Meaningful	Sound Policies
	Health Care	Appreciated	Capable Managers
	Social Security	Satisfying	Competent Employees
	Unemployment Compensation	Learning	Congenial Co-workers
	Workers' Compensation	Enjoyable	Appropriate Status Symbols
	Discretionary Benefits	Challenging	Working Conditions
	Paid Time-Off		**Workplace Flexibility**
	Life Insurance		Flextime
	Retirement Plans		Compressed Workweek
	Disability Protection		Job Sharing
	Employee Stock Option Plans		Telecommuting
	Employee Services		Part-Time Work
	Premium Pay		

HR Web Wisdom

Employee Benefits

www.ifebp.org

It is important to stay abreast of the latest developments in employee benefits practice.

in recruiting and retaining employees, they do not generally serve as motivation for improved performance.[6] For instance, excellent performers do not receive more comprehensive health insurance coverage than average performers.

Employee benefits derive from two broad sources. First, the U.S. federal government requires that most employers contribute so that employees can receive certain benefits. We refer to these items as *legally required benefits*. Laws such as the Social Security Act of 1935 mandate a variety of programs designed to provide income to retired workers, disability income, survivor benefits, and health care for older Americans; and, these programs are administered by federal government agencies. Legally required benefits can take other forms such as workers' compensation insurance, which the employer purchases and administers. Moreover, some cities and states have legislation that enhance federal government benefits such as paid sick leave. Second, companies may choose to offer additional benefits on a discretionary basis—for example, educational benefits and retirement savings plans. We refer to choice benefits as *discretionary benefits*. Discretionary benefits are benefit payments made because of unilateral management decisions in non-union firms and from labor-management negotiations in unionized firms.

FYI

The cost of employee benefits differs for the government and private sectors (per hour worked for each employee):

- Local and state government: $17.90 ($2.68 for legally required benefits; $15.22 for discretionary benefits);
- Private sector: $10.06 ($2.60 for legally required benefits; $7.46 for discretionary benefits).[7]

10.2 Describe legally required benefits and the various kinds.

Legally Required Benefits

The U.S. government established programs to protect individuals from catastrophic events such as disability and unemployment. Legally required benefits are protection programs that attempt to promote worker safety and health, maintain family income streams, and assist families in crisis. The cost of legally required benefits to employers is quite high. As of March 2017, U.S. companies spent an average of $5,408 per employee annually to provide legally required benefits.[8] HR staffs and compensation professionals must follow a variety of laws as they develop and implement programs.

Legally required benefits historically provided a form of social insurance. Prompted largely by the rapid growth of industrialization in the United States in the early 19th and 20th centuries and the Great Depression of the 1930s, initial social insurance programs were designed to minimize the possibility that individuals who became unemployed or severely injured while working would become destitute. In addition, social insurance programs aimed to stabilize the well-being of dependent family members of injured or unemployed individuals. Furthermore, early social insurance programs enabled retirees to maintain subsistence income levels. These intents of legally required benefits remain intact today.

The most substantial legally required benefits include various kinds of Social Security benefits, unemployment insurance, workers' compensation, and employer-sponsored health care.

Social Security

The Social Security Act of 1935 created a retirement benefits program. Amendments to the act added other forms of protection, such as disability insurance (1965) and survivors' benefits (1939). The acronym—OASDI—stands for the Old-Age (that is, retirement), Survivor, and Disability Insurance programs. The government instituted Medicare in 1965.

Disability insurance protects employees against loss of earnings resulting from total incapacity. *Survivors' benefits* provide family members with payments when the employee dies. Family members include the widow or widower and unmarried children. Unmarried children may be eligible for survivors' benefits until they are 18-years-old. In some cases, students retain eligibility until they are 19. *Medicare* provides hospital and medical insurance protection for individuals 65 years of age and older and for those who have become disabled at an earlier age.

The Federal Insurance Contribution Act (FICA) requires that employees and employers pay a portion of the cost of OASDI and Medicare coverage. Both the employer and employee each pay 6.2 percent of an employee's pay for the Social Security portion and 1.45 percent for Medicare. FICA and Medicare (or HI for hospital insurance) designations in paychecks refer to these deductions. Self-employed individuals pay the entire amount (15.3 percent). The Social Security rate applies up to a maximum taxable wage of $127,200, which is subject to increase each year. Annual pay above the taxable wage base is not subject to FICA tax. The rate for Medicare applies to all earnings. Approximately 95 percent of the workers in this country pay into and may draw Social Security benefits. In 2017, approximately 61 million people were receiving at least one type of Social Security benefit.[9]

The age for receiving full Social Security retirement benefits is increasing slowly until it reaches 67. These changes will not affect Medicare, with full eligibility under this program holding at age 65.

Unemployment Insurance

unemployment insurance
Provides workers whose jobs have been terminated through no fault of their own monetary payments for up to 26 weeks, or until they find a new job.

Unemployment insurance provides workers whose jobs have been terminated through no fault of their own monetary payments until they find a new job, up to 26 weeks. The basic program is state-run with oversight from the U.S. Department of Labor. States pay the benefits; the federal government pays the states for administrative costs. Employers pay the Federal Unemployment Tax at a rate of 6.0 percent (2017 rate) on the first $7,000 each employee earns. The permanent Extended Benefits Program provides an additional 13 or 20 weeks of compensation to workers who exhaust basic benefits in states where unemployment has worsened.

The intent of unemployment payments is to provide an unemployed worker time to find a new job equivalent to the one lost without suffering financial distress. Without this benefit, workers might have to take jobs for which they are underqualified. Unemployment compensation also serves to sustain consumer spending during periods of economic adjustment. In the United States, both federal and state statutes established unemployment insurance programs, and although the federal government provides guidelines, states administer them, and therefore benefits vary by state. Unlike Social Security retirement and Medicare benefits, only the employer pays unemployment tax.

Workers' Compensation

Self-employment and the employment of family members was common in agriculture-based economies. The industrialized economy, in contrast, mainly entailed ownership of manufacturing facilities that employed scores of workers. Many workers became seriously ill or injured while performing their jobs due to the absence of health and safety regulations. (The U.S. Congress passed the Occupational Safety and Health Act [OSHA] in the early 1970s.) In the 1800s and early 1900s, seriously injured and ill workers had virtually no recourse, because social insurance programs to protect injured and ill workers were nonexistent.[10] Thus, these workers faced impoverishment.

workers' compensation Provides a degree of financial protection for employees who incur expenses resulting from job-related accidents or illnesses.

Workers' compensation provides a degree of financial protection for employees who incur expenses resulting from job-related accidents or illnesses in the form of coverage of rehabilitation costs and temporary or permanent partial income replacement based on severity. As with unemployment insurance compensation, the various states administer individual programs, which are subject to federal regulations. Employers pay the entire cost of workers' compensation insurance, and their experience with job-related accidents and illnesses largely determines their premium expense. These circumstances should provide further encouragement to employers to be proactive with health and safety programs.

Health Care

Until the passage of the Patient Protection and Affordable Care Act (PPACA or ACA) of 2010, companies chose whether to offer health care plans. Since then, most must provide employees with affordable health care options. Failure to provide affordable health coverage results in costly penalties. We will discuss the ACA later in this section.

As noted earlier, health care coverage represents the most expensive employee benefit. In fact, according to data from the Organization for Economic Co-Operation and Development, the United States spends more per person on health care than any other country.[11] These costs threaten to go even higher.[12] The Office of Management and Budget indicated that the United States spent more than $3.2 trillion in health care per year in health-care costs.[13] Costs will likely increase 5.8 percent annually through 2025. Some companies have reduced or eliminated salary increases or bonuses, or both, to provide increasingly expensive medical benefits for employees.

A few factors have combined to create the high cost of health care:

- An aging population
- A growing demand for medical care
- Increasingly expensive medical technology

Companies can choose from the following ways to provide health-care coverage, and larger companies usually offer more than one option:

- Fee-for-service plans
- Alternative managed care plans
- Any health-care plan associated with consumer-driven health care

fee-for-service plans Insurance protection for three types of medical expenses: hospital expenses, surgical expenses, and physician's charges.

deductible Over a designated period, employees must pay for services before the insurance plan begins to pay for services.

out-of-pocket maximum The maximum amount an employee pays for health care during a calendar or plan year.

coinsurance The percentage of covered expenses paid by the insured. Most fee-for-service plans stipulate 20 percent coinsurance. This means that the insured will pay 20 percent of covered expenses, whereas the insurance company pays the remaining 80 percent.

FEE-FOR-SERVICE PLANS **Fee-for-service plans** provide protection against health care expenses in the form of a cash benefit paid to the insured or directly to the health care provider after the employee has received health care services. That is, these plans pay benefits on a reimbursement basis. Three types of eligible health expenses are hospital expenses, surgical expenses, and physician charges. Under fee-for-service plans, policyholders (employees) may generally select any licensed physician, surgeon, or medical facility for treatment.

Fee-for-service plans contain a variety of stipulations designed to control costs and to limit a covered individual's financial liability. Some of the common fee-for-service stipulations include deductibles, coinsurance, out-of-pocket maximums, and maximum benefits limits. We will consider some of these features. Over a designated period, employees must pay for services before the insurance plan begins to pay for services. This feature is referred to as a **deductible**. The deductible is usually a fixed amount ranging anywhere between $100 and $6,000 depending on the plan. Deductible amounts may also depend on annual earnings, expressed either as a fixed amount for a range of earnings or as a percentage of income.

Most insurance plans feature coinsurance, which becomes relevant after the insured pays the deductible. **Coinsurance** refers to the percentage of covered expenses paid by the insured. Most fee-for-service plans stipulate 20 percent coinsurance. This means that the plan will pay 80 percent of covered expenses, whereas the policyholder is responsible for the difference, in this case, 20 percent up to an out-of-pocket maximum amount.

managed care plans
Health care delivery that emphasizes cost control by limiting an employee's choice of doctors and hospitals. These plans also provide protection against health care expenses in the form of prepayment to health care providers.

prepaid medical services
HMOs are sometimes described as providing prepaid medical services because fixed periodic enrollment fees cover HMO members for all medically necessary services only if the services are delivered or approved by the HMO.

copayments
Fixed amount paid for medical services and the amount varies by type of service.

primary care physicians
Designated by HMOs to determine whether patients require the care of a medical specialist. This functions to control costs by reducing the number of medically unnecessary visits to expensive specialists.

consumer-driven health care
Refers to the objective of helping companies maintain control over costs while also enabling employees to make greater choices about health care.

high-deductible health insurance plans
Plans that require substantially higher deductibles compared to managed care plans and traditional fee-for-service plans.

health savings account (HSA)
Tax-free health spending and savings accounts available to individuals and families who have qualified high-deductible health insurance policies as determined by IRS regulation.

MANAGED CARE PLANS **Managed care plans** emphasize cost control by limiting an employee's choice of doctors and hospitals. The most common is Health Maintenance Organizations (HMO). HMOs provide **prepaid medical services** because fixed periodic enrollment fees cover HMO members for all medically necessary services only if the HMO approves or delivers services. HMOs generally provide hospital care, as well as services from physicians, surgeons, and other health care professionals.

HMO plans share several features in common with fee-for-service plans; however, HMOs differ from fee-for-service plans in three important ways. First, HMOs offer prepaid services, whereas fee-for-service plans operate on a reimbursement basis. Second, HMOs include the use of primary care physicians as a cost-control measure. Third, managed care plans rely on copayments rather than coinsurance to describe cost sharing between patients and insurance companies. **Copayments** refer to fixed amounts that vary by the service. For example, the copayment to visit the primary care physician tends to be lowest (e.g., $20) and emergency room visits are usually most expensive (e.g., $250).

HMOs designate some of their physicians, usually general or family practitioners, as primary care physicians. HMOs assign each member to a primary care physician or require each member to choose one. **Primary care physicians** determine when patients need the care of specialists. HMOs use primary care physicians to control costs by significantly reducing the number of unnecessary visits to specialists.

CONSUMER-DRIVEN HEALTH CARE PLANS Managed care plans became popular alternatives to fee-for-service plans mainly to help employers and insurance companies more effectively manage the costs of health care. As discussed, managed care plans by design imposed substantial restrictions on an employee's ability to make choices about from whom they could receive medical treatment—the gatekeeper role of primary care physicians—and the level of benefits they could receive based on designated in- and non-network providers.

Despite the cost control objectives of managed care, health care costs have continued to rise dramatically over the years while also restricting employee choice. Companies continue to find better ways to control the costs of health insurance. Increasingly, companies are adopting a **consumer-driven health-care plan (CDHP)** approach. This approach refers to the objective of helping companies maintain control over costs while also enabling employees to make wise choices about their health care. **High-deductible health insurance plans (HDHPs)** require substantially higher deductibles compared to managed care plans and traditional fee-for-service plans. What exactly distinguishes an HDHP from traditional health-care plans? For employee-only coverage, the minimum annual deductible is $1,300 with a maximum out-of-pocket limit at or below $6,550 in 2017. For family coverage, the deductible is $2,600 with a maximum out-of-pocket limit at or below $13,100. Generally, deductibles and copayments count toward the maximum out-of-pocket limit. Membership in these plans has increased steadily since 2006—from 7 percent to 28 percent in 2015.[14] They are a good way for employers to provide the same caliber of benefits to their employees while also reducing premiums and involving employees in managing the cost of coverage.

Companies may choose to combine a HDHP with a **health savings account (HSA)**. An HSA is a tax-free health spending and savings account available to individuals and families who have qualified high-deductible health insurance policies as determined by government regulations. HSAs are an important tool in the search to change consumers' health care spending behaviors and better manage health costs. It gives individuals a stake in managing their own health care dollars. Individuals and their employers deposit up to $6,550 a year in a pretax account to pay for deductibles for doctor visits, prescriptions, and other health expenses, as well as saving for future and long-term medical expenses. HSA-eligible health plans typically have lower premiums than other plans because of their higher deductibles. Another advantage is that even if a worker takes another job, the HSA stays with that individual.[15]

LEGISLATION PERTAINING TO HEALTH CARE With the high cost of medical care, an individual without health care insurance is vulnerable. The *Consolidated Omnibus Budget Reconciliation Act (COBRA)* of 1985 gives employees the opportunity to continue their coverage temporarily, which they would otherwise lose because of termination, layoff, or other changes in employment status. The act applies to employers with 20 or more employees. Under COBRA, individuals may keep their coverage, as well as coverage for their spouses and dependents, for up to 18 months after their employment ceases. Certain qualifying events can extend this coverage for up to 36 months. The individual, however, must pay for this health insurance.

The *Older Workers Benefit Protection Act* (*OWBPA*), the 1990 amendment to the Age Discrimination in Employment Act, placed additional restrictions on employer benefits practices. For instance, under certain circumstances, employers can require older employees to pay more for health care, disability, or life insurance than younger employees because these benefits generally become costlier with age; older workers may be more likely to incur serious illnesses, thus, insurance companies may charge employers higher rates.

The *Health Insurance Portability and Accountability Act* (*HIPAA*) of 1996 ensures that individuals will have ready access to coverage under a subsequent employer's health plan, regardless of their health or claims experience. In addition, HIPAA protects the transfer, disclosure, and use of health-care information. HIPAA requires written approval before a person's health care provider shares information with others.

The *Patient Protection and Affordable Care Act* (*PPACA* or *ACA*) of 2010, is often called "ObamaCare," named after former President Barack Obama who championed the law. The law created considerable political debate because it effectively reshaped major portions of the health care industry in the United States.[16] The act is based on the idea that when more people have health insurance—young, healthy people in addition to older, sicker people—risk will be spread out and costs will come down. Following are some of the major features of the law:

- All individuals are required to have health insurance coverage if they do not receive health coverage through their employer. Those who choose not to have insurance will pay a penalty.
- Employers are required to offer employees affordable health insurance or pay a penalty. Coverage is excessive if an employee premium contribution is above 9.5 percent of family income. To handle this situation, some companies are considering offering wage-based premiums where lower-wage earners pay less than those who are more highly paid.[17]
- Children can stay on their parents' policy until they are 26.
- Insurance companies cannot cancel a policy if the insured gets sick.
- An insurance company cannot deny coverage simply because of a pre-existing condition, which is a medical condition for which a diagnosis was made or treatment given prior to enrolling in a health-care plan.
- There is no maximum limit on insurance coverage.
- Pre-existing conditions are covered immediately.

It may appear odd to have a topic regarding smoke-free workplaces in the chapter on benefits, but the ACA justifies the placement. Insurance companies may charge tobacco users up to one and a half times the price that a nonuser pays for the same insurance plan. The law permits charging different rates because it is well documented that smokers increase health care costs because they tend to be ill more than nonsmokers are. The following paragraphs highlight the cost of smoking to organizations.

Ann Skye, wellness manager at Quintiles Transnational Corporation, said, "Smoking is the number one culprit in poor health, and its negative effects are indisputable. We feel it would be irresponsible for any employee wellness program not to aggressively address tobacco use."[18] Smoking is the biggest factor in controllable health care costs. According to the Centers for Disease Control and Prevention, cigarette smoking is the leading cause of preventable death in this country, accounting for roughly 480,000 deaths.[19] Numerous studies have concluded that workplace smoking is not only hazardous to employees' health, but also detrimental to the firm's financial health. Statistics show that cigarette smoking costs $156 billion in productivity losses in the workplace annually.[20] Employees who smoke consume more health-care resources, experience greater absenteeism, and tend to be less productive while at work.

Employers have grown increasingly intolerant of smokers and many workplaces are smoke-free, although about 36.5 million Americans continue to smoke.[21] Even though some smokers remain adamant that passive cigarette smoke is not harmful, the Surgeon General has concluded that there is no safe level of secondhand smoke exposure. The evidence that secondhand tobacco smoke causes serious harm becomes more concrete every day and may be an under-recognized cause of heart attack deaths. Having smoke-free workplace policies helps to fulfill an employer's legal obligation to provide a safe workplace under the Occupational Safety and Health Act's general duty clause, which requires organizations to furnish a workplace free from recognized hazards that are causing or are likely to cause death or serious physical harm. The policy also reduces the risk of litigation, potentially reduces workers' compensation premiums, and protects employees from harm.

According to the Centers for Disease Control, 50,000 people die from exposure to secondhand smoke each year.[22] A study released by the University of Minnesota Cancer Center revealed that nonsmoking employees had up to 25 times more nicotine in their bodies on days when they worked in restaurants and bars than on days they were not at work.[23]

Recently, companies are also using penalties against workers for unhealthy behaviors. The most common penalty is higher premium benefits and increased deductibles. At PepsiCo, smokers pay an annual $600 insurance surcharge, and Gannett Publishing charges an additional $60 per month. Some business owners have taken a personal stand against smoking in general, not just smoking in the workplace. Alaska Airlines, Union Pacific, and Turner Broadcasting have refused to hire smokers for more than 20 years.[24] Four employees from Weyco, a firm that manages benefit plans for workers on behalf of other companies, were fired after refusing to take a nicotine test to determine whether they had smoked. President Howard Weyers said, "Some call this a violation of privacy, pointing to the principle that what you do in your own home is your own business. But they forget the part about so long as it doesn't harm anyone else."[25] There potentially may be a problem with such a policy because 30 states and the District of Columbia have "lifestyle" statutes that limit an employer's ability to make adverse employment decisions based on what employees or applicants do while off duty. Some of those statutes may prevent an employer from terminating an employee or refusing to hire an applicant who smokes.[26]

10.3 Define *discretionary benefits* and explain the various types.

Discretionary Benefits

discretionary benefits
Benefit payments made because of unilateral management decisions in non-union firms and from labor–management negotiations in unionized firms.

Discretionary benefits are benefit payments made because of unilateral management decisions in non-union firms and from labor–management negotiations in unionized firms. An employee's desire for a specific benefit may change, requiring organizations to check the pulse of its workforce to determine the most sought after benefits. Discretionary benefits fall into three broad categories: *protection programs*, *paid time off*, and *services*. Protection programs provide family benefits, promote health, and guard against income loss caused by such catastrophic factors as unemployment, disability, or serious illnesses. Paid time off provides employees time off with pay for such events as vacation or holidays. Services provide such enhancements as tuition reimbursement and day-care assistance to employees and their families.

As we noted, social maladies prompted some federal and state legislation that created employee benefits. Quite different from these reasons are other factors that have contributed to the rise in discretionary benefits.

Most discretionary benefits originated in the 1940s and 1950s. During both World War II and the Korean War, the federal government mandated that companies not increase employees' wages or salaries, but it did not place restrictions on companies' employee benefits expenditures. Companies invested in expanding their offerings of discretionary benefits as an alternative to pay hikes as a motivational tool to enhance worker productivity.

Separate from the benevolence of employers, employee unions *directly* contributed to the increase in employee welfare practices through the National Labor Relations Act (NLRA) of 1935, which legitimized bargaining for employee benefits. Union workers tend to participate more in benefits plans than do non-union employees (94 percent versus 66 percent).[27] Unions also *indirectly* contributed to the rise in benefits offerings because non-union companies often fashion employment practices after union companies as an approach to minimize the chance that employees will seek union representation and may offer employees benefits that are comparable to the benefits received by employees in union settings.

FYI

Access to employee benefits differs based on full- and part-time work status:

	Health	Retirement	Life Insurance	Vacation
Full time	88%	81%	75%	87%
Part time	19%	38%	13%	35%[28]

Retirement Plans

Retirement income security is a major concern to individuals of all ages, but particularly to the members of the baby boom generation who are entering retirement in unprecedented numbers. Individuals rely on three sources for retirement income. Employer-sponsored retirement plans provide employees with income after they have met a minimum retirement age and have left the company. Second, as we discussed previously in this chapter, the Social Security OASDI program provides government-mandated retirement income to employees who have made sufficient contributions through payroll taxes. Third, individuals may use their initiative to take advantage of tax regulations that have created such retirement programs as individual retirement accounts (IRAs) and Roth IRAs. Our focus will be on employer-sponsored retirement plans.

According to the Employee Benefit Research Institute, the first plan in the United States, established in 1759, benefited widows and children of Presbyterian ministers.[29] Then, in the private sector, the American Express Company established a formal pension plan in 1875. Plans were adopted primarily in the railroad, banking, and public utility industries, and eventually became increasingly popular in the private sector. It is believed that more and more companies adopted retirement plans to attract and retain employees. Nevertheless, there were limits to which companies chose to retain employees. Approximately 30 years of service qualifies an employee for retirement benefits, and the mandatory retirement age was 65 in most states during the early twentieth century. According to economics professor Joanna Short, "Because of the lengthy service requirement and mandatory retirement provision, firms viewed pensions to reduce labor turnover and as a more humane way to remove older, less productive employees."[30] The most significant growth occurred after the government granted favorable tax treatment through the passage of the Revenue Act of 1921 and the Revenue Act of 1928. During World War II, government-imposed wage controls led companies to adopt discretionary employee benefits plans, which were excluded from those wage increase restrictions. As we will see in Chapter 11, the National Labor Relations Act of 1935 instituted retirement plans as a mandatory subject of bargaining subject between unions and management. This requirement contributed substantially to the growth of retirement plans in the union work setting.

qualified plans Welfare and pension plans that meet various requirements set forth by the Employee Retirement Income Security Act of 1974; these plans entitle employees and employers to favorable tax treatment by deducting the contributions from taxable income. Qualified plans do not disproportionately favor highly compensated employees.

nonqualified plans Welfare and pension plans that do not meet various requirements set forth by the Employee Retirement Income Security Act of 1974 (ERISA), disallowing favorable tax treatment for employee and employer contributions.

As noted, tax incentives encourage companies to offer pension programs. Some of the Employee Retirement Income Security Act (ERISA) of 1974 provisions set the minimum standards required to "qualify" pension plans for favorable tax treatment. Failure to meet any of the minimum standard provisions "disqualifies" pension plans for favorable tax treatment. **Qualified plans** meet these minimum standards. **Nonqualified plans** refer to pension plans that do not meet at least one of the minimum standard provisions; typically, highly paid employees benefit from participation in nonqualified plans.

vesting An employee's non-forfeitable rights to retirement plan benefits.

cliff vesting schedule Employers must grant employees 100 percent vesting after no more than three service years.

6-year graduated schedule Workers become 20 percent vested after 2 years and to vest at a rate of 20 percent each year thereafter until they are 100 percent vested after 6 years of service.

One of the minimum standards is vesting. **Vesting** refers to an employee's non-forfeitable rights to retirement plan benefits.[31] Keep in mind that an employee always possesses ownership of their contributions and any investment gains (accrued benefit). Vesting applies to the employer's accrued contribution on your behalf. Some employers may grant vesting rights immediately; however, most follow the ERISA guidelines. There are two options: cliff vesting schedule or 6-year graduated schedule. Under a **cliff vesting schedule** employers must grant employees 100 percent vesting after no more than three service years. That is, after 3 years of participation in the retirement plan, an employee has the right to receive all the accrued employer's contributions made on your behalf. Leaving one's job prior to vesting under this schedule is the same as falling off a cliff—an employee loses all the accrued employer contributions. On the other hand, companies may use a graduated vesting schedule. The **6-year graduated schedule** allows workers to become 20 percent vested after 2 years and to vest at a rate of 20 percent each year thereafter until they are 100 percent vested after 6 years of service.

Companies establish retirement plans following one of three design configurations: defined benefit plans, defined contribution plans, or hybrid plans that combine features of traditional defined benefit and defined contribution plans. We will review each type next.

defined benefit plan Retirement plan that provides the participant with a fixed benefit throughout retirement.

DEFINED BENEFIT PLANS A **defined benefit plan** is a formal retirement plan that provides the participant with a life-long fixed benefit throughout retirement. Although defined benefit formulas vary, typical factors include the participant's final years' average salary, years of service, and age. These generous plans provide 50 to 80 percent of an employee's final earnings. For instance, assume

HR Web Wisdom

Types of Retirement Plans

www.dol.gov/dol/topic/retirement/

Retirement information from the U.S. Department of Labor.

defined contribution plan
Retirement plan that requires specific contributions by an employee or an employer to a retirement or savings fund established for the employee.

401(k) plan
Defined contribution plan in which employees may defer income up to a maximum amount allowed.

matching contribution
Money the employer deposits into an employee's defined contribution account contingent on the employee contributing first.

cash balance plan
Retirement plan with elements of both defined benefit and defined contribution plans.

that a person's final average annual earnings are $50,000 in a plan that pays 50 percent. She or he would earn annual benefit equaling $25,000. Use of defined benefit plans has substantially declined in recent years. In 2015, only 15 percent of employees participated in defined benefit plans.[32] There are two key reasons for this low participation rate. First, the employer must ensure payment of benefits to retirees. In some years, larger contributions are required based on the level of investment performance. Second, longer life expectancies have contributed to the costliness of these plans.

DEFINED CONTRIBUTION PLANS The most popular option is the defined contribution with 44 percent employee participation.[33] A **defined contribution plan** permits employees to contribute to their accounts based on a chosen percentage of annual pay. At their discretion, the company makes matching contributions, which we will review shortly. Most *Fortune 100* companies offer employees only a defined contribution plan. Employees know in advance how much employers will contribute to a defined contribution plan; the amount of retirement income from a defined contribution plan will depend on the investment success of the investment fund.

There is a variety of defined contribution plans. The most common is the 401(k) plan. A **401(k) plan** is a defined contribution plan in which employees may defer income up to a maximum amount allowed. Sometimes, the employer chooses to add to employees' 401(k) accounts. A **matching contribution** is money the employer deposits into an employee's defined contribution account contingent on the employee contributing first. For instance, assume that an employer contributes 50 cents for each dollar contributed by an employee. Also, assume that an employee has an annual salary of $100,000 and contributes 10 percent to his or her defined contribution account ($10,000). Based on this match policy, the company would deposit $5,000 into the employee's account (50 percent × $10,000). You will have the opportunity to explore matching contributions in the *HR by the Numbers* feature at the end of this chapter.

CASH BALANCE PLANS For some organizations, a hybrid arrangement may be the desired approach to retirement plans. A **cash balance plan** is a plan with elements of both defined benefit and defined contribution plans. During economic recessions, 401(k) account balances substantially decline. Thus, many employers felt having employees assume 100 percent of the risks was too much. A middle ground uses a cash balance plan. When used as a stand-alone plan, a cash balance plan provides all the benefits that would otherwise be available under a standard defined benefit plan. It resembles a defined contribution plan because it uses an account balance to communicate the benefit amount. However, it is closer to being a defined benefit plan because the employer normally bears the responsibility for and the risks of managing the assets.[34]

Coca-Cola has a cash balance plan for all employees. Kevin Wagner, a senior retirement consultant in the Atlanta office of Watson Wyatt Worldwide, which worked with Coca-Cola in designing the cash balance plan, said, "It is refreshing to see a company understand the value of its defined benefit plan, which, at least in Coca-Cola's situation, brings great value to both the company and its employees."[35] Other companies that have converted to cash balance plans include Bank of America, Boeing, FedEx, Honeywell International, Massachusetts General Hospital, and 3M.

LEGISLATION PERTAINING TO RETIREMENT PLANS Two important laws influence retirement design, funding, and implementation: *Employee Retirement Income Security Act (ERISA)* of 1974 and *Pension Protection Act (PPA)* of 2006. ERISA regulates the implementation and administration of various employee benefits programs, particularly defined benefit programs. Since the law's passage, amendments extend to the design and operations of defined contribution and cash balance plans as well.

ERISA has several major objectives:

- To ensure that workers and beneficiaries receive adequate information about their benefits plans.
- To set standards of conduct for those managing employee-benefits plans and plan funds.
- To determine that adequate funds are being set aside to pay promised pension benefits.
- To ensure that workers receive pension benefits after they have satisfied certain minimum requirements (vesting).
- To safeguard pension benefits for workers whose pension plans are terminated (Pension Benefit Guarantee Corporation [PBGC]). The PBGC is a government agency that ensures that employees owed benefits under private-sector defined benefit pensions receive those benefits if a company terminates its plan.

The PPA strengthened protections for employees' company-sponsored retirement plans in at least two ways. First, this law should strengthen the financial condition of the PBGC by requiring that private sector companies that underfund their defined benefit plans pay substantially higher costs to ensure payment of retirement benefits.

Second, the PPA makes it easier for employees to participate in employer-sponsored defined contribution plans such as 401(k) plans. Millions of workers who are eligible to participate in defined contribution plans do not contribute to them. There are various reasons why employees choose not to participate, however, a prominent reason is that most individuals feel they do not have sufficient knowledge about choosing investment options (e.g., a high-risk mutual fund versus a fixed-rate annuity). In addition, once employees make the decision to participate in these plans and have been making regular contributions, they are not likely to stop. With these issues in mind, the PPA enables companies to enroll employees automatically in defined contribution plans and provides greater access to professional advice about investing for retirement. The act further requires that companies give multiple investment options to allow employees to select how much risk they are willing to bear. As an aside, risky investments usually have the greater potential for substantial gains or losses in value. Less risky investments usually have the potential for lower gains or losses.

Life Insurance and Disability Insurance

Employer-sponsored life insurance protects employees' families by paying a specified amount upon the employee's death. These plans often include accidental death and dismemberment claims, which pay additional benefits if death was the result of an accident or if the employee incurs accidental loss of a limb. The cost of group life insurance is relatively low, costing employers about $105 annually per employee.[36] Perhaps because of the low cost, approximately 95 percent of employers pay the entire life insurance premium.[37] Two of the more common life insurance plans are term life and whole life. **Term life insurance** provides protection to employees' beneficiaries only during a limited period based on a specified number of years subject to a maximum age. After that, the insurance automatically expires. **Whole life insurance** pays an amount to the designated beneficiaries of the deceased employee, but unlike term life policies, whole life plans do not terminate after beneficiaries receive payment.

term life insurance
Protection for providing monetary payments to an employee's beneficiaries upon the employee's death and offered only during a limited period based on a specified number of years or maximum age.

whole life insurance
A type of life insurance that provides protection to employees' beneficiaries during employees' employment and into the retirement years.

Workers' compensation protects employees from job-related accidents and illnesses. Some firms, however, provide additional protection that is more comprehensive. When short-term benefits run out, a firm's long-term plan may become active; such a plan may provide 50 to 70 percent of an employee's pretax pay. Long-term disability provides a monthly benefit to employees who because of illness or injury are unable to work for an extended period.

Paid Time-Off

Most employers recognize that employees need time away from the job for many purposes. Discussed in the following sections are vacations, sick pay and paid time off banks, parental leave, sabbaticals, volunteerism, and other forms of paid time off.

VACATION Vacation time serves important compensation goals. For instance, vacations help workers to be more creative and productive, reduce stress, brings families and friends closer, and improves job performance.[38] They may also encourage employees to remain with the firm.[39] Vacation time typically increases with seniority. For example, employees with 1 year of service might receive two weeks each year; 10 years' service, three weeks; and 15 years' service, four weeks.

Interestingly, many Americans do not take full advantage of their vacation benefits. A 2017 Alamo Rent A Car Family Vacation Survey revealed that 49 percent of U.S. workers felt guilt by coworkers for using vacation time.[40] Millennial employees were more prone to shaming by their peers than older employees (68 percent versus 37 percent). Some employees believe their employers do not want them to take vacations or are afraid to ask for time off. A Project: Time Off shed insight into why employees feel this way. Fewer than half of the managers surveyed talk to employees once a year or less frequently about vacation.[41] In addition, nearly half (45 percent) of managers themselves did not feel supported in taking time off. Many workers choose not to use any (or much) vacation because they believe that coworkers are not qualified to perform their jobs; and, on the flip side, others are concerned that coworkers will try to steal their jobs. As compared with other countries, the average 13 days Americans take annually is small. According to the Center for Economic and Policy Research, many countries, excluding the United States, have laws that provide for annual vacation. For example, the French take 30 days, British take 28 days, Danes take 25 days, Australians and Italians take 20 days, and Canadians and the Japanese take 10 days.[42] In the absence of a vacation law in the United States, companies choose whether to offer vacation. Typically, U.S. companies offer 10 to 14 vacation days per year.[43] In one survey, Americans lost more than 650 million days in unused vacation in 2016.[44] No doubt, the reasons we discussed account for much of this underutilization.

Companies consider various ways to encourage employees to use all their vacation benefits. For instance, some companies signal the importance of taking vacation by paying employees (additional money) to take vacation. HR professionals often refer to this approach as "paid, paid vacation." Not only do employees receive their pay while on vacation, but they also receive additional compensation. Two standout examples are software companies BambooHR and FullContact.[45] BambooHR reimburses employees up to $2,000 annually for the cost of plane tickets, hotel rooms, and vacation activities. FullContact provides each employee with $7,500 cash to spend on vacation. The following Watch It video describes this highly generous approach to vacations and the company's rationale for offering it.

Watch It I

If your instructor has assigned this, go to **www.pearson.com/mylab/management** to watch a video titled Best Boss Ever Pays Employees to Go on Vacation and respond to questions.

A few other companies offer unlimited paid vacation, including Grubhub, Netflix, LinkedIn, and the Virgin Group. Lindsey Ruthen, public relations associate at Grubhub, stated, "We do so to encourage work/life balance, and because we trust our employees to deliver great results and choose how their time is spent."[46] LinkedIn adopted an unlimited vacation policy as an element in the company's efforts to cultivate a unique corporate culture. Earlier, we said that many American employees do not take full advantage of vacation benefits. Therefore, why do these companies provide unlimited vacation benefits? These companies have created a longstanding culture of trust where employees are less likely to feel threatened by taking time off.[47] In principle, unlimited vacation sounds wonderful! In practice, the jury is still out on whether these plans will catch on or be successful where they already exist. These unlimited policies are simply too new to judge.

SICK PAY AND PAID TIME-OFF BANKS Each year, many firms allocate a certain number of paid sick days they may use when ill. Employees who are too sick to report to work continue to receive their pay up to the maximum number of days accumulated. As with vacation pay, the number of sick pay days often depends on seniority.

Some managers are critical of sick pay programs. At times, individuals have abused the system by calling in sick when all they wanted was an additional day of vacation. One approach in dealing with the problem of unscheduled absences is *paid time off banks*.[48] In lieu of sick leave, vacation time, and a personal day or two, a growing number of companies are providing **paid time off (PTO) banks**, a certain number of days off provided each year those employees can use for any purpose. PTO banks group all categories of time off such as sick leave, vacation, and personal days. Possible benefits from PTOs include simpler administration, high employee satisfaction, fewer creative excuses for time off, earlier notice of time-off needs, fewer last-minute absences, and fewer conflicts about time-off usage.

paid time off (PTO) banks
Means of dealing with the problem of unscheduled absences by providing a certain number of days each year that employees can use for any purpose.

FYI

The number of average annual days allotted in a PTO bank increases with years of service:

- 1 year: 15 days
- 5 years: 19 days
- 10 years: 22 days
- 15 years: 24 days[49]

Some companies are experimenting with different forms of PTO plans. A few companies use a so-called *results-only work environment (ROWE)*. This plan allows employees to work wherever and whenever they wish if they complete projects on time. It often provides the "perfect blend" to the younger generation or those who are young at heart where both work life and personal life can be enjoyed.[50] The attitude of many workers today is that if I can get it done, and get it done well, why does it matter where or when I work?[51] Employers Resource Council, a HR services company based in Mayfield Village, Ohio, gives employees all the time off that they want. There is no schedule and no limit for earned vacation and leave time. The firm's 30 employees must get their work done on time.[52]

Compared to many other countries, companies in the United States offer paid sick leave on a discretionary basis. However, times are changing. In recent years, several states have instituted laws governing paid sick leave and those laws specify the criteria for what constitutes illness. For instance, California law mandates how employees accrue and use paid sick leave benefits. Employers must include a carryover provision for unused sick leave from one calendar year to the next. That is, employees may use unused benefits in future years.

Paid sick laws are not limited to the states. Dozens of cities are jumping in. Seattle requires that employers with 5 to 49 employees provide 5 paid sick days per year, and additional days for larger employers. In San Francisco, employers with 10 or more employees must provide 9 paid sick days and 5 sick days in companies with fewer than 10 employees.

PARENTAL LEAVE The *Family and Medical Leave Act* (*FMLA*) of 1993 mandates that most companies provide employees up to 12 weeks of *unpaid* leave for family reasons, including illness or the birth or adoption of a child. In recent years, many companies voluntarily instituted paid parental leave policies, including Amazon.com Inc., Microsoft Corp., Netflix Inc., and Blackstone Group LP. Netflix offers one of the most generous family benefits, where employees may take up to one year of paid leave to care for a child.

Paid family leave traditionally benefited female workers because they played the role of primary caregiver. Increasingly, companies are working diligently to legitimize paternity leave. There continues to be a social stigma associated with fathers who choose to take time off (paid or unpaid) following the birth or adoption of a child. Unfortunately, a prevalent corporate norm devalues men who take such time off, in part, characterizing them as far less committed to their careers or career advancement. The following Watch It video describes Facebook CEO Mark Zuckerberg's decision to take an extended leave after the birth of his first child, setting an example to legitimize paternity leave by taking extended leave himself.

Watch It 2

If your instructor has assigned this, sign into **www.pearson.com/mylab/management** to watch a video titled Facebook CEO Takes 2 Months Paternity Leave and respond to questions.

sabbaticals
Temporary leaves of absence from an organization, usually at reduced pay.

SABBATICALS **Sabbaticals** are temporary leaves of absence from an organization, usually at reduced pay. Sabbaticals are customary in the academic community, focusing on faculty professional development. Private sector companies are beginning to consider the value of sabbaticals for employees. Approximately 20 percent of companies on *Fortune* magazine's list of the Top 100 Best Companies to Work For provide sabbaticals.[53] Increasingly, companies that offer sabbatical leave benefits focus on rejuvenation, helping employees "recharge their batteries" and return to work as refreshed and poised to be highly productive. According to Marla Kaplowitz, the North America CEO of media agency MEC, "A sabbatical is a way of recognizing that everyone needs a break at a certain point."[54] Sabbaticals come with a cost other than continuing to provide pay and benefits. According to Capterra's CEO, the cost of a sabbatical equals a 10 percent reduction in productivity on an annual basis, but only 2 percent over a five-year period.[55] He maintains that the benefit to the company and the employee's health and personal growth is a worthwhile expense. Eligibility criteria vary widely. At Clif Bar and Company, which manufactures organic food products (for example, protein bars), workers who complete seven years with the company are eligible to take an eight-week sabbatical with full pay.[56] Stonyfield Farm instituted a two-month paid sabbatical for anyone who has worked at least five years with the firm. Xerox has a Social Service Leave program where selected employees receive six-month paid leaves to provide service to the community.[57]

volunteerism
Time to support a meaningful cause.

VOLUNTEERISM **Volunteerism** refers to giving of one's time to support a meaningful cause. More and more companies are providing employees with paid time off to contribute to causes of their choice. In 2013, approximately 20 percent of companies offered paid time off for volunteer activities, trending up since 2007.[58] In many instances, companies tout this benefit as a form of work–life balance and a mechanism for the betterment of the community. Brokerage Company Charles Schwab provides employees with eight paid hours per year for this purpose. Managers have the discretion to provide additional paid time off for volunteer activities.[59] From a company's standpoint, a meaningful cause is associated with the work of not-for-profit organizations, such as the United Way, to help improve the well-being of people. Many meaningful causes throughout the world include improving literacy, providing comfort to terminally ill patients, serving food at homeless shelters, serving as a mentor to children who do not have one or more parents, and spending time with elderly or disabled residents of nursing homes who may no longer have living friends or family. Companies generally do not dictate the causes for which employees would receive paid time off, except they exclude political campaign and political action groups for eligibility because of possible conflicts of interest with company shareholders and management.

Companies favor providing paid time off for volunteer work for three reasons. First, volunteer opportunities allow employees to balance work and life demands. Second, giving employees the opportunity to contribute to charitable causes on company time represents positive corporate social responsibility, enhancing the company's overall image in the public eye. Third, paid time off to volunteer helps to promote retention. Employees are likely to feel that the employer shares similar values, possibly boosting commitment to the company. Salesforce made the *Fortune* magazine's annual rankings of the 100 best companies to work for. One employee said, "This is an extraordinarily special place that really cares about its employees, customers, and community. We are strongly encouraged to give back. I have done everything from volunteering in a soup kitchen, to working at a children's hospital in Morocco—all supported by the company."[60] For younger employees, company-sponsored volunteer benefits can help with recruitment. According to Sales Foundation's Suzanne DiBiana, "In Silicon Valley young graduates and employees are accepting jobs depending upon whether a company has a CSR [corporate social responsibility initiative] in place."[61]

OTHER TYPES OF PAID TIME OFF Although vacations, sick pay and PTO banks, volunteerism, and sabbaticals constitute the largest portion of paid time off benefits,[62] companies use numerous other types. Some companies routinely permit employees to take off during work hours to handle personal affairs without taking vacation time. When a worker participates in jury duty, some organizations continue to pay their salary; others pay the difference between jury pay and their salary. When the National Guard or military reserve are on duty, as has been the case in Afghanistan and Iraq, some companies pay employees a portion of their salary while on active duty. Further, during an election, many companies permit employees voting time. Still other firms permit bereavement time for the death of a close relative. Finally, there is the payment for time not worked while at the company such as rest periods, coffee breaks, lunch periods, cleanup time, and travel time. The Fair Labor Standards Act does not require employers to give workers a rest break, and only nine states require it.[63] In these states, usually the mandated break is 10 minutes for every four hours worked.

Employee Services

Organizations offer a variety of benefits that can be termed "employee services." These benefits encompass several areas, including childcare, educational assistance, food services/subsidized cafeterias, scholarships for dependents, relocation benefits, and benefits for domestic partner and individuals in same-sex marriages.

CHILDCARE A benefit offered by some firms is subsidized childcare. According to the National Conference of State Legislatures, an estimated 80 percent of employees miss work because of unexpected child-care coverage issues. Approximately every $1 invested in backup childcare yields $3 to $4 in returned productivity and benefit. At the Abbott Laboratories headquarters campus 30 miles north of Chicago, the company has built a $10 million state-of-the-art child-care center for more than 400 preschool children of Abbott workers. For parents who prefer a different arrangement, if their babysitter is sick, Abbott provides emergency backup service. Company child-care arrangements tend to reduce absenteeism, protect employee productivity, enhance retention and recruiting, promote the advancement of women, and make the firm an employer of choice.

EDUCATIONAL ASSISTANCE Educational assistance plans can go a long way in improving employee retention. In a recent survey of HR professionals, 58 percent said their organizations offered educational assistance for undergraduate education, and 54 percent offered graduate education assistance.[64] Some companies reimburse employees after they have completed a course with a grade of "C" or above while others provide for advance payment of these expenses. Still, other employers provide half the reimbursement up front and the rest on satisfactory completion of the course. United Technologies Corporation pays an employee's entire tuition and books up front. It also offers paid time off—as much as three hours a week, depending on the course load—to study. Internal Revenue Service regulations allow educational assistance benefits to be nontaxable up to $5,250 per year. Starbucks Coffee is an example of a company that offers generous educational assistance, named the "College Achievement Program." In 2015, the company announced a policy, permitting most employees (approximately 238,000) to earn a bachelor's degree from Arizona State University's online course offerings.

FOOD SERVICES/SUBSIDIZED CAFETERIAS There is generally no such thing as a free lunch. However, firms that supply food services or subsidized cafeterias provide an exception to this rule. What they hope to gain in return is increased productivity, less wasted time, enhanced employee morale, and in some instances, a healthier workforce. Most firms that offer free or subsidized lunches feel that they get a high payback in terms of employee relations. Northwestern Mutual is one such company. Free lunches are available in its cafeterias, where the menus list calories instead of prices. Keeping the lunch hour to a minimum is an obvious advantage, but employees also appreciate the opportunity to meet and mix with people they work with. Making one entree a heart-healthy choice and listing the calories, fat, cholesterol, and sodium content in food is also appealing to many employees.

SCHOLARSHIPS FOR DEPENDENTS Often companies provide scholarships for dependents of employees. Scholarship programs can help boost employee recruitment and retention. Franciscan Health Systems, a nonprofit health care provider in Tacoma, Washington, targets its awards primarily to employees' children who are interested in entering the health care field, although it also awards scholarships for study in other areas. NRG Energy conducts an annual competition for student scholarships up to $60,000 each. An independent committee selects participants to avoid the appearance of favoritism. Committee members include teachers, educators, and other academic professionals.

relocation benefits
Company-paid shipments of household goods and temporary living expenses, covering all or a portion of the real estate costs associated with buying a new home and selling the previously occupied home.

RELOCATION **Relocation benefits** are company-paid shipments of household goods and temporary living expenses, covering all or a portion of the real estate costs associated with buying a new home and selling the previously occupied home. Relocation packages vary but most companies will pay for household moving and packing expenses and temporary living expenses for up to six months until the home sells. Companies may also pay for weekly or bimonthly trips back home over the weekends. On average, companies spent approximately $13,000 per employee in 2014 on corporate relocation within the United States.[65]

Although relocating can be a hassle, it can also produce many benefits. Employees typically feel their employer has made an investment if they relocate and the firm pays all relocation expenses. Some companies have programs that help trailing spouses or partners secure employment. Other firms also provide outplacement help to spouses.

DOMESTIC PARTNER BENEFITS AND SAME-SEX MARRIAGE A challenge facing managers and HR professionals is deciding whether to offer domestic partner or civil union benefits. These arrangements may apply to same-sex or opposite-sex couples and one survey indicated that almost half of all firms offered benefits to opposite-sex domestic partners.[66] However, there has been much press about same-sex benefits. Unmarried domestic partners and those in registered civil unions are more often being included as qualified for coverage under employee benefit plans with larger companies. Of *Fortune 500* companies, about 81 percent offer same-sex partner benefits and 74 percent provide transgender-inclusive benefits.[67] Many companies are reimbursing gay and lesbian employees for the additional taxes they incur for their same-sex domestic partnership health care benefits. For example, New York-based Ernst & Young recently announced it would reimburse eligible employees for the tax, which averaged $1,100 per employee annually.[68]

Numerous counties, states, and municipalities offer domestic partner benefits and provide a basis for comparison of policies, legal hurdles, coverage, and costs. Many states, such as

California, Connecticut, New Jersey, Illinois, Iowa, New York, and Vermont, have joined this trend, as have hundreds of cities and counties. Employers require that employees who wish to enroll in an employer's domestic partner benefits meet eligibility requirements. Domestic partners must be of the same sex, have resided together for a year or more prior to application, and be financially interdependent. In addition, supporting documentation, including a Declaration of Domestic Partnership, is required, but once the domestic partner is added, dependent children are also eligible for coverage.[69] Companies use similar criteria for individuals who are in a registered civil union.

The Supreme Court's *Obergefell v. Hodges* ruling in June 2015 ensured in most cases that same-sex couples possess the same constitutional rights to marry and every state must recognize them. Now, companies are obliged to provide same-sex spouses benefits equal to spouses of opposite-sex marriages. The focus has been particularly on health care coverage.

The court's ruling has raised questions whether companies will continue to offer domestic partner benefits. A recent survey by the International Foundation of Employee Benefits Plans revealed that nearly 30 percent of companies surveyed said they are unlikely to continue to offer domestic partner benefits (and 20 percent for opposite-sex domestic partners).[70] Companies including Verizon, Delta Air Lines, IBM, and Corning eliminated domestic partner benefits. One reason for eliminating domestic partner benefits is equality that all individuals possess the constitutional right to marry regardless of sexual orientation.[71] There is concern among members of the LGBT community who feel that eliminating domestic partner benefits can have negative consequences. Sara Warbelow, legal director of the Human Rights Campaign warned, "If an LGBT employee is, in effect, 'outed' by being required to obtain a public marriage license in a state that doesn't provide explicit non-discrimination protections, it could place that employee and their family at risk of being denied credit, housing, and public accommodation." In 2017, 20 states did not have anti-discrimination laws protecting individuals based on sexual orientation, and three of these states did not include provisions protecting individuals based on gender identity.[72]

OTHER BENEFITS The number of possible service benefits is left to the imagination of companies and goal to attract and retain talent. Examples of additional service benefits include paid public transportation passes and employee discounts. A relatively new benefit is student loan repayment assistance. In 2015, student loan debt averaged more than $30,000 for undergraduate education.[73] Employers have many concerns about the negative impact of high student loan debt. First, there are concerns that employees do not have the resources to contribute to retirement savings plans. Second, retention worries increase because many employees are more likely to seek graduate level education in hopes of earning substantially more pay.[74] Finally, some believe that debt-laden employees are likely to feel substantial stress, possibly interfering with productivity. For instance, technology company NVIDIA is an example. Andrea Trudelle, director of global benefits, said, "As an employer, we want to see our employees lead happy and fruitful lives. Our intent was to improve employees' overall experience and help ease this burden so they can focus on other things."[75]

10.4 Explain workplace flexibility (work–life balance).

Workplace Flexibility (Work–Life Balance)

Effective work/life balance programs focus on solving any personal issues that can detract from an employee's work. For employers, creating a balanced work/life environment can be a key strategic factor in attracting and retaining the most talented employees. As Tina Tchen, executive director of the White House Council on Women and Girls, said, "Flexible work policies are an economic imperative for American families and companies."[76] Workplace flexibility is high on employees' lists of company benefits desired and continues to grow. It has moved from being a great benefit that a company can offer to a business necessity. By providing such an environment, employees are better able to fit family, community, and social commitments into their schedule. The homogeneous workforce that the United States once had is quite different now. Consider the following statistics and envision how the workplace profile has changed: 27 percent of single parents are men, 40 percent of the workforce is unmarried, one in five workers is 50 or older, and four million households are multi-generational. In addition, nearly 25 percent of Americans are caring for elders.[77]

For men and women seeking to balance their work and personal lives, time is nearly as important as money and may even be more important for some.[78] According to a Baylor University study, new mothers who return to work are more likely to stay on the job if they have greater control over their work schedules.[79] More employees are requesting workplace flexible benefits to achieve a better work and life balance. Marcee Harris Schwartz, the New York–based director of BDO USA's Flex program, said, "We do not think of flexibility as a set of options, or an employee benefit, or even a program. We really see it as a business strategy—a strategy that can help employees manage their own working life."[80] Some companies offer many of the factors typically associated with workplace flexibility. State Street Corporation, a multinational financial services provider with more than 29,000 employees in 26 countries, provides five options that give employees flexibility on when, how, and where they work.[81] These include flextime, compressed workweek, job sharing, two-in-a-box, telecommuting, and part-time work.

Flextime

flextime
Practice of permitting employees to choose their own working hours, within certain limitations.

Flextime is the practice of permitting employees to choose their own working hours, within certain limitations. Sometimes, companies offer flexible work hours in lieu of a salary increase, although guaranteed job security ranked number one. An important benefit of flextime is that it can bring better health to employees by reducing employee stress levels. For many old-economy managers who think they must see their employees every minute to make sure they are working, this may be difficult. Primarily, they believe flexible work arrangements could hamper collaboration because work schedules do not align.[82]

In a flextime system, employees typically work the same number of hours per day as they would on a standard schedule. However, they work these hours within what a bandwidth, which is the maximum length of the workday (see Figure 10-2). Core time is that part of the day when all employees must be present. *Flexible time* is the period within which employees may vary their schedules. A typical schedule permits employees to begin work between 6:00 A.M. and 9:00 A.M. and to complete their workday between 3:00 P.M. and 6:00 P.M. Marianne Mansfield, a case worker for the state of Massachusetts goes to work at 6:30 A.M. and is off at 3:00, P.M. a schedule she very much enjoys. This permits her to miss much of Boston's horrible traffic congestion.

Because flexible hours are highly valued today, providing a flexible work schedule gives employers an edge in recruiting new employees and retaining highly qualified ones.[83] In addition, flextime allows employees to expand their opportunities. For example, it may be easier for them to continue their education than if they were on a traditional work schedule. The public also seems to reap benefits from flextime. Transportation services, recreational facilities, medical clinics, and other services assist by reducing competition for service at conventional peak times. Yet, flextime is not suitable for all types of organizations. For example, its use may be severely limited in assembly-line operations and companies using multiple shifts.

Compressed Workweek

compressed workweek
Any arrangement of work hours that permits employees to fulfill their work obligation in fewer days than the typical five-day workweek.

The **compressed workweek** is an arrangement of work hours that permits employees to fulfill their work obligation in fewer days than the typical five-day, 8-hour-a-day workweek. A common compressed workweek is four 10-hour days. Another form of the compressed workweek is four 9-hour days and a half-day on Friday. Some hospitals permit their registered nurses to work three 12-hour days during a workweek. Still other firms are allowing employees to work longer, however, fewer days in the summer in exchange for a day off each week. There are endless different combinations of compressed workweeks.

Working under this arrangement, employees have reported greater job satisfaction. In addition, the compressed workweek offers the potential for better use of leisure time for family life,

FIGURE 10-2
Illustration of Flextime

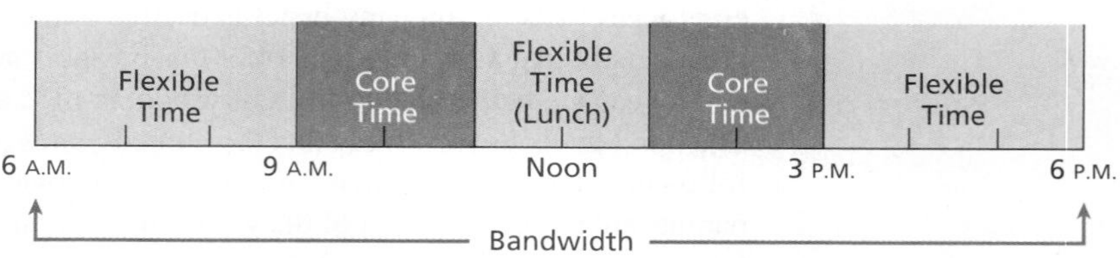

personal business, and recreation. Employers in some instances have cited advantages such as increased productivity and reduced turnover and absenteeism. Other firms, however, have encountered difficulty in scheduling workers' hours and at times employees become fatigued from working longer hours. In some cases, these problems have resulted in lower product quality and reduced customer service.

Job Sharing

job sharing
Two part-time people split the duties of one job in some agreed-on manner and are paid according to their contributions.

In **job sharing**, two part-time people split the duties of one job in some agreed-on manner and receive pay according to their contributions. It is an attractive option to people who want to work fewer than 40 hours per week.

Some have equated the benefits job sharing provides to that of running a marathon. Given equal athletic ability, two athletes running half a marathon back to back will invariably run faster than one runner going the entire distance alone will. Although the arrangements vary, the outcome is the same: Job sharing provides the flexibility to enjoy life. It provides an option to retain workers, particularly women who often opt out of the workforce to raise families. Often job sharers work as hard in, say, three days, as those working full time and are pleased they can combine work and motherhood or other interests.

There appears to be a growing trend as more companies offer job sharing. Two Ford Motor Company engineers used job sharing as a means of advancing their careers and still have time with their newborns. Julie Levine and Julie Rocco were joint program manager for the 2011 Explorer Crossover and each earned 80 percent of their full-time salaries and benefits. Rocco and Levine supervised 10 people. Rocco worked Monday, Wednesday, and Thursday, and Levine worked Tuesday, Wednesday, and Friday. Both worked about 40 hours a week each, which they consider part-time in the automobile industry.[84]

Job sharing also provides a means of encouraging older workers to remain on the job past retirement age. Sharing jobs has potential benefits that include the broader range of skills the partners bring to the job. For job sharing to work, however, the partners must be compatible, have good communication skills, and have a bond of trust with their manager. Job sharing also can pose challenges, including the need for additional oversight—such as conducting administrative tasks and performance reviews for two employees rather than one. However, if the option is the loss of two valued employees, the additional effort is certainly worth it.

HR Web Wisdom
Telecommuting
www.telework.gov/
Governmental Web site for employees who think they might like to telecommute (or are already doing so), for managers and supervisors who supervise teleworkers, and for agency telework coordinators.

Two-in-a-Box

Some companies are giving two executives the same responsibilities and the same title and letting them decide how the work is to be divided (Two-in-a-Box). Unlike job sharing, it is a full-time job for both executives. It certainly has some risk, as in the case of the 1998 DaimlerChrysler Corporation disaster of an attempt at Two-in-a-Box when one executive was unwilling to share authority, resulting in the resignation of the other executive. Problems certainly can occur as the egos of two executives meet, but it has proven successful in certain instances. A major advantage of this approach is that it can ease transition, permitting a newer manager to learn from a more experienced manager. It is also useful as managers confront the requirement of global traveling. One manager could be at the home office taking care of regular business while the other is traveling. For two-and-a-half years, two executives shared a job as heads of Cisco's routing group. The two had complementary skills and each gained experience from the other. Cisco typically combines a technically oriented manager with a business-oriented one.[85] The Two-in-a-Box approach requires work and constant communication, but for the right two executives, the benefits derived are worth it.

There are other examples of Two-in-a-Box. Aon Consulting is chaired by co-CEOs Kathryn Hayley and Baljit Dail.[86] German business software provider SAP AG appointed Bill McDermott and Jim Hagemann Snabe as co-CEOs.[87] Other companies that use co-CEOs include BlackBerry maker Research in Motion and restaurant chain P. F. Chang's China Bistro.

Telecommuting

telecommuting
Work arrangement whereby employees, called "teleworkers" or "telecommuters," can remain at home (or otherwise away from the office) and perform their work using computers and other electronic devices that connect them with their offices.

Telecommuting is a work arrangement whereby employees, called "teleworkers" or "telecommuters," can remain at home (or otherwise away from the office) and perform their work using computers and other electronic devices that connect them with their offices.

Telecommuting has become more popular in recent years. More than 4 million workers have telecommuting arrangements.[88] By 2020, up to 30 percent of the workforce will likely be telecommuting because of traffic congestion and frustration with commuting and high gas prices. According to a Gallup survey, 37 percent say they have telecommuted.[89] For self-motivated workers, telecommuting can increase worker productivity and improve job satisfaction and loyalty. Modern communications and information technologies permit people to work just about anywhere. Today, physical location is largely immaterial when it comes to working. Telecommuting is significantly changing not just the way people work, but also where they do it. One study indicates that employees who telecommute for most of the time are more satisfied with their jobs than those working primarily in an office.[90] Workers like telecommuting because there are fewer interruptions, less company politics, and less face-to-face communication. These benefits improve their work/life balance.

Despite the benefits, some companies are reconsidering the value of telecommuting arrangements and others have suspended those policies altogether. For instance, Yahoo CEO Marissa Meyer ended the company's telecommuting policy in 2013, reportedly after a review of "logins to the company server" showed that many people were not consistently online. IBM was a pioneer in legitimizing telecommuting arrangements; however, in 2017, the company terminated telecommuting arrangements for about 2,600 employees, particularly in the marketing area.[91] Michelle Peluso, IBM's chief marketing officer, stated, " . . . there is something about a team being more powerful, more impactful, more creative, and frankly hopefully having more fun when they are should to shoulder."[92]

Telecommuters generally are information workers. They accomplish jobs that require, for example, analysis, research, writing, budgeting, data entry, or computer programming. Teleworkers also include illustrators, loan executives, architects, attorneys, and publishers. Employees can accomplish both training and job duties without losing either efficiency or quality by using the Internet. Thanks largely to telecommuting, when the New York City transit union went on strike, knowledge workers could work from home, which greatly lessened the effect of the strike.

Another advantage of telecommuting is that it eliminates the need for office space. The expense of employees is not just their salaries and benefits, but also the overhead associated with office space. Deloitte LLP offers most of its 45,000 employees nationwide the option to telecommute as many as five days a week and have been doing this for 15 years. As leases come up for renewal, the firm can reduce office space and energy costs by 30 percent. Companies reconfigure facilities to accommodate mobile workers who do not need permanent offices.[93]

In addition, commuting distances are not a factor for teleworkers. The average time it takes to get to work continues to increase, which often contributes to tardiness and lost work hours. With telecommuting, firms may hire the best available employees located virtually anywhere in the world for many jobs. The ability to employ disabled workers and workers with young children further broadens the labor market. Finally, telecommuting is an alternative for executives who are unwilling to relocate. If the company is willing to permit the executive not to work out of headquarters, telecommuting may be the answer.

Part-Time Work

Historically, many have viewed part-time employees as second-class citizens. These workers reluctantly accepted a low-paying job until a full-time career break occurred. Today, increasing highly educated professionals are choosing part-time opportunities in their fields to address both job and personal needs. Alison Doyle, an About.com job search and employment expert, said, "Professional moms would be thrilled to lower their hours to spend more time with their children, and they don't mind giving up benefits to achieve that work/life balance."[94]

At Deloitte, managers discuss employee performance during twice-a-year evaluations focused not just on career targets but also on larger life goals. Employees can request to do more or less travel or client service. The employee can also request to move laterally into a new role—that may or may not come with a pay cut. About 10 percent of employees choose to "dial up" or "dial down" at any given time. The program is in response to Millennials demanding a better work/life balance and boomers looking to ease into retirement.[95]

HR BLOOPERS

The Job-Sharing Problem at SunTrust Bank

As the HR Manager at SunTrust Bank, Jerry James manages the company's generous benefit program that includes flexible work options. Many employees telecommute or take advantage of the company flextime policy. Generally, employees appreciate the flexible work options, but right now Jerry has a problem in the loan processing department. Two different employees from Loan Processing approached him several months ago about their desire for a flexible work option. Both employees had recently started families and both wanted part-time work, so Jerry suggested job sharing. No workers have requested this option before, but because these two employees did the same job for the company, Jerry thought it was a great idea. The two could share one job, and he could easily hire a new employee to take on the other job. However, after finishing another stressful call from one of the employees and reading a frustrated e-mail message from the other, Jerry knows they need some help working together. Jerry first recommended that they talk to their manager, but both employees told Jerry that they did not trust their manager to help them. The employees now do not seem to be even talking to each other at all and Jerry's discussion with their manager about their problems was not very helpful. The manager told Jerry he was surprised when these two employees requested the job sharing arrangement to begin with because they did not get along with each other very well. Now Jerry is not sure what to do.

If your professor has assigned this, go to **www.pearson.com/mylab/management** to complete the HR Bloopers exercise and test your application of these concepts when faced with real-world decisions.

10.5 Describe customized benefits plans.

customized benefit plan
Benefit plan that permits employees to make yearly selections to largely determine their benefit package by choosing between taxable cash and numerous benefits.

Customized Benefit Plans

Customized benefit plans permit employees to make yearly selections to determine their benefit package by choosing between taxable cash and numerous benefits.

Not long ago, firms offered a uniform package that generally reflected a typical employee based on tradition, budgets, and management choices. Today, the workforce has become considerably more heterogeneous, and this prototype is no longer representative. Companies must serve different interests in this increasingly diverse workforce.[96] With four generations of workers now in the workplace, customization and flexibility become important in developing a benefits package that meets the needs of everyone. Workers have considerable latitude in determining how much they will take in the form of salary, life insurance, pension contributions, and other benefits. Customized cafeteria plans permit flexibility in allowing each employee to determine the compensation components that best satisfy their needs.[97]

Obviously, organizations cannot permit employees to select all their benefits. For one thing, firms must provide the benefits required by law. In addition, it is probably wise to require that each employee have core benefits, especially in areas such as retirement and medical insurance. However, the freedom to select highly desired benefits would seem to maximize the value of an individual's compensation. Employees' involvement in designing their own benefit plans would also effectively communicate to them the cost of their benefits. In keeping the program current, management depends on an upward flow of information from employees to determine when benefit changes are needed.

The downside to customized benefit plans is that they are costly. Development and administrative costs for these plans exceed those for traditional plans. Even though customized benefit plans add to the organization's administrative burden, some firms apparently find that the advantages outweigh shortcomings.

10.6 Summarize the issues of communicating information about benefits plans.

Communicating Information about the Benefits Package

Employee benefits can help a firm recruit and retain a top-quality workforce. Organizations spend millions of dollars each year for benefits. Yet, many do not do a good job of communicating the value of this investment to the employees. Often organizations do not have to improve benefits to keep their best employees, rather, workers need to understand their benefits.

The HR director of Elm City Market discusses a variety of HR issues, including educating employees about their employee benefits options. The following Watch It video describes some of the benefit package components.

Watch It 3

If your instructor has assigned this, sign into **www.pearson.com/mylab/management** to watch a video titled Elm City Market: Designing and Administering Benefits and respond to questions.

ERISA provides still another reason for communicating information about a firm's benefits program. This act requires organizations with a pension or profit sharing plan to provide employees with specific data at specified times. The act further mandates that companies present the information in a manner that is easy to understand. In addition, under the Patient Protection and Affordable Care Act, employers must provide a benefits summary and coverage explanation to all applicants and enrollees at the time of initial enrollment and at the annual enrollment, in addition to the summary plan description required by ERISA.

PREPARING FOR EXAMS/QUIZZES

Chapter Summary by Learning Objectives

1. ***Define* indirect financial compensation (employee benefits).** *Indirect financial compensation (employee benefits)* includes all financial rewards that generally are not paid directly to the employee in the form of a wage, salary, or performance-based pay.
2. ***Describe legally required benefits and the various kinds.*** Legally required benefits currently account for nearly 10 percent of total compensation costs. These include Social Security, unemployment insurance, workers' compensation, and health insurance. Legally required benefits were often prompted by poor social or economic conditions. Companies can choose from a variety of health insurance set-ups based on its objectives. There are two long-standing approaches—fee-for-service plans and managed care plans. Some give employees a vast amount of choice over health care providers (fee-for-service plans), whereas others are more restrictive such as is the case for managed care plans. An emerging approach, consumer-driven health care, is the least costly to employers, but employees bear greater costs for health care services, often because these plans have high deductible features.

   Several laws regulate the practice of the employee benefits practices we reviewed in this section, such as the Consolidated Omnibus Budget Reconciliation Act, the Older Workers Benefit Protection Act, the Health Insurance Portability and Accountability Act, and the Patient Protection and Affordable Care Act. These laws define the obligation of employers and the rights of employees.
3. ***Define* discretionary benefits *and explain the various types.*** *Discretionary benefits* are benefit payments made because of unilateral management decisions in non-union firms and from labor/management negotiations in unionized firms.

   Discretionary benefits fall into three broad categories: *protection programs*, *paid time off*, and *services*. Protection programs provide family benefits, promote health, and guard against income loss caused by such catastrophic factors as unemployment, disability, or serious illnesses. Paid time off provides employees time off with pay for such events as vacation. Services provide such enhancements as tuition reimbursement and day-care assistance to employees and their families.

   Various laws regulate the practice of discretionary employee benefits practices we reviewed in this section. These include the Employee Retirement Income Security Act and the Pension Protection Act. These laws define the obligation of employers and the rights of employees.
4. ***Explain workplace flexibility (work–life balance).*** Workplace flexibility practices include flextime, the compressed workweek, job sharing, Two-in-a-Box, telecommuting, and part-time work.
5. ***Describe customized benefits plans.*** *Customized benefit plans* permit employees to make yearly selections to determine their benefit package by choosing between taxable cash and numerous benefits.
6. ***Summarize the issues of communicating information about benefits plans.*** Organizations spend millions of dollars each year for benefits. Yet, many do not do a good job of communicating the value of this investment to the employees. Often organizations do not have to improve benefits to keep their best employees, rather, workers need to understand the benefits that they receive.

Key Terms

indirect financial compensation (employee benefits) 279
unemployment insurance 281
workers' compensation 282
fee-for-service plans 282
deductible 282
coinsurance 282
out-of-pocket maximum 282
managed care plans 283
prepaid medical services 283
copayments 283
primary care physician 283
consumer-driven health care plans (CDHPs) 283

high-deductible health insurance plans (HDHPs) 283
health savings account (HSA) 283
discretionary benefits 285
qualified plans 286
nonqualified plans 286
vesting 286
cliff vesting schedule 286
6-year graduated schedule 286
defined benefit plan 286
defined contribution plan 287
401(k) plan 287
matching contribution 287
cash balance plan 287
term life insurance 288
whole life insurance 288
paid time off (PTO) banks 289
sabbaticals 290
volunteerism 291
relocation benefits 292
flextime 294
compressed workweek 294
job sharing 295
telecommuting 295
customized benefit plan 297

MyLab Management

If your instructor is using MyLab Management, go to **www.pearson.com/mylab/management** to complete the problems marked with this icon ✪.

Questions for Review

10-1. Define *indirect financial compensation (employee benefits)*.

10-2. What are the mandated or legally required benefits? Briefly describe each.

10-3. What are the basic categories of discretionary benefits? Describe each.

10-4. What items are included in the discretionary benefit of paid time off category?

10-5. Define each of the following:
- (a) fee-for-service plan
- (b) health maintenance organization (HMO)
- (c) consumer-driven health care plan
- (d) health savings account (HSA)

10-6. There are numerous forms of retirement plans. Describe each of the following:
- (a) defined benefit plan
- (b) defined contribution plan
- (c) 401(k) plan
- (d) cash balance plan

10-7. Define each of the following benefit laws:
- (a) Employee Retirement Income Security Act
- (b) Consolidated Omnibus Budget Reconciliation Act
- (c) Health Insurance Portability and Accountability Act
- (d) Family and Medical Leave Act
- (e) Older Workers Benefit Protection Act
- (f) Pension Protection Act
- (g) Patient Protection and Affordable Care Act

10-8. What are topics included within employee services?

✪ **10-9.** What is the purpose of a customized benefits plan?

10-10. What is the relationship between smoke-free workplaces and the Patient Protection and Affordable Care Act?

10-11. Define each of the following workplace flexibility practices:
- (a) flextime
- (b) compressed workweek
- (c) job sharing
- (d) telecommuting

10-12. What is the purpose of the staffing practice called Two-in-a-Box?

PREPARING FOR MY CAREER

ETHICS DILEMMA

A Poor Bid

You are vice-president of HR for a large construction company, and your company is bidding on an estimated $2.5 million public housing project. A local electrical subcontractor submitted a bid that you realize is 20 percent too low because labor costs have been incorrectly calculated. It is obvious to you that benefits amounting to more than 30 percent of labor costs have not been included. In fact, the bid was some $30,000 below those of the other four subcontractors. However, accepting it will improve your chance of winning the contract for the big housing project.

10-13. What would you do?

10-14. What factor(s) in this ethics dilemma might influence a person to make a less-than-ethics decision?

HRM Is Everyone's Business

Many employees feel entitled to receive employee benefits. While some laws require that companies provide benefits, it will be up to the organization to decide on which other benefits they will offer. As a manager or HR professional, you *might* oversee creating a benefits program, but employee requests will *certainly* require you to interpret policy to guide your responses. Whether you are dealing with the creation or interpretation of benefits, you will want to have access to accurate information so your organization's offerings serve as true benefits for employees and not a source of frustration and ambiguity.

Action checklist for managers and HR—helping employees understand and make use of their benefits

☑ Ensure that the employee benefits handbook is up to date and accurate. Make an online and paper version accessible.

☑ Set up workshops to help employees understand the elements of the benefits offered by the organization—highlight confusing aspects and aspects that are not well known. Particularly emphasize unique features.

☑ While many companies now have call centers that answer employees' questions about their benefits, stay current on company policies and legal requirements so that, when more complex benefits issues arise (e.g., health care coverage), the questions can be dealt with in a thoughtful and timely manner.

Managers take the lead

☑ Suggest ways to keep the "explaining your benefits" portion of new employee orientation engaging and interesting. HR (or the benefits specialist) should conduct the session.

☑ Keep track of the most common questions that employees raise. Keep HR apprised of this information, which will help shape informative sessions.

☑ When changing benefits, call employees together to discuss rationale and the tasks to make full use of the existing benefits.

HRM by the Numbers

Calculating 401(k) Matching Contributions

✪ *An additional HRM by the Numbers exercise can be found on MyLab Management.*

Companies decide whether to institute matching contributions. Ones that offer matching contributions do so for numerous reasons, including recruitment and retention of the most qualified individuals. Also, companies choose the formulas for making contributions and setting maximum limits. Here are three common approaches for determining matching contributions:

- **Full match:** The employer fully matches an employee's contribution to the 401(k) plan account up to an amount set by law. For illustrative purposes, an employee earning $50,000 annually contributes $2,000 to her 401(k). Then, the company's matching contribution equals $2,000.
- **Fixed dollar match:** The employer deposits $1 for every $1 the employee contributes to the plan up to a specified limit, for instance, 5 percent of pay. One employee contributes 3 percent of her $100,000 pay equaling $3,000: (3 percent × $100,000). The employer contributes the same amount. Another employee contributes 10 percent of his $100,000 pay equaling $10,000: (10 percent × $100,000). In this case, the company deposits $5,000: (5 percent × $100,000) because the plan specifies a 5 percent contribution maximum.
- **Variable dollar match:** The employer's contribution decreases as an employee's contribution increases. For example, an employer might deposit $1 for every $1 on the first 3 percent of pay contributed by the employee, and 50 cents per dollar on the next 3 percent of pay. An employee who earns $100,000 annually contributes 6 percent to the 401(k) plan, equaling $6,000: (6 percent × $100,000). The employer contributes a total of $4,500: [($1 × (3 percent × $100,000)) + ($0.50 × (3 percent × $100,000))].

Now, let's calculate the employer's matching contributions for three employees, Amanda, Shiyu and Onkar using each method. Amanda earns $35,000 annually and does not contribute anything to the 401(k) plan. Shiyu earns $125,000 annually and contributes 7 percent of pay to the 401(k) plan. Onkar earns $80,000 annually and contributes 2 percent of pay.

Questions

10-15. *Full match:* What is the employer's contribution for (a) Amanda, (b) Shiyu, and (c) Onkar? What is the total contribution (employee's contribution plus employer's matching contribution) to each employee's 401(k) account: (d) Amanda, (e) Shiyu, and (f) Onkar?

10-16. *Fixed dollar match:* 75 cents per each $1 employee contribution. What is the employer's contribution for (a) Amanda, (b) Shiyu, and (c) Onkar? What is the total contribution (employee's contribution plus employer's contribution) to each employee's 401(k) account: (d) Amanda, (e) Shiyu, and (f) Onkar?

10-17. *Variable dollar match:* $1 per each $1 employee contribution on the first 2 percent of pay and 75 cents per $1 employee contribution for the next 3 percent of pay. What is the employer's contribution for (a) Amanda, (b) Shiyu, and (c) Onkar? What is the total contribution (employee's contribution plus employer's contribution) to each employee's 401(k) account: (d) Amanda, (e) Shiyu, and (f) Onkar?

Working Together: Team Exercise

In small groups of three or four, come up with specific answers to the following questions. Talk through your perspectives with team members. Be prepared to share your ideas with the class.

Think about your work and non-work goals for the next five and ten years, respectively. Discuss these goals with group members and put together a list.

10-18. What are some of your work and non-work goals after you graduate from school for each time frame? Briefly describe them.
10-19. What are two employee benefits that will support the attainment of your goals during each time frame? Explain.

INCIDENT 1 Flextime

Kathy Collier is a supervisor of a government office in Washington, D.C. Morale in her office has been quite low recently. The workers have gone back to an 8:00 A.M. to 4:30 P.M. work schedule after having been on flextime for nearly two years.

When the directive came down allowing Kathy to place her office on flextime, she spelled out the rules carefully to her people. Each person was to work during the core period from 10:00 A.M. to 2:30 P.M.; however, they could work the rest of the eight-hour day at any time between 6:00 A.M. and 6:00 P.M. Kathy felt her workers were honest and well-motivated, so she did not bother to set up any system of control.

Everything went along well for a long time. Morale improved, and all the work seemed to get done. In November, however, an auditor from the General Accounting Office investigated and found that Kathy's workers were averaging seven hours a day. Two employees had been working only during the core period for more than two months. When Kathy's department manager reviewed the auditor's report, Kathy was told to return the office to regular working hours. Kathy was upset and disappointed with her people. She had trusted them and felt they had let her down.

Questions

10-20. What are the advantages and disadvantages of flextime?
10-21. What could Kathy have done to keep the situation from occurring?
10-22. Are there other workplace flexibility arrangements that Kathy might use to improve morale?

INCIDENT 2 Communicating Benefits at Seaview Property Management Company

With several changes in the company's health insurance options, Monique Solara knew that benefits open enrollment this year would be challenging. As the Manager of Employee Benefits at Seaview Property, Monique is responsible for administering Seaview's benefits program. The company recently announced changes to health insurance options as well as a reduction in the company's 401(k) matching contributions. Monique immediately received calls from several confused or angry employees. Because of the changes, some employees may need to change health care providers, which will be costlier to them. Other employees have concerns about their retirement benefits, particularly how much lower matching contributions will be.

Seaview offers a full menu of benefit options including three alternate health insurance plans and a generous 401(k) program. Even with the changes, Monique is confident that the value of Seaview's benefits program still exceeds competitors' offerings. However, she is not confident that employees understand how their benefits compare to other companies' benefits. In addition, she believes that employees generally feel entitled to their benefits, making any reductions a source of dissatisfaction.

The swift and negative response to the benefits changes reinforced Monique's belief as many employees complained that Seaview did not have a right to make such changes. Some employees even suggested the changes are illegal.

Prior to the recent changes, Monique thought the company's benefits communication was sufficient. New employees receive an informational packet that details the features of each benefit. There is extensive information about each health insurance option including lists of health care providers and an outline of specific coverage for common medical procedures. Then, during open enrollment each year, employees receive an updated packet of information listing any changes in the health insurance plans. Monique has included as much information as possible in both the new hire packets and the annual update packets. In fact, the packets have become quite bulky, which has raised concerns as many employees have mentioned they feel overwhelmed with the volume of information.

Monique is also concerned that the current information provided to the employees fails to help them understand the value of the benefits program. Seaview invests significantly in the benefits program and employee understanding is important for employee retention. Overall, Monique believes the current communication process is not effective, but she is unsure of the best communication strategy.

Questions

10-23. Why is it important to provide effective communication about employee benefits? Explain.
10-24. What is your opinion of Seaview's current benefits communication practices? Explain.
10-25. How can Seaview improve their benefits communication? Discuss.

MyLab Management

If your instructor is using MyLab Management, go to **www.pearson.com/mylab/management** for Auto-graded writing questions as well as the following Assisted-graded writing questions:

10-26. How does the use of discretionary benefits contribute to recruitment and retention?

10-27. Why is it important to communicate information about the benefits package?

Endnotes

1 Paul Fronstin and Ruth Helman, "Views on the Value of Voluntary Workplace Benefits: Findings from the 2015 Health and Voluntary Workplace Benefits Survey," *Employee Benefit Research Institute Notes* (November 2015), Vol. 36, No. 11: 1. Accessed April 4, 2017, at www.ebri.org/pdf/notespdf/EBRI_Notes_11_Nov15_WBS-PolFor.pdf.

2 Karen Wessels, Evren Esen, Jennifer Schramm, and Samantha DiNicola, "SHRM Survey Findings: 2016 Strategic Benefits—Leveraging Benefits to Retain and Recruit Employees," *Society for Human Resource Management* (November 30, 2016). Accessed March 31, 2017, at www.shrm.org/hr-today/trends-and-forecasting/research-and-surveys/Documents/SHRM-Survey-Findings-Strategic-Benefits-Leveraging-Benefits-to-Retain-and-Recruit-Employees.pdf.

3 U.S. Bureau of Labor Statistics, "Employer Costs for Employee Compensation—March 2017," (USDL 17-0770). Accessed August 1, 2017, at www.bls.gov.

4 Ibid.

5 Ibid.

6 Joseph J. Martocchio. (2018). *Employee Benefits: A Primer for Human Resource Professionals*, 6th ed. Burr Ridge, IL: McGraw-Hill/Irwin.

7 U.S. Bureau of Labor Statistics, "Employer Costs for Employee Compensation—March 2017," (USDL 17-0321). Accessed August 1, 2017, at www.bls.gov.

8 U.S. Bureau of Labor Statistics, "Employer Costs for Employee Compensation—March 2017," (USDL 17-0770). Accessed August 1, 2017, at www.bls.gov.

9 U.S. Social Security Administration. *Monthly Statistical Snapshot, January 2017*. Accessed March 17, 2017, at www.ssa.gov.

10 Melvyn Dubofsky and Joseph A. McCartin, "Labor in America: A History," (ninth edition). New York: Wiley-Blackwell, 2017.

11 Organization for Economic Co-Operation and Development, "Total Expenditures on Health per Capita." Accessed March 20, 2017, at www.oecd.org/els/health-systems/health-statistics.htm.

12 Matt Bolch, "Realities Drive Change in Health Care Delivery," *Financial Executive* 28 (January/February 2012): 36–39.

13 Centers for Medicare & Medicaid Services, "NHE Fact Sheet," Accessed March 12, 2017, at www.cms.gov/research-statistics-data-and-systems/statistics-trends-and-reports/nationalhealthexpenddata/nhe-fact-sheet.html.

14 Kaiser Family Foundation and Health Research & Educational Trust, "Employer Health Benefits 2016 Annual Survey," Accessed March 20, 2017, at http://files.kff.org/attachment/Report-Employer-Health-Benefits-2016-Annual-Survey.

15 Rhea Brittany Luebke, "Create a Retirement Savings Strategy Using a Health Savings Account," *Journal of Financial Service Professionals* 66 (January 2012): 27–29.

16 Lori Chordas, "New Year, New Rules," *Best's Review* 112 (January 2012): 52–53.

17 Nancy Hatch Woodward, "Earn Less, Pay Less," *HR Magazine* 57 (March 2012): 67–70.

18 "Even in Difficult Times, Employees See the Value of Smoking Cessation Programs," *Managed Care Outlook* 22 (June 1, 2009): 10–12.

19 "Tobacco-Related Mortality," *Centers for Disease Control* online (December 1, 2016). Accessed April 4, 2017, at www.cdc.gov/tobacco/data_statistics/fact_sheets/health_effects/tobacco_related_mortality/.

20 "Economic Trends in Tobacco," *Centers for Disease Control* online (March 3, 2017). Accessed April 4, 2017, at www.cdc.gov/tobacco/data_statistics/fact_sheets/economics/econ_facts/.

21 "Fast Facts," *Centers for Disease Control* online (February 9, 2017). Accessed April 4, 2017, at www.cdc.gov/tobacco/data_statistics/fact_sheets/.

22 "Tobacco-Related Mortality," *Centers for Disease Control* online (December 1, 2016). Accessed April 4, 2017, at www.cdc.gov/tobacco/data_statistics/fact_sheets/health_effects/tobacco_related_mortality/.

23 Paul McIntyre, "A Smoking Ban Isn't About Your Bottom Line, It's About Protecting Your Workers' Health," *Nation's Restaurant News* 39 (December 5, 2005): 24–34.

24 Joanne Deschenaux, "Is a 'Smoker-Free' Workplace Right for You?" *HR Magazine* 56 (July 2011): 42–45.

25 Monica Dobie, "Quit Smoking or Lose Your Job," *World Tobacco* (May 2005): 20–21.

26 Susan K. Lessack, "Where There's Smoke . . . Can You Fire (or Refuse to Hire)?" *HR Specialist: Employment Law* 40 (May 2011): 7.

27 U.S. Bureau of Labor Statistics, "Employee Benefits in the United States, March 2017," (USDL 17-1013). Accessed August 2, 2017, at www.bls.gov.

28 Ibid.

29 Employee Benefits Research Institute, "Pension Plans" (Chapter 4) *in Fundamentals of Employee Benefits Programs*. Washington, DC, 1997.

30 Joanna Short, "Economic History of Retirement in the United States." In R. Whaples (ed.), *EH.Net Encyclopedia*, October 1, 2002. Accessed March 2, 2017, https://eh.net/encyclopedia/economic-history-of-retirement-in-the-united-states/.

31 I.R.C. §§411(a) (2), 411(a) (5); Treas. Reg. §1.411(a)-3T; ERISA §203(a).

32 U.S. Bureau of Labor Statistics, "National Compensation Survey: Employee Benefits in the United States, March 2016," (Bulletin 2785). Accessed March 21, 2017, at www.bls.gov/ncs/ebs/benefits/2016/ebbl0059.pdf.

33 Ibid.

34 Lisa Murton Beets, "Cash Balance Pension Plans," *Smart Business Columbus* 20 (January 2012): 42.

35 Jerry Geisel, "Coca-Cola Makes Move to Cash Balance Plan," *Business Insurance* 43 (February 23, 2009): 3.

36 U.S. Bureau of Labor Statistics, "Employer Costs for Employee Compensation—March 2017," (USDL 17-0770). Accessed August 1, 2017, at www.bls.gov.

37 Ibid.

38 "Get Out of Town," *Benefits Magazine* 49 (February 2012): 74.

39 Frank L. Giancola, "Vacation Benefits Maligned, Manipulated, and Misunderstood," 50 (September 2013): 1–4.

40 Alamo Rent A Car, "Vacation Shaming On the Rise: Alamo Rent A Car's Annual Study Reveals Guilt Among Vacationing Millennials," (March 7, 2017). Accessed March 21, 2017, at www.alamo.com/en_US/car-rental/scenic-route/family-travel/2017-family-vacation-survey.html?mcid=pressrelease:685.

41 "The High Price of Silence: Analyzing the Business Implications of an Under-Vacationed Workforce," *Project: Time Off*. Accessed March 21, 2017, at www.projecttimeoff.com/sites/default/files/High_Price-of_Silence_FINAL.pdf.

42 Rebecca Ray, Milla Sanes, and John Schmitt, *No-Vacation Revisited* (January 19, 2017). Accessed March 1, 2017, at http://eqxdesign.com/read/2017/1/19/no-vacation-nation-revisited-by-the-center-for-economic-policy-and-research.

43 U.S. Bureau of Labor Statistics, "National Compensation Survey: Employee Benefits in the United States, March 2016," (Bulletin 2785). Accessed March 21, 2017, at www.bls.gov/ncs/ebs/benefits/2016/ebbl0059.pdf.

44 "The High Price of Silence: Analyzing the Business Implications of an Under-Vacationed Workforce," *Project: Time Off*. Accessed March 21, 2017, at www.projecttimeoff.com/sites/default/files/High_Price-of_Silence_FINAL.pdf.

45 Jeanne Sahadi, "These Companies Offer Paid Vacation . . . And Pay for Your Vacation," *MoneyCNN Marketwatch* (July

28, 2016). Accessed February 23, 2017, at http://money.cnn.com/2016/07/26/pf/companies-that-pay-for-employee-vacations/.

46 Thomas C. Frohlich, "7 Companies with Unlimited Vacation," *24/7 Wall St.* online (December 19, 2015). Accessed March 21, 2017, at http://247wallst.com/special-report/2015/12/13/7-companies-with-unlimited-vacation/2/.

47 David Burkus, "How to Make Unlimited Vacation Time Work at Your Company," *Harvard Business Review* online (June 15, 2015). Accessed March 21, 2017, at www.hbr.org.

48 Martocchio, *Employee Benefits*.

49 U.S. Bureau of Labor Statistics, "Employer Costs for Employee Compensation—March 2017," (USDL 17-0770). Accessed August 1, 2017, at www.bls.gov.

50 Jason Blumer, "The Perfect Blend: A Firm's Path to Ensuring Work-Life Balance," *CPA Practice Advisor* 22 (February 2012): 21.

51 Justin G. Roy and Sullivan Kreiss, "Ten Tips for Retaining the Next Generation," *Offshore* 72 (January 2012): 10–11.

52 Joseph Coombs, "Flexibility Still Meeting Resistance," *HR Magazine* 56 (July 2011): 72.

53 Lucinda Shen, "These 19 Great Employers Offer Paid Sabbaticals," *Fortune* online (March 7, 2016). Accessed April 3, 2017, at www.fortune.com.

54 Rachel. Feintzeig, "Cure for Office Burnout: Mini Sabbaticals," *Fortune* online (October 28, 2014). Accessed January 10, 2016, www.fortune.com.

55 Kate Harrison, "The Most Popular Employee Perks of 2014," *Fortune* online (February 19, 2014). Accessed January 4, 2016, www.fortune.com.

56 Jillian Berman, "Why Clif Bar Offers Sabbaticals and Other Conventional Work Perks," *Huffington Post* (August 26, 2013). Accessed September 11, 2013, at www.huffingtonpost.com.

57 Gary M. Stern, "Recharging Employees with More Free Time," *Investor's Business Daily* (January 7, 2013): A08.

58 Society for Human Resource Management (2013). "2013 Employee Benefits: An Overview of Employee Benefits Offerings in the U.S." Accessed February 5, 2015, at www.shrm.com.

59 Sarah Halzack, "Paid Time Off for Volunteering Gains Traction as a Way to Retain Employees. *The Washington Post* online (August 11, 2013). Accessed February 28, 2017, at www.washingtonpost.com.

60 Fortune Editors, "The 50 Best Workplaces for Giving Back," *Fortune* online (February 9, 2017). Accessed March 1, 2017, at http://fortune.com/2017/02/09/best-workplaces-giving-back/.

61 Ryan Scott, "The Best Volunteer Programs Do This," *Forbes* online (June 15, 2015). Accessed February 28, 2017, at www.forbes.com.

62 U.S. Bureau of Labor Statistics, *National Compensation Survey*.

63 U.S. Department of Labor, "Minimum Paid Rest Period Requirements Under State Law for Adult Employees in Private Sector," (January 1, 2017). Accessed March 21, 2017, at www.dol.gov/whd/state/rest.htm.

64 Jennifer Schramm, "Undereducated," *HR Magazine* 56 (September 2011): 136.

65 Worldwide ERC, "U.S. Domestic Transfers: Relocation Statistics," (2015). Accessed March 1, 2017, at www.worldwideerc.org/Resources/Research/Pages/Facts-and-Statistics.aspx.

66 "Domestic Partner Benefits After the Supreme Court Decision: 2015 Survey Results," *International Foundation of Employee Benefit Plans* (2015). Accessed February 28, 2017, at www.ifebp.org/bookstore/domestic-partnership-survey/Pages/default.aspx.

67 Human Rights Campaign, "Corporate Equality Index 2017," *The Human Rights Campaign Foundation* (2016). Accessed March 3, 2017, at http://assets.hrc.org//files/assets/resources/CEI-2017-FinalReport.pdf?_ga=1.197800748.2055824107.1490191225.

68 Rebecca Vesely "Some Companies Offer Tax Relief for Domestic Partners," *Workforce Management* 91 (February 2012): 15.

69 "Regional Briefs," *Managed Care Outlook* 24 (June 15, 2011): 4–5.

70 "Domestic Partner Benefits After the Supreme Court Decision: 2015 Survey Results," International Foundation of Employee Benefit Plans (2015). Accessed February 28, 2017, at www.ifebp.org/bookstore/domestic-partnership-survey/Pages/default.aspx.

71 Rachel Emma Silverman, "What Employers Need to Know About Supreme Court Gay Marriage Ruling," *The Wall Street Journal* online (June 26, 2015). Accessed March 22, 2017, at www.wsj.com.

72 American Civil Liberties Union, "Non-Discrimination Laws: State by State Information—Map. Accessed March 22, 2017, at www.aclu.org/map/non-discrimination-laws-state-state-information-map.

73 Katie Lobosco, "Students Are Graduating with $30,000 in Loans," *Money CNN* online (October 18, 2016). Accessed March 1, 2017, at http://money.cnn.com.

74 Chris Duchesne, "New Benefits Arte Key to Hiring the Best People for Your Organization," *Workspan* (October 2016): 19–22.

75 Ibid.

76 "Work/Life Policies Enhance Business," *HR Magazine* 57 (January 2012): 69.

77 "Work-Family Conflicts Affect Employees at All Income Levels," *HR Focus* 87 (April 2010): 9.

78 Henry G. Jackson, "Flexible Workplaces: A Business Imperative," *HR Magazine* 56 (October 2011): 10.

79 "Working Moms Need Flexibility," *OfficePro* 71 (August/September 2011): 5.

80 "Employers Embracing Programs as Morale Booster, Business Strategy," *HR Focus* 88 (September 2011): 1–4.

81 Alison Quirk, "The Business Case for Flex," *HR Magazine* (April 2012): 44–45.

82 Susan Dominus, "Rethinking the Work-Life Equation," *New York Times Magazine* online, February 16, 2016, accessed April 4, 2017, at www.nytimes.com; WorldatWork and FlexJobs, "Trends in Workplace Flexibility," WorldatWork, September 2015; Robin D. Richards, "The 2015 Workplace Flexibility Study," *Workplace Trends* (February 3, 2015). Accessed April 1, 2017, at https://workplacetrends.com/the-2015-workplace-flexibility-study/; Nicholas Bloom, "To Raise Productivity, Let More Employees Work from Home," *Harvard Business Review* online, (January–February 2014. Accessed March 2, 2016, at http://www.hbr.org.

83 Justin G. Roy, "Ten Tips for Retaining the Next Generation," *Power Engineering* 116 (January 2012): 11–12.

84 Jamie LaReau, "Ford's 2 Julies Share Devotion—and Job," *Automotive News* 85 (October 25, 2010): 4–26.

85 Scott Thurm, "Power-Sharing Prepares Managers," *Wall Street Journal* (December 5, 2005): B4.

86 Ed Frauenheim, "Co-CEOs: Two at the Top," *Workforce Management* 88 (May 18, 2009): 40–42.

87 "SAP AG Reports Departure of CEO and Appointment of Co-CEOs," *Telecomworldwire (M2)* (February 8, 2010).

88 Kate Lister, "Latest Telecommuting Statistics," *Global Workplace Analytics*, January 2016. Accessed March 22, 2017, at http://globalworkplaceanalytics.com/telecommuting-statistics.

89 Jeffrey M. Jones "In U.S. Telecommuting for Work Climbs to 37%," *Gallup* online (August 19, 2015) Accessed March 2, 2017, at www.gallup.com/poll/184649/telecommuting-work-climbs.aspx.

90 "The Virtual Office Gains Momentum," *Trends Magazine* (January 2011): 16–19.

91 Chris Weller, "IBM was a Pioneer in the Work-From-Home Revolution—Now It's Cracking Down," *Business Insider* online (March 27, 2017). Accessed April 2, 2017, at www.businessinsider.com/ibm-slashes-work-from-home-policy-2017-3.

92 Shaun Nichols, "IBM's Marissa Mayer Moment? Staff Told to Work in 1 of 6 Main Offices or Face the Axe," *The U.K. Register* online (February 8, 2017). Accessed April 4, 2017, at www.theregister.co.uk/2017/02/08/ibm_no_more_telecommuting/.

93 Dori Meinert, "Make Telecommuting Pay Off," *HR Magazine* 56 (June 2011): 32–37.

94 Adrienne Fox, "Part-Timers," *HR Magazine* 55 (August 2010): 28–33.

95 Laura Fitzpatrick, "We're Getting off the Ladder," *Time* 173 (May 25, 2009): 45.

96 Todd Henneman, "Workers Pick Their Perfect Perquisites," *Workforce Management* 91 (January 2012): 9.

97 Martocchio, *Employee Benefits*.

Part Five

Labor Relations, Employee Relations, Safety, and Health

Chapter 11

Labor Unions and Collective Bargaining

Chapter 12

Internal Employee Relations

Chapter 13

Employee Safety, Health, and Wellness

11 Labor Unions and Collective Bargaining

LEARNING OBJECTIVES After completing this chapter, students should be able to:

11.1 Explore the role of labor unions.

11.2 Describe the basic union structure and organized labor's strategies for a stronger movement.

11.3 Discuss laws affecting collective bargaining.

11.4 Summarize the formation of bargaining units and the collective bargaining process.

11.5 Describe the grievance procedure in a union environment.

11.6 Explain union decertification.

MyLab Management

Improve Your Grade!

If your professor is using MyLab Management, visit **www.pearson.com/mylab/management** for videos, simulations, and writing exercises.

Learn It

If your professor has chosen to assign this, go to **www.pearson.com/mylab/management** to see what you should particularly focus on and to take the Chapter 11 Warm-Up.

labor unions
Organizations that exist to represent the interests of employees in the workplace and to ensure fair treatment when conflicts arise between one or more employee and management.

collective bargaining
The process in which labor union leadership enters into good faith negotiations with management representatives over terms of employment such as work hours, pay, and job security.

collective bargaining agreement
Written document that describes the terms of employment reached between management and unions.

Labor unions and the process of collective bargaining are important considerations in the human resources (HR) field, which, as we described in Chapter 1, is the business function of managing people. **Labor unions** refer to organizations that exist to represent the interests of employees in the workplace and to ensure fair treatment when conflicts arise between one or more employee and management. Labor union leadership enters into good faith negotiations with management representatives over terms of employment such as work hours, pay, and job security. **Collective bargaining** refers to the process of negotiation. The result of a successful collective bargaining process is the **collective bargaining agreement** or contract, which specifies the negotiated terms.

In this chapter, we will explore a variety of important issues pertaining to labor unions. These include why labor unions exist and why employees join unions, the organizational structure of unions, laws affecting the relationship between unions and management, the collective bargaining process, grievance procedures, and how members can decertify unions if members do not feel that their best interests are being served.

11.1 Explore the role of labor unions.

The Role of Labor Unions

Labor unions in the United States came about out of necessity. Family agricultural farms and small family craft businesses were the bases for the U.S. economy before the early part of the twentieth century. The turn of the twentieth century marked the beginning of the Industrial Revolution in the United States. During the Industrial Revolution, the economy's transition from agrarian and craft businesses to large-scale manufacturing, or factory systems, began. Increasingly, individuals were becoming employees of large factories instead of self-employed farmers or small business owners. Factory owners, also referred to as *capitalists*, sought profits. Profits refer to the money that capitalists enjoy after deducting the costs of doing business (for example, raw materials, employee wages). Highly efficient workforces were therefore an essential part of the capitalist's profit motive.

The profit motive and the sheer size of factory employment gave rise to divisions of labor based on differences in worker skill, effort, and responsibilities. In other words, many people held positions performing the same job (for example, multiple employees perform the work specified in the job description for assembler) and the job types were diverse (for example, management,

production, and clerical). The growth in the size of the workplace necessitated practices to guide such activities as hiring, training, setting wages, handling grievances, and terminating employment for work rule violations or poor job performance. Factory owners sought out the expertise of mechanical engineers to promote efficient production systems and productive workers. The work of these engineers defined the scientific management movement. Ultimately, scientific management practices contributed to labor cost reductions by replacing inefficient production methods with efficient production methods.

Although a variety of unions had existed for decades, management was not obligated to recognize them. The industrialization of the U.S. economy when business owners sought out efficiency while sacrificing the welfare of workers and the economic devastation during the Great Depression placed workers at a disadvantage. Workers were subject to poor pay, unsafe working conditions, and virtually no job security. During the Great Depression, scores of businesses failed and most workers became chronically unemployed, giving management even greater power because many workers would accept substandard employment terms as an alternative to unemployment. Some workers banded together to negotiate better terms of employment, but employers were not willing to listen because collective action could jeopardize employers' control over the terms of employment. Still, employees experienced poor working conditions, substandard wage rates, and excessive work hours. As we discuss shortly, Congress enacted the National Labor Relations Act (NLRA) of 1935 to remove barriers to free commerce and to restore equality of bargaining power between employees and employers.

Throughout the years that followed, unions successfully negotiated favorable terms of employment for its members as well as job security provisions in collective bargaining agreements, particularly during economic recessions. However, as we discuss shortly, unionization has declined dramatically over the past several decades along with the need for greater compromise.

Why Employees Join Unions

Individuals join unions for many different reasons, which tend to change over time, and may involve job, personal, social, or political considerations. It would be impossible to discuss them all, but the following are some of the major reasons. From an HR professional's standpoint, the issues associated with employees' dissatisfaction with management are most relevant.

Every job holds the potential for real dissatisfaction. Everyone has a boiling point that can cause him or her to consider a union as a solution to actual or perceived problems. Union organizers look for arbitrary or unfair management decisions and then emphasize the advantages of union membership as a means of solving these problems. We describe some other common reasons for employee dissatisfaction next.

COMPENSATION AND EMPLOYEE BENEFITS Employees want their compensation to be fair and equitable. Wages are important because they provide both the necessities and standard of living. If employees are dissatisfied with their wages, they may look to a union for assistance in improving their standard of living. An important psychological aspect of compensation involves the amount of pay an individual receives in relation to that of other workers performing similar work (employee equity). If an employee perceives that management has shown favoritism by paying someone else more to perform the same or a lower-level job, the employee will likely become dissatisfied. Union members know precisely the basis of their pay and how it compares with that of others.

Employees who are covered under a collective bargaining agreement enjoy higher wages and are more likely to participate in a variety of employee benefit programs. In 2017, private sector employers whose employees were covered by a union contract spent an average $48.94 per employee per hour worked for wages and benefits.[1] This compares to $31.58 for nonunion employees. Of this amount, the average hourly wage rate was $29.34 and $22.44 in union and nonunion settings, respectively. Figure 11-1 shows the percentage of workers in private industry who had access to various employee benefits in 2017. In every case, union workers were more likely to have benefits than nonunion employees were. As the data show, there is a nearly 24 percent wage gap between union and nonunion employees. The amount varies by occupational group and some are higher. For example, the wage gap between nonunion workers in the installation, maintenance and repair occupation is 31 percent.[2]

FIGURE 11-1
Percentage of Employees Who Have Access to Employee Benefits in Union and Nonunion Settings

Employee Benefits	Union (%)	Nonunion (%)
Retirement	92	64
Medical Care	93	65
Medical Care (share of premiums)		
Employer pays	87	77
Employee pays	13	23
Life Insurance	79	67
Paid Leave		
Paid sick leave	79	67
Paid vacation	89	75
Paid holidays	89	76

Source: U.S. Bureau of Labor Statistics, *Employee Benefits in the United States–March 2017* (USDL 17–1013). Accessed August 1, 2017, at http://www.bls.gov.

JOB SECURITY Historically, young employees have been less concerned with job security than older workers have. Young employees seem to think, "If I lose this job, I can always get another." However, if they witness management consistently terminating older workers to make room for younger, lower paid employees, they may begin to think differently about job security. If the firm does not provide its employees with a sense of job security, workers may turn to a union.

ATTITUDE OF MANAGEMENT People like to feel that they are important. They do not like to be considered a commodity that can be bought and sold. Employees do not like to be subjected to arbitrary actions by management. In some firms, management is insensitive to the needs of its employees. In such situations, employees may perceive that they have little or no influence in job-related matters. Workers who feel that they are not part of the organization are prime targets for unionization. Tesla automobile workers complained to the United Autoworkers union about excessive overtime and unsafe working conditions at the Freemont, California plant, and they are requesting help with starting a union. CEO Elon Musk rejected workers claims, asserting, "The safety and job satisfaction of our employees here at Tesla has always been extremely important to us. We have a long history of engaging directly with our employees on the issues that matter to them, and we will continue to do so because it's the right thing to do."[3] Organizations that treat people with dignity and respect are typically difficult to organize, however, the contrasting perspectives in this example raise the likelihood that employees will join a union, particularly because they are clearly not satisfied with management's approach to addressing their concerns.

Prevalence of Unions

The U.S. Labor Department's Bureau of Labor Statistics reported that the percentage of wage and salary workers who were union members was 10.7 percent.[4] The number of wage and salary workers belonging to unions is at approximately 14.6 million. In 1983, the first year for which comparable union data are available, the union membership rate was 20.1 percent and there were 17.7 million union workers. Clearly, the unionization rate is declining and fewer employees receive union protection.

In 2016, 7.2 million public-sector employees belonged to a union, compared with 7.4 million union workers in the private sector. Public-sector workers had a union membership rate of 34.4 percent—more than five times higher than that of the private-sector workers rate of 6.4 percent. Private-sector industries with high unionization rates included utilities (24.5 percent) and construction (13.9 percent), whereas low unionization rates occurred in food service and drinking places (1.6 percent), agriculture and related industries (1.3 percent), and in financial services (1.2 percent). Indeed, the statistics show a noteworthy decline in unionization. There are many possible reasons for this trend, and we consider five.

First, in decades past, unions often intimidated workers to become members even if they did not care to do so. Unions used such tactics to boost their membership, thus, their power to negotiate with employers over terms of employment. Quite simply, it is more difficult to ignore the voices of the many rather than the few. Over time, legislation outlawed unions' use of intimidation, after which the prevalence of unions began to decline.

Second, historically, unions provided a voice to protect the rights of disadvantaged groups, including women, older workers, and racial minorities. However, starting in the 1960s, anti-discrimination laws such as Title VII of the Civil Rights Act instituted protections. The array of legislation lessened the role of unions.

Third, globalization of business has contributed to the decline in unionization in a variety of ways. For example, higher quality automobile imports (such as Toyota and Honda automobiles) than U.S. automobile manufacturers required greater investments quality control and workforce flexibility, which unions tend to resist. Unions resist giving management too much discretion over employee assignments and pay out of concern that they would treat them unfairly, however, the survival of companies required that unions accept flexibility. Unions' willingness to permit greater management discretion raised questions about the ability of unions to protect workers.

Globalization through offshoring activities threatens unionization. Offshoring can be thought of as the migration of all or a significant part of the development, maintenance, and delivery of services to a company located in another country. With rare exception, employees do not move with the jobs. Traditionally, the reason given for offshoring is to reduce costs. Many of the lost jobs in the United States were unionized, which, as we showed, are most costly to employers than nonunion jobs. Moreover, the absence of or less restrictive labor laws (e.g., minimum wage laws) in other countries generally permit U.S. companies to lower employment costs.

Fourth, large companies such as Boeing, which have highly unionized workforces, are establishing new facilities in states where unionization rates are low. German automobile manufacturer Volkswagen built a state-of-the-art factory in Tennessee, which possess right-to-work laws. **Right-to-work laws** prohibit management and unions from entering into agreements requiring union membership as a condition of employment. At the beginning of 2017, 28 states had right-to-work laws, of which seven were passed since 2011.

right-to-work laws
Laws that prohibit management and unions from entering into agreements requiring union membership as a condition of employment.

Fifth, unionization is substantially higher in the public or government sector than in the private sector. Still, public sector unionization faces challenges throughout the country. Traditionally, there was much less resistance to unionize in the public sector than in the private sector. However, the tide is changing. For example, Wisconsin Governor Scott Walker signed a law in 2011 that eliminated most union rights for government workers. The state lost nearly 100,000 public sector union members between 2011 and 2016.[5]

Management's attitude may be reflected in even small actions. Employees may begin to feel they are being treated more as machines than as people. Supervisors may fail to give reasons for unusual assignments and may expect employees to dedicate their lives to the firm without providing adequate rewards. The prevailing philosophy may be, "If you don't like it here, leave." A management philosophy that does not consider the needs of employees as individuals makes the firm ripe for unionization. Management must keep in mind that unions will be less likely to gain a foothold if they are not abusive of power. Companies that are pro-employees are not likely to be unionized.

11.2 Describe the basic union structure and organized labor's strategies for a stronger movement.

Union Structure and Labor Strategies

The labor movement has developed a multilevel organizational structure. This complex of organizations ranges from local unions to the two principal federations—the AFL-CIO and the Change to Win Coalition. Structured unions then pursue strategies to build membership and representation of workers in as many workplaces as possible.

Structure of Unions

local union
Basic element in the structure of the U.S. labor movement.

craft union
Bargaining unit, such as the Carpenters and Joiners Union, which is typically composed of members of a trade or skill in a specific locality.

LOCAL UNION The basic element in the structure of the U.S. labor movement is the **local union** (or, the *local*). To the individual union member, the local is the most important level in the structure of organized labor. Through the local, individuals deal with the employer on a day-to-day basis. A local union may fill a social role in the lives of its members, sponsoring dances, festivals, and other functions. It may be the focal point of the political organization and activity of its members.

There are two basic kinds of local unions: craft and industrial. A **craft union**, such as the Carpenters and Joiners Union, is typically composed of members of a trade or skill in a specific locality. Members usually acquire their job skills through an apprenticeship-training program. An **industrial union** generally consists of all the workers in a plant or group of plants. The type of work they do and the level of skill they possess are not a condition for membership in the union. An example of an industrial union is the United Auto Workers.

industrial union
Bargaining unit that generally consists of all the workers in a plant or group of plants.

The local union's functions are many and varied. Administering the collective bargaining agreement and representing workers in handling grievances are two very important activities. Other functions include keeping the membership informed about labor issues, promoting increased membership, maintaining effective contact with the national union, and when appropriate, negotiating with management at the local level.

NATIONAL UNION The most powerful level in the union structure is the national union. As stated previously, most locals affiliate with national unions. A **national union** is composed of local unions, which it charters. As such, it is the parent organization to local unions. The local union, not the individual worker, holds membership in the national union. Each local union provides financial support to the national union based on its membership size. The Service Employees International Union (SEIU) is the largest and fastest-growing national union in North America, with 2.1 million members in the United States, Canada, and Puerto Rico. According to the SEIU Web site, the SEIU has more than 1.1 million members in the health care field, including nurses, LPNs, doctors, lab technicians, nursing home workers, and home care workers. The International Brotherhood of Teamsters indicates that it has about 1.4 million members.

national union
Organization composed of local unions, which it charters.

The national union is governed by a national constitution and a national convention of local unions, which usually meets every two to five years. Elected officers, aided by an administrative staff, conduct the day-to-day operations of the national union. The national union is active in organizing workers within its jurisdiction, engaging in collective bargaining at the national level, and assisting its locals in their negotiations. In addition, the national union may provide numerous educational and research services for its locals, dispense strike funds, publish the union newspaper, provide legal counsel, and actively lobby at national and state levels.

AMERICAN FEDERATION OF LABOR AND CONGRESS OF INDUSTRIAL ORGANIZATIONS The **American Federation of Labor and Congress of Industrial Organizations (AFL-CIO)** is the central trade union federation in the United States. It is a loosely knit organization of national unions that has little formal power or control. The member national unions remain completely autonomous and decide their own policies and programs.

American Federation of Labor and Congress of Industrial Organizations (AFL-CIO)
Central trade union federation in the United States.

HR Web Wisdom
Change to Win Coalition
www.changetowin.org
Topics related to "What they say they stand for, campaigns, strategic organizing, key facts, and who we are" are included on the Web site.

The AFL-CIO is a voluntary federation of 55 national and international labor unions representing 12.5 million members according to its Web site, including about 3 million members in Working America, its community affiliate. It represents the interests of labor and its member national unions at the highest level. The federation does not engage in collective bargaining; however, it provides how member unions can cooperate to pursue common objectives and attempt to resolve internal problems faced by organized labor. The federation is financed by its member national unions and is governed by a national convention, which meets every two years.

The structure of the AFL-CIO is complex. National unions can affiliate with one or more of the trade and industrial departments. These departments seek to promote the interests of specific groups of workers who are in different unions but have common interests. The federation's major activities focus on improving the image of organized labor and lobbying on behalf of labor interests. In addition, politically educating constituencies is crucial, as is resolving disputes between national unions and policing internal affairs of member unions.

CHANGE TO WIN COALITION The **Change to Win Coalition** is a union federation consisting of unions that broke from the AFL-CIO and formally launched a rival labor federation representing 6 million workers from seven labor unions. The mission of the Change to Win Coalition is, "to unite the 50 million American workers who work in industries that cannot be outsourced or shipped overseas into strong unions that can win them a place in the American middle class—where their jobs provide good wages, decent working conditions and a voice on the job."[6]

Change to Win Coalition
Union federation consisting of seven unions that broke from the AFL-CIO and formally launched a rival labor federation representing about 6 million workers from 7 labor unions.

The coalition, led by the SEIU, focuses its energies on new membership growth and not as much on lobbying. Also, included in the new coalition are Unite Here, the United Food and Commercial Workers International Union, United Brotherhood of Carpenters and Joiners of America, the United Farm Workers of America, and the Laborers' International Union of North America. The coalition wanted to direct its efforts at workers in industries in which employers could not easily outsource jobs. The primary targets for organizing included industries in cleaning, health care, hotels and restaurants, retailing, and transportation, whereas the AFL-CIO focused on electoral politics as a strategy to promote the labor movement. For example, the AFL-CIO typically invests resources into helping union-friendly politicians being elected into political office.

Organized Labor's Strategies for Promoting a Stronger Labor Movement

Even though the labor movement has suffered setbacks over the past few decades, it is likely that union membership would have been even lower if the following strategies had not been used.

STRATEGICALLY LOCATED UNION MEMBERS The importance of the jobs held by union members significantly affects union power. For instance, an entire plant may have to be shut down if unionized machinists performing critical jobs decide to strike. Thus, a few strategically located union members may exert a disproportionate amount of power. The type of firm that is unionized can also determine a union's power. Unionization of truckers or dockworkers can affect the entire country, and subsequently, enhance the union's power base. This is precisely what the longshoremen did in the Baltimore, Maryland, strike of 2013, which affected about 15,000 individuals employed in port-related businesses and several tens of thousands more employees who work for the port. Through control of key industries, a union's power may extend to firms that are not unionized.

PULLING THE UNION THROUGH One union tactic that has worked effectively at times is to put pressure on the end user of a company's product to have a successful organizing attempt. The United Automobile, Aerospace and Agricultural Implement Workers of America authorized a strike against four Johnson Controls Inc. (JCI) factories that made interior parts for some of the country's best-selling vehicles. The quick two-day strike cost workers little lost income, but it hurt General Motors Corporation by shutting down production of their popular Chevy Trail Blazer sport utility vehicle. Worried about lost sales in a profitable segment and desiring to preserve good relations with the UAW, GM played an active behind-the-scenes role by pressuring JCI to settle the dispute. The result was a major UAW victory.

Committee on Political Education (COPE)
Political arm of the AFL-CIO.

POLITICAL INVOLVEMENT The political arm of the AFL-CIO is the **Committee on Political Education (COPE)**. Founded in 1955, its purpose is to support politicians who are friendly to the cause of organized labor. The union recommends and assists candidates who will best serve its interests. In presidential and congressional elections, union support may have a significant impact. Union members also encourage their friends and families to support those candidates. Joshua Freeman, professor of labor history at the City University of New York Graduate Center, said, "Unions have gotten weaker, but that weakness is not reflected in the political arena. They are very effective in mobilizing their members and families. It's now fairly common to have one out of four votes in an election coming from a union household."[7] The union's political influence increases as the size of the voting membership grows. With friends in government, the union is in a stronger position to maneuver against management. Political involvement means more than endorsing candidates at all levels of politics, and then attempting to deliver the union membership's vote. Unions give money to candidates who pledge to help pass pro-labor legislation. During the 2016 election season, labor unions spent nearly $110 million to support elections, representing a 38 percent increase spent during the 2012 election season.[8] The SEIU donated $19 million, the National Education Association donated $18.1 million, and the AFL-CIO spent $14.6 million.[9]

union salting
Process of training union organizers to apply for jobs at a company and, once hired, working to unionize employees.

UNION SALTING **Union salting** is the process of training union organizers to apply for jobs at a company and, once hired, working to unionize employees. A "union salt" is an employee who serves this role. Traditionally, union salting is a common activity used by blue-collar labor unions within the construction and building industries. Unions in other sectors, including the hotel and restaurant industries, have adopted union salting activities. For instance, James Walsh, author of *Against the House: The Dramatic World of an Undercover Union Organizer*, described his success as a union salt organizing worker at two Florida casinos. Walsh made two important points pertaining to achieving success.[10] First, one person cannot achieve salting. He needed fellow employees who commanded their peers' respect and were influential. Identifying leaders required him to socialize with coworkers. He took time to "hang out" with coworkers to get to know them and some of their workplace concerns. Second, union salters sometimes reveal their intentions, but often they do not.[11] Walsh chose not to reveal his intentions because many workers would fear losing their jobs if asked to speak about their concerns, especially if management found out. Naturally, company management would be displeased to know if one or more employee was trying to organize workers.

There has been a variety of court cases regarding legal protections for union salts. In general, a company cannot terminate these employees solely because they also work for a union. However, if productivity suffers, a company may justifiably terminate a worker's employment.

flooding the community
Process of the union inundating communities with organizers to target a business.

FLOODING THE COMMUNITY **Flooding the community** is the process of the union inundating communities with organizers to target a business in an organizing attempt. With their flooding campaigns, unions typically choose companies in which nonunionized employees have asked for help in organizing. Generally, national unions recruit and train organizers. They are typically young, ambitious, college-educated people with a passion for the U.S. labor movement. Organizers meet with employees in small groups and even visit them at home. They know every nuance of a company's operations and target weak managers' departments to appeal to dissatisfied employees who may be willing to organize.

public awareness campaigns
Labor maneuvers that do not coincide with a strike or organizing campaign to pressure an employer for better wages, benefits, and the like.

PUBLIC AWARENESS CAMPAIGNS **Public awareness campaigns** involve labor maneuvers that do not coincide with a strike or an organizing campaign to pressure an employer for better wages, benefits, and the like. Increasingly, these campaigns serve as an alternative to strikes because more employers are willing to replace their striking employees. Employers have less recourse against labor campaigns that involve joining political and community groups that support union goals or picketing homes of a company's board of directors. They are also defenseless in dealing with the union's initiating proxy challenges to actions negative to labor, writing letters to the editors of the local newspapers, and filing charges with administrative agencies such as the Occupational Safety and Health Administration and the National Labor Relations Board (NRLB). These types of public awareness campaigns, which are not tied directly to labor gains, are often effective methods of developing union leverage. In some cases, the goal is creating public awareness to improve workplace conditions without the necessity of unionizing. For instance, Working America, a community affiliate of the AFL-CIO, launched the Massage Advocacy Group Project in 2015, in Portland, Oregon, to educate the public about the health benefits of massage as well as expose undesirable employment arrangements experienced by most therapists. Massage therapist Arwyn Daemyir said, "We are speaking about low wages, long hours, and unfair workplace practices, and being asked to do work that isn't paid for."[12] Generally, massage therapists receive pay for the time they are providing massages, but not for other work expected by employers, including laundry and front office tasks. Ultimately, campaign organizers hope that public awareness will encourage employers to provide fairer employment terms.

BUILDING ORGANIZING FUNDS To encourage workers to come together, the AFL-CIO often asks its affiliates to increase organizing funds. The federation may also increase funding to its Organizing Institute, which trains organizers, and even launches advertising campaigns to create wider public support for unions. National unions also create organizing funds.

UNIONS COLLABORATING WITH HIGH SCHOOLS Some high schools are pairing up with labor unions to prepare students for a career. Ten students from Saydel High School's construction shop class have entered a pilot program that allows them direct entry into the United Association of Plumbers and Steamfitters Local Union 33 once they graduate. At Local 33, apprentices receive training in plumbing, heating, air conditioning, medical gas, high purity piping, and water treatment. Greg Foshe, business manager of Local 33, said, "The goal of this program is to bring people into the union at a younger age. When students go from high school directly into their trade, they are going from learning situation to learning situation, creating a fast track educational experience."[13]

ORGANIZING YOUNGER WORKERS Union organizers often pursue a strategy of recruiting younger workers, and it may be coming at the right time because the lowest union membership rate is occurring among this group. In fact, according to the Bureau of Labor Statistics, the lowest union membership rate occurred among those ages 16 to 24 (4.4 percent).[14] In the past, senior organizers often considered younger organizers as second-class citizens. Consider what Rachael Hunt, a young union organizer, said, "Too many times, more experienced trade unionists have spoken to me as if I were a blank slate: ready to mold and be shaped to meet older organizers' viewpoints and goals. This same top-down, stale, bureaucratic organizational model that is crippling unions is also its biggest barrier to recruiting young people."[15] Richard Trumka, AFL-CIO president, said the following about including the ideas of younger workers: "I'm not suggesting that the labor movement ought to abandon all its traditions. But what I am saying is that nostalgia for the past is no strategy for the future. Tradition should always have a vote; we just can't let it have a veto."[16]

card check
Organizing approach by labor in which employees sign a nonsecret card of support if they want unionization, and if 50 percent of the workforce plus one worker signs a card, the union is formed.

ORGANIZING THROUGH THE CARD CHECK The **card check** is an organizing approach by labor in which employees sign a non-secret card of support if they want unionization, and if 50 percent of the workforce plus one worker signs a card, the union is formed. This organizing method's success depends on management not objecting to the use of card check. It permits workers to decide in a non-secret election their union status. Essentially, organizations decide to remain neutral and peacefully permit their employees to decide whether they want to unionize and not interfere as the union passes out authorization cards.

In 2013, the UAW launched a card-check campaign at the Volkswagen manufacturing facility in Tennessee. The card check procedure avoids holding a secret ballot by having workers sign cards to join a union. Most workers in a bargaining unit must sign cards, which are then certified, before the company recognizes the union. The union failed when eight workers represented by the National Right to Work Legal Defense Foundation filed charges with the NLRB alleging that the UAW had lied to workers and bullied them into signing cards.[17] The NLRB dismissed the charges; however, many workers protested the card-check approach, which pressured Volkswagen to hold a secret-ballot election. Some card check campaigns lead to unionization. In 2008, the Teamsters union launched a nationwide card-check campaign. Bargaining units from across the country signed authorization cards and were recognized as a union.[18] The largest was the drivers and dockworkers employed by UPS Freight, which added more than 9,900 members.[19]

11.3 Discuss laws affecting collective bargaining.

Laws Affecting Collective Bargaining

A variety of laws influence the collective bargaining process and outcomes. Some are geared specifically toward the process and others are laws that we have previously discussed that influence outcomes.

National Labor Relations Act

The National Labor Relations Act (NLRA) of 1935 (also known as the Wagner Act) is one of the most significant labor/management relations statutes ever enacted. The act declared legislative support, on a broad scale, for the right of employees to organize and engage in collective bargaining. Section 7 conveys the spirit of the Wagner Act, which defines the substantive rights of employees:

> *Employees shall have the right to self-organization, to form, join, or assist labor organizations, to bargain collectively through representatives of their own choosing, and to engage in other concerted activities, for collective bargaining or other mutual aid or protection.*

HR Web Wisdom
National Labor Relations Board
www.nlrb.gov
The NLRB is a federal agency that administers the National Labor Relations Act.

The NRLA created the National Labor Relations Board (NLRB). At the time, the board helped the labor movement, which at times resulted in heated and sometimes violent management resistance.[20] The NLRB was given two principal functions: (1) to establish procedures for holding bargaining unit elections and to monitor the election procedures (representation elections); and (2) to investigate complaints and prevent unlawful acts involving unfair labor practices. Much of the NLRB's work is delegated to 33 regional offices throughout the country. The President makes appointments to the NLRB, which require Senate confirmation. They decide on detailed rules governing union and management behavior, then on how to conduct elections.

Section 8 is a key part of the NLRA because it defines unfair labor practices. Unfair labor practices may result from an employer or union's actions. The act specifies five possible unfair employer labor practices:

- Interfering with, restraining, or coercing employees in the exercise of their right to self-organization.
- Dominating or interfering in the affairs of a union.

HR BLOOPERS

Stopping Unionization at Packer Industries

It appears that the rumors about a union organizing effort at Packer Industries are true. Jay Golden, the Director of HR, just confirmed with a supervisor that the employees have started signing authorization cards. Jay suspected this was coming because he had received an increased number of complaints about pay and working conditions over the last several months. He learned that a small group of employees is leading efforts to build interest in a union and Jay is very concerned. He is convinced that a union would create long-term challenges for the company and his instincts tell him he should do whatever is necessary to discourage employees from organizing. The company's CEO agrees with Jay and together they have started efforts to convince employees that they are better off without the union. The CEO started by holding a mandatory meeting where she made it very clear that if the union is certified, they can all count on a reduction in pay and benefits. Jay also has identified one of the leaders of the unionizing efforts. He has decided to transfer him to the second shift where there are fewer employees for him to talk to about the union. Jay is sure that this employee's transfer will make it clear to all employees that Packer Industries will do whatever it takes to prevent them from unionizing.

If your professor has assigned this, go to **www.pearson.com/mylab/management** to complete the HR Bloopers exercise and test your application of these concepts when faced with real-world decisions.

- Discriminating concerning hire or tenure or any condition of employment for encouraging or discouraging union membership.
- Discriminating against or discharging an employee who has filed charges or given testimony under the act.
- Refusing to bargain with chosen representatives of employees.

The law prohibits unions from engaging in unfair labor practices. Primarily, unions cannot force employees to waive their rights as defined in Section 7. In addition, unions may not encourage employer discrimination against employees who have been denied union membership unless such a denial was the result of failure to pay union membership dues.

Following passage of the Wagner Act, union membership increased from approximately 3 million to 15 million between 1935 and 1947.

Labor-Management Relations Act

In 1947, with public pressure mounting, Congress passed the Labor-Management Relations Act (Taft-Hartley Act). The Taft-Hartley Act extensively revised the NLRA. A new period began in the evolution of public policy regarding labor. The pendulum had begun to swing toward a more balanced position between labor and management.

Some of the important changes introduced by the Taft-Hartley Act included the following:

- Modifying Section 7 to include the right of employees to refrain from union activity as well as engage in it.
- Prohibiting the closed shop and narrowing the freedom of the parties to authorize the union shop.
- Broadening the employer's right of free speech.
- Providing that employers need not recognize or bargain with unions formed by supervisors.
- Giving employees the right to initiate decertification petitions.
- Providing for government intervention in national emergency strikes.

Another significant change extended the concept of unfair labor practices to unions. Labor organizations were to refrain from the following:

- Restraining or coercing employees in the exercise of their guaranteed collective bargaining rights.
- Causing an employer to discriminate in any way against an employee to encourage or discourage union membership.
- Refusing to bargain in good faith with an employer regarding wages, hours, and other terms and conditions of employment.

- Engaging in certain types of strikes and boycotts.
- Requiring employees covered by union-shop contracts to pay initiation fees or dues in an amount which the board finds excessive or discriminatory under all circumstances.
- *Featherbedding*, or requiring that an employer pay for services not performed.

FYI

In fiscal year 2016, the NLRB received 21,326 complaints of unfair labor practices and only 6,010 were settled during the same period.[21]

One of the most controversial elements of the Taft-Hartley Act is its Section 14b, which permits states to enact right-to-work legislation. In the 22 states without right-to-work laws, it is legal for an employer to agree with the union that a new employee must join the union after a certain period (generally 30 days), or be terminated. This is referred to as a "union-shop agreement." Right-to-work laws prohibit management and unions from entering into agreements requiring union membership as a condition of employment. These laws are state statutes or constitutional provisions that ban the practice of requiring union membership or financial support as a condition of employment. They establish the legal right of employees to decide for themselves whether to join or financially support a union.

Antidiscrimination Laws and Executive Orders

In Chapter 3, we discussed a variety of federal laws and executive orders that are designed to protect employees from illegal discrimination. Some of these federal laws include the Age Discrimination in Employment Act, the Pregnancy Discrimination Act, and the Equal Pay Act. We also noted that a variety of state and local laws provide similar or enhanced protection. These laws and executive orders made it easier for unions to protect the rights of many members.

11.4 Summarize the formation of bargaining units and the collective bargaining process.

Bargaining Unit Formation and the Collective Bargaining Process

Before a union can negotiate a contract, it must first be formed or certified. The primary law governing the relationship of companies and unions is the NLRA, as amended. Collective bargaining is one of the key parts of the act. Section 8(d) of the act defines collective bargaining, which we described as the process of negotiation between union representatives and representatives of management to agree on a collective bargaining agreement or contract. The act specifies that both the employer and representatives of employees meet at reasonable times to confer in good faith with respect to wages, hours, and other terms related to conditions of employment, or to negotiate an agreement.

Once the NLRB certifies the union, labor and management can engage in collective bargaining. Most union/management agreements in the United States are for a three-year period though contracts may be in effect for as long as seven or eight years. The bargaining structure can affect the conduct of collective bargaining. The four major structures are one company dealing with a single union, several companies dealing with a single union, several unions dealing with a single company, and several companies dealing with several unions. Most contract bargaining is carried out under the first type of structure. The process can become quite complicated when several companies and unions are involved in the same negotiations. However, even when there is only one industry involved and one group of workers with similar skills, collective bargaining can be very difficult.

bargaining unit
Group of employees, not necessarily union members, recognized by an employer or certified by an administrative agency as appropriate for representation by a labor organization for purposes of collective bargaining.

Forming a Bargaining Unit

The act further provides that the designated representative of the employees shall be the exclusive representative for all the employees in the unit for purposes of collective bargaining. A **bargaining unit** consists of a group of employees, not necessarily union members, recognized by an employer or certified by an administrative agency as appropriate for representation by a labor organization for purposes of collective bargaining.

FIGURE 11-2
Steps That Lead to Forming a Bargaining Unit

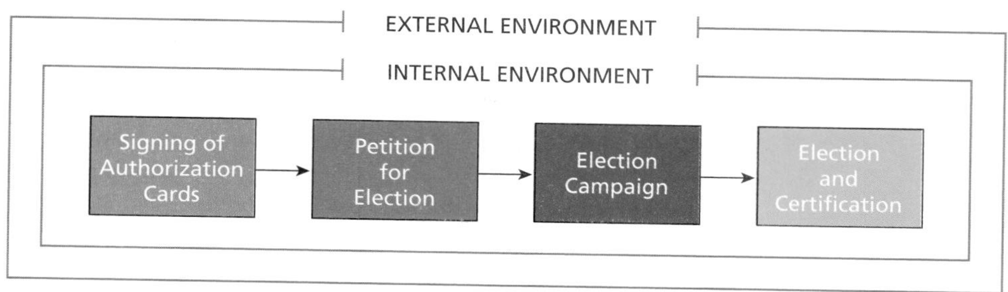

A unit may cover the employees in one plant of an employer, or it may cover employees in two or more plants of the same employer. Although the act requires the representative to be selected by the employees, it does not require any procedure to be used so long as the choice clearly reflects the desire of most employees in the bargaining unit. The employee representative is normally chosen in a secret-ballot election conducted by the NLRB. When workers desire to become the bargaining representative for a group of employees, several steps leading to certification must be taken (Figure 11-2).

Prior to observing the distribution of authorization cards, there are usually signs of an upcoming union organizing attempt. Some indications might be an increase in the number or intensity of employee complaints on wages, hours, working conditions, or management practices; unusual or more frequent employee challenges to management authority; and, an increase in the number of formal complaints to government agencies such as the U.S. Occupational Safety and Health Administration, U.S. Department of Labor, and state or federal equal employment agencies.

authorization card
Document indicating that an employee wants to be represented by a labor organization in collective bargaining.

SIGNING OF AUTHORIZATION CARDS A prerequisite to becoming a recognized bargaining unit is to determine whether there is sufficient interest on the part of employees to justify the unit. Evidence of this interest is expressed when at least 30 percent of the employees in a work group sign an authorization card (Table 11-1). The **authorization card** is a document indicating that an employee wants to be represented by a labor organization in collective bargaining. Most union organizers will not proceed unless at least 50 percent of the workers in the group sign cards.

PETITION FOR ELECTION After the authorization cards have been signed, a petition for an election may be made to the appropriate regional office of the NLRB. When the petition is filed, the NLRB will investigate. The purpose of the investigation is to determine, among other things, the following:

- Whether the board has jurisdiction to conduct an election.
- Whether there is a sufficient showing of employee interest to justify an election.
- Whether a question of representation exists (for example, the employee representative has demanded recognition, which has been denied by the employer).

TABLE 11-1

Example of an Authorization Card

YES, I WANT THE UNION

I, the undersigned, and employee of

(Name of Company)

Hereby authorize the (Name of the Union) to act as my collective bargaining agent with the company for wages, hours, and other terms and conditions of employment.

NAME ______________________ DATE ______________________

ADDRESS ____

CITY ______________________ STATE ______________ ZIP ______________

JOB TITLE ____

SIGN HERE ____

NOTE: THIS AUTHORIZATION IS TO BE SIGNED AND DATED IN EMPLOYEE'S OWN HANDWRITING. YOUR RIGHT TO SIGN THIS CARD IS PROTECTED BY LAW.

- Whether the election will include appropriate employees in the bargaining unit (for instance, the board is prohibited from including plant guards in the same unit with the other employees).
- Whether the representative named in the petition is qualified (for example, a supervisor or any other management representative may not be an employee representative).
- Whether there are any barriers to an election in the form of existing contracts or prior elections held within the past 12 months.[22]

If these conditions have been met, the NLRB will ordinarily direct that an election be held. A 2015 rule permits elections to be held as soon as 13 days after the union's petition.[23] Election details are left largely to the agency's regional director.

ELECTION CAMPAIGN Both union and management usually promote their causes actively during an election. Unions will continue to encourage workers to join the union, and management may begin a campaign to tell workers the benefits of remaining union free. The supervisor's role during the campaign is crucial. Supervisors need to conduct themselves in a manner that avoids violating the law and committing unfair labor practices. Specifically, they should be aware of what can and cannot be done during the pre-election campaign period. Throughout the campaign, supervisors should keep upper management informed about employee attitudes.

Theoretically, both union and management may tell their stories without interference from the other side. At times, the campaign becomes quite intense. Election results are invalid if the NLRB identifies conduct that interfered with the employees' freedom of choice. Examples of such conduct include the following:

- An employer or a union threatens loss of jobs or benefits to influence employees' votes or union activities.
- An employer or a union misstates key facts in the election campaign when the other party does not have a chance to reply.
- Either an employer or a union incites racial or religious prejudice by inflammatory campaign appeals.
- An employer fires employees to discourage or encourage their union activities or a union causes an employer to take such an action.
- An employer or a union makes campaign speeches to assembled groups of employees on company time within 24 hours of an election.

ELECTION AND CERTIFICATION The NLRB monitors the secret-ballot election on the date set. Its representatives are responsible for making sure that only eligible employees vote and for counting the votes. Following a valid election, the board will issue a certification of the results to the participants. If a majority of the employees voting in the bargaining unit has chosen a union, it will receive a certificate showing that it is now the official bargaining representative of the employees in the unit. However, the right to represent employees does not mean they have the right to dictate terms to management that would adversely affect the organization. The bargaining process does not require either party to make concessions, it only compels them to bargain in good faith in collective bargaining.

Collective Bargaining Process

The collective bargaining process is fundamental to union and management relations in the United States. Regardless of the current state of labor/management relations, the general aspects of the collective bargaining process are the same and are illustrated in Figure 11-3. Depending on the type of relationship encountered, the collective bargaining process may be relatively simple, or it may be a long, tense struggle for both parties. Regardless of the complexity of the bargaining issues, the ability to reach agreement is the key to any successful negotiation.

As you can see, both external and internal environmental factors can influence the process. The first step in the collective bargaining process is preparing for negotiations. This step is often extensive and ongoing for both union and management. After the issues to be negotiated have been determined, the two sides confer to reach a mutually acceptable contract. Although breakdowns in negotiations can occur, both labor and management have at their disposal tools and arguments that can be used to convince the other side to accept their views. Eventually, however, management and the union usually reach an agreement that defines the rules for the duration of the contract.

FIGURE 11-3
Collective Bargaining Process

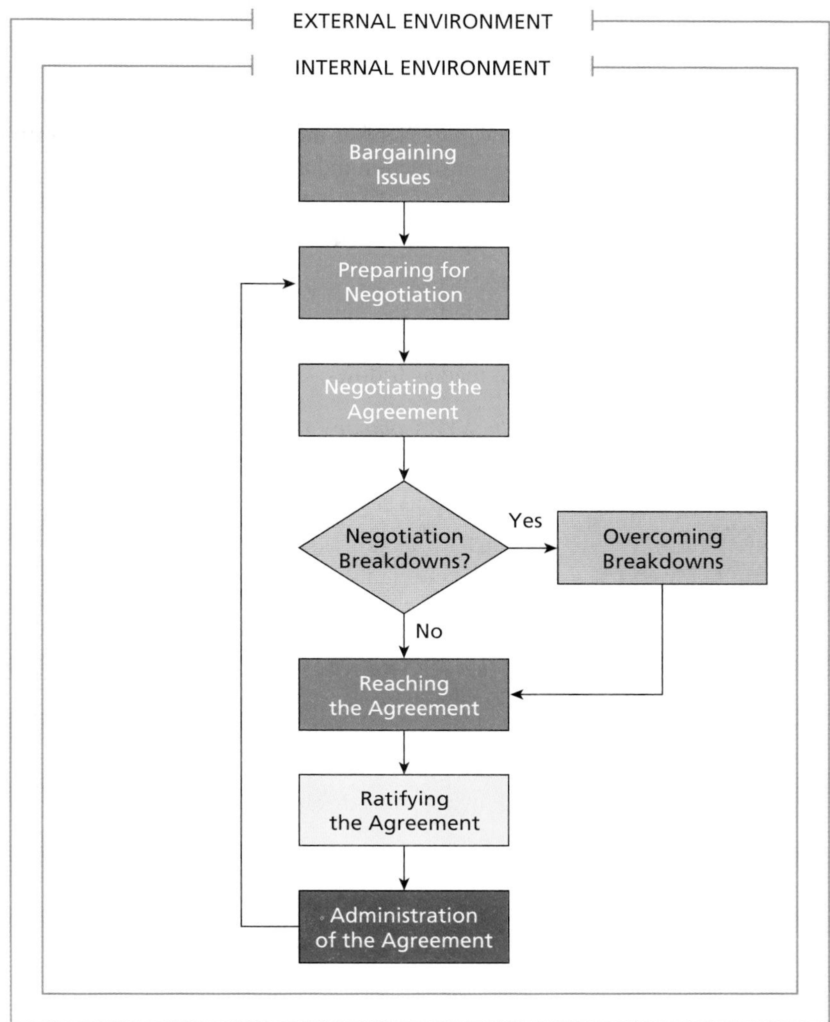

The next step is for the union membership to ratify the agreement. There is a feedback loop from "Administration of the Agreement" to "Preparing for Negotiation." Collective bargaining is a continuous and dynamic process, and preparing for the next round of negotiations often begins the moment a contract is ratified.

Bargaining Issues

Because of the complex issues facing labor and management today, negotiating teams must carefully prepare for the bargaining sessions. Prior to meeting at the bargaining table, the negotiators should thoroughly know the culture, climate, history, present economic state, and wage and benefits structure of both the organization and similar organizations. Because the length of a typical labor agreement is three years, negotiators should develop a contract that is successful both now and in the future. This consideration should prevail for both management and labor, although it rarely does. During the term of an agreement, the two sides usually discover contract provisions that need to be added, deleted, or modified. These items become proposals to be addressed in the next round of negotiations.

mandatory bargaining issues
Bargaining issues that fall within the definition of wages, hours, and other terms and conditions of employment.

permissive bargaining issues
Issues that may be raised, but neither side may insist that they be bargained over.

Bargaining issues can be divided into three categories: mandatory, permissive, and prohibited. **Mandatory bargaining issues** fall within the definition of wages, hours, and other terms and conditions of employment. These issues generally have an immediate and direct effect on workers' jobs. A refusal to bargain in these areas is grounds for an unfair labor practice charge. At times, collective bargaining toward new wage, rules, and benefits agreements may drag on for a long time. **Permissive bargaining issues** may be raised, but neither side may insist that they be bargained over. For example, management may want to bargain over health benefits for retired workers, but the union may choose not to bargain over the issue. Another permissive bargaining issue might be the union wanting management to provide child-care arrangements. **Prohibited bargaining issues**, such as the issue of the closed shop, an arrangement whereby union membership is a prerequisite, are statutorily outlawed. The Taft-Hartley Act made the closed shop illegal. However, the act was modified 12 years later by the Landrum-Griffin Act to permit a closed shop in the construction industry. This is the only exception allowed.

prohibited bargaining issues
Issues that are statutorily outlawed from collective bargaining.

Despite much dissimilarity, certain topics are included in virtually all labor agreements. Each topic discussed in the following section may be an issue in negotiations.

RECOGNITION This section usually appears at the beginning of the labor agreement. Its purpose is to identify the union that is recognized as the bargaining representative and to describe the bargaining unit—that is, the employees for whom the union speaks. A typical recognition section might read as follows:

> *The XYZ Company recognizes the ABC Union as the sole and exclusive representative of the bargaining unit employees for collective bargaining regarding wages, hours, and other conditions of employment.*

MANAGEMENT RIGHTS A section that is often but not always written into the labor agreement spells out the rights of management. If no such section is included, management may reason that it retains control of all topics not described as being able to be bargained in the contract. The precise content of the management rights section will vary by industry, company, and union. When included, management rights generally involve three areas:

- Freedom to select the business objectives of the company
- Freedom to determine the uses to which the material assets of the enterprise will be devoted
- Power to take disciplinary action for cause

Management essentially possesses the right to determine the work to be done and where, when, and how it is to be done; the number of employees who will do the work; supervise and instruct employees in doing the work; correct employees whose work performance or personal conduct fails to meet reasonable standards; and, hire, dismiss, and promote workers based on performance.

closed shop
Arrangement making union membership a prerequisite for employment.

union shop
Requirement that all employees become members of the union after a specified period of employment (the legal minimum is 30 days) or after a union-shop provision has been negotiated.

maintenance of membership
Employees who are members of the union when the labor agreement is signed or who later voluntarily join must continue their memberships until the termination of the agreement as a condition of employment.

agency shop
Labor agreement provision requiring, as a condition of employment, that each nonunion member of a bargaining unit pay the union the equivalent of membership dues as a service charge in return for the union acting as the bargaining agent.

open shop
Employment on equal terms to union members and nonmembers alike.

UNION SECURITY Union security is typically one of the first items negotiated in a collective bargaining agreement. The objective of union security provisions is to ensure that the union continues to exist and perform its functions. A strong union security provision makes it easier for the union to enroll and retain members. Some basic forms of union security clauses are next described.

A **closed shop** is an arrangement whereby union membership is a prerequisite for employment. As noted previously, closed shops are illegal in every industry except for the construction industry.

A **union shop** arrangement requires that all employees become members of the union after a specified period of employment (the legal minimum is 30 days) or after a union-shop provision has been negotiated. Employees must remain members of the union as a condition of employment for the duration of the contract. The union shop is generally legal in the United States, except in states that have right-to-work laws.

With **maintenance of membership**, employees who are members of the union at the time the labor agreement is signed, or who later voluntarily join must continue their memberships until the termination of the agreement as a condition of employment. This form of recognition is also prohibited in most states that have right-to-work laws.

An **agency shop** provision does not require employees to join the union; however, the labor agreement requires that, as a condition of employment, each nonunion member of the bargaining unit pay the union the equivalent of membership dues as a kind of tax, or service charge, in return for the union acting as the bargaining agent. The NLRA requires the union to bargain for all members of the bargaining unit, including nonunion employees. The agency shop is outlawed in most states that have right-to-work laws.

An open shop describes the absence of union security, rather than its presence. The **open shop**, strictly defined, is employment on equal terms to union members and nonmembers alike. Under this arrangement, no employee is required to join or contribute to the union financially.

checkoff of dues
Agreement by which a company agrees to withhold union dues from members' paychecks and to forward the money directly to the union.

Another type of security that unions attempt to achieve is the checkoff of dues. A checkoff agreement may be used in addition to any of the previously mentioned shop agreements. Under the **checkoff of dues** provision, the company agrees to withhold union dues from members' paychecks and to forward the money directly to the union. Because of provisions in the Taft-Hartley Act, each union member must voluntarily sign a statement authorizing this deduction. Dues check-off is important to the union because it eliminates much of the expense, time, and hassle of collecting dues from each member every pay period or once a month.

COMPENSATION This section typically constitutes a large portion of most labor agreements. Virtually any item that can affect compensation may be included in labor agreements. Some of the items frequently covered include the following:

The *wage rate schedule* refers to the base rates to be paid each year of the contract for each job are included in this section. At times, unions can obtain a cost-of-living adjustment (COLA), or escalator clause, in the contract to protect the purchasing power of employees' earnings. Another section of the agreement may cover *hours of work, overtime pay, hazard pay, and premium pay*, such as shift differentials.

For some firms, *jury pay* amounts to the employee's entire salary when he or she is serving jury duty. Others pay the difference between the amount employees receive from the court and the compensation that would have been earned. The procedure covering jury pay is typically stated in the contract.

Layoff or severance pay sections specify the amount that employees in various jobs or seniority levels will be paid if they are laid off or terminated is a frequently included item.

Recognized *holidays* and the amount of pay that a worker will receive if he or she must work on a holiday is specified here. In addition, the pay procedure for times when a holiday falls on a worker's normal day off is provided.

The *vacation* section spells out the amount of vacation that a person may take based on seniority. Any restrictions as to when the vacation may be taken are also stated.

grievance
Employee's dissatisfaction or feeling of personal injustice relating to his or her employment.

grievance procedure
Formal, systematic process that permits employees to express complaints without jeopardizing their jobs.

GRIEVANCE PROCEDURE Virtually all labor agreements include some form of grievance procedure. A **grievance** can be broadly defined as an employee's dissatisfaction or feeling of personal injustice relating to his or her employment. A **grievance procedure** (discussed later in this chapter) is a formal, systematic process that permits employees to express complaints without jeopardizing their jobs.

seniority
The length of time an employee has been associated with the company, division, department, or job.

EMPLOYEE SECURITY This section of the labor agreement establishes the procedures that cover job security for individual employees. Seniority is a key topic related to employee security. **Seniority** is the length of time an employee has been associated with the company, division, department, or job. Seniority may be determined companywide, by division, by department, or by job. Agreement on seniority is important because the person with the most seniority, as defined in the labor agreement, is typically the last to be laid off and the first to be recalled. The seniority system also provides a basis for promotion decisions. When qualifications are met, employees with the greatest seniority will likely be considered first for promotion to higher-level jobs.

JOB-RELATED FACTORS Many of the rules governing employee actions on the job are also included. Some of the more important factors are company work rules, work standards, and rules related to safety. This section varies, depending on the nature of the industry and the product manufactured.

Preparation for Negotiations

union steward
An individual who is both an official of the union and a company employee who represents and defends the interests of fellow employees.

The union must continuously gather information regarding membership needs to isolate areas of dissatisfaction. The union steward is normally in the best position to collect such data.[24] A **union steward** is both an official of the union and a company employee who represents and defends the interests of fellow employees. Union stewards are elected by their peers and are well informed regarding union members' attitudes. The union steward constantly funnels information up through the union's chain of command, where the data are compiled and analyzed. Union leadership attempts to uncover any areas of dissatisfaction because the general union membership must approve any agreement before it becomes final. Because they are elected, union leaders will lose their positions if the demands they make of management do not represent the desires of the general membership.

Management also spends long hours preparing for negotiations. All aspects of the current contracts are considered, including flaws that should be corrected. When preparing for negotiations, management should listen carefully to first-line managers. These individuals administer the labor agreement on a day-to-day basis and must live with errors made in negotiating the contract. An alert line manager is also able to inform upper management of the demands unions may plan to make during negotiations.

Management also attempts periodically to obtain information regarding employee attitudes. Surveys are often administered to workers to determine their feelings toward their jobs and job environment. Union and management representatives like to know as much as possible about employee attitudes when they sit down at the bargaining table.

Another part of preparation for negotiations involves identifying various positions that both union and management will take as the negotiations progress. Each usually takes an initially extreme position, representing the optimum conditions union or management would prefer. The two sides will likely determine absolute limits to their offers or demands before a breakdown in negotiations occurs. They also usually prepare fallback positions based on combinations of issues. Preparations should be detailed because clear minds often do not prevail during the heat of negotiations.

A major consideration in preparing for negotiations is the selection of the bargaining teams. The makeup of the management team usually depends on the type of organization and its size. Normally, labor relations specialists, with the advice and assistance of operating managers, conduct bargaining. Sometimes, top executives are directly involved, particularly in smaller firms. Larger companies use staff specialists (a HR manager or industrial relations executive), managers of principal operating divisions, and in some cases, an outside consultant, such as a labor attorney.

The responsibility for conducting negotiations for the union is usually entrusted to union officers. At the local level, rank-and-file members who are elected specifically for this purpose will normally supplement the bargaining committee. In addition, the national union will often send a representative to act in an advisory capacity or even to participate directly in the bargaining sessions. The real task of the union negotiating team is to develop and obtain solutions to the problems raised by the union's membership.

Negotiating the Agreement

There is no way to ensure speedy and mutually acceptable results from negotiations. At best, the parties can attempt to create an atmosphere that will lend itself to steady progress and productive results. For example, the two negotiating teams usually meet at an agreed-on neutral site, such as a hotel. When a favorable relationship can be established early, eleventh-hour (or last-minute) bargaining can often be avoided. It is equally important for union and management negotiators to strive to develop and maintain clear and open lines of communication. Collective bargaining is a problem-solving activity; consequently, good communication is essential to its success. Negotiations should be conducted in the privacy of the conference room, not in the news media. Often in the media, the unions belittle management and naturally management strikes back. The results can be harmful, often to both sides. If the negotiators feel that publicity is necessary, joint releases to the media may avoid unnecessary conflict.

The negotiating phase of collective bargaining begins with each side presenting its initial demands. Because a collective bargaining settlement can be expensive for a firm, the cost of various proposals should be estimated as accurately as possible. Some changes can be quite expensive, and others cost little or nothing, but the cost of the various proposals being considered must always be carefully deliberated. The term *negotiating* suggests a certain amount of give-and-take, the purpose of which is to lower the other side's expectations. For example, the union might bargain to upgrade its members' economic and working conditions and the company might negotiate to maintain or enhance profitability.

One of the costliest components of any collective bargaining agreement is a wage increase provision. An example of the negotiation of a wage increase is shown in Figure 11-4. In this example, labor initially demands a 40-cent-per-hour increase. Management counters with an offer of only 10 cents per hour. Both labor and management, as expected, reject each other's demand. Plan B calls for labor to lower its demand to a 30-cents-per-hour increase. Management counters with an offer of 20 cents. The positions in plan B are feasible to both sides, as both groups are in the bargaining zone. Wages within the bargaining zone are those that management and labor

FIGURE 11-4
Example of Negotiating a Wage Increase

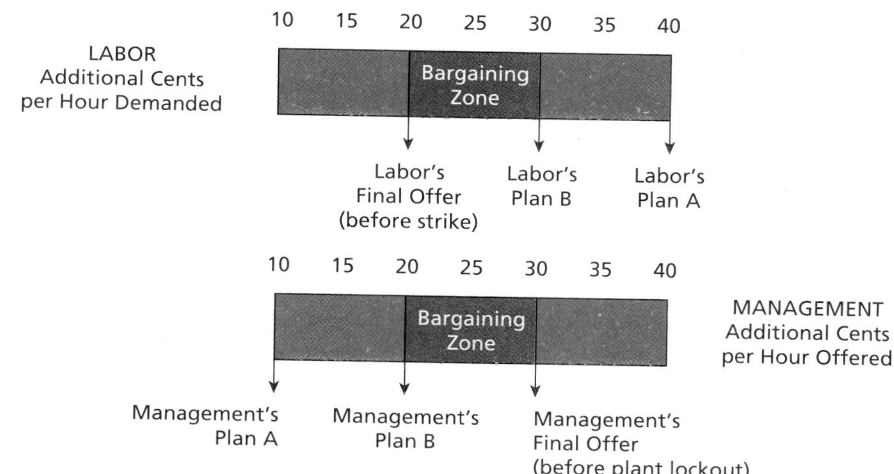

can both accept, in this case, an increase of between 20 cents and 30 cents per hour. The exact amount will be determined by the power of the bargaining unit and the skills of the negotiators.

The realities of negotiations are not for the weak of heart and at times are like a high-stakes poker game. A certain amount of bluffing and raising the ante takes place in many negotiations. The ultimate bluff for the union is when a negotiator says, "If our demands are not met, we are prepared to strike." Management's version of this bluff would be to threaten a lockout. Each of these tactics will be discussed later as a means of overcoming breakdowns in negotiations. The party with the greater leverage can expect to extract the most concessions.

Finding solutions to conflict can be win/win or win/lose. In the case of win/win, both parties to a conflict receive something of value even if it is not what each party wanted. For example, workers and management are at odds over a request for a higher hourly pay rate from $15 to $25. Management claims that raising wages to the $25 level could threaten job security if company sales declined by any amount. If workers and management can agree to a compromise increase (say, a pay raise to $20 per hour), then this would be a win/win situation. This is a win/win situation because workers received a pay raise and management provided more to employees while limiting compensation cost increases. Had management not agreed to any raise, the situation would have been win/lose because labor costs would have been contained at the expense of employee morale. In the Watch It Video, the importance of finding a win/win outcome to resolve conflict is discussed.

Watch It I
If your professor has assigned this, sign into **www.pearson.com/mylab/management** to watch a video titled Rudi's Bakery: Conflict and Negotiation and to respond to questions.

Even though one party in the negotiating process may appear to possess the greater power, negotiators often take care to keep the other side from losing face. They recognize that the balance of power may switch rapidly. By the time the next round of negotiations occurs, the pendulum may be swinging back in favor of the other side. Even when management appears to have the upper hand, it may make minor concessions that will allow the labor leader to claim gains for the union. Management may demand that workers pay for grease rags that are lost if the loss of these rags has become excessive. To obtain labor's agreement to this demand, management may agree to provide new uniforms for the workers if the cost of these uniforms would be less than the cost of lost rags. Thus, labor leaders, although forced to concede to management's demand, could show the workers that they have obtained a concession from management. Each side usually does not expect to obtain all the demands presented in its first proposal. Labor can lose a demand and continue to bring it up in the future. Demands for benefits that the union does not expect to receive when they are first made are known as **beachhead demands**.

beachhead demands
Demands that the union does not expect management to meet when they are first made.

Overcoming Breakdowns in Negotiations

At times negotiations break down, even though both labor and management may sincerely want to arrive at an equitable contract settlement. Several means of removing roadblocks may be used to get negotiations moving again.

THIRD-PARTY INTERVENTION Often, an outside person can intervene to help when an agreement cannot be reached and the two sides reach an impasse. The reasons behind each party's position may be quite rational, or the breakdown may be related to emotional disputes that tend to become distorted during the heat of negotiations. Regardless of the cause, something must be done to continue the negotiations. The two basic types of third-party intervention are mediation and arbitration.

mediation
Neutral third party enters the negotiations and attempts to facilitate a resolution to a labor dispute when a bargaining impasse has occurred.

In **mediation**, a neutral third party enters the negotiations and attempts to facilitate a resolution to a labor dispute when a bargaining impasse has occurred. A mediator serves a facilitator role. The objective of mediation is to persuade the parties to resume negotiations and reach a settlement. For instance, the Stop & Shop supermarket and the United Food and Commercial Workers (UFCW) union could not find common ground in setting terms for wages and employee benefits. Most union members authorized a strike, which prompted Stop & Shop management to agree to have a mediator facilitate negotiations. Daniel P. Clifford, president of UFCW Local 1459 indicated, "They hope to avoid a complete breakdown in negotiations and reach a settlement as we all do."[25]

A mediator has no power to force a settlement but can help in the search for solutions, make recommendations, and work to open blocked channels of communication. Successful mediation depends to a substantial degree on the tact, diplomacy, patience, and perseverance of the mediator. The mediator's fresh insights are used to get discussions going again. Mediation is voluntary at every step of the process. The mediator serves as an informal coach, helping to ensure that the discussions are fair and effective.

The principal organization involved in mediation efforts, other than some state and local agencies, is the Federal Mediation and Conciliation Service (FMCS). The Taft-Hartley Act established the FMCS as an independent agency. Either one or both parties involved in negotiations can seek the assistance of the FMCS, or the agency can offer its help if it feels that the situation warrants it. Federal law requires that the party wishing to change a contract must give notice of this intention to the other party 60 days prior to the expiration of a contract. If no agreement has been reached 30 days prior to the expiration date, the FMCS must be notified.

arbitration
Process in which a dispute is submitted to an impartial third party for a binding decision; an arbitrator acts as a judge and jury.

rights arbitration
Arbitration involving disputes over the interpretation and application of the various provisions of an existing contract.

interest arbitration
Arbitration that involves disputes over the terms of proposed collective bargaining agreements.

In **arbitration**, a dispute is submitted to an impartial third party for a binding decision; an arbitrator acts as a judge and jury. There are two principal types of union management disputes: rights disputes and interest disputes. Disputes over the interpretation and application of the various provisions of an existing contract are submitted to **rights arbitration**, which will be discussed shortly under the heading of "Grievance Procedure in a Union Environment." This type of arbitration is common in the United States.

The other type of arbitration, **interest arbitration**, involves disputes over the terms of proposed collective bargaining agreements. In the private sector, the use of interest arbitration as an alternative for impasse resolution has not been a common practice. Unions and employers rarely agree to submit the basic terms of a contract (such as wages, hours, and working conditions) to a neutral party for disposition. They prefer to rely on collective bargaining and the threat of economic pressure (such as strikes and lockouts) to decide these issues.

HR Web Wisdom

American Arbitration Association www.adr.org/

Provides services to individuals and organizations who wish to resolve conflicts out of court.

For either rights or interest arbitration, the disputants are free to select any person as their arbitrator, so long as they agree on the selection. Most commonly, however, the two sides make a request for an arbitrator to either the American Arbitration Association (AAA) or the FMCS. The AAA is a nonprofit organization with offices in many cities. Both the AAA and the FMCS maintain lists of arbitrators. When considering potential arbitrators, both management and labor will study the arbitrator's previous decisions to detect any biases. Obviously, neither party wants to select an arbitrator who might tend to favor the other's position.

After the arbitrator has been selected and has agreed to serve, a time and place for a hearing will be determined. The issue to be resolved will be presented to the arbitrator in a document that summarizes the question(s) to be decided. It will also point out any contract restrictions that prohibit the arbitrator from making an award that would change the terms of the contract.

At the hearing, each side presents its case. Arbitration is an adversarial proceeding, so a case may be lost because of poor preparation and presentation. The arbitrator may conduct the hearing much like a courtroom proceeding. Witnesses, cross-examination, transcripts, and legal counsel may all be used. The parties may also submit or be asked by the arbitrator to submit formal written statements. After the hearing, the arbitrator studies the material submitted and testimony given and is expected to reach a decision within 30 to 60 days. The decision is usually accompanied by a written opinion giving reasons for the decision.

The courts will generally enforce an arbitrator's decision unless: (1) the arbitrator's decision is shown to be unreasonable or capricious in that it did not address the issues; (2) the arbitrator exceeded his or her authority; or (3) the award or decision violated a federal or state law. In one arbitration case that ultimately went to the Supreme Court, the arbitrator's decision appeared to run counter to public policy of prohibiting workers who had tested positive for drugs from operating heavy machinery or being permitted to return to work. However, the Supreme Court wrote, "We recognize that reasonable people can differ as to whether reinstatement or discharge is the more appropriate remedy here. But both employer and union have agreed to entrust this remedial decision to an arbitrator."[26]

UNION STRATEGIES FOR OVERCOMING NEGOTIATION BREAKDOWNS There are times when a union believes that it must exert extreme pressure to get management to agree to its bargaining demands. Strikes and boycotts are the primary means that the union may use to overcome breakdowns in negotiations.

FYI

In 2016, there were 15 major labor strikes, idling 99,000 workers over a combined 1.54 million days.[27]

strike
Action by union members who refuse to work to exert pressure on management in negotiations.

When union members refuse to work to exert pressure on management in negotiations, their action is referred to as a **strike**. For instance, in 2016, 36,000 Verizon employees walked off the job after negotiations with management failed. Outsourcing jobs was one of the main reasons for workers' decision to strike. At the time, the U.S. Bureau of Labor Statistics indicated that the Verizon strike was the largest number of employees to strike in a single company. A strike halts production, resulting in lost customers and revenue, which the union hopes will force management to submit to its terms. In Korea, Hyundai workers conducted 21 partial strikes in 2016 that caused a production loss of about 117,000 vehicles costing the company more than $2.5 billion.[28] Some strikes can have far-reaching consequences for other firms and their customers. For example, when port workers on the west coast went on strike, many cargo ships were prohibited from reaching port and thousands of empty transport trucks remained empty. Many firms ranging from car dealers to retail companies experienced dwindling inventories of imported goods and the inability to serve all customer demand. The following Watch It video briefly describes the Los Angeles port strike and its effects.

Watch It 2

If your professor has assigned this, sign into **www.pearson.com/mylab/management** to watch a video titled LA Port Strike and to respond to questions.

The timing of a strike is important in determining its effectiveness. An excellent time is when business is thriving and the demand for the firm's goods or services is expanding. However, the union might be hard-pressed to obtain major concessions from a strike if the firm's sales are down and it has built up a large inventory. In this instance, the company would not be severely damaged.

Contrary to many opinions, unions prefer to use the strike only as a last resort. During a strike, workers have little income. The strike fund may only pay for items such as food, utilities, and motor fuel. In recent years, many union members have been even more reluctant to strike because of the fear of being replaced. When a union goes on an economic strike and the company hires replacements, the company does not have to lay off these individuals at the end of the strike. For example, Edw. C. Levy Co., headquartered in Detroit, Michigan, hired permanent replacements for the 130 members of the International Union of Operating Engineers Local 150 who struck the contractor's operations at Mittal Steel Company's Burns Harbor plant.[29]

Companies have typically been free to hire replacement workers on a temporary or permanent basis. A recent NLRB ruling limits a company's choice. Companies have latitude to hire permanent workers to ensure continuous operations rather than as punishment to striking workers. For example, the NLRB ruled that American Baptist Homes' decision to hire replacement workers was unlawful. The attorney for American Baptist Homes said that the company hired replacement workers because it, "wanted to teach the strikers and the union a lesson. They wanted to avoid any future strikes, and this was the lesson that they were going to be taught."[30]

A union's treasury is often depleted by payment of strike benefits to its members. In addition, members suffer because they are not receiving their normal pay. Striking workers during one General Motors strike got paid about $150 a week strike pay instead of the roughly $1,000 a week that they normally took home. Although strike pay helps, union members certainly cannot maintain a normal standard of living with these minimal amounts.

Sometimes during negotiations (usually at the beginning), the union may want to strengthen its negotiating position by taking a strike vote. Members often give overwhelming approval to a strike. This vote does not necessarily mean that there will be a strike, only that the union leaders now have the authority to call one if negotiations reach an impasse. A favorable strike vote can add a sense of urgency to efforts to reach an agreement.

Successful passage of a strike vote has additional implications for union members. Virtually every national union's constitution contains a clause requiring the members to support and participate in a strike if one is called. If a union member fails to comply with this requirement, he or she can be fined as high as 100 percent of wages if union pickets remain outside the company. However, the Supreme Court has ruled that an employee on economic strike may resign from the union and avoid being punished by the union. In today's economy, union members are using more subtle measures, such as sick-outs and work slowdowns, to avoid the impact of a strike while still bringing pressure on the company to meet union demands.

boycott
Agreement by union members to refuse to use or buy the firm's products.

The boycott is another of labor's weapons to get management to agree to its demands. A **boycott** involves an agreement by union members to refuse to use or buy the firm's products. A boycott exerts economic pressure on management, and the effect often lasts much longer than that of a strike. Once shoppers change buying habits, their behavior will likely continue long after the boycott has ended. At times, significant pressures can be exerted on a business when union members, their families, and their friends refuse to purchase the firm's products. This approach is especially effective when the products are sold at retail outlets and are easily identifiable by brand name. For instance, 7,000 members of Teamsters Local 688 boycotted grocery chain Schnuck Markets Inc. after the company laid off more than 200 warehouse workers to outsource those jobs.[31]

secondary boycott
Union attempt to encourage third parties (such as suppliers and customers) to stop doing business with a firm; declared illegal by the Taft-Hartley Act.

The practice of a union attempting to encourage third parties (such as suppliers and customers) to stop doing business with the company is known as a **secondary boycott**. The Taft-Hartley Act declared this type of boycott to be illegal.

MANAGEMENT STRATEGIES FOR OVERCOMING NEGOTIATION BREAKDOWNS There are times when management believes that it must exert extreme pressure to get the union to back away from a demand. The lockout and operating the firm by placing management and nonunion workers in the striking workers' jobs are the primary means management may use to overcome breakdowns in negotiations.

lockout
Management keeps employees out of the workplace and runs the operation with management personnel or replacements.

Management may use the lockout to encourage unions to come back to the bargaining table. In a **lockout**, management keeps employees out of the workplace and runs the operation with management personnel or replacements. In 2016, Honeywell's South Bend manufacturing plant locked out more than 300 union workers for 9 months.[32] The company initiated the lockout because the union rejected new contract terms that did not specify how much health insurance will cost them. Some of the highest-profile lockouts have involved professional sports teams. The National Hockey League and the National Basketball Association used a lockout to get players to return to negotiations. Unable to work, the employees are not paid; the fear of a lockout may bring labor back to the bargaining table. A lockout is particularly effective when management is dealing with a weak union, when the union treasury is depleted, or when the business has excessive inventories. The lockout is also used to inform the union that management is serious regarding certain bargaining issues.

A course of action that a company can take if the union goes on strike is to operate the firm by placing management and nonunion workers in the striking workers' jobs. The type of industry involved has considerable effect on the impact of this maneuver. If the firm is not labor-intensive and if maintenance demands are not high, such as at a petroleum refinery or a chemical plant, this practice may be quite effective. When appropriate, management may attempt to show how using nonunion employees can increase production. At times, management personnel will live in the plant and have food and other necessities delivered to them. This situation occurred when the 900 members of Local 470 of the International Association of Machinists struck at the PPG Plant in Lake Charles, Louisiana. Management continued to run the plant with management and contract labor personnel. The union members struck because of an increase in insurance payments and a new hiring-in rate for entry-level workers. Prior to the strike, the local had taken a strike vote, and an overwhelming number of workers had voted in favor of the strike. Later in negotiations, the union permitted members to vote on whether to accept or reject management's proposal. It was rejected by most workers. Then management sent registered letters to all union members suggesting that they were not willing to maintain the current work situation, and the company was considering hiring replacement workers. Another vote was taken and the contract was accepted. Prior to the final vote, approximately 100 workers had resigned from the union and crossed the picket line.

Reaching the Labor-Management Agreement

The document that emerges from the collective bargaining process is known as a "labor/management agreement" or "contract." It regulates the relationship between employer and employees for a specified period. It is still an essential but difficult task because each agreement is unique, and there is no standard or universal model.

Ratifying the Labor-Management Agreement

Most collective bargaining leads to an agreement without a breakdown in negotiations or disruptive actions. Typically, agreement is reached before the current contract expires. After the negotiators have reached a tentative agreement on all contract terms, they prepare a written agreement covering those terms, complete with the effective and termination dates. The approval process for management is often easier than for labor. The president or CEO has usually been briefed regularly on the progress of negotiations. Any difficulty that might have stood in the way of obtaining approval has probably already been resolved with top management by the negotiators.

However, the approval process is more complex for the union. Until most members voting in a ratification election approve it, the proposed agreement is not final. At times, union members reject the proposal and a new round of negotiations must begin. Many of these rejections might not occur if union negotiators were better informed about members' desires.

Administration of the Labor-Management Agreement

Negotiating, as it relates to the total collective bargaining process, may be likened to the tip of an iceberg. It is the visible phase, the part that makes the news. The larger and perhaps more important part of collective bargaining is administration of the agreement, which the public seldom sees. The agreement establishes the union/management relationship for the duration of the contract. Usually, neither party can change the contract's language until the expiration date, except by mutual consent. However, the main problem encountered in contract administration is uniform interpretation and application of the contract's terms. Administering the contract is a day-to-day activity. Ideally, the aim of both management and the union is to make the agreement work to the benefit of all concerned. At times, this is not an easy task.

Management is primarily responsible for explaining and implementing the agreement. This process should begin with meetings or training sessions not only to point out significant features but also to provide a clause-by-clause analysis of the contract. First-line supervisors must know their responsibilities and manage disagreements when they arise. In addition, supervisors and middle managers should be encouraged to notify top management of any contract modifications or new provisions required for the next round of negotiations.

The HR manager or industrial relations manager plays a key role in the day-to-day administration of the contract. He or she gives advice on matters of discipline, works to resolve grievances, and helps first-line supervisors establish good working relationships within the terms of the agreement. After becoming unionized, the HR manager's function tends to change rather significantly. It may even be divided into separate HR and industrial relations departments. In such situations, the vice president of HR may perform all HR management tasks except for dealing with union-related matters. All nonunion employees would go to the HR professional for assistance needed. The vice president of industrial relations would likely deal with all union-related matters.

The issues we have discussed thus far have largely been focused on the private sector. There are some differences in collective bargaining between the private and public sectors. We briefly highlight some of the differences next.

Public Sector Collective Bargaining

Executive Order 10988 established the basic framework for collective bargaining in federal government agencies. Title VII of the Civil Service Reform Act of 1978 regulates most of the labor–management relations in the federal service. It establishes the Federal Labor Relations Authority, which is modeled after the NLRA. The intent of the Federal Labor Relations Act is to bring the public-sector model in line with that of the private sector. Requirements and mechanisms for recognition and elections, dealing with impasses, and handling grievances are covered in the act. Collective bargaining for federal unions has traditionally been quite different from private-sector bargaining because wages were off the table. President Franklin D. Roosevelt recognized that the bargaining relationship that exists in the private sector cannot also exist in the public sector saying it, "cannot be transplanted into the public service. . . . The employer is the whole people."[33] Title V of the U.S. Code, the law that dictates rules for federal employees, did not allow bargaining over wage issues, except for the U.S. Postal Service.

There is no uniform pattern to state and local bargaining rights. More than two-thirds of the states have enacted legislation granting public-sector collective bargaining rights to some groups (e.g., teachers, police, and firefighters). However, the diversity of state labor laws makes it difficult to generalize about the legal aspects of collective bargaining at the state and local levels.

In the public sector, most governmental jurisdictions prohibit their employees from striking. This fact was vigorously pointed out in the 1981 strike by air traffic controllers when President Ronald Reagan used replacement workers to end the first declared national strike against the federal government. The Professional Air Traffic Controllers Organization (PATCO) sacrificed a substantial pay increase, a generous benefit package, and its existence in its attempt to legitimize strikes in the public sector.[34] Thus, interest arbitration is used more than in the private sector, although there is no uniform application of this method. A procedure used in the public sector is **final-offer arbitration**, which has two basic forms: package selection and issue-by-issue selection. In package selection, the arbitrator must select one party's entire offer on all issues in dispute. In issue-by-issue selection, the arbitrator examines each issue separately and chooses the final offer of one side or the other on each issue. Final-offer arbitration is often used to determine the salary of a professional baseball player. Both players and management present a dollar figure to an arbitrator. The arbitrator chooses one figure or the other.

final-offer arbitration
An arbitration procedure used in the public sector whereby the arbitrator must select one party's offer either as a package or issue-by-issue selection.

11.5 Describe the grievance procedure in a union environment.

Grievance Procedure in a Union Environment

As previously defined, a *grievance procedure* is a formal, systematic process that permits employees to express complaints without jeopardizing their jobs. A grievance procedure under a collective bargaining agreement is normally well defined. It is usually restricted to violations of the terms and conditions of the agreement. Other conditions that may give rise to a grievance include the following:

- A violation of law
- A violation of the intent of the parties as stipulated during contract negotiations
- A violation of company rules
- A change in working conditions or past company practices
- A violation of health or safety standards

Grievance procedures have many common features. However, variations may reflect differences in organizational or decision-making structures or the size of a plant or company. Some general principles based on widespread practice can serve as useful guidelines for effective grievance administration:

- Grievances should be settled promptly.
- Procedures and forms used for airing grievances must be easy to use and well understood by employees and their supervisors.
- Direct and timely avenues of appeal from rulings of line supervision must exist.

The multi-step grievance procedure is the most common type. In the first step, the employee usually presents the grievance orally and informally to the immediate supervisor in the presence of the union steward. This step offers the greatest potential for improved labor relations, and a large majority of grievances is settled here. The procedure ends if the grievance is resolved at this initial step. If the grievance remains unresolved, the next step involves a meeting between the plant manager or HR manager and higher union officials, such as the grievance committee or the business agent or manager. Prior to this meeting, the grievance is written out, dated, and signed by the employee and the union steward. The written grievance states the events, as the employee perceives them, cites the contract provision that allegedly has been violated, and indicates the settlement desired. If the grievance is not settled at this meeting, it moves to the third step, which typically involves the firm's top labor representative (such as the vice president of industrial relations) and high-level union officials. At times, depending on the severity of the grievance, the president may represent the firm. Arbitration is the final step in most grievance procedures. In arbitration, the parties submit their dispute to an impartial third party for binding resolution. Most agreements restrict the arbitrator's decision to application and interpretation of the agreement and the final decision is binding on both parties. If the union decides in favor of arbitration, it notifies management. At this point, the union and the company select an arbitrator.[35]

When arbitration is used to settle a grievance, a variety of factors may be considered to evaluate the fairness of the management actions that caused the grievance. Some factors include:

- Nature of the offense
- Due process and procedural correctness
- Double jeopardy
- Past record of grievant
- Length of service with the company
- Knowledge of rules
- Warnings
- Lax enforcement of rule
- Discriminatory treatment

The large number of interacting variables in each case makes the arbitration process difficult. The arbitrator must possess exceptional patience and judgment in rendering a fair and impartial decision.

Labor relations problems can escalate when a supervisor is not equipped to handle grievances at the first step. Because the union steward, the aggrieved party, and the supervisor usually handle the first step informally, the supervisor must be fully prepared. The supervisor should obtain as many facts as possible before the meeting because the union steward is likely to have also done his or her homework.

The supervisor needs to recognize that the grievance may not reflect the real problem. For instance, the employee might be angry with the company for modifying its pay policies, even though the union agreed to the change. To voice discontent, the worker might file a grievance for an unrelated minor violation of the contract.

Any disciplinary action administered may ultimately be taken to arbitration, when such a remedy is specified in the labor agreement. Employers have learned that they must prepare records that will constitute proof of disciplinary action and the reasons for it. Although the formats of written warnings may vary, all should include the following information:

- Statement of facts concerning the offense
- Identification of the rule that was violated
- Statement of what resulted or could have resulted because of the violation
- Identification of any previous similar violations by the same individual
- Statement of possible future consequences should the violation occur again
- Signature and date

FIGURE 11-5
Example of a Written Warning

Date: August 1, 2013
To: Wayne Sanders
From: Judy Bandy
Subject: Written Warning

We are quite concerned because today you were thirty minutes late to work and offered no justification for this. According to our records, a similar offense occurred on July 25, 2013. At that time, you were informed that failure to report to work on time is unacceptable. I am, therefore, notifying you in writing that you must report to work on time. It will be necessary to terminate your employment if this happens again.

Please sign this form to indicate that you have read and understand this warning. Signing is not an indication of agreement.

____
Name

____
Date

An example of a written warning is shown in Figure 11-5. In this instance, the worker has already received an oral reprimand. The individual is also warned that continued tardiness could lead to termination. It is important to document oral reprimands because they may be the first step in disciplinary action leading ultimately to arbitration.

11.6 Explain union decertification.

Union Decertification

decertification
Reverse of the process that employees must follow to be recognized as an official bargaining unit.

Until 1947, once a union was certified, it was certified forever. However, the Taft-Hartley Act made it possible for employees to decertify a union. **Decertification** is the reverse of the process that employees must follow to be recognized as an official bargaining unit. It results in a union losing its right to act as the exclusive bargaining representative of a group of employees. As union membership has declined, the need for decertification elections has also diminished.

FYI

In a recent 10-year period, employees held 2,398 decertification elections and voted to decertify the union in 1,448 of them.[36]

Members of a union's bargaining unit typically choose to decertify a union when it feels that the union is not creating an advantage such as in wage rates, benefits, and other employment-related matters. Bargaining unit members may also choose to decertify a union when it disagrees how money is spent. For example, in 2014, the police union in New Haven, Connecticut, overwhelmingly voted to decertify from AFSCME Council 15. Union members were dissatisfied with the use of the lump-sum payments it made to the union (for its members' education and legal representation of police officers if needed) because the Union spent a portion of these payments to subsidize activities for small police forces rather than to the exclusive benefit of its members.[37]

The rules established by the NLRB spell out the conditions for filing a decertification petition; it is essentially the reverse of obtaining union recognition. At least 30 percent of the bargaining unit members must petition for an election. As might be expected, this task by itself may be difficult because union supporters are likely to oppose the move. Few employees know about decertification and fewer still know how to start the process. In addition, although the petitioners' names are supposed to remain confidential, many union members are fearful that their signatures on the petition will be discovered. The timing of the NLRB's receipt of the decertification petition is also critical. The petition must be submitted between 60 and 90 days prior to the expiration of the current contract. When all these conditions have been met, the NLRB regional director will schedule a decertification election by secret ballot.

The NLRB carefully monitors the events leading up to the election. Current employees must initiate the request for the election. This is what happened regarding professional football when the National Football League Players Association (NFLPA) decertified in March 2011. If the NLRB determines that management initiated the action, it will not certify the election. After a petition has been accepted, however, management can support the decertification election attempt. If most votes cast is against the union, the employees will be free from the union. Strong union supporters are all likely to vote. Thus, if a substantial number of employees is indifferent to the union and chooses not to vote, decertification may not occur.

In the Watch It video, UPS provides a balanced perspective on the value of union representation from the standpoint of costs and benefits to employees and the company. Ultimately, employees maintain a choice with or without a union. If employees were dissatisfied with union representation, they could easily choose to decertify it.

 **Watch It 3**

If your professor has assigned this, sign into **www.pearson.com/mylab/management** to watch a video titled UPS: Union Management and to respond to questions.

PREPARING FOR EXAMS/QUIZZES

Chapter Summary by Learning Objectives

1. ***Explore the role of labor unions.*** Labor came about out of necessity. Employers often set unfavorable terms of employment (for example, low wages) and unsafe working conditions. The collective effort of employees provided them with greater power to negotiate better terms of employment.

   Employees join unions because of dissatisfaction with management, the need for a social outlet, the need for avenues of leadership, forced unionization, and social pressure from peers.

   The latest figures from the Labor Department's Bureau of Labor Statistics showed that the percentage of wage and salary workers who were members of a union was 10.7 percent. The number of wage and salary workers belonging to unions is at approximately 14.6 million. In 1983, the first year for which comparable union data are available, the union membership rate was 20.1 percent and there were 17.7 million union workers. The unionization rate is declining steadily.

   In 2016, 7.2 million public-sector employees belonged to a union, compared with 7.4 million union workers in the private sector. Public-sector workers had a union membership rate of 34.4 percent—more than five times higher than that of the private-sector workers rate of 6.4 percent. Private-sector industries with high unionization rates included utilities (24.5 percent) and construction (13.9 percent), whereas low unionization rates occurred in food service and drinking places (1.6 percent), agriculture and related industries (1.3 percent), and in financial services (1.2 percent).

2. ***Describe the basic union structure and organized labor's strategies for a stronger movement.*** The basic element in the structure of the U.S. labor movement is the local union. The national union is the most powerful level, and the American Federation of Labor and Congress of Industrial Organizations (AFL-CIO) is the central trade union federation in the United States. It is a loosely knit organization of national unions that has little formal power or control. The member national unions remain completely autonomous and decide their own policies and programs.

   Organized labor's new strategies for a stronger movement include strategically located union members, pulling the union through, political involvement, union salting, flooding the community, public awareness campaigns, building organizing funds, collaborating with high schools, and organizing through the card check.
3. ***Discuss laws affecting collective bargaining.*** The National Labor Relations Act of 1935 (also known as the Wagner Act) is one of the most significant labor/management relations statutes ever enacted. The act declared legislative support, on a broad scale, for the right of employees to organize and engage in collective bargaining. The Taft-Hartley Act extensively revised the National Labor Relations Act. A new period began in the evolution of public policy regarding labor.
4. ***Summarize the formation of bargaining units and the collective bargaining process.*** The steps involved include signing authorization cards, petitioning for election, campaigning, winning the election, and being certified.

   The negotiating phase of collective bargaining begins with each side presenting its initial demands. The term *negotiating* suggests a certain amount of give-and-take. The party with the greater leverage can expect to extract the most concessions.

   Bargaining issues can be divided into three categories: mandatory, permissive, and prohibited. Certain topics are included in virtually all labor agreements. These are recognition, management rights, union security, compensation, grievance procedure, employee security, and job-related factors.

   The union must continuously gather information regarding membership needs to isolate areas of dissatisfaction. Management also spends long hours preparing for negotiations. The negotiating phase of collective bargaining begins with each side presenting its initial demands. The term *negotiating* suggests a certain amount of give-and-take. The party with the greater leverage can expect to extract the most concessions.

   Breakdowns in negotiations can be overcome through third-party intervention (mediation and arbitration), union tactics (strikes and boycotts), and management recourse (lockouts and continued operation without striking workers).

   The document that emerges from the collective bargaining process is known as a "labor/management agreement" or "contract."

   The approval process for management is often easier than for labor. The president or CEO has usually been briefed regularly on the progress of negotiations. However, the approval process is more complex for the union. Until most members voting in a ratification election approve it, the proposed agreement is not final.

   The larger and perhaps more important part of collective bargaining is administration of the agreement, which the public seldom sees. The agreement establishes the union/management relationship for the duration of the contract.
5. ***Describe the grievance procedure in a union environment.*** A grievance procedure under a collective bargaining agreement is normally well defined. It is usually restricted to violations of the terms and conditions of the agreement.
6. ***Explain union decertification.*** Decertification is essentially the reverse of the process that employees must follow to be recognized as an official bargaining unit.

Key Terms

MyLab Management

If your instructor is using MyLab Management, go to **www.pearson.com/mylab/management** to complete the problems marked with this icon ✪.

Questions for Review

11-1. What are organized labor's strategies for a stronger movement?

✪ **11-2.** What is the status (prevalence) of unions today?

11-3. Define the following terms:
  (a) local union
  (b) craft union
  (c) industrial union
  (d) national union

11-4. What is the difference between the NLRA and the Labor-Management Relations Act?

✪ **11-5.** Why has the NLRB recently been thrust into the forefront of labor relations?

11-6. What steps must a union take in establishing the collective bargaining relationship? Briefly describe each step.

11-7. What are the steps involved in the collective bargaining process?

✪ **11-8.** Distinguish among mandatory, permissive, and prohibited bargaining issues.

11-9. What are topics included in virtually all labor agreements?

11-10. Define each of the following:
  (a) closed shop
  (b) union shop
  (c) agency shop
  (d) maintenance of membership
  (e) checkoff of dues

11-11. What are the primary means by which breakdowns in negotiations may be overcome? Briefly describe each.

11-12. What is involved for both management and labor in ratifying the agreement?

11-13. What is involved in the administration of a labor agreement?

11-14. How is the collective bargaining process different in the public sector?

11-15. What is typically involved in the grievance procedure in a unionized organization?

11-16. Define *decertification*. What are the steps in decertification?

PREPARING FOR MY CAREER

P I A Personal Inventory Assessment

✪ *An additional Personal Inventory Assessment can be found on MyLab Management.*

Gaining Power and Influence

This self-assessment helps you understand your proficiency with four closely related skills: gaining power, exercising influence, resisting unwanted influence, and increasing formal authority. If you are not currently employed in a work organization, do your best to apply these questions to another type of role.

ETHICS DILEMMA

A Strategic Move

You are the plant manager for a medium-sized manufacturing company that has been experiencing growing employee tensions, and there has been a lot of talk among workers about forming a union. You have even seen what appear to be authorization cards being passed out around the plant. Sandy Marshall, one of the workers in your plant, has been seen talking to many of the workers, obviously about forming a union. Sandy is influential with the workers throughout the plant and appears to be a natural leader. You believe that if Sandy continues to promote the union, she will have a major impact among the workers in organizing the union. You have a supervisory position that has just come open. It pays a lot more than what Sandy currently makes. You think, "If I make her a supervisor, she won't be able to use her influence to help get the union started." However, another worker in your department is more qualified and has been with the firm several years longer than Sandy, although he is less influential with other workers throughout the plant.

11-17. What would you do?

11-18. What factor(s) in this ethics dilemma might influence a person to make a less than ethical decision?

HRM Is Everyone's Business

The National Labor Relations Act (NLRA) bestows upon most employees the right to organize and form a bargaining unit. Both employees and management must comply with the provisions of the NLRA. During an organizing campaign, HR professionals and managers must understand how to comply with NLRA regulations.

Action checklist for managers and HR—understand HR managers', other managers', and employees' roles during organizing campaigns

HR takes the lead

- ☑ HR professionals should carefully educate managers about employees' rights and responsibilities during an organizing campaign.
- ☑ Tell managers how they may proactively communicate with employees about active campaigns. For instance, signing a union authorization card does not obligate employees to vote for a union in an election.
- ☑ Maintain an open-door policy that permits managers and employees the opportunity to inquire about union-related activities that they observe in the workplace and options for responding to the situation. For example, employees are not obligated to speak to union organizers.

Managers take the lead

- ☑ Managers should create a list of their and employees' rights and responsibilities. During a union organizing campaign, they should communicate management's position on union representation. For example, it is acceptable to tell employees that the company is opposed to unionization. In addition, managers must ensure employees that they will not be penalized for participating in organizing activities. Examples of penalties include pay reductions and termination.
- ☑ Employee dissatisfaction with the fairness of a company's employment policies and procedures as well as pay and benefits are among the reasons for seeking union representation. Managers should listen to employees' concerns and discuss them with HR professionals and higher management. Perhaps conducting a survey of local pay rates will facilitate an understanding of whether the company should consider awarding pay adjustments.
- ☑ Managers should never offer to improve working conditions, award larger pay raises, promise additional paid time off, or grant favors on the condition that employees vote against union representation. Such actions unlawfully influence employees' rights to seek representation.

HRM by the Numbers

Costing Union and Nonunion Wages and Benefits

✪ *An additional HRM by the Numbers exercise can be found on MyLab Management.*

We learned that compensation costs are typically higher in union settings than in nonunion settings. Below is a table that illustrates the costs of wages and salaries as well as some employee benefits for union and nonunion employees. These values are expressed as employer costs per hour worked for employee compensation. Answer the questions that follow the table.

Compensation Component	Union Costs	Nonunion Costs
Wages and salaries	28.61	22.27
Paid leave		
Vacation	1.75	1.12
Holiday	1.02	0.65
Sick	0.52	0.26
Personal	0.17	0.13
Insurance		
Life	0.08	0.04
Health	5.98	2.15
Short-term disability	0.17	0.05
Long-term disability	0.12	0.04

Compensation Component	Union Costs	Nonunion Costs
Retirement and savings		
Defined benefit	3.09	0.34
Defined contribution	1.27	0.68
Legally required benefits		
Social Security	1.87	1.47
Medicare	0.48	0.37
Federal unemployment insurance	0.03	0.03
State unemployment insurance	0.23	0.17
Workers' compensation	1.02	0.40

Questions

11-19. What are the hourly compensation costs for: (a) wages and salaries; (b) paid time off; (c) insurance; (d) retirement and savings; and (e) legally required benefits in union settings? What are the hourly compensation costs for: (f) wages and salaries; (g) paid time off; (h) insurance; (i) retirement and savings; and (j) legally required benefits in nonunion settings?

11-20. For each of the five categories listed in the table, what is the percent cost difference between union and nonunion settings?

11-21. Let's say that a company is interested in knowing the *annual* total compensation costs in the (a) union; and (b) nonunion setting. Assume that for the purposes of calculating annual costs, each employee works 40 hours per week, 52 weeks per year. Calculate these costs for a workforce of 3,000 employees in each setting.

Working Together: Team Exercise

In small groups of three or four, come up with specific answers to the following questions. Talk through your perspectives with team members. Be prepared to share your ideas with the class.

Think about the role of unions based on the ideas discussed in this chapter. From the employee's perspective, come up with a list of advantages and disadvantages to joining a union. Do the same, looking at it from the employer's perspective.

11-22. What are the top two advantages and two disadvantages from an employee's perspective? Explain.

11-23. What are the top two advantages and two disadvantages from an employer's perspective? Explain.

INCIDENT 1 Break Down the Barrier

Yesterday, Angelica Angulo received a job offer as a server with GEM Hotel Corporation, located in Las Vegas, Nevada. She had recently graduated from high school in Milford, a small town in New Mexico. Because Angelica had no college aspirations upon graduation, she had moved to Las Vegas to look for a job.

Angelica's immediate supervisor spent only a brief time with her before turning her over to Laurie Rader, an experienced server, for training. After they had talked, Laurie asked, "Have you given any thought to joining our union? You'll like all of our members."

Angelica had not considered this. Moreover, she had never associated with union members, and her parents had never been members either. At Milford High, her teachers had never talked about unions. The fact that this union operated as an open shop meant nothing to her. Angelica replied, "I don't know. Maybe. Maybe not."

The day progressed much the same way, with several people asking Angelica the same question. They were all friendly, but there seemed to be a barrier that separated Angelica from the other workers. One worker looked Angelica right in the eyes and said, "You're going to join, aren't you?" Angelica still did not know, but she was beginning to lean in that direction.

After the end of her shift, Angelica went to the washroom. Just as she entered, Stephanie Clements, the union steward, also walked in. After they exchanged greetings, Stephanie said, "I hear that you're not sure about joining our union. You, and everyone else, reap the benefits of the work we've done in the past. It doesn't seem fair for you to be rewarded for what others have done. Tell you what, why don't you join us down at the union hall tonight? We'll discuss it more then."

Angelica nodded yes and finished cleaning up. "That might be fun," she thought.

Questions

11-24. Why does Angelica have the option of joining or not joining the union? Hint: Nevada is a right-to-work state.

11-25. What are the pros and cons regarding Angelica joining the union?

11-26. How are the other workers likely to react toward Angelica if she chooses not to join? Discuss.

INCIDENT 2 We're Listening

Akio Watanabe is the director of customer service at Innovative Solutions, a software development company. When he assumed this role 10 years ago, serious customer service complaints were occurring frequently and the company began losing business to competitors. Akio identified the reasons for poor customer service and he developed a plan to turn things around. The plan was a success. Employee morale was high. Everything was looking up! For now, at least.

Six months later, Zofia Nowicki, one of the senior customer service supervisors, scheduled a meeting with Akio. Akio greeted Zofia and exclaimed, "The customer service department is operating like a well-oiled machine!"

Zofia replied, "That has definitely been the case until recently." She went on to explain, "As you know, we've implemented mandatory overtime and have informed employees not to schedule more than three consecutive days of vacation at a time."

Akio stated, "Well, Zofia, that doesn't seem to be creating a problem. After all, our customer service ratings are at an all-time high. And, besides, the overtime pay should help ease financial pressures they may feel at home."

"We shouldn't expect that to last very long. In fact, there are many disgruntled employees," Zofia explained. In a worried voice, she expressed concern that employees often gathered in small groups and stopped talking when she approached. "Akio, that is highly unusual!"

"Zofia, aren't you being overly sensitive?"

She replied, "Well, I thought so at first. Then, I found a brochure on a table from a labor union that has had much success in organizing workers at similar companies."

"What do you propose we do, Zofia? If employees successfully unionize, wages, and benefits costs will rise, and we will have less flexibility to schedule overtime. We won't have the resources to hire additional customer service representatives if our labor costs go up." In a panicked tone, he lamented, "Our customer service ratings will plummet."

Questions

11-27. Why are employees considering union representation?

11-28. If you were Akio, what would you do now?

MyLab Management

If your instructor is using MyLab Management, go to **www.pearson.com/mylab/management** for Auto-graded writing questions as well as the following Assisted-graded writing questions:

11-29. How has globalization influenced the prevalence of unions in the United States?

11-30. What are the primary reasons employees join labor unions?

Endnotes

1 U.S. Bureau of Labor Statistics, "Employer Costs for Employee Compensation—March 2017," (USDL 17-0770). Accessed August 1, 2017, at www.bls.gov.

2 Ibid.

3 Alan Ohnsman, "Musk Draws 'Fake News' Rebuke from UAW as Union Eyes Tesla Factory," *Forbes* online (February 10, 2017). Accessed April 1, 2017, at www.forbes.com.

4 U.S. Bureau of Labor Statistics, "Union Members—2016," (USDL 17-0107). Accessed March 30, at www.bls.gov.

5 Barry T. Hirsch and David Macpherson, "Union Membership, Coverage, Density and Employment by State, 1983–2016. *Union Membership and Coverage Database from the CPS*. Accessed April 1, 2017, at Unionstats.com.

6 Change to Win, "About Us." Accessed March 3, 2017, at www.changetowin.org/about.

7 "Army Corps Projects Defy Unions' Upbeat Labor Agreement Tally," *Concrete Products* 113 (October 2010): 8.

8 Lucinda Shen, "Labor Unions Up Political Spending for Hillary Clinton and Democrats," *Fortune* online (October 18, 2016). Accessed April 1, 2017, at www.fortune.com.

9 Dave Jamieson and Paul Blumenthal, "Labor Unions Spent a Record Amount on the Elections. But Not as Much as These 5 People," *The Huffington Post* online (November 8, 2016). Accessed March 30, 2017, at www.huffington-post.com.

10 Bourree Lam, "Life as an Undercover Union Organizer," *The Atlantic* online (March 21, 2016). Accessed March 10, 2017, at www.the-atlantic.com.

11 "Union Organizing: What Does the Term "Salting" as a Union Organizing Tactic Mean? *Society for Human Resource Management* online (January 10, 2017). Accessed March 1, 2017, at www.shrm.org.

12 Karen Menehan, "Massage Therapists Launch Fair Workplace Campaign," *Massage Magazine* online (February 24, 2016). Accessed April 1, 2017, at www.massagemag.com/massage-therapists-launch-fair-workplace-campaign-34817/.

13 "Unions Takes Proactive Approach to Training," *Plant Engineering* 63 (October 2009): 8.

14 U.S. Bureau of Labor Statistics, "Union Members—2016," (USDL 17-0107). Accessed March 30, at www.bls.gov.

15 Rachel Haut, Natalie Kelly, and Max Mishler, "Youth Activism in the Labor Movement," *New Labor Forum* 18 (Winter 2009): 98–107.

16 Richard. L. Trumka, "Selling Unions to Young Workers," *Vital Speeches of the Day* 75 (October 2009): 475–478.

17 "Volkswagen's Union Gamble: The German Car Maker Invites the UAW into Its Tennessee Plant," *Wall Street Journal* (February 13, 2014). Accessed February 28, 2014, at www.wsj.com.

18 "UPS Freight Workers Become Teamsters," *Toledo Business Journal* 24 (April 2008): 24–28.

19 "Teamsters Ratify UPS Freight Contract," *Florida Shipper* 33 (April 21, 2008): 13.

20 Stephanie Armour and Holly Rosenkrantz, "A Backlash Looms for the Federal Labor Board," *Bloomberg Businessweek* (February 14, 2011): 26–27.

21 "Charges and Complaints," *National Labor Relations Board*. Accessed March 31, 2017, at www.nlrb.gov/news-outreach/graphs-data/charges-and-complaints/charges-and-complaints.

22 *A Guide to Basic Law and Procedures under the National Labor Relations Act* (Washington, D.C.: U.S. Government Printing Office, October 1978): 11–13.

23 Dennis G. Collins and Kevin T. McLaughlin, "Key Steps to Prepare for a Union-Organizing

Campaign," Society for Human Resource Management online (February 23, 2016). Accessed March 15, 2017, at www.shrm.org.

24 T. L. Stanley, "Union Stewards and Labor Relations," *Supervision* 71 (February 2010): 3–6.

25 Jim Kinney, "Federal Mediators to Intervene in Dispute Between Stop & Shop, Labor Union," *MassLive* online (March 3, 2016). Accessed March 31, 2017, at www.masslive.com/business-news/index.ssf/2016/03/stop_shop_union_to_resume_negotiations_n.html.

26 "Arbitrator's Decision Upheld," *Business Insurance* 34 (December 4, 2000): 2.

27 U.S. Bureau of Labor Statistics, "Work Stoppages in 2017," (USDL 17-0180). Accessed March 31, 2017, at www.bls.gov.

28 Frank Ahrens, "Hyundai Battles Striking Workers as Global Ambitions Surge," *Forbes* online (October 5, 2016). Accessed April 1, 2017, at www.forbes.com.

29 Andrea Holecek, "Levy Co. Replaces Striking Steel Workers, Fires Others," *The Times* (March 29, 2006).

30 Allen Smith, "NLRB Limits Rights to Permanently Replace Strikers," *Society for Human Resource Management* online (June 10, 2016). Accessed February 22, 2017, at www.shrm.org.

31 Lisa Brown, "Teamsters to Boycott Schnucks Stores in Layoff Dispute," *St. Louis Post Dispatch* online (June 16, 2016). Accessed March 30, 2017, at www.stltoday.com.

32 Bob Blake, Lockout Over at Honeywell Plant in South Bend," *South Bend Tribune* online (February 26, 2017). Accessed March 31, 2017, at www.southbendtribune.com.

33 Nina Easton, "Labor Unions: Flailing in D.C. and Making Enemies on Main Street," *Fortune* 163 (March 21, 2011): 68.

34 Michael R. Carrell and Christina Heavrin, *Labor Relations and Collective Bargaining: Cases, Practices, and Law* (Upper Saddle River, NJ: Prentice Hall, 2010): 241.

35 Charles A. Borell, "How Unions Can Improve Their Success Rate in Labor Arbitration," *Dispute Resolution Journal* 61 (February 2006): 28–38.

36 "Decertification Petitions—RD," *National Labor Relations Board*. Accessed April 2, 2017, at www.nlrb.gov.

37 Rich Scinto, "AFSCME Down to 1 Big-City Policy Union Following New Haven Decertification," *New Haven Register* (February 26, 2014). Accessed April 1, 2014, at www.nhregister.com.

12 Internal Employee Relations

LEARNING OBJECTIVES After completing this chapter, students should be able to:

12.1 Explain the concept of employment at will.

12.2 Describe the concept of discipline and summarize disciplinary action.

12.3 Explain employment termination of various occupational groups.

12.4 Explain the use of ombudspersons and alternative dispute resolution.

12.5 Describe transfers, promotions, resignations, and retirements as factors involved in internal employee relations.

MyLab Management

Improve Your Grade!

If your professor is using MyLab Management, visit **www.pearson.com/mylab/management** for videos, simulations, and writing exercises.

Learn It

If your professor has chosen to assign this, go to **www.pearson.com/mylab/management** to see what you should particularly focus on and to take the Chapter 12 Warm-Up.

The status of most workers is not permanently fixed in an organization. Employees constantly move upward (promotion), laterally (transfers), downward (demotion), and out of the organization (separation and termination). At times, employees may violate work rules that require management intervention or employees may possess a grievance based on their claim of inappropriate application of policy or other inappropriate behavior. To ensure that workers with the proper skills and experience are available at all levels, constant and concerted efforts are required to maintain good internal employee relations. **Internal employee relations** comprise the human resources (HR) management activities associated with the movement of employees within the company and the relationship between employees and employers within the company. Such topics include discipline and disciplinary action, termination, demotion, downsizing, transfers, promotions, resignations, and retirement.

internal employee relations
Those human resource management activities associated with the movement of employees within the organization.

Employment at will is first discussed as a factor affecting internal employee relations, particularly for employee groups who are not represented by a labor union. Understanding employment at will provides a basis for understanding why movement of employees is more likely in nonunion settings than in union settings.

12.1 Explain the concept of employment at will.

Employment at Will

employment at will
Unwritten contract created when an employee agrees to work for an employer but no agreement exists as to how long the parties expect the employment to last.

Employment at will is a legal doctrine that specifies that employment may be terminated by either the employer or employee for any reason. "The employment at will doctrine avows that, when an employee does not have a written employment contract and the term of employment is of definite duration, the employer can terminate the employee for good cause, bad cause, or no cause at all."[1] For unionized workers, a collective bargaining agreement sets aside an employer's ability to use employment at will provisions because the terms of employment are managed in accordance with the provisions of the collective bargaining agreement. Certainly, there are numerous hiring standards to avoid such as race, religion, sex, national origin, age, sexual orientation, gender identity, and disabilities. Notwithstanding, various employment standards to avoid that are based on laws, court decisions, and executive orders, approximately two of every three U.S. workers depend almost entirely on the continued goodwill of their employer. Individuals falling into this category are known as "at-will employees."

FYI

Montana is the only state that does not recognize the employment at will doctrine. Instead, the state presumes that employers can fire employees only for just cause (discussed later in this chapter).

There are three exceptions to the at will doctrine, which have been established by courts of law. The first is an implied contract exception. Implied contracts can be formed through an employer's representation of continued employment in writing or through oral statements. Written statements made in employment handbooks that specify continued employment based on continued satisfactory job performance are an example of an implied contract. A manager or supervisor who makes similar oral statements to employees is also an example of an implied contract. Employers can do certain things to help protect themselves against litigation for wrongful discharge based on a breach of implied employment contract. Statements in documents such as employment applications and policy manuals that suggest job security or permanent employment should be avoided if employers want to minimize charges of wrongful discharge. Telling a person during a job interview that he or she can expect to hold the job as long as they want could be considered a contractual agreement and grounds for a lawsuit. Normally, a person should not be employed without a signed acknowledgment of the at will disclaimer. In addition, the policy manual should have it noticeably stated in bold, larger-than-normal print, so it is clear to the employee that this is an at will relationship. Other guidelines that may assist organizations in avoiding wrongful termination suits include clearly defining the worker's duties, providing good feedback on a regular basis, and conducting realistic performance appraisals on a regular basis. Most states recognize this exception.

Second, employers generally cannot exercise at will termination if such a termination violates a state's public policy. For example, workers' compensation programs are governed by rules in every state. Terminating an employee for filing a workers' compensation claim after becoming injured while on the job cannot be made on at will grounds. Most states recognize this exception.

Third, only a few states recognize something referred to as an implied covenant of good faith and fair dealing in the employment relationship. Terminating employment without *just cause*, which we discuss later in this chapter, would be considered an act of bad faith and unfair dealing. An example of employer bad faith would be terminating a long-service employee who consistently has demonstrated exceptional job performance and follows work rules. In the following Watch It video, a former Allegiant Air pilot discusses an in-flight emergency and his response that ultimately led to his termination.

Watch It I

If your professor has assigned this, sign into **www.pearson.com/mylab/management** to watch a video titled Pilot Files Wrongful Termination Lawsuit Against Allegiant Air and to respond to questions.

12.2 Describe the concept of discipline and summarize disciplinary action.

discipline
State of employee self-control and orderly conduct that indicates the extent of genuine teamwork within an organization.

disciplinary action
Invoking a penalty against an employee who fails to meet established standards.

Discipline and Disciplinary Action

Discipline is the state of employee self-control and orderly conduct that indicates the extent of genuine teamwork within an organization. A necessary but often trying aspect of internal employee relations is the application of **disciplinary action**, which is invoking a penalty against an employee who fails to meet established standards. Even though disciplinary action may be tense, unpleasant, and fraught with conflict, at times it must be done. Don Crosby, vice-president of international and corporate HR at McDonald's, said, "It's the hardest thing a manager has to do. It's also rocky terrain for many executives, who simply do not know when or how to hold the stick, swinging it haphazardly and inconsistently, striking too hard, too soft, or not at all."[2]

Effective disciplinary action addresses the employee's wrongful behavior, not the employee as a person. Incorrectly administered disciplinary action is destructive to both the employee and the organization. Thus, disciplinary action should not be applied haphazardly. Disciplinary action is not usually management's initial response to a problem. Normally, there are positive ways to convince employees to adhere to company policies, which are necessary to accomplish organizational goals. However, managers must administer disciplinary action at times when company rules are violated.

Disciplinary Action Process

The disciplinary action process is dynamic and ongoing. Because one person's actions can affect others in a work group, the proper application of disciplinary action fosters acceptable behavior by other group members. Conversely, unjustified or improperly administered disciplinary action can have a detrimental effect on other group members.

The disciplinary action process is shown in Figure 12-1. The external environment affects every area of HR management, including disciplinary actions. Changes in the external environment, such as technological innovations, may render a rule inappropriate and may necessitate creating new rules. Laws and government regulations that affect company policies and rules are also constantly changing. For instance, the Occupational Safety and Health Act (OSHA) caused many firms to establish safety rules.

Changes in the internal environment of the firm can also alter the disciplinary action process. Through organization development, the firm may change its employer brand. Because of this shift, first-line supervisors may begin to handle disciplinary action more positively. Organization policies can also have an impact on the disciplinary action process. Think how a new smoke-free workplace policy might affect the workplace and the possible need for disciplinary action.

The disciplinary action process deals largely with infractions of rules. Notice in Figure 12-1 that rules are established to better facilitate the accomplishment of organizational goals. Rules are specific guides to behavior on the job. The dos and don'ts associated with accomplishing

FIGURE 12-1
Disciplinary Action Process

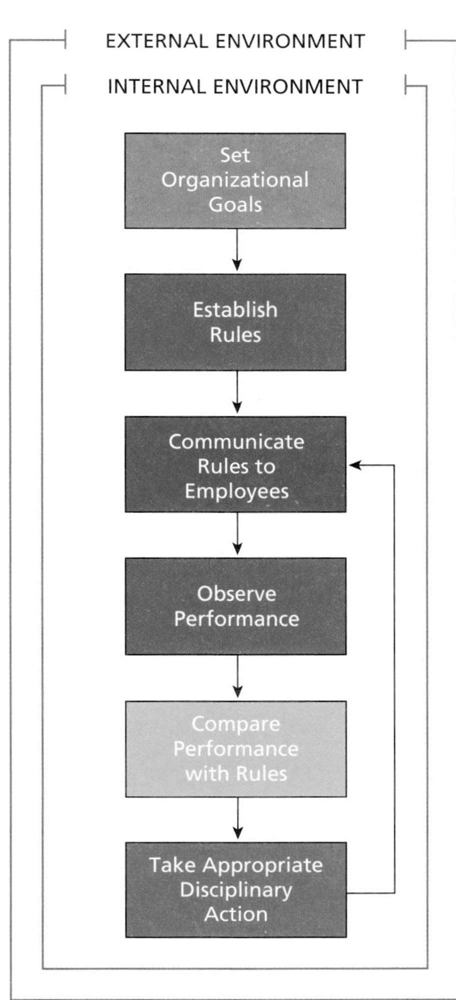

tasks may be highly inflexible. For example, a company may forbid the use of tobacco products anywhere on company property.

After management has established rules, it must communicate these rules to employees. The manager then observes the performance of workers and compares performance with rules. If employee behavior does not vary from acceptable practices, there is no need for disciplinary action, but when an employee's behavior violates a rule, corrective action may need to be taken. Taking disciplinary action against someone often creates an uncomfortable psychological climate. However, managers can still sleep well at night after taking disciplinary action if the rules have been clearly articulated to everyone.

The purpose of disciplinary action is to alter behavior that can have a negative impact on achievement of organizational objectives, not to chastise the violator. The word *discipline* comes from the word *disciple*, and when translated from Latin, it means, *to teach*. Thus, the intent of disciplinary action should be to ensure that the recipient sees disciplinary action as a learning process rather than as something that inflicts pain.

Note that the process shown in Figure 12-1 includes feedback from the point of taking appropriate disciplinary action to communicating rules to employees. When disciplinary action is taken, all employees should realize that certain behaviors are unacceptable and should not be repeated.[3] However, if appropriate disciplinary action is not taken, employees may view the behavior as acceptable and repeat it.

Approaches to Disciplinary Action

Several approaches to the administration of disciplinary action have been developed. Three of the most important concepts are the hot stove rule, progressive disciplinary action, and disciplinary action without punishment.

hot stove rule
An approach to disciplinary action that have four consequences which are analogous to touching a hot stove.

HOT STOVE RULE According to the **hot stove rule**, disciplinary action should have the following consequences, which are analogous to touching a hot stove:

- *Burns immediately.* If disciplinary action is to be taken, it must occur immediately so that the individual will understand the reason for it.
- *Provides warning.* It is also extremely important to provide warning that punishment will follow unacceptable behavior. As individuals move closer to a hot stove, its heat warns them that they will be burned if they touch it; therefore, they can avoid the burn if they so choose.
- *Gives consistent punishment.* Disciplinary action should also be consistent in that everyone who performs the same act will be punished accordingly. As with a hot stove, each person who touches it with the same degree of pressure and for the same period is burned to the same extent.
- *Burns impersonally.* Disciplinary action should be impersonal. The hot stove burns anyone who touches it—without favoritism.

If the circumstances surrounding all disciplinary action were the same, there would be no problem with this approach. However, situations are often quite different, and many variables may be present in each disciplinary action case. For instance, does the organization penalize a loyal 20-year employee the same way as an individual who has been with the firm for less than six weeks? Supervisors often find that they cannot be completely consistent and impersonal in taking disciplinary action and they need a certain degree of flexibility. Because situations do vary, progressive disciplinary action may be more realistic and more beneficial to both the employee and the organization.

progressive disciplinary action
Approach to disciplinary action designed to ensure that the minimum penalty appropriate to the offense is imposed.

PROGRESSIVE DISCIPLINARY ACTION **Progressive disciplinary action** is intended to ensure that the minimum penalty appropriate to the offense is imposed. The progressive disciplinary model was developed in response to the National Labor Relations Act (NLRA). The goal of progressive disciplinary action is to communicate formerly problem issues to employees in a direct and timely manner so that they can improve their performance. Its use involves answering a series of questions about the severity of the offense. The manager must ask these questions, in sequence, to determine the proper disciplinary action, as illustrated in Figure 12-2. After the manager has determined that disciplinary action is appropriate, the proper question is, "Does this violation warrant more than

FIGURE 12-2
Progressive Disciplinary Action Approach

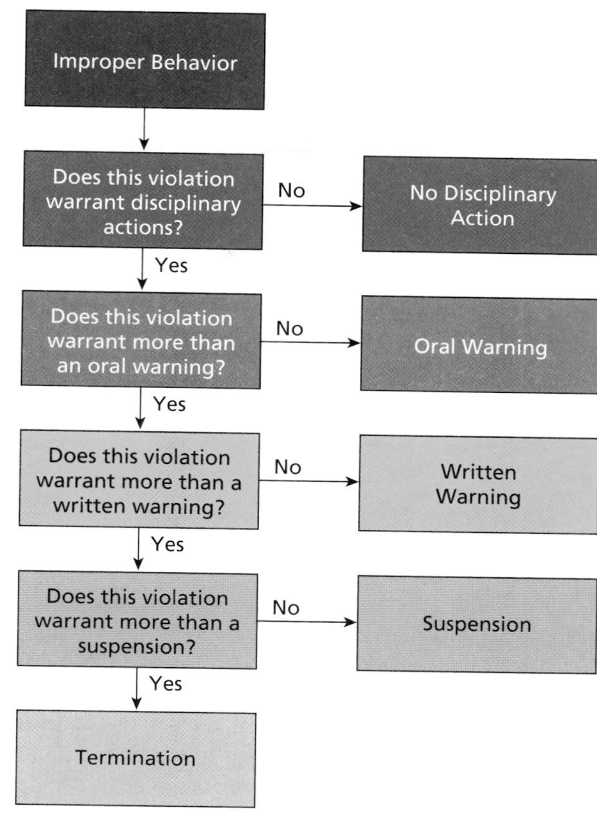

an oral warning?" If the improper behavior is minor and has not previously occurred, perhaps only an oral warning will be sufficient. In addition, an individual may receive several oral warnings before a *yes* answer applies. The manager follows the same procedure for each level of offense in the progressive disciplinary process. The manager does not consider termination until each lower-level question is answered *yes*. However, major violations, such as assaulting a supervisor or another worker, may justify moving through each level of question to the immediate termination of the employee. It is important for the worker to know what can result if improvement does not result.[4]

HR Web Wisdom

Progressive Disciplinary Action

http://hrdailyadvisor.blr.com/?s=discipline

Numerous articles related to disciplinary action and progressive disciplinary action.

To assist managers in recognizing the proper level of disciplinary action, some firms have formalized the procedure. One approach to establish progressive disciplinary action guidelines in a factory environment is shown in Table 12-1. In this example, a worker who is absent without authorization will receive an oral warning the first time it happens and a written warning the second time; the third time, the employee will be terminated. Fighting on the job is an offense that normally results in immediate termination. Specific guidelines for various offenses should be developed to meet the needs of the organization. For example, the wearing of rings or jewelry for aircraft mechanics is strictly prohibited. There would likely be no such rule in an office environment. The rule should fit the need of the situation.

disciplinary action without punishment
Process in which a worker is given time off with pay to think about whether he or she wants to follow the rules and continue working for the company.

DISCIPLINARY ACTION WITHOUT PUNISHMENT The process of giving a worker time off with pay to think about whether he or she wants to follow the rules and continue working for the company is called **disciplinary action without punishment**. The approach throws out formal punitive disciplinary action policies for situations such as chronic tardiness or a bad attitude in favor of affirming procedures that make employees want to take personal responsibility for their actions and be models for accomplishment of the corporate mission. When an employee violates a rule, the manager issues an oral reminder. Repetition brings a written reminder, and the third violation results in the worker having to take one, two, or three days off (with pay) to think about the situation. During the first two steps, the manager tries to encourage the employee to solve the problem. If the third step is taken, upon the worker's return, the worker and the supervisor meet to agree that the employee will not violate rules again or the employee will leave the firm.

TABLE 12-1

Suggested Guidelines for Disciplinary Action

Offenses Requiring First, an Oral Warning; Second, a Written Warning; and Third, Termination
Negligence in the performance of duties
Unauthorized absence from job
Inefficiency in the performance of job
Offenses Requiring a Written Warning and Then Termination
Sleeping on the job
Failure to report to work one or two days in a row without notice
Negligent use of property
Offenses Requiring Immediate Termination
Theft
Fighting on the job
Falsifying time card
Failure to report to work three days in a row without notice

When disciplinary action without punishment is used, it is especially important that all rules be explicitly stated in writing. At the time of orientation, new workers should be told that repeated violations of different rules would be viewed in the same way as several violations of the same rule. This approach keeps workers from taking undue advantage of the process. Walmart has a form of disciplinary action without punishment they call "Decision-Making Day." It provides a paid day off for the employee to decide to either improve or leave the company. It is Walmart's most severe discipline before termination.[5]

Problems in the Administration of Disciplinary Action

As might be expected, administering disciplinary action is not a pleasant task, but it is a manager's job to do. Although the manager is in the best position to take disciplinary action, many would rather avoid it even when it is in the company's best interest. Such reluctance often stems from breakdowns in other areas of HR management. For instance, if a manager has consistently rated an employee high on annual performance appraisals, the supervisor's rationale for taking disciplinary action against a worker for mediocre performance would be weak. In a possible termination situation, it could be that the employee's productivity has dropped substantially. It might also be that the employee's productivity has always been low, yet the supervisor had trouble justifying to upper-level management that the person should be terminated. Rather than run the risk of a decision being overturned, the supervisor retains the ineffective worker.

Occasionally, there may be lawsuits involving members of protected groups who claim that the disciplinary action was taken against them because they are members of a protected group. One of the best ways for a company to protect itself against lawsuits claiming discrimination or harassment is to ensure that it has proper, written policies barring unfair treatment of its staff and a system for ensuring that the policies are followed. Disciplinary actions should be fully documented, and managers should be trained in how to avoid bias claims.[6] Also, although discrimination laws prohibit employers from making employment decisions based on an employee's membership in a protected class, basing decisions solely on performance helps prevent violation of these laws.

A supervisor may be perfectly justified in administering disciplinary action, but there is usually a proper time and place for doing so. For example, taking disciplinary action against a worker in the presence of others may embarrass the individual and defeat the purpose of the action. Even when they are wrong, employees resent disciplinary action administered in public. By disciplining employees in private, supervisors prevent them from losing face with their peers.

In addition, many supervisors may be too lenient early in the disciplinary action process and too strict later. This lack of consistency does not give the worker a clear understanding of the penalty associated with the inappropriate action. A supervisor will often endure an unacceptable situation for an extended period. Then, when a decision is finally made to act, he or she is apt to overreact and come down excessively hard. However, consistency does not necessarily mean that the same penalty must be applied to two different workers for the same offense. For instance, managers would be consistent if they always considered the worker's past record and length of service.

12.3 Explain employment termination of various occupational groups.

Employment Termination

termination
Most severe penalty that an organization can impose on an employee.

Termination is the most severe penalty that an organization can impose on an employee, therefore, it should be the most carefully considered form of disciplinary action. The experience of being terminated is traumatic for employees regardless of their position in the organization. They can experience feelings of failure, fear, disappointment, and anger. It is also a difficult time for the person making the termination decision. Knowing that termination may affect not only the employee but also an entire family increases the trauma. Not knowing how the terminated employee will react also may create considerable anxiety for the manager who must do the firing. An individual who is terminated may respond with a wide range of emotions ranging from workplace violence to being very unemotional in the matter.

"Just Cause" as a Standard for Choosing to Terminate Employment

just cause
A standard for determining whether to terminate an employee and the standard is based on whether an employee violated company policy or work rules and the severity of the violation.

Just cause is a standard for determining whether to terminate an employee and the standard is based on whether an employee violated company policy or work rules and the severity of the violation. Employers that embrace the at will doctrine are not compelled to justify a termination decision. However, in an employment contract, just cause separates the basis for termination from that of a mass layoff because of economic reasons or exercise of at will rights by requiring a reason for termination.

In union settings, most collective bargaining agreements require just cause for discipline and discharge. If a union files a grievance over the termination of a union member, the employer typically has the burden to show just cause existed for the termination during a labor arbitration hearing. We discuss labor arbitration later in the alternative dispute resolution section of this chapter. In the nonunion settings, just cause is protection for the employer and employee. For example, assume that a company includes a severance pay policy. In most policies, companies withhold severance pay when termination is for just cause. Just cause provides protection to employers by justifying not making severance pay whose termination is for just cause, and it provides protection to employees by justifying receipt of severance pay whose termination does not meet just cause standards.

In 1972, Professor Carroll R. Daugherty, who served as a labor arbitrator, put forth seven tests to help future arbitrators decide whether employee termination or other adverse actions in union settings, such as demotion, met just cause standards. Although established for use by arbitrators, the questions provide useful guidance for management whose companies have just cause employment provisions. Prior to deciding to terminate an employee, management can review whether the just cause standard will likely be upheld if the termination is subsequently challenged by the former employee. The seven tests follow:

1. Did the company give to the employee forewarning or foreknowledge of the possible or probably disciplinary consequences of the employee's conduct?
2. Was the company's rule or managerial [sic] reasonably related to: (a) the orderly, efficient, and safe operation of the company's business; and (b) the performance that the company might properly expect of the employee?
3. Did the company, *before* administering discipline to an employer, try to discover whether the employee did in fact violate or disobey a rule or order of management?
4. Was the company's investigation conducted fairly and objectively?
5. At the investigation, did the company "judge" obtain substantial and compelling evidence or proof that the employee was guilty as charged?
6. Has the company applied its rules, orders, and penalties even-handedly and without discrimination to all employees?
7. Was the degree of discipline administered by the company in a case reasonably related to: (a) the seriousness of his employee's proven offense; and (b) the record of the employee in his service with the company?[7]

Considerations in Communicating the Termination Decision

Most of the time, when the decision is made to terminate a worker, the employee should not be surprised because he or she should have been given explicit warnings and counseling prior to being fired. The worker should have been advised of specific steps needed to take to keep the job. Support should have been provided to show what needed to be done. The worker also should have been given a reasonable period to comply with the supervisor's expectations.

Experts suggest that firings should be on Mondays because it lets the dismissed workers start looking for a job right away.[8] Further, firing a worker at the end of the day leaves little chance for discussion among the remaining staff that may interrupt the workplace. HR professionals and managers should try to plan the termination and not make it based on emotions. Certain steps should be followed in the termination process. In the first place, the worker's manager normally and HR representative should personally communicate the decision and present a termination letter. There are various considerations for preparing termination letters.[9] Letters should state that the person's employment *has been* terminated, not *will be* terminated. In addition, HR professionals include in the letter essential information about collecting their last paycheck, any severance pay, payout of unused vacation or sick leave, and instructions to apply for health benefits under COBRA.

Second, the termination process should be kept short, using nonaccusatory language. Third, the manager should not go into the reason for the dismissal and should not answer any questions regarding the decision.[10] In some states, when an employee is involuntarily terminated, the employer must pay all earned and unpaid wages within 24 hours after the employee demands it. To avoid any potential dispute over when a demand was made, most employers simply have the final paycheck available at the termination meeting. Also, select a location where there will be no interruptions. If the employee becomes argumentative, managers may need to get up and leave once the worker has been fired. For that reason, a manager's office is normally not used.[11] Finally, most managers believe that it is best to have a witness because the person being fired may interpret your statements in the worst possible light.[12]

Termination of Employees at Various Levels

Regardless of the similarities in the termination of employees at various levels, distinct differences do exist regarding nonmanagerial/nonprofessional employees, executives, and middle and lower-level managers and professionals.

NONMANAGERIAL/NONPROFESSIONAL EMPLOYEES Individuals in this category are neither managers nor professionally trained individuals, such as engineers or accountants. They generally

HR BLOOPERS

Effective Discipline at Berries Groceries

As Katie Smith travels to one of the Berries Groceries store locations, she is worried about the meeting she is about to have with one of the deli clerks. As the HR Manager for the chain of grocery stores, Katie is working to improve the overall performance and retention of the mostly part-time grocery staff. The store manager of this location called Katie about the employee and he asked her to sit in on a disciplinary meeting to give the employee a written warning. Last week, the deli clerk had failed to follow the proper procedures when closing the deli counter at the end of the day, and thus, some food had spoiled and needed to be thrown out. The manager told Katie that this employee and other employees have failed to follow the proper procedures in the past, but he has never given any disciplinary action before this incident. However, this time there was a significant amount of food product that went to waste, and he felt that he could use this disciplinary action to set an example for all employees so they know that they need to start following the procedure. He said he tells every employee the closing procedures when they are hired and that he should not have to remind them every time they close the deli. Katie understands the importance of ensuring that employees follow proper food handling procedures but has an uneasy feeling that this meeting is not going to go well.

If your professor has assigned this, go to **www.pearson.com/mylab/management** to complete the HR Bloopers exercise and test your application of these concepts when faced with real-world decisions.

include employees such as steelworkers, truck drivers, salesclerks, and wait staff. If the firm is unionized, the termination procedure is typically well defined in the labor/management agreement. For example, drinking on the job might be identified as a reason for immediate termination. Absences, on the other hand, may require three written warnings by the supervisor before termination action can be taken.

When the firm is union-free, these workers can generally be terminated more easily because the worker is most likely an at will employee. In most union-free organizations, violations justifying termination are often included in the firm's employee handbook. At times, especially in smaller organizations, the termination process is informal with the first-line supervisor telling workers what actions warrant termination. Regardless of the size of the organization, management should inform employees of the actions that warrant termination.

TERMINATION OF MIDDLE- AND LOWER-LEVEL MANAGERS AND PROFESSIONALS Typically, the most vulnerable and perhaps the most neglected groups of employees about termination have been middle- and lower-level managers and professionals. Employees in these jobs may lack the political influence that a terminated executive has. Although certainly not recommended, termination may have been based on something as simple as the attitude or feelings of an immediate superior on a given day.

EXECUTIVES Unlike workers at lower-level positions, CEOs do not have to worry about their positions being eliminated. Their main concern is pleasing the board of directors because hiring and firing the CEO is a board's main responsibility. Often the reason for terminating a CEO is that the board of directors lost confidence in the executive. Tenure has become increasingly shaky for new CEOs because the turnover in large corporations is high. According to John Challenger, CEO of the outplacement firm Challenger, Gray & Christmas, Inc., "It's not a job for someone who thinks they're going to stay in one spot for a long career right now," he says. "Tenures are short, particularly in big public companies."[13]

Executives usually have no formal appeal procedure. The reasons for termination may not be as clear as for lower-level employees. Some of the reasons include the following:

- *Economic downturns.* At times, business conditions may force a reduction in the number of executives.
- *Reorganization/downsizing.* To improve efficiency or because of merging with another company, a firm may reorganize or downsize, resulting in the elimination of some executive positions.
- *Philosophical differences.* A difference in philosophy of conducting business may develop between an executive and the board. To maintain consistency in management philosophy, the executive may be replaced.
- *Decline in productivity.* The executive may have been capable of performing satisfactorily in the past but, for various reasons, can no longer perform the job as required.

This list does not include factors related to illegal activities such as sexual harassment or insider trading. Under those circumstances, the firm has no moral obligation to the terminated executive.

An organization may derive positive benefits from terminating executives, but such actions also present a potentially hazardous situation for the company. Terminating a senior executive is an expensive proposition, often in ways costlier than just the separation package. The impact on the organization should be measured in relationships, productivity, strategic integrity, and investor confidence, as well as dollars. Many corporations are concerned about developing a negative public image that reflects insensitivity to the needs of their employees. They fear that such a reputation would impede their efforts to recruit high-quality managers. Also, terminated executives have, at times, made public statements detrimental to the reputation of their former employers.

Demotion as an Alternative to Termination

demotion
Process of moving a worker to a lower level of duties and responsibilities, which typically involves a reduction in pay.

Demotion is the process of moving a worker to a lower level of duties and responsibilities, which typically involves a reduction in pay. Demotion may be a legitimate career option that had nothing to do with disciplinary action. However, in this section, demotion is addressed as a disciplinary action option. Emotions may run high when an individual is demoted. The demoted person may suffer loss of respect from peers and feel betrayed, embarrassed, angry, and disappointed. The employee's productivity may also decrease further. For these reasons, demotion should be used cautiously. If demotion is chosen instead of termination, efforts must be made to preserve the self-esteem of the individual. The person may be asked how he or she would like to handle the demotion announcement. A positive image of the worker's value to the company should be projected.

The handling of demotions in a unionized organization is usually spelled out clearly in the labor–management agreement. Should a decision be made to demote a worker for unsatisfactory performance, the union should be notified of this intent and given the specific reasons for the demotion. Often the demotion will be challenged and carried through the formal grievance procedure. Documentation is necessary for the demotion to be upheld. Even with the problems associated with demotion for cause, it is often easier to demote than to terminate an employee. In addition, demotion is often less devastating to the employee. For the organization, however, the opposite may be true if the demotion creates lingering ill will and an embittered employee.

Downsizing, discussed next, is different from termination, however, the results for workers involved is the same—they no longer have a job.

Downsizing

downsizing
Reverse of a company growing; it suggests a one-time change in the organization and the number of people employed (also known as *restructuring* or *rightsizing*).

Downsizing, also known as *restructuring* or *rightsizing*, is essentially the reverse of a company growing; it suggests a one-time change in the organization and the number of people employed. Typically, both the organizational structure and the number of people in the organization shrink for improving organizational performance. The retail industry has experienced large downsizing. For instance, retailer JCPenney announced that it would close approximately 140 stores in 2017.[14] In addition, once-prominent shoe retailer Payless ShoeSource Inc. filed for bankruptcy.[15] Retailers such as these whose business is based on physical stores have lost ground to online retailers such as Amazon. JCPenney hopes to reduce costs, using some of those savings to bolster their online shopping presence.

Companies that have downsized should not forget about the workers that remain. Communication channels should be open to let those remaining workers know what and why the downsizing occurred. Often those who remain suffer *survivor's guilt* or *survivor syndrome*, and open communication can do much to get by the feeling. Often it is a good idea to have a venting session where workers can express their concerns. Questions should be answered clearly and candidly.

Planning is crucial as a company prepares for downsizing. Often there may be age and other discrimination claims if downsizing results in a disproportionately adverse impact on members of a protected class. At times, older workers with higher salaries than their younger counterparts become targets for cost-cutting measures and age discrimination claims occur. It is important to analyze the breakdown of downsized workers to ensure that all protected groups of workers are not disproportionately affected. It is equally imperative that an employer use objective, job-related criteria to decide which positions will be affected. In addition, the downsizing organization should be prepared to deal with government requirements such as the Consolidated Omnibus Budget Reconciliation Act (COBRA) and Employee Retirement Income Security Act (ERISA).

Workers should understand when they are hired how the system will work in the event of layoffs. When the firm is unionized, the layoff procedures are usually stated clearly in the labor/management agreement. Seniority usually is the basis for layoffs, with the least-senior employees laid off first. The agreement may also have a clearly spelled-out *bumping procedure*. When senior-level positions are eliminated, the people occupying them have the right to bump workers from lower-level positions, if they have the proper qualifications for the lower-level job. When bumping occurs, the composition of the workforce is altered.

Union-free firms should also establish layoff procedures prior to facing layoff decisions. In union-free firms, productivity and the needs of the organization are typically key considerations. When productivity is the primary factor, management must be careful to ensure that productivity, not favoritism, is the actual basis for the layoff decision. Therefore, it is important to define accurately productivity considerations well in advance of any layoffs.

NEGATIVE ASPECTS OF DOWNSIZING When downsizing is chosen, companies typically describe the positive results, such as improving the bottom line. Many believe that the guaranteed results of employee downsizing on organizational market returns, profitability, and other financial outcomes are at best evasive.[16] There also is a negative side to downsizing. Following are some examples:

- During layoffs, employers and employees must realize that there is a natural grieving period and a desire to go back to the way things used to be. Friendships may be lost, and there is day-to-day uncertainty about the future. It is difficult to think about contributing to the bottom line when you do not know if tomorrow will be your day to be cut.[17]
- Layers are pulled out of a firm, making advancement in the organization more difficult. Thus, more and more individuals find themselves plateaued.
- Workers begin seeking better opportunities because they believe they may be the next in line to be laid off. Often the best workers find other jobs and there is an increase in voluntary departures.[18]
- Employee loyalty is often significantly reduced. For workers who remain after downsizing, the loyalty level is often low.
- Institutional memory or corporate culture is lost.
- Workers who remain after downsizing are also faced with the realization of having to do additional work (some call it "ghost work"). Jim Link, staffing agency Randstad's managing director for HR, said, "The piling-on of responsibilities is at an all-time high."[19]
- When demand for the products or services returns, the company often realizes that it has cut too deeply. It then begins looking for ways to get the job done.

WORKER ADJUSTMENT AND RETRAINING NOTIFICATION ACT The Worker Adjustment and Retraining Notification (WARN) Act requires covered employers to give 60 days' notice before a plant closing or mass layoff that will affect at least 100 full-time employees, not counting employees who work an average of less than 20 hours per week.[20] As an example of how the process works: Century Aluminum of West Virginia ceased operations on February 20, 2009. It had issued a federal WARN notice in December 2008 to its 679 employees.[21] Therefore, no penalty was imposed on the company.

There are severe monetary sanctions for failing to comply with the requirements of WARN. The penalties for WARN notice violations include liability to each affected worker for back pay and benefits for up to 60 days. For example, more than 800 former employees of solar energy company Solyndra received a $3.5 million settlement because the company initiated a mass layoff.[22] The company failed to provide the required 60-day warning notice to employees that it would close. However, if an unforeseeable business circumstance leads to closing earlier than 60 days, the WARN does not apply. Such was the case with Hale-Halsell Company. Six days after the retailer United Supermarket, Hale-Halsell's biggest customer, severed ties with the company, and the wholesaler announced 200 layoffs.[23]

outplacement
A procedure whereby laid-off employees are given assistance in finding employment elsewhere.

OUTPLACEMENT In **outplacement**, laid-off employees are given assistance in finding employment elsewhere. The use of outplacement began at the executive level, but it has also been used at other organizational levels. Through outplacement, the firm tries to soften the impact of displacement. Barbara Barra, executive vice-president of operations for the consulting firm Lee Hecht Harrison, said, "There is a strong correlation between how a company treats departing employees and its ability to attract and retain top talent now and in the future, particularly when the economy rebounds."[24] Some of the services provided by outplacement include a discussion of pension options, Social Security benefits, expenses for interviews, and wage/salary negotiations. Usually career guidance is provided as well as instructions on how to conduct a self-appraisal directed toward recognizing skills, knowledge, experience, and other qualities recruiters may require in a new job. Tutoring in how to search for a job is usually available, and there is often help available in how to interview in the new employment environment.

When organizational change takes place, there will be a psychological impact on both the individuals who were dismissed and those who remain. Companies use outplacement to take care of employees by moving them successfully out of the company. This proactive response will also likely have a positive influence on those who remain with the company after downsizing. More employers are offering outplacement help to preserve their employer brand and reputation.

severance pay
Compensation designed to assist laid-off employees as they search for new employment.

SEVERANCE PAY **Severance pay** is compensation designed to assist laid-off employees as they search for new employment. (As a reminder, we reviewed golden parachute arrangements in Chapter 9, which are severance packages for executives under certain circumstances.) Although no federal law requires U.S. companies to pay severance, a recent study revealed characteristics of severance packages for companies that do. More than 50 percent indicated "Salary Grade/ Level" as a factor; 40 percent stated full-time employment status and pre-negotiated employment agreements are factors as well.[25] Even so, U.S. employees earn the least amount of severance pay worldwide, regardless of their job level or tenure.[26] When offered, typically one to two weeks of severance pay for every year of service is provided, up to some predetermined maximum. The employee's organizational level generally affects the amount of severance pay provided. For example, nonmanagers may get eight or nine weeks of pay even if their length of service is greater than eight or nine years. Middle managers may receive severance pay amounts based on the number of years worked.

There are many compelling reasons to pay severance to employees who are involuntarily terminated. Many managers think that treating ousted workers well sends an important message to those who remain behind. There may be a feeling that "we all could be in that situation someday." A major reason a firm offers severance today is that something in return is provided. The departing worker must waive all rights to sue the company, but the waiver has to be voluntary.[27] In a recent survey, nearly three-quarters of some 400 HR professionals answered *yes* when asked if they required workers who were laid off to sign a form releasing their organization from liability for employment actions.[28] From the employee's viewpoint, severance is paid so that they will not sue the organization.[29] "It's not love; it's not a gift—it's a business transaction," notes Alan Sklover, author of *Fired, Downsized, or Laid Off*.[30]

Recent developments might lead companies to reconsider whether to provide severance pay to employees. In 2014, the U.S. Supreme Court ruled (*U.S. v. Quality Stores Inc.*) that severance pay is subject to Federal Insurance Contribution Act (FICA) tax. In Chapter 10, we said that FICA requires that employees and employers pay a portion of the cost of Old Age, Survivors, and Disability Insurance (OASDI) and Medicare coverage. Arguably, paying a tax on money that is awarded to former employees can create a substantial cost burden for companies.

12.4 Explain the use of ombudspersons and alternative dispute resolution.

Ombudspersons and Alternative Dispute Resolution

Not all internal employee relations situations are as severe as termination and layoffs. An ombudsperson or alternative dispute resolution may be used to resolve these disputes. We will consider these topics next.

Ombudspersons

ombudsperson
Complaint officer who has access to top management and who hears employee complaints, investigates, and recommends appropriate action.

An **ombudsperson** is a complaint officer who has access to top management and who hears employee complaints, investigates, and recommends appropriate action. Employers use ombudspersons in their organizations to help defuse problems before they become lawsuits or scandals. The more internal mechanisms a corporation must deal with internal problems, the less likely these problems are to wind up in court. Ombudspersons are impartial, neutral counselors who can give employees confidential advice about problems ranging from abusive managers to allegations of illegal corporate activity. Ombudspersons are used so that all workers may seek informal, confidential assistance to work through problems without losing control over how their concerns will be addressed. The ombudsperson is typically independent of line management and reports near or at the top of the organization.

Melissa Cameron is the ombudsperson for Bayer Corporation North American operations. The firm's 16,600 employees can contact her confidentially to blow the whistle on bad behavior or discuss other workplace issues. She said, "If you find even one or two cases a year that are substantiated, you have more than paid for my salary in terms of addressing a situation on the front end rather than going through litigation."[31]

Alternative Dispute Resolution

alternative dispute resolution (ADR)
Procedure whereby the employee and the company agree ahead of time that any problems will be addressed by an agreed-upon means.

As the number of employment-related lawsuits increases, companies have looked for ways to protect themselves against the costs and uncertainties of the judicial system. **Alternative dispute resolution (ADR)** is a procedure whereby the employee and the company agree ahead of time that any problems will be addressed by an agreed-upon means.

ADR is based on the use of a jury waiver, which is a contractual provision in which an employee waives the right to a trial by jury in a legal proceeding brought against an employer.[32] Types of ADR include arbitration, mediation, negotiated rulemaking, neutral fact-finding, and minitrials. Except for binding arbitration, the goal of ADR is to provide a forum for the parties to work toward a voluntary, consensual agreement, as opposed to having a judge or other authority decide the case. Mediation is the preferred method for most people. ADR cases run the gamut from racial, gender, and age discrimination to unfair firings. The idea behind ADR is to resolve conflicts between employer and employee through means less costly and contentious than litigation. A successful program can save a company thousands of dollars in legal costs and hundreds of hours in managers' time. Just as important, perhaps, it can protect a company from the demoralizing tension and bitterness that employee grievances can spread through a workforce. Compared to litigation, ADR processes are less adversarial, faster and more efficient, relatively lower in cost, and private. In the Watch It video, attorneys from the Gordon Law Group discuss the realities of conflict in the workplace between employees as well as between the employer and employee that occur from time to time. They also refer to approaches to find resolution to conflict.

 **Watch It 2**

If your professor has assigned this, sign into **www.pearson.com/mylab/management** to watch a video titled Gordon Law Group and to respond to questions.

HR Web Wisdom

Alternative Dispute Resolution

www.opm.gov/er/adrguide/toc.asp

Office of Personnel Management, Alternative Dispute Resolution: A Resource Guide.

When parties agree to mediate, they can reach a settlement in 96 percent of the cases. A presidential executive order requires federal agencies to: (1) promote greater use of mediation, arbitration, early neutral evaluation, agency ombudspersons, and other alternative dispute resolution techniques; and (2) promote greater use of negotiated rulemaking.

The Supreme Court rendered an opinion in *Circuit City v. Adams* that greatly enhanced an employer's ability to enforce compulsory ADR agreements. The Court held that the ADR was valid and enforceable and made clear that ADR applied to the clear majority of employees and was available to employers seeking to enforce compulsory arbitration agreements. However, in 2012, the National Labor Relations Board (NLRB) held that a Florida-based home builder committed an unfair labor practice under federal labor law by maintaining a mandatory arbitration agreement that waived the rights of employees to participate in class or collective actions. Only time will tell how this decision will affect ADR.

12.5 Describe transfers, promotions, resignations, and retirements as factors involved in internal employee relations.

More Considerations for Internal Employee Relations

HR professionals either may initiate or approve requests for employment status changes. These include transfers, promotions, resignations, and retirements.

Transfers

transfer
Lateral movement of a worker within an organization.

The lateral movement of a worker within an organization is called a **transfer**. A transfer may be initiated by the firm or by an employee. The process does not and should not imply that a person is being either promoted or demoted. Transfers serve several purposes, five of which we describe here. First, firms often find it necessary to reorganize. Offices and departments are created and abolished in response to the company's needs. In filling positions created by reorganization, the company may have to move employees without promoting them. A similar situation may exist when an office or department is closed. Rather than terminate valued employees, management may transfer them to other areas within the organization. These transfers may entail moving an employee to another desk in the same office or to a location halfway around the world.

Second, transfers make positions available in the primary promotion channels. At times, productive but unpromotable workers may clog promotion channels. Other qualified workers in the organization may find their opportunities for promotion blocked. When this happens, a firm's most capable future managers may seek employment elsewhere. To keep promotion channels open, the firm may decide to transfer employees who are unpromotable but productive at their organizational level.

Third, transfers may satisfy employees' personal needs. The reasons for wanting a transfer are numerous. An individual may need to accompany a transferred spouse to a new location or work closer to home to care for aging parents, or the worker may dislike the long commute to and from work. Factors such as these may be of sufficient importance that employees may resign if a requested transfer is not approved. Rather than risk losing a valued employee, the firm may agree to the transfer.

Fourth, transfers may also be an effective means of dealing with personality clashes. Some people just cannot get along with one another. Because each of the individuals may be a valued employee, a transfer may be an appropriate solution to the problem. Nevertheless, managers must be cautious regarding the "grass is always greener on the other side of the fence" syndrome. When some workers encounter a temporary setback, they immediately ask for a transfer before they even attempt to work through the problem.

Fifth, because of a limited number of management levels, it is becoming necessary for managers to have a wide variety of experiences before achieving a promotion. Individuals who desire upward mobility often explore possible lateral moves so that they can learn new skills.

Promotions

promotion
Movement of a person to a higher-level position in an organization.

A **promotion** is the movement of a person to a higher-level position in the organization. The term *promotion* is one of the most emotionally charged words in the field of HR management. An individual who receives a promotion normally receives additional financial rewards and the ego boost associated with achievement and accomplishment. Most employees feel good about being promoted. Nevertheless, for every individual who gains a promotion, probably others were not selected. If these individuals wanted the promotion badly enough or their favorite candidate was overlooked, they may slack off or even resign. If the consensus of employees directly involved is that the wrong person was promoted, considerable resentment may result.

Numerous laws, court cases, and executive orders apply when individuals are hired. These same hiring standards apply to promotion decisions. Promotion decisions should not discriminate against employees because of age, race, religion, national origin, color, sex, pregnancy, or disability.[33]

Resignations

Even when an organization is totally committed to making its environment a good place to work, workers will still resign. Some employees cannot see promotional opportunities, or at least not enough, and will therefore move on. A certain amount of turnover is healthy for an organization and is often necessary to afford employees the opportunity to fulfill career objectives. When turnover becomes excessive, however, the firm must do something to slow it. The most qualified employees are often the ones who resign because they are more mobile. On the other hand, marginally qualified workers never seem to leave. If excessive numbers of a firm's highly qualified and competent workers are leaving, a way must be found to reverse the trend.

exit interview
Means of revealing the real reasons employees leave their jobs; it is conducted before an employee departs the company and provides information on how to correct the causes of discontent and reduce turnover.

ANALYZING VOLUNTARY RESIGNATIONS When a firm wants to determine why individuals leave, it can use the exit interview or the postexit questionnaire. An **exit interview** is a means of revealing the real reasons employees leave their jobs and it is conducted before an employee departs the company. An important question pertains to whether employees felt they had received a good realistic job preview.[34] Determining why employees leave a company can provide an opportunity for the firm to make changes to reduce turnover rates and reduce the associated costs.[35] Well-designed exit interviews that are executed appropriately should help provide HR professions and other company leaders with the following information and understanding:[36]

- Uncover issues related to HR (e.g., pay, benefits, development opportunities, and succession planning)
- Understand employees' perceptions of the work itself
- Gain insight into managers' leadership styles and effectiveness
- Learn about HR benchmarks (e.g., salary, benefits) at competing organizations
- Foster innovation by soliciting ideas for improving the organization
- Create lifelong advocates for the organization

FYI

A survey of companies in more than 35 countries revealed that 75 percent conducted exit interviews.

Often, the reason an employee leaves the job is misleading. Leigh Branham, author of *The 7 Hidden Reasons Employees Leave: How to Recognize the Subtle Signs and Act before It's Too Late*, believes that employees will cite pay as the reason they quit their jobs, 60 to 80 percent of the time. His research suggests that only 12 to 15 percent of employees leave for this reason.[37] Perhaps departing employees are reluctant to burn bridges by revealing the real reason for leaving because they may need a reference from their supervisor in the future and fear reprisal. However, only after determining the *real* reason for leaving can a firm develop a strategy to overcome the problem.

At times, women who are on the fast track are not candid about why they quit. A consulting firm was hired to discover why top-performing women were quitting in high numbers, saying in their exit interviews that they wanted to spend more time with their kids. However, the employers later learned that these women had returned to work with another firm, some starting their own firms and working longer hours. In anonymous interviews, the women who had quit explained the problem. Most said they had left their jobs because they could not see a future for themselves there. The wanting-to-spend-more-time-with-kids story was just cover—so they could maintain good relations with their former bosses.[38]

Often a third party, such as a person in the HR department or an outsource party will conduct the exit interview. A third party may be used because employees may not be willing to air their problems with their former bosses. Outsourcing the exit interviews may be beneficial because employers believe that the person who is leaving will be more honest when he or she is not speaking to a company employee. Over time, properly conducted exit interviews can provide considerable insight into why employees leave. Patterns are often identified that uncover weaknesses in the firm's management system. Knowledge of the problem permits corrective action to be taken. In addition, exit interviews help to identify training and development needs and identify areas in which changes need to be made. They may also be used to identify hidden biases of managers who are hurting the productivity of the unit.[39]

post-exit questionnaire
Questionnaire sent to former employees several weeks after they leave the organization to determine the real reason they left.

Another means of determining the real reason employees are leaving the organization is by administering a **post-exit questionnaire**, which is sent to former employees several weeks after they leave the organization. Usually, they have already started work at their new company. Ample blank space is provided so that a former employee can express his or her feelings about and perceptions of the job and the organization. Because the individual is no longer with the firm, he or she may respond more freely to the questions. However, there are several major weaknesses in the use of the post-exit questionnaire. Participation rates are often low because former workers may not care enough to respond and they may be difficult to reach after they have departed.[40] Also, the interviewer is not present to interpret and probe for more information.

ATTITUDE SURVEYS: A MEANS OF RETAINING QUALITY EMPLOYEES Exit and post-exit interviews can provide valuable information to improve HR management practices. The problem, however, is that these approaches are reactions to events that were detrimental to the organization.

attitude survey
Survey that seeks input from employees to determine their feelings about topics such as the work they perform, their supervisor, their work environment, flexibility in the workplace, opportunities for advancement, training and development opportunities, and the firm's compensation system.

An alternative, proactive approach is administering attitude surveys. **Attitude surveys** seek input from employees to determine their feelings about topics such as the work they perform, their supervisor, their work environment, flexibility in the workplace, opportunities for advancement, training and development opportunities, and the firm's compensation system. They can provide valuable information to management, but they should not be a substitute for day-to-day discussion between managers and workers.[41] Because some employees will want their responses to be confidential, every effort should be made to guarantee their anonymity. To achieve this, it may be necessary to have the survey administered by a third party. Regardless of how the process is handled, attitude surveys have the potential to improve management practices. For this reason, they are widely used throughout industry today. Joseph Cabral, senior vice-president and chief HR officer for the North Shore-LIJ Health System in Long Island, New York, says, "North Shore has been surveying its 38,000 employees annually for the past three years, but it recently went to a quarterly survey to provide more real-time and actionable results and to allow comparisons across worksites and departments."[42]

Employees should be advised of the purpose of the survey. The mere act of giving a survey communicates to employees that management is concerned about their problems, wants to know what they are, and wants to solve them, if possible. Analyzing survey results of various subgroups and comparing them with the firm's total population may indicate areas that should be investigated and problems that need to be solved. For instance, the survey results of the production night shift might be compared with the production day shift. Should problems show up, management must be willing to make the suggested changes. If the survey does not result in some improvements, the process may be a deterrent to employees and future surveys may not yield helpful data. If you are not going to do anything because of the survey, do not bother to administer it.

offboarding
Facilitates employee departure from the company by assisting in the completion of exit tasks, including exit interviews, forms completion, the return of company property, and ensuring that employees receive the appropriate extended benefits.

OFFBOARDING **Offboarding** facilitates employee departure from the company by assisting in the completion of exit tasks, including exit interviews, forms completion, the return of company property, and ensuring that employees receive the appropriate extended benefits.[43] Topics such as the worker's 401(k) and COBRA need to be addressed. Teresa Grote, practice director of composite solutions for Ascendum, an information technology company, said, "I think that in our highly litigious society today, making sure that you go through proper offboarding is probably equally, if not more, important than proper onboarding."[44]

Retirements

phased retirement
Any arrangement that allows people to move from full-time work to retirement in steps.

Many long-term employees leave an organization by retiring. However, many of today's employees are not planning for a traditional retirement, in which they have an immediate and abrupt end to their working career at a specific age, such as 65. Some want to work past the normal retirement age because they are healthy and want to keep active; others must work because their retirement account has dwindled and they cannot afford to retire. **Phased retirement** is any arrangement that allows people to move from full-time work to retirement in steps. In addition, 20 percent of employers say that phased retirement is critical to their company's HR strategy today. That number nearly triples to 61 percent when employers look ahead five years. Allen Steinberg, a principal at Hewitt Associates, said, "Employers will be losing key talent at a time when attracting and retaining skilled workers will be more important."[45] However, a recent study found that major corporations do not have phased retirement programs for older workers who can continue adding value.[46] In fact, a Society for Human Resource Management Survey found that only five percent of firms offer such programs.[47] Another survey revealed that 42 percent of companies are considering them.[48]

The Pension Protection Act of 2006 permits limited phased retirement by allowing in-service pension plan withdrawals to begin at age 62 rather than 65. A benefit of phased retirement is that it permits a company to reduce labor costs without hurting morale. It also lets an organization hold on to its experienced workers so they can share their knowledge with a less-experienced workforce. The federal government's phased retirement program requires participants to spend about 20 percent of their time mentoring employees who plan to assume their job duties once they leave.[49] Employees at Lee Memorial can work as few as 16 hours a week and still be eligible for benefits. Mercy Health's phased retirement plan allows workers aged 50 and older to reduce the number of hours worked while keeping their benefits.[50] CVS Caremark has set up a "snowbird" employment program to retain valuable employees. The program allows pharmacists to transfer south to places such as Florida for the winter, following the business's customers. Other benefits CVS Caremark provides the more mature workforce include part-time work, training, and flexible scheduling.[51]

Sometimes employees will be offered early retirement before reaching the organization's normal length-of-service requirement. Historically, early retirement has been viewed as an attractive solution when workforce reductions had to be made. Early retirement plans, which gained popularity in the 1980s, appealed to older workers facing layoffs. Early retirement is still being used, but companies often reserve the right to reject a highly productive worker's request.

PREPARING FOR EXAMS/QUIZZES

Chapter Summary by Learning Objectives

1. ***Explain the concept of employment at will.*** *Employment at will* is an unwritten contract created when an employee agrees to work for an employer but no agreement exists as to how long the parties expect the employment to last.
2. ***Describe the concept of discipline and summarize disciplinary action.*** *Discipline* is the state of employee self-control and orderly conduct present within an organization.

   Disciplinary action occurs when a penalty is invoked against an employee who fails to meet established standards.

   After management has established rules, it must communicate these rules to employees. The manager then observes the performance of workers and compares performance with rules. If employee behavior does not vary from acceptable practices, there is no need for disciplinary action, but when an employee's behavior violates a rule, corrective action may be necessary.

   Three of the most important concepts are the hot stove rule, progressive disciplinary action, and disciplinary action without punishment. As might be expected, administering disciplinary action is not a pleasant task, but it is a job that managers sometimes must do. Although the manager is in the best position to take disciplinary action, many would rather avoid it even when it is in the company's best interest. Such reluctance often stems from breakdowns in other areas of HR management.
3. ***Explain employment termination of various occupational groups.*** *Termination* is the most severe penalty that an organization can impose on an employee, therefore, it should be the most carefully considered form of disciplinary action. Regardless of the similarities in the termination of employees at various levels, distinct differences exist regarding non-managerial/non-professional employees, executives, and middle and lower-level managers and professionals.

   Demotion is the process of moving a worker to a lower level of duties and responsibilities, which typically involves a reduction in pay. If demotion is chosen instead of termination, efforts must be made to preserve the self-esteem of the individual.

   Downsizing, also known as *restructuring* or *rightsizing*, is essentially the reverse of a company growing; it suggests a one-time change in the organization and the number of people employed.
4. ***Explain the use of ombudspersons and alternative dispute resolution.*** An *ombudsperson* is a complaint officer with access to top management who hears employee complaints, investigates, and recommends appropriate action.

   Alternative dispute resolution is a procedure whereby the employee and the company agree ahead of time that any problems will be addressed by an agreed-upon means.
5. ***Describe transfers, promotions, resignations, and retirements as factors involved in internal employee relations.*** The lateral movement of a worker within an organization is called a *transfer*.

   A *promotion* is the movement of a person to a higher-level position in the organization. Even when an organization is totally committed to making its environment a good place to work, workers will still resign.

   Many long-term employees leave an organization by retiring. Much of today's employees are not planning for a traditional retirement, in which they have an immediate and abrupt end to their working career at a specific age, such as 65. Some want to work past the normal retirement age because they are healthy and want to keep active; others must work because their retirement account has dwindled and they cannot afford to retire.

Key Terms

internal employee relations 339
employment at will 339
discipline 340
disciplinary action 340
hot stove rule 342
progressive disciplinary action 342
disciplinary action without punishment 343
termination 345
just cause 345
demotion 347
downsizing 348
outplacement 349
severance pay 350
ombudsperson 350
alternative dispute resolution (ADR) 351
transfer 351
promotion 352
exit interview 353
postexit questionnaire 354
attitude survey 354
offboarding 354
phased retirement 354

MyLab Management

If your instructor is using MyLab Management, go to **www.pearson.com/mylab/management** to complete the problems marked with this icon ✪.

Questions for Review

12-1. Define *internal employee relations*.

12-2. What is meant by the term *employment at will*?

12-3. What is the difference between discipline and disciplinary action?

12-4. What are the steps to follow in the disciplinary action process?

12-5. Describe the following approaches to disciplinary action:
(a) hot stove rule
(b) progressive disciplinary action
(c) disciplinary action without punishment

✪**12-6.** What are the problems associated with the administration of disciplinary action?

12-7. How does termination often differ regarding non-managerial/non-professional employees, executives, and middle and lower-level managers and professionals?

12-8. Define *demotion*. Why should it be used cautiously?

12-9. Define *downsizing*. What are some problems associated with downsizing?

12-10. Define *outplacement* and *severance pay*.

12-11. Define *ombudsperson* and *alternative dispute resolution (ADR)*. Why might a firm want to use an ombudsperson or alternative dispute resolution?

12-12. Distinguish between transfers and promotions.

✪**12-13.** Briefly describe the techniques available to determine the real reasons that an individual decides to leave the organization.

12-14. Define *offboarding*. Why is it important?

12-15. Define *phased retirement*. Why do so many employees desire to have a phased retirement?

PREPARING FOR MY CAREER

P I A Personal Inventory Assessment

✪ *An additional Personal Inventory Assessment can be found on MyLab Management.*

Workplace Discipline Indicator

This instrument assesses the way you prefer to discipline employees. If you have not yet worked a job where you supervised employees, approach this assessment by considering how you would expect to be treated if disciplined at work.

ETHICS DILEMMA

To Fire or Not to Fire

You are a first-line supervisor for Kwik Corporation, a medium-sized manufacturer of automotive parts. Workers in your company and your department are quite close, and you view them as family. The work in your department can be quite dangerous. It is especially important that all workers wear their safety glasses because in the past there have been some serious injuries.

The company has a rule that states that any employee who does not follow the stated policy will receive a written reprimand on the first offense and will be terminated on the second violation. You have had to terminate several workers in the past because of similar violations. The other day, Allen Smith, one of your best and most influential employees, violated the safety glasses rule and you gave him a reprimand. You hated to do that because he is by far your best worker and he often helps you if you have a problem with the other workers. He has also been with the company for a long time. You would be lost without him. You walk up to Allen's workstation and observe him not wearing his safety glasses again. He knows that he has been caught and quickly puts his glasses on and says in a pleading voice, "Please don't fire me. I promise it will never happen again. I have just had a lot on my mind lately."

12-16. What would you do?

12-17. What factor(s) in this ethics dilemma might influence a person to make a less-than-ethical decision?

HRM Is Everyone's Business

Every employee possesses the responsibility to follow work rules and perform well. Unfortunately, violations occur. In these situations, management is responsible for ensuring that appropriate disciplinary action is taken.

Action checklist for managers and HR—understand HR managers' and other managers' roles in the disciplinary process

HR takes the lead

- ☑ HR professionals should carefully educate managers about workplace policies, for example, absence from work, performance expectations, professional conduct, and dress code.
- ☑ Tell managers how they may proactively communicate policies to employees. It is not sufficient to refer employees to a handbook.
- ☑ Maintain an open-door policy for managers who choose to discuss concerns about employees who have or may have violated workplace rules, and alternative courses of action.

Managers take the lead

- ☑ Managers should discuss proper conduct and the disciplinary policy with employees. Clearly communicate the desire to have every employee be knowledgeable about workplace expectations and to take responsibility for meeting them.
- ☑ Except in extreme cases involving documented safety violations, managers should not immediately assume guilt. Rather than accuse an employee of wrongdoing, ask for their side of the story first.
- ☑ When discipline is warranted, discuss the plan for addressing it with HR. Ask for their participation in the process.

HRM by the Numbers

Why Employees Leave

✪ *An additional HRM by the Numbers exercise can be found on MyLab Management.*

Employees choose to leave a company for many reasons and some employees leave for involuntary reasons. Calculating turnover rates to quantify employee departures by reason can help companies identify possible weaknesses in their work practices or company culture. For instance, significant turnover resulting from mediocre performance should prompt a company to review its selection and training practices. Valued employees may leave the company for other jobs to enhance career advancement or compensation. For example, a compensation survey will reveal the competitiveness of pay and benefits offerings relative to the competition, possibly shedding light on those departures.

Companies calculate turnover rates for a desired reference period (e.g., monthly, quarterly, annually) based on the following information: (a) the number of workers leaving during the chosen reference period; and (b) average number of workers employed during the reference period. The turnover rate is calculated as: a/b. Use the data in the table to calculate turnover rates for the questions that follow.

		Involuntary			Voluntary			Total
	Average Number of Employees	Poor Performance	Work Rule Violation	At Will Termination	New Job	Return to School	Stay-at-Home Parent	Monthly Turnover
First quarter								
January	1,750	33	11	20	30	40	1	135
February	1,725	15	4	0	10	0	0	29
March	1,770	1	2	0	35	0	0	38
Average number of employees	1,748							
Second quarter								
April	1,755	20	3	0	10	0	6	39
May	1,715	30	10	25	39	32	11	147
June	1,775	3	0	0	4	0	3	10
Average number of employees	1,748							
Third quarter								
July	1,740	11	13	20	10	0	5	59
August	1,695	1	2	35	0	15	3	56
September	1,685	2	3	0	11	0	1	17
Average number of employees	1,707							
Fourth quarter								
October	1,630	24	1	15	23	0	7	70
November	1,615	20	0	0	1	0	1	22
December	1,605	0	0	0	2	10	2	14
Average number of employees	1,617							
Annual turnover by reason (number of employees)		160	49	115	175	97	40	636

Note: The total number of employees who leave the company each month is not the sole determinant of the average number of employees per month. The company may also hire new employees. For this exercise, we are focusing exclusively on turnover.

In addition, the average number of employees per quarter is rounded down to the nearest integer (less than .5) and up to the nearest integer (.5 or more).

Questions

12-18. Calculate the overall turnover rate for each quarter: (a) first quarter; (b) second quarter; (c) third quarter; and (d) fourth quarter.

12-19. What is the total annual turnover rate?

12-20. Calculate the annual turnover rate for: (a) all involuntary reasons combined; and (b) all voluntary reasons combined. Which rate is higher?

Working Together: Team Exercise

In small groups of three or four, come up with specific answers to the following questions. Talk through your perspectives with team members. Be prepared to share your ideas with the class.

Assume that you are working as the assistant manager of a gas station. An employee told you in confidence that she saw a coworker place a handful of lottery tickets in his backpack without paying for them. Only you and the employee who allegedly stole lottery tickets are working during an evening shift. This is the first time you have worked with this employee and you know very little about him. Also, you did not participate in hiring him.

12-21. Would you address this allegation of theft during your work shift? Explain.

12-22. Besides you and the employee who allegedly stole lottery tickets, who else should be involved and in what capacity? Explain.

INCIDENT 1 Employment at Will

Aaradhya Patel is the HR manager for Apothec Pharmaceuticals. She is working with district sales managers who are completing annual performance reviews of pharmaceutical representatives. The most important performance criterion is dollar sales volume for the previous year's calendar quarters. Each representative is expected to achieve at least $750,000 in quarterly sales.

Aaradhya is meeting with James Johnson, an Apothec district sales manager, to discuss his team member's sales performance. James recommends firing Richard Smith and Stephen Mayers. Richard's current year quarterly sales ranged between $615,000 and $680,000. Stephen's current year quarterly sales ranged between $625,000 and $675,000. In years past, both employees' sales were off the charts. In addition to previously demonstrating exemplary sales performance, both Richard and Stephen have consistently received top marks from the physicians who buy Apothec's products. This past year was no exception.

Aaradhya informed James that he could fire only Stephen. Although their performances were similarly below standard, there were important differences in employment terms. Until five years ago, newly hired Apothec sales representatives signed contracts. The performance expectations section explicitly states that an employee whose performance falls below standard shall be given one year to meet expectations; otherwise, face possible employment termination. Since then, Apothec no longer issues contracts. Offer letters clearly specify at-will employment. Richard was hired eight years ago, and Stephen was hired four years ago.

James expressed disappointment. He had already identified two ideal candidates to replace Richard and Stephen, and was eager to make job offers. Aaradhya informed James that the matter was settled for Richard. And, she encouraged James to consider the entirety of Stephen's performance record since joining Apothec.

Questions

12-23. Do you agree with Apothec's decision to eliminate employment contracts? Discuss.

12-24. Do you think James should act on his recommendation to fire Stephen? Explain.

12-25. What are some of the financial and nonfinancial costs associated with employment contracts? At-will employment? Explain.

INCIDENT 2 To Heck with Them!

Isabelle Anderson is the North Carolina plant manager for Hall Manufacturing Company, a company that produces a line of relatively inexpensive painted wood furniture. Six months ago, Isabelle became concerned about the turnover rate among workers in the painting department. Manufacturing plant turnover rates in that part of the South generally averaged about 30 percent, which was the case at Hall. The painting department, however, had experienced a turnover of nearly 200 percent in each of the last two years. Because of the limited number of skilled workers in the area, Hall had introduced an extensive training program for new painters, and Isabelle knew that the high turnover rate was costly.

Isabelle conducted exit interviews with many of the departing painters. Many of them said that they were leaving for more money, others mentioned better benefits, and some cited personal reasons for quitting. But there was nothing to help Isabelle pinpoint the problem. Isabelle had checked and found that Hall's wages and benefits were competitive with, if not better than, those of other manufacturers in the area. She then called in Nelson Able, the painting supervisor, to discuss the problem. Nelson's response was, "To heck with them! They will do it my way or they can hit the road. You know how this younger generation is. They work to get enough money to live on for a few weeks and then quit. I don't worry about it. Our old-timers can take up the slack." After listening to Nelson for a moment, Isabelle thought that she might know what caused the turnover problem.

Questions

12-26. Interpret a turnover rate of 200 percent. What does it mean? (Hint: Refer to the HR By the Numbers Feature for the formula as a guide.)

12-27. Do you believe that the exit interviews were accurate? Explain your answer.

12-28. What do you believe was the cause of the turnover problem?

MyLab Management

If your instructor is using MyLab Management, go to **www.pearson.com/mylab/management** for Auto-graded writing questions as well as the following Assisted-graded writing questions:

12-29. What might be some limitations of at will employment from the company's and employee's perspectives?

12-30. What are the challenges to employers that are associated with the just cause standard?

Endnotes

1 Charles J. Muhl, "The Employment-at-Will Doctrine: Three Major Exceptions," *Monthly Labor Review* (January 2001): 3.

2 Vadim Liberman, "The Perfect Punishment," *Conference Board Review* 46 (January/February 2009): 32–39.

3 Michael S. Lavenant, "The Art of Employee Discipline: How to Retain Control & Increase Production," *Nonprofit World* 28 (July/August 2010): 22–23.

4 "What It Means to You," *Legal Alert for Supervisors* 5 (September 1, 2009): 2.

5 David B. Ritter and Mari Kaluza, "Lesson from Walmart: How to Cut Risk when a Co-worker Harasses," *HR Specialist: Illinois Employment Law* 5 (May 2011): 6.

6 "Document All Disciplinary Actions, Including Why and When You Decided to Act," *HR Specialist: New Jersey Employment Law* 6 (May 2011): 3.

7 Carroll R. Daugherty, "Seven Tests for Learning Whether Employer Had Just Cause for Disciplining an Employee," as reproduced in the labor arbitration case Whirlpool Corp., 58 LA 421 (1972).

8 Jada A. Graves, "How to Fire Someone Compassionately," *U.S. News and World Reports* (August 22, 2013). Accessed April 4, 2014, at www.money.usnews.com.

9 Dick Grote, "A Step-by-Step Guide to Firing Someone," *Harvard Business Review* online (February 17, 2016). Accessed April 11, 2017, at www.hbr.org.

10 "Don't Pile on Reasons for Firing; You're Spoiling for Retaliation Fight in Court," *HR Specialist: Texas Employment Law* 5 (April 2010): 2.

11 "10 Steps to Stress-free, Lawsuit-free Termination Meetings," *HR Specialist: New York Employment Law* 7 (July 2009): 6.

12 "Three Keys to Keep Terminations from Turning into Lawsuits," *Legal Alert for Supervisors* 5 (March 15, 2010): 3.

13 Steve Schaefer, "Watch Your Backs, CEOs: The Margin for Error is Shrinking," *Forbes* (July 19, 2012). Accessed March 31, 2014, at www.forbes.com.

14 Khadeeja Safdar and Suzanne Kapner, "Six Retail Chains, Six Survival Strategies," *The Wall Street Journal* online (February 28, 2017). Accessed March 30, 2017, at www.wsj.com.

15 Patrick Fitzgerald, "Shoe Retailer Payless Files for Chapter 11 Bankruptcy," *The Wall Street Journal* online (April 4, 2017). Accessed April 10, 2017, at www.wsj.com.

16 Shirley M. Mayton, "Survivor Coping," *OD Practitioner* 43 (Winter 2011): 42–47.

17 Susan Storm Smith, "In a Time of Layoffs, Keep Human Resources Humane," *BusinessWeek Online* (March 19, 2009): 11.

18 Pat Galagan, "The Biggest Losers: The Perils of Extreme Downsizing," *T+D* 64 (November 2010): 27–29.

19 Vickie Elmer, "The Invisible Promotion," *Fortune* 163 (February 7, 2011): 31–32.

20 "The Worker Adjustment and Retraining Notification Act," *U.S. Department of Labor Employment and Training Administration Fact Sheet.* Accessed February 1, 2017, at www.doleta.gov/programs/factsht/warn.htm.

21 "Century Closes W.Va. Smelter," *Metal Producing & Processing* 47 (March/April 2009): 4.

22 Megan Leonhardt, "Solyndra to Pay $3.5M to Settle WARN Act Claims," *360.com* website (August 13, 2012). Accessed April 4, 2017, at www.law360.com/articles/369272/solyndra-to-pay-3-5m-to-settle-warn-act-claims.

23 Lauren Williamson, "Grocer Gave Fair WARNing," *InsideCounsel* 20 (April 2009): 77.

24 "Severance, Outplacement Receive More Attention," *HR Focus* 86 (June 2009): 12.

25 "Survey Shows Severance Amounts Unchanged in Three Years," *2016 Severance Report*, ClearRock, Inc. (2016). Accessed April 11, 2017, at http://clearrock.com/survey-shows-severance-amounts-unchanged-three-years/.

26 "Survey Finds Severance Pay Declines for U.S. Employees," *Report on Salary Surveys* 9 (January 2009): 4.

27 Anne E. Moran, "Waivers and Severance Arrangements: EEOC Announcement Offers Reminders for Employers," *Employee Relations Law Journal* 35 (2010): 72–80.

28 Rita Zeidner, "Most Employers Require Waivers for Severance Pay," *HR Magazine* 54 (January 2009): 27.

29 "How Employers Are Handling Severance," *Managing Benefits Plans* 10 (February 2010): 12–15.

30 "8 Keys to Negotiating Severance," *Executive Leadership* 24 (June 2009): 8.

31 "5 Questions: Melissa Cameron, Ombudsman, North American Operations, Bayer Corp," *Workforce Management* 88 (October 19, 2009): 8.

32 James J. Rooney, "Jury Waivers: Your New Alternative to Arbitration Agreements?" *HR Specialist: New York Employment Law* 7 (January 2012): 6.

33 "Choosing Employees for Promotion: A 6-step Legal Process," *HR Specialist: New York Employment Law* 4 (August 2009): 4.

34 Sue Sommercille and Amy-Kate Snowise, "Get the Most Out of Your Exit Interviewing," *Human Resources Magazine* 16 (June/July 2011): 28–29.

35 Patricia M. Buhler, "The Exit Interview: A Goldmine of Information," *Supervision* 72 (August 2011): 11–13.

36 Everett Spain and Boris Groysberg, "Making Exist Interview Count," *Harvard Business Review* online (April 2016). Accessed March 1, 2017, at www.hbr.org.

37 Kenya McCullum, "The Retention Intention," *OfficePro* 69 (2009 Special Edition): 8–11.

38 Sharon Meers and Joanna Strober, "When Women Don't Tell the Truth," *Conference Board Review* 46 (Summer 2009): 9–10.

39 "Use Exit Interviews to Spot Boss's Hidden Bias," *HR Specialist* 9 (May 2011): 3.

40 Terence E. Shea, "Getting the Last Word," *HR Magazine* 55 (January 2010): 24–25.

41 Wendy Phaneuf, "Gaining Insight: What Employee Opinion Surveys Can Tell You," *Security: Solutions for Enterprise Security Leaders* 48 (July 2011): 23.

42 Lin Grensing-Pophal, "To Ask or Not to Ask," *HR Magazine* 54 (February 2009): 53–55.

43 John Lamb, "Offboarding: Completing the Cycle Efficiently," *Employee Benefit Advisor* 9 (June 2011): 60–61.

44 Elizabeth Galentine, "Parting Ways Pleasantly," *Employee Benefit News* 23 (June 2009): 42–43.

45 Miller Stephen, "Phased Retirement Keeps Boomers in the Workforce," *HR Magazine* (December 2008): 61–62.

46 "Firms Don't Focus on Aging Staffers," *Investor's Business Daily* (January 9, 2012): 1.

47 Nancy Collamer, "Phase A Full-Time Job into Part-Time, Then, Retirement," *Forbes* online (March 21, 2017). Accessed April 4, 2017, at www.forbes.com.

48 Tom Anderson, "Employers Offer Older Workers Flexible Retirement," *CNBC* online (August 21, 2016). Accessed April 1, 2017, at www.cnbc.com.

49 Nicole Ogrysko, "Less Than 100 Federal Employees Have Signed Up for Phased Retirement," *Federal News Radio* online (August 16, 2016). Accessed April 17, 2017, at http://federalnewsradio.com.

50 "Key Steps to Recruiting & Retaining Older Workers," *H&HN: Hospitals & Health Networks* 82 (January 2008): 55–56.

51 Tamara Lytle, "Benefits for Older Workers," *HR Magazine* 57 (March 2012): 52–58.

13 Employee Safety, Health, and Wellness

LEARNING OBJECTIVES After completing this chapter, students should be able to:

13.1 Explain the nature and role of safety, health, and wellness.

13.2 Discuss workplace safety programs.

13.3 Summarize the problems associated with workplace bullying and violence.

13.4 Discuss the negative effects of employee stress and burnout.

13.5 Explain substance abuse, substance-abuse-free workplaces, and how to implement a drug-testing program.

13.6 Describe employee wellness programs and employee assistance programs.

MyLab Management

Improve Your Grade!

If your professor is using MyLab Management, visit **www.pearson.com/mylab/management** for videos, simulations, and writing exercises.

Learn It

If your professor has chosen to assign this, go to **www.pearson.com/mylab/management** to see what you should particularly focus on and to take the Chapter 13 Warm-Up.

Many workplaces have features that could threaten the *safety* and *health* of employees if not managed properly. For example, in manufacturing settings, metal presses mold liquid steel into components for engine manufacturing. The temperature of liquefied steel exceeds 1,000°F, which would melt human flesh in an instant. In other manufacturing settings, exposures to substances, such as silica, that have carcinogenic qualities are known to substantially raise lung cancer risks. Safety and health is also a prevalent concern in other settings such as in protective services (e.g., the precarious environments in which firefighters and police officers work) and in health care settings (e.g., doctors, nurses, and lab technicians who meet patients with contagious viruses or blood-borne illnesses).

Besides the influence of a hazardous work environment, employee *wellness* concerns may manifest in different ways. For example, some employees may have difficulties performing their jobs effectively because of stressful work environments (e.g., intense production scheduling) or emotional stress that results from problems outside the workplace (e.g., the fallout from divorce). Sometimes, behaviors outside the workplace (e.g., the use of illicit drugs or overeating) could negatively affect wellness, and subsequently, job performance.

Human resources (HR) practice takes place in a physical and social work environment that often has an impact on workers' safety, health, and wellness. Our focus in this chapter is on exploring employee safety, health, and wellness and how companies manage these concerns.

13.1 Explain the nature and role of safety, health, and wellness.

Nature and Role of Safety, Health, and Wellness

safety
Protection of employees from injuries caused by work-related accidents.

health
Employees' freedom from physical or emotional illness.

In our discussion, **safety** involves protecting employees from injuries caused by work-related accidents. Included within the umbrella definition of safety are factors related to musculoskeletal disorders, stress injuries, and workplace and domestic violence. **Health** refers to employees' freedom from physical or emotional illness. Problems in these areas can seriously affect a worker's productivity and quality of work life. They can dramatically lower a firm's effectiveness and employee morale. In fact, job-related injuries and illnesses are more common than most people realize. For a variety of reasons, which we discuss throughout this chapter, HR professionals play a crucial role in promoting a safe and healthful work environment and addressing ways to support physical and mental wellness. Strictly from a business perspective, HR professionals guard the welfare of its valuable human capital without whom the company cannot achieve its strategic objectives. Also, HR professionals invest time and energy to ensure compliance with government health and safety standards.

We begin with the role of promoting occupational safety and health, which is mandated by the Occupational Safety and Health Act of 1970. Afterward, we address employee wellness concerns and programs.

Occupational Safety and Health Administration

The Occupational Safety and Health Act of 1970 created the Occupational Safety and Health Administration (OSHA). The mission of OSHA is to promote and ensure workplace safety and health in the United States and to reduce workplace fatalities, injuries, and illnesses. OSHA is committed to ensuring—so far as possible—that every working person in the nation has a safe and healthful working environment. It believes that providing workers with a safe workplace is central to their ability to enjoy health, security, and the opportunity to achieve the American dream. Addressing safety and health issues in the workplace also saves the employer money and adds value to the business. To handle this workload, OSHA has approximately 2,100 inspectors responsible for the health and safety of 130 million workers, employed at more than 8 million worksites around the United States.[1] These figures translate to about one compliance officer for every 59,000 workers.

general duty clause
As used by OSHA, employers are required to furnish, to each employee, a place of employment that is free from recognizable hazards that are causing, or likely to cause, death or serious physical harm to the employee.

Employers have a responsibility under the **general duty clause** of the Occupational Safety and Health Act to furnish a workplace free from recognized hazards that are causing or are likely to cause death or serious physical harm. To prove a violation of the general duty clause, OSHA must demonstrate: (1) that a condition or activity in the workplace presented a hazard; (2) that the employer or its industry recognized this hazard; (3) that the hazard was likely to cause death or serious physical harm; and (4) that a feasible and effective means existed to eliminate or materially reduce the hazard. In 2016, two workers employed by Green Bay Manufacturing, a muffler component manufacturer based in Green Bay, Wisconsin, were severely injured when the safety lock of a molding machine failed. These workers sustained debilitating injuries within 10 days of each other. One worker's hand was crushed and the other's injury required a partial amputation of his left middle finger. OSHA proposed penalties in excess of $200,000 for violating the act's general duty clause by failing to re-evaluate its machine safety procedures and exposing workers to hazards even after the injuries.[2]

Employers possess other rights and responsibilities under OSHA. Likewise, employees possess rights and responsibilities. Figure 13-1 summarizes these rights and responsibilities on an official OSHA poster, which employers are required to display in the workplace.

In 1913, the U.S. Bureau of Labor Statistics documented about 23,000 industrial deaths in a workforce of 38 million, which is a rate of about 61 deaths per 100,000 workers.[3] The number of fatal work injuries in the United States in 2015 was 4,836 based on a substantially larger workforce. In 2015, the worker death rate was 3.4 deaths per 100,000 workers.[4]

FYI

The highest number of fatal occupational injuries in 2015:

- All transportation accidents: 2,054
- Roadway accidents: 1,264
- Fall, slip, trip: 800
- Contact with objects and equipment: 722
- Violence and other injuries by persons or animals: 703[5]

Since its beginning in 1970, OSHA has helped to cut workplace fatalities by more than 60 percent and occupational injury and illness by 40 percent. At the same time, U.S. employment has more than doubled from 56 million workers at 3.5 million work sites to more than 160 million workers at 8 million worksites. The agency has helped standardize reasonable worker protections. Rules defining confined spaces, machine guards, or hard hat zones have allowed many plant managers and site supervisors to think more about productivity, not accidents. One of the most frequently mentioned hazards that OSHA addresses must do with missing or inadequate fall protection.[6]

Even though OSHA would like a successful partnership relationship to exist, at times penalties must be given. Financial penalties serve as reminders to companies of the benefits of

FIGURE 13-1
Job Safety and Health—It's the Law!

Job Safety and Health

It's the law!

OSHA®
Occupational Safety and Health Administration
U.S. Department of Labor

EMPLOYEES:

- You have the right to notify your employer or OSHA about workplace hazards. You may ask OSHA to keep your name confidential.
- You have the right to request an OSHA inspection if you believe that there are unsafe and unhealthful conditions in your workplace. You or your representative may participate in that inspection.
- You can file a complaint with OSHA within 30 days of retaliation or discrimination by your employer for making safety and health complaints or for exercising your rights under the *OSH Act*.
- You have the right to see OSHA citations issued to your employer. Your employer must post the citations at or near the place of the alleged violations.
- Your employer must correct workplace hazards by the date indicated on the citation and must certify that these hazards have been reduced or eliminated.
- You have the right to copies of your medical records and records of your exposures to toxic and harmful substances or conditions.
- Your employer must post this notice in your workplace.
- You must comply with all occupational safety and health standards issued under the *OSH Act* that apply to your own actions and conduct on the job.

EMPLOYERS:

- You must furnish your employees a place of employment free from recognized hazards.
- You must comply with the occupational safety and health standards issued under the *OSH Act*.

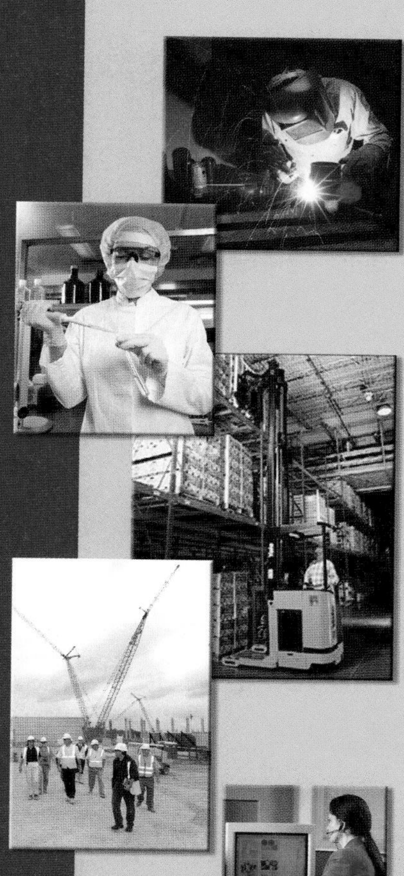

Free assistance in identifying and correcting hazards or complying with standards is available to employers, without citation or penalty, through OSHA-supported consultation programs in each state.

This free poster available from OSHA –
The Best Resource for Safety and Health

1-800-321-OSHA (6742)
www.osha.gov

OSHA 3165-02 2012R

maintaining safe and healthy working conditions. A serious hazard citation has a maximum penalty of $12,471 in 2016 (indexed annually for inflation).[7] A serious violation occurs when there is substantial probability that death or serious physical harm could result from a hazard about which the employer knew or should have known.[8] A willful or repeated violation might have a maximum amount of $124,709 per violation. Calculated instance by instance, if ten employees were exposed to one hazard the employer intentionally did not eliminate, the penalty amount would immediately jump to as much as $1,247,090. For example, an electronic cigarette manufacturer received penalties amounting to $184,500 for various OSHA violations.[9] Of this total, two willful citations carried a penalty of $112,500 because the company did not provide protective gloves when workers handled products containing nicotine and eye protection when they handled corrosive chemicals and concentrated nicotine.

OSHA has implemented the Severe Violator Enforcement Program that increases inspections at work sites where "recalcitrant employers" have repeatedly violated safety regulations and endangered workers. It also requires a mandatory follow-up inspection to make sure required changes were made. Auto parts manufacturer Sunfield Inc., received a $3.42 million fine for 46 egregious willful, two willful, one repeat, and eight safety violations.[10] The company failed to train workers on how to safely operate heavy equipment, did not service the equipment, and failed to disconnect machinery from a power supply before maintenance and service.

OSHA and Whistle-Blowers

A little-known fact is that OSHA is charged with more than just enforcing health and safety matters. Within the Department of Labor, OSHA enforces the whistle-blower protection provisions of 21 statutes, covering not just workplace safety but also the environment, consumer products, the financial system, and other areas. For instance, the Sarbanes-Oxley Act has a provision that makes it illegal to fire or otherwise discriminate against a corporate officer for trying to report possible accounting irregularities to higher corporate officials or enforcement agencies. The U.S. Department of Labor administers this portion of the Sarbanes-Oxley Act, not the U.S. Securities and Exchange Commission. The whistle-blower provision of the Dodd-Frank Act prohibits employers from retaliating against employees who raise various protected concerns or provide protected information to the employer or to the government. OSHA Assistant Secretary Dr. David Michaels said, "Whistle-blowers play a vital role in ensuring the integrity of our financial system, as well as the safety of our food, air, water, workplaces and transportation systems. The ability of workers to speak out and exercise their legal rights without fear of retaliation is crucial to many of the legal protections and safeguards that all Americans value."[11] Between 2006 and 2016, the number of OSHA whistle-blower complaints increased nearly 70 percent from 1,195 to 2,030.[12] The increase may be due to individuals possessing more confidence in their legal rights. Alternatively, there are simply more potential violations. Or, it could be a combination of both, which is the most likely case.

Recently OSHA ruled that the National Railroad Passenger Corp. (Amtrak) violated the whistle-blower protection provisions of OSHA by discharging a supervisory special agent. While employed, the agent expressed unease about railroad safety, fraud and abuse involving an Amtrak contractor, and he supported another employee's safety concerns.[13] OSHA ordered Amtrak to reinstate the employee, pay the former employee a total $892,551 for back wages ($723,332) and interest ($34,218), punitive damages ($100,000), compensatory damages ($35,000), and reasonable attorneys' fees.

In 2012, OSHA ordered AirTran Airways, a subsidiary of Southwest Airlines Company, to reinstate a former pilot who was fired after reporting numerous mechanical concerns. The agency also has ordered that the pilot be paid more than $1 million in back wages plus interest and compensatory damages. An investigation by OSHA's Whistle-Blower Protection Program found reasonable cause to believe that the termination was an act of retaliation in violation of the whistle-blower provision of the Wendell H. Ford Aviation Investment and Reform Act for the 21st Century.

In another case, OSHA recently ordered a Florida trucking company to reinstate a driver fired for refusing to drive two unsafe trucks. The department ruled that Zurla Trucking, a 42-driver company, violated the Surface Transportation Assistance Act. It was required to pay back wages, plus interest, and compensatory damages and $125,000 in punitive damages. Zurla also had to remove adverse references related to the firing from the employee's records. However, most of the attention regarding health and safety relates to OSHA.

As one last example, OSHA ordered Head Rush Technologies, a sporting goods manufacturer, to pay $125,000 in back wages and other damages to a former employee who, while employed, suggested to the company's chief executive officer that the company conduct more extensive research on product safety. However, the company claimed that it discharged the employee for insubordination. OSHA did not accept the company's explanation and ruled that it retaliated against the employee in violation of the Consumer Product Safety Improvement Act.[15]

As these cases illustrate, OSHA prohibits any person from discharging or in any manner retaliating against any employee because the employee has exercised rights under OSHA. Rights provided by the act include employee participation in safety and health activities such as complaining to OSHA and seeking an OSHA inspection, participating in an OSHA inspection, participating or testifying in any proceeding related to an OSHA inspection, and reporting a work-related injury, illness, or fatality. Under OSHA, retaliation is generally defined as any action that would dissuade a reasonable employee from engaging in protected activity. Depending on the circumstances of the case, "adverse" action can include:

- Firing or laying off
- Blacklisting
- Demoting
- Denying overtime or promotion
- Disciplining
- Denial of benefits
- Failure to hire or rehire
- Intimidation
- Making threats
- Reassignment affecting prospects for promotion
- Reducing pay or hours[14]

OSHA and the Small Business

OSHA provides a Web-based step-by-step occupational health and safety guide that can help determine the government requirements that apply to small businesses. The guide is intended to help small business employers meet the legal requirements imposed by OSHA and achieve an in-compliance status before an OSHA inspection. It covers the basics of an occupational safety and health plan for small business owners, tips on how to self-assess the workplace, employee training strategies, and more.

It also has an on-site consultation service that provides small businesses with free advice from trained state government staff. The service is separate from any enforcement programs that the OSHA operates and is entirely confidential. Sessions identify and uncover potential workplace hazards and are intended to help small business owners improve their workplace safety and health systems. Small businesses that participate can qualify for a one-year exemption from routine OSHA inspections.

HR BLOOPERS

Health and Safety Problems at XIF Chemicals

XIF Chemicals is finally able to significantly grow its market share in the specialty chemical marketplace. The company has had a few problems with safety violations in their laboratories, but HR Director Janet Haven believes that they have finally achieved compliance and can now focus on what is important—new product development. She needs to make one more staffing change and then everything should be in order. Today she is going to inform laboratory employee Joe Jones that the company is transferring him to another division. Joe is a good worker, but he has just caused too many problems in the laboratory. While the laboratory manager has assured Janet that they are following all safety regulations, Joe has once again placed a call to OSHA to complain about some concern with chemical storage and request an inspection. Joe claims he shared his concern with the laboratory manager who ignored him. Janet trusts that the manager has followed all safety regulations so she feels Joe's concerns are unfounded. In fact, in a follow-up call Janet made to him, Joe couldn't tell her what specific safety regulation was being violated. So, Janet has decided the best option is to have Joe move to a position where he has less access to the chemicals that cause him such a concern.

If your professor has assigned this, go to **www.pearson.com/mylab/management** to complete the HR Bloopers exercise and test your application of these concepts when faced with real-world decisions.

The Economic Impact of Safety

Job-related deaths and injuries of all types extract a high toll not only in human misery but also in economic loss. According to a Liberty Mutual Workplace Safety Index, workplace illnesses and injuries, causing absences of more than five days, cost U.S. firms nearly $60 billion, an average of more than $1 billion per week.[16] The leading cause of workplace injuries and their associated costs are overexertion (e.g., lifting, carrying, pushing, pulling, etc.). The significant financial costs are often passed along to the consumer in the form of higher prices. Thus, job-related deaths and injuries affect everyone, directly or indirectly. Safety risks can be significant for employers. In addition to workers' compensation costs, OSHA can levy major fines. Indirect costs related to turnover and lost productivity add to the expense.

Companies have come a long way in recognizing the importance and cost benefits of safety. Workplaces are safer, thanks to efforts of employers, insurance companies, unions, and state and federal agencies. Safety professionals strive for lower workers' compensation costs, as do insurance companies, who work to keep both their clients' and their own costs down. However, death and injuries continue to occur.

13.2 Discuss workplace safety programs.

Workplace Safety Programs

Every employer needs to have a comprehensive safety program in place regardless of the degree of danger involved. Safety programs may accomplish their purposes in two primary ways: one focusing on *unsafe employee actions* and the other on *unsafe working conditions*.

Unsafe Employee Actions

Training and orientation of new employees emphasizing safety is especially important. The early months of employment are often critical because it has been proven that work injuries decrease with length of service. The first approach in a safety program is to create a psychological environment and employee attitudes that promote safety. A *corporate culture* needs to exist in which employees are involved and engaged and can provide input on changes to their workplace. Many firms expect a positive link between employee engagement and involvement and safety performance. A comprehensive study of more than 82,000 business units and 1.8 million employees in 230 organizations, across 49 industries and in 73 countries supports this expectation. The top 25 percent of companies surveyed demonstrated 70 percent fewer safety incidents than companies in the bottom 25 percent.[17] Accident rates decline when workers consciously or subconsciously think about safety. This attitude must permeate the firm's operations, and a strong company policy emphasizing safety and health is crucial. Although there is danger that everyone's responsibility will become no one's responsibility, a truly safe environment takes the effort of everyone from top management to the lowest-level employee. Every individual in a firm should be encouraged to come up with solutions to potential safety problems, and the firm's managers must take the lead. Management's unique role is clear because OSHA places primary responsibility for employee safety on the employer.

Unsafe Working Conditions

The second approach to safety program design is to develop and maintain a safe physical working environment. Here, altering the environment becomes the focus for preventing accidents. Even if Joe, a machine operator, has been awake all night with a sick child and can barely keep his eyes open, the safety devices on his machine will help protect him. Management should create a physical environment in which accidents cannot occur. It is in this area that OSHA has had its greatest influence.

Developing Safety Programs

Workplace accident prevention requires safety program planning. Plans may be relatively simple, as for a small retail store, or more complex and highly sophisticated, as for a large automobile assembly plant. Regardless of the organization's size, the support of top management is essential if safety programs are to be effective.

Table 13-1 shows some of the reasons for top management's support of a safety program. This information suggests that the lost productivity of a single injured worker is not the only factor to consider. Every phase of HR management is involved. The firm may have difficulty recruiting if it

TABLE 13-1

Reasons for Management's Support of a Safety Program

- **Personal loss.** The physical pain and mental anguish associated with injuries are always unpleasant and may even be traumatic for an injured worker. Of still greater concern is the possibility of permanent disability or even death.
- **Financial loss to injured employees.** Most employees are covered by company insurance plans or personal accident insurance. However, an injury may result in financial losses not covered by insurance.
- **Lost productivity.** When an employee is injured, there will be a loss of productivity for the firm. In addition to obvious losses, there are often hidden costs. For example, a substitute worker may need additional training to replace the injured employee. Even when another worker is available to move into the injured employee's position, efficiency may suffer.
- **Higher insurance premiums.** Workers' compensation insurance premiums are based on the employer's history of insurance claims. The potential for savings related to employee safety provides a degree of incentive to establish formal programs.
- **Possibility of fines or imprisonment.** Since the enactment of the Occupational Safety and Health Act, a willful and repeated violation of its provisions may result in serious penalties for the employer.
- **Social responsibility.** Many executives feel responsible for the safety and health of their employees. Several firms had excellent safety programs years before OSHA existed. They understand that a safe work environment is not only in the best interests of the firm, but also that providing one is the right thing to do.

gains a reputation for being an unsafe place to work. Employee relations erode if workers believe that management does not care enough about them to provide a safe workplace. Firms will see an increase in compensation costs when they must pay a premium to attract and retain qualified applicants. Maintaining a stable workforce may become difficult if employees perceive their workplace as hazardous. To overcome these problems, safety training must be a continuous process to ensure a safe workplace.

job hazard analysis (JHA)
Multistep process designed to study and analyze a task or job and then break down that task into steps that provide a means of eliminating associated hazards.

JOB HAZARD ANALYSIS **Job hazard analysis (JHA)** is a multistep process designed to study and analyze a task and then breaks down that task into steps that provide a means of eliminating associated hazards. JHA can have a major impact on safety performance. It results in a detailed written procedure for safely completing many tasks within a plant. A successful JHA program features several key components: management support, supervisor and employee training, written program, and management oversight. It is an effective and useful tool to isolate and address safety issues and risks.

OSHA has issued a comprehensive booklet to assist in JHA. The booklet explains what JHA is and offers guidelines to help firms conduct their own step-by-step analysis.[18]

SUPERFUND AMENDMENTS REAUTHORIZATION ACT (SARA), TITLE III SARA requires businesses to communicate more openly about the hazards associated with the materials they use and produce and the wastes they generate. Although SARA has been around since 1986, some firms still do not have a satisfactory program in place. The hazard communication standard often leads the list of OSHA violations because the top category for OSHA citations is for no written hazard communication program. Dealing with this standard appears to be relatively simple and inexpensive, except when organizations ignore its provisions.

EMPLOYEE INVOLVEMENT One way to strengthen a safety program is to include employee input, which provides workers with a sense of involvement. To prevent accidents, each worker must make a personal commitment to safe work practices. A team concept, in which employees watch out for each other as a moral obligation, is a worthy goal. Supervisors can show support for the safety program by conscientiously enforcing safety rules and by closely conforming to the rules themselves. Participation in such teams helps form positive attitudes, and employees develop a sense of ownership of the program. Involved employees may become concerned not only with safety issues but also with ways to improve productivity.

SAFETY ENGINEER In many companies, one staff member coordinates the overall safety program. Titles such as *safety engineer* and *safety director* are common. One of the safety engineer's primary tasks is to provide safety training for company employees. This involves educating line managers about the merits of safety and recognizing and eliminating unsafe situations. Although the safety engineer operates essentially in an advisory capacity, a well-informed and assertive person in this capacity may exercise considerable influence in the organization. Some major corporations also have *risk management departments* that anticipate losses associated with safety factors and prepare legal defenses in the event of lawsuits.

Accident Investigation

Accidents can happen even in the most safety-conscious firms. Whether an accident results in an injury, an organization should carefully evaluate each occurrence to determine its cause and to ensure that it does not recur. The safety engineer and the line supervisor usually jointly investigate accidents. One of the responsibilities of any supervisor is to prevent accidents. To do so, the supervisor must learn, through active participation in the safety program, why accidents occur, how they occur, where they occur, and who is involved. Supervisors gain a great deal of knowledge about accident prevention by helping to prepare accident reports. OSHA Form 300 is a log of work-related injuries and illnesses. The log is used in the evaluation of safety programs, discussed next. Most employers electronically transmit records of occupational injuries and illnesses directly to OSHA.

Evaluation of Safety Programs

Perhaps the best indicator of a successful safety program is a reduction in the injury frequency rate. OSHA's formula is:

Injury Frequency Rate = ((number of recordable injuries / total hours worked by all company employees during the calendar year) × the total number of hours worked by a reference group of full-time employees per calendar year). The U.S. Bureau of Labor Statistics bases the reference group calculation on 10,000 full-time employees working 40 hours per week, 50 weeks per year. Thus, the total number of hours worked by full time employees in the reference group is 20,000,000, calculated as 10,000 reference full-time employees × 40 hours per week × 50 weeks per calendar year. The user can adjust the reference to a smaller or larger number that is more fitting for the size of the workforce, such as 1,000 employees or even 100 employees. Also, it is important to note that injury frequency rates can be calculated for the company overall or smaller units within the company such as department or physical location.

Other OSHA metrics currently in use include total cases, nonfatal cases without lost workdays, total lost workday cases, cases with days away from work, and measure of fatalities. In addition to program-evaluation criteria, an effective reporting system helps to ensure that accidents are reported and receive attention. This is important because almost half of workplaces inspected by OSHA are for underreported numbers of employee injuries or illnesses.[19] With the start of a new safety program, the number of accidents may decline significantly because some supervisors may fail to report certain accidents to make the statistics for their units look better. Proper evaluation of a safety program depends on the accurate reporting and recording of data.

Organizations must use the conclusions derived from an evaluation for them to be of any value in improving the safety program. Gathering data and permitting this information to collect dust on the safety director's desk will not solve problems or prevent accidents. Accident investigators must transmit evaluation results upward to top management and downward to line managers to generate improvements.

Musculoskeletal Disorders

musculoskeletal disorders (MSDs)
Conditions that affect the body's muscles, joints, tendons, ligaments, and nerves.

Musculoskeletal disorders (MSDs) are non-fatal conditions that affect the body's muscles, joints, tendons, ligaments, and nerves. Work-related MSDs, including tendonitis, carpal tunnel syndrome, and back pain, cost U.S. companies $61.2 billion annually just to cover lost productivity.[20] According to the U.S. Bureau of Labor Statistics, 356,910 MSD cases accounted for 31 percent of all injury and illness cases in 2015.[21] The median days away from work were 12 days. The highest incidence rate occurred for nursing assistants (171 cases per 10,000 full-time workers).

FYI

The highest and lowest incidence rates of nonfatal occupational injuries per 10,000 full-time workers in 2015:

- Police and sheriff's patrol officers: 497.7
- Medical and clinical laboratory technicians: 144.5[22]

carpal tunnel syndrome (CTS)
Caused by pressure on the median nerve that occurs because of a narrowing of the passageway that houses the nerve.

A major musculoskeletal disorder is **carpal tunnel syndrome (CTS)** caused by pressure on the median nerve that occurs because of a narrowing of the passageway that houses the nerve. People who have CTS may experience pain, numbness, or tingling in the hands or wrist, a weak grip, the tendency to drop objects, sensitivity to cold, and in later stages, muscle deterioration, especially in the thumb.

CTS tends to develop in people who use their hands and wrists repeatedly in the same way. Illustrators, carpenters, assembly-line workers, and people whose jobs involve work on personal computers are the ones most commonly affected. Workers in an office environment often experience CTS. If employees keyboard 40 words per minutes, they press 12,000 keys per eight-hour day with approximately eight ounces of force needed to press each key. Using these estimates, employees working full-time will exert approximately 16 tons of force each day.[23]

CTS is preventable, or at least its severity can be reduced. Managers can provide ergonomic furniture, especially chairs, and ensure that computer monitors are positioned at eye level and keyboards at elbow level. Employees can also cooperate by reporting early symptoms of CTS. Also, it helps to often rest the hand and wrist in a neutral position trying not to perform the exact activities that caused the syndrome. Often taking nonsteroidal anti-inflammatory drugs will help. Certainly, any physical therapy aimed at exercising the hand muscle-tendon units should be stopped until after symptoms have disappeared. Other suggested actions include keeping wrists straight, taking exercise breaks, alternating tasks, shifting positions periodically, adjusting chair height, working with feet flat on the floor, and being conscious of posture. Many of these actions suggest the need for ergonomics.

Ergonomics

ergonomics
Process of designing the workplace to support the capabilities of people and job or task demands.

A specific approach to dealing with health problems such as MSDs and enhancing performance is ergonomics. **Ergonomics** is the process of designing the workplace to support the capabilities of people and job or task demands. Through ergonomics, the goal is to fit the machine and work environment to the person, rather than require the person to make the adjustment. Ergonomics includes all attempts to structure work conditions so that they maximize energy conservation, promote good posture, and allow workers to function without pain or impairment. Failure to address ergonomic issues results in fatigue, poor performance, and MSDs. In fact, ergonomic disorders are the fastest-growing category of work-related illness.

There is a clear economic payoff in using ergonomics. Blue Grass Energy, a Kentucky distribution cooperative, implemented a proactive and mandatory stretching program for its field crews, purchased battery-operated tools, and tested back-saving technology and has minimized lost labor hours resulting from injuries in the field. All the line workers are required to stretch their muscles before each strenuous work day, resulting in a dramatic decline in pulled hamstrings and other muscles and back injuries.[24] Other companies have discovered that improving the work environment boosts morale, lowers injury rates, and yields a positive return on investment. A sound ergonomic approach to avoiding workplace injuries is prevention.

The workforce of the future is expected to be increasingly mobile. With mobile devices, employees can work virtually anywhere. Ergonomics engineers are concerned that this group is setting itself up for musculoskeletal problems, which can range from discomfort to the development of tendonitis. Margo Fraser, executive director of the Association of Canadian Ergonomists, said, "Workers who find they are pulling laptops out in coffee shops and fast-food restaurants must also remember they are not just sitting in non-ergonomic chairs, but ones that are "anti-ergonomic," purposefully designed to keep people from sitting in them for hours at a time."[25]

Herman Miller is a manufacturer of ergonomically well-designed office equipment, including chairs and work surfaces. As you will see in the Watch It video, Herman Miller provides ergonomics training to its clients. This company also makes investments in safety training for its employees to promote safety within as well as helping them to serve as more effective consultants to clients.

Watch It I

If your professor has assigned this, sign into **www.pearson.com/mylab/management** to watch a video titled Herman Miller: Safety and to respond to questions.

Another threat to the safety and security of people on the job is workplace bullying and violence, discussed next.

13.3 Summarize the problems associated with workplace bullying and violence.

Workplace Bullying and Violence

Unfortunately, workplace bullying and violence has become a fact of life in some workplaces, and these activities threaten the safety of employees, family members, and customers. Increasingly, most companies are adopting ways to ensure worker safety against bullying and violence. We discuss these issues next.

Workplace Bullying

workplace bullying
Acts of continual hostile conduct that deliberately hurt another person emotionally, verbally, or physically.

The definition of workplace violence has been expanded to include bullying because it has become more common, is costly, and is a possible predictor of physical violence. **Workplace bullying** includes acts of continual hostile conduct that deliberately hurt another person emotionally, verbally, or physically. There are basically two types of bullying—physical and psychological. Physical bullying involves intimidation or threatening actions.[26] Screaming, pushing, shoving, or invading a person's personal space provide examples of physical bullying. Psychological bullying involves activities such as jokingly ridiculing a person in a harmful manner or even staring at somebody in a hostile way. Most companies include bullying behaviors within their workplace violence policy. Usually employees will accept a firm's expectations if they are clearly stated.

Experts use the term *status-blind harassment* to separate workplace bullying from workers protected under federal and state statutes. Adeola Adele, EPLI product leader for Marsh's FINPRO group, says, "Workplace violence starts with bullying." She tells of a case in which an individual shot his coworkers. The worker had been bullied at work, and no one would listen.[27]

Some researchers make the case that a definition of bullying should include social hostility, which includes gossiping or social rejection. According to one survey, this is the most common type of bullying committed by women, who are responsible for more than 40 percent of workplace bullying.[28]

It is often seen as a means of gaining power over another person through repeated aggressive behavior. Bullying may cause severe psychological pain for victims and for coworkers who witness the attacks.[29] According to a study by the National Institute for Occupational Safety and Health, bullying tends to occur when there is a lack of trust of management, a poor organizational climate, higher absenteeism and turnover rates, reduced productivity, and higher litigation costs.[30] In recent years, employers have noted increased workplace rudeness, which may lead to increased bullying.[31] According to one study, 35 percent of employees report being bullied.[32] In another study, 75 percent of employees report being bullied at work or witnessing it.[33] Currently, several states have proposed legislation regarding bullying in the workplace; however, none of those states has passed legislation.

Often, managers and supervisors, not nonsupervisory employees, tend to be bullies. Men are more often bullies than are women.[34] Who are the victims? One study revealed that employees who are well regarded by management for their contributions are common targets.[35] Also, this study showed that victims tend to be "nice" people, including those who are helpful and nurturing to coworkers.

At this time, there are no legal protections against bullying unless it were to involve physical contact with the victim or to violate existing equal employment opportunity laws that prohibit discrimination such as sexual harassment by creating a hostile work environment. Nevertheless, it is in an employer's best interests to ensure that bullying does not occur. Apart from the serious impact on victims, the employer is likely to experience unwanted turnover, higher absenteeism, and higher insurance costs.[36] A critical intangible consequence is earning a bad institutional reputation, which could turn current or prospective customers away and make it difficult to recruit talent.

The landscape for bullying is expanding, creating greater challenges for firms. Growing social media, texting, and e-mail use has given way to work- and nonwork-related *cyberbullying*. According to Teresa Daniel, author of *Stop Bullying at Work: Strategies and Tools for HR, Legal*

& Risk Management Professionals, "The idea is to trash people we don't particularly like is not new, but cellphones, computers and social media make it so much easier to inflict widespread damage through the spread of rumors, outright lies or compromising photos."[37] Unfortunately, bullying in the digital age is easier.[38] The bully can avoid direct confrontation because activity is not limited to being physically present in the same location. In addition, cyberbullying enables bullies to cross outside work boundaries anytime of any day. More disturbing, some bullies maintain anonymity by using an unidentified account. Like face-to-face bullying, cyberbullying that creates a hostile work environment is likely illegal. In *Isenhour v. Outsourcing of Millersburg*, a female operations manager allegedly harassed a male accounts receivable representative when she sent him sexually explicit texts and asked him for graphic photos of himself. The judge ruled there was sufficient evidence for a jury to decide whether the male employee was subject to a hostile work environment, thus, violating Title VII of the Civil Rights Act (Chapter 3). An interesting fact: Some of the texts were sent outside work hours; still, the judge considered explicit texting at any time likely to be sexual harassment.

It is quite important for a company to develop a culture that does not accept any type of bullying. Firms should strive to make civility part of the culture.[39] Workplace bullying is not likely to occur in a culture in which leaders send the message that each employee is valued, respected, and appreciated. Creating a culture of civility may require careful planning and a change in thinking and behaviors for corporate leaders. There is much work to be done. One survey revealed that 61 percent of respondents indicated their employer failed to respond to abusive conduct.[40] The following Watch It video shows employees who were once bullied in the workplace and the negative impact of bullying on their wellbeing. In addition, the narrator offers suggestions for managing bullying in the workplace from the perspective of those being bullied and management.

 **Watch It 2**

If your professor has assigned this, sign into **www.pearson.com/mylab/management** to watch a video titled Bullying on the Job and to respond to questions.

Workplace Violence

workplace violence
Physical assault, threatening behavior, verbal abuse, hostility, or harassment directed toward employees at work or on duty.

All too often, HR professionals are receiving wake-up calls about the potential for workplace violence. Recently, an employee killed two fellow workers at a Kraft Foods Inc. plant in Philadelphia, and in another instance, a truck driver shot and killed eight coworkers, then himself, at a beer distributor in Connecticut. OSHA defines **workplace violence** as physical assault, threatening behavior, verbal abuse, hostility, or harassment directed toward employees at work or on duty. The fact that OSHA has included verbal abuse in the definition of workplace violence has HR professionals concerned that the general duty clause could even be cited for obscene language.[41]

According to the U.S. Bureau of Labor Statistics, violence accounted for nearly 15 percent of all workplace injuries in 2015, and, as noted earlier, 703 people were killed.[42] Sadly, homicide is among the top five causes of death. Regardless of who commits the crime, there is the horror of random workplace violence.

There is no way to estimate the physical and psychological damage to other employees, who are only onlookers to the violent behavior. The issue facing most large employers is not *if* they will ever deal with an act of workplace violence, but *when*.

VULNERABLE EMPLOYEES Employees at gas stations and liquor stores, taxi drivers, police officers, and convenience store managers working night shifts face the greatest danger from workplace violence. However, no workplace is immune from violence. Hospital managers overwhelmingly say that the biggest threat emergency department workers face is patient violence. Most hospitals now have security guards stationed in their emergency departments, particularly at times such as Saturday nights, when violence seems to escalate.

There are numerous reasons for violent acts committed by employees or former employees. Among the most common are personality conflicts, marital or family problems, drug or alcohol abuse, and firings or layoffs. For instance, a disgruntled former television station employee fatally shot a reporter and cameraman on live television nearly two years after being fired for continually demonstrating belligerent and threatening behavior.[43]

Domestic violence, unfortunately, also is a relevant topic for HR professionals' consideration. Spillover from domestic violence is a threat to employees and their coworkers because one of the easiest places to the find the victim is at his or her workplace.[44] The U.S. Bureau of Labor Statistics reported that homicide by a relative or domestic partner accounted for 43 percent of female workers' deaths in 2015.[45] For example, Robert Reza slipped into the Emcore manufacturing plant in Albuquerque, New Mexico, and shot six employees—killing two—before taking his own life because he was angry with his girlfriend, a plant employee.[46] Domestic violence can have an impact on a firm's bottom line, costing about $5 billion each year in lost productivity (approximately $729 million) and health care costs (more than $4 billion).[47] A company's legal liability also drives up the total cost of domestic violence. Therefore, business organizations have a huge stake in the problem of domestic violence.

Judith A. Lampley, general counsel of the Equal Employment Advisory Council, said, "The biggest mistake an employer can make is to ignore the issue."[48] The *general duty clause* of the Occupational Safety and Health Act requires a firm to furnish a workplace free from recognized hazards that are causing or are likely to cause death or serious physical harm. This includes protecting not only an intended victim of domestic violence, but also coworkers, who can become victims when angry partners bring weapons to a workplace. An employer could potentiality face claims by the victim, coworkers, third parties, and even the person who caused the domestic violence.

Legal Consequences of Workplace Violence

In addition to the horror of workplace violence, there is also the ever-present threat of legal action. Civil lawsuits claiming *negligent hiring* or *negligent retention* are a constant threat. *Negligent hiring* is the liability an employer incurs when it fails to conduct a reasonable investigation of an applicant's background, and then assigns a potentially dangerous person to a position in which he or she can inflict harm. **Negligent retention** is the liability an employer may incur when a company keeps persons on the payroll whose records indicate a strong potential for wrongdoing and fails to take steps to defuse a possibly violent situation. If an employer ignores warning signs leading up to a violent incident, it could be held legally liable. As previously mentioned, under OSHA's *general duty clause*, employers are required to furnish, to each employee, a place of employment that is free from recognizable hazards that are causing, or likely to cause, death or serious harm to the employee.

negligent retention
Liability an employer may incur when a company keeps persons on the payroll whose records indicate a strong potential for wrongdoing and fails to take steps to defuse a possibly violent situation.

Laws passed since the early 1980s recognize the seriousness of domestic violence. In 1984, the Family Violence Prevention and Services Act was passed to help prevent domestic violence and provide shelter and related assistance for victims. The Violence Against Women Act was passed in 1994, creating new federal criminal laws and establishing additional grant programs within the Department of Health and Human Services and the Department of Justice (DOJ). The Violence Against Women and DOJ Reauthorization Act of 2005 required a study to be prepared to determine the prevalence of domestic violence, dating violence, sexual assault, and stalking among men, women, youth, and children. At least 29 states plus the District of Columbia have laws that allow people who leave jobs because of domestic violence to become eligible for unemployment benefits. Also, some states such as Florida, California, Colorado, Hawaii, Illinois, Kansas, and Maine, give domestic violence victims the right to take time off. Florida law permits employees to take up to three days leave from work in any 12-month period for a variety of activities connected with domestic violence issues.

INDIVIDUAL AND ORGANIZATIONAL CHARACTERISTICS TO MONITOR Some firms that have experience with workplace violence are trying an alternative approach. Instead of trying to screen out violent people, they are attempting to detect employees who commit minor aggressive acts and exhibit certain behaviors. These individuals often go on to engage in more serious behaviors.

Once identified, these people are required to meet with trained staff members for counseling if needed. This approach may require more commitment on the part of the firm, but the alternative cost of violence may make this expenditure reasonable in the long run.

Although there are no sure signs an employee will commit an act of violence, certain behaviors can signal a problem, such as erratic behavior, increased irritability or hostility, reduced quality of work, poor organizational and time management skills, absenteeism, and a look of physical exhaustion. There are usually signs preceding workplace violence. Workers who shoot and kill their coworkers are likely to be employees who recently experienced a negative change in employment status, including those who have been fired, whose contracts have not been renewed, or who have been suspended because of a dispute with management. In one instance, a Domino's Pizza employee was discharged and later arrested after setting fires at two stores, causing more than $1 million in damages. The worker entered the buildings using keys he had not been required to turn in.[49] All terminations should require employees to return all company property issued, such as keys, access cards and ID badges, and uniforms. Workers who are fired for a violent conflict should be escorted off company property. If possible, a heightened security alert should be made at the perimeter for several hours afterward in the event the employee returns to "get even."

PREVENTIVE ACTIONS The best protection employers can offer is to establish a zero-tolerance policy for workplace violence by and against employees.[50] However, there is no way an employer can completely avoid risk when it comes to violence. Incidences of some unbalanced person coming in and shooting people happen randomly, and organizations can do little to anticipate or prevent them. However, there are things that can be done to reduce the risk. There are basically two parts to violence prevention. First, there must be a process in place to help with early detection of worker anger. Second, supervisors and HR staff need to be trained in how to skillfully handle difficult employment issues.

A firm can take certain actions to minimize violent acts and to avoid lawsuits. It should have policies that ban weapons on company property, including parking lots, and under suspicious circumstances, require employees to submit to searches for weapons or examinations to determine their mental fitness for work. A firm should also have a policy stating that it will not tolerate any incidents of violence or even threats of violence, and it should encourage employees to report all suspicious or violent activity to management. In addition, many firms are equipping receptionists and those responsible for checking workers into the facility with panic buttons to enable them to alert security officers instantly.

Can the selection process predict applicants who will be prone to violence? The answer is "No." On the other hand, the profiles of individuals *not* prone to violence tend to have certain things in common. The most important characteristic and one with the highest correlation is that an applicant has no history of substance abuse. Other positive factors include being outwardly focused and having outside interests and friendships rather than being mainly self-involved. Finally, applicants with a good work history often are a strong predictor of a person not inclined to violence.

To confirm these characteristics, the firm must conduct a thorough background investigation prior to hiring. Gordon Basichis, cofounder of Corra Group, an international corporate security firm, said, "At first glance, a person's background check for misdemeanors may not look so bad, but it can get worse because sexual and violent crimes, especially domestic ones, can get plea-bargained down or dropped by family members."[51]

An increasingly dire safety concern is having an active-shooter situation. A spate of school and workplace shootings must compel organizations to develop and implement an active-shooter plan. A survey of 900 organizations revealed that 69 percent of the respondents cited active shooters as one of the major threats to workplace safety, yet, 39 percent indicated their organization does not have a communication plan in place, and 70 percent stated their organization is not fully prepared to handle these situations.[52] Effective active-shooter plans educate employees how to cope with and respond to emergency situations. The U.S Department of Homeland Security published guidelines for creating and implementing effective plans (Figure 13-2).

FIGURE 13-2
Active Shooter Pocket Guide Information

HOW TO RESPOND
WHEN AN ACTIVE SHOOTER IS IN YOUR VICINITY

1. RUN
- Have an escape route and plan in mind
- Leave your belongings behind
- Keep your hands visible

2. HIDE
- Hide in an area out of the shooter's view
- Block entry to your hiding place and lock the doors
- Silence your cell phone and/or pager

3. FIGHT
- As a last resort and only when your life is in imminent danger
- Attempt to incapacitate the shooter
- Act with physical aggression and throw items at the active shooter

CALL 911 WHEN IT IS SAFE TO DO SO

HOW TO RESPOND
WHEN LAW ENFORCEMENT ARRIVES

- Remain calm and follow instructions
- Put down any items in your hands (i.e., bags, jackets)
- Raise hands and spread fingers
- Keep hands visible at all times
- Avoid quick movements toward officers such as holding on to them for safety
- Avoid pointing, screaming or yelling
- Do not stop to ask officers for help or direction when evacuating

INFORMATION
YOU SHOULD PROVIDE TO LAW ENFORCEMENT OR 911 OPERATOR

- Location of the active shooter
- Number of shooters
- Physical description of shooters
- Number and type of weapons held by shooters
- Number of potential victims at the location

COPING
WITH AN ACTIVE SHOOTER SITUATION

- Be aware of your environment and any possible dangers
- Take note of the two nearest exits in any facility you visit
- If you are in an office, stay there and secure the door
- Attempt to take the active shooter down as a last resort

Contact your building management or human resources department for more information and training on active shooter response in your workplace.

PROFILE
OF AN ACTIVE SHOOTER

An active shooter is an individual actively engaged in killing or attempting to kill people in a confined and populated area, typically through the use of firearms.

CHARACTERISTICS
OF AN ACTIVE SHOOTER SITUATION

- Victims are selected at random
- The event is unpredictable and evolves quickly
- Law enforcement is usually required to end an active shooter situation

CALL 911 WHEN IT IS SAFE TO DO SO

13.4 Discuss the negative effects of employee stress and burnout.

stress
Body's nonspecific reaction to any demand made on it.

Employee Stress and Burnout

Stress is the body's non-specific reaction to any demand made on it. It affects people in different ways and therefore is highly individualized. Certain events may be quite stressful to one person but not to another. Moreover, the effect of stress is not always negative. For example, mild stress improves productivity, and it can be helpful in developing creative ideas. For many students, a small bit of stress before an exam improves performance. However, excessive stress may have the opposite effect.

Many believe their stress has increased over the past five years. Several factors account for this rise, including increased workloads, terrorism, corporate scandals, and economic conditions.

Although much of the world has reduced the number of hours worked each year per person over the past decade, Americans have done just the opposite. Each year, more than 550 million working days are lost in the United States because of absenteeism resulting from stress.[53] And the costs are staggering. Overall, absenteeism cost employers $500 billion.[54] If people work longer hours, they often do not have time to refresh, resulting in a deterioration of their personal lives.

Potential Consequences of Stress

Although everyone lives under a certain amount of stress, if it is severe enough and persists long enough, it can be harmful. In fact, stress can be as disruptive to an individual as any accident. It can result in poor attendance, excessive use of alcohol or other drugs, poor job performance, or even overall poor health. There is increasing evidence indicating that severe, prolonged stress is related to the six leading causes of death, including heart disease, cancer, lung ailments, accidents, cirrhosis of the liver, and suicide.[55] This is in addition to the everyday headaches, back spasms, overeating, and other annoying ailments the body has developed in response to stress. Stress tops the list of changeable health risks that contribute to health care costs, ahead of other top risks such as current and past tobacco use, obesity, lack of exercise, high blood-glucose levels, depression, and high blood pressure.

Stressful Jobs

Many workers could identify with Jet Blue flight attendant Steven Slater when he imploded on the job and exited down the plane's emergency slide.[56] After a rude passenger's bag hit his head, he used the plane's intercom to curse the customer, thanked the other passengers, grabbed two beers, activated the emergency chute, left the plane, and went home. There are probably many workers who would like to take similar actions in their workplaces. John Challenger, chief executive officer of Challenger, Gray & Christmas, a Chicago-based outplacement firm, said, "Slater tapped into a vein of anger that a lot of people have toward their employers. They are mad about all the layoffs they've gone through at work. They are mad about having their benefits cut."[57] Stress and workload strains are real challenges now. Estimates are that one in three people in the United States is living with extreme stress, with a large percentage of all doctor visits being related to stress.

The National Institute for Occupational Safety and Health has studied stress as it relates to work and found that some jobs are generally perceived as being more stressful than other jobs. The 12 most stressful jobs are listed in Table 13-2. The common factor among these jobs is lack of employee control over work.[58] Workers in such jobs may feel that they are trapped, treated more like machines than people. Workers who have more control over their jobs, such as college professors and master craft persons, hold some of the less stressful jobs.

The fact that certain jobs are identified as more stressful than others has important managerial implications. Managers are responsible for recognizing significantly deviant behavior and referring employees to health professionals for diagnosis and treatment. Telling signs of stress may include a reduction in the quantity and quality of work, frequent short periods of absence, increased alcohol consumption, poor time keeping, or becoming tearful or withdrawn. Under excessive stress, a person's dominant trait may become even more obvious. For example, if the individual is a private person, he or she withdraws from colleagues; if the person is upbeat, he or she becomes hyperactive. Ideally, stress should be dealt with before this occurs. To do so, managers must be aware of potential sources of stress. These sources exist both within and outside the organization. Regardless of its origin, stress possesses devastating potential.

Burnout

burnout
Incapacitating condition in which individuals lose a sense of the basic purpose and fulfillment of their work.

Burnout, although rarely fatal, is an incapacitating condition in which individuals lose a sense of the basic purpose and fulfillment of their work. It is a special form of stress in which individuals become exhausted either physically or mentally or both. Seemingly the body or the mind can no longer handle the overwhelmingly high demands placed on it. Burnout differs from stress in that it causes people who have previously been highly committed to their work to become disillusioned and lose interest and motivation. Individuals who experience burnout often experience emotional exhaustion and lose interest in work.[59] When this occurs, they may lose their motivation to perform. Burnout is the most common factor leading to the decision to *check out* temporarily.

TABLE 13-2

Most and Least Stressful Jobs 2017

The 10 Most Stressful Jobs (1 = greatest amount of stress)

1. Enlisted military personnel
2. Firefighter
3. Airline pilot
4. Police officer
5. Event coordinator
6. Newspaper reporter
7. Corporate executive (senior)
8. Public relations executive
9. Taxi driver
10. Broadcaster

The Least Stressful Jobs (1 = greatest amount of stress)

1. Diagnostic medical sonographer
2. Compliance officer
3. Hair stylist
4. Audiologist
5. University professor (tenured)
6. Medical records technician
7. Jeweler
8. Operations research analyst
9. Pharmacy technician
10. Medical laboratory technician

Source: CareerCast.com, "The Most Stressful Jobs," and "The Least Stressful Jobs of 2017." Accessed April 14, 2017, at www.careercast.com/jobs-rated/most-stressful-jobs-2017 and www.careercast.com/jobs-rated/least-stressful-jobs-2017.

Burnout is frequently associated with people whose jobs require them to work closely with others under stressful and tension-filled conditions. However, any employee may experience burnout, and no one is exempt. The dangerous part of burnout is that it is contagious. A highly cynical and pessimistic burnout victim can quickly transform an entire group into burnouts. Virtual teams that exist over the long term (more than a year) often run a strong risk of declining performance because of team burnout.

Burnout's price tag is high: it results in reduced productivity, higher turnover, and generally lousy performance. Employee burnout costs the U.S. economy between $125 million and $190 million annually in healthcare spending alone.[60] People often become physically and psychologically weakened from trying to deal with it. Although some employees try to hide their problems, shifts in their behavior may indicate dissatisfaction. They may start procrastinating or go to the opposite extreme of taking on too many assignments. They may lose things and become increasingly disorganized. Good-natured individuals may turn irritable. They may become cynical, disagreeable, pompous, or even paranoid. Their motivation toward a project may not be the same as it used to be, and they may dread doing work that they used to enjoy. It is very important that the problem be dealt with quickly. Some means of dealing with burnout include keeping expectations realistic, reducing workload, finding means to relax at work, and developing and maintaining interests outside work.

13.5 Explain substance abuse, substance-abuse-free workplaces, and how to implement a drug-testing program.

Substance Abuse, Substance-Abuse-Free Workplaces, and Drug-Testing Programs

Failure to test for drugs can sometimes have a disastrous effect on companies large and small. For instance, Cake for You is a small specialty bakery. Its service includes making and delivering wedding cakes to receptions. In hiring a delivery driver, Cake for You owners always carefully determined that job candidates had a valid driver's license. The owners were quite pleased with their new employee, Mike. He was prompt, neatly attired, and seemed to have a pleasant demeanor. Unfortunately, while making a delivery one morning, Mike was involved in, and in fact caused, a four-vehicle accident that resulted in one fatality. The investigation revealed that Mike was high on marijuana. Had the owners of the firm included drug testing as part of their screening process, they might not be facing a huge lawsuit. In certain industries, such as transportation, for example, drug use on the job is especially hazardous and potentially devastating to the firm. Think of the damage that could be caused by a 40-ton truck careening out of control. Under ideal conditions, a fully loaded truck in daylight on a dry road cannot stop in less than 300 feet, or the length of a football field.

substance abuse
Use of illegal substances or the misuse of controlled substances such as alcohol and drugs.

Substance abuse involves the use of illegal substances or the misuse of controlled substances such as alcohol and drugs. About 14 million people who are employed either full-time or part-time abuse alcohol or drugs.[61] These workers use more sick days and are late more often. They remain in jobs for shorter lengths of time, and their health care costs are twice that of other employees.[62] According to the Substance Abuse and Mental Health Services Administration, drug-using employees are 3.6 times as likely to be involved in workplace accidents and 5 times as likely to file workers' compensation claims.[63] Further, research indicates that between 10 and 20 percent of the nation's workers who die on the job test positive for alcohol or drugs.[64] Even so, few issues generate more controversy today than substance-abuse testing. Yet, alcohol and drug abuse are workplace issues.

Alcohol Abuse

alcoholism
Medical disease characterized by uncontrolled and compulsive drinking that interferes with normal living patterns.

Although our society often attaches a stigma to alcoholism, in 1956, the American Medical Association described it as a treatable disease. **Alcoholism** is a medical disease characterized by uncontrolled and compulsive drinking that interferes with normal living patterns. The National Council on Alcoholism & Drug Dependence reports that 40 percent of workplace fatalities and 47 percent of workplace injuries are related to alcohol consumption. Stress plays a key role in a person becoming an alcoholic. It is a significant problem that affects people at every level of society, and it can both result from and cause excessive stress. When under stress, people with a particular genetic arrangement are inclined to act impulsively, increasing their danger of problem drinking.[65] As a person starts to drink excessively, the drinking itself produces greater stress. A vicious cycle is created as this increased stress is dealt with by more drinking. Early signs of alcohol abuse are especially difficult to identify. Often the symptoms are nothing more than an increasing number of days absent from work. Alcohol abusers are also much more likely to be using other substances.[66]

Drug Abuse

Drug users are increasingly gravitating to the workplace. Four percent overall of workplace drug tests (based on 9.5 million urine samples) were positive, indicating the usage of an illegal drug.[67] Although the percentage is small, the number of individuals is staggering—approximately 380,000. Imagine having an additional 380,000 employees in the workplace. As it stands, drug use in the workplace costs employers approximately $81 billion each year in lost productivity, according to the U.S. Department of Labor. The National Institute of Drug Abuse cites that employees at risk for illegal on-the-job substance use have been shown to have three times more sick days, three times the tardiness rate, three times more accidents, and are five times more likely to file workers' compensation claims than individuals not engaging in illegal substance use.[68] Because most of *Fortune 500* companies conduct pre-employment drug screening, a large number of employed drug users work for smaller businesses, many of which do not use drug testing. In fact, 71 percent of companies with 2,500 or more employees require pre-employment drug tests, whereas less than 40 percent of businesses with fewer than 100 employees even had a pre-employment drug-testing policy.[69]

It has also been estimated that more than 120 million prescriptions for controlled substance painkillers are dispensed annually. These substances include powerful painkillers that also carry an elevated risk of addiction.[70] Prescription drugs can be as addictive, impairing, and destructive as common street drugs.

Substance-Abuse-Free Workplace and Drug Testing

The Drug-Free Workplace Act of 1988 requires some federal contractors and all federal grantees to agree that they will provide drug-free workplaces as a condition of receiving a contract or grant from a federal agency (details of the act may be seen in Table 13-3). The U.S. Department

TABLE 13-3

Drug-Free Workplace Act of 1988

The Drug-Free Workplace Act of 1988 requires some federal contractors and all federal grantees to agree that they will provide drug-free workplaces as a condition of receiving a contract or grant from a federal agency.

Organizations, with contracts from any U.S. federal agency, must comply with the provisions of the act if the contract is in the amount of $100,000 or more. Organizations must do the following:

(A) publish a statement notifying employees that the unlawful manufacture, distribution, dispensation, possession, or use of a controlled substance is prohibited in the person's workplace. The statement should also notify employees of any punitive actions that will be taken.

(B) establish a drug-free awareness program to inform employees about
  (i) the dangers of drug abuse in the workplace;
  (ii) the policy of maintaining a drug-free workplace;
  (iii) any available drug counseling, rehabilitation, and employee assistance programs; and
  (iv) the penalties that many be imposed on employees for drug abuse violations.

(C) make it a requirement that each employee be given a copy of the workplace substance abuse policy.

If a contractor is found not to have a drug-free workplace, each contract awarded by any federal agency shall be subject to suspension of payments under the contract or termination of the contract, or both. The contractor may also be ineligible for award of any contract by any federal agency, and for participation in any future procurement by any federal agency, for a period not to exceed 5 years.

of Transportation (DOT) requires drug and alcohol testing for drivers of commercial vehicles, as well as employees that perform "safety-sensitive duties." Unless public safety and security are at risk, employers decide if drug testing is performed.

Firms have tackled the drug-abuse problem head-on by establishing a drug-free workplace program. But, some cautions should be taken. Some philosophies and practices that can undermine the effectiveness of drug-free workplace programs may be seen in Table 13-4.

The steps for establishing a substance-abuse-free workplace may be seen in Figure 13-3. Note that the first step is to establish a drug- and alcohol-free policy. The U.S. Department of Labor offers a Drug-Free Workplace Advisor that provides guidance on how to develop a drug- and alcohol-free workplace. At Texas Instruments, the policy is simple and straightforward, "There will be no use of any illegal drug."

The second step is to provide education and training for supervisors and workers. At a minimum, supervisor training should include a review of the drug-free workplace policy, the supervisor's specific responsibilities in implementing the policy, and ways to recognize and deal with employees who have job performance problems that could be related to alcohol and drug use. Managers must learn to recognize impaired or intoxicated employees and those who may be addicted. Possible signs that suggest an employee may be a substance abuser includes excessive absenteeism, radical mood swings, and a decline in personal appearance. However, the existence

TABLE 13-4

Philosophies and Practices That Can Undermine the Effectiveness of Drug-Free Workplace Programs

- Focusing only on illicit drug use and failing to include alcohol—the number-one drug of abuse in our society
- Accepting drug use and alcohol abuse as part of modern life and a cost of doing business
- Over-reliance on drug testing
- Focusing on termination of users rather than rehabilitation
- Reluctance of supervisors to confront employees on the basis of poor performance
- Reinforcing an individual's denial regarding the impact of his or her alcohol and drug use
- Restricting benefits or access to treatment of alcoholism and addiction
- Allowing insurers to restrict access to treatment programs

Source: www.dol.gov/elaws/asp/drugfree/drugs/screen5.asp?selection_list= (accessed April 19, 2014).

FIGURE 13-3
Developing a Substance-Abuse-Free Workplace

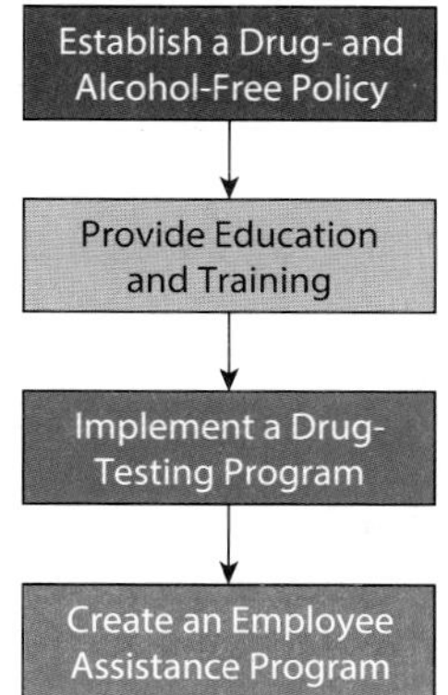

of these indicators alone is not adequate to determine the presence or absence of *any* condition. The supervisor should never try to diagnose, make accusations, or treat such problems. The indicators provide the supervisor a basis for making a referral to a person who can help the employee, such as an employee assistance program.

Employees should also be educated as to the purpose and ramifications of the drug- and alcohol-free environment. The purpose of this training is to familiarize employees with the drug-free workplace program and provide general education awareness about the dangers of alcohol and drug abuse. Employees should be informed about the requirements of the organization's drug-free workplace policy, the prevalence of alcohol and drug abuse and their impact on the workplace, how to recognize the connection between poor performance and alcohol or drug abuse, the progression of the disease of alcohol and drug addiction, and what types of assistance may be available. The program should send a clear message that use of alcohol and drugs in the workplace is prohibited. Employees are encouraged to voluntarily seek help with alcohol and drug problems. It should be noted that individuals who are in recovery from a problem with alcohol or with legal or illegal drugs are protected from discrimination under the Americans with Disabilities Act.[71]

There are hundreds of illegal substances that people abuse. These include cocaine, amphetamines, heroin and other opiates, ecstasy, LSD, PCP, inhalants, alcohol, steroids, and marijuana. Marijuana use has become a more complex challenge for HR professionals. Four states and the District of Columbia permit the recreational use of marijuana, several states deem marijuana use as legal, and marijuana use for medicinal purposes is legal when prescribed by a physician in more than 20 other states.[72] For instance, in *Coats v. Dish Network LLC*, Dish Network fired Brandon Coats, a quadriplegic employee with a valid medical prescription for marijuana, after failing a random drug test.[73] Coats filed a wrongful termination lawsuit against the company because he used marijuana exclusively outside of work hours. Although medicinal marijuana use is legal in Colorado where Coats worked, DISH Network argued that marijuana use is illegal under federal law. The Colorado Supreme Court supported the company's argument, upholding the lawfulness of Coats' termination. Wrongful termination lawsuits in other states ruled against former employees' claims that companies should provide reasonable accommodation for marijuana use under the Americans with Disabilities Act. In general, courts ruled that marijuana use does not fall within the law's definition of a qualified individual with a disability.

FYI

Workplace drug testing revealed heroin usage has increased 146 percent between 2011 and 2015.[74]

The third step in establishing a substance abuse-free workplace is to implement a drug-testing program. Proponents of drug-testing programs contend that they are necessary to ensure workplace safety, security, and productivity. A drug-free workplace program should balance the rights of employees and the rights of employers, balance the need to know and rights to privacy, balance detection and rehabilitation, and balance the respect for employees and the safety of all. The difficulty is not in formulating the policy, but rather in implementing it. Also, remember that the Americans with Disabilities Act protects an employee in a substance-abuse rehabilitation program.

Urine, blood, oral fluids, or hair samples are possible drug-testing methods, with most employers relying on urine testing. However, the majority regard blood tests as the forensic benchmark against which to compare others. The problem with this approach is that it is invasive and requires trained personnel for administration and analysis. The use of hair samples is unique in that drug traces will remain in the hair and will not likely diminish over time. Human hair samples are easy to collect, store, and transport, and they are difficult to change. Although urine and blood testing can detect only current drug use, advocates of hair sample analysis claim it can detect drug use from 3 days to 90 days after drug consumption. This would prohibit an applicant from compromising the test by short-term abstinence. A new method can detect drugs and other substances from the sweat in fingerprints, permitting mobile drug testing with immediate results.[75]

When the oral fluid method is used, the collection pad is saturated and the individual places the swab in a collection vial, snaps off the handle, seals the container, and hands it over for analysis. Oral fluid testing is especially well-suited to cases of reasonable suspicion and post-accident testing. Oral fluid is a great deterrent because it can be done immediately in the workplace and it does not give an individual an opportunity to adulterate or substitute a urine specimen.[76] From a prospective employee's viewpoint, oral fluid and hair testing may be less embarrassing than a urine test. For example, it is humiliating for a candidate to hear, "We're really happy to have you on board. But, will you take this cup and fill it?"

The final step in obtaining a substance-abuse-free workplace is the creation of wellness programs and employee assistance programs.

13.6 Describe employee wellness programs and employee assistance programs.

Employee Wellness and Employee Assistance Programs

wellness programs
Designed to promote the mental and physical well-being of employees and family members.

employee assistance program (EAP)
Comprehensive approach that many organizations have taken to deal with burnout, alcohol and drug abuse, and other emotional disturbances.

Wellness programs are designed to promote the mental and physical well-being of employees and family members.[77] Oftentimes, employers create employee assistance programs as a structure within which to offer wellness initiatives. **Employee assistance programs (EAPs)** help employees cope with personal problems that may impair their personal lives or job performance. Examples of such problems include alcohol or drug abuse, domestic violence, the emotional impact of AIDS and other diseases, clinical depression, and eating disorders.[78] EAPs also assist employers in helping troubled employees identify and solve problems that may be interfering with their jobs or personal lives.

Wellness Programs

Wellness programs are becoming more widespread as more employers become conscious of the impact employee health has on performance. Employers that start wellness programs not only help lower health-related costs, but also find that employees are more engaged and productive at work.[79] A recent study found that medical costs fall by about $3.27 for every dollar spent on wellness programs, and that the costs of absenteeism declined by $2.73 for every dollar spent.[80] Further program growth is being prompted by the shift toward wellness and prevention in the design of employer-sponsored health care benefits and by federal health care reform legislation. Barry Hall, global wellness research leader at Buck Consultants LLC's Boston office, said, "Wellness is currently the biggest area of growth in benefits, and it's primarily fueled by employer demand."[81] The Patient Protection and Affordable Care Act provides employers with additional incentives to help workers stay healthy. The cap on health insurance premium discounts increased from 20 percent to 30 percent in 2014. Employers can use these discounts to entice employees to participate and meet certain goals in company wellness programs. Under certain situations, employers can move the incentive up to 50 percent. Small businesses with fewer than 100 employees are now eligible for grants to implement new wellness programs.

The traditional view that health is dependent on medical care and is the absence of disease is changing. Today, it is clear that optimal well-being is often achieved through environmental safety, organizational changes, and healthier lifestyles. Laura Karkula, vice-president of Wellness Products at OptumHealth, said, "The research shows that companies that deploy health and wellness programs and take the approach of building an overall culture of health have a stronger commitment to those values."[82] Health and wellness programs have also been shown to encourage employees to remain at their companies longer. Important factors in making these programs successful include active strong leadership, especially from the CEO.[83]

There is growing evidence that in addition to containing direct medical costs, effective health programs boost productivity, reduce absenteeism, lower turnover and recruiting costs, and improve morale. Infectious diseases, over which a person has little control, are not the problem they once were. From 1900 to 1970, the death rate from major infectious diseases dropped dramatically. However, the death rate from major chronic diseases, such as heart disease, cancer, and stroke, has significantly increased. Today, heart disease and stroke are the top two killers worldwide. Chronic obstructive pulmonary disease and lung cancer are also growing threats to life. Healthy lifestyle measures such as not smoking, eating healthy foods, and exercising more may help prevent these diseases.

Chronic lifestyle diseases are much more prevalent today than ever before. The good news is that people have a great deal of control over many of them. These are diseases related to smoking, excessive stress, lack of exercise, obesity, and alcohol and drug abuse. Increased recognition of this has prompted employers to become actively involved with their employees' health and to establish wellness programs. Focusing on health care is inherently reactive; focusing on health is proactive, and potentially, a game changer.

There has been a shift toward an approach to improving health that includes involving workers in identifying problems and developing solutions. Wellness programs often expand their focus to include other health issues, such as diet, stress, substance abuse, employee assistance programs, and smoking cessation.

In developing a wellness program, firms should first conduct a health-risk assessment by surveying their employees to determine which workers could benefit from lifestyle change. Then, a wellness program to address appropriate employee health needs can be implemented. Sometimes getting everyone on board to take a health-risk assessment is difficult and incentives such as gift cards and use of big-screen televisions and travel opportunities are used as grand prizes. At Integris Health, employees who completed a health-risk assessment received preferred pricing on benefits, but those who completed the assessment and brought it to a physician during a preventive care visit collected an extra incentive.[84] Penalties such as increased insurance premiums are also being used to increase employee participation in wellness programs.[85] Beth Umland, director of research for health and benefits at Mercer LLC in New York City, said, "Premium discounts are becoming a real mainstay incentive and the amount of premium discounts is growing."[86]

Once companies have identified high-risk employees and the health issues they face, they can determine what programs are needed and offer incentives for participation in activities such as smoking cessation classes or joining Weight Watchers. At Lincoln Plating, everyone gets quarterly health-risk appraisals that include blood-pressure screening and body weight, body fat, and flexibility measurements. Each employee reviews the quarterly results with the wellness manager or occupational nurse and sets individual wellness objectives.

The growth in wellness programs has created new leaders with titles such as wellness manager, health and wellness manager, well-being director, wellness coordinator, wellness specialist, and wellness champion. Most of the employees report to a company's top HR or employee benefits executive who is responsible for defining the wellness mission and working to improve health and well-being.[87]

Social Networking and Wellness

Employers increasingly are adopting social networking to strengthen the success of their wellness programs. In his research, Dr. Nicholas Christakis of the Harvard Medical School found that good health is pervasive. When someone loses weight or quits smoking, their friends and family are more likely to also do so. He said, "The implication of this research is that interventions can leverage this phenomenon to purposefully spread healthy behaviors."[88] Social networking brings employees together and works to increase peer support. Social networking also generates participation rates higher than any traditional form of wellness initiative. Using social network tools such as Twitter and Facebook, employees can tell others how well they are doing regarding quitting smoking or losing weight. Jamie Curtis, vice-president of business development with Spectrum Health Systems, said, "If employees are given access to a social platform as part of a Wellness program, they feel more empowered to participate."[89] Once workers quit smoking or lose weight, they are certain to tell others, creating a sort of competition. Can you imagine the impact before and after pictures of a person who has lost weight would have on other friends? Such might be the same case with a Tweet that says, "I lost another 10 pounds."

Limeade Inc. of Washington offers social media–based wellness programs that permit employees to engage in healthy activities. The system permits workers to track their progress and share tips with colleagues. Limeade CEO Henry Albrecht said, "Our programs are social because the science of behavioral change shows that people make changes when they have support of friends and peers."[90]

Employee Assistance Programs

The Drug-Free Workplace Act also requires federal employees and employees of firms under government contract to have access to employee assistance program services. Compared to wellness programs, an EAP is a more comprehensive approach that many organizations have taken to deal with numerous problem areas such as burnout, alcohol and drug abuse, and other emotional disturbances.

As you would imagine, EAPs grew rapidly in number following that act. Returns on investment in EAPs will vary but one estimate is that a mature, well-run program will return a minimum of three dollars for every dollar spent on it. Advantages claimed for EAPs include lower absenteeism, decreases in workers' compensation claims, and fewer accidents.

Whether managed in-house or outsourced, EAPs have traditionally focused first on mental health, including substance-abuse counseling. Today, companies are aware that the advantages of an EAP extend well beyond assistance for alcohol or drug-related problems. Many have expanded to include financial and legal advice, referrals for day care and elder care, and a host of other services, including assistance with marital or family difficulties, job performance problems, stress, and grief. EAPs are also being used to help with managing critical events in the workplace such as mass shooting in domestic violence cases. In an EAP, most or all the costs (up to a predetermined amount) are borne by the employer. The EAP concept includes a response to personal psychological problems that interfere with both an employee's well-being and overall productivity. The purpose of EAPs is to provide emotionally troubled employees with the same consideration and assistance given employees with physical illnesses. Just having an EAP sends a message that the employer cares, and this can provide considerable encouragement for employees.

A primary concern with an EAP is getting employees to use the program. Some employees perceive that there is a stigma attached to *needing help*. Supervisors must receive training designed to provide specialized interpersonal skills for recognizing troubled employees and encouraging them to use the firm's EAP. Addicted employees are often experts at denial and deception, and they can fool even experienced counselors.

PREPARING FOR EXAMS/QUIZZES

Chapter Summary by Learning Objectives

1. ***Explain the nature and role of safety, health, and wellness.*** *Safety* involves protecting employees from injuries because of work-related accidents. *Health* refers to the employees' freedom from physical or emotional illness. *Wellness* programs are designed to promote the mental and physical well-being of employees and family members. The role of OSHA is to ensure a safe and healthful workplace for every U.S. worker.

   Within the Department of Labor, OSHA enforces the whistle-blower protection provisions of 21 statutes, covering not just workplace safety but also the environment, consumer products, the financial system, and other areas.

   Small businesses are not exempt from the mandate to provide a safe and healthful work environment. OSHA provides online resources and free consulting assistance to help small businesses comply with OSHA requirements.

   Job-related deaths and injuries of all types extract a high toll not only in human misery, but also in economic loss. The significant financial costs are often passed along to the consumer in the form of higher prices. Thus, job-related deaths and injuries affect everyone, directly or indirectly. Safety risks can be significant for employers. In addition to workers' compensation costs, OSHA can levy major fines.

2. ***Discuss workplace safety programs.*** Safety programs may be designed to accomplish their purposes in two primary ways. The first approach is to create a psychological environment and attitude that promote safety. The second approach to safety program design is to develop and maintain a safe physical working environment.

   There many ways to evaluate the effectiveness of workplace safety programs. Perhaps the best indicator of a successful safety program is a reduction in the injury frequency rate. Other OSHA metrics currently in use include total cases, nonfatal cases without lost workdays, total lost workday cases, cases with days away from work, and measure of fatalities.

Preventing musculoskeletal disorders is an important objective of workplace safety programs. *Musculoskeletal disorders (MSDs)* are conditions that affect the body's muscles, joints, tendons, ligaments, and nerves. Work-related MSDs, including tendonitis, carpal tunnel syndrome, and back pain, cost U.S. businesses billions of dollars annually just to cover the lost productivity costs associated with these ailments. A major musculoskeletal disorder is *carpal tunnel syndrome (CTS)* caused by pressure on the median nerve that occurs because of a narrowing of the passageway that houses the nerve.

Ergonomics is the study of human interaction with tasks, equipment, tools, and the physical environment. Through ergonomics, the goal is to fit the machine and work environment to the person, rather than require the person to make the adjustment.

3. ***Summarize the problems associated with workplace bullying and violence.*** *Workplace bullying* includes acts of continual hostile conduct that deliberately hurt another person emotionally, verbally, or physically. Companies have expanded the definition of workplace violence to include bullying because they recognize that it is common, costly, and a possible forerunner to acts of physical violence.

OSHA defines *workplace violence* as physical assault, threatening behavior, verbal abuse, hostility, or harassment directed toward employees at work or on duty. Workplace violence affects more than two million workers each year.

Spillover from domestic violence is a threat to both women and their companies. Domestic violence has become an epidemic in this country.

4. ***Discuss the negative effects of employee stress and burnout.*** *Stress* is the body's nonspecific reaction to any demand made on it. Stress may be coped with through numerous means.

Although everyone lives under a certain amount of stress, if it is severe enough and persists long enough, it can be harmful. In fact, stress can be as disruptive to an individual as any accident. It can result in poor attendance, excessive use of alcohol or other drugs, poor job performance, or even overall poor health.

The National Institute for Occupational Safety and Health has studied stress as it relates to work and found that some jobs are generally perceived as being more stressful than other jobs. The common factor among these jobs is lack of employee control over work.

Burnout, although rarely fatal, is an incapacitating condition in which individuals lose a sense of the basic purpose and fulfillment of their work.

5. ***Explain substance abuse, describe substance abuse-free workplaces, and how to implement a drug-testing program.*** *Substance abuse* involves the use of illegal substances or the misuse of controlled substances such as alcohol and drugs. The Drug-Free Workplace Act of 1988 requires some federal contractors and all federal grantees to agree that they will provide drug-free workplaces as a condition of receiving a contract or grant from a federal agency.

The first step for establishing a substance-abuse-free workplace is to establish a drug- and alcohol-free policy. The second step is to provide education and training for supervisors and workers. The third step in establishing a substance-abuse-free workplace is to implement a drug-testing program. The final step in obtaining a substance-abuse-free workplace is the creation of an employee assistance program.

6. ***Describe employee wellness programs and employee assistance programs.*** *Wellness programs* are designed to promote the mental and physical well-being of employees and family members. These programs are becoming more widespread as more employers become conscious of the impact employee health has on performance. Today, the prevailing opinion is that optimal health can generally be achieved through environmental safety, organizational changes, and changed lifestyles.

Employers increasingly are adopting social networking to strengthen the success of their wellness programs. If used effectively and thoughtfully, these strategies have the potential to create high participation rates, long-term engagement, sustainable behavior change, and significant health outcomes for employee populations.

An *employee assistance program* is a comprehensive approach that many organizations develop to deal with marital or family problems; job performance problems; stress, emotional, or mental health issues; financial troubles; alcohol and drug abuse; and grief.

Key Terms

safety 363
health 363
general duty clause 364
job hazard analysis (JHA) 369
musculoskeletal disorders (MSDs) 370
carpal tunnel syndrome (CTS) 371
ergonomics 371
workplace bullying 372
workplace violence 373
negligent retention 374
stress 376
burnout 377
substance abuse 379
alcoholism 379
wellness programs 382
employee assistance program (EAP) 382

MyLab Management

If your instructor is using MyLab Management, go to **www.pearson.com/mylab/management** to complete the problems marked with this icon ✪.

Questions for Review

13-1. Define *safety* and *health*.

13-2. What is the purpose of the Occupational Safety and Health Act?

✪ **13-3.** What relationship does OSHA have with small businesses?

13-4. What are the primary ways in which safety programs are designed? Discuss.

13-5. What is the purpose of job hazard analysis?

13-6. Why are companies concerned with musculoskeletal disorders? What is carpal tunnel syndrome?

13-7. Define *ergonomics*. What is the purpose of ergonomics?

13-8. Define *workplace bullying*. What are the basic forms of workplace bullying?

✪ **13-9.** What effect does workplace and domestic violence have on an organization?

13-10. What laws were passed because of domestic violence?

13-11. Define *stress*. Why should a firm attempt to identify stressful jobs?

13-12. What is the purpose of substance-abuse-free workplaces in organizations?

13-13. What are the steps for establishing a substance-abuse-free workplace?

✪ **13-14.** Why are firms adopting social networking to strengthen the success of their wellness programs?

13-15. What are *employee assistance programs* and *wellness programs*?

PREPARING FOR MY CAREER

P I A Personal Inventory Assessment

✪ *An additional Personal Inventory Assessment can be found on MyLab Management.*

Stress Management

This self-assessment is designed to help you understand how well you manage stress. It also provides insights into your overall well-being.

ETHICS DILEMMA

In Confidence

Margaret Tierney recently joined Sweet Scents Candle Manufacturing as an HR generalist. Prior to joining the company, Margaret worked as an HR generalist at a large bank. Recognizing that there are differences between manufacturing and financial services companies, Margaret knew it was important to become familiar with the candle manufacturing process, the working conditions, and the employees on the manufacturing line.

Margaret worked in the corporate office across town from the manufacturing facility. She scheduled some time to meet with Samuel Kemper, plant manager, at the manufacturing facility. Upon Margaret's arrival, Samuel greeted her at the plant's entrance. "Margaret, welcome aboard!" He went on to say, "I've planned your entire visit. We'll tour the factory together and I will introduce you to some of the supervisors."

"Thank you, Samuel." She asked, "Have you scheduled time for me to walk along the line on my own afterwards?" I would like the opportunity to say hello to some of the workers."

Samuel replied, "Oh, Margaret, I know that you are very busy. Perhaps you can talk with the w[illegible] another time." He went on to say, "We are operating at full capac[illegible] demand, thus, I don't recom-m[illegible] interru[illegible] [illegible]rly next year."

The tour commenced. Margaret learned quite a lot about the manufacturing process. Samuel and the supervisors explained the steps as they walked the line. At one point during the tour, Samuel was paged to the front office. While away, Margaret pondered Samuel's response to her intention to chat with workers. She found herself feeling ill at ease. After all, she is the employees' HR representative.

With that in mind, Margaret spoke to a few workers. Two of them, Melissa and Robert, seemed nervous. Margaret asked if everything was OK. Melissa and Robert looked at each other, Robert shrugged his shoulders, and he turned to Margaret. Robert asked, "Can we tell you something in confidence?"

"Of course," Margaret replied. After some hesitation, Robert said "We've been so busy that regular maintenance has not been performed and many of the fire extinguishers require recharging."

Margaret asked, "Haven't you brought these concerns to your supervisor's attention?" Melissa chimed in, "Yes, I did, and I was warned never to bring this up again." She went on to say, "My supervisor suggested I would be fired if I did. I can't afford to lose my job. I'm a widow raising a young child."

Just as Margaret was about to discuss the matter further, Robert whispered, "Here comes Mr. Kemper." Then, Melissa and Robert immediately returned to their work stations.

As Samuel approached, he said to Margaret, "Let's continue with the tour. You're very busy and we should get you out the door to avoid rush hour traffic."

On the drive back to her office, Margaret thought about how to respond to the situation and had some ideas. However, Melissa's and Robert's identities would likely be revealed in the process because they are well known in the plant for raising safety concerns. Thus, Melissa risked breeching her promise of confidentiality. She is now unsure about what to do.

13-16. What would you do if you were in Margaret's shoes?

13-17. What additional factor(s) in this ethics dilemma might influence a person to make a less-than-ethical decision?

HRM Is Everyone's Business

Emergency situations in the workplace arise when least expected. Companies have an obligation to protect employee welfare, and having emergency plans in place is the first step. Examples of emergency plans focus on responses to fire, violence, environmental hazards (such as chemical spills or release of toxic fumes), and injuries. Both HR professionals and managers play an essential role in developing, implementing, and evaluating these plans.

Action checklist for managers and HR—communicating with workers during an emergency

HR takes the lead

- ☑ HR professionals review and discuss every emergency plan in detail with managers.
- ☑ Tell managers how to proactively share the plans with their employees. Make attendance at emergency plan review workshops a mandatory requirement.
- ☑ Invite safety experts (e.g., law enforcement, firefighters) to discuss the plans with managers and employees.

Managers take the lead

- ☑ Encourage employees to provide feedback on the plans.
- ☑ When reviewing plans with HR, offer recommendations for clarifying information. Share appropriate information learned from employees.
- ☑ Educate employees about their roles and responsibilities in promoting safety and responding to emergency situations. Encourage employees to raise safety concerns with managers or HR professionals, even if not certain that a problem truly exists.

HRM by the Numbers

Calculating Workplace Injury Frequency Rates

✪ *An additional HRM by the Numbers exercise can be found on MyLab Management.*

All companies have a vested interest in maintaining safe and healthful workplaces and there are various activities to achieve this goal. Identifying where problems are prevalent is a good start. HR professionals should regularly review departmental safety records as well as calculate injury rates. The following table displays workplace injury data for two years along with additional pertinent information.

	2016		2017	
Location	**Number of Accidents**	**Number of Employees**	**Number of Accidents**	**Number of Employees**
Manufacturing				
New York	3	525	2	550
Illinois	14	475	9	425
California	5	650	0	500
Warehouse				
New York	6	675	4	725
Illinois	9	525	9	575
California	4	850	7	1,000
Company Total	41	3,700	31	3,775

Note: The basis for calculating the injury frequency rate is 100 employees who work full time annually (40 hours per week, 50 weeks per year).

Questions

13-18. Calculate the 2016 injury frequency rates for: (a) manufacturing overall; (b) warehouse overall; and (c) company overall; and, the 2017 injury frequency rates for: (d) manufacturing overall; (e) warehouse overall; and (f) company overall.

13-19. Calculate the percent change in injury frequency rates between 2016 and 2017 for: (a) manufacturing overall; (b) warehouse overall; and (c) company overall. Which areas showed an increase, decrease, or no change between 2016 and 2017?

13-20. If the company set a goal of reducing the 2017 injury rates by 10 percent for 2018, how many accidents would there be for: (a) manufacturing overall; (b) warehouse overall; and (c) company overall. Assume the 2017 staffing levels carry over to 2018.

Working Together: Team Exercise

In small groups of three or four, come up with specific answers to the following questions. Talk through your perspectives with team members. Be prepared to share your ideas with the class.

Think about a job you or a friend or relative have held. Briefly describe the job tasks and the working conditions.

13-21. What are possible safety concerns? Explain.

13-22. How can the jobholder avoid work-related injury or illness? Discuss.

INCIDENT 1 Something Isn't Quite Right

Liam Murphy was a model employee. He never missed a day of work, he always arrived on time, his performance exceeded expectations, and Liam always gave a helping hand to coworkers. In fact, Liam received the Employee of the Year award five times in the last six years.

Liam's coworkers have noticed that he has not been himself lately. Liam often comes to work late, he hasn't been getting all his work completed, and what he completes is filled with errors. Liam has also been withdrawn. In the past, he cheerfully greeted his coworkers. Now, he barely talks to anyone. Upon arriving at work, Liam goes directly to his office and closes the door. He rarely responds to e-mails, which is unlike him.

Two coworkers, Belinda and Marcus, discussed the changes they have seen in Liam. Belinda asked Marcus, "Have you noticed that Liam seems unhappy and keeps his distance from us?" She added, "That simply is not the Liam we have come to know and love."

Marcus replied, "Yes, I have noticed the changes, and I'm worried." Scratching his head, he then said, "On occasion, I write an email to Liam asking for his advice. He rarely replies."

"Enough is enough. Let's talk to Liam now," Belinda insisted. Marcus agreed and both went to Liam's office. They found Liam staring out the window and he barely acknowledged their presence. Belinda approached Liam and noticed the smell of alcohol on his breath. His eyes were bloodshot.

Belinda gently put her hand on Liam's left shoulder and said, "Liam, Marcus and I would like to talk to you." She added, "You just don't seem to be yourself. Everybody has been whispering about the changes in you."

Liam took a step back from Belinda and said defensively, "Leave me alone. I'm perfectly fine."

"No, Liam. You are not fine," Marcus asserted. He added, "Please, let us help you."

Uncharacteristic of Liam, he screamed, "Get out of my office! Get out of my office right now!" Belinda and Marcus were startled and immediately left Liam's office.

Questions

13-23. What do you think is likely to be Liam's problem? Discuss.

13-24. What should Belinda's and Marcus' next steps be?

13-25. How might use of an employee assistance program help in this situation?

INCIDENT 2 A Commitment to Safety?

Wanda Zackery was extremely excited a year ago when she joined Landon Electronics as its first safety engineer. She had graduated from Florida State University with a degree in electrical engineering and had a strong desire to enter business. Wanda had selected her job at Landon Electronics over several other offers. She believed that it would provide her with a broad range of experiences that she could not receive in a strictly engineering job. Also, when the company president, Martha Lincoln, interviewed her, she promised her that the firm's resources would be at her disposal to correct any safety-related problems.

[illegible] first few months at Landon were hectic but exciting. She imme- [illegible] [illegible]erous safety problems. One of the most danger- [illegible] [illegible]ety guards on all exposed equipment. [illegible] [illegible]ding expected costs, to make needed minimum changes. She estimated that it would take approximately $50,000 to complete the necessary conversions. Wanda then presented the entire package to Ms. Lincoln. She explained the need for the changes to her, and Ms. Lincoln cordially received her presentation. She said that she would like to think it over and get back to her.

But that was six months ago! Every time Wanda attempted to get some action on her proposal, Ms. Lincoln was friendly but still wanted some more time to consider it. In the meantime, Wanda had become increasingly anxious. Recently, a worker had barely avoided a serious injury. Some workers had also become concerned. She heard through the grapevine that someone had telephoned the regional office of OSHA.

Her suspicions were confirmed the very next week when an OSHA inspector appeared at the plant. No previous visits had ever been made to the company. Although Ms. Lincoln was not overjoyed, she permitted the inspector access to the company. Later, she might have wished that she had not been so cooperative. Before the inspector left, he wrote violations for each piece of equipment that did not have the necessary safety guards. The fines could total nearly $125,000 if the problems were not corrected right away. The inspector cautioned that repeat violations could cost approximately $1.25 million and possible imprisonment.

As the inspector was leaving, Wanda received a phone call. "Wanda, this is Ms. Lincoln. Get up to my office right now. We need to get your project under way."

Questions

13-26. Discuss Ms. Lincoln's level of commitment to occupational safety.

13-27. Is there a necessary trade-off between Landon's need for low expenses and the workers' need for safe working conditions? Explain.

13-28. Safety programs may accomplish their purposes in two primary ways: one focusing on ***unsafe employee actions*** and the other on ***unsafe working conditions***. Which areas of Wanda's proposal was she directing her efforts? Discuss.

MyLab Management

If your instructor is using MyLab Management, go to **www.pearson.com/mylab/management** for Auto-graded writing questions as well as the following Assisted-graded writing questions:

13-29. What are the purposes of wellness programs?

13-30. Why should a firm be concerned with employee burnout?

Endnotes

1 "Commonly Used Statistics," *Occupational Safety and Health Administration* online. Accessed April 13, 2017, at www.osha.gov/oshstats/commonstats.html.

2 "Green Bay Manufacturer Faces More than $219K in Proposed Penalties after Two Workers Suffer Severe Injuries within 10 Days," *OSHA News Release–Region 5* (January 18, 2017). Accessed April 13, 2017, at www.osha.gov/pls/oshaweb/owadisp.show_document?p_table=NEWS_RELEASES&p_id=33714.

3 Samuel Greengard, "Playing it Safe: The Roaring '20s & Now," *Workforce Management* 91 (January 2012): 1.

4 "Commonly Used Statistics," Occupational Safety & Health Administration. Accessed April 13, 2017, at www.osha.gov.

5 U.S. Bureau of Labor Statistics, "National Census of Fatal Occupational Injuries, 2015" (December 16, 2016, USDL 16-2304). Accessed April 1, 2017, at www.bls.gov.

6 Ibid.

7 "OSHA Penalty Adjustments to Take Effect After August 1, 2016). *Occupational Safety and Health Administration* online. Accessed April 13, 2017, at www.osha.gov/Publications/OSHA3879.pdf.

8 "Recycling Company Cited for Baling Machine Death," *Industrial Safety & Hygiene News* 46 (January 2012): 16.

9 U.S. Department of Labor, "US Labor Department's OSHA Fines Lakewood, NJ, Manufacturer Nearly $185,000 for Exposing Workers to Chemical, Other Hazards," *OSHA Regional News Release* (March 27, 2013, OSHA 13-030). Accessed April 10, 2014, at www.osha.gov.

10 Tom Musick, "OSHA's Top 10 Most Cited Violations," *Safety+Health* online (November 26, 2016). Accessed April 13, 2017, at http://safetyandhealthmagazine.com.

11 "OSHA to Improve Whistleblower Protections," *Material Handling & Logistics* 66 (August 2011): 8.

12 U.S. Department of Labor, "The Whistleblower Protection Programs: Whistleblower Investigation Data," Accessed April 13, 2017, at www.whistleblowers.gov/factsheets_page.html#stats.

13 U.S. Department of Labor, "OSHA Orders Amtrak to Reinstate, Pay $892K to Employee Discharged in Violation of Federal Railroad Safety Act," *OSHA Regional News Release* (January 18, 2017, OSHA 2017-12-BOS). Accessed April 12, 2017, at http://www.osha.gov.

14 Occupational Safety & Health Administration, "Protection from Discrimination." Accessed April 5, 2014, at www.osha.gov.

15 U.S. Department of Labor, "OSHA Finds Boulder Sporting Goods Manufacturer Retaliated Against Worker Who Reported Concerns about Free-Fall Equipment Safety," *OSHA Regional News Release* (November 15, 2016, OSHA 16-216-DEN). Accessed April 2, 2017, at www.osha.gov.

16 Liberty Mutual Research Institute for Safety, *2017 Liberty Mutual Workplace Safety Index*. Accessed April 7, 2017, at www.libertymutualgroup.com.

17 Brandon Rigoni and Bailey Nelson, "Engaged Workplaces Are Safer for Employees," *Gallup* online (May 24, 2016). Accessed March 15, 2017, at www.gallup.com/businessjournal/191831/engaged-workplaces-safer-employees.aspx.

18 Occupational Safety & Health Administration, "Job Hazard Analysis." Accessed June 2, 2014 at www.osha.gov/Publications/osha3071.pdf.

19 Dave Zielinski, "What's Safe? Employers Underreport Injuries and Illnesses," *HR Magazine* 57 (February 2012): 12.

20 Swati Deshkar, "Ergonomics Investment," *Professional Safety* 55 (October 2010): 48–50.

21 U.S. Bureau of Labor Statistics, "Nonfatal Occupational Injuries and Illnesses Requiring Days Away from Work, 2015" (November 10, 2016, USDL 16-2130). Accessed April 2, 2017, at www.bls.gov.

22 U.S. Bureau of Labor Statistics, "Nonfatal Occupational Injuries and Illnesses Requiring Days Away from Work, 2015" (November16, 2016, USDL 16-2134). Accessed April 1, 2017, at www.bls.gov.

23 Cynthia Roth, "The Importance of Ergonomics for the Safety Professional," *EHS Today* 4 (February 2011): 45–47.

24 Dathan Lane, "Ergonomics Protection," *Transmission & Distribution World* 63 (April 2011): 64F–64I.

25 Lawrence Cummer, "Office? I Don't Need an Office," *Backbone* (April 2011): 20–21.

26 Susanne Sclafane, "Do You Work with a Jerk?" *National Underwriter/Property & Casualty Risk & Benefits Management* 115 (March 28, 2011): 14–15.

27 Susanne Sclafane, "What Employers Need to Know about Workplace Bullying," *National Underwriter/Property & Casualty Risk & Benefits Management* 115 (April 11, 2011): 22.

28 "The Next Step in Curbing Workplace Bullying?" *Security Director's Report* 10 (October 2010): 2–4.

29 Jacqueline Munson and Christopher Thompson, "Addressing Bullying at Work," *Profiles in Diversity Journal* 14 (January/February 2012): 78.

30 "Bullying Proves the Point—You Should Be a Team Player," *Security Director's Report* 12 (January 2012): 1–15.

31 Kristy Armand, "Standing Up to the Office Bully," *Thrive Magazine* (January 2012): 28–29.

32 Carl R. Kjeldsberg, "Workplace Bullying," American Psychological Association (online). Accessed April 13, 2017, at www.apaexcellence.org/resources/special-topics/workplace-bullying.

33 Christine Comaford, "75% of Workers Are Affected by Bulling—Here's What to Do about It," *Forbes* online (August 27, 2016). Accessed April 13, 2017, at www.forbes.com.

34 Workplace Bullying Institute, "2014 WBI U.S. Workplace Bullying Survey" (2014). Accessed April 11, 2017, at http://workplacebullying.org/multi/pdf/WBI-2014-US-Survey.pdf.

35 "Who Gets Targeted? Why Me?" Workplace Bullying Institute. Accessed April 5, 2017, at http://www.workplacebullying.org/individuals/problem/who-gets-targeted/.

36 Workplace Bullying Institute, 2014.

37 Aliah D. Wright, "What HR Can Do about Cyberbullying in the Workplace," *Society for Human Resource Management* (May 13, 2016). Accessed April 13, 2017, at www.shrm.org.

38 Denise R. Friedman, "Cyberbullying in the Workplace: Is This Where We Are Headed?" *Psychology Today* online (June 1, 2016). Accessed April 3, 2017, at www.psychology-today.com/blog/always-more-learn/201606/cyberbullying-in-the-workplace-is-where-we-are-headed.

39 Donna M. Owens, "Incivility Rising," *HR Magazine* 57 (February 2012): 33.

40 Workplace Bullying Institute, 2014.

41 Arthur G. Sapper, "Sticks and Stones," *HR Magazine* 56 (September 2011): 115–118.

42 U.S. Bureau of Labor Statistics, "National Census of Fatal Occupational Injuries, 2015" (December 16, 2016, USDL 16-2304). Accessed April 1, 2017, at www.bls.gov.

43 Erik Eckholm and Richard A. Oppel Jr. "Virginia Shooting Spotlights Riddle of Workplace Safety," *The New York Times* online (August 27, 2015). Accessed January 30, 2017, at http://nytimes.com.

44 "Preventing Serious Domestic Violence Spillover Events," *Security Director's Report* 10 (January 2010): 1–13.

45 U.S. Bureau of Labor Statistics, "National Census of Fatal Occupational Injuries, 2015" (December 16, 2016, USDL 16-2304). Accessed April 1, 2017, at www.bls.gov.

46 Kathryn Hawkins, "Domestic Violence & the Workplace," *OfficePro* 70 (October 2010): 16–19.

47 Norbert Alicea, "HR: Domestic Violence and the Workplace," *BenefitsPro* online (September 1, 2016). Accessed April 11, 2017, at http://healthadvocate.com/downloads/stories/2016/1512045-HR-Domestic_Violence_and_the_Workplace.pdf.

48 "Employer Policies on Domestic Violence Paramount, Experts Assert," *HR Focus* 88 (February 2011): 3–5.

49 "Making Difficult Terminations as Safe as Possible," *Security Director's Report* 11 (March 2011): 1–15.

50 Kathryn Tyler, "Safer Separations," *HR Magazine* 56 (December 2011): 43.

51 Juliette Fairley, "Strategies that Avoid Workplace Violence, a Rising Threat," *Business Insurance* 44 (November 11, 2010): 31.

52 Ben Dipietro, "The Morning Risk Report: Companies Lack Active-Shooter Plans," *The Wall Street Journal* online (August 31, 2016). Accessed January 31, 2017, at www.wsj.com.

53 Emma Seppala and Kim Cameron, "Proof That Positive Work Cultures Are More Productive," *Harvard Business Review* online (December 1, 2015). Accessed March 14, 2017, at www.hbr.org.

54 Ibid.

55 Cris W. Cannon, "The Reality of Stress and the Need for Management," *Managed Care Outlook* 23 (August 15, 2010): 1–8.

56 "Flight Attendant Incident Puts the Spotlight on Workplace Stress," *EHS Today* 3 (September 2010): 18.

57 Devin Leonard, "Mad as Hell," *Bloomberg Businessweek* (August 16, 2010): 5–6.

58 Katherine Hobson, "Beware: Your Job May Be Killing You," *U.S. News & World Report* 147 (February 2010): 50.

59 Steven Berglas, "Can You Prevent Burnout?" *Forbes* 187 (March 14, 2011): 66.

60 Eric Garton, "Employee Burnout Is a Problem with the Company, Not the Person," *Harvard Business Review* online (April 6, 2017). Accessed April 14, 2017, at www.hbr.org.

61 Linda B. Dwoskin, Melissa Bergman Squire, and Jennifer F. Burdick, "Substance Abuse in the Workplace: ADA and FMLA Issues to Consider, Part I," *Employee Benefit Plan Review* 66 (January 2012): 27–32.

62 Robert J. Grossman, "What to Do about Substance Abuse," *HR Magazine* 55 (November 2010): 32–38.

63 "Are Your Workers Accidents Just Waiting to Happen?" *Safety Compliance Letter* (February 2012): 7–11.

64 T. L. Stanley, "Workplace Substance Abuse: A Grave Problem," *Supervision* 70 (June 2009): 18–21.

65 "Genes Linked to Alcoholism," *Investor's Business Daily* (April 15, 2011): 1.

66 "Facts about Recovery," *Psychology Today* (2012 Best in Treatment): 16–17.

67 Lauren Weber, "Greater Share of U.S. Workers Testing Positive for Illicit Drugs," *The Wall Street Journal* online (September 14, 2016). Accessed February 20, 2017, at www.wsj.com.

68 Paul Meskanick, "Critical Success Factors for Recruitment Process Outsourcing (RPO)," *Offshore* 69 (June 2009): 8–11.

69 Bill Leonard, "Poll: Majority Favors Drug Testing Applicants," *HR Magazine* 56 (November 2011): 87.

70 "Employers Reluctant to Play Role in Preventing Abuse of Painkillers," *HR Focus* 88 (April 2011): 1–4.

71 Jonathan Segal, "Elephant in the Living Room," *HR Magazine* 57 (March 2012): 95–98.

72 "HR Managers Tightening Drug Policies Since Legalization of Pot," *Denver Post* online (December 15, 2015 and updated on October 2, 2016). Accessed April 15, 2017, at www.denverpost.com.

73 Mark Berman, "Colorado Supreme Court Says Companies Can Fire Workers for Using Medical Marijuana in Their Off Hours," *The Washington Post* online (June 15, 2015). Accessed April 1, 2017, at www.washingtonpost.com.

74 Lauren Weber, "Greater Share of U.S. Workers Testing Positive for Illicit Drugs," *The Wall Street Journal* online (September 14, 2016). Accessed February 20, 2017, at www.wsj.com.

75 "Fingerprint Drug Testing Seen," *Investor's Business Daily* (November 11, 2011): 2.

76 Catherine McGuire, "What's New in Oral Drug Testing," *Safety Compliance Letter* (January 2012): 7–11.

77 Joseph J. Martocchio, *Employee Benefits: A Primer for Human Resource Professionals* (2018). Burr Ridge, IL: McGraw-Hill.

78 Ibid.

79 Jim Purcell, "Meet the Wellness Programs That Save Companies Money," *Harvard Business Review* online (April 20, 2016). Accessed April 14, 2017, at www.hbr.org.

80 Katherine Baicker, David Cutler, and Zirui Song, "Workplace Wellness Programs Can Generate Savings," *Health Affairs* (2010) *29*(2): 304–311.

81 Susan J. Wells, "Navigating the Expanding Wellness Industry," *HR Magazine* 56 (March 2011): 45–50.

82 "Employees Value Wellness Programs, But Opportunities Exist for Employers to Do Even More," *Managed Care Outlook* 24 (March 1, 2011): 1–9.

83 Sandra Price, "Ante Up for Wellness," *HR Magazine* 57 (February 2012): 40–42.

84 "With Incentives, Wellness Program Makes Employees Accountable," *Managing Benefits Plans* 11 (July 2011): 16.

85 "More Employers Using Wellness Incentives, Experts Say," *Managing Benefits Plans* 14 (February 2012): 11–13.

86 Susan J. Wells, "Wellness Rewards," *HR Magazine* 57 (February 2012): 67–69.

87 Susan J. Wells, "New Calling: Wellness Officer," *HR Magazine* 56 (February 2011): 43–49.

88 "Using Social Networks to Bolster Your Wellness Programs," *Managing Benefits Plans* 11 (June 2011): 6–8.

89 Jamie Curts, "Social Well-Being," *Smart Business Indianapolis* 8 (September 2011): 18.

90 Lisa Beyer, "Companies Are Turning to Technology to Help to Keep Workers Well," *Workforce Management* 90 (October 2011): 6.

Part six

Operating in a Global Environment

Chapter 14

Global Human Resource Management

14 Global Human Resource Management

LEARNING OBJECTIVES After completing this chapter, students should be able to:

14.1 Discuss the evolution of global business and the context for global human resource management.

14.2 Summarize global staffing practices.

14.3 Describe global performance management and human resource development practices.

14.4 Discuss global compensation practices.

14.5 Explain global safety, health, and employee and labor relations.

14.6 Discuss globalization issues for small to medium-sized businesses.

MyLab Management

Improve Your Grade!

If your professor is using MyLab Management, visit **www.pearson.com/mylab/management** for videos, simulations, and writing exercises.

Learn It

If your professor has chosen to assign this, go to **www.pearson.com/mylab/management** to see what you should particularly focus on and to take the Chapter 14 Warm-Up.

The current state of globalization has resulted in a high level of interconnections between the economies of various parts of the world. U.S. employers will increasingly conduct business with entities in a variety of other countries as former underdeveloped parts of the world experience tremendous economic, trade, and standard of living growth. In addition, the move from traditional manufacturing to knowledge- and service-based employment also means that jobs as well as markets are more likely to be dispersed geographically. As the need for employers to interact globally increases, human resource (HR) management professionals are going to have increased opportunities to develop programs for U.S. employees in foreign assignments, as well as for indigenous employees in foreign offices of the parent company. In this chapter, we provide a glimpse of HR practices around the world.

14.1 Discuss the evolution of global business and the context for global human resource management.

Evolution and Context of Global Business and Human Resource Management

Throughout this book, we've spent considerable time studying the U.S. domestic business environment and how HR management fits within this context. As we will see, studying business on a global scale adds greater complexity because we are incorporating the norms that vary between countries. In addition, these added features influence differences in approaches to managing human resources.

Evolution of Global Business

The environment confronted by businesses today is so vastly different from doing business in one or two countries of only a few decades ago. The world is becoming more of a multinational community in which the interdependencies between countries and between organizations are increasing dramatically. It is now one large marketplace consisting of more than 7.5 billion people speaking 6,900 languages, with thousands of governments all having different regulations and tax requirements. There are millions of organizations. The top 500 companies generate more than $27 trillion in value worldwide.[1] In fact, only 29 percent of the total number of consumers worldwide resides in the United States.[2]

The magnitude of the global economy is expressed in the *gross domestic product (GDP)*, which describes the size of a country's economy. Size is expressed as the market value of all final

goods and services produced within the country over a specified period. GDP figures are reported at each nation's GDP at purchasing power parity (PPP) exchange rates. That is, these figures indicate the sum value of all goods and services produced in the country valued at prices prevailing in the United States. The five largest GDPs total more than $58 trillion: China, $21.2 trillion; United States, $19.2 trillion; India, $8.7 trillion; Japan, $4.9 trillion; and Germany, $3.9 trillion.[3]

With globalization, everybody in the organization, and especially in the HR department, has had to change focus, change attitude, and adjust the approach in the way an organization operates. Not long ago, General Electric was "American," and Sony was "Japanese," but today these companies are truly global. Years ago, a lot of U.S. multinational corporations had operations in Canada or perhaps Mexico, but not in many other countries. Now, U.S. firms such as Coca-Cola, Procter & Gamble, and Texas Instruments do most of their business and employ most of their workers outside the United States. Countless products of U.S. companies are made outside the country. Many non-U.S. companies make products here, such as Toyota American, which manufactures cars in Kentucky. Companies still regularly do business in Canada and Mexico, but many now have operations in Hong Kong, Singapore, Japan, the United Kingdom, France, Germany, and Southeast Asia, to name a few. More and more U.S. global corporations are doing business in former Eastern Bloc countries. Vietnam, a country with which the United States was at war throughout the 1960s until the mid-1970s, now has U.S. firms operating there. Stewart McCardle, vice president of global financial services for Weichert Relocation Resources Inc., said, "U.S. companies are placing employees throughout Africa, the Middle East and Eastern Europe. In South America, it's not just Brazil or Argentina, but also Chile and Colombia."[4]

Today, globalization is not limited only to large organizations. It is now important for both large and small firms. Going global can provide a company with an assortment of rewards. The major benefit is that having a global customer base provides some protection against domestic business cycles. Companies that export tend to be more profitable, better organized, and more competitive than companies that are exclusively domestically focused.

Most companies initially become global without making substantial investments in foreign countries by exporting, licensing, or franchising. Ultimately, they may become a multinational or global corporation.

exporting
Selling abroad, either directly or indirectly, by retaining foreign agents and distributors.

EXPORTING **Exporting** entails selling abroad, either directly or indirectly, by retaining foreign agents and distributors. It is a way that many small businesses enter the global market. When deciding to enter the global arena, exporters need to identify and understand their target markets. Companies must determine whether the market or country needs their products or services, whether there are any import tariffs or quotas, and the local pricing structures. Also, exporters must understand and manage other countries' cultures and governmental policies.[5]

FYI

The total worldwide value of exports was $16.23 trillion in 2016. The top three exporting countries were:

- China: $2.01 trillion
- United States: $1.47 trillion
- Germany: $1.28 trillion[6]

licensing
Arrangement whereby an organization grants a foreign firm the right to use intellectual properties such as patents, copyrights, manufacturing processes, or trade names for a specific period.

franchising
Option whereby the parent company grants another firm the right to do business in a prescribed manner.

LICENSING **Licensing** is an arrangement whereby an organization grants a foreign firm the right to use intellectual properties such as patents, copyrights, or trade names for a specific period. The use of a licensing arrangement is expanding in emerging markets. For example, 7-Eleven has granted licenses to use its trademark in Indonesia.

FRANCHISING **Franchising** is an option whereby the parent company grants another firm the right to do business in a prescribed manner. For example, Subway shops must follow marketing procedures established by the headquarters. Franchising arrangements involve integration of operations with trademark usage. The growth of franchising in the world is phenomenal. Franchisees must follow stricter operational guidelines than licensees. Twenty years ago, only giants such as McDonald's were meaningfully engaged in international franchising, but now international expansion has become a popular choice for many small U.S. franchises.[7] More than 500 U.S. franchises operate internationally. Approximately 16 percent of U.S. franchises generate between 25 percent and 30 percent of revenue from international activities.[8] High demand U.S. franchise categories include food and beverage, health and beauty, wellness and fitness, professional services, education, apparel/textile, and retail. KFC saw the benefit of being an early entrant into global markets and has more than 15,000 KFCs located outside the United States.[9]

In determining whether international franchising is justified, the company must evaluate the amount of time, effort, risk, and legal proceedings related to selling a franchise internationally. It also must determine whether the product is valued in the targeted country. Also, the unique culture of the country should be a part of the decision-making process. Most franchise companies should bend and change to the cultural experiences of each individual country. Many countries such as Australia, Brazil, China, France, Indonesia, Italy, Japan, Malaysia, Mexico, Russia, South Korea, Spain, and Venezuela have their own specific regulations.[10] Most U.S. companies rely heavily on contractual relationships, however, in many other countries, people conduct business based on relationships first rather than relying on a contract. For example, in countries such as Singapore, Australia, and the United Kingdom, it is best to focus on the specifics of the contract and provide detailed information when negotiating with prospects or their attorneys. In most Latin American countries, the Middle East, and China, it is important to first build a solid relationship with the investor.[11]

multinational corporation (MNC)
Firm that is based in one country (the parent or home country) and produces goods or provides services in one or more foreign countries (host countries).

MULTINATIONAL CORPORATION Companies can vary greatly in their degree of global involvement. A **multinational corporation (MNC)** is a firm that is based in one country (the parent or home country) and produces goods or provides services in one or more foreign countries (host countries). An MNC directs manufacturing and marketing operations in several countries; these operations are coordinated by a parent company, usually based in the firm's home country. For example, General Motors is a U.S. corporation, headquartered in Detroit, Michigan, with manufacturing plants located in the United States, China, Mexico, and South Korea. Volkswagen is a German corporation, headquartered in Wolfsburg, Germany, with manufacturing facilities in many other countries, including the United States.

global corporation
Organization that has corporate units in several countries that are integrated to operate as one organization worldwide.

GLOBAL CORPORATION A **global corporation** is an organization that has corporate units in many countries that are integrated to operate as one organization worldwide. The global corporation operates as if the entire world were one entity. Global corporations sell essentially the same products throughout the world with components that may be made or designed in different countries. Expectations are that as the world becomes more globally open, the globalization of corporations will become much more commonplace. Not many years ago, Procter & Gamble was primarily a U.S. business investing heavily in food brands. Now it is a truly global corporation with more than 300 brands in more than 180 countries crossing the Americas, Europe, the Middle East and Africa, and Asia.[12] Approximately 56 percent of the company's sales were made outside the United States.[13] Its corporate leaders are an extremely diverse group, representing many cultures and backgrounds. Another global company, Johnson & Johnson has 250 businesses in 60 countries.[14]

CH2MHILL is a global engineering company that oversees complex projects around the world, including the expansion of the Panama Canal. As the Watch It Video indicates, company leadership carefully anticipates and studies contextual factors that impact how business should be practiced in diverse cultural settings.

Watch It 1

If your professor has assigned this, sign into **www.pearson.com/mylab/management** to watch a video titled CH2MHILL: Management in the Global Environment and to respond to questions.

Context of Global Business

The world is experiencing an increasing global workforce. Global HR problems and opportunities are enormous and are expanding. Individuals dealing with global HR matters face a multitude of challenges beyond that of their domestic counterparts. These considerations range from cultural to political barriers to demographic considerations in the workforce and international aspects such as compensation. Before upper management decides on a global move, it is vitally important that the critical nature of HR issues be considered. Companies that engage in the global economy place even greater emphasis on strategic HR. The functional areas associated with effective global HR management are similar to the ones they experience domestically, as shown in Figure 14-1. Although the six functions are the same, the global external environmental factors may significantly impact the way they are implemented. Sound global HR management practices are required for successful performance in each area. As with domestic HR, the functional areas are not separate and distinct, but are highly interrelated. We will discuss the functional areas after giving some consideration to the setting in which global HR happens.

HR practice in the United States is influenced by many factors that we have highlighted at various points throughout the previous chapters. Some of these factors include country political and economic structure, the legal system, national cultural norms, and characteristics of the labor force. When practicing HR within any one country, these factors are relatively constant. For example, the United States has many worker protections such as antidiscrimination laws. Global HR practitioners require, at minimum, an appreciation of the variation in these four factors to understand how to best structure and implement the six HR functions that we revisit later in the chapter.

COUNTRY POLITICS AND ECONOMIC STRUCTURE A country's political system and its economic structure are highly related. In this section, we consider the United States and China given the substantial size of their economies and their prominence in global business. The United States political system is based on democracy. Democratic governments are formed by participation of all eligible citizens through voting directly on issues (for example, election of the U.S. president) or indirectly through elected representatives (for example, members of Congress and the Senate). Two political parties—the Democratic and Republican parties—dominate the composition of U.S. government. These parties often have differing opinions on how HR management should be accomplished. Democrats tend to favor government regulation that protects the rights of employees, for instance, the Fair Labor Standards Act. Republicans, on the other hand, tend not to favor government regulation, believing that businesses should have as much flexibility as possible to operate successfully. For example, many in the Republican Party do not support an

FIGURE 14-1
Environment of Global Human Resources Management

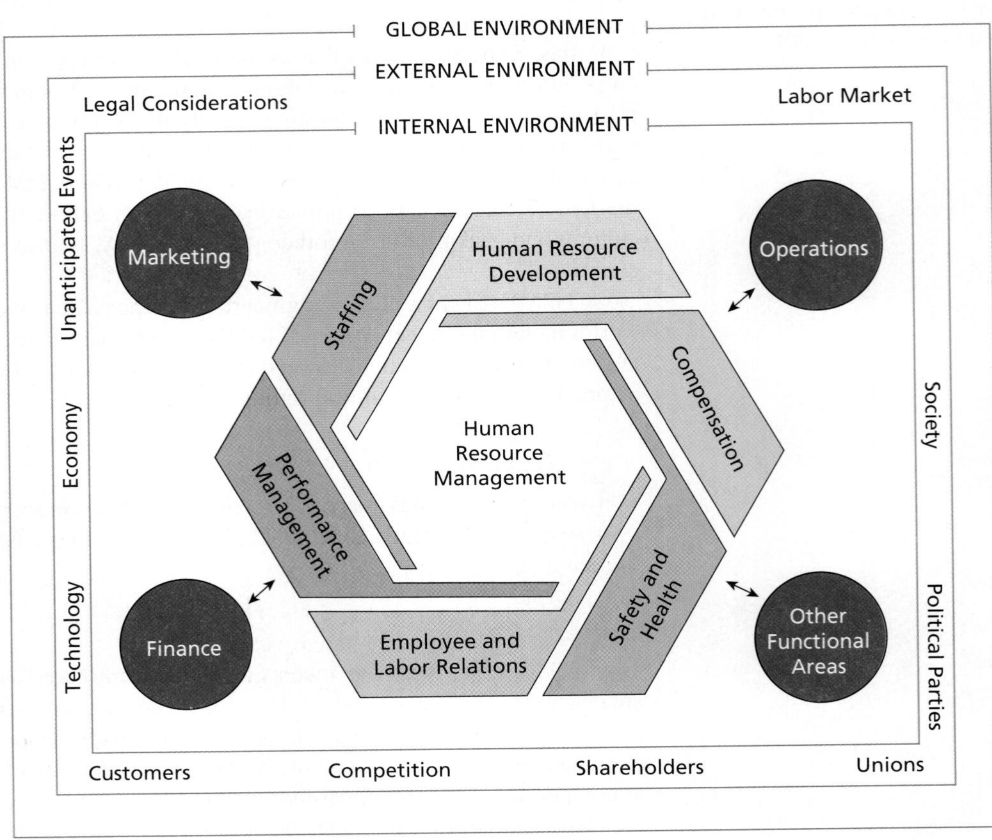

increase in the federal minimum wage pay rate because of higher labor costs, which would surely undercut profitability. The U.S. economy is based on the idea of *capitalism*. Under capitalism, the government does not possess ownership of all land, businesses, or natural resources. This economic system relies on market forces in which supply and demand for products, services, and labor determine monetary value.

China's political system is based on *communism*. Communism is set on the principle of community ownership. That is, all property, businesses, and natural resources are community owned, but these items are controlled by the single political party (Communist Party). Also, in communist societies, the government provides necessities. In principle, citizens elect individuals to serve in the Communist Party, but that is rarely the case. In recent decades, China's economy has become more diverse. While maintaining communist control, economic growth has been fueled by market forces and capitalism. As a result, a growing segment of the population has gained considerable wealth and is adopting similar lifestyles as in the United States that is based on income and wealth. Still, one of the key challenges for the government has been to sustain adequate job growth for tens of millions of workers laid off from state-owned enterprises, migrants, and new entrants to the workforce.

LEGAL SYSTEM The growing complexity of the political and legal landscapes in the global environment is one of the most important trends affecting global business. Managers working for global businesses contend with a growing tide of employment legislation that cuts across national boundaries. Legal and political forces are unique to each country, and sometimes the laws of one contradict those of another, or are ignored altogether. For example, Americans may encounter laws that are routinely ignored by host countries, creating somewhat of a dilemma. The growing complexity of legal compliance in the global environment is one of the most important trends affecting global business. Managers working for global businesses contend with a growing tide of employment legislation that cuts across national boundaries. Legal and political forces are unique to each country, and sometimes, the laws of one contradict those of another. For instance, the French authorities acknowledge that their data-protection laws are in direct conflict with the U.S. Sarbanes-Oxley Act, but they insist that multinationals comply with French law. Further, the nature and stability of political and legal systems vary across the globe. U.S. firms enjoy relatively stable legal and political systems, and the same is true in many of the developed countries. In other nations, however, the legal and political systems are much less stable. Some governments are subject to coups, dictatorial rule, and corruption, which can substantially alter both the business and legal environments. Legal systems can also become unstable, with contracts suddenly becoming unenforceable because of internal politics.

HR regulations and laws vary greatly among countries. In the United States, United Kingdom, and Canada, the list of hiring standards to avoid is quite lengthy and precise. In India, it is legal for an advertisement for an Indian airline flight attendant to read, "18-27 years old, different height minimums for males and females, status unmarried, unblemished complexion and good eyesight."[15] As previously mentioned, merely conducting a background check is different from one country to another. In many Western European countries, laws on labor unions and employment make it difficult to lay off employees. Because of political and legal differences, it is essential that a comprehensive review of the political and legal environment of the host country is conducted before beginning global operations.

Some have asked the question, "Does operating under local laws and customs free a company of all ethical considerations?" Google certainly understands the problems that can occur when attempting to go global. To do business in China, Google had to submit its search results to government censorship, which was an undesirable concession. Still, company leaders felt the benefits to the Chinese people would exceed the evils of the censored results and went ahead with it. But after repeated squabbling with the Chinese government and evidence of hacking into the Gmail accounts of dissidents in late 2009 and in March 2010, Google removed its search engine from China.[16] Each company should evaluate what it would do in instances such as Google encountered.

Americans may encounter laws that are routinely ignored by host countries, creating somewhat of a dilemma. For example, the laws in some countries that require a minimum age for factory workers are often not enforced. A U.S. Department of Labor report revealed continued child labor abuses in the apparel and textile industries.[17]

cultural values
The norms for behaviors and beliefs.

NATIONAL CULTURAL NORMS Cultural differences create challenges for managing HR. **Cultural values** pertain to the norms for behaviors and beliefs. National culture is steeped in a country's history, and we can describe it based on a society's social traditions, political and economic philosophy, and legal system. More recently, researchers and practitioners have tried to understand how cultural values influence workplace practices. We often rely on six categories to describe national culture.[18] These include power distance, individualism/collectivism, masculine/feminine, uncertainty avoidance, pragmatism/normative, and indulgence/restraint. We focus on the first three because those dimensions are among the most widely discussed in the global HR context.

Power distance describes the extent to which power is unequally distributed. High power distance cultures reinforce hierarchical control, and members generally do not expect justification for the actions taken by those in power. Low power distance cultures embrace greater equality and justification for actions, particularly where actions create a disadvantage to an individual or group. Germany is well known for a culture that rates low in power distance whereas the United Arab Emirates is culture that strongly captures a high-power distance orientation.

Individualism refers to the extent to which an individual focuses on his or her own welfare relative to others. Collectivism describes a concern for the welfare of the larger group such as family, coworkers, or other groups. The United States and Canada are highly individualistic cultures, whereas Chile, China, and Mexico value collectivistic norms.

Masculine cultures place high value on achievement, material award, and assertiveness. Feminine cultures espouse cooperation, modesty, and quality of life. Japan is an example of a highly masculine culture, whereas Norway and Finland embody the values of a feminine culture.

The following Watch It video provides additional perspective on China's culture. History and religion play an important role in shaping culture. In addition, cultural character influences how to conduct business.

Watch It 2

If your professor has assigned this, sign into **www.pearson.com/mylab/management** to watch a video titled Impact of Culture on Business: Spotlight on China and to respond to questions.

Although Hofstede's work was published decades ago, the dimensions of cultural values still hold. Nevertheless, it is important to recognize the obvious statement that not all people are alike. Our interactions with individuals from the same culture may differ because a variety of factors, such as personality, influence how people interact with each other. For example, we previously described Americans as being proactive. Indeed, this is a fair characterization of most Americans. But, by nature, some may not live up to this expectation because they are inherently introverted. Introverted people tend to be focused more on internal thoughts, feelings, and moods rather than on seeking out interactions with others. Personality variables are measured on a continuum. Introversion is typically considered as part of a continuum along with extraversion, or individuals who generally seek out interactions with others.

LABOR FORCE CHARACTERISTICS AND DYNAMICS As in the United States, the characteristics of the labor force worldwide holds implications for global HR practice. For example, China's work force is aging dramatically, much like in the United States.[19] However, the Chinese government's one-child policy has left a substantial gap in younger generations; thus, a shrinking labor pool. For decades, the Chinese government imposed a policy in which couples could have up to one child. Recently, the government has begun to relax this policy by allowing some couples to have as many as two children.[20] For entirely different reasons, Japan is facing a similar labor shortage because of cultural values that increasingly disfavor romantic relationships.[21] Economic growth in India has been affected by the widespread return of unskilled factory workers from large cities to rural farming locations.[22] Low wages, high costs, and significant rates of inflation have made it difficult for those individuals to meet basic financial obligations. Government policies that provide substantial subsidies to residents create an attractive alternative. Factories struggle to maintain or expand production given the impracticalities of city life.

Educational attainment is an important consideration. The Hays Global Skills Index report warns that many countries throughout the world are facing a labor shortage of highly skilled workers that will continue for years to come.[23] A McKinsey Global Institute report indicates that gaps between labor supply and demand for labor will increase between 3 percent and 11 percent based on country.[24] At the same time, the supply of low-skilled workers will far exceed the demand for their services. Inadequate primary educational systems in many countries are a major contributor to these trends.

The role of gender plays a significant role in influencing employment. The global assignment of women and members of racial and ethnic minorities can involve cultural and legal issues. Regrettably, female talent is underused in most emerging countries. Occupational segregation is prevalent worldwide. Women are overrepresented in clerical and support jobs (63 percent) and underrepresented in management jobs (33 percent).[25] This situation may be partly explained by family-related constraints and pressures, as well as work-related issues that combine to force women to either settle for dead-end jobs or leave the workforce. For example, in Saudi Arabia, women are not permitted to drive.[26] Often, global careers are affected when a worker decides to return to China to take care of her family. In the United Arab Emirates, a single woman cannot board a plane or stay in a hotel unless a male relative is willing to accompany her. In India, a woman returning from a global assignment often is given less-challenging roles or projects or receives lower performance ratings.[27]

Many women who want to work face barriers, oftentimes, on religious grounds. In Chapter 3, we referred to a U.S. Supreme Court decision (*EEOC v. Abercrombie & Fitch*) that prohibits an employer from refusing to hire an applicant motivated by religious bias or unwillingness to make reasonable accommodation for religious beliefs. That decision was based on a Muslim woman who was refused employment because of her religious practice of wearing a hijab. Similar religious biases exist throughout the world. For instance, a company in Belgium fired a female employee because she wore a hijab at work. An advocate General with the European Court of Justice asserted that prohibiting head scarves does not constitute religious discrimination, a violation of European regulations, "if that ban is founded on a general company rule prohibiting visible political, philosophical and religious symbols in the workplace, and not on stereotypes or prejudice against one or more particular religions or against religious beliefs in general."[28]

The news isn't all bad. There are some positive trends that have emerged regarding women working in the global environment. According to a recent study, nearly three million female university graduates enter the Chinese workforce each year. Of the total Graduate Management Admission Test applicants, 40 percent are male and 60 percent are female. The study also discovered that 76 percent of Chinese women aspire to top-level positions compared to only 52 percent in the United States.[29] In addition, women in Asian countries are encouraged in educational pursuits. According to Maria Saab, a research fellow at the New America Foundation, "Women are graduating from universities and graduate programmes at higher rates than men and are better positioned for senior management positions when they open up [and] this growth can also be traced back to the promotion of women within communist regimes."[30]

Women are rapidly moving into the management ranks in some countries. In 2016, women held 45 percent of senior management jobs in Russia. In Asia, women have a significant presence on senior leadership teams: the Philippines (39 percent), Thailand (37 percent), and Indonesia (36 percent).[31] China is not far behind at 30 percent female representation in senior management roles.

FYI

Women represent 39.4 percent of the labor force worldwide. Female representation varies by country, for example:

- Rwanda and Mozambique: 54.4 percent
- United States: 45.8 percent
- China: 43.8 percent
- United Arab Emirates: 12.4 percent[32]

We now turn our attention to the six functional HR functional areas in a global context: staffing, human resources development (training), performance management, compensation, safety and health, and employee and labor relations.

14.2 Summarize global staffing practices.

Global Staffing

Companies must choose from various types of global staff members and may use specific approaches to global staffing. Global staff members may be selected from among three different types: expatriates, host-country nationals, and third-country nationals.

Expatriate

expatriate
Employee who is not a citizen of the country in which a firm's operations are located but is a citizen of the country in which the organization is headquartered.

An **expatriate** is an employee who is not a citizen of the country in which the firm operations are located but is a citizen of the country in which the organization is headquartered. The U.S. expatriate population has grown rapidly because of the large numbers of workers who are being sent to China and India. An example of an expatriate is a U.S. citizen who is employed by General Electric (headquartered in the United States) and is assigned to a position in Italy.

Until recently, many U.S. expatriates accepted assignments in Asia on a short-term basis because the compensation incentives were significant. Their interests fit well with a company's objectives of setting up operations (months rather than years). There has been a shift toward placing expatriates on a long-term basis (years rather than months), particularly given the interest of younger expatriates from around the world who are seeking "adventure," prefer to assimilate to the culture over extended periods, gravitate toward learning the language, and are willing to take assignments without lucrative monetary inducements. There are various reasons for this shift. For instance, the unemployment rate in Singapore has been extremely low, leading companies to seek talent from outside. Also, many companies there believe that importing global talent provides a greater diversity of perspectives that better suit the global business environment.[33]

Host-Country National

host-country national (HCN)
Employee who is a citizen of the country where the subsidiary is located.

A **host-country national (HCN)** is an employee who is a citizen of the country where the subsidiary is located. An example would be a U.S. citizen working for a Japanese company in the United States. Normally, the bulk of employees in international businesses will be HCNs. Companies that are staffed by locals not only are typically less expensive but also offer advantages from a cultural and business standpoint. In most industries, HCNs comprise more than 98 percent of the workforce in the foreign operations of North American and Western European MNCs. Halliburton is a leading energy services company headquartered in the United States with 50,000 employees working in 70 countries, representing 140 nationalities.[34] Halliburton's workforce, including managers, is overwhelmingly made up of citizens of the host country.[35] Hiring local people and operating the company like local companies whenever possible is good business. The ultimate goal of most foreign operations is to turn over control to local management.

Third-Country National

third-country national (TCN)
Citizen of one country, working in a second country, and employed by an organization headquartered in a third country.

A **third-country national (TCN)** is a citizen of one country, working in a second country, and employed by an organization headquartered in a third country. An example would be an Italian citizen working for a French company in Germany.

Approaches to Global Staffing

Using the three basic types of global staff, there are four major approaches to global staffing: ethnocentric, polycentric, regiocentric, and geocentric staffing. These approaches reflect how the organization develops its HR policies and the preferred types of employees for different positions.

ethnocentric staffing
Staffing approach in which companies primarily hire expatriates to staff Staffing approach in which companies primarily hire expatriates to staff higher-level foreign positions.

ETHNOCENTRIC STAFFING With **ethnocentric staffing**, companies primarily hire expatriates to staff higher-level foreign positions. This would be the case with Rich Products Corporation, based in Buffalo, New York, with $3.5 billion in annual sales. Rich sells food products in more than 112 countries and employs 9,000 workers worldwide.[36] Judy Campbell, vice president, international HR, said, "Our strategy has always been to focus on local talent development. We have never had more than six expats in any of our international locations."[37] This strategy assumes that home-office perspectives and issues should take precedence over local perspectives and issues and that expatriates will be more effective in representing the views of the home office. The corporate HR department is primarily concerned with selecting and training managers for foreign assignments, developing appropriate compensation packages, and handling adjustment issues when managers return home. Generally, expatriates are used to ensure that foreign operations are linked effectively with parent corporations.

polycentric staffing
Staffing approach in which host-country nationals are used throughout the organization, from top to bottom.

POLYCENTRIC STAFFING When HCNs are used throughout the organization, from top to bottom, it is referred to as **polycentric staffing**. In developed countries such as Japan, Canada, and the United Kingdom, there has been more reliance on local executives and less on traditional expatriate management. The ultimate goal of most foreign operations is to turn over control to local management. The use of the polycentric staffing model assumes that HCNs are better equipped to deal with local market conditions. Organizations that use this approach will usually have a fully functioning HR department in each foreign subsidiary responsible for managing all local HR issues. Corporate HR managers focus primarily on coordinating relevant activities with their counterparts in each foreign operation. Most global employees are usually HCNs because this helps to clearly establish that the company is making a commitment to the host country and not just setting up a foreign operation. HCNs often have much more thorough knowledge of the culture, the politics, and the laws of the locale, as well as how business is done. There is no standard format in the selection of HCNs. The following Watch It video illustrates the importance of polycentric staffing as an element of the Save the Children nonprofit organization's strategy.

Watch It 3

If your professor has assigned this, sign into **www.pearson.com/mylab/management** to watch a video titled Save the Children: Global Human Resource Management and to respond to questions.

regiocentric staffing
Staffing approach that is like the polycentric staffing approach, but regional groups of subsidiaries reflecting the organization's strategy and structure work as a unit.

REGIOCENTRIC STAFFING **Regiocentric staffing** is like the polycentric approach, but regional groups of subsidiaries reflecting the organization's strategy and structure work as a unit. There is some degree of autonomy in regional decision making, and promotions are possible within the region but rare from the region to headquarters. Each region develops a common set of employment practices.

geocentric staffing
Staffing approach that uses a worldwide integrated business strategy.

GEOCENTRIC STAFFING **Geocentric staffing** is a staffing approach that uses a worldwide integrated business strategy. The firm attempts to always hire the best person available for a position, regardless of where that individual comes from. The geocentric staffing model is most likely to be adopted and used by truly global firms. Usually, the corporate HR function in geocentric companies is the most complicated because every aspect of HR must be dealt with in the global environment.

Recruiting Host-Country Nationals

One of the biggest mistakes that can be made in the multinational arena is to assume that the recruiting approaches that work in the parent company will also be effective in recruiting HCNs. For example, an error that many recruiters make is believing that all countries in Europe are similar or the same. Thinking that Italy is like France simply because of their close geographic proximity is like believing that the United States is like Mexico because they are neighbors in North America. The use of technology in global recruiting also varies considerably. For example, although Scandinavian companies in Norway, Sweden, and Denmark were among the first to promote Internet use for recruiting, recruiters in France, Italy, and much of southern Europe do not use it as much.[38]

Selecting Expatriates

Expatriates are often selected from those already within the organization, and the process involves four distinct stages: self-selection, creating a candidate pool, technical skills assessment, and making a mutual decision.

In stage one, self-selection, candidates determine whether they are right for a global assignment, whether their spouses and children are interested in relocating internationally, and whether this is the best time for a move. In the case of self-selection, the candidates assess themselves on all the relevant dimensions for a job and then decide whether to pursue a global assignment. The self-assessment extends to the entire family. One survey found that 55 percent of employees facing dual-career issues are less likely to put themselves forward as a candidate for a global assignment.[39] When candidates are selected for expatriate assignments, spouses, partners, and entire families also need to be "selected." Basically, candidates must decide whether to go to the next step in the selection process.

Stage two involves creating a candidate database organized according to the firm's staffing needs. Included in the database is information such as the year the employee is available to go overseas, the languages the employee speaks, the countries the employee prefers, and the jobs for which the employee is qualified.

Stage three involves scanning the database for all possible candidates for a given global assignment; then the list is forwarded to the assigning department. There, each candidate is assessed on technical and managerial readiness relative to the needs of the assignment. In the final stage, one person is identified as an acceptable candidate based on his or her technical or managerial readiness and is tentatively selected.

If the decision is made to employ expatriates, certain selection criteria should be carefully considered in stages two and three. It takes a special blend of person to add up to an outstanding expatriate who can be productive and accepted in an unfamiliar setting. Expatriate selection criteria should include cultural adaptability, strong communication skills, technical competence, professional or operational expertise, global experience, country-specific experience, interpersonal skills, language skills, family flexibility, and country- or region-specific considerations. However, according to one survey by Cartus, a workforce development provider, when considering employees for international assignments, 72 percent of companies chose technical competence and 65 percent chose job experience.[40]

Background Investigation

Conducting a background investigation on potential employees is especially important in the global environment. According to the HireRight, a pre-employment screening company in Irvine, California, 25 percent of global companies either conduct employee screening or have plans to start, an increase from 11 percent in 2009.[41] Conducting background investigations when working in the global environment is equally, or even more, important, but differences across cultures and countries often put up barriers. Each country has its own laws, customs, and procedures for background screenings. For instance, Japanese law covers a person working at the Tokyo office of a U.S.-based company and includes privacy statutes that prohibit criminal checks on Japanese citizens. The United Kingdom does not allow third parties such as background-checking firms to have direct access to criminal records held by local police. Instead, the job applicant and the recruiting organization must sign and submit a formal request to a specific agency responsible for handling criminal records. It can take up to 40 business days to get information back. Some countries have not instituted background check laws or procedures. In 2017, the United Arab Emirates began background checks of expatriates, who total more than 4 million of the labor force.[42] After a spate of criminal activity from expatriates, the government recognized that it is not sufficient to limit employment background checks to Emirati. For instance, HireRight tells the story of a person who had been in the United States for two years and had applied for a job with a multinational firm. There were no gaps in the individual's employment history that would suggest he had ever been in jail. However, further checking revealed that he had been convicted of murder in his home country and in accord with a practice that was legal at the time, had paid a proxy to serve his prison term while he remained free and in the workforce.[43]

HR BLOOPERS

United Architect's Expatriate Problems

On the flight back from United Architect's London office, Nate Brown is trying to figure out how to handle his current challenge. As the HR Director of the multinational firm, Nate was in London to meet with an expatriate that has requested a transfer home. The architect moved to London six months ago for a three-year assignment and now she says it just isn't going to work out. The firm transferred her to London rather quickly and didn't follow their usual selection and orientation process because of the tight timeframe. The London office had just secured a new project and they needed an architect from the U.S. office to join them immediately to get the project started. The architect that was selected told Nate that her husband had some concerns about taking the assignment because he would not be able to work while in London and he is at a critical point in his career. Further, although the architect had traveled for the firm previously, she had never traveled abroad. However, she agreed to take the assignment because she thought it would be good for her career. Now she is having problems getting along with her London colleagues and reports that she just is not happy living in London. Nate also believes her husband is pressuring her to move back home as well. The project is at a critical point and Nate knows it will be extremely difficult to find a new architect for the project now.

If your professor has assigned this, go to **www.pearson.com/mylab/management** to complete the HR Bloopers exercise and test your application of these concepts when faced with real-world decisions.

Root Capital is a small business that invests in small agricultural businesses in Africa and South America. As described in the Watch It video, company leadership faces challenges in hiring local talent that meets its business objectives. Also, working across multiple national cultures, Root Capital faces challenges in maintaining employee cohesion across the distant locations.

Watch It 4

If your professor has assigned this, sign into **www.pearson.com/mylab/management** to watch a video titled Root Capital: Human Resource Management and Operations and to respond to questions.

14.3 Describe global performance management and human resource development practices.

Global Performance Management and Human Resource Development

Some training and development professionals believe that performance appraisal as well as training and development strategies that work for a U.S. audience can be equally effective abroad. Unfortunately, nothing could be further from the truth. Also, global training and development is needed because people, jobs, and organizations are often quite different. Next, various aspects of global HR development will be discussed.

Performance Management

Two major influences on the effectiveness of performance appraisal practices throughout the world are information asymmetry and cultural values.[44] *Information asymmetry* refers to a difference in the quality and amount of information available to two or more individuals or groups. For example, let's assume that a company's headquartered in the United States instructed an employee to increase the staffing of its factory in New Delhi, India, by 10 percent in 2018. The headquarters will adopt this goal as a performance criterion come time to conduct the expatriate's performance appraisal. At the end of the year, the staffing increased by only 4 percent, which leads the company headquarters to judge the expatriate's performance as negative. The expatriate has learned from immersion in his job that illiteracy or substandard pay relative to the cost of living contributed dramatically to the result. However, the corporate headquarters does not have intimate knowledge of local conditions in New Delhi and simply attributed the outcome to an ineffective expatriate.

Cultural norms influence the adoption of performance appraisal practices as well as an employee's reaction to appraisal. In China and Japan, performance feedback is uncommon because the normative practice of "saving face" is well-ingrained in those cultures. Giving negative performance feedback would cast the employee in a negative light, which is something that the Japanese and Chinese seek to avoid at all costs.

There is some evidence to suggest that performance appraisal practices performed by companies within high power distance cultures rely on the manager or supervisor as the single source of judgment.[45] Where power distance is lower, it is not unusual for companies to solicit performance information from multiple sources, including subordinates. In individualistic cultures, performance appraisal seeks to differentiate employees based on performance. In contrast, performance appraisals in collectivist cultures generally do not focus on individual performance because negative performance information could hurt the solidarity of group members.

Expatriate Human Resource Development

The training of employees going on a global assignment has often been bleak but appears to be improving. The development process should start as soon as workers are selected—before they begin the global assignment. Organizations are recognizing that expatriate employees and their families face special situations and pressure that training and development activities must prepare them to deal with. Employees and their families must have an effective orientation program and a readjustment-training program. In addition, the employee must have a program of continual development. Figure 14-2 illustrates the ideal expatriate preparation and development program, which includes pre-move orientation and training, continual development, and repatriation orientation and training.

FIGURE 14-2
The Expatriate Preparation and Development Program

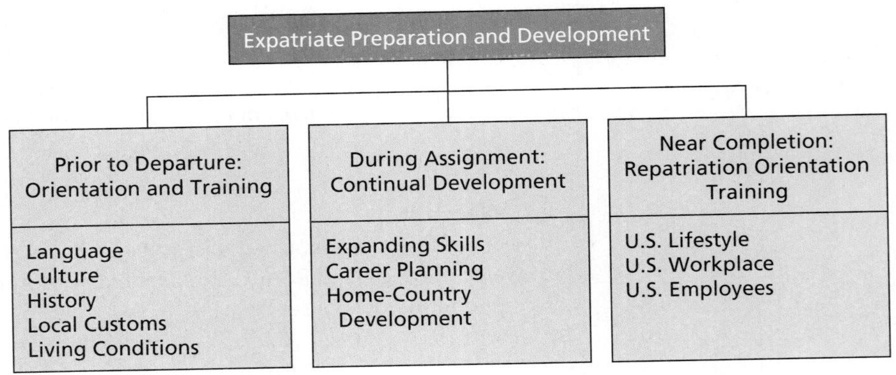

Pre-Move Orientation and Training

Pre-move orientation and training of expatriate employees and their families are essential before the global assignment begins. The pre-move orientation needs to be aggressively undertaken so that the expatriate understands cultural dos and don'ts and is immersed in the language. Obviously, providing an expatriate a cultural "dummies" guide and a basic phrasebook for speaking the language is not enough. Continuing employee development, in which the employee's global skills are fitted into career planning and corporate development programs, makes the eventual transition to the host home country less disruptive. Marc Sokol, senior vice president at Personnel Decisions International, said, "The cost of failure is very high. If you leave it to self-study, then you're rolling the dice."[46]

Some companies hire life coaches to lead predeparture training, recognizing that language preparation alone, for example, is not sufficient to help expatriates and family members cope in a new culture. Katherine Barton, a London-based life coach said, "They [employers] are realizing that it's not just about the culture, but about the transition that employees go through abroad."[47] This is the case for both first-time expatriates and seasoned expatriates moving to a new location. Author Pattie McCarthy, a relocation expert, indicated that managing unhappiness is essential to promoting adjustment, "Relocating is enormously difficult, and coaching can really help people because the basis of coaching is figuring out what you are unhappy with and changing it."[48]

Many organizations have established a formal *buddy system* to alleviate the stress new expatriates and their families normally endure and to reduce the time it takes for expatriates to operate at peak productivity. Buddies often inform expatriates of host-office norms and politics, invite them into their homes, introduce them to friends and networks, and help bolster their credibility in the office.

> **FYI**
>
> The rates of expatriate failure range up to 40 percent in developed countries, and up to 70 percent in underdeveloped countries.[49]

Continual Development: Online Assistance and Training

Companies now offer online assistance and training in areas such as career services, cross-cultural training, and employee assistance programs. The Internet offers global employees assistance 24 hours a day, seven days a week. Technology is a timesaving and cost-effective solution for the stress experienced by employees who are on assignment or doing business travel. With a satellite phone, individuals can communicate with one another in undeveloped countries. The distance problems from headquarters cannot be overcome without e-mail and voice mail, but, for some issues, Skype can be used if there is an Internet connection. Satellite phones throughout the world can also have Internet access, but the price goes up because additional hardware is required. Even if the assignment is a short-term business trip, technology can be used to provide ongoing contact and support with the home country. For example, online career services can give expatriates and their spouses the opportunity to upgrade skills while on assignment.

repatriation
Process of bringing expatriates home.

Repatriation Orientation and Training

Orientation and training are also necessary prior to **repatriation**, which is the process of bringing expatriates home. Repatriation is often the weak link in global HR management. Returning expatriates have not always had a pleasant experience. Even though a company may spend considerable money in sending managers overseas, too many returning managers report dissatisfaction with the process.[50] Many companies do not specify in advance how the international experience will fit into an employee's career progression. In fact, numerous expatriates were not even guaranteed a job on their return.[51] Further, expatriates often come home to a company that has undergone significant change from such events as mergers, acquisitions, reorganizations, and workforce contraction or expansion, which can create an unfamiliar environment.[52]

International businesses spend upward of two to three times of an expatriate's base salary only to have 16 percent resign within two years of their return.[53] Reasons given for leaving include they were not being properly prepared to return to their work and were not able to use skills they learned abroad. Employers should make every effort to find a place in the organization that will use the expatriate's experience gained during the assignment. Also, the returning expatriate should be given a job with at least the same degree of responsibility and authority.

To counter the challenges of repatriation, firms need to have a formal in-house repatriation program in place. A dialogue regarding expectations and career planning on return will help to manage expectations. Also, the exchange should continue after the employee has returned home. In addition, acknowledgment and recognition of the significant overseas contribution is a courtesy that the returning employee has earned and richly deserves. Ideally, there should be a clear career path or position identified for the expatriate employee on his or her return. An effective repatriation training program should support the assignees in defining their new or strengthened skills and knowledge and instruct them on how to posture themselves in the corporate environment to which they have returned.

Global E-learning

Globalization has created a special need for e-learning, and companies are embracing it to train the global workforce. In the past, a training program for a *Fortune 200* company in Asia would likely cost between $250,000 and $500,000 for travel and related expenses. Many believe that live, instructor-led training is still more effective, but the question that must be asked is, "how much more effective?" E-learning allows companies to keep the money and still receive a good training product. Industry analysts predict that the corporate expenditures on global e-learning will increase approximately 11.4 percent between 2016 and 2020.[54] New technology and the novel applications of existing technology emerge from time to time. Some of the trends include mobile learning, gamification, video-based training, and competency-based learning.[55]

The most obvious deterrent to any global e-learning implementation is the failure to recognize the impact of cultural differences on the program's success.[56] Not analyzing the culture or failing to recognize important cultural differences can seriously damage success. One study found that only 25 percent of e-learning implementation plans addressed cultural differences that affect management. Cultural accessibility is required so all learners can achieve the same learning outcomes by putting in the same amount of effort. A problem that evolves in implementing global e-learning is that the e-learning program is embedded with the culture of the person(s) who developed the program.[57]

Research showed that 91 percent of employees of global corporations said that English is "required" or "important" in their jobs, and that the need is increasing dramatically. Eighty-nine percent of employees said they are more likely to climb the corporate ladder if they can communicate in English. Many companies offer courses only in English or in English and one other language, usually Spanish. An English-only focus works for firms that routinely conduct their business all over the world in English. But others need courses in more than one language. Companies that want to offer courses in several languages usually turn to translators. Financial services provider GE Capital relies on translation companies to offer Web-based courses in English, French, German, and Japanese.[58]

Hilton's team members are scattered the world over. In a sector that sees high turnover rates, it is also hard to imagine that a classroom trainer could keep up with the demands of hundreds of new workers requiring training. Hilton, along with many multinational companies, realized that it could save money through online courses. Hilton first introduced e-learning when the company launched its Hilton University with 60 generic business skills programs and 21 finance programs. Over the years, Hilton put in place an additional 40 business skills courses and significantly increased the number of generic online courses offered. Hilton came a long way in a short period, from 5,000 course completions after the first year to more than 40,000 completions in the third year.[59]

Virtual Teams in a Global Environment

Virtual teams are becoming commonplace in many global organizations. A recent survey revealed that 85 percent of employees work on virtual teams, and 41 percent of never met face-to-face in the same location.[60] In addition, nearly half of the survey respondents said that more than half of their team members include members from other countries.[61] With virtual teams, team members do not have to meet face-to-face to be effective, thereby eliminating "dead time" caused by traveling. These teams operate across boundaries of time and geography and have become a necessity of everyday working life.

Virtual teams enable companies to accomplish things more quickly and efficiently. The times when virtual team members are in one place are few, especially when members are located across the globe. This often makes global teams more difficult to manage effectively. Communication is the key to keeping teams working effectively together.[62]

Some of the difficulties that virtual teams confront regarding communication are discussed next. Without face-to-face communication, team members often do not feel as connected or committed to the team. The virtual work environment does not provide opportunities to build trust that comes from proximity.[63] However, there are numerous considerations for building and maintaining trust. A willingness to give up some control is necessary. Professor Amy Wrzesniewski conducted a study in which she gave team members documents with different information that they could not share with each other. This requirement necessitated that individuals rely on their team members' interpretation of their own information. Wrzesniewski said, "The second you don't trust your team or think that they don't have your group's best interests in mind with respect to their conduct, people tend to take a collective step back." She added, "It's no longer a group that functions as tightly as it could."[64] Obviously, face-to-face communication is best for providing feedback followed by video, telephone, instant messaging, e-mail, and bulletin boards. E-mail and bulletin boards are generally best for tasks that require little collaboration such as information sharing. When teams need to solve complex problems or make decisions, technology such as videoconferencing or telepresence can be an asset.[65]

Communication problems between team members appear to be directly proportional to the number of time zones that separate them. An effective virtual leader rotates the time frames when conference calls for team meetings are going to be held so that the same people are not always inconvenienced. If it is only a couple of zones, teammates will be in their offices earlier or later than one another, but their workdays still overlap enough to allow phone calls. If the distance stretches from 9 to 12 time zones, workdays do not overlap at all, and e-mail and voice mail must be used.[66] There is also the language problem to contend with. Because English is becoming the world language, those for whom English is a second language may be at a disadvantage. Many Asians are concerned with saving face if they do not understand something. They may be hesitant to ask questions that would reveal their ignorance, thus widening the communication gap. On the other hand, those who are fluent only in English may be at a disadvantage when working with their international colleagues who move easily between their native languages, English, French, and Mandarin.[67]

There are some general rules to follow in selecting virtual team members. Chad Thompson, Aon Hewitt's senior consultant with the talent and rewards practice, believes that the best virtual workers are those who thrive on interdependent working relationships. He also believes that employees who do not mind or who like ambiguity in their job responsibilities and who have strong communication skills also tend to succeed in virtual work environments. Workers who have been labeled as "lone wolves" usually do not function well in a virtual team because they do not collaborate well.[68]

Virtual team members do not have the luxury of getting together over lunch or just communicating informally in the office. To overcome this lack of informal getting to know each other, Facebook, a discussion board, a team calendar, or a chat room might be beneficial. Team members can then connect with each other in ways other than meetings and establish a stronger group bond.[69]

14.4 Discuss global compensation practices.

Global Compensation

Companies that are successful in the global environment align their HR programs in support of their strategic business plans. A major component is the way the compensation program supports business structure, organization, and both global and regional operations.

Compensation for Host-Country Nationals

Certainly, in compensation-related matters, organizations should think globally but act locally. The realities of global business—in which each country has its own culture and different service expectations—must be reflected in the way employees are serviced.[70] Brad Boyson, head of HR and corporate services for Hamptons MENA, a property company with operations throughout the Middle East, believes that prudent HR professionals should, "benchmark on local conditions and add as needed."[71]

One reason that organizations relocate to other areas of the world is probably the high-wage pressures in the home country that threaten their ability to compete on a global basis. Globally, the question of what constitutes a fair day's pay is not as complicated as it is in the United States; normally, it is slightly above the prevailing wage rates in the area. The same is often true of benefits and nonfinancial rewards. Variations in laws, living costs, tax policies, and other factors all must be considered when a company is establishing global compensation packages. For example, Puerto Rico has laws that require paying severance pay and a Christmas bonus. Employers in Nigeria are required to provide a life insurance policy for employees at a rate of three times their salary. In Italy, a mandatory benefit is paid when an employee leaves an organization, regardless of whether this is because of resignation, termination, or retirement. In Belgium, employers offering a defined contribution pension scheme must provide a guaranteed investment return of 3.25 percent.[72]

Some countries have employment laws that feature specific criteria for terminations, including those related to layoffs, shutdowns, mergers and acquisitions, and discharge for cause. Other termination laws call for notice periods, severance requirements, payout of paid time off and incentive compensation, benefits continuation, and employee consent and grievance procedures.[73]

The company will want to create a precise picture of employment and working conditions to establish appropriate practices in each country. Some of the factors that should be considered include minimum-wage requirements, which often differ from country to country and even from city to city within a country; working-time information, such as annual holidays, vacation time and pay, paid personal days, standard weekly working hours, probation periods, and overtime restrictions and payments; and hiring and termination rules and regulations covering severance practices.

Culture often plays a part in determining compensation. North American compensation practices encourage individualism and high performance; continental European programs typically emphasize social responsibility; the traditional Japanese approach considers age and company service as primary determinants of compensation. In other countries, there is no guarantee that additional compensation will ensure additional output. It has been found that, in some countries, additional pay has resulted in employees' working less. As soon as employees have earned enough to satisfy their needs, time spent with family or on other noncompany activities is perceived as more valuable than additional cash. In former communist countries, people were used to a system in which pay and performance were not related. Under the old system, good employees were paid the same as poor performers. This practice is changing. Many communist countries' governments have loosened regulations that permit foreign for-profit companies to operate on their soils. Increasingly, as communist countries' governments have loosened regulations economies have incorporated noteworthy elements of market-driven business activities (e.g., U.S. profit-oriented joint venture companies in China), pay-for-performance practices have become more prevalent.

In countries such as France and Greece, where the best graduates often choose government positions with secure paychecks for life, it is quite difficult to attract good employees with pay schemes that include high bonuses for achieving specific objectives. In places such as Hong Kong, where people value risk and are motivated by personal financial gains, employees who have achieved a significant professional result expect a financial form of recognition (raise, bonus, or commission) within a matter of weeks. They are likely to look for another employer if they must wait until their next annual performance review. Whereas people in the United States derive great status from high pay, nations in large parts of Europe and Asia shun conspicuous wealth. In Italy, where teamwork is more valued than individual initiative, sales incentives for top sales professionals working in small teams can be demotivating. The recipient of a large award may feel awkward when receiving larger than a fair share of the reward pie.

Because of these and other cultural differences, it is difficult to design a global, one-size-fits-all pay scheme that attracts the best talent in all countries. In particular, pay-for-performance schemes often need to be adapted to local preferences, depending on whether income security or higher risks and returns are preferred.

Expatriate Compensation

Expatriate compensation provides exceptional challenges compared to home-country employment, such as developing packages that are reasonably cost-effective while still attractive and motivating. For expatriate managers and professionals, the situation is more complex than simply paying at or slightly above local host-country compensation rates. The largest expatriate costs historically have included overall remuneration, housing, cost-of-living allowances, and physical relocation. Most companies ensure that expatriates' compensation accounts for additional costs that may be associated with moving to and living in another country. The **balance sheet approach** provides expatriates the standard of living they normally enjoy in the United States or the expatriate's home country. Thus, the United States or the home country is the standard for all payments. This approach has strategic value to companies for two important reasons. First, this approach protects expatriates' standards of living. Without it, companies would have a difficult time placing qualified employees in international assignments. Second, the balance sheet approach enables companies to control costs because it relies on objective indexes that measure cost differences between the United States and foreign countries.

balance sheet approach
Provides expatriates the standard of living they normally enjoy in the United States or the expatriate's home country.

Employees receive allowances whenever the costs in the foreign country exceed the costs in the United States. Expense categories include housing and utilities, goods and services, discretionary income, and taxes. Allowance amounts vary according to the lifestyle enjoyed in the United States. Companies can obtain pertinent information about costs for foreign countries from at least three information sources. First, they can rely on expatriates who have spent considerable time on assignment or foreign government contacts. Second, private consulting companies (e.g., Towers Watson) or research companies (e.g., Bureau of National Affairs) can conduct custom surveys. Third, most U.S. companies consult the *U.S. Department of State Indexes of Living Costs Abroad, Quarters Allowances, and Hardship Differentials*, which is published quarterly by the U.S. Department of State.

In the past few years, additional challenges have hit companies as they have attempted to go global. First, the devaluation of the U.S. dollar has had a major impact on expatriate compensation. Also, there have been changes to the U.S. tax code that affect expatriate lifestyle. These challenges come at a time when global business is expanding. Meeting these challenges will affect how effectively the United States competes in the global market. In the past, expatriates regularly received a premium for taking an overseas assignment. Today, overseas jobs with rich expatriate packages are becoming less prevalent.[74]

14.5 Explain global safety, health, and employee and labor relations.

Global Safety, Health, and Employee and Labor Relations

As with the other HR functions, differences in safety, health, and employee and labor relations create challenges for HR professionals. We review each of these in turn.

Safety and Health

Special needs are often encountered when global safety and health issues are encountered. Global health care provider CIGNA International has teamed up with CIGNA Behavioral Health to offer employee assistance programs (EAPs) for expatriate employees of multinational firms. The EAP allows CIGNA International participants to access a multilingual support and counseling network. Employees and their dependents can receive assistance through telephone or personal visits for a wide range of behavioral health and work/life concerns. The program is designed to help employees better manage stress and anxiety, depression, and substance abuse, as well as to help them to lead healthy lifestyles.

Specific to global assignments are emergency evacuation services and global security protection. An international firm was preparing to evacuate 15 expatriate employees and dependents from a country that had suffered an earthquake. When it came time to meet at the departure point, 25 people showed up. Those arranging for the evacuation had not known that two technical teams were in the country supporting clients at the time.

Often, evacuation and care of injured employees is done through private companies. Medical emergencies are frightening under any circumstances, but when an employee becomes sick or injured abroad, it can be a traumatic experience. If the travelers are assigned to more remote or less-developed areas, companies should be aware that in many medical facilities, needles are often reused, equipment is not properly used, and there is a lack of basic medical supplies. Also, employees and their families living abroad must constantly be aware of security issues. Many firms provide bodyguards who escort executives everywhere. Some firms even have disaster plans to deal with evacuating expatriates if natural disasters, civil conflicts, or wars occur.

Global companies continue to face global safety risks. That is one of the lessons learned after the 1984 disaster in Bhopal, India, affected Union Carbide's worldwide operations. The Bhopal disaster was the worst industrial disaster in history. It was caused by the accidental release of 40 metric tons of methyl isocyanate (MIC) from a Union Carbide India, Limited (UCIL), pesticide plant located in the heart of the city of Bhopal, in the Indian state of Madhya Pradesh. UCIL was a joint venture between Union Carbide and a consortium of Indian investors. The accident in the early hours produced heavier-than-air toxic MIC gas, which rolled along the ground through the surrounding streets, killing thousands outright and injuring anywhere from 150,000 to 600,000 others, at least 15,000 of whom died later from their injuries. Some sources give much higher fatality figures.[75]

Health and safety professionals with international experience say one of the most important trends sweeping through successful multinational companies is the shift to a single safety management system that applies to all their operations throughout the world. Although the example of Bhopal revealed the risks of safety failures, experts emphasize that taking a global approach to safety and health is not only about avoiding problems. It opens a wealth of opportunities to improve performance. Although events on the scale of Bhopal are rare, many companies have discovered that the way they treat their workers anywhere on the planet can pose a risk to their corporate reputation.

Employers should also be concerned with health issues for HCNs. In many instances, employee health has deteriorated because of an increase in chronic disease and lifestyle-related health issues, not only in developed countries, but also in emerging economies such as Mexico, China, and India. Twenty years ago, less than 10 percent of Mexican adults were obese; today, 68 percent are overweight and the problem is becoming increasingly widespread in younger people. It is estimated that 57.2 percent of the Indian population will have diabetes by 2025. China and the Philippines are troubled by inconsistent health care, especially among the poor.[76]

Global Employee Relations

Moving the discussion of disciplinary action into the international arena often presents different situations. For instance, the punishment for an employee who stole $10,000 in the United States would likely lead to termination. This is not the case in Japan. A Japanese judge ruled that the $10,000 was too small an amount to justify termination and the worker was reinstated.[77]

The concept of employment at will is generally accepted in the United States. Remember that employment at will is an unwritten contract created when an employee agrees to work for an employer but no agreement exists as to how long the parties expect the employment to last. When it comes to discharging a worker who is not performing, it is much harder to do in Europe than in North America and other parts of the world. In fact, Europe may have the most employee-friendly laws. Even though they face global competition, unions in several European countries have resisted changing their laws and removing government protections. In many Western European countries, laws on labor unions and employment make it difficult to lay off employees. Laws make it hard to fire workers, so companies are reluctant to hire. It is also difficult to discipline a worker for poor performance in China. Laws tend to come down on the side of the employees when addressing disciplinary action.

In India, as soon as a company hires more than 100 employees, it is legally impossible to terminate anyone without permission of the government and then it must be because of criminal wrongdoing. Such laws have long discouraged foreign investors, held back manufacturing, and prevented the nation from experiencing industrial growth like China's.

Because of the differences in how governments view disciplinary action in the global environment, it is difficult for a global company to establish a standardized policy on disciplinary action. The company will want to create a precise picture of employment and working conditions to establish appropriate practices in each country. Some of the factors that should be considered include hiring and termination rules and regulations covering severance practices.[78]

Global Labor Relations

Obviously, the strength and nature of unions differ from country to country, with unions ranging from nonexistent to relatively strong. In fact, unionism in private companies is a declining phenomenon in nearly all developed countries. Codetermination, which requires firms to have union or worker representatives on their boards of directors, is common in European countries. Even though they face global competition, unions in several European countries have resisted changing their laws and removing government protections. Laws make it hard to fire workers, so companies are reluctant to hire. Generous and lengthy unemployment benefits discourage the jobless from seeking new work. Motorola paid a net pretax charge of about $83 million in related severance fees for jobs cut in Germany. Wage bargaining remains centralized, and companies have little flexibility to fashion contracts that fit their needs. High payroll taxes raise labor costs, and their laws mandating cumbersome layoff procedures increase the cost of the product.

On the other hand, in some South American countries, such as Chile, collective bargaining for textile workers, miners, and carpenters is prohibited. And unions are generally allowed only in companies of 25 workers or more. This practice has encouraged businesses to split into small companies to avoid collective bargaining, leaving workers on their own.

In China, the All-China Federation of Trade Unions (ACFTU) is the only government-recognized union. The ACFTU is putting pressure on foreign-invested enterprises to establish unions and sign collective contracts with their employees. Under the People's Republic of China (PRC) Trade Union Law, the employer, not employees, contributes union dues if the company is not unionized. The pressure to unionize through the collection of union dues is likely to continue with the support of ACFTU.[79]

There were 2,663 labor strikes in 2016, which is more than double the number in 2014.[80] Non-payment of wages accounts for most labor disputes in China.[81] For instance, a succession of strikes occurred at several factories in Guangdong and China's coastal regions. Workers at Honda Motor Company factories in several Guangdong cities demanded higher wages and better working conditions. Honda gave in, providing a 24 percent pay increase, which prompted work stoppages at several other facilities.[82]

Humiliation caused by a series of suicides at Foxconn, a subsidiary of Taiwan's Hon Hai Precision Industry Company, forced the company to give a 30 percent pay increase. The suicides were apparently in response to poor working conditions at the firm.[83] The new generation of Chinese factory workers, born during the 1980s and 1990s, are more sensitive to social issues and workplace rights than their parents. Previous generations might have taken any job available, even for low salaries, but, these young workers are seeking jobs that not only pay well but also provide a better life for their families, provide career development, and treat employees with respect.

14.6 Discuss globalization issues for small to medium-sized businesses.

Globalization for Small to Medium-Sized Businesses

International sales have become a vital and growing part of the market for small to medium-sized businesses.[84] A recent study found that nearly a quarter of U.S. small firms receive some sales from overseas, and another 6 percent is expected to join their ranks for a combined total of approximately one million small- to medium-sized business owners who engage in international sales in the near future.[85] Globalization, the Internet, and e-commerce have made it easier than ever for small businesses to reach the 95 percent of consumers that do not live in the United States. Exporting gives small businesses the opportunities to tap into new markets, increase sales, generate economies of scale, and improve inventory management, as well as help maintain U.S. competitiveness and create jobs.

As noted earlier in an FYI feature, U.S. exports totaled $1.47 trillion in 2016. Small- and medium-size businesses are important contributors to export activity. These firms accounted for 98 percent of exporters and approximately one-third of total export values.[86] To achieve this goal, the Small Business Administration (SBA) has programs available to help small businesses expand into exporting. In 2015, SBA supported about 1,500 export loans to small business, totaling more than $1.4 billion.[87] Export loan providers include the following:[88]

- *Export Working Capital Loans* are short-term loans of 12 months or less. These loans provide a line of credit for suppliers, inventory, or production of goods. As a result of the Small Business Jobs Act, the SBA guarantee on these loans is 90 percent, with the maximum size of the loan being $4.5 million.
- *Export Express Loans* help small businesses that need capital fast to take advantage of a possible overseas sale. They can help cover marketing materials, translation, or travel costs for a trade mission. These loans can get approval by the SBA within 36 hours. The Small Business Jobs Act increased loan sizes up $500,000 and are 90 percent guaranteed up to $350,000. There is also a 75 percent guarantee for loans larger than $350,000.
- *International Trade Loans* help businesses invest in real estate and working capital to support exporting over the long term. These loans can be used for expansion, renovation, and modernization of facilities or in some cases refinancing existing loans. Usually, these loans are needed when a few big orders from abroad start to flow in, and the business needs to expand to a larger location or buy equipment to meet demand. International Trade Loans can be for up to $5 million. They carry a 90 percent guarantee, and maturity is usually 10 to 15 years for machinery or 25 years for real estate.[89]

There are numerous examples where the SBA has been helpful. An Export Working Capital Loan helped Nidek Medical Products, Inc., a manufacturer of medical nebulizers and oxygen concentrators for 25 years with 40 employees. The company was focusing largely on international sales and had established distribution warehouses in South America and Europe. But carrying the receivables for export sales had created a cash crunch and put the company's finances in jeopardy. With assistance from the SBA, the company received a $1.3 million Export Working Capital Loan that solved its cash flow difficulties.

The move into global markets can be intimidating for leaders of smaller businesses, but HR professionals in these companies can help. They can learn more about the cultural and human capital factors that will have the biggest effect on new international initiatives. They can work with government and business groups to navigate the legal and bureaucratic environments that can make it difficult for businesses to get started in new markets.[90]

PREPARING FOR EXAMS/QUIZZES

Chapter Summary by Learning Objectives

1. ***Discuss the evolution of global business and the context for global human resource management.*** Most companies initially become global without making substantial investments in foreign countries by exporting, licensing, or franchising. A multinational corporation is a firm that is based in one country (the parent or home country) and produces goods or provides services in one or more foreign countries (host countries). A global corporation has corporate units in many countries that are integrated to operate as one organization worldwide.

   The world is experiencing an increasing global workforce. Global HR problems and opportunities are enormous and are expanding. Individuals dealing with global HR matters face a multitude of challenges beyond that of their domestic counterparts.

   HR practice in the United States is influenced by many factors. Some of these factors include country political and economic structure, the legal system, national cultural norms, and characteristics of the labor force. When practicing HR within any one country, these factors are relatively constant. For example, the United States has many worker protections such as antidiscrimination laws. Global HR practitioners require, at minimum, an appreciation of the variation in these four factors to understand how to best structure and implement HR practices in other countries.

2. ***Summarize global staffing practices.*** Companies must choose from various types of global staff members and may use specific approaches to global staffing. Global staff members may be selected from among three different types: expatriates, host-country nationals, and third-country nationals. There are four major approaches to global staffing: ethnocentric, polycentric, regiocentric, and geocentric.
3. ***Describe global performance management and human resource development practices.*** Some training and development professionals believe that performance appraisal as well as training and development strategies that work for a U.S. audience can be equally effective abroad. Unfortunately, nothing could be further from the truth. Also, global training and development is needed because people, jobs, and organizations are often quite different. The ideal expatriate preparation and development program includes pre-move orientation and training, continual development, and repatriation orientation and training.
4. ***Discuss global compensation practices.*** Globally, the question of what constitutes a fair day's pay for host-country nationals is not as complicated as it is in the United States; normally, it is slightly above the prevailing wage rates in the area. The same is often true of benefits and non-financial rewards.

   Expatriate compensation provides exceptional challenges compared to home-country employment, such as developing packages that are reasonably cost-effective while still attractive and motivating. For expatriate managers and professionals, the situation is more complex than simply paying at or slightly above local host-country compensation rates.
5. ***Explain global safety, health, and employee and labor relations.*** U.S.-based global operations are often safer and healthier than host-country operations but frequently not as safe as similar operations in the United States. A government's role in defining the circumstances under which an employer may discipline or fire employees, and the strength and nature of unions differ from country to country, with unions ranging from nonexistent to relatively strong.
6. ***Discuss globalization issues for small and medium-sized businesses.*** There has been a growing push among business organizations and the government to help small- and medium-sized businesses increase their exports. The SBA has programs available to help small businesses expand into exporting.

Key Terms

exporting 394
licensing 394
franchising 394
multinational corporation (MNC) 395
global corporation 395
cultural values 398
expatriate 400
host-country national (HCN) 400
third-country national (TCN) 400
ethnocentric staffing 400
polycentric staffing 401
regiocentric staffing 401
geocentric staffing 401
repatriation 405
balance sheet approach 408

MyLab Management

If your instructor is using MyLab Management, go to **www.pearson.com/mylab/management** to complete the problems marked with this icon ✪.

Questions for Review

14-1. How has global business evolved?

14-2. Define the following terms:
- (a) exporting
- (b) licensing
- (c) franchising
- (d) multinational corporation
- (e) global corporations

✪**14-3.** What are some global issues confronting women?

14-4. What are the various types of global staff members?

14-5. What is the general process for selecting expatriates?

✪**14-6.** Why is pre-move orientation and training of expatriates so important?

✪**14-7.** Why is repatriation orientation and training needed?

14-8. What is the importance of e-learning in the global environment?

14-9. What difficulties do virtual teams have in the global environment?

✪**14-10.** What is meant by the statement regarding compensation for host-country nationals, "Organizations should think globally but act locally"?

14-11. What has been the status of expatriate compensation in recent years?

14-12. What are factors to consider in global health and safety?

14-13. What are factors to consider in global employee and labor relations?

✪**14-14.** What are some problems and opportunities related to small- and medium-sized businesses in the global environment?

PREPARING FOR MY CAREER

P I A Personal Inventory Assessment

An additional Personal Inventory Assessment can be found on MyLab Management.

Multicultural Awareness Scale

This instrument assesses an individual's awareness of other cultures and cultural contexts. Specifically, how comfortable or aware you are with other cultures.

ETHICS DILEMMA

Meeting Customer Demand at Any Cost

Vivid Computers, a manufacturer of desktop and laptop computers, distinguishes itself from the competition with the most life-like graphics based on proprietary technology. The company outsources manufacturing of the all-important graphics cards to two companies. Pacific Coastal Manufacturing is in California and the other, Atlantic Ridge Manufacturing, is in a small island country where there are virtually no protective labor laws in place.

Demand for Vivid's computers has been explosive. Pacific Coastal has been operating at full capacity for some time now. Mandating substantial overtime or extended workweeks would violate local employment laws, resulting in enormous fines. Thus, Vivid turned its focus on Atlantic Ridge to ramp up production. The components manufacturer extended the workweek from five to seven days, added a third work shift, and instituted mandatory overtime at the regular pay rate, boosting each worker's weekly hours from 40 to 60. These changes have been in effect for nearly 18 months, which is enabling Vivid to keep up with demand.

Since the rule changes, more than half of the Atlantic Ridge workforce has been exhibiting telltale signs of undue stress. Sometimes, workers cope by taking time off from work. However, company managers routinely threaten to fire workers who take time off. In a three-month period, five workers experienced fatal heart attacks while on the job and three committed suicide at their work stations. There were no such catastrophic events prior to the work rule changes.

Marta O'Leary, Atlantic Ridge's operations manager, reported the unsustainable pace to Vivid's corporate office on multiple occasions, and she explained that the tragic events were undoubtedly the result of longer work hours. Bradley Fontaine, Vivid's vice president of worldwide operations, was not sympathetic to these concerns. Instead, he focused on the Atlantic Ridge plant's stellar productivity. Bradley also offered Marta a substantial salary increase and generous incentive pay opportunities tied to the plant's continued high productivity levels. Marta was stunned by Bradley's response to the situation.

14-15. What would you do?

14-16. What factor(s) in this ethics dilemma might influence a person to make a less than ethical decision?

HRM Is Everyone's Business

Expatriate deployment requires substantial interactions between HR professionals and the managers who wish to staff overseas jobs with expatriates. There are many issues besides selection that HR professionals and managers must consider before moving forward.

Action checklist for managers and HR—selecting and preparing employees for expatriate assignments

HR takes the lead

- ☑ HR professionals must first understand how a manager's plan to deploy an expatriate will fulfill business objectives and the necessary qualifications required to meet those objectives. The discussion could reveal that employing a host country national (HCN) makes better sense from a cost perspective and the HCN's knowledge of idiosyncratic business customs.
- ☑ Draft a selection procedure to identify the most qualified and willing employees to take overseas assignments. Selection decisions are not limited to an employee's qualifications. Family considerations addressing overall quality of life are essential—educational resources for children, housing, community, and employment opportunities for a partner or spouse.
- ☑ Customize preparatory activities, including cultural training and accommodation of family members, well in advance of departure. Language training may be necessary where the host country language differs.

- ☑ Craft a communication plan for regular interaction with the expatriate throughout the duration of the assignment to help ensure adjustment and connectedness with company developments.
- ☑ Anticipate the expatriate's return by identifying suitable job assignments. The assignment should be appropriately challenging and capitalize on the employee's added value from completing the overseas assignment.

Managers take the lead

- ☑ Managers should communicate their need for making an expatriate assignment. Essential information includes business objectives, costs and benefits to the company, quality of life considerations, expected length of the assignment, necessary skill sets, and working conditions.
- ☑ Recommend willing qualified candidates for the assignment and review qualifications in the context of established selection criteria.
- ☑ Explain how the expatriate's skill development and accomplishments can be fully utilized and identify career-enhancing options in advance of the expatriate's return to the home country.

HRM by the Numbers

An additional HRM by the Numbers exercise can be found on MyLab Management.

Illustrating the Balance Sheet Approach

A colleague will be soon departing for a one-year assignment (365 days) in Doha, Qatar. Most companies rely on the balance sheet approach to ensure that the employee does not incur more costs than they do at home because of the location change. For now, you are interested in estimating some of the factors, including your colleague's annual base pay and some of the various allowances he will receive while on assignment in Doha. Currently, his U.S. annual base pay is $125,000. The company routinely raises base pay 5 percent to reflect added responsibilities. The company also awards a 20 percent annual cost-of-living allowance and 10 percent annual hardship allowance (based on the higher annual base pay rate), an annual housing allowance equal to $29,500, and a $50 per diem (*daily* food allowance).

Questions

14-17. Calculate your colleague's annual base pay rate while on assignment in Doha.

14-18. Calculate, on an annual basis, the: (a) cost-of-living allowance; (b) hardship allowance; (c) housing allowance; and (d) per diem.

14-19. Based on your calculations in questions 14-17 and 14-18, how much will the company spend for this one-year assignment in Doha?

Working Together: Team Exercise

In small groups of three or four, come up with specific answers to the following questions. Talk through your perspectives with team members. Be prepared to share your ideas with the class.

Preparing employees for overseas assignments takes careful consideration. Assume that you work for a financial services company that is planning to open an office in Mumbai, India six months from now. A team of five managers will supervise the office opening, and they will be there for six months. Only one manager has previously worked in India. All five managers will work directly with the local management. Your job is to prepare this team for their assignment.

14-20. What are some of the topics appropriate for inclusion in a pre-departure training program? Discuss.

14-21. What are some of the issues you would address in advance of the expatriates' return? Explain.

INCIDENT 1 My Darling

Matilda has held several positions at McGill Enterprises in Chicago during the past 10 years. Most recently, she served as the U.S. call center manager. McGill is planning to open a call center in another country and offered Matilda the top spot. Matilda enthusiastically accepted this assignment and moved to her new location last month. Her first goal is to fill supervisory job vacancies. James Greenwood was the first candidate.

Matilda greeted James enthusiastically, "Welcome, James!" Then, she extended her hand to shake his. James did not do the same. Instead, he moved closer to Matilda and gave her a hug and a light peck on the cheek. Then, James responded to Matilda's verbal greeting, "It's so good to finally meet you, my darling."

As James sat down, he said, "Tell me about your family." He added, "Are they well?"

Matilda was shocked because she always took the lead in the interview process. She usually broke the ice by chatting about neutral subjects such as the weather or traffic conditions.

"Thank you, James, for taking the time to meet with me." Matilda added, "I don't see a good fit for you in our organization." Then, she asked James to leave.

Later that day, Matilda contacted Ashley Lamare, McGill's director of human resources, to discuss her experience. A long pause followed after Matilda relayed her story. Then, Ashley asked, "Matilda, did James do anything inappropriate?"

Surprised by Ashley's response, Matilda said, "Yes, Ashley. He called me "my darling," and then asked about my family." She added, "He hugged me, too!"

Ashley explained that using terms of endearment such as "my darling," "sweetheart," and "my love," are part of the regional dialect and typically are not suggestive of sexual interest or disrespect. In fact, both men and women use similar terms when greeting friends or others in the workplace, regardless of gender. Also, a gentle hug is a customary greeting in the workplace, much like the handshake.

"How was I supposed to know that?" Matilda responded defensively.

Ashley stated, "There is a lot of information about business etiquette and cultural norms on the Internet." She added, "Matilda, you are a manager and should know to take the initiative to learn local customs."

Questions

14-22. Do you believe that Matilda overreacted to James? Why or why not?

14-23. Should Ashley have taken responsibility to educate Matilda before she left on assignment? Or, was it Matilda's responsibility to educate herself? Explain.

14-24. Now educated about the location's cultural norms, Matilda decides to call James. What should she say to him? Explain.

INCIDENT 2 Was There Enough Preparation?

"Hi, Sam. How are the preparations going for your assignment in Japan?"

"Well, Elvis, I really feel prepared for the assignment, and the high level of apprehension I first experienced is gone."

"What exactly did the preparation program involve, Sam?"

"The experience was really exhaustive. First, I spent a good deal of time in a comprehensive orientation and training program. The program covered training and familiarization in the language, culture, history, living conditions, and local customs of Japan. Then, to make the transition back to home easier and better for my career, I have developed a plan with my boss that includes several trips back here to remain a key part of this operation. Also, my career development training will include the same training as the other managers in the home office. Finally, I was completely briefed on repatriation orientation and training that I would experience when I returned. Also, I was fully briefed on the compensation package, which appears to be fairly generous."

"That is great, Sam. Have you found a place to live yet?"

"Not yet, Elvis, but my wife and children are leaving in three days to meet with the company's relocation person to consider the various possibilities."

"How did the family like the orientation training, Sam?"

"Well, my wife ordered some Japanese language tapes, and I think she read all of the information that was covered in the class. She and the children will be fine because they have time to adapt; they don't have to hit the ground running like I do."

Questions

14-25. Do you believe that Sam's family is adequately prepared for the move to Japan? Why or why not?

14-26. Should the company's orientation program have included training for Sam's family? Discuss.

14-27. Is repatriation orientation and training necessary for Sam's family on their return to the United States?

MyLab Management

If your instructor is using MyLab Management, go to **www.pearson.com/mylab/management** for Auto-graded writing questions as well as the following Assisted-graded writing questions:

14-28. What are the approaches to global staffing?

14-29. What are some global employee and labor relations problems?

Endnotes

1 Fortune Global 500, 2016. Accessed April 24, 2017, at beta.fortune.com/global500/.

2 "The 25 Largest Consumer's Markets . . . . and the Outlook for 20015," *International Business Guide* online. Accessed April 24, 2017, at www.internationalbusinessguide.org/25-largest-consumers-markets-outlook-2015/.

3 "Country Comparison: GDP (Purchasing Power Parity)," *CIA World Factbook* online. Accessed April 24, 2017, at www.cia.gov/library/publications/the-world-factbook/rankorder/2001rank.html.

4 Eric Krell, "Be Global Risk Manager," *HR Magazine* 57 (March 2012): 81–84.

5 Jaime Santiago, "Exporting, Anyone?" *Caribbean Business* 39 (April 28, 2011): 21.

6 Central Intelligence Agency. "Country Comparison: Exports," *The World Factbook*. Accessed April 28, 2017, at www.cia.gov/library/publications/the-world-factbook/rankorder/2078rank.html.

7 Jose Pagliery, "The Hot Business of Exporting America's Franchises," *CNN Money* (July 12, 2013). Accessed April 1, 2014, at www.money.cnn.com.

8 "Franchising," *Export.gov*. Accessed April 10, 2017, at http://2016.export.gov/industry/franchising/.

9 Kay Marie Ainsley, "How American Fast Food Franchises Expanded Abroad," *The Balance* online (June 27, 2016). Accessed April 24, 2017, at www.thebalance.com/how-american-fast-food-franchises-expanded-abroad-1350955.

10 Margaret McEntire, "Best Practices for International Franchising: Be Aware of Cultural Differences," *Franchising World* 43 (March 2011): 29.

11 Bachir Mihoubi, "Dealing with the Complexities of International Expansion," *Franchising World* 43 (March 2011): 11–14.

12 Procter & Gamble, "Where We Operate." Accessed April 3, 2017, at www.pg.com/en_US/downloads/media/Fact_Sheets_Operate.pdf..

13 Procter & Gamble, "2016 P&G Annual Report." Accessed April 3, 2017, at www.pginvestor.com/.

14 Johnson & Johnson, "About Johnson & Johnson." Accessed April 24, 2017, at www.jnj.com/about-jnj.

15 Kathryn Tyler, "What Are Global Cultural Competencies?" *HR Magazine* 56 (May 2011): 44–46.

16 Kaveh Waddell, "Why Google Quite China—and Why It's Heading Back," *The Atlantic* online (January 19, 2016). Accessed April 1, 2017, at www.theatlantic.com; Steven Levy, "Google and Its Ordeal in China," *Fortune* 163 (May 2, 2011): 94–100.

17 U.S. Department of Labor, *Findings on the Worst Forms of Child Labor,* September 30, 2015.

18 The Hofstede Centre, "National Cultural Dimensions." Accessed March 31, 2014, at www.geert-hofstede.com.

19 "China's Working Population Fell Again," *The Wall Street Journal* (January 21, 2014). Accessed April 15, 2014, at www.wsj.com.

20 "China Birth Rate Up After One-Child Rule Change," *BBC News* online (January 23, 2017). Accessed April 24, 2017, at www.bbc.com.

21 "Japan's Sexual Apathy Is Endangering the Global Economy," *The Washington Post* (April 14, 2014). Accessed April 14, 2014, at www.washingtonpost.com.

22 Raymond Zhong and Saptarishi Dutta, "As Growth Slows in India, Rural Workers Have Fewer Incentives to Move to Cities," *The Wall Street Journal* (April 13, 2014). Accessed April 14, 2014, at www.wsj.com.

23 Hays, PLC "The Global Skills Landscape: A Complex Puzzle," *The Hays Global Index* (2016). Accessed April 24, 2017, at www.hays-index.com/wp-content/uploads/2016/09/Hays-GSI-Report-2016.pdf.

24 Richard Dobbs, Anu Madgavkar, et al., McKinsey Global Institute, *The World at Work: Jobs, Pay, and Skills for 3.5 Billion People* (June 2012).

25 "Progress of the World's Women 2015-2016," United Nations. Accessed April 24, 2017, at http://progress.unwomen.org.

26 Sewell Chan, "Let Women Drive, a Prince in Saudi Arabia Urges," *The New York Times* online (November 30, 2016). Accessed April 24, 2017, at www.nytimes.com.

27 Sylvia Ann Hewlett and Ripa Rashid, "The Battle for Female Talent in Emerging Markets," *Harvard Business Review* 88 (May 2010): 101–106.

28 Sewell Chan, "E.U. Legal Opinion Upholds Employer's Ban on Head Scarves," *The New York Times* online (May 31, 2016). Accessed April 25, 2017, at http://nytimes.com.

29 Ann Pace, "Chinese Women Flood the Global Talent Ranks," *T+D* 65 (June 2011): 20.

30 "Women in Business: Turning Promise into Practice," *Grant Thornton International Business* Report 2016. Accessed April 25, 2017, at www.grantthornton.am/en/publications/ibr/reports_2016.

31 Ibid.

32 The World Bank, "Labor Force, Female (% of Total Labor Force)," Accessed April 28, 2017, at http://worldbank.org.

33 "Rashmi Dalai, "Does Asia Still Need 'Traditional' Western Expats?" *The Wall Street Journal* online (September 15, 2015). Accessed February 27, 2017, at www.wsj.com.

34 Halliburton, "Corporation Profile." Accessed April 24, 2017, at www.halliburton.com.

35 Cindy Bigner, "Halliburton Finds the Best Talent in Every Country and Culture," *Profiles in Diversity Journal* 13 (May/June 2011): 47.

36 Rich Product Corporation, "About Us." Accessed April 25, 2017, at www.richs.com/about/.

37 Fay Hansen, "Looking South," *Workforce Management* 87 (April 21, 2008): 21–26.

38 Jeremy Eeskanazi, "When in Rome, Recruit Like the Romans Do: An Environmental Scan of the European Recruiting Landscape," *Journal of Corporate Recruiting Leadership* 5 (June 2010): 3–9.

39 Lorraine Bello and Galen Tinder, "Dual Career Implications on Workforce Mobility: The Evolution of the Relocating Spouse/Partner," *Benefits & Compensation Digest* 46 (September 2009): 36–39.

40 Ann Pace, "Training for the Leap Overseas," *T+D* 63 (August 2009): 18.

41 "Addressing 5 Gaps in Investigative Screening Programs," *Security Director's Report* 10 (October 2010): 4–6.

42 "Security Checks on Foreign Workers in UAE Soon," *Gulf News* online (January 10, 2017). Accessed April 25, 2017, at http://gulfnews.com.

43 Pamela Babcock, "Foreign Assignments," *HR Magazine* 50 (October 2005): 91–98.

44 Steven H. Appelbaum, Michel Roy, Terry Gilliland, "Globalization of Performance Appraisals: Theory and Applications," *Management Decision, 49* (2011): 570–585.

45 Hilla Peretz and Yitzhak Fried, "National Cultures, Performance Appraisal Practices, and Organizational Absenteeism and Turnover: A Study Across 21 Countries," *Journal of Applied Psychology, 97* (2012): 448–459.

46 Michael Laff, "Offshore Acclimation," *T+D* 63 (May 2009): 22–23.

47 Sara Toth Stub, "Coaching Grows as Expats Seek Help Managing Change," *The Wall Street Journal* online (August 16, 2017). Accessed April 25, 2017, at www.wsj.com.

48 Ibid.

49 Tim Burgess, "International Assignment Failure and Tracking Methods," *The Forum for Expatriate Management* online (August 20, 2016). Accessed April 28, 2017, at www.forum-expat-management.com/users/18563-tim-burgess/posts/11414-international-assignment-failure-and-tracking-methods.

50 Avan R. Jassawalla and Hermant C. Sashittal, "Thinking Strategically about Integrating Repatriated Managers in MNCs," *Human Resource Management* 48 (September/October 2009): 769–792.

51 Michelle V. Rafter, "Return Trip for Expats," *Workforce Management* 88 (March 16, 2009): 1–3.

52 Alice Andors, "Happy Returns," *HR Magazine* 55 (March 2010): 61–63.

53 Ronald Alsop, "When Expats Return Home, What's Next?" (January 16, 2014). *BBC*. Accessed June 2, 2014, at www.bbc.com. O Mishra Jitendra, "Repatriation," *Advances in Management* 4 (January 2011): 7–19.

54 "Elearning Market Trends and Forecast 2017-2021," *Docebo* (Web site). Accessed April 25, 2017, at www.docebo.com.

55 Roth, J. "5 Amazing eLearning Trends of 2016," *eLearning Industry* (Web site). Accessed April 24, 2017, at https://elearningindustry.com/5-amazing-elearning-trends-2016.

56 Andrea Edmundson, "When Cultural Values Interfere with Globalized E-learning," *MultiLingual* 21 (June 2010): 28–30.

57 Andrea Edmundson, "Culturally Accessible E-learning: An Overdue Global Business Imperative," *T+D* 63 (April 2009): 40–45.

58 Deepak Desai, "Globalization and the English Skills Gap," *Chief Learning Officer* 7 (June 2008): 62–63.

59 Hanif Sazen, "Keeping It Fresh," *e.learning age* (June 2005): 28–29.

60 "Trends in Global Virtual Teams: Virtual Teams Survey Report - 2016," RW^3 Culture Wizard (2016). Accessed May 1, 2017, at http://cdn.culturewizard.com/PDF/Trends_in_VT_Report_4-17-2016.pdf.

61 Ibid.

62 Lara Schlenkrich and Christopher Upfold, "A Guideline for Virtual Team Managers: The Key to Effective Social Interaction and Communication," *Electronic Journal of Information Systems Evaluation* 12 (2009): 109–118.

63 Marissa Garff, "The Virtual Reality," *T+D* 65 (August 2011): 22.

64 "Five Lessons for Global Virtual Teams," *Yale School of Management* (January 26, 2016). Accessed May 1, 2017, at http://som.yale.edu/news/2016/01/five-lessons-global-virtual-teams.

65 Darleen DeRosa, "Hello, Is Anybody Out There? Six Steps to High-Impact V-Meetings," *T+D* 65 (August 2011): 28–29.

66 "Leading the Virtual Team," *Associations Now* (May 2008): 18.

67 Elliott Masie, "A Global Learning Language," *Chief Learning Officer* 11 (January 2012): 10.

68 Bill Leonard, "Managing Virtual Teams," *HR Magazine* 56 (June 2011): 38–42.

69 Billie Williamson, "Managing Virtually: First, Get Dressed," *BusinessWeek Online* (June 17, 2009): 19.

70 Jeff Miller, "The Touchstones of Successful Global Benefits Outsourcing," *Benefits Quarterly* (2011 Second Quarter): 24–27.

71 David Tobenkin, "Learn the Landscape," *HR Magazine* 56 (May 2011): 51–54.

72 Vicki Taylor, "Benefits around the World," *Employee Benefits* (February 2006): Special Section, 8–9.

73 Yvette Lee, Lesa Albright, and Ruhal Dooley, "Tele-terminating, Terminating Employees Abroad, Recruiting Diversity," *HR Magazine* 55 (June 2010): 31–32.

74 Hashi Syedain, "From Expats to Global Citizens," *People Management* (January 2012): 22–26.

75 Wikipedia, "Bhopal Disaster." Accessed February 14, 2010, at http://en.wikipedia.org/wiki/Bhopal_disaster.

76 Randall Stram, "Globally, Wellness Programs Lead to Healthier Employees," *Benefits Magazine* 48 (March 2011): 22–25.

77 V. L., "When You Don't Get to Make the Rules," *Conference Board Review* 46 (January/February 2009): 37.

78 Neil B. Krupp, "Global Compensation Planning—Establishing and Maintaining a Competitive Edge in the International Marketplace," *Compensation & Benefits Management* 18 (Spring 2002): 54–56.

79 Lesli K. Ligorner and Todd Shengqiang Liao, "Unionization and Collective Bargaining: New Tools for Social Harmony," *China Business Review* 37 (November/December 2010): 28–31.

80 Hudson Lockett, "China Labour Unrest Spreads to 'New Economy'," *Financial Times* (February 1, 2017). Accessed March 20, 2017, at www.ft.com.

81 Simon Denyer, "Strikes and Workers' Protests Multiply in China, Testing Party Authority," *The Washington Post* online (February 25, 2016). Accessed April 15, 2017, at www.washington-post.com.

82 Luming Chen and Samuel Estreicher, "A New Labor Era: Higher Costs and Greater Pressures," *China Business Review* 38 (April–June 2011): 26–29.

83 "The Next China," *Economist* 396 (July 31, 2010): 48–50.

84 Graziella Sicoli, "Evolving Dynamics in the Process of Business Internationalization," *Global Journal of Business Research* 6 (2012): 117–124.

85 "International Small Businesses Need Facebook, Twitter," *Channel Insider* (June 23, 2011): 1.

86 U.S. Census Bureau, "A Profile of U.S. Importing and Exporting Companies, 2013–2014," (CB16-47, April 5, 2016). Accessed May 1, 2017, at www.census.gov/foreign-trade/Press-Release/edb/2014/edbrel.pdf.

87 U.S. Small Business Association, "Summary of Performance and Financial Information: Fiscal Year–2015." Accessed May 1, 2017, at www.sba.gov/sites/default/files/files/SBA-SPFI-Report-2015.pdf.

88 U.S. Small Business Association, "SBA Export Loan Programs." Accessed May 1, 2017, at www.sba.gov/loans-grants/see-what-sba-offers/sba-loan-programs/general-small-business-loans-7a.

89 U.S. Small Business Association, "SBA Export Loan Programs." Accessed May 1, 2017, at www.sba.gov/loans-grants/see-what-sba-offers/sba-loan-programs/general-small-business-loans-7a/special-types-7a-loans/sba-export-loan-programs.

90 Jennifer Schramm, "Think Globally," *HR Magazine* 56 (June 2011): 56.

Glossary

Achievement tests A test of current knowledge and skills.

Active job seekers Individuals committed to finding another job, whether presently employed or not.

Adverse impact Takes place when an employment decision, practice or policy has a disproportionately negative effect on a protected group. Oftentimes, it may be thought of as *unintentional discrimination.*

Affirmative Action Refers to the expectation and program requirements that companies make a positive effort to recruit, hire, train, and promote employees from groups who are underrepresented in the labor force.

Affirmative action program (AAP) Approach developed by organizations with government contracts to demonstrate that workers are employed in proportion to their representation in the firm's relevant labor market.

Agency shop Labor agreement provision requiring, as a condition of employment, that each non-union member of a bargaining unit pay the union the equivalent of membership dues as a service charge in return for the union acting as the bargaining agent.

Alcoholism Medical disease characterized by uncontrolled and compulsive drinking that interferes with normal living patterns.

AllianceQ Group of *Fortune 500* companies, along with more than 3,000 small- and medium-sized companies, that have collaborated to create a pool of job candidates.

Alternative dispute resolution (ADR) Procedure whereby the employee and the company agree ahead of time that any problems will be addressed by an agreed-on means.

American Federation of Labor and Congress of Industrial Organizations (AFL-CIO) Central trade union federation in the United States.

Applicant pool Number of qualified applicants recruited for a particular job.

Apprenticeship training Training method that combines classroom instruction with on-the-job training.

Aptitude tests A test of how well a person can learn or acquire skills or abilities.

Arbitration Process in which a dispute is submitted to an impartial third party for a binding decision; an arbitrator basically acts as a judge and jury.

Assessment center Selection technique that requires individuals to perform activities similar to those they might encounter in an actual job.

Attitude survey Survey that seeks input from employees to determine their feelings about topics such as the work they perform, their supervisor, their work environment, flexibility in the workplace, opportunities for advancement, training and development opportunities, and the firm's compensation system.

Authorization card Document indicating that an employee wants to be represented by a labor organization in collective bargaining.

Availability forecast Determination of whether the firm will be able to secure employees with the necessary skills, and from what sources.

Baby boomers People born just after World War II through the mid-1960s.

Balance sheet approach Provides expatriates the standard of living they normally enjoy in the United States or the expatriate's home country.

Bargaining unit Group of employees, not necessarily union members, recognized by an employer or certified by an administrative agency as appropriate for representation by a labor organization for purposes of collective bargaining.

Base pay The monetary compensation employees earn on a regular basis for performing their jobs. Hourly pay and salary are the main forms of base pay.

Beachhead demands Demands that the union does not expect management to meet when they are first made.

Behavior change Change in job-related behaviors or performance that can be attributed to training.

Behavior modeling Training and development method that permits a person to learn by copying or replicating behaviors of others to show managers how to handle various situations.

Behavioral encouragement plans Individual incentive pay plans that reward employees for specific such behavioral accomplishments as good attendance.

Behavioral interview Structured interview where applicants are asked to relate actual incidents from their past relevant to the target job.

Behavioral observation scale (BOS) A specific kind of behavioral system for evaluating job performance by illustrating positive incidents (or behaviors) of job performance for various job dimensions.

Behavioral systems Performance appraisal methods that focus on distinguishing between successful and unsuccessful behaviors.

Behaviorally anchored rating scale (BARS) method Performance appraisal method that combines elements of the traditional rating scale and critical incident methods; various performance levels are shown along a scale with each described in terms of an employee's specific job behavior.

Benchmarking Process of monitoring and measuring a firm's internal processes, such as operations, and then comparing the data with information from companies that excel in those areas.

Bias errors Evaluation errors that occur when the rater evaluates the employee based on a personal negative or positive opinion of the employee rather than on the employee's actual performance.

Blended training The use of multiple training methods to deliver training and development.

Board interview An interview approach in which several of the firm's representatives interview a candidate at the same time.

Bottom-up forecast Forecasting method in which each successive level in the organization, starting with the lowest, forecasts its requirements, ultimately providing an aggregate forecast of employees needed.

Boycott Agreement by union members to refuse to use or buy the firm's products.

Broadbanding Compensation technique that collapses many pay grades (salary grades) into a few wide bands to improve organizational effectiveness.

Burnout Incapacitating condition in which individuals lose a sense of the basic purpose and fulfillment of their work.

Business games Training and development method that permits participants to assume roles such as president, controller, or marketing vice-president of two or more similar hypothetical organizations and compete against each other by manipulating selected factors in a particular business situation.

Capital The factors that enable companies to generate income, higher company stock prices, economic value, strong positive brand identity, and reputation. There is a variety of capital that companies use to create value, including financial capital (cash) and capital equipment (state-of-the-art robotics used in manufacturing).

Card check Organizing approach by labor in which employees sign a non-secret card of support if they want unionization, and if 50 percent of the workforce plus one worker sign a card, the union is formed.

Career General course that a person chooses to pursue throughout his or her working life.

Career development Formal approach used by the organization to ensure that people with the proper qualifications and experiences are available when needed.

Career path A flexible line of movement through which a person may travel during his or her work life.

Career planning Ongoing process whereby an individual sets career goals and identifies the means to achieve them.

Caregiver (family responsibility) discrimination Discrimination against employees based on their obligations to care for family members.

Carpal tunnel syndrome (CTS) Common repetitive stress injury caused by pressure on the median nerve that occurs as a result of a narrowing of the passageway that houses the nerve.

Case study Training and development method in which trainees are expected to study the information provided in the case and make decisions based on it.

Cash balance plan Retirement plan with elements of both defined benefit and defined contribution plans.

Change to Win Coalition Union federation consisting of seven unions that broke from the AFL-CIO and formally launched a rival labor federation representing about 6 million workers from seven labor unions.

Checkoff of dues Agreement by which a company agrees to withhold union dues from members' paychecks and to forward the money directly to the union.

Classification method Job evaluation method in which classes or grades are defined to describe a group of jobs.

Clawback policy Allows the company to recover compensation if subsequent review indicates that payments were not calculated accurately or performance goals were not met.

Cliff vesting schedule Employers must grant employees 100 percent vesting after no more than three service years. That is, after three years of participation in the retirement plan, an employee has the right to receive all the accrued employer's contributions made on the employee's behalf.

Closed shop Arrangement making union membership a prerequisite for employment.

Coaching Often considered a responsibility of the immediate boss, who provides assistance much like a mentor, but the primary focus is about performance.

Code of ethics Establishes the rules that the organization lives by. The code of ethics helps employees know what to do when there is not a rule for something.

Cognitive ability tests Tests that determine general reasoning ability, memory, vocabulary, verbal fluency, and numerical ability.

Coinsurance The percentage of covered expenses paid by the insured. Most fee-for-service plans stipulate 20 percent coinsurance. This means that the insured will pay 20 percent of covered expenses, whereas the insurance company pays the remaining 80 percent.

Collective bargaining The process in which labor union leadership enters into good faith negotiations with management representatives over terms of employment such as work hours, pay, and job security.

Collective bargaining agreements Written documents that describe the terms of employment reached between management and unions.

Committee on Political Education (COPE) Political arm of the AFL-CIO.

Company stock The total equity or worth of the company.

Company stock shares Equity segments of equal value, which increase with the number of stock shares held.

Comparison systems A type of performance appraisal method; requires that raters (e.g., supervisors) evaluate a given employee's performance against other employees' performance attainments. Employees are ranked from the best performer to the poorest performer.

Compensation policy Policies that provide general guidelines for making compensation decisions.

Compensation survey A means of obtaining data regarding what other firms are paying for specific jobs or job classes within a given labor market.

Competencies An individual's capability to orchestrate and apply combinations of knowledge, skills, and abilities consistently over time to perform work successfully in the required work situations.

Competency modeling All of the competencies necessary for success in a group of jobs that are set within an industry context.

Competency-based pay Compensation plan that rewards employees for the capabilities they attain.

Compressed workweek Any arrangement of work hours that permits employees to fulfill their work obligation in fewer days than the typical five-day workweek.

Construct validity Test validation method that determines whether a test measures certain constructs, or traits, that job analysis finds to be important in performing a job.

Consumer-driven health care plans Refers to the objective of helping companies maintain control over costs, while also enabling employees to make greater choices about health care.

Content validity Test validation method whereby a person performs certain tasks that are required by the job or completes a paper-and-pencil test that measures relevant job knowledge.

Contingent workers Described as the "disposable American workforce" by a former Secretary of Labor, have a nontraditional relationship with the worksite employer, and work as part-timers, temporaries, or independent contractors.

Contrast errors A rating error in which a rater (e.g., a supervisor) compares an employee to other employees rather than to specific explicit performance standards.

Copayments The fixed amounts that vary by the service. For example, the copayment to visit the primary care physician tends to be lowest (e.g., $20) and emergency room visits are usually most expensive (e.g., $250).

Corporate career Web sites Job sites accessible from a company home page that list available company positions and provide a way for applicants to apply for specific jobs.

Corporate culture System of shared values, beliefs, and habits within an organization that interacts with the formal structure to produce behavioral norms.

Corporate social responsibility (CSR) Implied, enforced, or felt obligation of managers, acting in their official capacity, to serve or protect the interests of groups other than themselves.

Corporate sustainability Concerns with possible future impact of an organization on society, including social welfare, the economy, and the environment.

Corporate university Training and development delivery system provided under the umbrella of the organization.

Cost-of-living adjustment (COLA) Escalator clause in a labor agreement that automatically increases wages as the U.S. Bureau of Labor Statistics cost-of-living index rises.

Country's culture Set of values, symbols, beliefs, languages, and norms that guide human behavior within the country.

Craft union Bargaining unit, such as the Carpenters and Joiners Union, which is typically composed of members of a trade or skill in a specific locality.

Criterion-related validity Test validation method that compares the scores on selection tests to some aspect of job performance determined, for example, by performance appraisal.

Critical incident technique (CIT) Performance appraisal method that requires keeping written records of highly favorable and unfavorable employee work actions.

Cross-training Type of training for educating team members about the other members' jobs so that they may perform them when a team member is absent, is assigned to another job in the company, or has left the company altogether.

Cultural values The norms for behaviors and beliefs.

Customized benefit plan Benefit plan that permits employees to make yearly selections to largely determine their benefit package by choosing between taxable cash and numerous benefits.

Decertification Reverse of the process that employees must follow to be recognized as an official bargaining unit.

Defined benefit plan Retirement plan that provides the participant with a fixed benefit upon retirement.

Defined contribution plan Retirement plan that permits employees to contribute to their accounts based on a chosen percentage of annual pay. At their discretion, the company makes matching contributions.

Demotion Process of moving a worker to a lower level of duties and responsibilities, which typically involves a reduction in pay.

Development Learning that goes beyond today's job and has a more long-term focus.

Direct financial compensation (monetary compensation) Pay that a person receives in the form of wages, salaries, commissions, and bonuses.

Disciplinary action Invoking a penalty against an employee who fails to meet established standards.

Disciplinary action without punishment Process in which a worker is given time off with pay to think about whether he or she wants to follow the rules and continue working for the company.

Discipline State of employee self-control and orderly conduct that indicates the extent of genuine teamwork within an organization.

Discretionary benefits Benefit payments made as a result of unilateral management decisions in nonunion firms and from labor/management negotiations in unionized firms.

Disparate treatment Occurs when an employer treats some employees less favorably than others because of race, religion, sex, national origin, or age. It may be thought of as *intentional discrimination*.

Diversity Any perceived difference among people: age, race, religion, functional specialty, profession, sexual orientation, geographic origin, lifestyle, tenure with the organization or position, and any other perceived difference.

Diversity management Ensuring that factors are in place to provide for and encourage the continued development of a diverse workforce by melding actual and perceived differences among workers to achieve maximum productivity.

Downsizing Reverse of a company growing; it suggests a one-time change in the organization and the number of people employed (also known as restructuring or rightsizing).

Dual-career family A situation in which both spouses or partners have jobs and family responsibilities.

Dual-career path Career path that recognizes that technical specialists can and should be allowed to contribute their expertise to a company without having to become managers.

E-learning Training and development method for online instruction using technology-based methods such as DVDs, company intranets, and the Internet.

Employee assistance program (EAP) Comprehensive approach that many organizations have taken to deal with burnout, alcohol and drug abuse, and other emotional disturbances.

Employee referral An employee of the company recommends a friend or associate as a possible member of the company; this continues to be the way that top performers are identified.

Employee requisition Document that specifies job title, department, the date the employee is needed for work, and other details.

Employee stock plans The right to purchase shares of company stock.

Employer branding Firm's corporate image or culture created to attract and retain the type of employees the firm is seeking.

Employment at will Unwritten contract created when an employee agrees to work for an employer but no agreement exists as to how long the parties expect the employment to last.

Employment interview Goal-oriented conversation in which an interviewer and an applicant exchange information.

Equal Employment Opportunity (EEO) The set of laws and policies that requires all individuals' rights to equal opportunity in the workplace, regardless of race, color, sex, religion, national origin, age, or disability.

Ergonomics Process of designing the workplace to support the capabilities of people and job or task demands.

Errors of central tendency Error that occurs when raters (e.g., supervisors) judge all employees as average or close to average.

Ethics Discipline dealing with what is good and bad, or right and wrong, or with moral duty and obligation.

Ethnocentric staffing Staffing approach in which companies primarily hire expatriates to staff higher-level foreign positions.

Event recruiting Recruiters going to events being attended by individuals the company is seeking.

Executive A top-level manager who reports directly to a corporation's CEO or to the head of a major division.

Executive order (EO) Directive issued by the president that has the force and effect of law enacted by Congress as it applies to federal agencies and federal contractors.

Exempt employees Employees categorized as executive, administrative, professional, or outside salespersons.

Exit interview Means of revealing the real reasons employees leave their jobs; it is conducted before an employee departs the company and provides information on how to correct the causes of discontent and reduce turnover.

Expatriate Employee who is not a citizen of the country in which the firm operations are located but is a citizen of the country in which the organization is headquartered.

Exporting Selling abroad, either directly or indirectly, by retaining foreign agents and distributors.

Factor comparison method Job evaluation method that assumes there are five universal factors consisting of mental requirements, skills, physical requirements, responsibilities, and working conditions; the evaluator makes decisions on these factors independently.

Fee-for-service plans Provide protection against health care expenses in the form of a cash benefit paid to the insured or directly to the health care provider after the employee has received health care services. These plans pay benefits on a reimbursement basis. Three types of eligible health expenses are hospital expenses, surgical expenses, and physician charges.

Final-offer arbitration An arbitration procedure used in the public sector whereby the arbitrator selects one party's offer either as a package or issue-by-issue selection.

First-impression effect An initial favorable or unfavorable judgment about an employee's which is ignored or distorted.

Flextime Practice of permitting employees to choose their own working hours, within certain limitations.

Flooding the community Process of the union inundating communities with organizers to target a business in an organizing attempt.

Forced distribution method Performance appraisal method in which the rater is required to assign individuals in a work group to a limited number of categories, like a normal frequency distribution.

Formal assessment The use of established external approaches to facilitate evaluation of an issue at hand.

401(k) plan Defined contribution plan in which employees may defer income up to a maximum amount allowed.

Franchising Option whereby the parent company grants another firm the right to do business in a prescribed manner.

Free agents People who take charge of all or part of their careers by being their own bosses or by working for others in ways that fit their needs or wants.

Gain sharing Plans that describe group incentive systems that reward employees with an incentive payment based on improved company performance for increased productivity, increased customer satisfaction, lower costs, or better safety records.

General duty clause As used by OSHA, employers are required to furnish, to each employee, a place of employment that is free from recognizable hazards that are causing, or likely to cause, death or serious physical harm to the employee.

General Schedule Classification of federal government jobs into 15 classifications (GS-1 through GS-15), based on such factors as skill, education, and experience levels. In addition, jobs that require high levels of specialized education (e.g., a physicist), significantly influence public policy (e.g., law judges), or require executive decision making are classified in three additional categories: Senior Level (SL), Scientific & Professional (SP) positions, and the Senior Executive Service (SES).

Generalist A person who may be an executive and performs tasks in a variety of HR-related areas.

Generation X Label affixed to the 40 million American workers born between the mid-1960s and late 1970s.

Generation Y Comprises people born between the late 1970s and mid-1990s.

Generation Z or Digital Natives Internet-assimilated children born between 1995 and 2009.

Genetic tests Tests given to identify predisposition to inherited diseases, including cancer, heart disease, neurological disorders, and congenital diseases.

Geocentric staffing Staffing approach that uses a worldwide integrated business strategy.

Glass ceiling Invisible barrier in organizations that impedes women and minorities from career advancement.

Global corporation Organization that has corporate units in a number of countries that are integrated to operate as one organization worldwide.

Golden parachute contract Perk that protects executives if another company acquires their firm or if the executive is forced to leave the firm for other reasons.

Graphoanalysis Use of handwriting analysis as a selection factor.

Grievance Employee's dissatisfaction or feeling of personal injustice relating to his or her employment.

Grievance procedure A formal, systematic process that permits employees to express complaints without jeopardizing their jobs.

Group interview Meeting in which several job applicants interact in the presence of one or more company representatives.

Halo error (positive halo error) Evaluation error that occurs when a manager generalizes one positive performance feature or incident to all aspects of employee performance, resulting in a higher rating.

Health Employees' freedom from physical or emotional illness.

Health savings accounts (HSAs) Tax-free health spending and savings accounts available to individuals and families who have qualified high-deductible health insurance policies as determined by IRS regulation.

High-deductible health insurance plans (HDHPs) Plans that require substantially higher deductibles compared to managed care plans and traditional fee-for-service plans.

Horn error (negative halo error) Evaluation error that occurs when a manager generalizes one negative performance feature or incident to all aspects of employee performance, resulting in a lower rating.

Host-country national (HCN) Employee who is a citizen of the country where the subsidiary is located.

Hot stove rule An approach to disciplinary action that have four consequences which are analogous to touching a hot stove.

Hourly pay (wage) One type of base pay. Employees earn hourly pay for each hour worked.

HR outsourcing (HRO) Process of hiring external HR professionals to do the HR work that was previously done internally.

Human capital As defined by economists, refers to sets of collective skills, knowledge, and ability that employees can apply to create economic value for their employers.

Human capital theory A theory premised on the idea that employees' knowledge and skills generate productive capital known as human capital. Employees can develop knowledge and skills from formal education or on-the-job experiences.

Human resource development (HRD) Major HRM function consisting not only of training and development, but also of individual career planning and development activities, organization development, and performance management and appraisal.

Human resource ethics Application of ethical principles to HR relationships and activities.

Human resource information system (HRIS) Any organized approach for obtaining relevant and timely information on which to base HR decisions.

Human resource management (HRM) Utilization of individuals to achieve organizational objectives.

Human resource manager or human resource management professional Individual who normally acts in an advisory or staff capacity, working with other managers to help them deal with HR matters.

Human resource planning Systematic process of matching the internal and external supply of people with job openings anticipated in the organization over a specified period.

Illegal discriminatory bias A bias error for which a supervisor rates members of his or her race, gender, nationality, or religion more favorably than members of other classes.

Interindustry wage or compensation differentials Pattern of pay and benefits associated with characteristics of industries.

In-basket training Training and development method in which the participant is asked to establish priorities for and then handle a number of business papers, e-mail messages, memoranda, reports, and telephone messages that would typically cross a manager's desk.

Incentive pay Compensation, other than base wages or salaries, that fluctuates according to employees' attainment of some standard (e.g., a pre-established formula, individual or group goals, or company earnings).

Indirect financial compensation (employee benefits) Refers to extrinsic compensation other than hourly wages or annual salary. This form of compensation includes a wide variety of rewards of monetary value such as such as paid vacation and medical care.

Industrial union Bargaining unit that generally consists of all the workers in a particular plant or group of plants.

Interest arbitration Arbitration that involves disputes over the terms of proposed collective bargaining agreements.

Interindustry wage or compensation differentials Pattern of pay and benefits associated with characteristics of industries.

Internal employee relations Those HR management activities associated with the movement of employees within the organization.

Internet recruiter Person whose primary responsibility is to use the Internet in the recruitment process (also called cyber recruiter).

Internship Special form of recruitment that involves placing a student in a temporary job with no obligation either by the company to hire the student permanently or by the student to accept a permanent position with the firm following graduation.

Job Group of tasks that must be performed for an organization to achieve its goals.

Job analysis Systematic process of determining the skills, duties, and knowledge required for performing jobs in an organization.

Job bidding Procedure that permits employees who believe that they possess the required qualifications to apply for a posted position.

Job description Document that provides information regarding the essential tasks, duties, and responsibilities of a job.

Job design Process of determining the specific tasks to be performed, the methods used in performing these tasks, and how the job relates to other work in an organization.

Job enlargement Increasing the number of tasks a worker performs, with all of the tasks at the same level of responsibility.

Job enrichment Changes in the content and level of responsibility of a job so as to provide greater challenges to the worker.

Job evaluation Process that determines the relative value of one job in relation to another.

Job fair Recruiting method engaged in by a single employer or group of employers to attract a large number of applicants to one location for interviews.

Job hazard analysis (JHA) Multi-step process designed to study and analyze a task or job and then break down that task into steps that provide a means of eliminating associated hazards.

Job-based pay Employee compensation for jobs employees currently perform.

Job-knowledge tests Tests designed to measure a candidate's knowledge of the duties of the job for which he or she is applying.

Job posting Procedure for informing employees that job openings exist.

Job rotation (cross-training) Moves employees from one job to another to broaden their experience.

Job sharing Two part-time people split the duties of one job in some agreed-on manner and are paid according to their contributions.

Job specification A document that outlines the minimum acceptable qualifications a person should possess to perform a particular job.

Jobs Network of employment Web sites where any company can list job openings for free.

Just cause A standard for determining whether to terminate an employee and the standard is based on whether an employee violated company policy or work rules and the severity of the violation.

Just-in-time training (on-demand training) Training provided anytime, anywhere in the world when it is needed.

Keyword résumé Résumé that contains an adequate description of the job seeker's characteristics and industry-specific experience presented in keyword terms to accommodate the computer search process.

Keywords Words or phrases that are used to search databases for résumés that match.

Labor market Potential employees located within the geographic area from which employees are recruited.

Labor unions Organizations that exist to represent the interests of employees in the workplace and to ensure fair treatment when conflicts arise between one or more employee and management.

Lateral skill path Career path that allows for lateral moves within the firm, taken to permit an employee to become revitalized and find new challenges.

Learning The extent to which an employee understands and retains principles, facts, and techniques.

Learning organization Firm that recognizes the critical importance of continuous performance-related training and development and takes appropriate action.

Leniency error Giving an undeserved high performance appraisal rating to an employee.

Licensing Arrangement whereby an organization grants a foreign firm the right to use intellectual properties such as patents, copyrights, manufacturing processes, or trade names for a specific period of time.

Likes and dislikes survey Procedure that helps individuals in recognizing restrictions they place on themselves.

Line managers Individuals directly involved in accomplishing the primary purpose of the organization.

Local union Basic element in the structure of the U.S. labor movement.

Lockout Management keeps employees out of the workplace and runs the operation with management personnel or replacements.

Maintenance of membership Employees who are members of the union at the time the labor agreement is signed or who later voluntarily join must continue their memberships until the termination of the agreement as a condition of employment.

Managed care plans Health care delivery that emphasizes cost control by limiting an employee's choice of doctors and hospitals. These plans also provide protection against health care expenses in the form of prepayment to health care providers.

Management development Consists of all learning experiences provided by an organization resulting in upgrading skills and knowledge required in current and future managerial positions.

Management incentive plans Bonuses to managers who meet or exceed objectives based on sales, profit, production, or other measures for their division, department, or unit.

Management-by-objectives (MBO) Performance appraisal technique. Supervisors and employees determine objectives for employees to meet during the rating period and employees appraise how well they have achieved their objectives. MBO is used mainly for managerial and professional employees and typically evaluates employees' progress toward strategic planning objectives.

Mandatory bargaining issues Bargaining issues that fall within the definition of wages, hours, and other terms and conditions of employment.

Market lag policies Pay policy that distinguishes companies from the competition by compensating employees less than most competitors. Lagging the market indicates that market levels fall below the market match line.

Market lead policies Pay policy that distinguishes companies from the competition by compensating employees more highly than most competitors. Leading the market denotes market levels above the market match line.

Market match policies Average pay that most employers provide for a similar job in a particular area or industry.

Matching contribution Money the employer deposits into an employee's defined contribution account contingent on the employee contributing first.

Mediation Neutral third party enters the negotiations and attempts to facilitate a resolution to a labor dispute when a bargaining impasse has occurred.

Mentoring Approach to advising, coaching, and nurturing for creating a practical relationship to enhance individual career, personal, and professional growth and development.

Merit bonuses Lump sum monetary awards based on employees' past job performances. Employees do not continue to receive nonrecurring merit increases every year. Employees must instead earn them each time.

Merit pay Pay increase added to employees' base pay based on their level of performance.

Mission Unit's continuing purpose, or reason for being.

Multinational corporation (MNC) Firm that is based in one country (the parent or home country) and produces goods or provides services in one or more foreign countries (host countries).

Musculoskeletal disorders (MSDs) Conditions that affect the body's muscles, joints, tendons, ligaments, and nerves.

NACElink Network An alliance among the National Association of Colleges and Employers, DirectEmployers Association, and Symplicity Corporation; a national recruiting network and suite of Web-based recruiting and career services automation tools serving the needs of colleges, employers, and job candidates.

National union Organization composed of local unions, which it charters.

Negative halo effect See *horn error*.

Negligent hiring Liability a company incurs when it fails to conduct a reasonable investigation of an applicant's background, and then assigns a potentially dangerous person to a position where he or she can inflict harm.

Negligent retention Liability an employer may incur when a company keeps persons on the payroll whose records indicate strong potential for wrongdoing and fails to take steps to defuse a possible violent situation.

Network career path Method of career progression that contains both a vertical sequence of jobs and a series of horizontal opportunities.

Niche sites Web sites that cater to highly specialized job markets such as a particular profession, industry, education, location, or any combination of these specialties.

Nominal hourly compensation The face value of a dollar.

Nonexempt employees Employees not categorized as executive, administrative, professional, or outside salespersons, and required to receive overtime pay for work beyond the completion of standard work hours.

Nonfinancial compensation Derives from within an employee's self. For example, nonfinancial compensation can come from the satisfaction that a person receives from the job itself or from the psychological or environment in which the person works.

Nonqualified plans Welfare and pension plans that do not meet at least one requirement set forth by the Employee Retirement Income Security Act of 1974 (ERISA), disallowing favorable tax treatment for employee and employer contributions.

Norm Frame of reference for comparing an applicant's performance with that of others.

Objectivity Condition that is achieved when everyone scoring a given test obtains the same results.

Offboarding Facilitates employee departure from the company by assisting the completion of exit tasks, including exit interviews, forms completion, the return of company property, and ensuring that employees receive the appropriate extended benefits.

Ombudsperson Complaint officer with access to top management who hears employee complaints, investigates, and recommends appropriate action.

Online higher education Educational opportunities including degree and training programs that are delivered, either entirely or partially, via the Internet.

On-the-job-training (OJT) An informal training and development method that permits an employee to learn job tasks by performing them.

Open shop Employment on equal terms to union members and non-members alike.

Organization development (OD) Planned and systematic attempts to change the organization, typically to a more behavioral environment.

Organizational analysis Training needs assessment activity, which focuses on the firm's strategic mission, goals, and corporate plans are studied, along with the results of strategic HR planning.

Organizational fit Management's perception of the degree to which the prospective employee will fit in with the firm's culture or value system.

Organizational results Typically, training outcomes such as enhanced productivity, lower costs, and higher product or service quality.

Orientation Initial training and development effort for new employees that informs them about the company, the job, and the work group.

Outplacement A procedure whereby laid-off employees are given assistance in finding employment elsewhere.

Outsourcing Process of hiring an external provider to do the work that was previously done internally.

Out-of-pocket maximum The maximum amount an employee pays for health care during a calendar or plan year.

Paid time off (PTO) banks Means of dealing with the problem of unscheduled absences by providing a certain number of days each year that employees can use for any purpose.

Paired comparisons Supervisors compare each employee to every other employee, identifying the better performer in each pair.

Passive job seekers Potential job candidates, who are typically employed, satisfied with their employer, and content in their current role but if the right opportunity came along, they might like to learn more.

Pay compression Occurs whenever a company's pay spread between newly hired or less qualified employees, and more qualified job incumbents is small. In extreme cases, less experienced employees are paid as much as or more than employees who have been with the organization a long time because of a gradual increase in starting salaries and limited salary adjustments for long-term employees.

Pay grade Grouping of similar jobs to simplify pricing jobs.

Pay mix compensation policies Combination of direct (core compensation) and indirect financial compensation (employee benefits) components that make up an employee's total compensation package.

Pay range Minimum and maximum pay rate with enough variance between the two to allow for a significant pay difference.

Pay structures Pay rate differences for jobs of unequal worth and the framework for recognizing differences in employee contributions.

Performance appraisal (PA) Formal system of review and evaluation of individual or team task performance.

Performance management (PM) Goal-oriented process directed toward ensuring that organizational processes are in place to maximize the productivity of employees, teams, and ultimately, the organization.

Permissive bargaining issues Issues may be raised, but neither side may insist that they be bargained over.

Perquisites (perks) Special benefits provided by a firm to a small group of key executives and designed to give the executives something extra.

Person analysis A training needs assessment activity that focuses on finding answers to questions such as, "Who needs to be trained? What do they need to do differently from what they're doing today? What kind of knowledge, skills, and abilities (KSAs) do employees need?"

Personality Individual differences in characteristic patterns of thinking, feeling, and behaving.

Personality tests Self-reported measures of traits, temperaments, or dispositions.

Person-focused pay Compensation for developing the flexibility, knowledge, and skills to perform a number of jobs effectively.

Phased retirement Any arrangement that allows people to move from full-time work to retirement in steps.

Piecework Incentive pay plan in which employees are paid for each unit they produce.

Point method Job evaluation method where the raters assign numerical values to specific job factors, such as knowledge required, and the sum of these values provides a quantitative assessment of a job's relative worth.

Polycentric staffing Staffing approach in which host-country nationals are used throughout the organization, from top to bottom.

Position Collection of tasks and responsibilities performed by one person.

Positive halo effect See *halo error.*

Postexit questionnaire Questionnaire sent to former employees several weeks after they leave the organization to determine the real reason they left.

Preliminary screening In employee selection, a review to eliminate those who obviously do not meet the position's requirements.

Prepaid medical services HMOs are sometimes described as providing prepaid medical services because fixed periodic enrollment fees cover HMO members for all medically necessary services only if the services are delivered or approved by the HMO.

Primary care physicians Designated by HMOs to determine whether patients require the care of a medical specialist. This functions to control costs by reducing the number of medically unnecessary visits to expensive specialists.

Profession Vocation characterized by the existence of a common body of knowledge and a procedure for certifying members.

Professional employer organization (PEO) A company that leases employees to other businesses.

Profit sharing Plans that pay a portion of company profits to employees, separate from base pay, cost-of-living adjustments, or permanent merit pay increases. These plans award cash to employees, typically on a quarterly or annual basis.

Progressive disciplinary action Approach to disciplinary action designed to ensure that the minimum penalty appropriate to the offense is imposed.

Prohibited bargaining issues Issues that are statutorily outlawed from collective bargaining.

Promotion Movement of a person to a higher-level position in an organization.

Promotion from within (PFW) Policy of filling vacancies above entry-level positions with current employees.

Public awareness campaigns Labor maneuvers that do not coincide with a strike or organizing campaign to pressure an employer for better wages, benefits, and the like.

Qualified plans Welfare and pension plans that meet various requirements set forth by the Employee Retirement Income Security Act of 1974; these plans entitle employees and employers to favorable tax treatment by deducting the contributions from taxable income. Qualified plans do not disproportionately favor highly compensated employees.

Quality circles Groups of employees who voluntarily meet regularly with their supervisors to discuss problems, investigate causes, recommend solutions, and take corrective action when authorized to do so.

Rating errors In performance appraisals, differences between human judgment processes versus objective, accurate assessments uncolored by bias, prejudice, or other subjective, extraneous influences.

Reactions Training evaluation criterion focused on the extent to which trainees liked the training program related to its usefulness, and quality of conduct.

Real hourly compensation Measure of the purchasing power of a dollar.

Realistic job preview (RJP) Method of conveying both positive and negative job information to the applicant in an unbiased manner.

Recruitment Process of attracting individuals on a timely basis, in sufficient numbers, and with appropriate qualifications to apply for jobs with an organization.

Recruitment methods Specific means used to attract potential employees to the firm.

Recruitment sources Where qualified candidates are located.

Reengineering Fundamental rethinking and radical redesign of business processes to achieve dramatic improvements in critical, contemporary measures of performance such as cost, quality, service, and speed.

Reference checks Validations from individuals who know the applicant that provide additional insight into the information furnished by the applicant and allow verification of its accuracy.

Referral plans Individual incentive pay plans for rewarding the referral of new customers or recruiting successful job applicants.

Regiocentric staffing Staffing approach that is similar to the polycentric staffing approach, but regional groups of subsidiaries reflecting the organization's strategy and structure work as a unit.

Reliability Extent to which a selection test provides consistent results.

Relocation benefits Company-paid shipment of household goods and temporary living expenses, covering all or a portion of the real estate costs associated with buying a new home and selling the previously occupied home.

Requirements forecast Determining the number, skill, and location of employees the organization will need at future dates in order to meet its goals.

Results-based performance appraisal Performance appraisal method in which the manager and subordinate jointly agree on objectives for the next appraisal period; in the past, a form of management by objectives.

Résumé Goal-directed summary of a person's experience, education, and training developed for use in the selection process.

Reverse mentoring A process in which older employees learn from younger ones.

Right-to-work laws Laws that prohibit management and unions from entering into agreements requiring union membership as a condition of employment.

Rights arbitration Arbitration involving disputes over the interpretation and application of the various provisions of an existing contract.

Role-playing Training and development method in which participants are required to respond to specific problems they may encounter in their jobs by acting out real-world situations.

Sabbaticals Temporary leaves of absence from an organization, usually at reduced pay.

Safety Protection of employees from injuries caused by work-related accidents.

Salary One type of base pay. Employees earn salaries for performing their jobs, regardless of the actual number of hours worked. Companies generally measure salary on an annual basis.

Say on pay Provision that gives shareholders in all but the smallest companies an advisory vote on executive pay.

Scanlon plan Gain sharing plan that provides a financial reward to employees for savings in labor costs resulting from their suggestions.

Secondary boycott Union attempt to encourage third parties (such as suppliers and customers) to stop doing business with a firm; declared illegal by the Taft-Hartley Act.

Selection Process of choosing from a group of applicants the individual best suited for a particular position and the organization.

Self-assessment Process of learning about oneself.

Seniority Length of time an employee has been associated with the company, division, department, or job.

Seniority pay Pay program in which pay increases are based on length of service.

Severance packages Refer to pay and benefits awarded to employees for a period of time after they leave the company. Oftentimes, buyouts include bonus payments that vary in amount based on salary and years of service.

Severance pay Compensation designed to assist laid-off employees as they search for new employment.

Shared service center (SSC) A center that takes routine, transaction-based activities dispersed throughout the organization and consolidates them in one place (also known as a center of expertise).

Shareholders Owners of a corporation.

Similar-to-me effect The tendency on the part of raters to judge favorably employees whom they perceive as like themselves.

Simulators Training and development delivery system comprised of devices or programs that replicate actual job demands.

Situational interview Gives interviewers better insight into how candidates would perform in the work environment by creating hypothetical situations candidates would be likely to encounter on the job and asking them how they would handle them.

6-year graduated schedule Allows workers to become 20 percent vested after two years and to vest at a rate of 20 percent each year thereafter until they are 100 percent vested after six years of service.

Skill-based pay System that compensates employees for their job-related skills and knowledge, not for their job titles.

Social audit Systematic assessment of a company's activities in terms of its social impact.

Specialist Individual who may be an HR executive, an HR manager, or a non-manager, and who is typically concerned with only one of the five functional areas of HR management.

Spillover effect Non-union companies' offer of similar compensation unionized companies with the goal of is reducing the likelihood that nonunion workforces will seek union representation.

Spot bonus Relatively small monetary gift provided employees for outstanding work or effort during a reasonably short period of time.

Staffing Process through which an organization ensures that it always has the proper number of employees with the appropriate skills in the right jobs, at the right time, to achieve organizational objectives.

Standardization Uniformity of the procedures and conditions related to administering tests.

Stock options Incentive plan in which employees can buy a specified amount of stock in their company in the future at or below the current market price.

Strategic planning Process by which top management determines overall organizational purposes and objectives and how they are achieved.

Strength/weakness balance sheet A self-evaluation procedure, developed originally by Benjamin Franklin, that assists people in becoming aware of their strengths and weaknesses.

Stress Body's non-specific reaction to any demand made on it.

Stress interview Form of interview in which the interviewer intentionally creates anxiety.

Strictness errors Being unduly critical of an employee's work performance.

Strike Action by union members who refuse to work in order to exert pressure on management in negotiations.

Structured interview Interview in which the interviewer asks each applicant for a particular job the same series of job-related questions.

Substance abuse Use of illegal substances or the misuse of controlled substances such as alcohol and drugs.

Succession planning Process of ensuring that qualified persons are available to assume key managerial positions once the positions are vacant.

Survey feedback Organization development method of basing change efforts on the systematic collection and measurement of subordinate's attitudes through anonymous questionnaires.

Task analysis A training needs assessment activity, which focuses on the tasks required to achieve the firm's purposes.

Team building Conscious effort to develop effective work groups and cooperative skills throughout the organization.

Team coordination training Team training focused on educating team members how to orchestrate the individual work that they do to complete the task.

Team training Training focused on teaching knowledge and skills to individuals who are expected to work collectively toward meeting a common objective.

Telecommuting Work arrangement whereby employees, called "teleworkers" or "telecommuters," are able to remain at home (or otherwise away from the office) and perform their work using computers and other electronic devices that connect them with their offices.

Term life insurance Protection for providing monetary payments to an employee's beneficiaries upon the employee's death, and offered only during a limited period based on a specified number of years or maximum age.

Termination Most severe penalty that an organization can impose on an employee.

Third-country national (TCN) Citizen of one country, working in a second country, and employed by an organization headquartered in a third country.

360-degree feedback evaluation method Popular performance appraisal method that involves evaluation input from multiple levels within the firm as well as external sources.

Total compensation Represents both the intrinsic and extrinsic rewards employees receive for performing their jobs.

Traditional career path Employee progresses vertically upward in the organization from one specific job to the next.

Training Activities designed to provide learners with the knowledge and skills needed for their present jobs.

Training and development (T&D) Heart of a continuous effort designed to improve employee competency and organizational performance.

Training and development needs assessment Helps companies determine whether training is necessary. It may be determined by conducting analyses on three levels, which include organization, task, and person.

Trait systems Type of performance appraisal method, requiring raters (e.g., supervisors or customers) to evaluate each employee's traits or characteristics (e.g., quality of work and leadership).

Transfer Lateral movement of a worker within an organization.

Transfer of training Training evaluation method focusing on the extent to which an employee generalizes knowledge and skill learned in training to the work place, as well as maintains the level of skill proficiency or knowledge learned in training.

Two-tier wage system A wage structure where newly hired workers are paid less than current employees for performing the same or similar jobs.

Unemployment insurance Provides workers whose jobs have been terminated through no fault of their own monetary payments for up to 26 weeks or until they find a new job.

Uniform Guidelines Provide a single set of principles that were designed to assist employers, labor organizations, employment agencies, and licensing and certification boards in complying with federal prohibitions against employment practices that discriminate on the basis of race, color, religion, sex, and national origin.

Union Consists of employees who have joined together for the purpose of negotiating terms of employment, such as wages and work hours.

Union salting Process of training union organizers to apply for jobs at a company and, once hired, working to unionize employees.

Union shop Requirement that all employees become members of the union after a specified period of employment (the legal minimum is 30 days) or after a union shop provision has been negotiated.

Unstructured interview Interview in which the job applicant is asked probing, open-ended questions.

Validity Extent to which a test measures what it claims to measure.

Vestibule system Training and development delivery system that takes place away from the production area on equipment that closely resembles equipment actually used on the job.

Vesting An employee's acquired non-forfeitable rights to pension benefits.

Virtual job fair Online recruiting method engaged in by a single employer or group of employers to attract a large number of applicants.

Volunteerism Time allotted to support a meaningful cause.

Wage See *hourly pay*.

Wage curve Fitting of plotted points to create a smooth progression between pay grades (also known as the pay curve).

Wellness programs Designed to promote the mental and physical well-being of employees and family members.

Whole life insurance A type of life insurance that provides protection to employees' beneficiaries during employees' employment and into the retirement years.

Workers' compensation Provides a degree of financial protection for employees who incur expenses resulting from job-related accidents or illnesses.

Work standards method Performance appraisal method that compares each employee's performance to a predetermined standard or expected level of output.

Workplace bullying Acts of continual hostile conduct that deliberately hurt another person emotionally, verbally, or physically.

Workplace violence Physical assault, threatening behavior, verbal abuse, hostility, or harassment directed toward employees at work or on duty.

Work-sample tests Tests that require an applicant to perform a task or set of tasks representative of the job.

Zero-base forecast Forecasting method that uses the organization's current level of employment as the starting point for determining future staffing needs.

Name Index

Company Index

Subject Index